Tobacco Taxation in Latin America and the Caribbean

A CALL FOR TOBACCO TAX REFORM

OECD
BETTER POLICIES FOR BETTER LIVES

Please cite this publication as:
OECD (2024), *Tobacco Taxation in Latin America and the Caribbean: A Call for Tobacco Tax Reform*, OECD Publishing, Paris, https://doi.org/10.1787/080cd662-en.

ISBN 978-92-64-72396-2 (print)
ISBN 978-92-64-55030-8 (PDF)
ISBN 978-92-64-36824-8 (HTML)
ISBN 978-92-64-82671-7 (epub)

Photo credits: Cover design by Baseline Arts Ltd using images from © Africa Studio/Shutterstock.com.

Corrigenda to OECD publications may be found at: https://www.oecd.org/en/publications/support/corrigenda.html.

Foreword

The Organisation for Economic Co-operation and Development (OECD) has undertaken a project on tobacco taxation in the Latin America and the Caribbean (LAC) region with the financial support of Bloomberg Philanthropies. The project sought to identify ways of improving the effectiveness of tobacco taxation and stimulating dialogue on tobacco taxation policy between Finance and Health Ministries in the LAC region. The project was carried out by the OECD's Centre for Tax Policy and Administration (CTPA) in tandem with the OECD's Directorate for Employment, Labour, and Social Affairs. Deliverables include a report on tobacco taxation in the LAC region, a regional workshop on tobacco taxation, and technical support on tobacco taxation for countries in LAC.

The report, one of the project outputs, was produced by the Tax Policy and Statistics Division of the CTPA. Within the CTPA, the work on the report was led by Bert Brys and authored by, in alphabetical order, Bert Brys, Jean-Baptiste Carpentier, Céline Colin, Caroline Maschka and Mariona Mas Montserrat.

The Health Division of the OECD's Directorate for Employment, Labour, and Social Affairs provided significant input. Their inputs were led by Michele Cecchini and written by Alexa Segal, with contributions from Aliénor Lerouge, Fabien Lenthy, Marion Devaux, and Sabine Vuik.

The authors would like to thank the delegates of Working Party No.2 on Tax Policy Analysis and Tax Statistics in its Inclusive Framework format for their inputs and feedback. The project team acknowledges the comments received from the Ministries of Finance of Brazil, Costa Rica, the Dominican Republic, Jamaica, Mexico, Peru, Saint Kitts and Nevis and Uruguay, and the Revenue agency of Mexico.

The authors would also like to thank participants in the 2023 and 2024 meetings of the OECD Expert Group on the Economics of Public Health (EGEPH), where preliminary versions of the report were presented. A particular thank you goes to representatives from the Ministries of Health and other participating governmental organizations from Brazil, Costa Rica, Mexico and the United States, as well as experts from Chile.

Colleagues Kurt Van Dender, Daniel Fichmann and Stéphane Buydens from the CTPA, and Stefano Scarpetta, Mark Pearson, Francesca Colombo, Chris James and Caroline Penn from the OECD's Directorate for Employment, Labour, and Social Affairs provided useful contributions and comments. The authors are grateful to Hazel Healy and Antonia Vanzini from the CTPA for their assistance with editing and report communication and to Sahnur Soykan for organisational support. Meral Gedik prepared the report for publication.

The authors would also like to thank colleagues from the Pan American Health Organisation, the World Bank, the World Health Organisation, the University Adolfo Ibáñez and Johns Hopkins University for their valuable feedback.

The report was approved by Working Party No.2 on Tax Policy Analysis and Tax Statistics in its Inclusive Framework format in August 2024. This report was also reviewed by the Health Committee and its Expert Group on the Economics of Public Health. It is published under the responsibility of the Secretary General of the OECD. The opinions expressed and arguments employed herein do not necessarily reflect the official views of OECD member countries. The report was prepared for publication by the OECD Secretariat.

Table of contents

FIGURES

TABLES

BOXES

Abbreviations and acronyms

BP	Best practice
CAF	Customs administration fee
CIF	Cost, insurance and freight
Cofins	*Contribuições para os Financiamento da Seguridade Social*
COPD	Chronic obstructive pulmonary disease
CPI	Consumer price index
CTPA	OECD's Centre for Tax Policy and Administration
EFP	Ex-factory price
ENDS	Electronic nicotine delivery systems
ENNDS	Electronic non-nicotine delivery systems
FCTC	Framework Convention on Tobacco Control
FET	*Fondo especial del tabaco*
FRP	Final retail price
GATS	Global adult tobacco survey
GDP	Gross domestic product
HTP	Heated tobacco products
IAE	*Impuesto adicional de emergencia sobre cigarrillos*
ICE	*Impuesto a los consumos específicos*
ICMS	Tax on the movement of goods and services
IECT	*Impuestos específico al consumo de cigarrillos y otros productos de tabaco*
IEPS	*Impuesto especial sobre producción y servicios*
IMESI	*Impuesto específico interno*
IMF	International Monetary Fund
Inder	Tax for the rural development Institute
IPI	*Imposto sobre productos industrializados*
LAC	Latin America and the Caribbean
LCU	Local currency unit

MERCOSUR	*Mercado Común del Sur* (Southern Common Market)
MPOWER	Monitoring tobacco consumption and the effectiveness of preventive measures
	Protect people from tobacco smoke
	Offer help to quit tobacco use
	Warn about the dangers of tobacco
	Enforce bans on tobacco advertising, promotion and sponsorship
	Raise taxes on tobacco
OECD	Organisation for Economic Co-operation and Development
PAHO	Pan American Health Organization
PIS/Pasep	*Programas de Integração Social e de Formação do Patrimônio do Servidor Público*
PPP	Purchasing power parity
RYO	Roll-Your-Own
SCF	Standard compliance fee
SCT	Special consumption tax
SRP	Suggested retail price by the manufacturer/importer
SSB	Sugar-sweetened beverages
VAT	Value added tax
WHO	World Health Organization
WTO	World Trade Organization

Executive summary

Tobacco use prevalence remains high in Latin America and the Caribbean (LAC), resulting in significant health, economic and social costs. In 2021, over 350 000 individuals died from tobacco use and second-hand smoke, and over 40% of respiratory cancers in LAC were attributable to tobacco use. The smoking-attributable medical costs can reach up to 1.5% of GDP per year. These striking figures call for policy action. While countries in LAC have made significant progress with tobacco control policies, there is still significant scope for tobacco tax reform in the region.

This report introduces a framework to assess countries' tobacco tax policy performance based on a selection of best practices. The framework complements existing tools, including the World Health Organisation's (WHO) MPOWER matrix and Johns Hopkins University's cigarette tax scorecard, both of which evaluate tobacco tax progress over time. The framework intends to pave the way for country-specific tobacco tax reform analysis and recommendations. It shows that, while most countries signed the WHO Framework Convention on Tobacco Control (FCTC) and implemented its key guiding principles as of 2003, progress has stalled since. There is an urgent need for a new wave of tobacco tax reforms in the LAC region to improve the effectiveness of both tobacco tax policy and administration.

Over the past decades, countries in LAC have gradually, albeit partially, aligned their tobacco tax policy with best practices. Countries have started to rely more on excise taxes than on other indirect taxes to raise the price of tobacco products. Volume-based (i.e. specific) tobacco excise taxes are more common than price-based (i.e. ad valorem) tobacco excise taxes. Uniform rates are more widespread than tiered rates. Many countries index their specific taxes to inflation, but none adjust them to real income growth. All traditional tobacco products (cigarettes, cigars, cigarillos and roll-your-own tobacco) are taxed, although not necessarily in the same way. Tobacco sale regulations are in place in most countries.

Nevertheless, many countries have significant scope to improve their tobacco tax policy design and administration. Most of tobacco tax shares remain below the WHO's recommended threshold of 75% of the retail price. Ad valorem tobacco taxes are often levied on a narrow base without an excise tax floor that ensures that a minimum amount of tobacco excise tax is paid. When they are not banned, new tobacco and nicotine products are often not taxed or taxed at rates too low to prevent their take-up by young people. Tax rates vary significantly across tobacco products, which might incentivise consumers to switch from expensive to cheaper tobacco products rather than to reduce or quit smoking.

Tobacco products remain affordable on average in LAC and have become more affordable over time. The main objective of tobacco taxes is to increase the price of tobacco products such that smokers reduce or quit smoking. For this tax-induced incentive to be effective, tobacco excise taxes need to be sufficiently high, which will also limit the possibilities for tobacco businesses to absorb the tax instead of passing it through to retail prices.

Tobacco excise taxes have the potential to raise significant revenues. Revenues from indirect taxes on tobacco range from 0.01% (in Barbados) to 2.58% (in Chile) of total tax revenue. Tobacco excise taxes raise 0.50% of total tax revenue in LAC on average, which is about one-third of average annual smoking-attributable medical costs. Countries with higher tobacco use prevalence raise more tax revenues. The average tobacco excise tax collected per pack of legal cigarettes sold increased from USD 1.2 to 2.0 (expressed in purchasing power parity) between 2008 and 2016 due to significant increases in the tobacco tax rates. However, the tax ratio has increased only slightly since then, reflecting the absence of ambitious tobacco tax reforms in recent years.

Concerns about revenue losses from tobacco excise hikes are overstated. First, the demand for tobacco products is inelastic as smokers tend to adjust their behaviour only slowly over time. A tobacco tax increase will tend to raise tax revenues in the short run, even if tobacco use decreases. In the longer run, tobacco tax increases can result in a drop in revenues, but the reduction in health, economic and social costs would be far larger than the loss in tax revenues, thereby resulting in a positive impact for the government budget. Second, concerns that tobacco tax increases would strengthen illicit trade should not prevent tobacco tax reform either. Instead, these concerns call for accompanying measures to contain illicit trade.

The report identifies key tobacco tax reform priorities across countries in LAC, including:

- Increase specific tobacco excise tax levels and index them to inflation and real income growth to reduce the affordability of tobacco products.
- In countries with an ad valorem tobacco tax component, introduce a minimum tax or price floor, and levy the ad valorem tax on the suggested or actual retail price rather than on the ex-factory price. Use information from the value added tax administration to ensure that the tobacco tax base is aligned with the retail price.
- Align the design of excise taxes across tobacco products to achieve a similar tax burden, especially between highly substitutable tobacco products, to prevent smokers from switching from expensive to cheaper tobacco products rather than to reduce or quit smoking.
- Where the sales of new emerging tobacco and nicotine products are not banned, tax them at similar levels than cigarettes to reduce their take up, especially among young people.
- Account for the strategic response of tobacco businesses when designing tobacco tax policy. Evaluate the impact of tobacco tax increases on pre-tax and retail prices over time and follow-up with additional tax measures as necessary.
- Select the tobacco excise tax point that facilitates most the tobacco excise tax administration, align the tobacco excise tax structure with the taxing point and introduce measures to limit fraud:
  - Use modern fiscal markings.
  - Collect more detailed tobacco transaction information within the excise tax declarations.
  - Enforce mandatory licencing for all parts of the tobacco value chain.
- Levy the value added tax on the tobacco excise tax-inclusive price.
- Implement Article 5.3 of the WHO FCTC so that direct and indirect (tax and non-tax) subsidies are not provided to tobacco companies to prevent these subsides from undermining the effectiveness of tobacco tax policies.

Finally, this report calls for an enhanced national and regional dialogue to advance the tobacco tax reform agenda. Ministries of Finance and Ministries of Health need to strengthen their cooperation to ensure that tobacco tax policies are effective in significantly reducing tobacco use. Other parts of government might have to participate in such a dialogue, including tax and customs authorities, given their important role in enforcing tobacco excise taxes. At the regional level, countries have an untapped reform potential to exchange information on tobacco-related information to avoid weak tobacco control policies in one country, while creating a hurdle for effective tobacco tax policies in other countries.

Overview

Countries in Latin America and the Caribbean (LAC) have made significant progress in tackling the adverse impact of tobacco use on their societies. Smoking prevalence and tobacco-related death rates have declined in most countries in the LAC region in the past two decades. Many factors, including the implementation of effective tobacco control policies and strict regulation that prevents smoking in public spaces and advertisement bans for tobacco products, have contributed to this positive outcome.

However, there remain significant tobacco-related health challenges for individuals and societies. Tobacco use has substantial economic costs. Tobacco users often face higher health expenses due to tobacco-related illnesses and reduced resilience to cope with diseases, such as cardiovascular or lung diseases, COVID-19, etc. At the societal level, smoking-related diseases incur pre-mature deaths, productivity and welfare losses, and impose a heavy burden on health systems in the LAC region.

Carefully designed tobacco tax reforms will help governments reach both their health and tax revenue objectives. By incentivising smokers to quit or reduce smoking (including smoking initiation), tobacco taxes lower smoking-related individual and societal costs and send a signal to set societies on a path towards tobacco-free generations. Tobacco taxes have revenue potential that can contribute to the financing of health systems. This revenue potential is underutilised in LAC, despite the large investment needs in health systems highlighted during the COVID-19 pandemic. In the longer run, tobacco taxes reduce tobacco consumption which has a positive impact on tobacco-related diseases and public health expenditure.

While progress in tobacco tax reform has been significant, there remains substantial scope for further tobacco tax reform. According to the World Health Organisation (WHO), increasing tobacco taxes and prices is the single most effective and cost-effective measure for reducing tobacco use. Over the last decades, countries in the LAC region have made significant tobacco tax reform progress. For instance, many countries have now largely aligned the design of their tobacco excise taxes with the WHO's tobacco tax policy best practices. However, more recently, tobacco tax reform progress has stalled, and there remains significant scope in many LAC countries to improve the design and administration of tobacco taxes.

This report supports efforts to put tobacco taxation on the policy agenda and to set in motion ambitious tobacco tax reforms in LAC countries. The report provides an overview of the health impacts of tobacco consumption, the tax revenue that is raised by tobacco taxes, the design and administration of tobacco taxation, the tobacco tax reforms that LAC countries have implemented, the impact of tobacco taxes on tobacco prices and the affordability of tobacco products. The analysis builds on information collected at the country level and published by academics, national institutions, and international and regional organisations. Information from this report can be used to benchmark a LAC country against other countries in the region, or to compare the region with tobacco taxation practices in other parts of the world. Such a benchmarking exercise can be used to enhance the dialogue between Health Ministries, Finance Ministries, tax administrations, revenue agencies and customs authorities, to discuss the relevance of tobacco taxation from a budget perspective, to strengthen the design and administration of tobacco taxation and to start regional tobacco tax cooperation.

Chapter 1 of the report sets the scene. The chapter focuses on the consumption trends in tobacco products in LAC countries, both among adults and young individuals. It outlines the adverse effects of tobacco consumption, including the burden it places on public health, the substantial health expenditures it incurs, and the losses in productivity it entails. Additionally, it evaluates the current state of tobacco control policies in the region. The chapter discusses the efficacity of tobacco tax policies in raising cigarette prices, and the role of tobacco excise taxes (defined as taxes levied on tobacco products produced for sale within a country, or imported and sold in that country, at a specific stage of production or distribution).

Chapter 2 focuses on tobacco tax revenue, building on data from the OECD Revenue Statistics database, the WHO and national data sources. The chapter focuses on tobacco excise tax revenue in countries in LAC and presents a series of correlations between tobacco excise tax revenue and other indicators of tobacco use and tax policy.

Chapter 3 provides an overview of tobacco tax policy design in countries in LAC. The chapter describes the design of excise taxes on tobacco products, focusing on a wide range of factors, including: the tax structure, the tax base, tax rates, indexation mechanisms, tax floors and tax caps and tobacco excise revenue earmarking practices. The chapter discusses the design of other indirect taxes that are levied on tobacco products, including the value added tax (VAT), import duties and other indirect taxes. The chapter also provides information on the authorities that are involved in the design of tobacco tax policy in each country, the tobacco excise tax administration as well as the tobacco sale regulations that support tobacco tax policy. The chapter looks at all types of tobacco products (cigarettes, cigars, cigarillos, Roll-Your-Own tobacco, new tobacco and nicotine products) and places greater emphasis on cigarette taxation as this is the first tobacco product consumed in LAC.

Chapter 4 discusses the need for tobacco tax reform in LAC. The chapter starts by an overview of the implementation of tobacco tax policy best practices in LAC countries. It evaluates the extent to which past country tobacco excise tax reforms are aligned with the WHO tobacco tax policy best practices. The chapter then points at the reasons why LAC countries have significant scope to introduce tobacco tax reforms, both at the domestic and regional level, and what are some tobacco tax reform options.

Chapter 5 shows that many tobacco excise tax reforms took place before 2011, and that the pace and scale of tobacco excise tax reform in LAC has decreased since 2012. The chapter discusses measures to further reduce smoking prevalence. In particular, countries will have to take into account the behavioural responses of the tobacco sector to tobacco tax reforms, better align tobacco tax administration and tax policy design, put the affordability of tobacco products at the centre of their tobacco tax reforms, ensure that Ministries of Finance and Health, tax administration, revenues agencies and customs authorities cooperate on a recurrent basis, and engage in a regional tobacco tax cooperation.

Chapter 6 presents country profiles for the following 18 countries: Argentina, Bolivia, Brazil, Chile, Colombia, Costa Rica, the Dominican Republic, Ecuador, El Salvador, Guatemala, Honduras, Jamaica, Mexico, Nicaragua, Panama, Paraguay, Peru and Uruguay. Subject to data availability, each country profile provides information on tobacco use prevalence, MPOWER measures, taxes and prices of the most sold brand of cigarettes, trends in retail prices of cigarettes by brand category, affordability of cigarettes, the design of tobacco excise taxes across tobacco products, tobacco tax reforms, tobacco excise tax revenue, the average excise tax revenue collected per pack of 20 cigarettes sold, and the change in the main tobacco tax policy indicators.

1 Setting the scene

This chapter presents consumption trends of tobacco, both among adults and young individuals in countries in Latin America and the Caribbean (LAC). The chapter outlines the adverse effects of tobacco consumption, including the burden it places on public health, the substantial health expenditures it incurs, and the losses in productivity it entails. The chapter evaluates the current state of tobacco control policies within the region and discusses the impact of tobacco taxes in raising cigarette prices.

1.1. Tobacco consumption in LAC countries

Tobacco use remains widespread in LAC countries, particularly among males (Figure 1.1). Approximately 12% of people in LAC currently use tobacco, with males having a prevalence three-fold that of females. The highest tobacco use rates for males in the LAC region are observed in Chile, where nearly one in three males use tobacco (31%), followed by Argentina (29%). In contrast, the lowest rates among males are found in Panama (8%). The prevalence for females mirrors the pattern seen in males, with Chile and Argentina having the highest rates of tobacco use among females. However, countries with the lowest rates of tobacco use for females are Barbados, Guatemala, Honduras, Belize, El Salvador and Panama (prevalence rates below 2%).

Figure 1.1. Tobacco use

Percentage of the population aged 15 years and over who currently use any tobacco product (smoked and/or smokeless tobacco) on a daily or non-daily basis, 2022

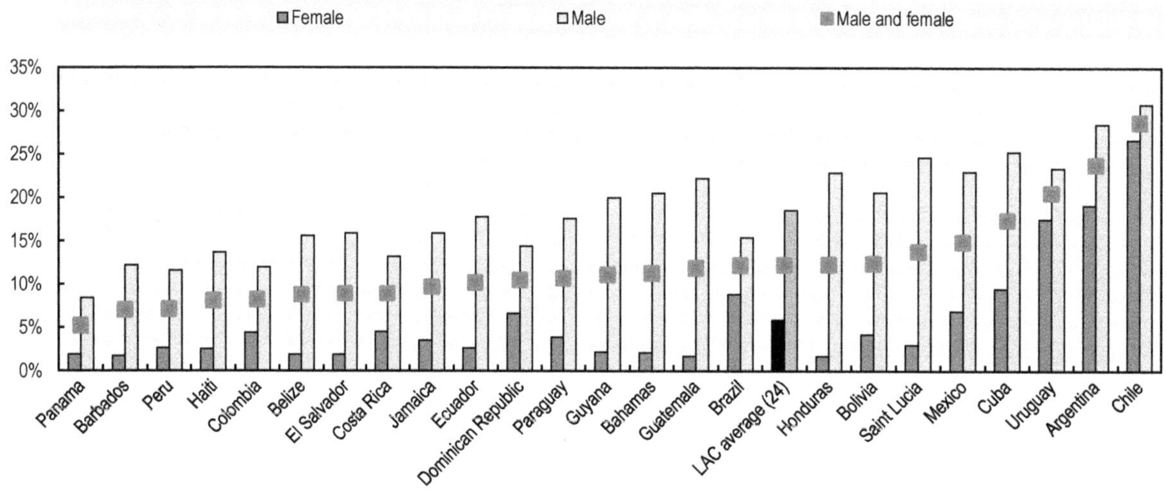

Note: Tobacco products include cigarettes, pipes, cigars, cigarillos, waterpipes (hookah, shisha), bidis, kretek, heated tobacco products, and all forms of smokeless (oral and nasal) tobacco. Tobacco products exclude e-cigarettes (which do not contain tobacco), e-cigars, e-hookahs, and e-pipes. The rates are age-standardized to the World Health Organisation (WHO) standard population. The LAC average was calculated as the weighted average of the countries included in the figure, according to the World Bank 2022 population data.
Source: WHO Global Health Observatory Data Repository (WHO, 2024[1]) using population data from (World Bank, 2022[2]).

Cigarettes are the most consumed tobacco product in LAC countries. In 2022, on average 86% of tobacco users in LAC smoked cigarettes (Figure 1.2). The rate is lower in the Dominican Republic where cigarette smoking represents 65% of tobacco use, which might be attributed to the popularity of other tobacco products such as cigars and pipes.

Figure 1.2. Prevalence of cigarette smokers among tobacco users

Percentage of the population that currently smoke cigarettes as % of all tobacco users, on a daily or non-daily basis, aged 15 years and older, 2022

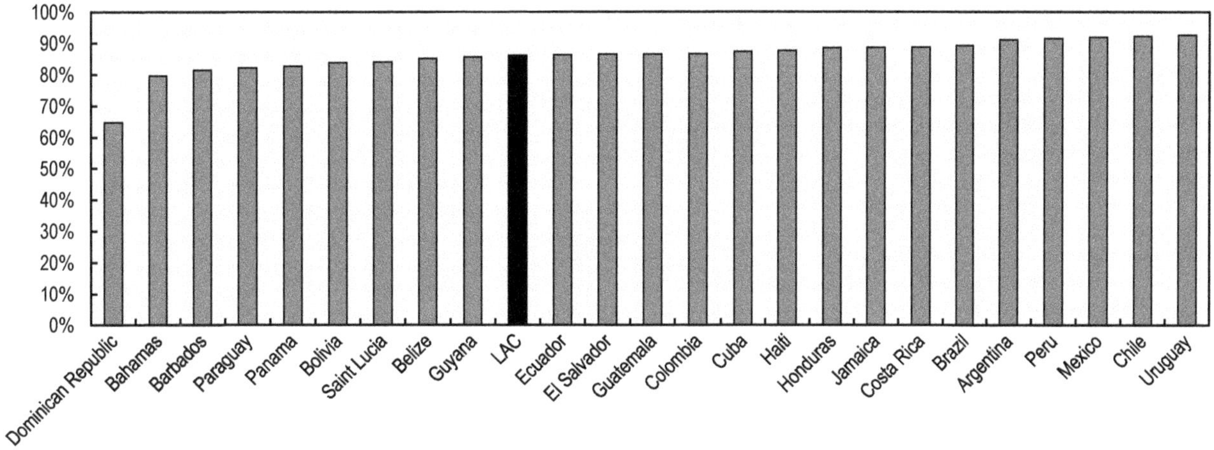

Note: LAC countries with data on tobacco consumption in 2022. The numerator is current cigarette smoking prevalence; the denominator is current tobacco use prevalence, which includes cigarettes, pipes, cigars, cigarillos, waterpipes (hookah, shisha), bidis, kretek, heated tobacco products, and all forms of smokeless (oral and nasal) tobacco. Tobacco products exclude e-cigarettes (which do not contain tobacco), e-cigars, e-hookahs, and e-pipes. The rates are age-standardized to the WHO standard population. The LAC average was calculated as the average of the countries included in the figure.
Source: WHO Global Health Observatory Data Repository (WHO, 2024[11]).

In LAC countries, the average number of cigarettes smoked varies significantly (Figure 1.3). Retail data from 2022 indicates a four-fold difference between countries with the highest and lowest per-smoker cigarette consumption. On average, countries with a higher prevalence of tobacco use also have a higher number of cigarettes smoked per capita (noting that the data shows only legal sales per number of smokers while smokers may smoke both legal and illicit cigarettes). As such, while an average current smoker aged 15 or older in Bolivia smokes about 1 300 cigarettes per year, an average current smoker in Argentina – which is one of the countries with the highest prevalence of tobacco use – smokes 5 225 cigarettes per year (i.e. over 14 cigarettes per day, every day of the year).

Evidence from six LAC countries for which the Global Adult Tobacco Survey (GATS) is available shows that most current tobacco users aged 15 and older are daily consumers (Figure 1.4). In Brazil and Uruguay, 90% and 85%, respectively, of current smokers characterise themselves as daily smokers. Conversely, in Mexico and Panama, a different pattern emerges whereby there are slightly more occasional smokers than daily smokers (i.e. while a significant proportion of current smokers in these countries do smoke daily, a large proportion use tobacco more occasionally).

Figure 1.3. Cigarette volume sales among tobacco users in Latin American countries

Cigarettes consumed annually per current smoker aged 15 years and older, 2022

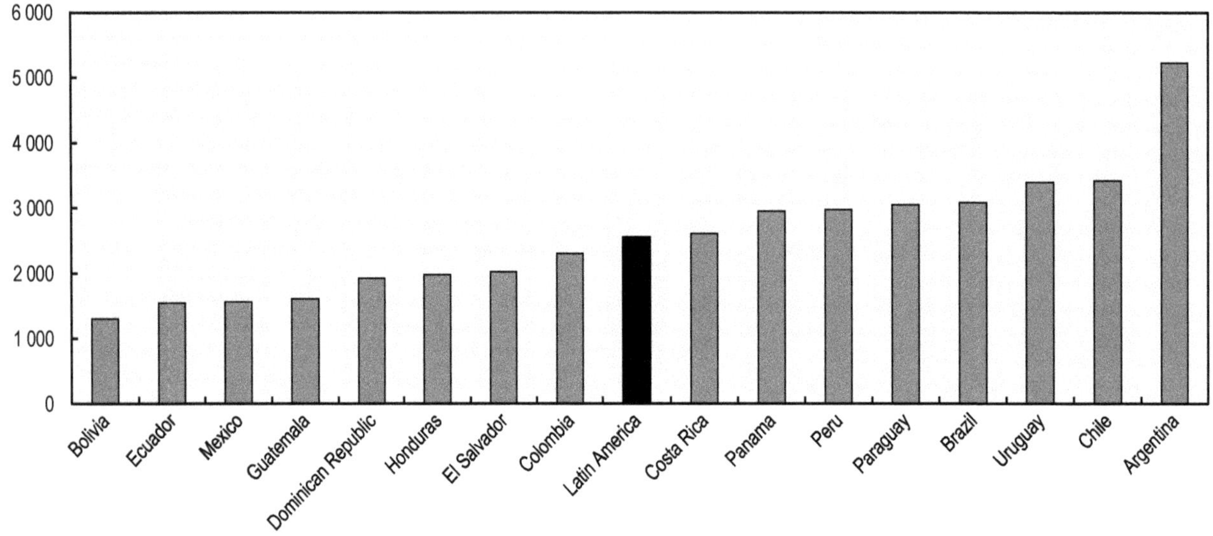

Source: Euromonitor International Tobacco Industry edition, 2023 © All rights reserved (Euromonitor International, 2023[3]).

Figure 1.4. Prevalence of daily tobacco users

Percentage of daily smokers among all current tobacco users aged 15 and above

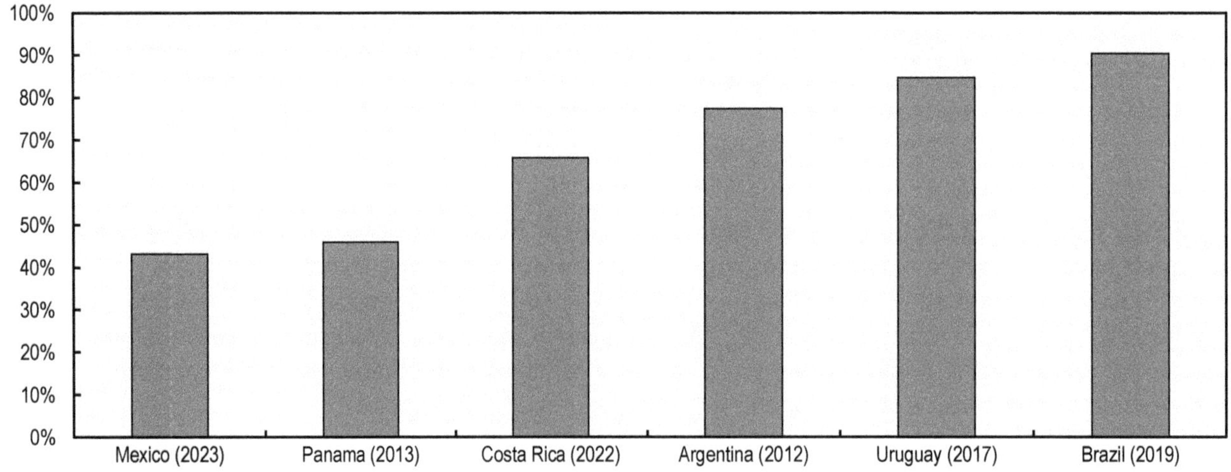

Note: Data was recorded from each country's respective Global Adult Tobacco Survey (GATS) and therefore includes adults, aged 15 and older, tobacco users; except for Brazil, where those surveyed were over 18 years old.
Source: Global Adult Tobacco Survey Argentina 2012 (Government of Argentina, 2013[4]); Pesquisa Nacional de Saúde 2019 (Government of Brazil, 2021[5]); Global Adult Tobacco Survey Costa Rica 2022 (Government of Costa Rica, 2023[6]); Global Adult Tobacco Survey Mexico 2023 (Government of Mexico, 2023[7]); Global Adult Tobacco Survey Panama 2013 (Government of Panama, 2013[8]); Global Adult Tobacco Survey Uruguay 2017 (Government of Uruguay, 2017[9]).

The level of nicotine dependence varies by country. Nicotine dependence is typically measured with two indicators: the number of cigarettes consumed per day and the length of time elapsed between the moment the smoker awakens and the moment at which the first tobacco product is consumed. Of the six LAC countries that have available GATS data on the average number of cigarettes consumed per day for current daily smokers, Mexico had the lowest (average of 8.3 cigarettes per current daily smoker) and Panama and Uruguay had the highest (14.8 and 15.2 respectively) (Figure 1.5). Looking at the other measure of dependency, daily tobacco smokers in Brazil appear to be the most dependent (60% of daily smokers use tobacco within the first 30 minutes of waking), followed by Costa Rica and Panama. Daily smokers in Mexico and Argentina seem to depend less on tobacco as nearly 57% of them in each country, wait at least 60 minutes after waking to smoke.

Figure 1.5. Nicotine dependence

Nicotine dependence in daily tobacco smokers aged 15 and older

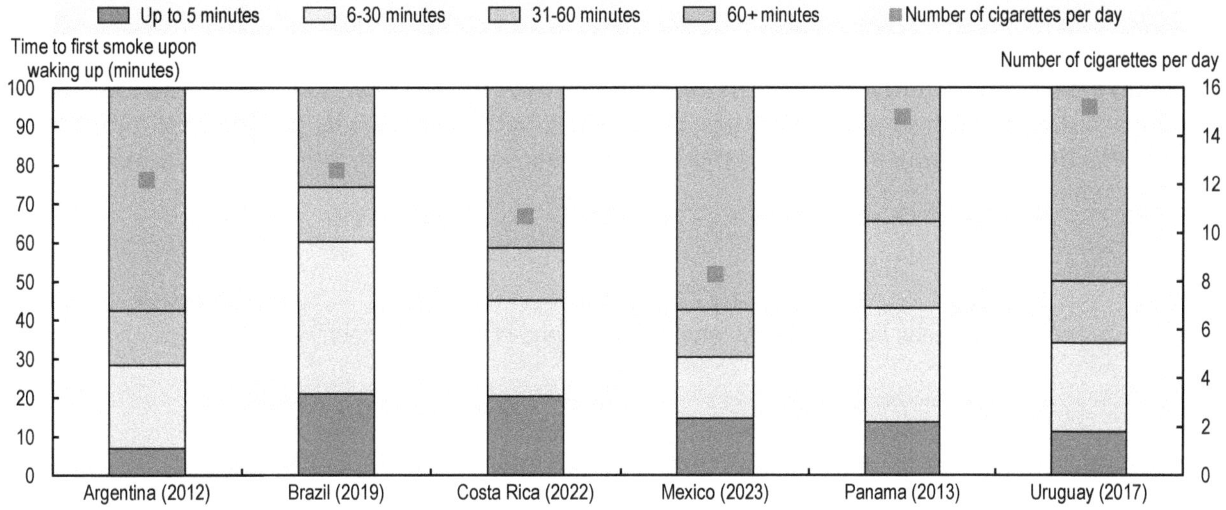

Note: Data was recorded from each country's respective GATS and therefore includes adults, aged 15 and older, tobacco users; except for Brazil, where those surveyed were over 18 years old. The 2019 report from Brazil and the 2022 report from Costa Rica did not capture the time to first smoke, so the data from the 2008 GATS Brazil and 2015 GATS Costa Rica was used for that metric.

Source: Global Adult Tobacco Survey Argentina 2012 (Government of Argentina, 2013[4]); Global Adult Tobacco Survey Brazil 2008 (Government of Brazil/ PAHO, 2010[10]); Pesquisa Nacional de Saúde 2019 (Government of Brazil, 2021[5]); Global Adult Tobacco Survey Costa Rica 2022 (Government of Costa Rica, 2023[6]); Global Adult Tobacco Survey Costa Rica 2015 (Government of Costa Rica, 2017[11]); Global Adult Tobacco Survey Mexico 2023 (Government of Mexico, 2023[7]); Global Adult Tobacco Survey Panama 2013 (Government of Panama, 2013[8]); Global Adult Tobacco Survey Uruguay 2017 (Government of Uruguay, 2017[9]).

Nicotine dependence does not exhibit a consistent pattern by sex across LAC countries. Surveys in Argentina and Panama show higher nicotine dependence among adult males compared to females, while in Brazil and Costa Rica, females exhibit higher dependence levels (Government of Argentina, 2013[4]; Government of Brazil/ PAHO, 2010[10]; Government of Costa Rica, 2017[11]; Government of Mexico, 2023[7]; Government of Panama, 2013[8]; Government of Uruguay, 2017[9]). The surveys for Uruguay and Mexico did not provide conclusive evidence of a consistent pattern of nicotine dependence based on sex.

There is a correlation between the age of smokers, socioeconomic family characteristics and nicotine dependence. Daily smokers aged 65 years and older are more likely to engage in smoking within 30 minutes of waking (48%), compared to the average smoking population (40% - figure based on the GATS from each country and averaged across countries). In addition, in general, surveys indicate that daily smokers with low household incomes and/or lower levels of education tend to exhibit higher levels of nicotine dependency. However, Mexico seems to be an exception because while there is still a slight distinction by educational attainment, the pattern is reversing, and tobacco use is lower among the lower income than the high income (U.S. National Cancer Institute/ WHO, 2016[12]). In Mexico, those with no formal education smoke an average of 8.3 cigarettes per day, with 43.5% of them smoking within the first 30 minutes of waking. In contrast, smokers with a university education smoke an average of 7.7 cigarettes per day, and only 21% smoking within the first 30 minutes of waking (Government of Mexico, 2023[7]). Findings corroborate a 2016 review documenting an inverse relationship between income and tobacco use in LAC countries (Bardach et al., 2016[13]).

The demand for cigarettes in LAC countries is relatively inelastic. This means that the quantity of cigarettes demanded does not change significantly with the change in price. In most LAC countries, the own-price elasticity for cigarettes is likely below -0.5, with a short-term elasticity of -0.31 and a long-term elasticity of -0.43 (Guindon, Paraje and Chaloupka, 2018[14]).[1] A price elasticity of -0.31 means that a 10% increase in the price of cigarettes would lead to a decrease of 3.1% in the quantity demanded.

1.2. Evolution of tobacco consumption in the LAC region

There have been significant decreases in tobacco use over the past two decades in the LAC region. In 2005, about 20% of individuals over the age of 15 used tobacco, but this rate decreased to 12% by 2022 (Figure 1.6). During this period, the rate of reduction in tobacco use among males was 34%, while among females, it was 45%.

Figure 1.6. Evolution of tobacco use

Tobacco use prevalence trends by sex among people aged 15 and older in LAC countries

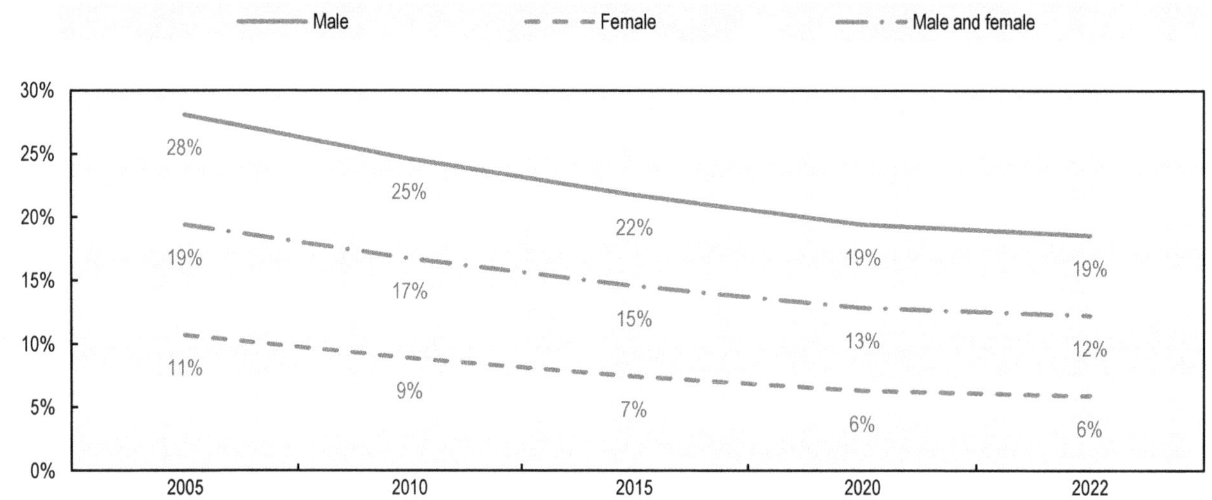

Note: The average prevalence for tobacco use per year includes Argentina, Bahamas, Barbados, Belize, Bolivia, Brazil, Chile, Colombia, Costa Rica, Cuba, the Dominican Republic, Ecuador, El Salvador, Guatemala, Guyana, Haiti, Honduras, Jamaica, Mexico, Panama, Paraguay, Peru, Saint Lucia and Uruguay. Tobacco products include cigarettes, pipes, cigars, cigarillos, waterpipes (hookah, shisha), bidis, kretek, heated tobacco products, and all forms of smokeless (oral and nasal) tobacco. Tobacco products exclude e-cigarettes (which do not contain tobacco), e-cigars, e-hookahs, and e-pipes. The rates are age-standardized to the WHO standard population.
Source: Data for prevalence was extracted from the WHO Global Health Observatory Data Repository (WHO, 2024[1]).

However national surveys suggest not all LAC countries are experiencing meaningful decreases in tobacco use. Despite macro-level declines in tobacco use over the last 17 years, significant strides remain to be achieved within each country, especially due to the recent stalling in the decrease in tobacco use from 2020 to 2022, as shown in the figure above. An example of this phenomenon includes Chile, where the overall prevalence of tobacco use declined from 35.2% in 2018 to 32.5% in 2020. However, at the same time, the prevalence of tobacco use for daily users and the prevalence of individuals who have ever used tobacco did not decrease (Government of Chile, 2021[15]). Further, there was a statistically significant increase in smoking intensity – measured as the number of smoking days per month (from 21 days in 2018 to 22 days in 2020) (Government of Chile, 2021[15]).

The COVID-19 pandemic has had a negative impact on smoking prevalence in various countries. The pandemic contributed to elevated levels of stress, disruption and social isolation, potentially contributing to a rise in smoking prevalence, or a lack of decline (Sarich et al., 2022[16]). This has contributed not only to a slower decline in prevalence rates, and some countries have experienced an increase in tobacco use prevalence among certain strata of population (i.e. high-income populations in Mexico).

1.3. Tobacco use among young people

There exists a significant variation (by nearly 20 percentage points) in the prevalence of young people who are tobacco users across LAC countries (Figure 1.7). In half of the LAC countries, tobacco use prevalence among young people is higher than amongst the adult population. At the same time, the prevalence of tobacco use among young people in most LAC countries follows the same trend of adults, as LAC countries with low rates of adult tobacco use also tend to experience lower levels among young people. For instance, like the adult population in the LAC region, numerous countries in the LAC report a tobacco use prevalence below 15% for young people aged 13 to 15. The countries with the lowest proportion of young people who use tobacco in LAC include El Salvador, Peru, and Costa Rica. Conversely, some countries exhibit a high prevalence of tobacco use among young people, akin to the adult population. The LAC countries with the highest proportion of young people using tobacco are found in Argentina and Chile, where 20% and 25%, respectively of people aged 13 to 15 are tobacco users.

The average age of initiation of smoking does not seem to be correlated with the prevalence of tobacco use amongst young people (aged 13 to 15) in LAC countries. At the same time, while the age of initiation for daily smokers hovers around 16 to 18, the risk of starting daily smoking begins in pre-adolescence. A 2023 report of three Latin American countries, including Argentina, Brazil and Mexico, shows a positive likelihood of initiation around aged 12 or 13, with a peak at age 17 (Franco-Churruarin and González-Rozada, 2023[17]). The average age of daily smoking initiation is 18.8 in Mexico, 17.0 in Argentina, 17.0 in Brazil, 16.9 in Panama, 16.3 in Uruguay and 16.1 in Costa Rica (Franco-Churruarin and González-Rozada, 2023[17]; Government of Costa Rica, 2017[11]; Government of Mexico, 2023[7]; Government of Panama, 2013[8]; Government of Uruguay, 2017[9]).

Figure 1.7. Prevalence of tobacco use by age

Prevalence of tobacco use amongst young people (13-15 years old) versus adult population (aged 15 and older), 2022

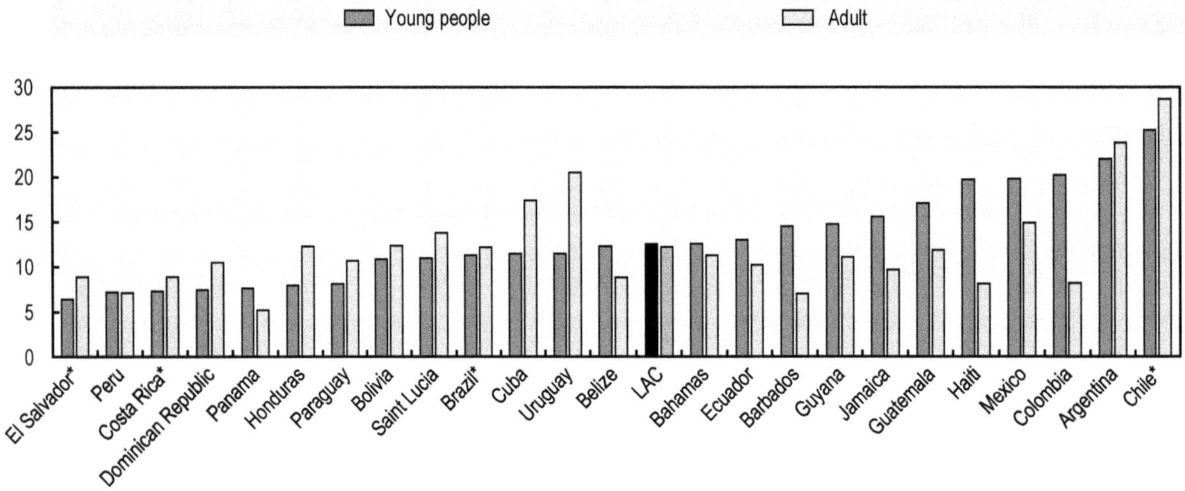

Note: Tobacco products include cigarettes, pipes, cigars, cigarillos, waterpipes (hookah, shisha), bidis, kretek, heated tobacco products, and all forms of smokeless (oral and nasal) tobacco. Tobacco products exclude e-cigarettes (which do not contain tobacco), e-cigars, e-hookahs, and e-pipes. Data for adults are age-standardized to the WHO standard population. The LAC average was calculated as the average of the countries included in the figure.
Source: WHO Global Health Observatory Data Repository (WHO, 2024[11]). Countries with an asterisk did not have data on prevalence for young people from the Global Health Observatory, so were extracted from Health at a Glance: Latin America and the Caribbean (OECD/The World Bank, 2023[18]).

Electronic cigarette usage stands out as a prevalent form of nicotine product among LAC youth (Figure 1.8). On average, 8% of individuals aged 13 to 15 currently consume nicotine in the form of electronic cigarette (e-cigarette[2]) in LAC. Trinidad and Tobago have the highest prevalence of e-cigarette use during the past 30 days (nearly 18% of youth use e-cigarettes), followed by Paraguay (12%) (Figure 1.8). Traditional cigarettes are the second-most common method of nicotine consumption amongst young people, with 7.7% of youth aged 13 to 15 opting for this form of nicotine. Argentina, Mexico, and Haiti have the highest prevalence of cigarette smoking among young people aged 13-15, ranging from 14% to 18%. Conversely, Antigua and Barbuda, the Dominican Republic, and Paraguay have the lowest prevalence of cigarette smoking among young people, all under 3%. Smokeless tobacco has a smaller prevalence compared to cigarette smoking and e-cigarettes, with Venezuela and Dominica having the highest prevalence of smokeless tobacco for children, at around 8% each (Figure 1.8).

Figure 1.8. Nicotine delivery product used by young people

Prevalence of current tobacco use (in the past 30 days) among young people aged 13-15, by nicotine product

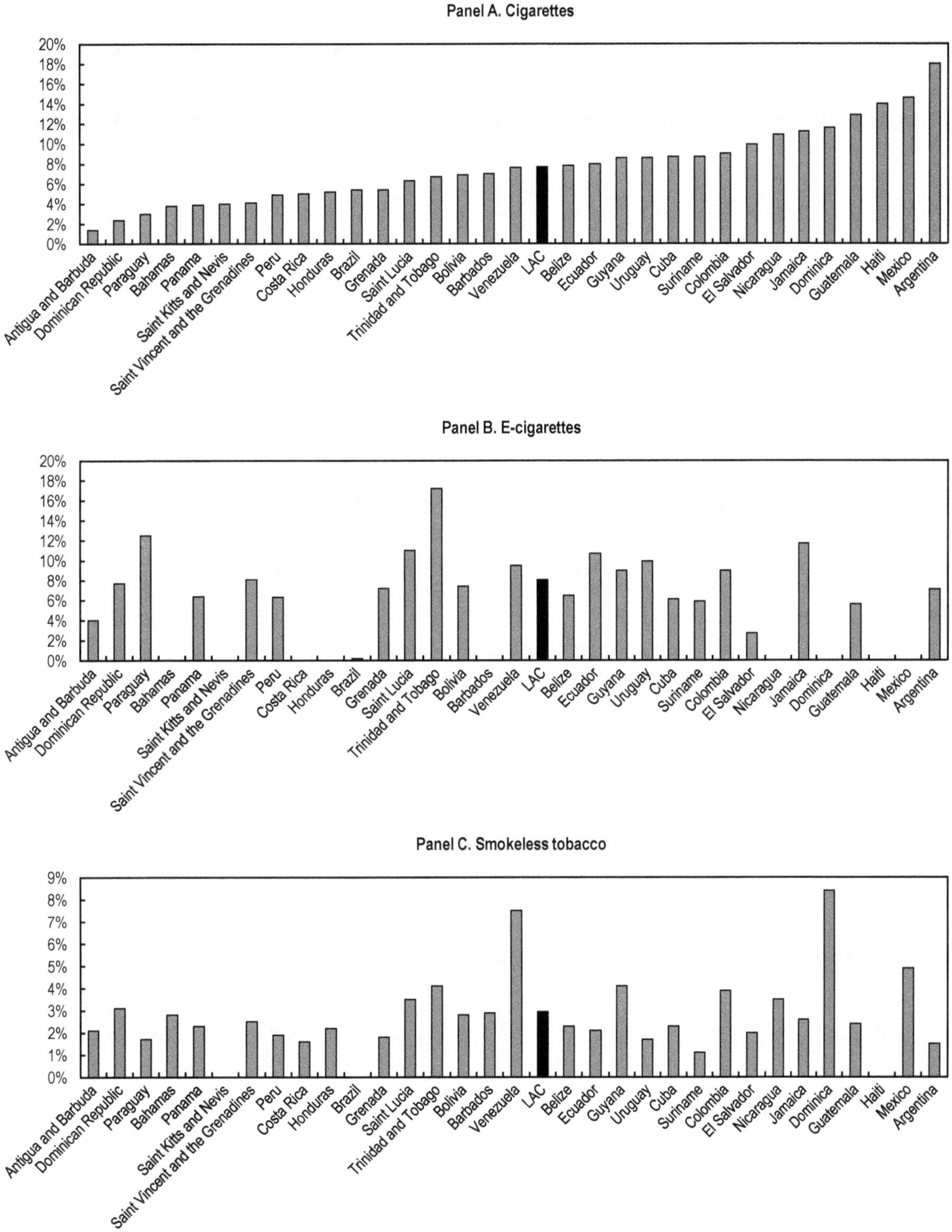

Note: All data came from the most updated Global Youth Tobacco Survey for young people aged 13-15. Data ranges from 2009 until 2019.
Source: Data for prevalence was extracted from the WHO Global Health Observatory Data Repository (WHO, 2024[1]).

1.4. Negative impacts of tobacco use

Tobacco consumption is the leading cause of preventable death and disability and a major driver of health costs and lost productivity. Users of tobacco are at risk of a variety of poor health outcomes over their life course, including non-communicable diseases. As there is no proven safe level of tobacco consumption (United States government, 2017[19]), tobacco smoking has adverse effects on both the individual- and population-level. Different types of costs are attributable to tobacco smoking, specifically:

- Health burden including cardiovascular diseases, chronic obstructive pulmonary disease (COPD) and cancers;
- Health expenditure caused by smoking-related diseases or second-hand smoke. In addition, addressing nicotine addiction is also cause of additional treatment costs;
- Productivity losses generated by reduced workforce participation due to increased ill health and mortality caused by tobacco-related diseases, both for the caregiver and individual themself.

1.4.1. The health burden of tobacco use

Every year, over 350 000 individuals die from tobacco use and second-hand smoke in the LAC region (Table 1.1). Estimates suggest that second-hand smoke alone is responsible for over 52 000 deaths every year, equating to approximately 3% of adult deaths in the LAC region. While the number of deaths attributed to tobacco use and second-hand smoke varies greatly across the region due to differing population sizes in each country, some countries have higher proportions of deaths from second-hand smoke than others. For example, Guatemala, Nicaragua, and Chile all have rates above 20%, meaning that 20% of tobacco-related deaths in these countries are attributed to second-hand smoke. In contrast, countries with the smallest fraction of deaths from second-hand smoke include Barbados, Uruguay, and the Dominican Republic, each at around 11%. Estimates also suggest that nearly 70 million smokers are at risk of tobacco-related death and disease in the region (Astudillo, Cruces and Puig, 2022[20]).

Table 1.1. Deaths attributed to tobacco use

2021

	Number of deaths attributed to tobacco consumption	Number of deaths attributed to second-hand smoke	Percentage of tobacco-related deaths caused by second-hand smoke	Total deaths
Antigua and Barbuda	31	6	16%	37
Argentina	30 745	5 313	15%	36 058
Bahamas	137	23	14%	160
Barbados	119	15	11%	134
Belize	106	18	14%	124
Bermuda	51	7	12%	58
Bolivia	3 090	614	17%	3 703
Brazil	134 182	20 638	13%	154 820
Chile	7 142	1 826	20%	8 967
Colombia	13 226	2 711	17%	15 937
Costa Rica	1 575	237	13%	1 812
Cuba	15 271	2 430	14%	17 701
Dominica	32	6	16%	37
Dominican Republic	6 362	765	11%	7 127
Ecuador	3 605	628	15%	4 234
El Salvador	1 549	351	18%	1 900
Grenada	39	8	16%	47
Guatemala	3 057	885	22%	3 942
Guyana	311	65	17%	375
Haiti	2 934	691	19%	3 624
Honduras	4 139	913	18%	5 052
Jamaica	1 259	229	15%	1 487
Mexico	39 509	8 020	17%	47 529
Nicaragua	1 280	341	21%	1 621
Panama	991	161	14%	1 151
Paraguay	3 955	592	13%	4 548
Peru	6 800	1 127	14%	7 927
Saint Kitts and Nevis	19	4	17%	23
Saint Lucia	76	11	12%	87
Saint Vincent and the Grenadines	49	10	16%	59
Suriname	332	63	16%	395
Trinidad and Tobago	892	196	18%	1 088
Uruguay	3 801	479	11%	4 280
Venezuela	14 085	2 881	17%	16 966
Total	300 749	52 261	16%	353 010

Source: Global Burden of Disease Collaborative Network. Global Burden of Disease Study 2021 (Institute for Health Metrics and Evaluation, 2024[21]).

Tobacco consumption poses a significant health challenge in the LAC region. The ten most common causes of death due to tobacco use include ischemic heart disease, COPD, tracheal, bronchus, and lung cancer, stroke, lower respiratory infections, diabetes mellitus, larynx cancer, aortic aneurysm, oesophageal cancer and stomach cancer (Figure 1.9). This group of conditions contribute to 88% of the tobacco-associated deaths in the region. In the LAC region, nearly 70 000 tobacco users die each year from ischemic heart disease (26% of tobacco-related deaths per year), followed by COPD (16%) and tracheal, bronchus and lung cancers (14%).

Figure 1.9. Tobacco-related cause of death among tobacco users

Ten most prevalent tobacco-related causes of death in LAC countries, 2021

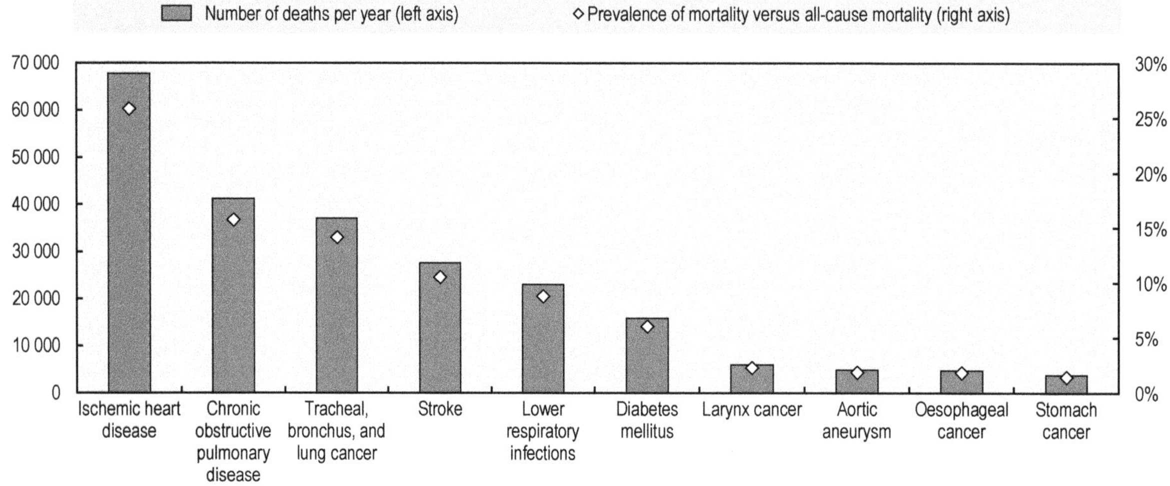

Note: The left-hand side y-axis illustrates the number of deaths per year. The right-hand side y-axis illustrates the percentage of the condition as a fraction of all-cause mortality in 2021, encompassing all ages and both sexes in aggregated LAC counties.
Source: Global Burden of Disease Collaborative Network. Global Burden of Disease Study 2021 (Institute for Health Metrics and Evaluation, 2024[21]).

While ischemic heart disease is the most common cause of death for tobacco users, tobacco smoking is the primary contributing risk factor for lung cancer and a variety of other respiratory illnesses, such as COPD. In LAC countries, over 40% of the cases of respiratory cancers are attributable to tobacco use (Figure 1.10), though this figure varies between 21% in Haiti to 62% in Uruguay and Paraguay. This pattern mirrors what is observed in the prevalence of tobacco use, seen in Figure 1.1, whereby the countries with the lowest prevalence of tobacco use also have the lowest rates of respiratory cancers and vice versa.

Figure 1.10. Tracheal, bronchus, and lung cancers attributable to tobacco use

Percent of tracheal, bronchus, and lung cancers attributable to tobacco use, 2021

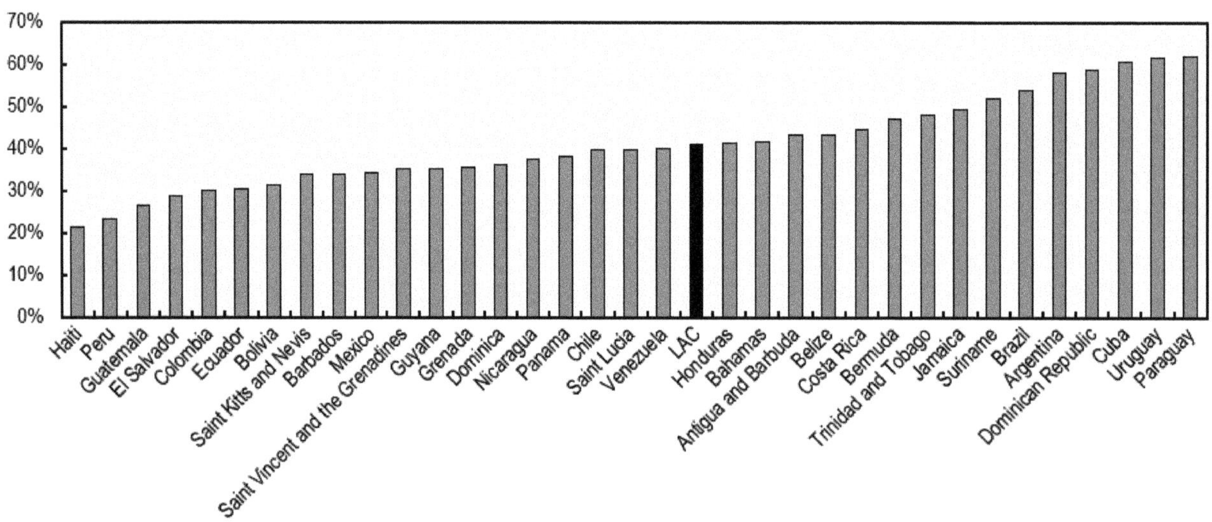

Source: Global Burden of Disease Collaborative Network. Global Burden of Disease Study 2021 (Institute for Health Metrics and Evaluation, 2024[21]).

1.4.2. The impact of tobacco-related diseases on health expenditure

Health expenditure primarily results from the treatment of the conditions associated with tobacco use. The health expenditure associated with tobacco use encompasses expenses for hospitalisation, outpatient care, medications and therapies for individuals affected by tobacco-related diseases. Moreover, addressing nicotine addiction incurs additional treatment costs, encompassing counselling services, nicotine replacement therapy, and medications like nicotine patches or prescription drugs designed to assist individuals in quitting smoking. Further, apart from the health expenses incurred by smokers themselves, there are also costs associated with providing health to individuals exposed to second-hand smoke, particularly children and non-smoking adults. There are also environmental costs that are associated with tobacco use – ranging from the impact of tobacco production and manufacturing to the management of waste throughout and after production. These means that many estimates do not account for a range of additional costs, leading to significant underestimation of tobacco costs, particularly in countries with extensive tobacco cultivation.

Annual smoking-attributable medical costs in LAC countries vary significantly from one country to another (Table 1.2). Uruguay, Paraguay, Chile, and Bolivia stand out with the highest smoking-attributable medical costs as a proportion of gross domestic product (GDP), amounting to 1.5% for Uruguay and 0.8% for the others (Pichon-Riviere et al., 2020[22]). Conversely, Honduras demonstrates the lowest per capita cost of smoking, with annual smoking-attributable medical costs equivalent to 0.3% of annual GDP, representing 3.5% of total health expenditure. This discrepancy correlates with variations in smoking intensity per capita, where Uruguay, Paraguay, and Chile have relatively high smoking intensity and/or tobacco use prevalence rates, while Honduras ranks lower (see Figure 1.3). Note that the low ranking of Honduras could be an artifact of the capacity of the health infrastructure and, therefore, may not accurately represent the true costs needed to address smoking-attributable medical expenses. Despite the catastrophic economic and public health impact of tobacco use in the LAC region, amounting to a predicted annual USD 27 billion, only about a third of the cost is covered through tobacco taxes, on average (see also Box 1.1).

Table 1.2. Smoking-attributable medical costs

Percent of total health expenditure and GDP represented by smoking-attributable medical costs, proportion recovered through tobacco taxes, per capita cost of smoking-attributable medical costs in 2015

	Annual smoking-attributable medical costs				Proportion of annual smoking-attributable medical costs recovered through tobacco excise taxes
	Total costs, USD millions	Per capita cost, USD	As a proportion of total health expenditure	As a proportion of GDP	
Argentina	3 817	88	7.3%	0.6%	55%
Bolivia	250	23	11.8%	0.8%	6%
Brazil	11 830	567	5.7%	0.7%	26%
Chile	1 901	106	9.4%	0.8%	79%
Colombia	1 709	35	9.7%	0.6%	10%
Costa Rica	242	50	5.7%	0.4%	26%
Ecuador	476	30	5.6%	0.5%	41%
Honduras	56	7	3.5%	0.3%	52%
Mexico	4 768	37	8.0%	0.4%	47%
Paraguay	301	45	10.7%	0.8%	20%
Peru	796	25	8.0%	0.4%	9%
Uruguay	800	233	16.7%	1.5%	26%
All 12 countries	**26 946**	**51**	**6.9%**	**0.6%**	**36%**

Note: All costs are in 2015 USD million. Information for this table was acquired from Table 1 and Table 3 of the source cited below.
Source: Adapted from (Pichon-Riviere et al., 2020[22]).

Box 1.1. Current tobacco taxes and economic losses associated with tobacco use

Two studies have computed the tax revenue and costs associated with tobacco use. They conclude that existing tobacco tax revenues account for only a fraction of the economic costs attributed to tobacco use.

A 2023 study concluded that current tobacco taxes cover 15% of the economic losses in the LAC region (using data from eight selected countries: Argentina, Brazil, Chile, Colombia, Costa Rica, Ecuador, Mexico and Peru). This study estimated that while all eight countries were far from recovering the costs generated by tobacco consumption through tobacco taxation, recovery shares ranged from as low as 4.4% in Peru to 29.2% in Chile. Costs accounted for in this study included productivity losses due to premature death and disability, caregiver's costs, and medical costs (Pichon-Riviere et al., 2023[23]).

Another study concluded that tax revenue generated from cigarette sales accounted for 36% of the estimated health costs attributed to smoking in 12 LAC countries in 2015 (Argentina, Bolivia, Brazil, Chile, Colombia, Costa Rica, Ecuador, Honduras, Mexico, Paraguay, Peru and Uruguay) (Table 1.2). Expenses covered both medical costs and reductions in quality of life linked to prevalent tobacco-related diseases (Pichon-Riviere et al., 2020[22]).

As such, increasing cigarette prices through taxation would yield significant health and economic benefits. For example, it was calculated that implementing a 50% increase in cigarette prices through taxation across 12 LAC countries would potentially prevent over 300 000 deaths, reduce the occurrence of 1.3 million disease events, and gain 9 million healthy life-years, and lead to savings of USD 27 billion in health expenses over the next decade (Pichon-Riviere et al., 2020[22]). The cumulative economic value of such an initiative would amount to USD 44 billion in the LAC region (Pichon-Riviere et al., 2023[23]).

Source: (Pichon-Riviere et al., 2020[22]); (Pichon-Riviere et al., 2023[23]).

1.4.3. Productivity losses associated with tobacco use

The lost human capital that results from tobacco-attributable morbidity and mortality are as large as the health costs at a societal level (WHO, 2022[24]). This includes the broader social and economic consequences of smoking, such as reduced productivity due to absenteeism at work with negative economic consequences for both the employer and the employee. Estimates suggest that these other costs account for more than 50% of the total economic burden associated with tobacco use (Pichon-Riviere et al., 2023[23]) (Figure 1.11). A study of eight LAC countries that account for health and economic costs concluded that the economic losses associated with tobacco use equate to USD 50 billion (Pichon-Riviere et al., 2023[23]). The size of this economic loss attributable to tobacco represents 1.4% of the combined GDP of Argentina, Brazil, Chile, Colombia, Costa Rica, Ecuador, Mexico, and Peru (countries accounting for 80% of the Latin American population).

Figure 1.11. Annual economic cost attributable to tobacco use

Annual economic cost attributable to tobacco use by source, as a percentage of total cost, 2020

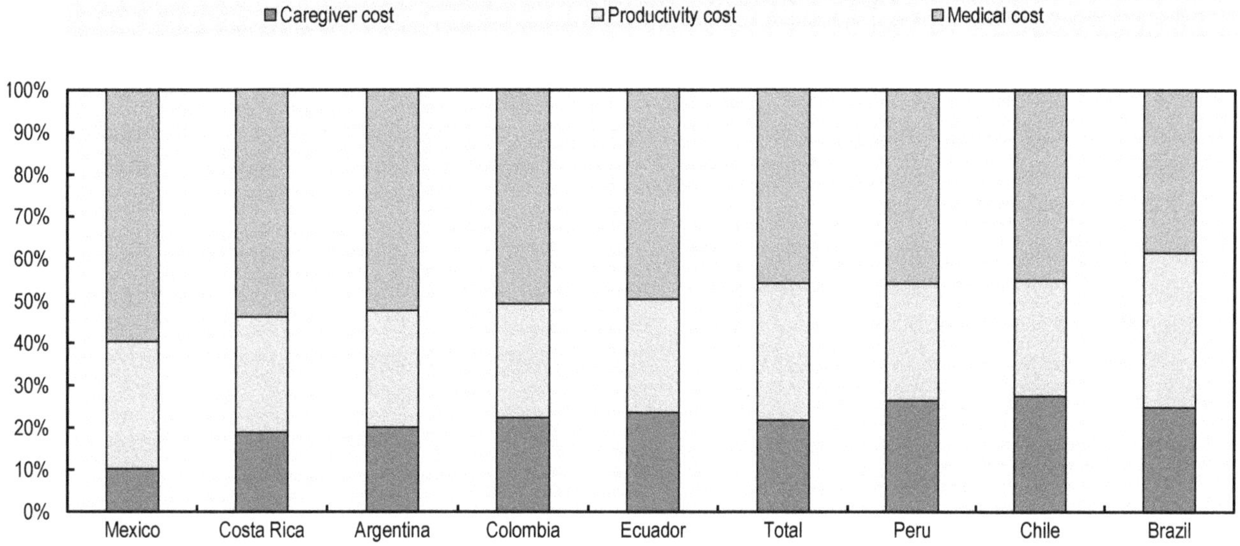

Source: Data adapted from (Pichon-Riviere et al., 2023[23]).

1.5. Tobacco control policies in LAC countries

Many factors have contributed to the decrease in tobacco use in the LAC region. Among these factors are widespread anti-smoking campaigns, public health initiatives, and smoking bans which have improved awareness of the health risks associated with tobacco use, increased the price, and decreased the accessibility of tobacco products (Rodriguez-Iglesias and Chaloupka, 2018[25]; Sandoval et al., 2022[26]). Some countries have also combined interventions in comprehensive tobacco control programmes which included policies such as graphic warnings on tobacco packaging, smoking bans in public spaces, and increased tobacco taxes (WHO, 2019[27]).

Tax and non-tax measures are complementary and interact to determine overall success of government tobacco interventions. While taxes are the most effective method to reduce tobacco use, non-tax measures are also necessary for effective and long-term success in tobacco use cessation (Hutchinson et al., 2022[28]; Paraje, Muñoz and Pruzzo, 2023[29]). As such, although the rest of this report focuses primarily on tobacco policy in the form of taxation, it does not mean that non-tax reforms are not needed.

The WHO Framework Convention on Tobacco Control (WHO FCTC) establishes guidelines aimed at addressing the tobacco epidemic and implementing tobacco control measures. Assessing the degree of WHO FCTC implementation can serve as a benchmark for a country's performance in this regard. The MPOWER policy package offers a means to benchmark countries based on their adherence to these guidelines (Box 1.2) (WHO, 2020[30]).

Box 1.2. WHO Framework Convention on Tobacco Control (FCTC) and MPOWER policy package

The WHO FCTC was developed in 2005 in response to the globalization of the tobacco epidemic. It aims to tackle some of the causes of that epidemic, including complex factors with cross-border effects, such as trade liberalization and direct foreign investment, tobacco advertising, promotion and sponsorship beyond national borders, and illicit trade in tobacco products. It is the first international public health treaty negotiated under WHO auspices and contains guidelines and requirements for the implementation of the most cost-effective tobacco control measures available necessary for reducing the tobacco epidemic.

Some of the key interventions that Parties to the WHO FCTC are required to implement include the importance of tobacco taxes and price measures (Article 6); protection from second-hand smoke in all indoor workplaces and public places and public transportation (Article 8); large graphic health warnings on the packaging of tobacco products (Article 11); and a comprehensive ban on tobacco advertising, sponsorship, and promotion (Article 13).

These measures can be considered the starting point for the comprehensive implementation of the Convention. The treaty also addresses several other issues, including the disclosure and regulation of ingredients in tobacco products, forbidding the sale of tobacco products by or to minors, treatment for tobacco addiction, research, and exchange of information among countries and promoting public awareness.

While the WHO's FCTC guidelines provide the foundation for countries to implement and manage tobacco control, the MPOWER policy package was developed in 2007 to provide the tools necessary for action on tobacco control. The MPOWER measures are used to assist in the country-level implementation of effective interventions to reduce the demand for tobacco. The acronym represents the following:

Monitoring tobacco use and prevention policies.

Protecting people from tobacco smoke.

Offer help to quit tobacco use.

Warn about the dangers of tobacco.

Enforce bans on tobacco advertising, promotion, and sponsorship.

Raise taxes on tobacco.

As of 2023, 183 parties have ratified the FCTC treaty. All LAC countries except Argentina, Cuba, the Dominican Republic and Haiti are Parties of the WHO FCTC. The implementation of tobacco control measures has progressed in recent years, especially in low- and middle-income countries where the heaviest burden of smoking is concentrated. Currently, over half of the world's population benefits from large graphic health warnings on tobacco packages, and one-third have access to cessation services provided at best-practice levels.

Source: WHO 2021 global progress report on implementation of the WHO Framework Convention on Tobacco Control (WHO, 2022[24]); WHO report on the global tobacco epidemic (WHO, 2021[31]); OECD Health at Glance 2021 (OECD, 2021[32]).

The MPOWER policy package facilitates the assessment of effective tobacco control policies across countries. All the columns of Table 1.3 report the level of implementation in the country for each of the six policies identified in the MPOWER strategy. Each MPOWER policy area is scored per criteria outlined in Annex Table 1.A.1 where the colour scheme signifies performance levels, with the darkest blue denoting the implementation of a best practice, followed by lighter blues, corresponding to a lower performance category in the respective policy area.

Table 1.3. MPOWER policy package

Status of the WHO FCTC in LAC countries and a summary of applying the MPOWER policy package, 2022 data release

	M	P	O	W		E	R	
Country	Monitoring	Smoking bans*	Cessation services	Health warnings	Mass media	Advertising bans*	Taxation	Cigarettes less affordable since 2012
Antigua and Barbuda		6				8	14.9%	↔
Argentina		8				6	76.5%	↔
Bahamas		–				...	53.6%	Yes
Barbados		10				–	43.0%	↔
Belize		–				–	33.6%	↔
Bolivia							31.5%	...
Brazil		7				8	80.2%	No
Chile		8				9	80.3%	Yes
Colombia		5				6	65.2%	Yes
Costa Rica		8				8	55.1%	↔
Cuba		5				–	10.0%	↔
Dominica		–				–	26.1%	Yes
Dominican Republic		3				–	44.7%	↔
Ecuador		5				7	64.0%	Yes
El Salvador		5				7	45.7%	Yes
Grenada		–				–	44.0%	No
Guatemala		5				...	49.0%	↔
Guyana		3				5	24.9%	↔
Haiti		–				–	27.1%	...
Honduras		6				...	38.3%	Yes
Jamaica		5				...	38.8%	↔
Mexico		8				4	67.6%	↔
Nicaragua		6				...	75.7%	Yes
Panama		10				10	56.5%	↔
Paraguay		7				5	19.2%	↔
Peru		8				...	73.3%	↔
Saint Kitts and Nevis		–				–	19.8%	↔
Saint Lucia		6				–	43.1%	↔
Saint Vincent and the Grenadines		–				–	23.2%	↔
Suriname		3				7	49.3%	Yes
Trinidad and Tobago		5				8	27.5%	Yes
Uruguay		10		☆		9	65.5%	↔
Venezuela		8				9	73.4%	...

Notes: For the definitions and the colours of the classification of the interventions, see Annex 1.A to this chapter.

Data for each indicator was assessed by the WHO on 31 December 2022. Exceptions to this cutoff date were tobacco product prices and taxes (cut-off date 31 July 2022) and anti-tobacco mass media campaigns (cut-off date 30 June 2022).

* Numbers represent levels of compliance (out of 10 possible, where 0 represents the lowest and 10 represents the highest score) = 8-10 represent complete compliance; 3-7 represent moderate compliance; 0-2 represent minimal compliance.

☆ Plain packaging is mandated.

... Data not reported/not available.

– Data not required/not applicable.

The measure R applies to cigarettes only while the other measures apply to all tobacco products.

Affordability of cigarettes: Yes = Cigarettes less affordable – per capita GDP needed to buy 2 000 cigarettes of the most sold brand increased on average between 2012 and 2022; No = Cigarettes more affordable – per capita GDP needed to buy 2 000 cigarettes of the most sold brand declined on average between 2012 and 2022. ↔ = No trend changes in affordability of cigarettes between 2012 and 2022.
Source: Adapted from WHO report on the global tobacco epidemic (WHO, 2023[33]).

Countries in LAC have made substantial progress in implementing the MPOWER policy package. Of the 33 countries in the LAC region, 25 countries have achieved the highest level of application of at least one measure of the MPOWER policy package (Table 1.3). Brazil outperforms the other LAC countries, with the highest application across all MPOWER measures. Uruguay follows with five MPOWER measures, then Chile, Costa Rica, Mexico, and Panama follow, each attaining the highest application on four of the MPOWER policy measures. Conversely, the countries with the lowest achievement across the MPOWER policy package are the Bahamas, Belize, Dominica, the Dominican Republic, Grenada, Haiti, Saint Kitts and Nevis, and Saint Vincent and the Grenadines.

Only seven LAC countries have fully implemented tobacco consumption monitoring policies (measure M). This means that only these seven countries possess surveillance systems that provide up-to-date, regular, and comprehensive data regarding tobacco consumption among both adult and youth populations. Monitoring tobacco use has been hampered by the COVID-19 pandemic as data collection efforts were hindered between the years of 2020 to 2022, as was the release of results for surveys completed before and during the pandemic (WHO, 2023[33]). This clarifies the decrease in the number of countries achieving higher MPOWER implementation levels in the 2022 data compared to the 2020 data. While only five countries, including Barbados, Belize, Dominica, Haiti, and Saint Kitts and Nevis, lacked recent representative data on tobacco use prevalence among adults and youth in the 2020 report, the 2022 survey reveals that 10 countries lacked such data. These countries are Barbados, Belize, Dominica, the Dominican Republic, Grenada, Guatemala, Guyana, Honduras, Saint Kitts and Nevis, and Suriname (Table 1.3).

Most countries in the LAC region have successfully established smoke-free environments (measure P). Compared to other WHO regions, the LAC region has implemented measure P at the highest level of application (as of 31 December 2022) (WHO, 2023[33]). Countries with the highest standards in this category have completely smoke-free public places, indoor workplaces, and public transportation. There are, however, seven countries (Bahamas, Belize, Dominica, Grenada, Haiti, Saint Kitts and Nevis, and Saint Vincent and the Grenadines) that do not have bans to ensure that at least two types of public spaces and workplaces are completely smoke-free. The most common public spaces for which no smoking ban is enforced among these seven countries include health facilities, educational facilities, and universities (WHO, 2023[33]).

Only about 10% of LAC countries reach best practice in cessation services (measure O). Only four countries (Brazil, Costa Rica, Jamaica, and Mexico) have a national quit line, and offer nicotine replacement treatment and other cessation services cost-covered. The majority of countries fall into the two middle categories of implementation, meaning that nicotine replacement treatment and/or some cessation services are available though neither are cost-covered or that nicotine replacement treatment and/or some cessation services are available and at least one of them is cost-covered (WHO, 2023[33]). Four countries provide no cessation services (Antigua and Barbuda, Dominica, Grenada, and Haiti).

The LAC region has succeeded in the packaging and labelling of tobacco products and the implementation of anti-tobacco national mass media campaigns (measure W with two subcategories for health warnings and mass media). Nineteen LAC countries that achieved best practice in this measure have warnings that cover an average of at least 50% of the front and the back of the packaging with all the appropriate characteristics. Conversely, nine countries (Bahamas, Belize, Dominica, the Dominican Republic, Grenada, Guatemala, Haiti, Saint Kitts and Nevis, Saint Vincent and the Grenadines) fall into the lowest implementation category for this measure. This implies that these countries lack mandatory tobacco warnings or have small warnings (averaging less than 30% on the front and back). Additionally, they have not executed a national anti-tobacco campaign lasting at least three weeks between July 2020 and June 2022.

Less than one-third of LAC countries have achieved the highest level of implementation for comprehensive monitoring and enforcement of bans on tobacco advertising, promotion, and sponsorship (measure E). While nine countries in the LAC region implement measures relating to tobacco advertising, promotion, and sponsorship at the highest level of application, 16 countries have a complete absence of a ban or enforce a ban that does not at least cover national television, radio, and print media.

Only four LAC countries have achieved the highest level of implementation for the share of indirect taxes in the retail price of tobacco products (measure R). To reach best practice, the indirect tax share that consists of tobacco excise taxes but also other indirect taxes such as the value added tax (VAT), should reach at least 75% of the retail price. Only four countries (Argentina, Brazil, Chile, and Nicaragua) have achieved best practice in this component (Table 1.3 and Figure 1.12). More than half of the countries (20) receive a low R score as the tax share stays below 50% of the retail price. Of these twenty countries, six countries including Antigua and Barbuda, Cuba, Guyana, Paraguay, Saint Kitts and Nevis, Saint Vincent and the Grenadines, have tax shares below 25% of the retail price, with Cuba having the lowest tax share at 10% (Table 1.3 and Figure 1.12).

1.6. Effectiveness of tobacco tax policy in raising cigarette prices

The MPOWER R underlying assumption is that a high tax share reflects a high level of taxes and, therefore, a high tax-inclusive price of cigarettes. As such, this indicator recognises that increased prices of tobacco as a result of high taxes is one of the most effective tools to reduce tobacco use (Ngo et al., 2022[34]; Sandoval et al., 2022[35]). High prices will create an incentive for smokers to quit or reduce smoking and deter potential smokers from starting. Additionally, higher prices make cigarettes less affordable and discourage youth from starting to smoke.

With a few exceptions, the indirect tax share in retail prices remains relatively low in countries in LAC, at least when compared to the WHO 75% tax share target. In 2022, the tobacco tax share was 46.7% of the retail price of the most sold brand of cigarettes on average across countries in LAC (Figure 1.12). While the weighted average price of cigarettes is usually preferred over the most sold brand of cigarettes to capture market shares, this data is not accessible for all LAC countries. Hence, the rest of the report uses most sold brands of cigarettes prices.

Surprisingly, LAC countries that meet the R target have lower cigarette prices than countries with more moderate tax shares (Figure 1.13). Countries with a tobacco tax share above 75% have, on average, lower cigarette prices (USD purchasing power parity PPP 5.9) than countries with tobacco tax shares between 25% and 75% (USD PPP 7.4 and 8.2, respectively). For instance, Brazil is the country with the second highest tobacco tax share (80%) (Figure 1.12) in the LAC region but is also the country with the second lowest cigarette retail prices (USD PPP 2.1) (Figure 1.13) with cigarettes remaining very affordable (Figure 1.14). Hence, there is no guarantee that cigarette will be expensive (i.e. with high prices) in countries that meet the 75% tax share target. This is why the cigarette tax scorecard was developed to consider jointly cigarettes prices, affordability, tax share and excise tax structure (Drope et al., 2024[36]).

On the other hand, LAC countries that are the worst R performers have the lowest cigarette prices in the region (Figure 1.13). LAC countries with a tobacco tax share below 25% are also the countries where, on average, cigarette prices are the lowest (USD PPP 4.6). For the under-performers, the tax share R indicator performs better in signalling the ineffectiveness of tobacco tax policies.

Figure 1.12. Share of indirect taxes of the most sold brand of cigarettes

Total indirect taxes as % of the retail price of the most sold brand of cigarettes, 2022

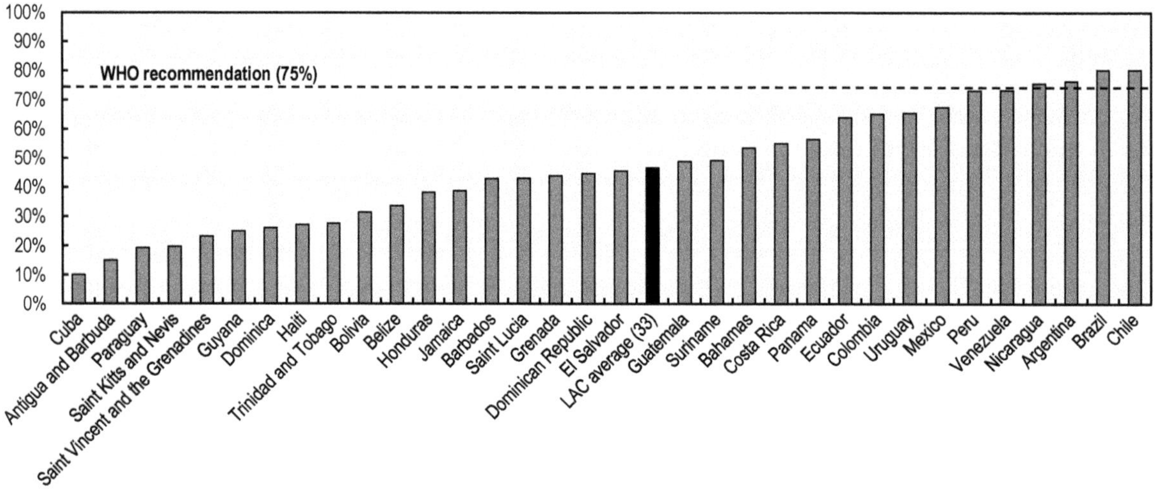

Note: Total indirect taxes include excise taxes, VAT, import duties, and any other indirect taxes. The most sold brand of cigarettes is determined based on national market share information and varies across countries.
Source: WHO report on the global tobacco epidemic (WHO, 2023[33]).

Figure 1.13. Breakdown of the retail price of the most sold brand of cigarettes

Total indirect taxes and pre-tax prices in USD PPP, for the most sold brand of cigarettes, 2022

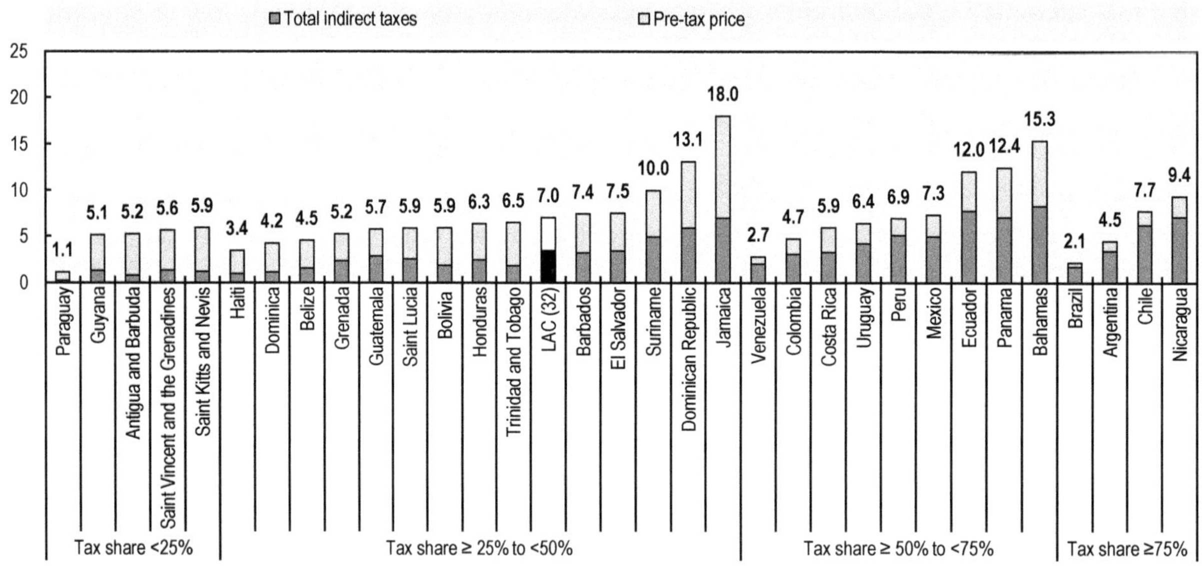

Note: Total indirect taxes include excise taxes, VAT, import duties, and any other indirect taxes. Pre-tax prices are defined as the retail price for a pack of 20 cigarettes of the most sold brand minus the indirect taxes levied on this brand. Prices in USD PPP are based on the implied PPP conversion rate from the International Monetary Fund (IMF) World Economic Outlook Database (October 2023). Cuba has been excluded due to missing USD PPP implied conversion rate. The most sold brand of cigarettes is determined based on national market share information and varies across countries.
Source: WHO report on the global tobacco epidemic (WHO, 2023[33]); IMF World Economic Outlook Database (IMF, 2023[37]).

In order to measure the effectiveness of tobacco tax policies and reforms, the MPOWER R indicator has to be complemented with an indicator that measures the affordability of tobacco products. There is not necessarily a positive correlation between the tax share and cigarette prices (Chaloupka et al., 2021[38]). Moreover, the tobacco tax share and cigarette prices do not provide sufficient information on consumer's capacity to buy cigarettes. The tax share and the price level should therefore be complemented with an indicator of affordability. Against this background, the implementation of the MPOWER policy package includes information on the change in the affordability indicator between 2012 and 2022 (WHO, 2023[33]). The extent to which cigarettes are affordable is typically measured as the required GDP per capita to buy 2 000 cigarettes of the most sold brand (or the cheapest or premium brand) of cigarettes in a country and in a particular year (Blecher, 2020[39]). Cigarette affordability varies significantly in countries in LAC (Figure 1.14).

Tax shares and cigarette affordability are not positively correlated, on the contrary. For instance, in countries where the tax share exceeds 50%, cigarettes from the most sold brand are more affordable (4.2% of GDP per capita is required to purchase 2 000 cigarettes) than in countries with a tax share between 25-50% (6.2% of GDP per capita is required to purchase 2 000 cigarettes) (Figure 1.14). However, in countries where the tax share is the lowest, tobacco products are also the most affordable for all types of brands (Figure 1.14 and Figure 1.15).

Figure 1.14. Cigarette affordability

Percentage of GDP per capita required to purchase 100 packs of 20 cigarettes of the most sold brand, 2022

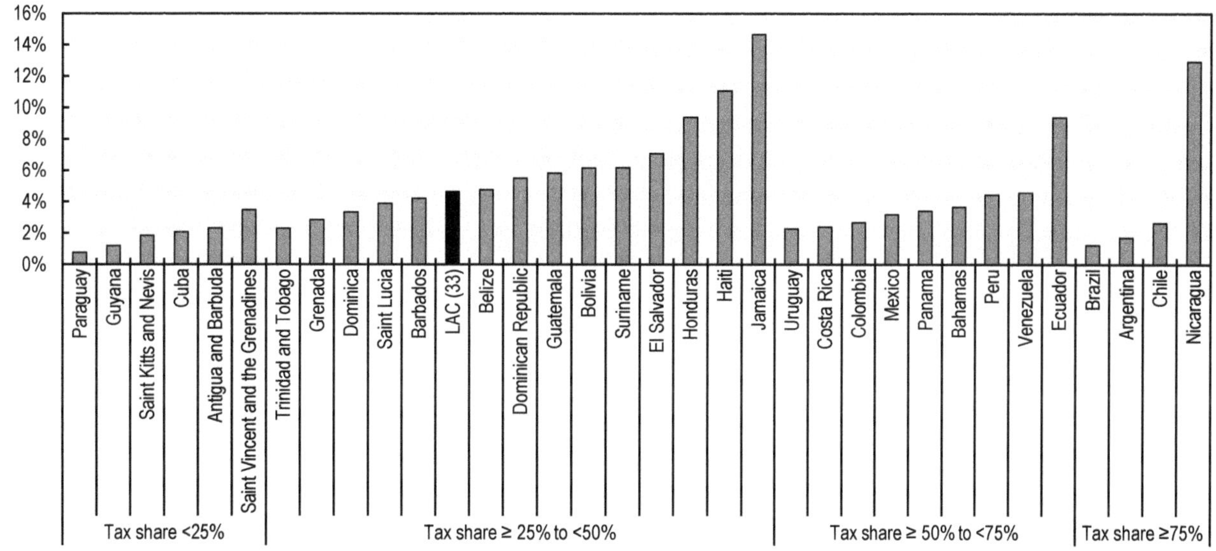

Note: The affordability indicator measures the percentage of the country's GDP per capita required to purchase 100 packs of 20 cigarettes. A higher percentage means lower affordability of cigarettes while a lower percentage means higher affordability. The most sold brand of cigarettes is determined based on national market share information and varies across countries.
Source: WHO report on the global tobacco epidemic (WHO, 2023[33]).

In countries with a larger tobacco tax share, tobacco markets are characterised, on average, by lower price dispersion (Figure 1.15). Higher price dispersion across cigarette brands provides smokers with more opportunities to trade down. Rather than to quit or reduce smoking, smokers (especially young people and lower-income population) might smoke cheaper products instead. In countries with a tax share above 50% are characterised, on average, by a lower degree of retail price dispersion than in countries where the tax share is between 25% and 50%, which can be explained by the more common ad valorem structures in countries with a tax share below 50% (see Table 3.1 in Chapter 3).

Figure 1.15. Cigarettes affordability of the cheapest, premium and most sold brands

Percentage of GDP per capita required to purchase 100 packs of 20 cigarettes, 2022

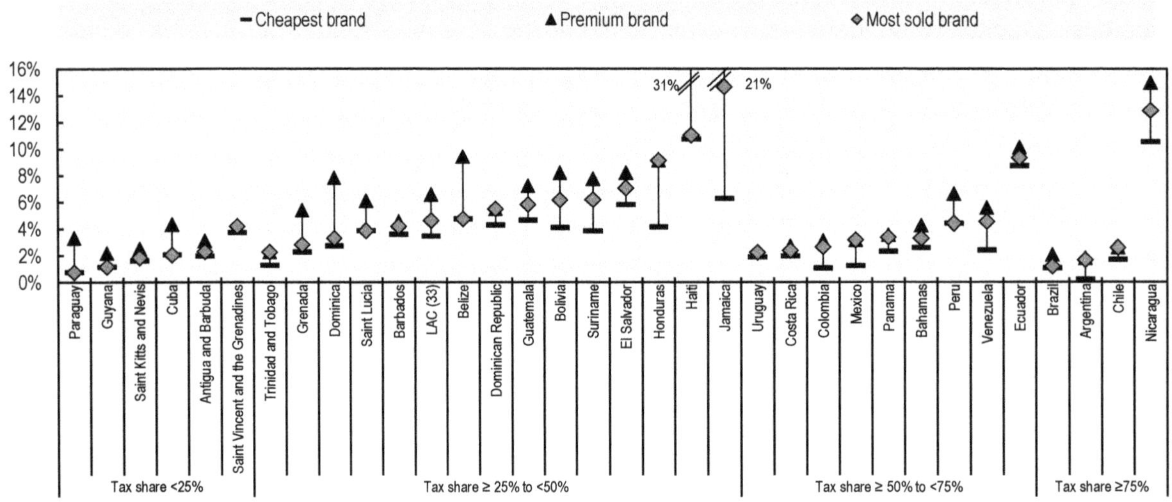

Note: The affordability indicator measures the percentage of the country's GDP per capita required to purchase 100 packs of 20 cigarettes. A higher percentage means lower affordability of cigarettes while a lower percentage means higher affordability. Affordability of the cheapest and premium brands are OECD calculations based on WHO report on the global tobacco epidemic (WHO, 2023[33]). The cheapest, most sold and premium brands of cigarettes are determined based on national market share information and can vary over time (i.e. the cheapest/most sold/premium brands of cigarettes in year 1 can be different from year 2) and across countries.
Source: Adapted from WHO report on the global tobacco epidemic (WHO, 2023[33]).

In most LAC countries, cigarettes have not become less affordable since 2012 (Table 1.4). Cigarettes have become less affordable in ten LAC countries between 2012 and 2022, but only in five countries (Bahamas, Colombia, Dominica, Honduras, Nicaragua) this can be linked to an increase in the tobacco tax share, while they became more affordable over the last ten years in two countries, including in Brazil despite the fact that the tax share in retail prices in Brazil exceeds the best practice of 75% (Table 1.3 and Figure 1.12). There are 14 countries in LAC where cigarettes have not become less affordable, and the tax share has not increased. Overall, this signals that there has been some progress albeit modest on average across the region.

The effectiveness of tobacco tax policy should be evaluated using a multitude of indicators rather than focusing only on the MPOWER R indicator. The relation between the changes in the tax share, retail prices and tobacco affordability are complex and depend on various factors, including tobacco tax reform, the tobacco industry's response (or the absence thereof) to tax reforms and general price strategies, and nominal income growth in a jurisdiction (both inflation and real income growth) (IARC, 2008[40]; Drope, Siu and Chaloupka, 2022[41]). The interaction of these factors, and their impact on affordability and the tax share, which are considered in the cigarette tax scorecard, are discussed in Table 1.5, and this analysis is deepened in Chapter 5. Two key observations can be made:

- If retail prices – either because of tax increases or pre-tax price increases – increase less than nominal income growth, cigarettes do not become less affordable.
- Tax shares might decline even if taxes have increased if the increase in pre-tax retail prices exceeds the tax increase.

Table 1.4. Evolution of the tobacco tax share and cigarette affordability

2012 to 2022

Cigarettes are less affordable since 2012 and the tax share has increased	Cigarettes are less affordable since 2012 but the tax share has not increased	Cigarettes are not less affordable since 2012 despite an increase in the tax share	Cigarettes are not less affordable since 2012 and the tax share has not increased
Bahamas	Chile	Argentina	Antigua and Barbuda
Colombia	Ecuador	Brazil	Barbados
Dominica	El Salvador	Paraguay	Belize
Honduras	Suriname	Peru	Costa Rica
Nicaragua	Trinidad and Tobago	Saint Lucia	Cuba
		Saint Vincent and the Grenadines	Dominican Republic
			Grenada
			Guatemala
			Guyana
			Jamaica
			Mexico
			Panama
			Saint Kitts and Nevis
			Uruguay

Note: Information included in this Table corresponds to the trends in tax share and affordability of the most sold brand of cigarettes. Tobacco tax share corresponds to the portion of total indirect taxes levied on a pack of 20 cigarettes, including excise taxes, VAT, import duties, and any other indirect taxes. The affordability indicator measures the percentage of the country's GDP per capita required to purchase 100 packs of 20 cigarettes. A higher percentage means lower affordability of cigarettes while a lower percentage means higher affordability. To assess whether affordability changed on average since 2012, the average annual percentage change in affordability was calculated as the least squares growth rate for all countries with four or more years of data. The affordability of cigarettes was considered unchanged if the least squares trend in the per capita GDP required to purchase 2 000 cigarettes (that is, 100 packs of 20 cigarettes) was not significant at the 5% level. Cigarettes were considered to have become less (more) affordable on average if the least squares trend in the per capita GDP required to purchase 2 000 cigarettes was positive (negative) and significantly different from zero at the 5% level.
Source: WHO report on the global tobacco epidemic (WHO, 2023[33]).

Table 1.5. Overview of the main features driving the evolution of the tobacco tax share and cigarette affordability

Scenario	Reason(s)
Cigarettes become less affordable and the tax share increases	• Tax increases exceed pre-tax price increases (if any) • Retail price increases exceed income growth
Cigarettes become less affordable while the tax share decreases	• Pre-tax price increases exceed tax increases (if any) • Retail price increases exceed income growth
Cigarettes become more affordable while the tax share increases	• Tax increases exceed pre-tax price increases (if any) • Retail price increases remain below income growth
Cigarettes become more affordable and the tax share decreases	• Pre-tax price increases exceed tax increases (if any) • Retail price increases remain below income growth

Source: OECD.

References

Astudillo, K., G. Cruces and J. Puig (2022), *Four Strategies to Make Tobacco Taxation an Effective Tool to Reduce Consumption*, Inter-American Development Bank, https://blogs.iadb.org/gestion-fiscal/en/four-strategies-to-make-tobacco-taxation-an-effective-tool-to-reduce-consumption/ (accessed on 13 September 2023). [20]

Bardach, A. et al. (2016), "Income and smoking prevalence in Latin America: A systematic review and meta-analysis", *Rev Panam Salud Publica*, pp. 263-271, https://pubmed.ncbi.nlm.nih.gov/28001203/#:~:text=Low%20income%20was%20associated%20with,%25CI%201.17%2D2.30). [13]

Blecher, E. (2020), "Affordability of Tobacco Products: The Case of Cigarettes", *Tobacconomics*, https://tobacconomics.org/research/affordability-of-tobacco-products-the-case-of-cigarettes/. [39]

Chaloupka, F. et al. (2021), *Cigarette Tax Scorecard (2nd Edition)*, Tobacconomics, https://tobacconomics.org/research/cigarette-tax-scorecard-2nd-edition/. [38]

Drope, J. et al. (2024), *Tobacconomics cigarette tax scorecard (3rd ed.)*, Bloomberg School of Public Health, Johns Hopkins University, https://tobacconomics.org/research/cigarette-tax-scorecard-3rd-edition/. [36]

Drope, J., E. Siu and F. Chaloupka (2022), "Perseverance is innovation: the journey to successful tobacco tax reform", *Tobacco Control*, Vol. 31/2, pp. 241-242, https://doi.org/10.1136/tobaccocontrol-2021-057088. [41]

Euromonitor International (2023), *Euromonitor International's Tobacco Industry edition*, https://www.euromonitor.com/tobacco. [3]

Franco-Churruarin, F. and M. González-Rozada (2023), *Prevalence of daily smoking and initiation in Argentina, Brazil, and Mexico. A Tobacconomics Research Report.*, Tobacconomics, Health Policy Center, Institute for Health Research and Policy, University of Illinois Chicago, https://tobacconomics.org/files/research/888/regional-la-youth-smoking-report-v4.0.pdf. [17]

Government of Argentina (2013), *Global Adult Tobacco Survey Argentina 2012*, GATS Argentina Working Group, https://cdn.who.int/media/docs/default-source/ncds/ncd-surveillance/data-reporting/argentina/gats/arg_country_report_2012.pdf?sfvrsn=2a6b135e_5&download=true. [4]

Government of Brazil (2021), *Pesquisa Nacional de Saúde 2019*, Brazilian Institute of Geography and Statistics, https://www.ibge.gov.br/estatisticas/sociais/saude/9160-pesquisa-nacional-de-saude.html. [5]

Government of Brazil/ PAHO (2010), *Global Adult Tobacco Survey Brazil 2008*, National Cancer Institute, https://cdn.who.int/media/docs/default-source/ncds/ncd-surveillance/data-reporting/brazil/gats/gats-2008-brazil-report-en.pdf?sfvrsn=69bc0d3_5&download=true. [10]

Government of Chile (2021), *Décimo Cuarto Estudio Nacional de Drogas en Población General 2020*, National Service for the Prevention and Rehabilitation of Drug and Alcohol Consumption, https://www.senda.gob.cl/principales-resultados-del-decimo-cuarto-estudio-nacional-de-drogas-en-poblacion-general-2020/. [15]

Government of Costa Rica (2023), *GATS Global Adult Tobacco Survey Fact Sheet : Costa Rica 2022*, Ministry of Health, https://stacks.cdc.gov/view/cdc/148219 (accessed on 13 June 2024). [6]

Government of Costa Rica (2017), *2015 Global Adult Tobacco Survey, Costa Rica*, Ministry of Health, https://cdn.who.int/media/docs/default-source/ncds/ncd-surveillance/data-reporting/costa-rica/gats_costarica_2015_countryreport.pdf?sfvrsn=712df7f4_1&download=true (accessed on 10 October 2023). [11]

Government of Mexico (2023), *Encuesta Global de Tabaquismo en Adultos (GATS)*, National Commission on Mental Health and Addictions, https://www.gob.mx/salud/conadic/documentos/encuesta-global-de-tabaquismo-en-adultos-gats-2023-359138 (accessed on 13 June 2024). [7]

Government of Panama (2013), *Global Adult Tobacco Survey Panama 2013*, Ministry of Health/ Gorgas Memorial Institute of Health Studies, https://cdn.who.int/media/docs/default-source/ncds/ncd-surveillance/data-reporting/panama/pan_report2013.pdf?sfvrsn=4b125f53_1&download=true. [8]

Government of Uruguay (2017), *Global Adult Tobacco Survey Uruguay 2017*, Ministry of Public Health of Uruguay/ National Institute of Statistics, https://cdn.who.int/media/docs/default-source/ncds/ncd-surveillance/data-reporting/uruguay/gats_uruguay_2017_countryreport.pdf?sfvrsn=3349b05b_1&download=true. [9]

Guindon, G., G. Paraje and F. Chaloupka (2018), "The Impact of Prices and Taxes on the Use of Tobacco Products in Latin America and the Caribbean", *American Journal of Public Health*, Vol. 108/S6, pp. S492-S502, https://doi.org/10.2105/ajph.2014.302396r. [14]

Hutchinson, B. et al. (2022), "The case for investment in tobacco control: lessons from four countries in the Americas", *Revista Panamericana de Salud Pública*, Vol. 46, p. 1, https://doi.org/10.26633/rpsp.2022.174. [28]

IARC (2008), *Methods for Evaluating Tobacco Control Policies*, International Agency for Research on Cancer, https://www.iarc.who.int/wp-content/uploads/2018/07/Tobacco_vol12.pdf. [40]

IMF (2023), *World Economic Outlook Database*, International Monetary Fund, https://www.imf.org/en/Publications/WEO/weo-database/2023/October (accessed on 13 January 2024). [37]

Institute for Health Metrics and Evaluation (2024), *Results from the 2021 Global Burden of Disease (GBD) study*, Global Burden of Disease Collaborative Network, https://vizhub.healthdata.org/gbd-results/ (accessed on 26 June 2024). [21]

Ngo, A. et al. (2022), "As countries improve their cigarette tax policy, cigarette consumption declines", *Tobacco Control*, Vol. 33/e1, https://doi.org/10.1136/tc-2022-057486. [34]

OECD (2021), *Health at a Glance 2021: OECD Indicators*, OECD Publishing, Paris, https://doi.org/10.1787/ae3016b9-en. [32]

OECD/The World Bank (2023), *Health at a Glance: Latin America and the Caribbean 2023*, OECD Publishing, Paris, https://doi.org/10.1787/532b0e2d-en. [18]

Paraje, G., M. Muñoz and L. Pruzzo (2023), *Impacto de la ratificación del Convenio Marco para el Control del Tabaco sobre el número de fumadores en la Región de las Américas*, Tobaconomía, https://tabaconomia.uai.cl/wp-content/uploads/2023/06/Impacto-de-la-ratificacion-del-Convenio-Marco-final.pdf. [29]

Pichon-Riviere, A. et al. (2020), "The health and economic burden of smoking in 12 Latin American countries and the potential effect of increasing tobacco taxes: an economic modelling study", *The Lancet Global Health*, Vol. 8/10, pp. e1282-e1294, https://doi.org/10.1016/s2214-109x(20)30311-9. [22]

Pichon-Riviere, A. et al. (2023), "Health, economic and social burden of tobacco in Latin America and the expected gains of fully implementing taxes, plain packaging, advertising bans and smoke-free environments control measures: a modelling study", *Tobacco Control*, pp. tc-2022-057618, https://doi.org/10.1136/tc-2022-057618. [23]

Rodriguez-Iglesias, G. and F. Chaloupka (2018), *The Economics of Tobacco and Tobacco Control in Latin America*, Tobacconomics, https://tobacconomics.org/files/research/429/Economics-Tobacco-Control-Latin-America_2.3.pdf. [25]

Sandoval, R. et al. (2022), "Advances in Tobacco Control in the Region of the Americas, 2020", *Revista Panamericana de Salud Pública*, Vol. 46, p. 1, https://doi.org/10.26633/rpsp.2022.202. [26]

Sandoval, R. et al. (2022), "Lessons learned from fostering tobacco taxes in the Americas and implications for other health taxes", *Revista Panamericana de Salud Pública*, Vol. 46, p. 1, https://doi.org/10.26633/rpsp.2022.188. [35]

Sarich, P. et al. (2022), "Tobacco smoking changes during the first pre-vaccination phases of the COVID-19 pandemic: A systematic review and meta-analysis", *eClinicalMedicine*, Vol. 47, p. 101375, https://doi.org/10.1016/j.eclinm.2022.101375. [16]

U.S. National Cancer Institute/ WHO (2016), *The Economics of Tobacco and Tobacco Control*, National Cancer Institute Tobacco Control Monograph, U.S. Department of Health and Human Services, National Institutes of Health, National Cancer Institute, World Health Organization, https://cancercontrol.cancer.gov/sites/default/files/2020-08/m21_complete.pdf. [12]

United States government (2017), *Tobacco*, National Cancer Institute, https://www.cancer.gov/about-cancer/causes-prevention/risk/tobacco (accessed on 13 January 2024). [19]

WHO (2024), *Global Health Observatory: Age-standardized estimates of current tobacco use, tobacco smoking and cigarette smoking (Tobacco control: Monitor)*, World Health Organization, https://www.who.int/data/gho/data/indicators/indicator-details/GHO/gho-tobacco-control-monitor-current-tobaccouse-tobaccosmoking-cigarrettesmoking-agestd-tobagestdcurr (accessed on 20 February 2024). [1]

WHO (2023), *WHO report on the global tobacco epidemic 2023: Protect people from tobacco smoke*, World Health Organization, https://www.who.int/publications/i/item/9789240077164. [33]

WHO (2022), *2021 Global Progress Report*, World Health Organization, Secretariat of the WHO Framework Convention on Tobacco Control, https://fctc.who.int/publications/i/item/9789240041769. [24]

WHO (2021), *WHO report on the global tobacco epidemic 2021: Addressing new and emerging products*, World Health Organization, https://www.who.int/publications/i/item/9789240032095. [31]

WHO (2020), *The Global Strategy to Accelerate Tobacco Control 2019-2025: Focusing and intensifying efforts to implement the WHO Framework Convention on Tobacco Control*, World Health Organization, https://fctc.who.int/newsroom/news/item/11-11-2020-global-strategy-to-accelerate-tobacco-control-teaser-campaign (accessed on 31 March 2023). [30]

WHO (2019), *WHO global report on trends in prevalence of tobacco use 2000-2025, third edition*, World Health Organization, https://www.who.int/publications/i/item/who-global-report-on-trends-in-prevalence-of-tobacco-use-2000-2025-third-edition. [27]

World Bank (2022), *Population, total - Latin America & Caribbean*, World Bank, https://data.worldbank.org/indicator/SP.POP.TOTL?locations=ZJ-XJ (accessed on 27 June 2024). [2]

Annex 1.A. WHO FCTC MPOWER criteria legend

Annex Table 1.A.1. Outlining the WHO FCTC MPOWER criteria legend

M	P	O	W (Health warnings)	W (Mass media)	E	R
There are recent representative and periodic data for both adults and youths.	All public places, indoor workplaces, and public transportation are totally smoke-free (or at least 90% of the population is covered by subnational legislation).	There is a national quit line, nicotine replacement therapy, and some cessation services are available; the full costs are covered.	Large warning (covers an average of at least 50% of the front and the back of the packaging) with all the appropriate characteristics.	National campaign conducted with at least seven appropriate characteristics including airing on television and/or radio.	Ban on all forms of direct and indirect advertising (or at least 90% of the population covered by subnational legislation completely banning tobacco advertising, promotion and sponsorship).	Taxes represent ≥75% of the retail sale price of cigarettes.
There are recent and representative data for both adults and youths.	Six to seven types of public spaces and workplaces are completely smoke-free.	Nicotine replacement therapy or some cessation services are available; costs for at least one of them are covered.	Medium-sized warning (covers an average of 30%–49% of the front and back of the packaging) with all the appropriate characteristics, or a large warning, which lacks one to three of the appropriate characteristics.	National campaign conducted with five to six appropriate characteristics.	Ban on national television, radio and print media as well as on some but not all other forms of direct and/or indirect advertising.	Taxes represent ≥ 50% – <75 of the retail sale price of cigarettes.
There are recent and representative data for either adults or youths.	Three to five types of public spaces and workplaces are completely smoke-free.	Nicotine replacement therapy or some cessation services are available; costs are not covered.	Medium-sized warning that lacks one or more of the appropriate characteristics, or a large warning in which four or more appropriate characteristics are lacking.	National campaign conducted with one to four appropriate characteristics.	Ban on national television, radio and print media only.	Taxes represent ≥ 25 – <50% of the retail sale price of cigarettes.
No known data or no recent data or data that are not both recent and representative.	Complete absence of bans or up to two types of public spaces and workplaces are completely smoke-free.	None.	No warning or a small warning (on average less than 30% of the front and back).	No national campaign conducted between July 2020 and June 2022 with a duration of at least three weeks.	Complete absence of ban, or ban that does not cover national television, radio and print media.	Taxes represent <25% of the retail sale price of cigarettes.

Source: WHO report on the global tobacco epidemic (WHO, 2023[33]).

Notes

[1] Short-term and long-term elasticity refer to the responsiveness of the quantity demanded to price changes over time (i.e. how individuals adjust their behaviour in relation to price changes). In this context, short-term elasticity of cigarettes might be inelastic as consumers may not immediately find substitutes for a product. Especially because cigarette consumption differs from other goods due to its addictive nature, elasticities tend to be particularly low, especially in the short run. However, in the long-term, cigarettes might become more elastic as consumers may find new alternatives, or producers may modify production.

[2] E-cigarettes are electronic nicotine delivery systems (ENDS). They provide users with nicotine by transforming a liquid into vapor.

2 Tobacco tax revenue in Latin America and the Caribbean

This chapter provides an overview of tax revenue in countries in Latin America and the Caribbean (LAC). The chapter presents data on tobacco excise tax revenue, discusses its level over time, as well as revenue from other indirect taxes levied on tobacco products. The chapter explores relationships between tobacco excise tax revenue and other indicators of tobacco use and tobacco tax policy.

2.1. Tax revenue in LAC

In 2022, the average tax-to-GDP ratio in LAC was 21.5% (Figure 2.1). Revenue across the region ranges from 10.6% of gross domestic product (GDP) in Guyana to 33.3% of GDP in Brazil. Given the elevated fiscal deficits in the region (World Bank, 2024[1]), and the fact that, on average, central government gross debt remains above pre-pandemic levels (OECD et al., 2023[2]), there is a need for LAC countries to increase their tax revenue.

Figure 2.1. Tax-to-GDP ratio

Tax revenue as % of GDP, 2022

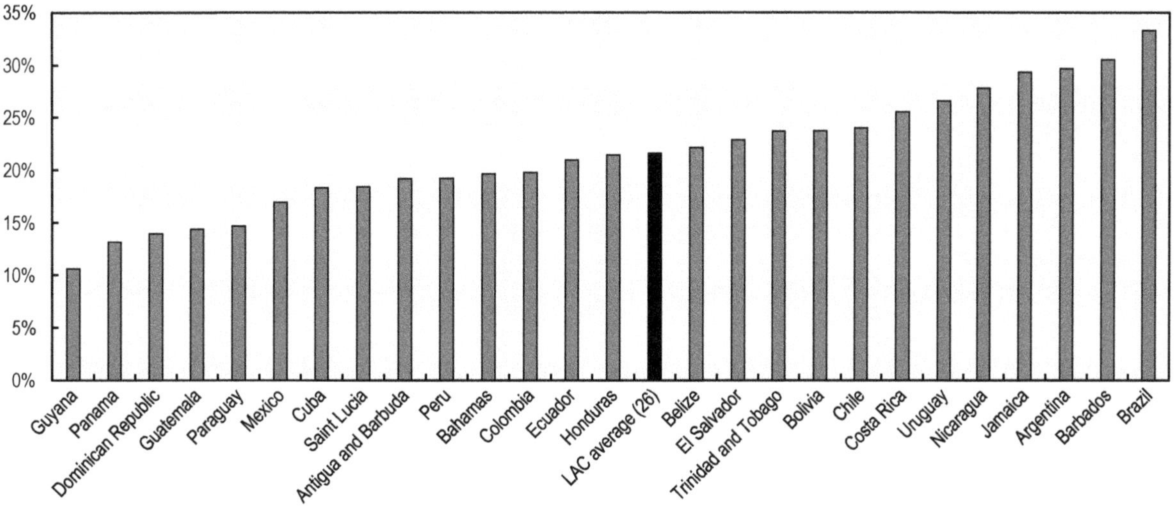

Note: The LAC average represents the unweighted average of 26 LAC countries that report tax revenue to OECD Revenue Statistics, excluding Venezuela due to data issues.
Source: OECD Revenue Statistics (OECD, 2024[3]).

Taxes on goods and services account, on average, for half of total tax revenue in LAC (Figure 2.2). The proportion of revenue derived from taxes on goods and services varies significantly, ranging from 10.9% of total tax revenue in Cuba to 79.1% in the Bahamas. Excise tax revenue, on average, make up 6.7% of total tax revenue but also vary considerably across countries in the LAC region (from 1.7% in Trinidad and Tobago to 15.0% in the Dominican Republic).

Figure 2.2. Tax mixes

Revenue of the main tax categories as % of total tax revenue, 2022

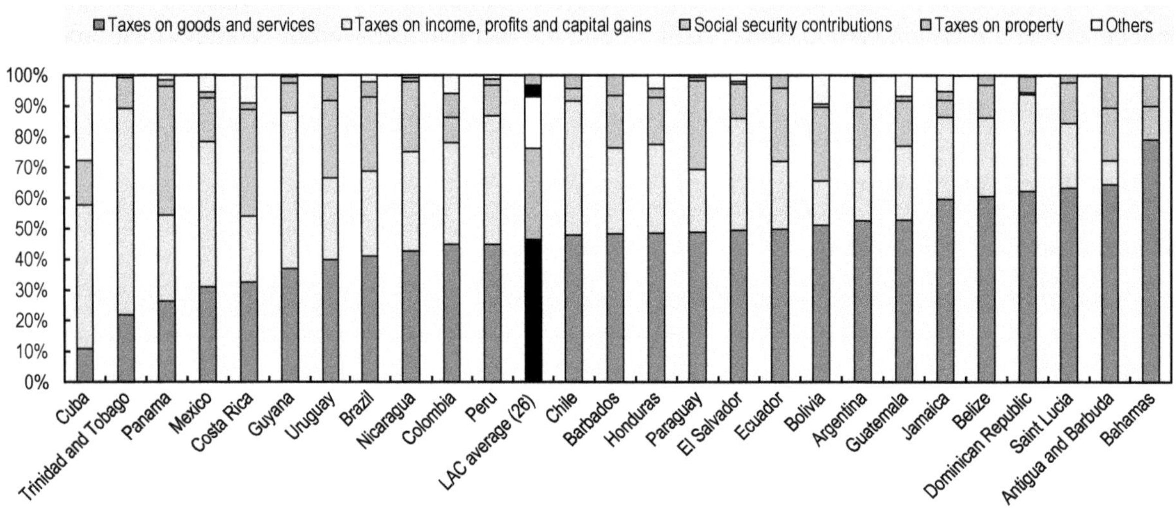

Note: The LAC average represents the unweighted average of 26 LAC countries that report tax revenue to OECD Revenue Statistics, excluding Venezuela due to data issues.
Source: OECD Revenue Statistics (OECD, 2024[3]).

Revenue from health excise taxes (i.e. excise taxes levied on alcohol, tobacco and sugar-sweetened beverages (SSBs)) varies substantially across LAC countries (Figure 2.3). Based on available data, health excise tax revenue ranges from 0.1% of GDP in Brazil (when considering for the tobacco only the Imposto sobre productos industrializados – IPI, which is the excise tax on tobacco, and no other indirect taxes, see Box 2.1) to 0.7% of GDP in the Dominican Republic.

In the LAC region, tobacco excise taxes tend to raise less revenue than alcohol excise taxes. In LAC, excise taxes on alcohol raise 0.24% of GDP in revenue on average, followed by excise taxes on tobacco (0.13% of GDP) and SSB (0.10% of GDP) (based on sample of 17 countries, see Figure 2.3). Out of the 16 LAC countries for which information is available, 12 countries raise higher excise tax revenue on alcohol than on tobacco. This differs from other regions in the world where revenue from tobacco excise taxes (0.5-0.6% of GDP in 2019) exceeds revenue from alcohol excise taxes (0.3% of GDP in 2019) (Blecher, Ozer and Bloom, 2023[4]).

Figure 2.3. Health excise tax revenue

Health excise tax revenue as % of GDP, latest year available

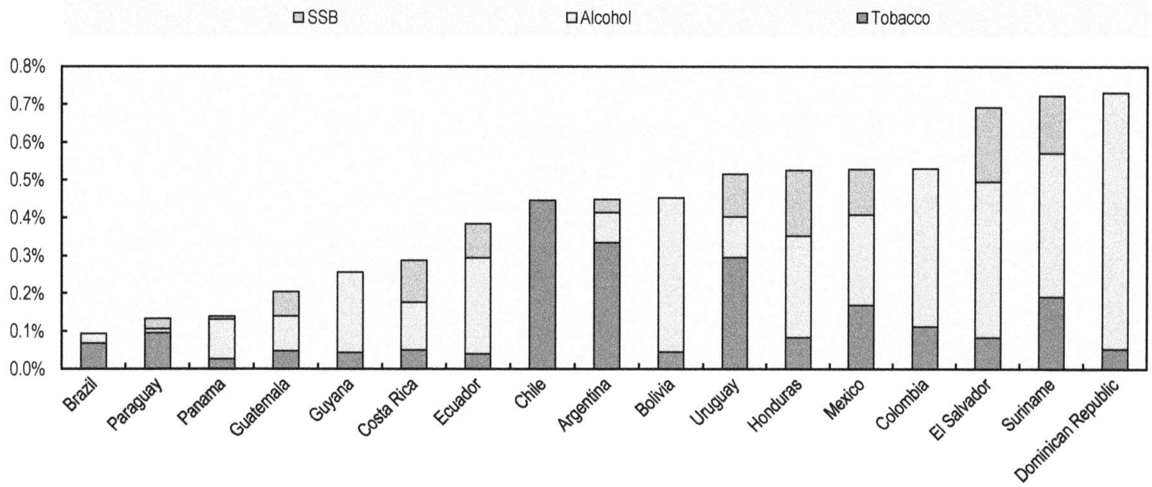

Note: For this report, health excise taxes are classified as excise taxes levied on alcohol, tobacco and SSBs, and do not include excise taxes levied on food. This figure includes revenue data from OECD Revenue Statistics and national sources for countries which report tax revenue raised from health excise taxes; it does not include data reported by the World Health Organisation (WHO) report on the global tobacco epidemic as the data do not cover non-tobacco health excise tax revenue. See Box 2.1 for more information on tobacco tax revenue (source of information and calculations) and country selection. For the following countries, revenue data reported for excise taxes on non-alcoholic beverages is classified as excise tax revenue from SSB: Argentina, Costa Rica, Ecuador, Paraguay, Suriname and Uruguay. Colombia introduced a SSB excise tax in 2022 (Law 2277 of 2022 Tax Reform) but excise tax revenue from SSB are not available yet. The Dominican Republic and Guyana do not have an SSB excise tax in place according to the Global SSB Tax Database (World Bank, 2023[5]). Chile levies an indirect tax on alcohol and SSB, respectively, classified as "Tasas especiales del impuesto al valor agregado" (or "value added tax special rates") under official tax revenue reports, and hence is not included in this figure on excise tax. For Bolivia and Brazil, the data sources used (national data for Bolivia and OECD Revenue Statistics for Brazil) report excise tax revenue on beverages in general with no clear distinction between alcohol and SSB. For both countries, the revenue reported under "Bebidas" (Bolivia) and "Beverages" (Brazil) has been classified as alcohol excise tax revenue and, hence, no excise tax revenue is shown under the SSB category. The latest year available is 2022 for Argentina, Brazil, Chile, Colombia, Costa Rica, the Dominican Republic, El Salvador, Guatemala, Guyana, Honduras, Mexico, Panama, Paraguay, Suriname and Uruguay; 2021 for Ecuador; 2020 for Bolivia.
Source: OECD Revenue Statistics (OECD, 2024[3]); National data.

2.2. Tobacco excise tax revenue in LAC countries

Tobacco taxes, which are indirect taxes levied on tobacco products, consist of four types of taxes: tobacco excise taxes, the value added tax (VAT) (and sales taxes, if any), import duties, and any other indirect taxes (see the note of Figure 2.4 for a definition of each tax). This section starts by looking at revenue raised by all tobacco taxes before focusing on tobacco excise revenue. According to the available data, revenue from tobacco taxes ranges from 0.01% of total tax revenue in Barbados (less than 0.01% of GDP) to 2.58% of total tax revenue in Chile (0.67% of GDP).

There is significant scope for countries in LAC to improve the quality of the tobacco tax revenue data they report. Box 2.1 provides detailed information on the sources and availability of tobacco tax revenue data and shows that there are significant differences across countries and sources. For instance, many countries do no report tobacco tax revenue across all tobacco tax types. About one third of countries in LAC do not report disaggregated tobacco tax revenue data (Box 2.1). Hence for these countries data in Figure 2.4 likely underestimate actual tobacco tax revenue. For countries for which data are available, inconsistencies across data sources can be observed (e.g., Argentina, Bolivia, Honduras, Nicaragua and Trinidad and Tobago). These issues underscore the need for improving the quality of tobacco tax revenue data at the country level.

In most LAC countries (22 out of 28) tobacco excise taxes constitute the largest share of the total taxes levied on tobacco products (Figure 2.4). Costa Rica, Dominica, Haiti and Saint Vincent and the Grenadines are the only countries where the VAT raises the largest share of tobacco tax revenue (Antigua and Barbuda is not considered because the country does not levy a tobacco excise tax).

Figure 2.4. Tobacco tax revenue

Tobacco tax revenue as % of total tax revenue, latest year available

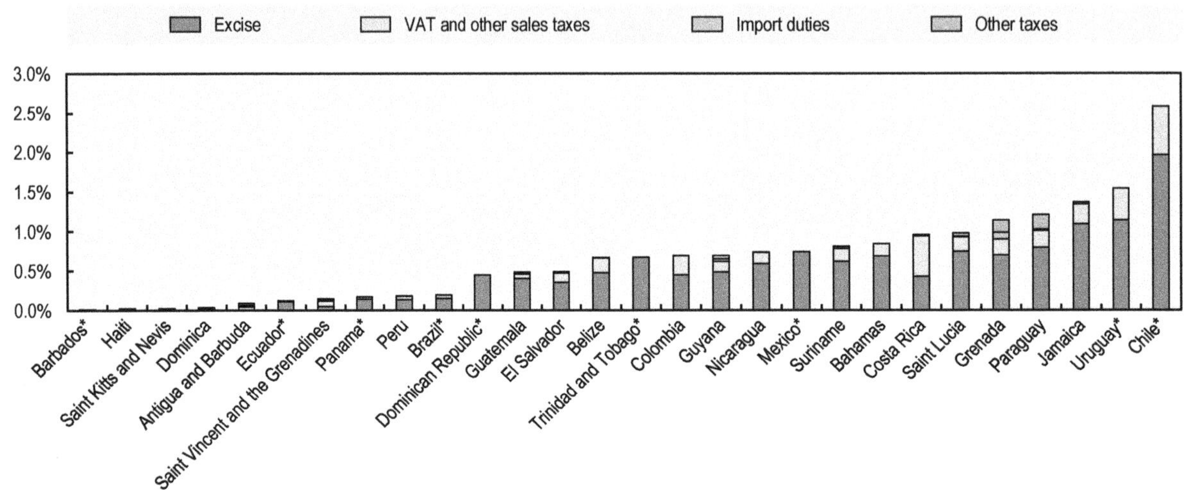

Note: This graph only includes tobacco tax revenue data published by the WHO, as this is the only source reporting tobacco tax revenue across different tax instruments. The total tax revenue data used in this figure are from the International Monetary Fund (IMF) World Economic Outlook (October 2023). Countries with a "*" do not report tobacco tax revenue data across all four tax instrument categories in the WHO report on the global tobacco epidemic (WHO, 2023[6]). Hence their tobacco tax revenue figures might be underestimated. In the case of Brazil, it includes revenue from the federal excise tax levied on tobacco product (the Imposto sobre productos industrializados, IPI) and from the Programas de Integração Social e de Formação do Patrimônio do Servidor Público (PIS/Pasep) which is an indirect tax (but not an excise tax). It does not include revenue from the Imposto sobre Operações relativas à Circulação de Mercadorias e sobre Prestações de Serviços de Transporte Interestadual (ICMS) which is another indirect tax for which data are not available. "Excise" refers to the sum of revenue from specific and ad valorem excise taxes (see Annex 3.A for definitions). "Other taxes" includes any other tax that is not an excise tax, import duty, VAT or sales tax, but that applies to either the quantity of tobacco or to the value of a transaction of a tobacco product. It excludes corporate taxes on tobacco companies or other direct taxes that tobacco companies may pay. The latest year available is 2022 for Nicaragua and Saint Kitts and Nevis; 2021 for Antigua and Barbuda, Belize, Brazil, Chile, Colombia, Costa Rica, Dominica, the Dominican Republic, Ecuador, El Salvador, Grenada, Guatemala, Mexico, Panama, Peru, Saint Lucia, Saint Vincent and the Grenadines, Suriname and Uruguay; 2020 for Bahamas, Jamaica, Paraguay and Trinidad and Tobago; 2019 for Guyana; 2015 for Haiti; 2014 for Barbados.
Source: WHO report on the global tobacco epidemic (WHO, 2023[6]); IMF World Economic Outlook Database (IMF, 2023[7]).

Comparatively low tobacco excise tax revenue signals that countries in LAC might have scope to raise more tobacco excise tax revenue (Goodchild, Sandoval and Belausteguigoitia, 2017[8]). Tobacco excise taxes raise, on average, 0.12% of GDP (0.50% of total tax revenue) in LAC (based on sample of 30 countries, see Figure 2.5). As pointed out before, this is below the average observed from an international sample of countries (0.5-0.6% of GDP; see (Blecher, Ozer and Bloom, 2023[4])). Tobacco excise tax revenue ranges from less than 0.01% of GDP in Barbados, Dominica, Haiti, and Saint Kitts and Nevis to 0.45% of GDP (1.86% of total tax revenue) in Chile.

Figure 2.5. Tobacco excise tax revenue

Tobacco excise tax revenue, latest year available

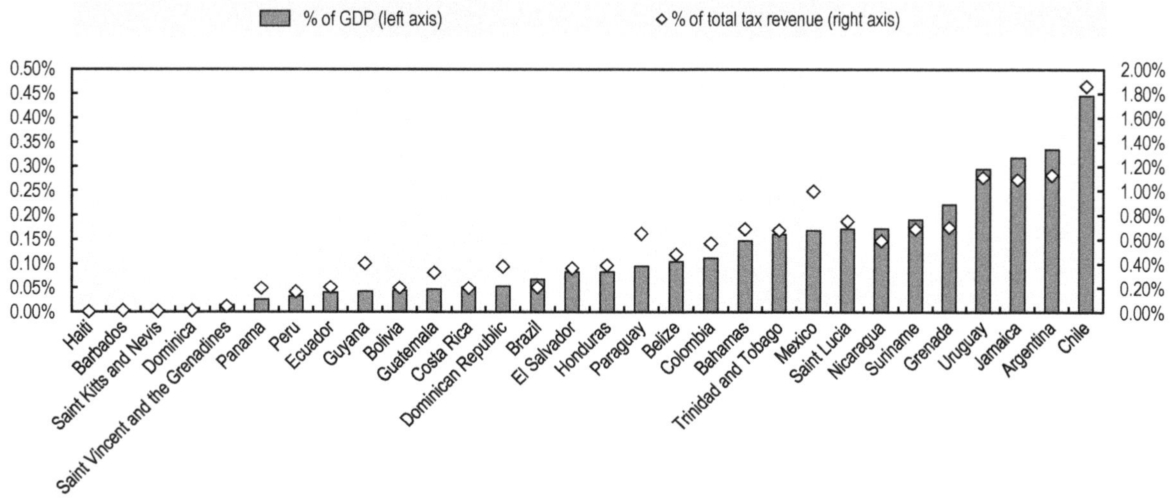

Note: See Box 2.1 for more information on tobacco tax revenue (source of information and calculations) and country selection. The latest year available is 2022 for Argentina, Brazil, Chile, Colombia, Costa Rica, the Dominican Republic, El Salvador, Guatemala, Guyana, Honduras, Mexico, Nicaragua, Panama, Paraguay, Peru, Saint Kitts and Nevis, Suriname, and Uruguay; 2021 for Belize, Dominica, Ecuador, Grenada, Saint Lucia, Saint Vincent and the Grenadines; 2020 for Bahamas, Bolivia, Jamaica and Trinidad and Tobago; 2015 for Haiti; 2014 for Barbados.
Source: OECD Revenue Statistics (OECD, 2024[3]); WHO report on the global tobacco epidemic (WHO, 2021[9]) and (WHO, 2023[6]); National data.

Tobacco excise tax revenue in LAC is declining (Figure 2.6). From 2012 to 2022, the average tobacco excise tax revenue (based on a sample of 16 countries for which data is available over the entire period) declined from 0.21% to 0.13% of GDP (from 1.06% to 0.60% of total tax revenue). It declined in 15 countries (Argentina, Brazil, Chile, Costa Rica, the Dominican Republic, El Salvador, Guatemala, Guyana, Honduras, Mexico, Panama, Paraguay, Peru, Suriname, and Uruguay) and increased in only one country (Colombia). In constant local currencies (with prices fixed for 2022), tobacco excise tax revenue declined in 11 countries (Brazil, Costa Rica, the Dominican Republic, El Salvador, Guatemala, Guyana, Honduras, Mexico, Panama, Suriname, and Uruguay) and increased in five countries (Argentina, Chile, Colombia, Paraguay, and Peru). This follows a longer-term trend of declining tobacco excise tax revenue (as a share of total tax revenue) observed in the region since 1990 (Rodriguez-Iglesias and Chaloupka, 2017[10]). To some extent, this trend is a reflection of the significant decrease in tobacco use over time in the LAC region (see Figure 1.6 in Chapter 1).

Figure 2.6. Trends in tobacco excise tax revenue

Tobacco excise tax revenue, average of 16 countries, 2012-2022

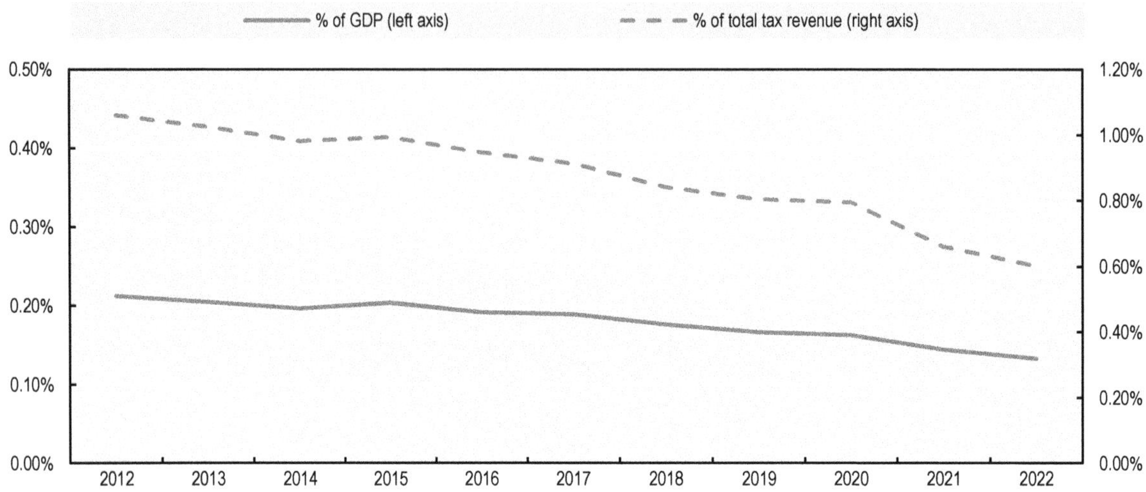

Note: Country selection is based on countries for which data on tobacco excise tax revenue from 2012 to 2022 was available. See Box 2.1 for more information on tobacco tax revenue (source of information and calculations) and country selection. The average tobacco excise tax revenue is calculated from an unweighted average of the 16 countries included in this Figure (Argentina, Brazil, Chile, Colombia, Costa Rica, the Dominican Republic, El Salvador, Guatemala, Guyana, Honduras, Mexico, Panama, Paraguay, Peru, Suriname, and Uruguay).
Source: OECD Revenue Statistics (OECD, 2024[3]); National data.

Box 2.1. Availability of data on tobacco tax revenue

In this chapter, the main sources for tobacco tax revenue data are:

- OECD Revenue Statistics which publishes tobacco excise tax revenue for 15 LAC countries.
- The WHO report on the global tobacco epidemic which publishes data on revenue from tobacco excise taxes for 30 LAC countries, and revenue for all non-excise tobacco tax instruments (VAT, import duties and other taxes) for 21 LAC countries. This chapter includes data from the 2021 and 2023 editions (WHO, 2021[9]) and (WHO, 2023[6]).
- National data, which is used for the five countries for which the OECD does not publish tobacco excise tax revenue: Bolivia (Plurinational State of Bolivia, 2021[11]), Mexico (Government of Mexico, 2023[12]), Peru, Paraguay (Government of Paraguay, 2023[13]), and Suriname (Government of Suriname, 2024[14]).

Three countries were not (or partially) included in the analysis:

- Cuba does not report disaggregated tobacco tax revenue in the OECD Revenue Statistics or in the WHO report on the global tobacco epidemic.
- Venezuela because of data issues.
- Antigua and Barbuda is excluded from tobacco excise tax analysis as there is no tobacco excise tax in place.

Some countries were excluded from parts of the analysis because of inconsistency in tobacco excise tax revenue data between sources:

- In four countries, inconsistencies between the WHO and OECD Revenue Statistics data was observed.
  - For Nicaragua and Trinidad and Tobago: WHO data were used as it more closely aligns with publicly available national data (hence, those countries are excluded from Figure 2.3, Figure 2.6 and Figure 2.7 which rely on OECD and national data).
  - For Argentina and Honduras: OECD data were used as it more closely aligns with national data (hence those countries are not represented in Figure 2.4 which uses WHO data).
- For Bolivia, inconsistency between the WHO and the national source was observed for 2019 (the latest year for which WHO reports tobacco excise tax revenue). National data was used in this chapter, and hence Bolivia is excluded from Figure 2.4 which relies only on WHO data.
- For some countries, specific observations are to be made:
  - Costa Rica: OECD Revenue Statistics provides data for the specific tax on tobacco ("Impuesto a los Productos de Tabaco") but does not provide disaggregated data for the ad valorem excise tax on tobacco ("Impuesto Selectivo de Consumo"). Data for the latter is only reported in a broad category "Other specific taxes on consumption". Hence, tobacco excise tax data available for Costa Rica are a lower bound estimate.
  - Brazil: Tobacco tax revenue data reported by the WHO only includes revenue collected by the federal excise tax levied on tobacco product (i.e. Imposto sobre productos industrializados, IPI). and from another indirect tax (i.e. the Programas de Integração Social e de Formação do Patrimônio do Servidor Público - PIS/Pasep). It does not include revenue from the Imposto sobre Operações relativas à Circulação de Mercadorias e sobre Prestações de Serviços de Transporte Interestadual (ICMS) which is another indirect tax for which data are not available. Hence, tobacco tax revenue data for Brazil are a lower bound estimate.

Data on GDP and total tax revenue that was used to compute indicators is from OECD Revenue Statistics (OECD, 2024[3]) or the IMF World Economic Outlook (IMF, 2023[7]). Tobacco tax revenue data from the WHO was paired with IMF data (for Bahamas, Barbados, Belize, Dominica, Grenada, Haiti, Jamaica, Nicaragua, Saint Kitts and Nevis, Saint Lucia, Saint Vincent and the Grenadines, Suriname and Trinidad and Tobago). Tobacco tax revenue data from the OECD and national sources (with the exception of Suriname as it is not covered by OECD Revenue Statistics) was paired with GDP and total tax revenue data from the OECD (for Argentina, Bolivia, Brazil, Chile, Colombia, Costa Rica, the Dominican Republic, Ecuador, El Salvador, Guatemala, Guyana, Honduras, Mexico, Panama, Paraguay and Uruguay). Figure 2.4 is an exception: it uses tobacco tax revenue data from the WHO, and total tax revenue data from the IMF.

Source: OECD.

2.3. Correlations between tobacco excise tax revenue and indicators of tobacco use and tax policy

The variation in tobacco tax revenue across countries can be correlated to a wide range of factors. The main factors that may contribute to the differences in tobacco excise tax revenue include a country's tax mix, the tobacco excise tax design, the administration of the tax, the intensity of illicit tobacco trade, prices of tobacco products (when there is an ad valorem component – an ad valorem tax being a tax on the value of a transaction at some point in the production or distribution chain), and the volume of tobacco that is consumed (Rodriguez-Iglesias and Chaloupka, 2017[10]; World Bank, 2019[15]; Blecher, Ozer and Bloom, 2023[4]). The figures in the remainder of this chapter explore correlations between tobacco excise tax revenue and other indicators of tobacco use and tobacco tax policy across LAC countries.

Tobacco excise tax revenue tends to be higher in countries for which indirect taxes are an important part of their tax mix. LAC countries that raise higher revenue from taxes on goods and services also tend to raise higher revenue from tobacco excise taxes (Figure 2.7). The correlation remains positive when outliers (Argentina, Chile and Uruguay) are not included.

LAC countries with a specific or mixed tobacco excise tax structures raise, on average, more tobacco excise tax revenue than countries with an ad valorem structure (Figure 2.8; Figure 2.12). This observation is aligned with other findings based on an international sample, where the average tobacco excise tax revenue corresponds to 0.6% for specific structures (specific tobacco excise levies a lump-sum amount per stick, pack, 1 000 sticks, or kilogram), and 0.7% for mixed structures (combination of a specific component with an ad valorem component) versus 0.2% of GDP for ad valorem structures (Blecher, Ozer and Bloom, 2023[4]). However, the World Bank finds larger differences in average tobacco excise tax revenue between tax structures across the world than this chapter's results for LAC.

Figure 2.7. Relationship between tobacco excise tax revenue and revenue from taxes on goods and services

Latest year available

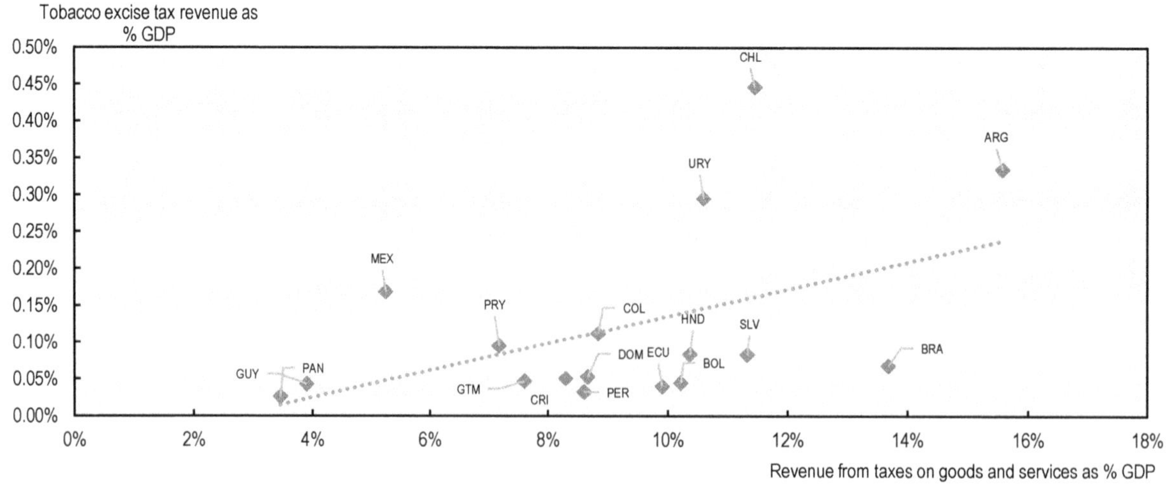

Note: The country selection was based on countries for which there is tobacco excise tax revenue data (from OECD Revenue Statistics or national sources) and data on tax revenue from goods and services (from OECD Revenue Statistics). See Box 2.1 for more information on tobacco tax revenue (source of information and calculations). The latest year available is 2022 for: Argentina, Brazil, Chile, Colombia, Costa Rica, the Dominican Republic, El Salvador, Guatemala, Guyana, Honduras, Mexico, Panama, Paraguay, Peru and Uruguay; 2021 for Ecuador; 2020 for Bolivia.
Source: OECD Revenue Statistics (OECD, 2024[3]); National data.

Figure 2.8. Tobacco excise tax revenue across excise tax structures for cigarettes

Tobacco excise tax revenue as % of GDP, latest year available

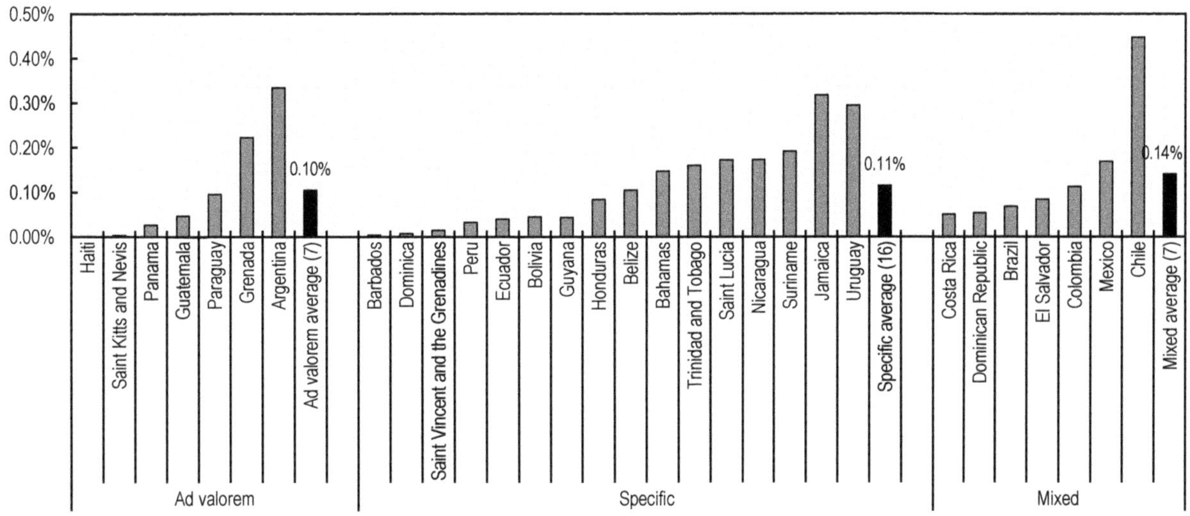

Note: See Box 2.1 for more information on tobacco tax revenue (source of information and calculations) and country selection. The latest year available is 2022 for Argentina, Brazil, Chile, Colombia, Costa Rica, the Dominican Republic, El Salvador, Guatemala, Guyana, Honduras, Mexico, Nicaragua, Panama, Paraguay, Peru, Saint Kitts and Nevis, Suriname, and Uruguay; 2021 for Belize, Dominica, Ecuador, Grenada, Saint Lucia, Saint Vincent and the Grenadines; 2020 for Bahamas, Bolivia, Jamaica, and Trinidad and Tobago; 2015 for Haiti; 2014 for Barbados.
Source: OECD Revenue Statistics (OECD, 2024[3]); WHO report on the global tobacco epidemic (WHO, 2023[6]); National data.

On average countries with higher tobacco excise tax as a share of cigarette retail price tend to raise more tobacco excise tax revenue (Figure 2.9), **but this correlation needs to be nuanced**. Analysis in Chapter 1 shows that the countries that meet the MPOWER R target are also the ones with the lowest tax-inclusive prices, which puts their tobacco tax revenue under pressure. Countries such as Argentina and Chile (and Uruguay to a lesser extent) that meet the MPOWER R target, have high excise tax revenue because of high tobacco prevalence (see Figure 1.1 in Chapter 1) despite having low cigarettes prices. In other countries with a low excise tax share and low prevalence (e.g. Jamaica), high excise tax revenue can be explained by high cigarettes prices (see Figure 1.13 in Chapter 1).

Figure 2.9. Relationship between tobacco excise tax revenue and the tobacco excise tax share in retail price

Latest year available

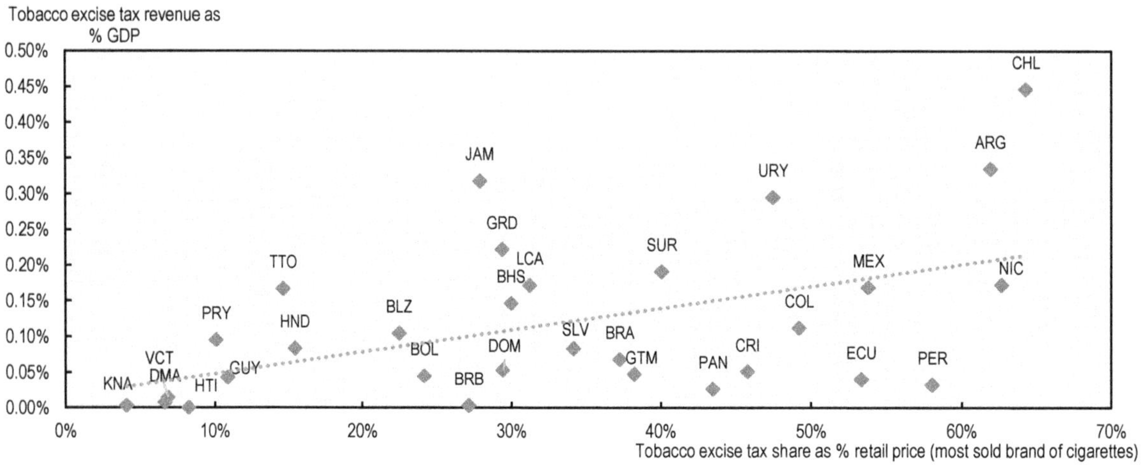

Note: See Box 2.1 for more information on tobacco tax revenue (source of information and calculations) and country selection. For tobacco excise tax revenue, the latest year available is 2022 for Argentina, Brazil, Chile, Colombia, Costa Rica, the Dominican Republic, El Salvador, Guatemala, Guyana, Honduras, Mexico, Nicaragua, Panama, Paraguay, Peru, Saint Kitts and Nevis, Suriname, and Uruguay; 2021 for Belize, Dominica, Ecuador, Grenada, Saint Lucia, Saint Vincent and the Grenadines; 2020 for Bahamas, Bolivia, Jamaica, and Trinidad and Tobago; 2015 for Haiti; 2014 for Barbados. Data for tobacco excise tax share as % of retail price (most sold brand of cigarettes) is only available every second year. Hence, for countries where there was no direct match of years with the latest year of tobacco excise tax revenue data, tax share data from the following year was used. The year used is 2022 for Belize, Dominica, Ecuador, Grenada, Saint Lucia, Saint Vincent and the Grenadines; 2016 for Haiti.

Source: OECD Revenue Statistics (OECD, 2024[3]); WHO report on the global tobacco epidemic (WHO, 2021[9]) and (WHO, 2023[6]); National data.

Tobacco use is positively correlated with tobacco excise tax revenue (Figure 2.10; Figure 2.11). A positive correlation between tobacco excise tax revenue and tobacco use prevalence is presented in Figure 2.10. Similarly, Figure 2.11 illustrates a positive correlation between tobacco excise tax revenue and legal cigarettes sales per capita. For countries with a similar tobacco use, measured either through prevalence rates or through cigarette sales per capita, significant differences in tobacco excise tax revenue can be observed. For example, tobacco excise tax revenue in countries with a tobacco use prevalence rate of approximately 10% varies between 0.04% of GDP (Ecuador) and 0.32% of GDP (Jamaica). This suggests that, for a similar tobacco use, countries with relatively low tobacco excise tax revenue could be foregoing significant tobacco tax revenue.

Figure 2.10. Relationship between tobacco excise tax revenue and tobacco use prevalence

Latest year available

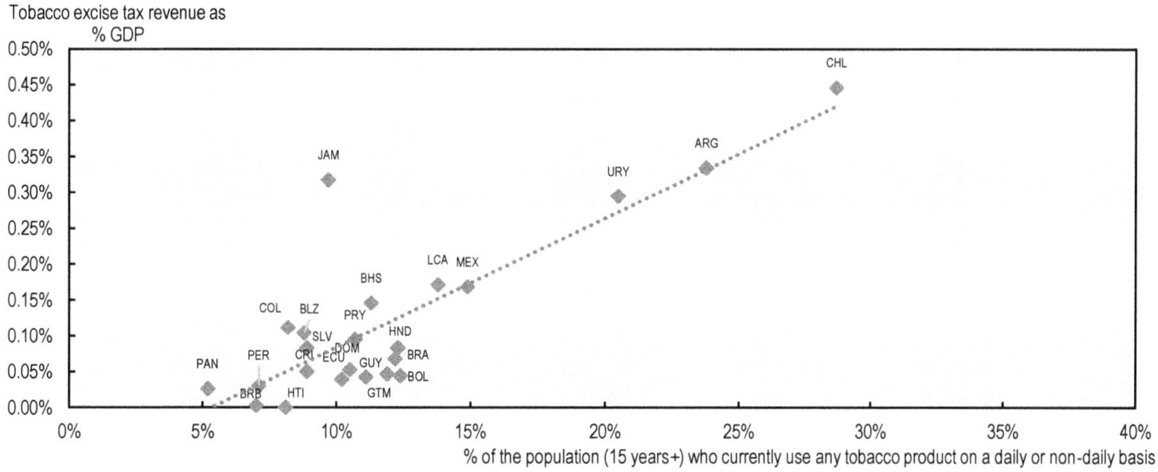

Note: See Box 2.1 for more information on tobacco tax revenue (source of information and calculations) and country selection. Dominica, Grenada, Nicaragua, Saint Kitts and Nevis, Saint Vincent and the Grenadines, Suriname and Trinidad and Tobago are excluded as the WHO Global Health Observatory does not report tobacco use prevalence rates. For tobacco excise tax revenue, the latest year available is 2022 for Argentina, Brazil, Chile, Colombia, Costa Rica, the Dominican Republic, El Salvador, Guatemala, Guyana, Honduras, Mexico, Panama, Paraguay, Peru, Suriname and Uruguay; 2021 for Belize, Ecuador, Saint Lucia; 2020 for Bahamas, Bolivia, Jamaica; 2015 for Haiti; 2014 for Barbados. Data on tobacco consumption are estimated for 2022. The definition of tobacco use: the percentage of the population aged 15 years and over who currently use any tobacco product on a daily or non-daily basis. Tobacco products include cigarettes, pipes, cigars, cigarillos, waterpipes (hookah, shisha), bidis, kretek, heated tobacco products, and all forms of smokeless (oral and nasal) tobacco. Tobacco products exclude e-cigarettes (which do not contain tobacco), e-cigars, e-hookahs, and e-pipes. The rates are age-standardized to the WHO standard population.

Source: OECD Revenue Statistics (OECD, 2024[3]); WHO report on the global tobacco epidemic (WHO, 2021[9]) and (WHO, 2023[6]); National data; Data for prevalence was extracted from the WHO Global Health Observatory Data Repository (WHO, 2024[16]).

Figure 2.11. Relationship between tobacco excise tax revenue and legal cigarette sales

Latest year available

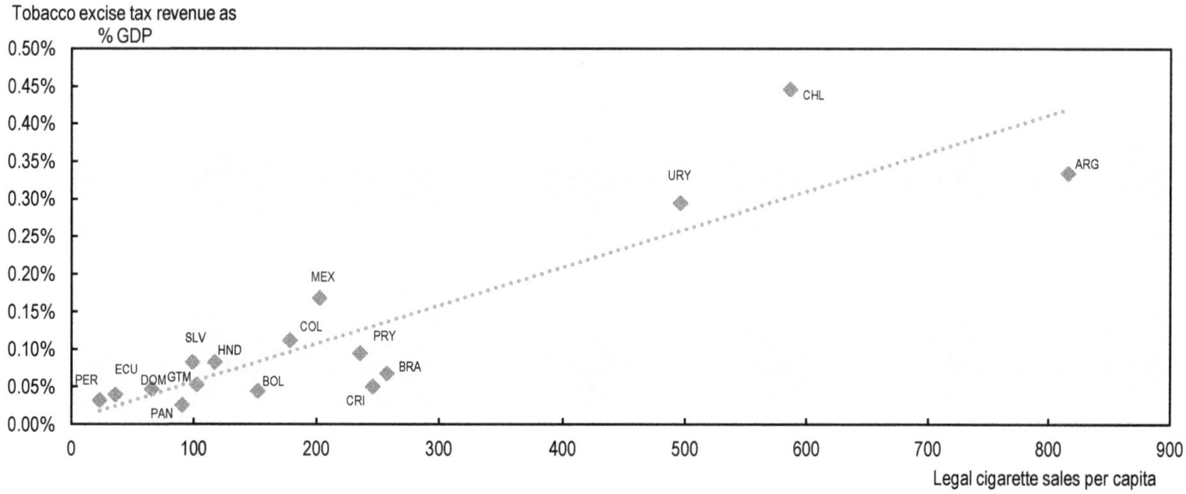

Note: See Box 2.1 for more information on tobacco tax revenue (source of information and calculations) and country selection. Country selection is based on countries which Euromonitor researches and applies both primary and secondary research techniques to build their market consensus. The latest year available is 2022 for Argentina, Brazil, Chile, Colombia, Costa Rica, the Dominican Republic, El Salvador, Guatemala, Honduras, Mexico, Panama, Paraguay, Peru and Uruguay; 2021 for Ecuador and 2020 for Bolivia. The country selection is provided by the availability of data on sales of cigarettes in Euromonitor International Tobacco Industry edition, 2023 © All rights reserved (Euromonitor International, 2023[17]).

Source: OECD Revenue Statistics (OECD, 2024[3]); National data; Euromonitor International Tobacco Industry edition, 2023 © All rights reserved (Euromonitor International, 2023[17]).

Whilst their main objective is to reduce tobacco consumption, tobacco excise taxes have the potential to raise more revenue on average in LAC (WHO, 2021[18]; Goodchild, Sandoval and Belausteguigoitia, 2017[8]). Figure 2.12 reflects substantial variation across LAC countries in the average excise tax revenue collected per pack of legal cigarettes sold, ranging from USD purchasing power parity (PPP) 0.5 in Bolivia to USD PPP 4.5 in Chile. Country-specific analysis is required to quantify the additional tobacco tax revenue that individual countries could raise but, overall, the differences across the region and the previous findings suggest that many countries could increase the tax revenue collected per pack of cigarettes. As previously observed in Figure 2.8, specific and mixed tobacco excise tax structures tend to generate more revenue than an ad valorem structure (WHO, 2021[18]).

Figure 2.12. Average excise tax revenue collected per pack of 20 cigarettes sold

Tobacco excise tax revenue in USD PPP collected per pack of legal cigarettes sold, latest year available

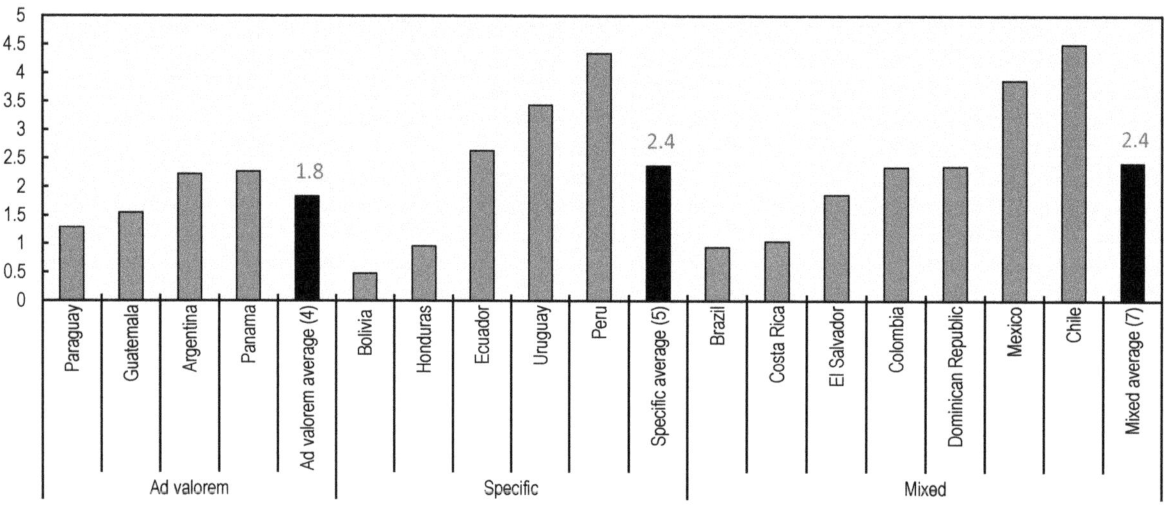

Note: See Box 2.1 for more information on tobacco tax revenue (source of information and calculations) and country selection. The latest year available is 2022 for Argentina, Brazil, Chile, Colombia, Costa Rica, the Dominican Republic, El Salvador, Guatemala, Honduras, Mexico, Panama, Paraguay, Peru and Uruguay; 2021 for Ecuador and 2020 for Bolivia. The country selection is based on Euromonitor International Tobacco Industry edition, 2023 © All rights reserved (Euromonitor International, 2023[17]).
Source: OECD Revenue Statistics (OECD, 2024[3]); National data; Euromonitor International Tobacco Industry edition, 2023 © All rights reserved (Euromonitor International, 2023[17]); IMF World Economic Outlook Database (IMF, 2023[7]).

References

Blecher, E., C. Ozer and D. Bloom (2023), *Knowledge Note: Unpacking the empirics behind health tax revenue*, World Bank, https://thedocs.worldbank.org/en/doc/f1f068e38935e2f5d92b7edf365d5089-0350032023/original/KN-4-Unpacking-the-empirics-behind-health-tax-revenues.pdf. [4]

Euromonitor International (2023), *Euromonitor International's Tobacco Industry edition*, https://www.euromonitor.com/tobacco (accessed on 1 August 2023). [17]

Goodchild, M., R. Sandoval and I. Belausteguigoitia (2017), "Generating revenue by raising tobacco taxes in Latin America and the Caribbean", *Revista Panamericana de Salud Pública*, pp. 1-7, https://doi.org/10.26633/rpsp.2017.151. [8]

Government of Mexico (2023), *Ingresos Presupuestarios del Gobierno Federal (Resumen Artículo 1 LIF) Pesos corrientes multianual (2000-2022), Millones de pesos (Flujos Acumulados)*, Secretariat of Finance and Public Credit, http://presto.hacienda.gob.mx/EstoporLayout/estadisticas.jsp (accessed on 13 August 2023). [12]

Government of Paraguay (2023), *Recaudacion en concepto de ISC*, Ministry of Finance, Asunción, Paraguay, https://www.set.gov.py/web/portal-institucional/estadisticas (accessed on 13 July 2023). [13]

Government of Suriname (2024), *Financieel Jaarplan 2024*, General Bureau of Statistics, https://statistics-suriname.org/financiele-notas-suriname/. [14]

IMF (2023), *World Economic Outlook Database*, International Monetary Fund, https://www.imf.org/en/Publications/WEO/weo-database/2023/October (accessed on 13 January 2024). [7]

OECD (2024), *Global Revenue Statistics Database*, Organisation for Economic Co-operation and Development, https://www.oecd.org/tax/tax-policy/global-revenue-statistics-database.htm (accessed on 13 August 2023). [3]

OECD et al. (2023), *Latin American Economic Outlook 2023: Investing in Sustainable Development*, OECD Publishing, Paris, https://doi.org/10.1787/8c93ff6e-en. [2]

Plurinational State of Bolivia (2021), *Boletín Económico: Ingresos Tributarios al Primer Semestre 2021*, Ministry of Economy and Public Finance, https://repositorio.economiayfinanzas.gob.bo/documentos/2018/VPT/DIRECCIONES/DGET/BOLETIN_BEIGT/2021/Boletin%20Economico%20de%20Ingresos%20Tributarios%201%20semestre%202021.pdf. [11]

Rodriguez-Iglesias, G. and F. Chaloupka (2017), *Best Practices for Tobacco Tax Policies in Latin America and the Caribbean*, Tobacconomics, Health Policy Center, Institute for Health Research and Policy, University of Illinois at Chicago, https://tobacconomics.org/uploads/misc/2018/08/Latin-America-and-Caribbean-Brief-FINAL-Web-Version.pdf. [10]

WHO (2024), *Global Health Observatory: Age-standardized estimates of current tobacco use, tobacco smoking and cigarette smoking (Tobacco control: Monitor)*, World Health Organization, https://www.who.int/data/gho/data/indicators/indicator-details/GHO/gho-tobacco-control-monitor-current-tobaccouse-tobaccosmoking-cigarrettesmoking-agestd-tobagestdcurr (accessed on 20 February 2024). [16]

WHO (2023), *WHO report on the global tobacco epidemic 2023: Protect people from tobacco smoke*, World Health Organization, https://www.who.int/publications/i/item/9789240077164. [6]

WHO (2021), *WHO report on the global tobacco epidemic 2021: Addressing new and emerging products*, World Health Organization, https://www.who.int/publications/i/item/9789240032095. [9]

WHO (2021), *WHO technical manual on tobacco tax policy and administration*, World Health Organization, https://www.who.int/publications/i/item/9789240019188. [18]

World Bank (2024), *Global Economic Prospects, January 2024*, World Bank, https://doi.org/10.1596/978-1-4648-2017-5. [1]

World Bank (2023), *Global SSB Tax Database*, World Bank, https://ssbtax.worldbank.org/ (accessed on 20 September 2023). [5]

World Bank (2019), *Confronting tobacco illicit trade: a global review of country experiences: Latin America and Carribean*, World Bank, https://documents1.worldbank.org/curated/en/677451548260528135/pdf/133959-REPL-PUBLIC-6-2-2019-19-59-24-WBGTobaccoIllicitTradeFINALvweb.pdf. [15]

3 Tobacco tax policy design in Latin America and the Caribbean

This chapter provides an overview of tobacco tax policy design across 19 countries in Latin America and the Caribbean (LAC). It describes tobacco excise tax structures, tax bases, tax rates, indexation mechanisms, excise tax floors and tax caps, and tobacco excise revenue earmarking practices. The chapter also outlines key aspects of the design of other indirect taxes levied on cigarettes. Finally, the chapter provides information on the authorities involved in tobacco tax policy design, key tobacco excise tax administration features, and tobacco sales regulations.

3.1. Excise taxes on tobacco products

A tobacco excise tax is a tax on tobacco products that are produced for sale within a country or imported and sold in that country, at a specific stage of production or distribution. This section provides information on the design of excise taxes in 19 countries in LAC: Argentina, Bolivia, Brazil, Chile, Colombia, Costa Rica, the Dominican Republic, Ecuador, El Salvador, Guatemala, Honduras, Jamaica, Mexico, Nicaragua, Panama, Paraguay, Peru, Uruguay and Venezuela. These countries were selected on the basis of the most comprehensive information available.

3.1.1. Excise tax structure

Tobacco products are subject to excise taxes in most LAC countries (Figure 3.1 and Table 3.1). All countries levy an excise tax on cigarettes. 17 countries levy an excise tax on cigars, cigarillos and Roll-Your-Own (RYO) tobacco. Honduras is the only country that levies an excise tax on cigarettes but not on other tobacco products. In the Dominican Republic, cigars and cigarillos are not subject to a tobacco excise tax. Only five countries levy an excise tax on heated tobacco products (HTPs), while three ban their sales (Brazil, Mexico, Panama). When sales of e-cigarettes (i.e. electronic delivery systems with nicotine – ENDS – and without nicotine – ENNDS) are not banned, only two countries have an excise tax (Costa Rica and Ecuador) while the majority of countries (ten) do not levy excise tax (Perucic et al., 2022[1]).

The excise tax structure – ad valorem, specific, or mixed – is generally the same across tobacco products. An ad valorem tobacco excise tax is a tax on the value of a transaction between two independent entities at some point in the production or distribution chain. A specific tobacco excise tax levies a lump-sum tax amount per stick, pack, per 1 000 sticks, or per kilogram (WHO, 2021[2]). A mixed excise tax structure combines a specific component together with an ad valorem component. 8 out of the 18 LAC countries with an excise tax on tobacco products other than cigarettes apply the same excise tax structure across tobacco products when the latter are taxed (Argentina, Colombia, El Salvador, Jamaica, Nicaragua, Panama, Paraguay and Venezuela) (Table 3.1).

For cigarettes, specific and mixed excise tax structures are the most common. Seven countries levy a specific excise tax on cigarettes and seven countries levy a mixed excise tax that combine a specific and an ad valorem component (Figure 3.1). In contrast, for cigars, cigarillos and RYO tobacco, most countries levy an ad valorem excise tax.

Very few countries levy an excise tax on new tobacco and nicotine products. A limited number of countries (Brazil, Mexico, Panama) ban the sales of HTPs. When the sales of HTPs are not banned, most countries (11) do not levy excise tax. HTPs are taxed in five countries in LAC (Colombia, Costa Rica, Ecuador, Paraguay and Peru). The excise tax structure is ad valorem in three countries (Costa Rica, Ecuador and Paraguay), mixed in Colombia and specific in Peru. More countries ban the sales of e-cigarettes (Argentina, Brazil, Mexico, Nicaragua, Panama, Uruguay and Venezuela) (WHO, 2023[3]). Ten LAC countries that do not ban nor tax e-cigarettes (Table 3.1). Costa Rica and Ecuador are the only countries in LAC with an excise tax on e-cigarettes (Table 3.1). In Ecuador, the excise tax applies only to electronic delivery systems containing nicotine (ENDS).

Tobacco products intended for export are not subject to excise taxes. This is aligned with the destination-based feature of an excise tax that is levied on domestic consumption and not on goods that are exported and consumed in another jurisdiction (see also Chapter 5).

Some LAC countries have tobacco excise tax exemptions (Box 3.1). Handmade tobacco products benefit from preferential excise tax treatment in two LAC countries, while the Dominican Republic allow non-profit organizations to import cigarettes at a zero-excise tax rate.

Figure 3.1. Excise tax structure by tobacco product

In number of countries, 2022

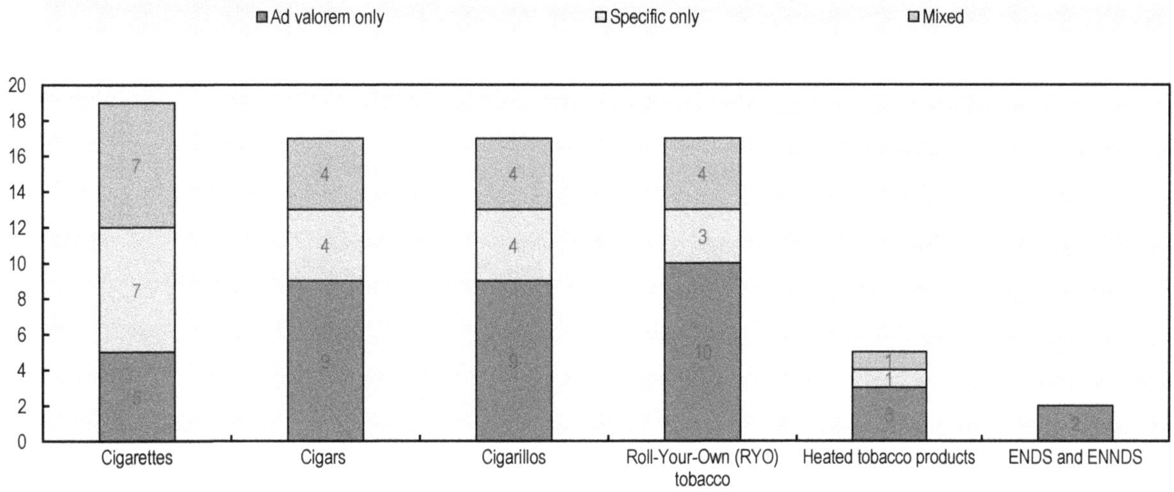

Note: The following countries are included: Argentina, Bolivia, Brazil, Chile, Colombia, Costa Rica, the Dominican Republic, Ecuador, El Salvador, Guatemala, Honduras, Jamaica, Mexico, Nicaragua, Panama, Paraguay, Peru, Uruguay and Venezuela. See Table 3.1 for country detailed information. Following the World Health Organisation (WHO) report on the global tobacco epidemic (WHO, 2021[4]), new tobacco and nicotine products in this report include electronic nicotine delivery systems (ENDS), electronic non-nicotine delivery systems (ENNDS) and heated tobacco products (HTP).
Source: National legislation listed in Annex Table 3.B.1.

Box 3.1. Tobacco excise tax exemptions

Tobacco products for export are commonly exempt from excise tax in the source country. The rationale behind the tobacco tax exemption in the source country is to avoid double taxation, as tobacco products will be subject to excise tax in the destination jurisdiction where the tobacco products will be consumed. The tax will typically be levied at the border (OECD, 2022[5]).

Handmade tobacco products benefit from preferential excise tax treatment in a few LAC countries. In Guatemala, handmade tobacco products (either domestically produced or imported) are exempt from excise tax. In Mexico, handmade tobacco products other than cigarettes are taxed at a rate of 30.4% levied on the final (observed) retail price (excluding VAT) and are not subject to the specific excise tax. In contrast, manufactured tobacco products are taxed at a rate of 160% levied on the ex-factory price (cigarettes) or the final VAT-exclusive retail price (non-cigarettes products). Manufactured tobacco products are also taxed with a specific excise tax.

In the Dominican Republic, non-profit organisations (i.e. institutions engaged in religious, educational, cultural, social assistance and other comparable activities) are not subject to excise tax when they import tobacco products.

Source: National legislation listed in Annex Table 3.B.1.

Table 3.1. Excise tax structure by tobacco product, 2022

	Cigarettes	Cigars	Cigarillos	RYO tobacco	Heated tobacco products (HTP)	ENDS and ENNDS
Argentina	Ad valorem	Ad valorem	Ad valorem	Ad valorem	No excise	Sales are banned
Bolivia	Specific	Specific	Specific	Ad valorem	No excise	No excise
Brazil	Mixed (special regime) Ad valorem (general regime)	Ad valorem	Ad valorem	Ad valorem	Sales are banned	Sales are banned
Chile	Mixed	Ad valorem	Ad valorem	Ad valorem	No excise	No excise
Colombia	Mixed	Mixed	Mixed	Mixed	Mixed	No excise
Costa Rica	Mixed	Mixed	Mixed	Mixed	Ad valorem	Ad valorem
Dominican Republic	Mixed	No excise	No excise	Ad valorem	No excise	No excise
Ecuador	Specific	Ad valorem	Ad valorem	Ad valorem	Ad valorem	Ad valorem (ENDS only)
El Salvador	Mixed	Mixed	Mixed	Mixed	No excise	No excise
Guatemala	Ad valorem	Specific	Specific	Specific	No excise	No excise
Honduras	Specific	No excise	No excise	No excise	No excise	No excise
Jamaica	Specific	Specific	Specific	No excise	No excise	No excise
Mexico	Mixed	Mixed (not-handmade) Ad valorem (handmade)	Mixed (not handmade) Ad valorem (handmade)	Mixed (not handmade) Ad valorem (handmade)	Sales are banned	Sales are banned
Nicaragua	Specific	Specific	Specific	Specific	No excise	Sales are banned
Panama	Ad valorem	Ad valorem	Ad valorem	Ad valorem	Sales are banned	Sales are banned
Paraguay	Ad valorem	Ad valorem	Ad valorem	Ad valorem	Ad valorem	No excise
Peru	Specific	Ad valorem	Ad valorem	Ad valorem	Specific	No excise
Uruguay	Specific	Ad valorem	Ad valorem	Specific	No excise	Sales are banned
Venezuela	Ad valorem	Ad valorem	Ad valorem	Ad valorem	No excise	Sales are banned

Note: Following the WHO report on the global tobacco epidemic (WHO, 2021[4]), new tobacco and nicotine products in this report include ENDS, ENNDS and HTP. Argentina, Brazil, Mexico, Nicaragua, Panama, Uruguay, and Venezuela do not levy an excise tax on e-cigarettes (ENDS and ENNDS) because their sales are banned (WHO, 2023[3]). Brazil, Mexico, and Panama do not levy an excise tax on HTP because their sales are banned (WHO, 2023[3]). In Brazil, two excise tax structures exist for cigarettes: the general regime (ad valorem) and the special regime (mixed). Most taxpayers opt for the special regime as this regime has lower effective tax rate compared to the general regime (Government of Brazil, 2020[6]). In Mexico, handmade tobacco products other than cigarettes are not subject to the specific excise tax (see Box 3.1). Therefore, the excise tax structure for those products is ad valorem only. In Uruguay, the standard rate of the excise tax on tobacco is 70% levied on the price fixed by the Ministry of Economy and Finance. Hence the Ministry of Economy and Finance considers the excise tax structure to be specific.
Source: National legislation listed in Annex Table 3.B.1.

3.1.2. Excise tax base

Tobacco excise tax bases vary across tobacco excise tax structure (see Annex 3.A). Tobacco excise taxes can be levied either on the value (ad valorem) or the quantity (specific) of the tobacco product. The tax base of ad valorem tobacco excise taxes can be: the ex-factory price (exclusive of other indirect taxes); the cost, insurance and freight (CIF) value for imported products (exclusive of other indirect taxes); the retail price suggested by the manufacturer/importer (excluding or including other indirect taxes); or the final (observed) retail price (excluding or including other indirect taxes). The tax base of specific excise tax is either: the number of sticks of tobacco product (single stick or 1 000 sticks); the number of individual packs; or the weight of the tobacco product.

In ad valorem only excise tax structures, the most common tax base across tobacco products is the suggested retail price (Figure 3.2), **although there are significant differences across cigarettes and other tobacco products**. Some countries tax the ex-factory price (or CIF value when the product is imported), but this base is less common than the suggested retail price. The suggested retail price includes the distributors and retailers profit margins, and hence leads to a larger tax base compared to the ex-factory price (see Annex 3.A). In mixed excise tax structures, there is no clear pattern for the choice of the tax base of the ad valorem component, but there are some countries that tax the final (observed) retail price of cigarettes as part of a mixed tax structure.

Most countries with an ad valorem tax exclude other indirect taxes from the excise tax base. Two-thirds of LAC countries with an ad valorem excise tax (either ad valorem only or mixed) exclude the value added tax (VAT), import duties, and others indirect taxes (and, in mixed structures, the specific excise component) from the excise tax base. This is observed across all tobacco products (Figure 3.2 and Figure 5.9 in Chapter 5). As a result, the tax base of the ad valorem tax in those countries is significantly narrower compared to countries that include other indirect taxes in the ad valorem excise tax base.

A limited number of LAC countries use the final retail price of tobacco products for the ad valorem excise tax base (Figure 3.2). In Brazil, Chile, and Colombia, the ad valorem excise tax on tobacco products is based on the tax-inclusive final retail prices. In Mexico, the ad valorem component is levied on the final (observed) tax-exclusive retail price for non-cigarette tobacco products (cigars, cigarillos and RYO tobacco), while it is levied on the ex-factory price net of tax for cigarettes. Domestic manufacturers (i.e. excise taxpayers) in Brazil and Chile declare retail prices to the tax authority via the track and trace system. The ad valorem tax rate is applied on those prices that include all other indirect taxes, including the VAT, import duties, specific excise taxes and other additional indirect taxes. In the case of Brazil, the ad valorem tax is included in its own tax base. In Mexico, each January, excise taxpayers have to provide to the tax administration the list of cigarettes on the market, their wholesale, retail and suggested retail prices and any price modification. Colombia is the only country that requires major retail stores to annually report tobacco products' retail prices to the Revenue Agency. The reported retail prices are used as the excise tax base, including all other indirect taxes. The retail prices reported for the preceding year are adjusted based on projected consumer price index (CPI) growth rates to establish the ad valorem tax base for the subsequent year.

Specific excise taxes in LAC are commonly levied as an amount per stick of tobacco product (Figure 3.3). Most of LAC countries with a specific excise tax (specific only or mixed) on tobacco products use the number of single sticks as the excise tax base. In most cases, the specific tax base is the number of single sticks, except in Bolivia, Honduras and Nicaragua where the specific tax is levied per 1 000 sticks of cigarettes. Other apply the specific component per individual pack of 20 cigarettes (or its equivalent if the individual pack contains less than 20 cigarettes). As RYO tobacco is cut tobacco without uniform packaging, the specific excise duty is often based on weight. However, in Costa Rica and Mexico the tax base is the stick as for other tobacco products. In those cases, equivalence factors are used to compute the tax liability per stick of RYO tobacco based on the average weight of a manufactured cigarette stick (0.6811 gram of tobacco in Costa Rica and 0.75 gram of tobacco in Mexico). Colombia and Peru are the only countries in LAC that levy a specific excise tax on HTPs. There are no countries in LAC which levy a specific excise tax on ENDS or ENNDS.

Figure 3.2. Ad valorem tax base by tobacco products and by excise tax structure

Number of countries, 2022

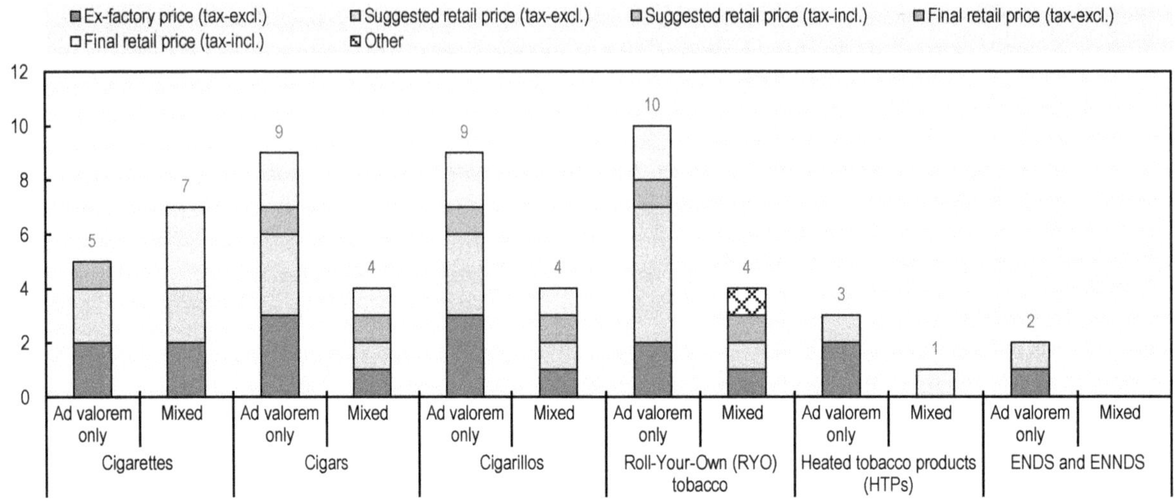

Note: The following countries are included: Argentina, Bolivia, Brazil, Chile, Colombia, Costa Rica, the Dominican Republic, Ecuador, El Salvador, Guatemala, Honduras, Jamaica, Mexico, Nicaragua, Panama, Paraguay, Peru, Uruguay and Venezuela. Following the WHO report on the global tobacco epidemic (WHO, 2021[4]), new tobacco and nicotine products in this report include ENDS, ENNDS and HTP. "Other" refers to the tax base for RYO tobacco products in Colombia which is 10% of the specific excise tax. In Brazil, the ad valorem excise tax base is narrowed as it is 15% of the tax-inclusive retail price.
Source: National legislation listed in Annex Table 3.B.1.

Figure 3.3. Specific tax base by tobacco products and by excise tax structure

Number of countries, 2022

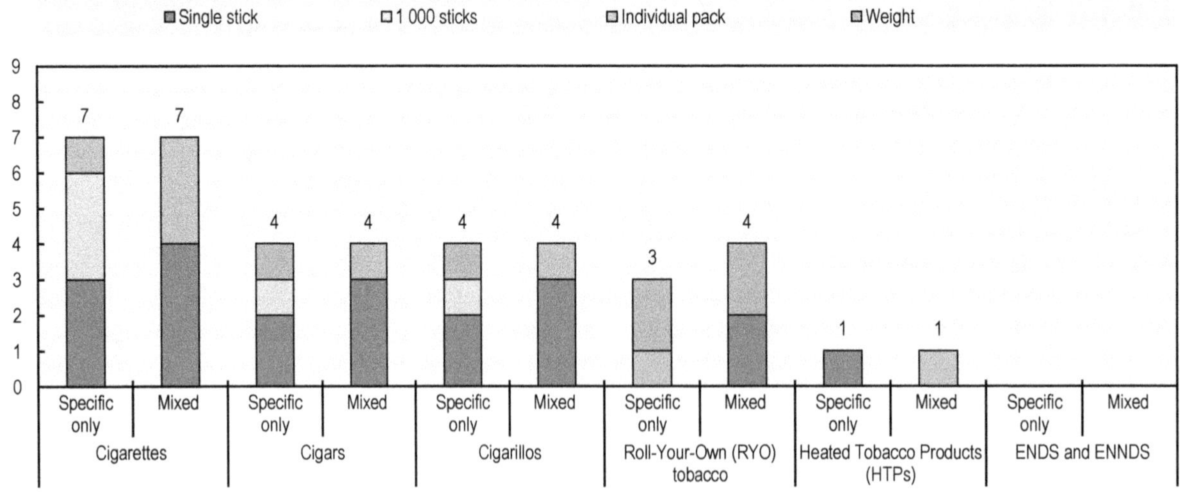

Note: Countries included in the figure are Argentina, Bolivia, Brazil, Chile, Colombia, Costa Rica, the Dominican Republic, Ecuador, El Salvador, Guatemala, Honduras, Jamaica, Mexico, Nicaragua, Panama, Paraguay, Peru, Uruguay and Venezuela. Following the WHO report on the global tobacco epidemic (WHO, 2021[4]), new tobacco and nicotine products in this report include ENDS, ENNDS and HTP.
Source: National legislation listed in Annex Table 3.B.1.

3.1.3. Excise tax rates

The choice for a tobacco excise tax structure has an impact on the tax rates that are set (see Chapter 5). Tobacco tax structures that rely on a single excise component (either specific or ad valorem) will require setting higher statutory rates compared to mixed structures to achieve a similar effective tobacco tax burden. The analysis included below will therefore examine tax rates of mixed excise tax structures separately from the rates in single component excise tax structures.

Cigarettes

In ad valorem only excise tax structures, statutory tax rates on cigarettes vary widely (Figure 3.4). Ad valorem rates range from 100% in Guatemala to 20% in Paraguay which is particularly low as it is levied on a narrow tax base (i.e. the ex-factory price compared to suggested retail price in Argentina, Panama and Venezuela).

In specific only excise tax structures, significant differences in tax rates can be observed for cigarettes (Figure 3.5). The specific tax for a pack of 20 cigarettes is around USD 2 in four out of the seven countries with a specific only excise tax. However, important differences in specific tax can be observed when taxes are expressed in USD purchasing power parity (PPP). Bolivia is the only country which continues to have a tiered system that levies two different rates based on the type of tobacco used in cigarettes (blond or brown).

Figure 3.4. Tax rates levied on cigarettes in ad valorem only excise tax structures

Statutory tax rates for a pack of 20 cigarettes in percentage of the tax base, 2022

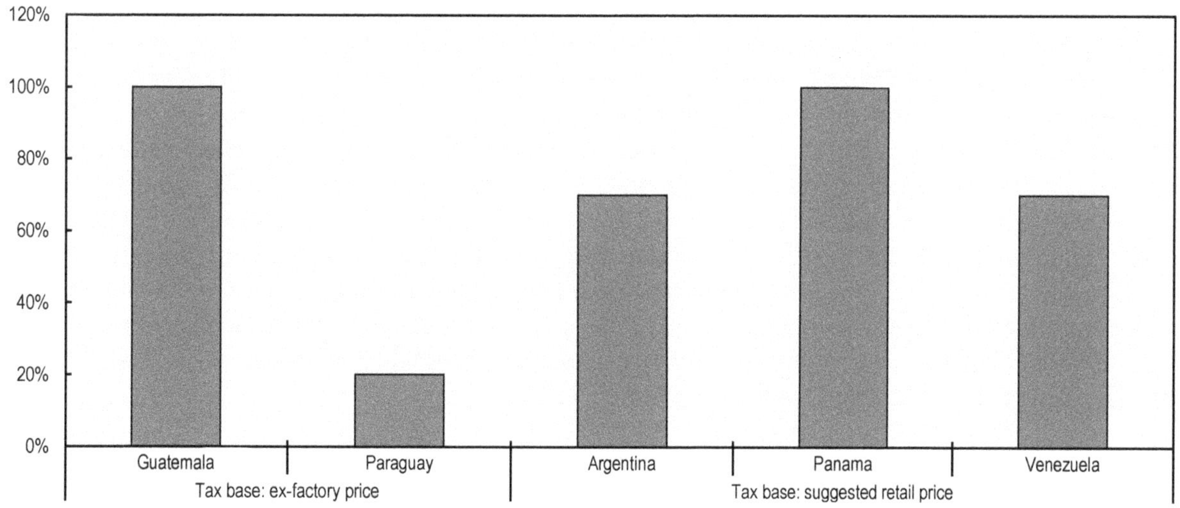

Note: Ad valorem tax bases are tax exclusive in all countries included in the figure, except in Venezuela where the ad valorem tax is levied on the tax-inclusive suggested retail price.
Source: National legislation listed in Annex Table 3.B.1.

Figure 3.5. Tax rates levied on cigarettes in specific only excise tax structures

Specific excise tax for a pack of 20 cigarettes in USD and USD PPP, 2022

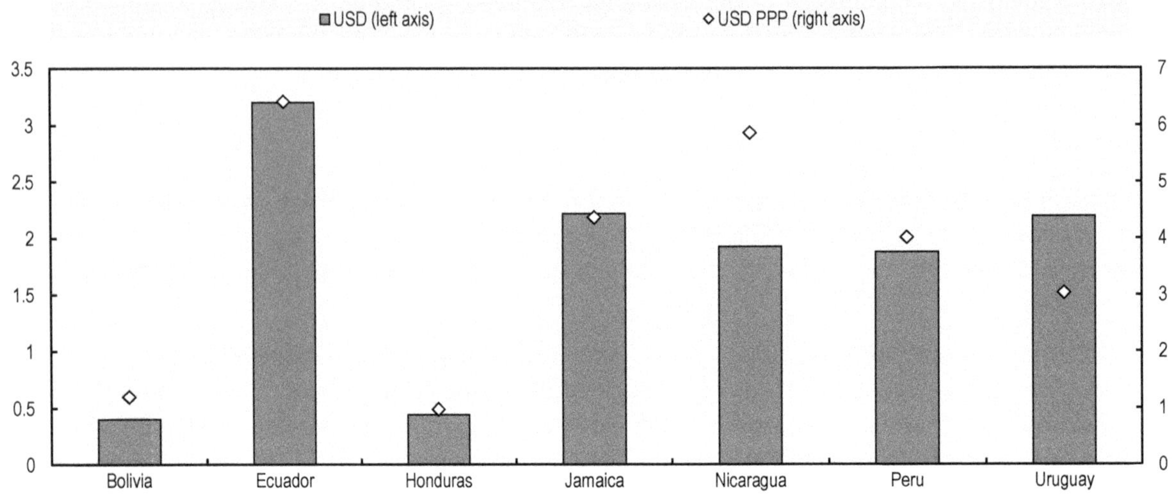

Note: For Bolivia, the figure shows the highest rate of the tiered system. Specific excise taxes in USD purchasing power parity (PPP) are based on the implied PPP conversion rate from the International Monetary Fund (IMF) World Economic Outlook Database (October 2023). Specific excise taxes have been standardized to a 20-unit pack to allow the comparison across countries with different tax bases.
Source: National legislation listed in Annex Table 3.B.1; IMF World Economic Outlook Database (IMF, 2023[7]).

Countries with mixed excise tax structures that have a relatively low ad valorem rate tend to have a higher specific tax (and vice versa). Compared to other countries with a mixed excise tax structure included in Figure 3.6, Chile, Colombia and the Dominican Republic levy relatively higher rates in USD PPP for the specific component (Figure 3.6 – Panel A) and lower rates for the ad valorem component (Figure 3.6 – Panel B). These three countries rely more on the specific component of their mixed systems. Costa Rica has relatively high rates for both the ad valorem and the specific tax component. The ad valorem component is levied on the ex-factory price of cigarettes net of taxes (or CIF value for imported products) which is a narrow base compared to the retail price. The high statutory rate (160%) of the ad valorem component in Mexico is also levied on the narrow tax base of the ex-factory price. The rate of the specific component in Brazil is the lowest across mixed tobacco excise tax structures. While the rate of the ad valorem rate component is relatively high (66.7%), its tax base (15% of the tax-inclusive retail price) is narrow. As a result, the share of the ad valorem component in Brazil represents only 10% of the (tax-inclusive) retail price (Government of Brazil, 2022[8]).

Figure 3.6. Tax rates levied on cigarettes in mixed excise tax structures, 2022

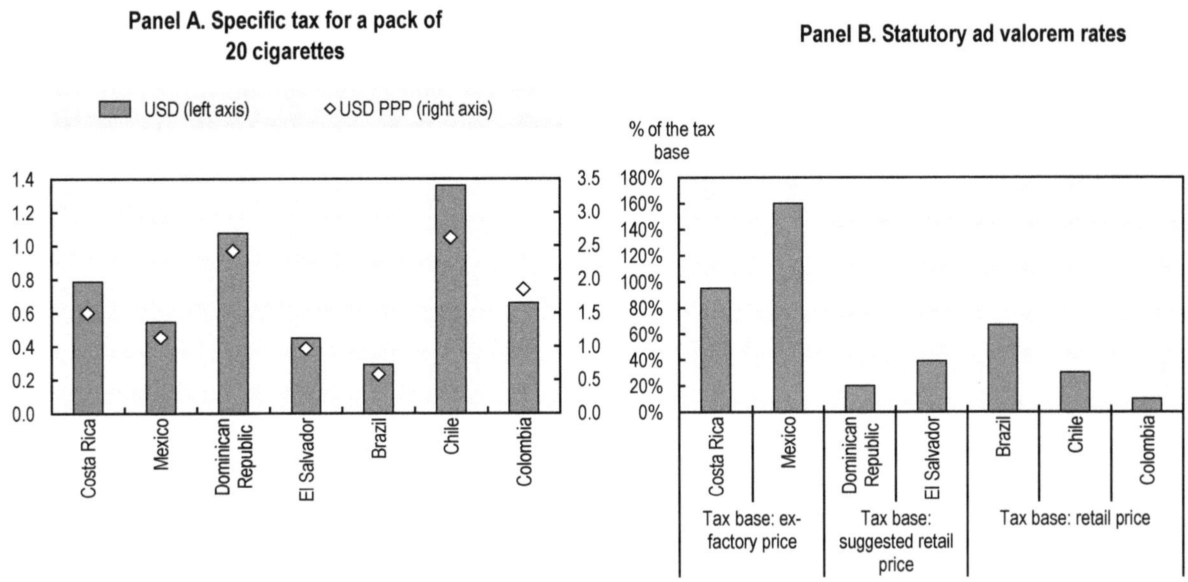

Note: Specific taxes in USD PPP are based on the implied PPP conversion rate from the IMF World Economic Outlook Database (October 2023). Specific excise taxes have been standardized to a 20-unit pack to allow the comparison across countries with different tax bases. The specific tax for Chile is the annual simple average of the monthly CPI-adjusted specific tax. Excise tax rates for Brazil correspond to the special excise tax regime (see Table 3.1). The ad valorem tax base is tax-exclusive in Costa Rica, the Dominican Republic, El Salvador and Mexico; and tax-inclusive in Brazil, Chile and Colombia. In Brazil, the ad valorem excise tax base is narrowed as it is 15% of the tax-inclusive retail price.
Source: National legislation listed in Annex Table 3.B.1; IMF World Economic Outlook Database (IMF, 2023[7]).

Non-cigarette tobacco products

Three countries do not tax all traditional tobacco products (Table 3.2). Honduras does not tax cigars, cigarillos and RYO tobacco. The Dominican Republic does not tax cigars and cigarillos. Jamaica does not tax RYO tobacco.

New tobacco and nicotine products are taxed in a limited number of LAC countries (Table 3.2). Among countries that do not ban the sale of HTP, eleven do not levy an excise tax on HTP (Argentina, Bolivia, Chile, the Dominican Republic, El Salvador, Guatemala, Honduras, Jamaica, Nicaragua, Uruguay and Venezuela). Among the five countries that levy an excise tax on HTP, three tax them with an ad valorem excise tax (Costa Rica, Ecuador and Paraguay), one with a mixed excise tax (Colombia) and one with a specific excise tax (Peru). The rate at which HTP are taxed is similar than the one applied to other non-cigarette tobacco products in three countries (Colombia, Ecuador and Paraguay). Regarding ENDS and ENNDS, ten countries do not ban their sales nor levy an excise tax on those products. Their sales are banned in seven countries (Argentina, Brazil, Mexico, Nicaragua, Panama, Uruguay, Venezuela). Only Costa Rica levies an ad valorem excise tax on both ENDS and ENNDS while the ad valorem tax in Ecuador is levied only on ENDS.

Seven countries have similar excise tax structures across tobacco products and similar (or close) excise tax rates. Those are Colombia (with higher rates for RYO tobacco), Costa Rica (with slightly lower rates for RYO tobacco), Jamaica (with RYO tobacco not taxed), Mexico (with tiered rates ranges for handmade non-cigarette products), Panama, Paraguay (including for new tobacco and nicotine products) and Venezuela. Four countries have a similar excise tax structure and rates across non-cigarette tobacco products but that differ from cigarette taxation (Argentina, Chile, Ecuador and Peru) (Table 3.2).

The tax structure or rates vary across tobacco products in some countries. For instance, in Brazil the ad valorem tax rate is the same for all non-cigarette products except for cigarillos that are taxed at a higher rate (300%). El Salvador has a mixed structure for all tobacco products with same rates applying except for cigars that are taxed significantly higher. In Guatemala, excise tax structures and rates vary. In Nicaragua, the excise tax structure is the same across non-cigarette tobacco products and is levied per kilogram. However, it varies significantly when the statutory rate is standardized to a 20-unit pack. In Bolivia, the excise tax structure is specific for all tobacco products, except for RYO tobacco which is ad valorem. Similarly, in Uruguay the excise tax levied on cigarettes and RYO tobacco is specific while it is ad valorem for cigars and cigarillos (Table 3.2).

Two LAC countries have tiered rates for non-cigarette tobacco products. In Guatemala, the specific tax for cigars has four tiers based on length and weight, with an additional tier rate for cigars imported from non-Central American countries. RYO tobacco is taxed with two tiered rates that vary based on the tobacco's origin (i.e. RYO tobacco imported from Central American countries is taxed at lower rates). In Mexico, handmade tobacco products benefit from a lower ad valorem rate (30.4% against 160% for manufactured tobacco products) and are not subject to the specific excise tax.

Table 3.2. Statutory tax rates on tobacco products

In USD PPP, current USD and percentage of the tax base, 2022

	Cigarettes		Cigars		Cigarillos		RYO tobacco		Heated tobacco products		ENDS and ENNDS	
	Specific tax rate per 20-unit pack USD PPP (USD)	Ad valorem	Specific tax rate per 20-unit pack USD PPP (USD)	Ad valorem	Specific tax rate per 20-unit pack USD PPP (USD)	Ad valorem	Specific tax rate per 20-unit pack USD PPP (USD)	Ad valorem	Specific tax rate per 20-unit pack USD PPP (USD)	Ad valorem	Specific tax rate per 20-unit pack USD PPP (USD)	Ad valorem
Argentina		70% (on SRP)		20% (on SRP)		20% (on SRP)		25% (on SRP)				
Bolivia	0.6 - 1.2 (0.2 - 0.4)		1.2 (0.4)		1.2 (0.4)			50% (on SRP)				
Brazil	0.6 (0.3)	66.7% (on 15% of FRP)		30% (on FRP)		300% (on FRP)		30% (on FRP)				
Chile	2.6 (1.4)	30% (on FRP)		53% (on FRP)		53% (on FRP)		59.7% (on FRP)				
Colombia	1.8 (0.7)	10% (on FRP)	1.8 (0.7)	10% (on FRP)	1.8 (0.7)	10% (on FRP)	3.9 (1.4)	10% (on other)	1.8 (0.7)	10% (on FRP)		
Costa Rica	1.5 (0.8)	95% (on EFP)	1.5 (0.8)	95% (on EFP)	1.5 (0.8)	95% (on EFP)	1.5 (0.8)	65% (EFP)		20% (EFP)		20% (EFP)
Dominican Republic	2.4 (1,1)	20% (on SRP)						20% (on SRP)				
Ecuador	6.4 (3.2)			150% (on SRP)		150% (on SRP)		150% (on SRP)		150% (on SRP)		150% (on SRP)
El Salvador	1.0 (0.5)	39% (on SRP)	1.0 (0.5)	100% (on SRP)	1.0 (0.5)	39% (on SRP)	1.3 (0.6)	39% (on SRP)				
Guatemala		100% (on EFP)	0.005 - 0.26 (0.003 - 0.13)		0.008 - 0.013 (0.004 - 0.006)		0.005 - 0.015 (0.003 - 0.08)					
Honduras	1.0 (0.4)											
Jamaica	4.4 (2,2)		4.4 (2,2)		4.4 (2,2)							

	Cigarettes		Cigars		Cigarillos		RYO tobacco		Heated tobacco products		ENDS and ENNDS	
	Specific tax rate per 20-unit pack USD PPP (USD)	Ad valorem	Specific tax rate per 20-unit pack USD PPP (USD)	Ad valorem	Specific tax rate per 20-unit pack USD PPP (USD)	Ad valorem	Specific tax rate per 20-unit pack USD PPP (USD)	Ad valorem	Specific tax rate per 20-unit pack USD PPP (USD)	Ad valorem	Specific tax rate per 20-unit pack USD PPP (USD)	Ad valorem
Mexico	1.1 (0.5)	160% (on EFP)	1.1 (0.5)	30.4% - 160% (on FRP)	1.1 (0.5)	30.4% - 160% (on FRP)	1.1 (0.5)	30.4% - 160% (on FRP)				
Nicaragua	5.9 (1.9)	...	55.1 (18.1)		10.9 (3.6)		2.9 (1.0)					
Panama		100% (on SRP)		100% (on SRP)		100% (on SRP)		100% (on SRP)				
Paraguay		20% (on EFP)		20% (on EFP)		20% (on EFP)		20% (on EFP)		20% (on EFP)		
Peru	4.0 (1.9)	...		50% (on EFP)		50% (on EFP)		50% (on EFP)	3.3 (1.6)			
Uruguay	3.0 (2.2)	...		70% (on EFP * 1.85)		70% (on EFP * 1.85	0.5 (0.3)					
Venezuela		70% (on SRP)		70% (on SRP)		70% (on SRP)		70% (on SRP)				

Note: Ad valorem tax base "EFP" means "Ex-factory price/CIF value"; "SRP" means "Suggested retail price by the manufacturer/importer"; "FRP" means "Final (observed) retail price"; "Other" refers to the ad valorem tax base for Roll-Your-Own (RYO) tobacco products in Colombia, which is 10% of the specific excise tax applied to RYO tobacco; blank cells mean that there is no excise tax for the corresponding tobacco product. In Mexico, handmade tobacco products other than cigarettes are not subject to the specific excise tax (see Box 3.1). Therefore, the excise tax structure for those products is ad valorem only. In Uruguay, the ex-factory price of cigars and cigarillos is multiplied by 1.85 to get the taxable base of the ad valorem excise tax. Following the WHO report on the global tobacco epidemic (WHO, 2021[4]), new tobacco and nicotine products in this report include ENDS, ENNDS and HTP. Specific taxes are converted into USD PPP with the implied PPP conversion rate available in the IMF World Economic Outlook Database (October 2023). Specific excise taxes have been standardized to a 20-unit pack to allow the comparison between countries with different tax bases. Specific tax in Nicaragua for non-cigarette tobacco products is levied on each kilogram. To compute the specific tax for a 20-unit pack, the median weight of cigars is assumed to be 14.1 grams while for cigarillos the median weight is 2.8 grams (Yassin S, 2022[9]). Specific tax for RYO tobacco products in Colombia and El Salvador is levied on each gram, while it is levied on each kilogram in Nicaragua. To compute the specific tax for an equivalent 20-unit pack of RYO tobacco in those countries, it is assumed that the median cigarette in terms of weight contains 0.75 gram of tobacco (Gallus et al., 2014[10]). In the case of Costa Rica and Mexico, national legislations listed in Annex Table 3.B.1 assume a median weight for a cigarette stick of 0.6811 grams and 0.75 grams respectively.
Source: National legislation listed in Annex Table 3.B.1; IMF World Economic Outlook Database (IMF, 2023[7]).

3.1.4. Indexation mechanisms

Regular adjustments of specific excise taxes on tobacco products are a common practice in LAC. The specific excise tax is adjusted regularly in 11 of the 14 LAC countries with a specific excise tax on cigarettes (Table 3.3). The aim is to ensure that the effective tax expressed in nominal monetary value does not erode over time as a result of inflation and, possibly, real income growth. Some countries, such as Colombia, Chile, the Dominican Republic, Honduras and Nicaragua introduced the indexation of the specific excise tax many years ago (2004 – 2010) while others, such as Mexico and Peru, only have started indexing the specific tax in 2019 (Table 3.3 and Figure 5.2 in Chapter 5). Most of the adjustments in the specific taxes are realised annually through the adoption of decrees rather than being carried out automatically at a fixed point in time. In the Dominican Republic, the specific tax is adjusted quarterly while in Chile it is automatically adjusted every month.

The most common practice is to annually index the specific component with inflation, typically using the growth in the consumer price index (CPI). Ten of the eleven countries that regularly adjust their specific tax use the CPI to determine the increase in the specific tax (Table 3.3). Countries do not impose a ceiling to the annual adjustment of the specific tax, except in Honduras where the annual increase of the specific tax cannot exceed 6%, irrespective of the actual change in the CPI.

Some countries differ from the standard CPI-indexing approach. In Colombia, the annual adjustment to the specific excise tax is, since 2019, equal to the annual growth in the CPI plus four percentage points. In Peru, the indexation mechanism has been reformed in 2020 and the specific excise tax is now indexed only with the increase in the price of cigarettes. Bolivia and Chile index their specific tax using a well-defined tax unit that is indexed itself for inflation. In Bolivia, the specific tax is indexed with the "Unidad de Fomento de Vivienda" that serves as a reference for financial operations, contracts and all types of legal acts in national currency. In Chile, the specific tax is expressed as a share of the "Unidad Tributaria Mensual" which has been implemented since 1974 to adjust all kinds of tax liabilities, fees and other penalties for inflation. No country indexes the specific tax to real income growth.

In Paraguay and Uruguay, tobacco excises are adjusted based on parameters that are not made public. Paraguay updates the ad valorem excise rate according to selected economic parameters. Starting from 2021, the ad valorem rate must be gradually adjusted aligned with the internal and external economic circumstances that the country faces. The Ministry of Finance takes the final decision to increase (or not) the ad valorem rate based on technical reports from the Central Bank and the economic team of the executive power ("Equipo Económico Nacional del Poder Ejecutivo") that are not publicly available. In Uruguay, the specific tax is annually updated via a presidential decree without the use of an explicit parameter that determines the tax increase.

Table 3.3. Specific excise tax adjustment mechanism for cigarettes, 2022

	A specific excise tax is applied (Yes/No)	Regular adjustment mechanism		Indexation with inflation		Indexation with real income growth	
		Yes/No	Frequency	Yes/No	Year of adoption (year of modification)	Yes/No	Frequency
Argentina	No						
Bolivia	Yes	Yes	Annually	Yes	2017	No	
Brazil	Yes	No		No		No	
Chile	Yes	Yes	Monthly	Yes	2010	No	
Colombia	Yes	Yes	Annually	Yes (+ 4 p.p.)	2006 (2016)	No	
Costa Rica	Yes	Yes	Annually	Yes	2012	No	
Dominican Republic	Yes	Yes	Quarterly	Yes	2004 (2012)	No	
Ecuador	Yes	Yes	Annually	Yes	2011 (2016)	No	
El Salvador	Yes	No		No		No	
Guatemala	No						
Honduras	Yes	Yes	Annually	Yes	2010	No	
Jamaica	Yes	No		No		No	
Mexico	Yes	Yes	Annually	Yes	2019	No	
Nicaragua	Yes	Yes	Annually	Yes	2009 (2012)	No	
Panama	No						
Paraguay	No						
Peru	Yes	Yes	Annually	Yes (cigarette CPI)	2001 (2019) (2020)	No	
Uruguay	Yes	Yes	Annually	No		No	
Venezuela	No						

Note: Blank cells mean that there is no adjustment mechanism.
Source: National legislation listed in Annex Table 3.B.1.

3.1.5. Excise tax floors and tax caps

The objective of an excise tax floor in countries with an ad valorem excise tax is to have a minimum tax on each unit of excisable product. Ad valorem excise taxes are levied on the price of the tobacco product (see Annex 3.A), which may result in a low tax liability for products that are sold at a low price. In such settings, tax authorities may wish to set an excise tax floor, defined as a minimum amount of tax that has to be paid when a tobacco product is purchased, regardless of the tobacco product's price. The excise tax floor ensures a consistent stream of tax revenue, that a minimum amount of tobacco tax has to be paid on all tobacco products, irrespective of their price, and reduces opportunities for smokers to “trade down” and buy cheaper tobacco products rather than quit or reduce smoking (WHO, 2021[2]).

Different mechanisms exist to implement an excise tax floor. The most common approach is to set a minimum excise tax liability, which imposes a minimum amount of tax on all excisable tobacco products regardless of their price (WHO, 2021[2]). Alternatively, some countries implement a price floor (i.e. minimum legal price below which retailers are prohibited from selling tobacco products) which, in practice, is equivalent to a minimum excise tax (i.e. the ad valorem rate is applied to the minimum tax base set by the price floor). Similarly, countries can rely on a minimum ad valorem tax base.

Five LAC countries implement a tobacco excise tax floor. Five out of the twelve LAC countries that levy an ad valorem excise tax on cigarettes apply a minimum tax (Table 3.4). Brazil enforces a price floor across all States. Since 2016, a pack of 20 cigarettes cannot be sold at a price below the price floor of BRL 5. Cigarettes are taxed with a specific tax of BRL 1.5 and an ad valorem rate (66.7% on 15% of the retail price). The minimum tax is, therefore, BRL 2 (i.e. tax amount and rates applied to the minimum price) (equivalent to USD 0.4 based on the 2022 exchange rate). Argentina is the only LAC country that applies a minimum specific tax to non-cigarette products and adjusts the excise tax floor for inflation (Table 3.4).

In Costa Rica and Guatemala, the calculation of the excise tax floor is complex. In Costa Rica, the amount of the tax floor corresponds to 85% of total ad valorem indirect taxes levied on the most sold brand of cigarettes (i.e. ad valorem excise tax, the VAT and the Tax for the Rural Development Institute, Inder). Consequently, the sum of the tax liabilities derived from these three ad valorem indirect taxes cannot be lower than the tax floor (Table 3.4). This amount is updated annually through discretionary measures. Guatemala sets a minimum excise tax base for cigarettes which cannot be lower than 75% of the suggested retail price net of taxes. The minimum excise tax liability is then determined by applying the statutory 100% ad valorem rate to this minimum tax base.

Some LAC countries apply a maximum tax rate above which the current tax rate cannot be increased. In Argentina, the excise tax legislation establishes a maximum tax rate of 75% (the excise tax rate in force is currently 70%). In Paraguay a tax range is in place: the minimum tax rate is 18% (14% before the 2019 tobacco tax reform) and the maximum is 24% (20% before the 2019 tobacco tax reform) levied on the ex-factory price net of taxes (the excise tax rate in force is currently 20%). In Uruguay the excise tax rate levied on the price floor cannot exceed 72% (the excise tax rate in place is currently 70%).

Table 3.4. Excise tax floors in LAC countries, 2022

	An ad valorem excise tax is applied (Yes/No)	An excise tax floor is applied (Yes/No)	Tobacco product	Tax base	Statutory tax rate, local currency unit	Specific tax per 20-unit pack USD PPP (USD)	Automatic adjustment mechanism (Yes/No and frequency)
Argentina	Yes	Yes	Cigarettes	Individual pack	169.3	2.5 (1.3)	Yes, quarterly
			Cigars	Single stick	77.5	23.1 (11.9)	Yes, quarterly
			Cigarillos	Individual pack	155.02	2.3 (1.2)	Yes, quarterly
			RYO tobacco	50 g	310.1	2.5 (1.3)	Yes, quarterly
Bolivia	No	No					
Brazil	Yes	Yes	Cigarettes	Minimum price	BRL 1.5 + 66.7% levied on 15% of the tax base	0.8 (0.4)	No
Chile	Yes	No					
Colombia	Yes	No					
Costa Rica	Yes	Yes	Cigarettes	Ad valorem excise tax base, VAT tax base and Inder tax base for the most sold brand	85%	1.5 (0.8)	Yes, annually
Dominican Republic	Yes	No					
Ecuador	Yes	No					
El Salvador	Yes	No					
Guatemala	Yes	Yes	Cigarettes	75% of the suggested retail price, net of the VAT and the excise tax	100%		No
Honduras	No	No					
Jamaica	No	No					
Mexico	Yes	No					

	An ad valorem excise tax is applied (Yes/No)	An excise tax floor is applied (Yes/No)	Tobacco product	Tax base	Statutory tax rate, local currency unit	Specific tax per 20-unit pack USD PPP (USD)	Automatic adjustment mechanism (Yes/No and frequency)
Nicaragua	No	No					
Panama	Yes	Yes	Cigarettes	Individual pack	1.5	3.4 (1.5)	No
Paraguay	Yes	No					
Peru	Yes	No					
Uruguay	No						
Venezuela	Yes	No					

Note: Specific taxes are converted into USD PPP with the implied PPP conversion rate available in the IMF World Economic Outlook Database (October 2023). Specific excise taxes have been standardized to a 20-unit pack to allow the comparison between countries with different tax bases. In Argentina, the minimum specific excise tax for RYO tobacco is levied on weight (i.e. 50 grams). To compute the specific tax for an equivalent 20-unit pack of RYO tobacco, it is assumed that the median cigarette in terms of weight contains 0.75 gram of tobacco (Gallus et al., 2014[10]). The amount of the tax floor in Costa Rica corresponds to 85% of total ad valorem indirect taxes levied on the most sold brand of cigarettes (i.e. ad valorem excise tax, the VAT and the Inder).
Source: National legislation listed in Annex Table 3.B.1; IMF World Economic Outlook Database (IMF, 2023[7]).

3.1.6. Tobacco excise revenue earmarking

Half of the 19 LAC countries allocate some or all of their tobacco excise tax revenue to particular public programs (Table 3.5). In those cases, earmarking is set by law and legally binding (i.e. hard earmarking). The most common approach is to assign a share of the excise tax revenue from tobacco products to one or several public programs. In contrast, some countries choose to allocate all their tobacco excise tax revenue. For example, Paraguay earmarks all tobacco excise tax revenue which is split across several public programs. Only Guatemala allocates all tobacco excise tax revenue to one public program.

Earmarked tobacco excise tax revenue in LAC is primarily used to finance health initiatives. Almost all LAC countries that earmark their tobacco excise tax revenue allocate a significant share to health-related funds and programs that aim at alleviating the harmful effects of tobacco use (i.e. cancer treatment and prevention) (Table 3.5). Hence, in those countries, earmarked tobacco excise tax revenue helps strengthening tobacco control measures.

Table 3.5. Earmarking of tobacco excise tax revenue in LAC countries, 2022

	Earmarking of the excise tax revenue			Earmarking revenue from additional indirect taxes and fees levied on cigarettes (Yes/No)
	Specific component (Yes/No)	Ad valorem component (Yes/No)	Allocation of the excise tax revenue	
Argentina		No		Yes
Bolivia	No			
Brazil	Yes	Yes	Subnational governments; farming-related funds	Yes
Chile	No	No		
Colombia	Yes	Yes	Subnational governments; social protection-related funds	
Costa Rica	Yes	No	Health-related funds; support for sport activities	Yes
Dominican Republic	No	No		
Ecuador	No			
El Salvador	Yes	Yes	Health-related funds	
Guatemala	No	Yes	Health-related funds	
Honduras	No			
Jamaica	Yes		Health-related funds	Yes
Mexico	Yes	Yes	Subnational governments	
Nicaragua	Yes		Sports, physical education and recreation	
Panama		Yes	Health-related funds; customs administration	
Paraguay		Yes	Farming-related funds; health-related funds; support for sport activities	
Peru	No			
Uruguay	Yes		Subnational governments; health-related funds	
Venezuela		No		

Note: Categories of revenue allocation are ordered according to its relative importance in the total allocation. Blank cells mean "does not apply". Additional indirect taxes and fees levied on cigarettes are those listed in Table 3.8. Hence, they do not include the VAT nor import duties. In Nicaragua, the State contributes to at least 10% of the budget of sport, physical education and recreation with revenues from excise on cigarettes, alcohol and soft drinks.
Source: National legislation listed in Annex Table 3.B.1 and Annex Table 3.B.5.

3.2. Other indirect taxes levied on cigarettes

This section examines the design of other indirect taxes, aside from excise taxes, levied on cigarettes. These are the VAT, import duties and other indirect taxes.

3.2.1. Value added tax

The VAT base in countries in LAC is typically broader than the ad valorem excise tax base. Amongst the 19 countries included in this chapter, 14 countries include tobacco excise taxes in the VAT base; i.e., the VAT is levied on the retail price that includes the tobacco excise taxes (Chile, Costa Rica, the Dominican Republic, Ecuador, El Salvador, Guatemala, Honduras, Jamaica, Mexico, Nicaragua, Panama, Paraguay, Peru and Uruguay) (Table 3.6). Only four out of twelve LAC countries which implement an ad valorem excise tax include the VAT and other indirect taxes in its tax base; i.e., the ad valorem tobacco excise tax is levied on a retail price that includes the VAT (Brazil, Chile, Colombia and Venezuela). Amongst the countries which implement a mixed excise tax, four countries (Costa Rica, the Dominican Republic, El Salvador, Mexico) exclude the specific tax from the ad valorem tax base. As result, most countries levy the VAT on top of the tobacco excise taxes, while only a few countries follow an opposite approach and levy the ad valorem excise tax on top of a VAT-inclusive price. More information on this topic is included in Table 5.1 in Chapter 5.

While most countries levy the standard VAT rate, some countries in LAC levy an increased VAT rate on cigarettes. VAT rates imposed on cigarettes range from 10% in Paraguay to 32% in the State of Sao Paulo in Brazil (Table 3.6). Countries apply the standard VAT rate, except in Honduras and Panama where the VAT rate for cigarettes is increased by 3 and 8 percentage points, respectively. In Brazil, the State sales tax rates levied on cigarettes are also increased compared to the standard rates. However, the increased rates vary widely across States. In the case of the State of Sao Paulo, the rate levied on cigarettes is 32% (vs. 18% for the standard rate).

Table 3.6. VAT or sales tax levied on cigarettes in LAC countries, 2022

	An ad valorem excise tax is applied		VAT or sales tax	
	Yes/No	Base includes other indirect taxes (Yes/No)	Base includes excise tax (Yes/No)	Statutory rate
Argentina	Yes	No	No	21% (Standard rate)
Bolivia	No		No	13% (Standard rate)
Brazil	Yes	Yes	No	32% (Increased rate)
Chile	Yes	Yes	Yes	19% (Standard rate)
Colombia	Yes	Yes	No	19% (Standard rate)
Costa Rica	Yes	No	Yes (ad valorem excise tax only)	13% (Standard rate)
Dominican Republic	Yes	No	Yes	18% (Standard rate)
Ecuador	No		Yes	12% (Standard rate)
El Salvador	Yes	No	Yes	13% (Standard rate)
Guatemala	Yes	No	Yes	12% (Standard rate)
Honduras	No		Yes	18% (Increased rate)
Jamaica	No		Yes	15% (Standard rate)
Mexico	Yes	No	Yes	16% (Standard rate)
Nicaragua	No		Yes	15% (Standard rate)
Panama	Yes	No	Yes	15% (Increased rate)
Paraguay	No	No	Yes	10% (Standard rate)
Peru	No		Yes	18% (Standard rate)

	An ad valorem excise tax is applied		VAT or sales tax	
	Yes/No	Base includes other indirect taxes (Yes/No)	Base includes excise tax (Yes/No)	Statutory rate
Uruguay	No		Yes	22% (Standard rate)
Venezuela	Yes	Yes	No	16% (Standard rate)

Note: Blank cells mean that the category does not apply for the respective country. In Brazil, the Tax on the Movement of Goods and Services (ICMS) is a state tax whose rates vary widely across states. The rate presented in this table corresponds to the ICMS' rate in the State of Sao Paulo. In Mexico, companies located in the southern and northern provinces of the country had a reduced VAT rate of 8% until 2024 (DOF 30/12/2020).
Source: National legislation listed in Annex Table 3.B.5.

3.2.2. Import duties

The tax base for import duties levied on cigarettes is the cost, insurance, and freight (CIF) value with large differences in tax rates across countries in LAC. The tax base of import duties applied to cigarettes is the CIF value in all countries covered in this chapter (Table 3.7). Statutory rates of cigarettes' import duties range from 6% in Chile and Peru to 67% in Mexico. In all countries, the statutory rate of import duties levied on cigarettes exceeds the import duties that apply to other imported goods and services. The exception is Chile, which implements a homogeneous import duty structure (6% rate applied uniformly to almost all the products).

In 6 out of the 19 countries, trade agreements grant preferential tax treatment to imported cigarette products. This allows the import of cigarettes at a reduced or zero rate of duty (Table 3.7). Central American countries tend to have a greater number of trade agreements that allow cigarettes to be imported with reduced or zero import duties than South American countries (Bolivia and Chile). Import duty differentiation can lead to unintended effects as the same tobacco product can have a different tax burden depending on its origin.

Table 3.7. Import duties levied on cigarettes and trade agreements, 2022

	Import duties levied on cigarettes		Import duties on all taxable goods and services		Trade agreements that grant cigarettes with lower import duties			
	Tax base	Statutory rate	Average import duty rates	Maximum import duty rate	Number of trade agreements	Import duty tax reduction	Number of trading partners	
							All	LAC
Argentina	Ex-factory price (CIF)	20%	13%	35%	0			
Bolivia	Ex-factory price (CIF)	40%	12%	40%	4	100%	11	11
Brazil	Ex-factory price (CIF)	20%	11%	55%	0			
Chile	Ex-factory price (CIF)	6%	6%	6%	1	100%	48	1
Colombia	Ex-factory price (CIF)	15%	6%	98%	0			
Costa Rica	Ex-factory price (CIF)	40%	6%	150%	11	50% - 100%	60	16
Dominican Republic	Ex-factory price (CIF)	20%	8%	99%	0			
Ecuador	Ex-factory price (CIF)	30%	11%	86%	0			
El Salvador	Ex-factory price (CIF)	30%	6%	164%	7	100%	42	11

	Import duties levied on cigarettes		Import duties on all taxable goods and services		Trade agreements that grant cigarettes with lower import duties			
	Tax base	Statutory rate	Average import duty rates	Maximum import duty rate	Number of trade agreements	Import duty tax reduction	Number of trading partners	
							All	LAC
Guatemala	Ex-factory price (CIF)	20%	6%	40%	7	50% - 100%	11	10
Honduras	Ex-factory price (CIF)	55%	6%	164%	0			
Jamaica	Ex-factory price (CIF)	40%	9%	100%	0			
Mexico	Ex-factory price (CIF)	67%	7%	75%	0			
Nicaragua	Ex-factory price (CIF)	15%	6%	164%	5	100%	47	10
Panama	Ex-factory price (CIF)	15%	5%	260%	0			
Paraguay	Ex-factory price (CIF)	20%	10%	35%	0			
Peru	Ex-factory price (CIF)	6%	2%	11%	0			
Uruguay	Ex-factory price (CIF)	20%	10%	35%	0			
Venezuela	Ex-factory price (CIF)	20%	14%	40%	0			

Note: The average import duty rate for all taxable goods and services corresponds to the simple average of the duty rates. The maximum duty rate refers to the highest ad valorem duty across all headings. A 100% import duty tax reduction implies that the import duty is zero, while a 50% import duty tax reduction implies that the standard rate is halved. Costa Rica and Guatemala have many trade agreements that establish zero-rated import duties for cigarettes, but only one in each country establishes a halved import duty rate for cigarettes.
Source: Based on WTO Tariff Download Facility (WTO, 2023[11]).

3.2.3. Other indirect taxes

Four LAC countries levy additional indirect taxes on cigarettes aside from excise tax, VAT and import duties. Those additional indirect taxes on cigarettes are all ad valorem and levied on the retail price suggested by the manufacturer or the importer (Table 3.8). The exception is the specific component of the tax for the Special Tobacco Fund (FET) in Argentina, which is calculated based on the average weighted price of cigarettes (updated each semester) divided by ARS 0.142. Also, the Customs Administration Fee (CAF) in Jamaica is specific (JMD 1 on each stick of cigarette).

The tax bases of these additional indirect taxes exclude some of the other indirect taxes levied on cigarettes (Table 3.8). In Argentina, the tax base of the Additional Emergency Tax (IAE) is tax inclusive, but the FET tax base excludes the IAE and the VAT. In Costa Rica, the tax base of the Tax for the Rural Development Institute (Inder) excludes the specific excise tax and the VAT. In Jamaica, the tax bases of the ad valorem taxes are all tax exclusive. Only in Brazil, the tax base of Programas de Integração Social e de Formação do Patrimônio do Servidor Público (PIS/Pasep) and Contribuições para os Financiamento da Seguridade Social (Cofins) are tax inclusive.

Revenue from the additional indirect taxes on cigarettes are earmarked. Revenue from the IAE tax in Argentina and the tax for Inder in Costa Rica support public programs for rural households and economic activities. The FET tax in Argentina finances tobacco farming-related initiatives. In Brazil, revenue from the PIS/Pasep and Cofins levied on cigarettes contribute to social protection funds. In Jamaica, the Environmental Levy finances programs to mitigate the environmental impact of manufacturing activities, while revenue from other fees on cigarette imports finance the customs administration.

Table 3.8. Additional indirect taxes and fees levied on cigarettes, 2022

	Name	Tax base	Statutory tax rate	Tax floor (Yes/No)	Automatic adjustment mechanism (Yes/No)	Earmarked (Yes/No)
Argentina	Impuesto Adicional de Emergencia sobre Cigarrillos (IAE)	Suggested retail price (tax inclusive)	7%	No	No	Yes
	Fondo Especial del Tabaco (FET)	Suggested retail price (excl. VAT and IAE but not the excise tax)	8.35%	No	No	Yes
		Average weighted retail price	Average weighted retail price/0.142	No	Yes	Yes
Brazil	Programas de Integração Social e de Formação do Patrimônio do Servidor Público (PIS/Pasep)	Suggested retail price (tax inclusive) multiplied by 3.42	0.65%	No	No	Yes
	Contribuições para os Financiamento da Seguridade Social (Cofins)	Suggested retail price (tax inclusive) multiplied by 2.9169	3%	No	No	Yes
Costa Rica	Impuesto a favor del Instituto de Desarrollo Rural (Inder)	Suggested retail price (excl. VAT and specific excise tax)	2.5%	No	No	Yes
Jamaica	Environmental Levy	CIF value (tax exclusive)	0.5%	No	No	Yes
	Standard Compliance Fee (SCF)	CIF value (tax exclusive)	0.3%	No	No	Yes
	Customs Administration Fee (CAF)	Number of sticks	1.00	No	No	Yes

Source: National legislation listed in Annex Table 3.B.5.

3.3. Authorities involved in the tobacco tax policy design

Central governments in LAC are, in general, responsible for the design of indirect taxes that are levied on tobacco products (Table 3.9). In all countries, tobacco excise tax design falls under the responsibility of the central government through the Ministry of Finance. This is similar for the VAT, except in Brazil where sales tax rates are set at State level. Recently, the sales tax regime in Brazil has been replaced by a dual VAT. In Argentina, Brazil, Paraguay, Uruguay and Venezuela apply the Southern Common Market (MERCOSUR for its acronyms in Spanish) import tariffs.

Table 3.9. Authorities involved in tobacco tax policy setting, 2022

	Excise tax setting	VAT setting	Import duty setting
Argentina	Central government	Central government	Regional trade agreement (MERCOSUR)
Bolivia	Central government	Central government	Central government
Brazil	Central government	Regional governments	Regional trade agreement (MERCOSUR)
Chile	Central government	Central government	Central government
Colombia	Central government	Central government	Central government
Costa Rica	Central government	Central government	Central government
Dominican Republic	Central government	Central government	Central government
Ecuador	Central government	Central government	Central government
El Salvador	Central government	Central government	Central government
Guatemala	Central government	Central government	Central government
Honduras	Central government	Central government	Central government

	Excise tax setting	VAT setting	Import duty setting
Jamaica	Central government	Central government	Central government
Mexico	Central government	Central government	Central government
Nicaragua	Central government	Central government	Central government
Panama	Central government	Central government	Central government
Paraguay	Central government	Central government	Regional trade agreement (MERCOSUR)
Peru	Central government	Central government	Central government
Uruguay	Central government	Central government	Regional trade agreement (MERCOSUR)
Venezuela	Central government	Central government	Regional trade agreement (MERCOSUR)

Source: National legislation listed in Annex Table 3.B.1 and Annex Table 3.B.5.

3.4. Tobacco excise tax administration

There is no generally accepted definition of tobacco tax administration. For the purposes of this report, tobacco tax administration is defined as the range of regulations, procedures, tools and resources necessary to enforce the provisions of tobacco excise tax laws. The enforcement of the provisions of tobacco excise tax laws generally involve: i) identifying and registering tobacco taxpayers; ii) reporting and paying excise tax liabilities; iii) assessing excise tax declarations; iv) monitoring and evaluating tax compliance and enforcement (Preece, 2008[12]; OECD, 2023[13]; WHO, 2021[2]).

The availability of comprehensive information on tobacco tax administration in LAC is scarce. Publicly available information does not provide enough detail for a comprehensive analysis of the approaches and tools used by LAC countries to implement the four main tax administration tasks outlined in the previous paragraph.

However, some key features of tobacco tax administration in LAC can been identified.

- **Tobacco excise duties are all collected at the point of manufacture and/or importation** (see also Chapter 5). In all LAC countries covered in this chapter, the tax legislation defines the tobacco manufacturer as the agent who is legally obliged to pay the tobacco excise taxes. In the case of imported tobacco products, the legal excise taxpayer is the importer. Excise duties on tobacco products have to be paid when the excisable good leaves the manufactory or the warehouse to be released for domestic consumption (see also Chapter 5 for a more in-depth discussion).
- **Tobacco excise duty declarations have to be filled regularly but the type of information that has to be filed tends to be limited** (Annex Table 3.C.1 in Annex 3.C). Almost all LAC countries request tobacco manufacturers/importers to file a tobacco excise tax declaration on a monthly basis. Excise duty payments are generally due within the following 15 calendar days. The excise tax declaration can be made digitally in almost all countries, except in Bolivia and Honduras where tobacco excise taxpayers must present paper-based declarations to the tax authority. In most cases, the excise tax declarations ask for limited information regarding the tobacco transactions. Excise tax returns typically require information on the total value and quantity of tobacco products released for consumption during the period, but do not require taxpayers to report the names of cigarette brands, number of packs, or retail prices (except in Colombia and Mexico).
- **Fiscal marking of tobacco products is limited** (Annex Table 3.C.2 in Annex 3.C). Only 8 out of 19 countries reported the use of fiscal marking through tax stamps or other banderols. Fiscal markings only apply to cigarettes, except in four countries where it applies also to other tobacco products. The use of a unique identifier that contains data for tracking and tracing purposes is restricted to six countries in LAC only (see also Chapter 5).
- **Excise tax returns are regularly assessed in most LAC countries for which there is available information** (Annex Table 3.C.3 in Annex 3.C). Tax authorities routinely assess excise tax returns

to ensure accuracy and completeness of declared information on tobacco transactions. In most cases, tax authorities cross-check excise tax declarations with VAT or income tax declarations. In Peru, the tax administration also uses third-party information (i.e. bank records or financial transactions) to assess excise tax returns. In the case of cigarettes, which are all imported in Peru, tax assessment is made by customs. In countries for which information is available, tax audits are common and risk analysis is used to detect potential areas of non-compliance. Some countries conduct physical controls at production or warehouse sites to compare and check volumes of tobacco products with excise tax declarations.

- **The implementation of the core monitoring tools to secure the tobacco supply chain is still nascent** (Table 3.10, Table 3.11). Licenses are mandatory for manufacturers/importers in all LAC countries, except in Peru. However, other parts of the value chain (i.e. tobacco growing, distribution and retailing of manufactured tobacco products) are mostly out of the scope of licensing systems in LAC. Ten LAC countries have enacted a law containing provisions for the implementation of a national track and trace system, but only four countries have enforced these provisions. Brazil has implemented the first track and trace system in LAC (2008), followed by Ecuador (2017), Chile (2019) and the Dominican Republic (2020), while Panama is in the process of implementing it (Joosens, 2023[14]). Only seven LAC countries have ratified the WHO Protocol to Eliminate Illicit Trade in tobacco products that would enable countries to strengthen international cooperation in enforcing tobacco taxes (see also Chapter 5).

Table 3.10. Mandatory licensing for operators involved in the supply of tobacco products, 2022

	Raw tobacco producers (Yes/No)	Manufacturers/ importers of tobacco products (Yes/No)	Distributors of tobacco products (Yes/No)	Retailers of tobacco products (Yes/No)
Argentina	Yes	Yes	Yes	No
Bolivia	No	Yes	Yes	No
Brazil	No	Yes	Yes	No
Chile	Yes	Yes	Yes	No
Colombia	No	Yes	No	No
Costa Rica	No	Yes	No	No
Dominican Republic	No	Yes	No	No
Ecuador	No	Yes	Yes	No
El Salvador	No	Yes	Yes	Yes
Guatemala	Yes	Yes	Yes	No
Honduras	No	Yes	Yes	No
Jamaica	No	Yes	No	No
Mexico	No	Yes	No	No
Nicaragua	No	Yes	Yes	Yes
Panama	No	Yes	Yes	Yes
Paraguay	No	Yes	Yes	No
Peru	No	No	No	No
Uruguay	No	Yes	No	No

Source: WHO Framework Convention on Tobacco Control (FCTC) implementation database (WHO, 2021[15]); Tobacco Control Laws database (Campaign for Tobacco-Free Kids, 2020[16]); National legislation listed in Annex Table 3.B.1.

Table 3.11. Availability of tools to track and trace tobacco products, 2022

	Year of ratification of the WHO Protocol to Eliminate Illicit Trade in tobacco products	Unique identifier		Track and Trace system		
		In place (Yes/No)	Contains data for tracking and tracing purposes (Yes/No)	Legislated (Yes/No)	Implemented (Yes/No)	Year of implementation
Argentina		No		Yes	No	
Bolivia		No		...		
Brazil	2018	Yes	Yes	Yes	Yes	2008
Chile		Yes	Yes	Yes	Yes	2019
Colombia		No		...		
Costa Rica	2017	No		Yes	No	
Dominican Republic		Yes	Yes	Yes	Yes	2020
Ecuador	2015	Yes	Yes	Yes	Yes	2017
El Salvador		No		...		
Guatemala		No		...		
Honduras		No		...		
Jamaica		No		...		
Mexico		Yes	Yes	No		
Nicaragua	2013	No		Yes	No	
Panama	2016	No		Yes	No	
Paraguay	2022	Yes	Yes	Yes	No	
Peru		No		No		
Uruguay	2014	No		Yes	No	

Note: Cells with "..." indicate that the information is not available. Blank cells indicate that the category does not apply. Unique identifier is a serialized unique identification marking for each package of product. These identifiers are a distinctive combination of numbers, letters or both. The representation of the identifier on the package can be human-readable (letters or numbers) or machine-readable (barcodes) (WHO, 2021[2]).
Source: WHO FCTC implementation database (WHO, 2021[15]); Annex 9.5 "Supplementary information on taxation" of the WHO report on the global tobacco epidemic (WHO, 2023[3]); National legislation listed in Annex Table 3.B.1.

3.5. Tobacco sale regulations

In most LAC countries, tobacco control legislation provides effective regulation that strengthens the effectiveness of tobacco tax policy. The tobacco industry uses many marketing strategies aimed at lowering the impact of tobacco taxes on prices (see also Chapter 5). Some include, for instance, selling tobacco products as single stick, offering promotional discounts through reduced-price coupons or buy-one-get-one-free offers, and selling packs of cigarettes with a smaller amount of sticks compared to regular packs of 20 cigarettes (hence at a lower cost). Recently, ingredients that facilitate nicotine uptake, such as flavouring (sweeter, menthol, etc.), were sometimes added to cigarettes to keep them attractive (Krüsemann et al., 2018[17]; Erinoso et al., 2020[18]). In most LAC countries, those practices are prohibited by tobacco control legislation, except the regulation on cigarette content which is only adopted in Brazil (Table 3.12).

In some LAC countries, tobacco control legislation still falls short in addressing marketing strategies adequately (Table 3.12). In the Dominican Republic, Ecuador and Jamaica, the sale of single cigarette sticks is not prohibited. Evidence suggests that prices of cigarettes sold as sticks are not adjusted upward in response to a tobacco tax increase in order to limit the behavioural response from low-income and younger smokers (Gallien, Occhiali and Ross, 2023[19]). The Dominican Republic and Jamaica do not impose a minimum number of cigarettes per pack. This absence of regulation, together with the possibility of selling sticks of cigarettes, increase the ability of the tobacco industry to provide smokers with lower priced products compared to the conventional pack of 20 cigarettes. Promotional discounts for tobacco products are not prohibited in Guatemala, Honduras, Jamaica and Peru. Therefore, tobacco sellers might be allowed to temporarily reduce the price of their products through different promotional mechanisms to keep tobacco products affordable.

Table 3.12. Sale bans and regulations on tobacco products, 2022

	Bans			Regulation	
	Sale of single stick of cigarettes (Yes/No)	Sale of new tobacco and nicotine products (Yes/No)	Promotional discounts for tobacco products (Yes/No)	Minimum number of cigarettes per pack (Yes/No)	Cigarettes content (Yes/No)
Argentina	Yes	Yes	Yes	Yes	No
Bolivia	Yes	No	Yes	Yes	No
Brazil	Yes	Yes	Yes	Yes	Yes
Chile	Yes	No	Yes	Yes	No
Colombia	Yes	No	Yes	Yes	No
Costa Rica	Yes	No	Yes	Yes	No
Dominican Republic	No	No	...	No	...
Ecuador	No	No	Yes	Yes	No
El Salvador	Yes	No	Yes	Yes	No
Guatemala	Yes	No	No	Yes	No
Honduras	Yes	No	No	Yes	No
Jamaica	No	No	No	No	No
Mexico	Yes	Yes	Yes	Yes	No
Nicaragua	Yes	Yes	...	Yes	...
Panama	Yes	Yes	Yes	Yes	No
Paraguay	Yes	No	Yes	Yes	No
Peru	Yes	No	No	Yes	No
Uruguay	Yes	Yes	Yes	Yes	No
Venezuela	Yes	Yes	Yes	Yes	No

Note: Cells with "..." indicate that the information is not available. Following the WHO report on the global tobacco epidemic (WHO, 2021[4]), new tobacco and nicotine products in this report include ENDS, ENNDS and HTP. Promotional discounts for tobacco products refer to "the sale of tobacco products at a discount rate – such as through reduced-price coupons or buy-one-get-one-free offers" (WHO, 2021[2]). Regulation on cigarette content cover any restriction on the use of ingredients that give a false impression of tobacco quality and that encourage tobacco use in accordance with Article 9 of the FCTC.
Source: WHO report on the global tobacco epidemic (WHO, 2023[3]); Tobacco Control Laws database (Campaign for Tobacco-Free Kids, 2020[16]).

References

Campaign for Tobacco-Free Kids (2020), *Tobacco Control Laws Database*, https://www.tobaccocontrollaws.org/ (accessed on 13 December 2023). [16]

Erinoso, O. et al. (2020), "Global review of tobacco product flavour policies", *Tobacco Control*, Vol. 30/4, pp. 373-379, https://doi.org/10.1136/tobaccocontrol-2019-055454. [18]

Gallien, M., G. Occhiali and H. Ross (2023), "An overlooked market: loose cigarettes, informal vendors and their implications for tobacco taxation", *Tobacco Control*, pp. tc-2023-057965, https://doi.org/10.1136/tc-2023-057965. [19]

Gallus, S. et al. (2014), "Roll-your-own cigarettes in Europe", *European Journal of Cancer Prevention*, Vol. 23/3, pp. 186-192, https://doi.org/10.1097/cej.0000000000000010. [10]

Government of Brazil (2022), *Preços e Impostos*, National Cancer Institute, https://www.gov.br/inca/pt-br/assuntos/gestor-e-profissional-de-saude/observatorio-da-politica-nacional-de-controle-do-tabaco/politica-nacional/precos-e-impostos (accessed on 13 May 2023). [8]

Government of Brazil (2020), *Relação dos optantes pelo Regime Especial de apuração e recolhimento do IPI*, Secretariat of the Federal Revenue, https://www.gov.br/receitafederal/pt-br/assuntos/orientacao-tributaria/regimes-e-controles-especiais/cigarros-relacao-dos-optantes-pelo-regime-especial-de-apuracao-e-recolhimento-do-ipi (accessed on 13 January 2024). [6]

IMF (2023), *World Economic Outlook Database*, International Monetary Fund, https://www.imf.org/en/Publications/WEO/weo-database/2023/October (accessed on 13 January 2024). [7]

Joosens, L. (2023), *Status of the tracking and tracing system required under the WHO FCTC Protocol to Eliminate Illicit Trade in Tobacco Products*, Smoke Free Partnership, https://www.smokefreepartnership.eu/news/sfp-news/the-status-of-the-tracking-and-tracing-system-required-under-the-who-fctc-protocol-to-eliminate-illicit-trade-in-tobacco-products (accessed on 13 December 2023). [14]

Krüsemann, E. et al. (2018), "Identification of flavour additives in tobacco products to develop a flavour library", *Tobacco Control*, Vol. 27/1, https://doi.org/10.1136/tobaccocontrol-2016-052961. [17]

OECD (2023), *Tax Administration 2023: Comparative Information on OECD and other Advanced and Emerging Economies*, OECD Publishing, Paris, https://doi.org/10.1787/900b6382-en. [13]

OECD (2023), "The OECD classification of taxes and interpretative guide", in *Global tax revenue database*, OECD Publishing, Paris, https://www.oecd.org/content/dam/oecd/en/topics/policy-sub-issues/global-tax-revenues/oecd-classification-taxes-interpretative-guide.pdf. [21]

OECD (2022), *Consumption Tax Trends 2022. VAT/GST and Excise, Core Design Features and Trends*, OECD Publishing, Paris, https://doi.org/10.1787/6525a942-en. [5]

OECD (2008), *OECD Glossary of Statistical Terms*, OECD Publishing, Paris, https://doi.org/10.1787/9789264055087-en. [20]

Perucic, A. et al. (2022), "Taxation of novel and emerging nicotine and tobacco products (HTPs, ENDS, and ENNDS) globally and in Latin America", *Revista Panamericana de Salud Publica/Pan American Journal of Public Health*, Vol. 46, https://doi.org/10.26633/RPSP.2022.175. [1]

Preece, R. (2008), "Key controls in the administration of excise duties", *World Customs Journal*, Vol. 2/1, https://worldcustomsjournal.org/Archives/Volume%202%2C%20Number%201%20(Apr%202008)/08%20key_controls_in_the_administration_of_excise_duties.pdf. [12]

WHO (2023), *WHO report on the global tobacco epidemic 2023: Protect people from tobacco smoke*, World Health Organization, https://www.who.int/publications/i/item/9789240077164. [3]

WHO (2021), *Framework Convention on Tobacco Control implementation database*, World Health Organization, https://untobaccocontrol.org/impldb/parties/ (accessed on 13 December 2023). [15]

WHO (2021), *WHO report on the global tobacco epidemic 2021: Addressing new and emerging products*, World Health Organization, https://www.who.int/publications/i/item/9789240032095. [4]

WHO (2021), *WHO technical manual on tobacco tax policy and administration*, World Health Organization, https://www.who.int/publications/i/item/9789240019188. [2]

WTO (2023), *Tariff Download Facility*, World Trade Organization, http://tariffdata.wto.org/default.aspx (accessed on 13 October 2023). [11]

Yassin S, G. (2022), "Appendix F. Cigar Physical Characteristics" Premium Cigars: Patterns of Use, Marketing, and Health Effects, https://www.ncbi.nlm.nih.gov/books/NBK586235/. [9]

Annex 3.A. Definitions of key tax terminology

Ad valorem excise tax: Tax on a selected good produced for sale within a country or imported and sold in that country. These taxes come in the form of a percentage of the value of a transaction between two independent entities at some point of the production/distribution chain (WHO, 2023[3]).

Affordability of cigarettes: Financial capacity of consumers to buy cigarettes, defined as the share of GDP per capita required to purchase 100 packs of 20 cigarettes of the most sold brand (WHO, 2023[3]).

Excises: Taxes levied on a limited range of defined goods at a specific stage of production or distribution (OECD, 2022[5]).

Ex-factory (producer) price: The amount receivable by the manufacturer from the purchaser for a unit of a good or service produced as output minus any VAT or similar deductible tax, invoiced to the purchaser. It excludes any transport charges invoiced separately by the manufacturer (OECD, 2008[21]).

Final (observed) retail price: Price of tobacco products charged to consumers in retail stores. Generally, the final retail price is tax inclusive.

C.I.F (Cost, Insurance and Freight) value: Value of a good delivered at the frontier of the importing country, including any insurance and freight charges incurred to that point, or the price of a service delivered to a resident, before the payment of any import duties or other taxes on imports or trade and transport margins within the country (OECD, 2008[21]).

Cross border shopping: Activity wherein private individuals buy goods abroad because of lower taxes and import them for their own consumption, without declaring them in full in order to avoid paying import duties (OECD, 2008[21]).

Differential rate (or tier): Different tax rates are applied based on one or more characteristics of the product. In the case of tobacco, the characteristics can vary, from price level to the type of tobacco leaf contained in the cigarette, the size of production volume, the packaging, among other parameters (WHO, 2021[2]).

Excise tax floor: Within an ad valorem excise tax structure, minimum amount of tax to pay irrespective of the product's price (WHO, 2021[2]).

Import duties: Customs duties and other import charges which are payable on goods of a particular type when they enter the economic territory (OECD, 2008[21]).

Indexation: Periodic adjustment of the values based on the movement of the consumer price index (or other price index) (OECD, 2008[21]).

Mixed excise structure: Combination of specific and ad valorem excise.

Pre-tax price: Retail price of a product minus the indirect taxes levied on this product (i.e. excise taxes, VAT, import duties and other).

Specific excise tax: Tax on a selected good produced for sale within a country or imported and sold in that country. These taxes come in the form of an amount per stick, pack, per 1 000 sticks, or per kilogram (WHO, 2023[3]).

Suggested retail price: Price suggested by manufacturers to retailers to sell their tobacco products to consumers. The suggested retail price is commonly declared by the manufacturer (or the importer) to the tax administration for the computation of the excise tax liability. In comparison to the ex-factory price, which accounts for all production costs and manufacturer's margins (as well as freight and insurance costs in the case of imported products), the suggested retail price also accounts for the distributors and retailers' profit margins.

Taxes: Compulsory unrequited payments to the general government or to a supranational authority. They are unrequited in the sense that benefits provided by government to taxpayers are not normally in proportion to their payments (OECD, 2023[22]).

Tobacco tax burden: The share of tobacco taxes (excise tax, value added tax, import duty and any other taxes levied) in the retail price of tobacco products (WHO, 2023[3]).

Uniform rate: One rate applied across all brands of the same product type (WHO, 2021[2]).

Value added tax (VAT): Broad-based tax on final consumption by households collected - but not borne - by businesses through a staged process (OECD, 2022[5]).

Annex 3.B. Detailed tables on tobacco excise tax design

Annex Table 3.B.1. National legislation of excise taxes levied on tobacco products, 2022

	Official name	Legislation
Argentina	Impuestos internos a los tabacos	Ley No. 27.430
Bolivia	Impuesto a los consumos específicos (ICE)	Decreto Supremo No. 3442
Brazil	Imposto sobre productos industrializados (IPI)	Decreto No. 8.656
Chile	Impuestos a productos específicos	Decreto Ley 828, reformado por Ley 20899
Colombia	Impuesto al consumo de cigarrillos y tabaco elaborado	Ley No.1819
Costa Rica	Impuesto a los productos de tabaco (specific)	Ley No. 9028 Decreto Ejecutivo No. 37.185
	Impuesto selectivo de consumo (ad valorem)	Ley No. 7.972
Dominican Republic	Impuesto selectivo al consumo	Ley No. 253-12 Reglamento No. 1-18
Ecuador	Impuesto a los consumos especiales	Ley Orgánica para el equilibrio de las finanzas públicas (Suplemento – Registro Oficial No. 744)
El Salvador	Impuesto sobre productos del tabaco	Decreto No. 539
Guatemala	Impuesto sobre tabaco y sus productos	Decreto No. 61-77
Honduras	Impuesto de producción y consumo	Decreto 17-2010
Jamaica	Special consumption tax (SCT)	General Consumption Tax act
Mexico	Impuesto especial sobre producción y servicios (IEPS)	Ley del Impuesto Especial sobre Producción y Servicios (DOF 22-12-2023)
Nicaragua	Impuestos específico al consumo de cigarrillos y otros productos de tabaco (IECT)	Ley No. 987 Ley No. 522 (for earmarking)
Panama	Impuesto selectivo al consumo	Ley No. 69
Paraguay	Impuesto selectivo al consumo	Decreto No. 6619/2022
Peru	Sistema específico del impuesto selectivo al consumo	Decreto Supremo No. 092-2018-EF Resolución Ministerial N0. 034-2020-EF/15
Uruguay	Impuesto específico interno (IMESI)	Decreto Nº 96/990 Texto Ordenado 1996 (Título 11) reformado
Venezuela	Impuesto sobre cigarrillos y manufacturas de tabaco	Decreto N° 1.417

Note: The legislation included in Annex Table 3.B.1 corresponds to the most recent reference text which sets the guiding principles of the excise taxes currently levied in each country.
Source: National legislation.

Annex Table 3.B.2. Excise tax bases by tobacco product, 2022

	Cigarettes		Cigars		Cigarillos		Roll-Your-Own (RYO) tobacco		Heated tobacco products (HTPs)		ENDS and ENNDS	
	Specific	Ad valorem	Specific	Ad valorem	Specific	Ad valorem	Specific	Ad valorem	Specific	Ad valorem	Specific	Ad valorem
Argentina		SRP excl. VAT		SRP excl. VAT		SRP excl. VAT		SRP excl. VAT				
Bolivia	1 000 sticks		1 000 sticks		1 000 sticks			SRP excl. VAT				
Brazil	Individual pack	15% of FRP incl. VAT		FRP incl. VAT		FRP incl. VAT		FRP incl. VAT				
Chile	Single stick	FRP incl. VAT		FRP incl. VAT		FRP incl. VAT		FRP incl. VAT				
Colombia	Individual pack	FRP incl. VAT	Individual pack	FRP incl. VAT	Individual pack	FRP incl. VAT	Gram	Other	Individual pack	FRP incl. VAT		
Costa Rica	Single stick	EFP excl. VAT	Single stick	EFP excl. VAT	Single stick	EFP excl. VAT	Single stick 0.6811 g	EFP excl. VAT		EFP excl. VAT		EFP excl. VAT
Dominican Republic	Individual pack	SRP excl. VAT						SRP excl. VAT				
Ecuador	Single stick			SRP excl. VAT		SRP excl. VAT		SRP excl. VAT		SRP excl. VAT		SRP excl. VAT
El Salvador	Single stick	SRP excl. VAT	Single stick	SRP excl. VAT	Single stick	SRP excl. VAT	Gram	SRP excl. VAT				
Guatemala		EFP excl. VAT	Single stick		Single stick		Net kilogram					
Honduras	1 000 sticks											
Jamaica	Single stick		Single stick		Single stick							
Mexico	Single stick	EFP excl. VAT	Single stick	FRP excl. VAT	Single stick	FRP excl. VAT	Single stick 0.75 g	FRP excl. VAT				
Nicaragua	1 000 sticks		Kilogram		Kilogram		Kilogram					
Panama		SRP excl. VAT		SRP excl. VAT		SRP excl. VAT		SRP excl. VAT				
Paraguay		EFP excl. VAT		EFP excl. VAT		EFP excl. VAT		EFP excl. VAT		EFP excl. VAT		
Peru	Single stick			EFP excl. VAT		EFP excl. VAT		EFP excl. VAT	Single stick			

Uruguay	Individual pack			EFP excl. VAT multiplied by 1.85		EFP excl. VAT multiplied by 1.85	Individual pack 45 g					
Venezuela		SRP incl. VAT		SRP incl. VAT		SRP incl. VAT		SRP incl. VAT				

Note: Ad valorem tax base "EFP" means "Ex-factory price/CIF value"; "SRP" means "Suggested retail price by the manufacturer/importer"; "FRP" means "Final (observed) retail price"; "VAT" means "Value added tax"; "Other" refers to the ad valorem tax base for Roll-Your-Own (RYO) tobacco products in Colombia, which is 10% of the specific excise tax applied to RYO tobacco; blank cells mean that there is no excise tax for the corresponding tobacco product. Following the WHO report on the global tobacco epidemic (WHO, 2021[4]), new tobacco and nicotine products in this report include ENDS, ENNDS and HTP. The excise tax levied on e-cigarettes in Ecuador applies only to those containing nicotine (i.e., ENDS). Argentina, Brazil, Mexico, Nicaragua, Panama, Uruguay, and Venezuela do not levy an excise tax on e-cigarettes (ENDS and ENNDS) because their sales are banned (WHO, 2023[3]). Brazil, Mexico, and Panama do not levy an excise tax HTPs because their sales are banned (WHO, 2023[3]). In Brazil, there are two different excise tax regimes for cigarettes that taxpayers can opt for. The general regime is ad valorem only while the special regime is mixed. Because the special regime results in a lower effective tax rate, most taxpayers opt for the special regime (Government of Brazil, 2020[6]). Thus, the special (mixed) regime represents the main excise tax regime enforced for cigarettes. Specific tax for RYO tobacco products in Costa Rica and Mexico is levied by stick of tobacco products. To compute the specific tax liability by single stick of RYO tobacco, the weight of a cigarette is assumed to be 0.6811 gram of tobacco in Costa Rica and 0.75 gram of tobacco in Mexico according to national legislation.
Source: National legislation listed in Annex Table 3.B.1.

Annex Table 3.B.3. Excise tax rates by tobacco product, 2022

	Cigarettes		Cigars		Cigarillos		Roll-Your-Own (RYO) tobacco		Heated tobacco products (HTPs)		ENDS and ENNDS	
	Specific tax per 20-unit pack USD PPP (local currency)	Ad valorem	Specific tax per 20-unit pack USD PPP (local currency)	Ad valorem	Specific tax per 20-unit pack USD PPP (local currency)	Ad valorem	Specific tax per 20-unit pack USD PPP (local currency)	Ad valorem	Specific tax per 20-unit pack USD PPP (local currency)	Ad valorem	Specific tax per 20-unit pack USD PPP (local currency)	Ad valorem
Argentina		70%		20%		20%		25%				
Bolivia	0.6 - 1.2 (1.6 - 3.0)		1.2 (3.0)		1.2 (3.0)			50%				
Brazil	0.6 (1.5)	66.7%		30%		300%		30%				
Chile	2.6 (1 186.9)	30%		52.6%		52.6%		59.7%				
Colombia	1.8 (2 800)	10%	1.8 (2 800)	10%	1.8 (2 800)	10%	3.9 (5 947)	10%	1.8 (2 800)	10%		
Costa Rica	1.5 (509.4)	95%	1.5 (509.4)	95%	1.5 (509.4)	95%	1.5 (509.4)	65%		20%		20%

Dominican Republic	2.4 (59.3)	20%						20%				
Ecuador	6.4 (3.2)			150%		150%		150%		150%		150%
El Salvador	1.0 (0.5)	39%	1.0 (0.5)	100%	1.0 (0.5)	39%	1.3 (0.6)	39%				
Guatemala		100%	0.005 - 0.26 (0.02 - 1.0)		0.008 - 0.013 (0.03 - 0.05)		0.005 - 0.015 (0.02 - 0.06)					
Honduras	1.0 (10.8)											
Jamaica	4.4 (340.0)		4.4 (340.0)		4.4 (340.0)							
Mexico	1.1 (11.0)	160%	1.1 (11.0)	30.4% - 160%	1.1 (11.0)	30.4% - 160%	1.1 (11.0)	30.4% - 160%				
Nicaragua	5.9 (69.0)		55.1 (648.6)		10.9 (128.8)		2.9 (34.5)					
Panama		100%		100%		100%		100%				
Paraguay		20%		20%		20%		20%		20%		
Peru	4.0 (7.2)			50%		50%		50%	3.3 (6.0)			
Uruguay	3.0 (90.2)						0.5 (13.4)					
Venezuela		70%		70%		70%		70%				

Note: Blank cells mean that there is no excise tax for the corresponding tobacco product. Following the WHO report on the global tobacco epidemic (WHO, 2021[4]), new tobacco and nicotine products in this report include ENDS, ENNDS and HTP. The excise tax levied on e-cigarettes in Ecuador applies only to those containing nicotine (i.e., ENDS). Argentina, Brazil, Mexico, Nicaragua, Panama, Uruguay, and Venezuela do not levy an excise tax on e-cigarettes (ENDS and ENNDS) because their sales are banned (WHO, 2023[3]). Brazil, Mexico, and Panama do not levy an excise tax on HTPs because their sales are banned (WHO, 2023[3]). In Brazil, there are two different excise tax regimes for cigarettes that taxpayers can opt for. The general regime is ad valorem only while the special regime is mixed. Because the special regime results in a lower effective tax rate, most taxpayers opt for the special regime (Government of Brazil, 2020[6]). Thus, the special (mixed) regime represents the main excise tax regime enforced for cigarettes. In Mexico, handmade tobacco products other than cigarettes benefit from a lower ad valorem tax rate (30.4%) against a standard tax rate of 160%, and are not subject to the specific excise tax (see Box 3.1). Specific taxes are converted into USD PPP with the implied PPP conversion rate available in the IMF World Economic Outlook Database (October 2023). Specific excise taxes have been standardized to a 20-unit pack to allow the comparison across countries with different tax bases. Specific tax in Nicaragua for non-cigarette tobacco products is levied by kilogram. To compute the specific tax for a 20-unit pack, the median weight of cigars is assumed to be 14.1 grams while for cigarillos the median weight is 2.8 grams (Yassin S, 2022[9]). Specific tax for Roll-Your-Own (RYO) tobacco products in Colombia and El Salvador is levied by gram. To compute the specific tax for an equivalent 20-unit pack of RYO tobacco, it is assumed that the median cigarette in terms of weight contains 0.75 gram of tobacco (Gallus et al., 2014[10]).

Source: National legislation listed in Annex Table 3.B.1; and IMF World Economic Outlook Database (IMF, 2023[7]).

Annex Table 3.B.4. Excise tax floors by tobacco product, 2022

	Cigarettes		Cigars		Cigarillos		Roll-Your-Own (RYO) tobacco		New tobacco and nicotine products	
	Tax base	Specific tax per 20-unit pack USD PPP (local currency)	Tax base	Specific tax per 20-unit pack USD PPP (local currency)	Tax base	Specific tax per 20-unit pack USD PPP (local currency)	Tax base	Specific tax per 20-unit pack USD PPP (local currency)	Tax base	Specific tax per 20-unit pack USD PPP (local currency)
Argentina	Individual pack	2.5 (169.3)	Single stick	23.1 (1 550.2)	Individual pack	2.3 (155.0)	50 g	2.5 (165.4)		
Brazil	Minimum price	0.8 (2.0)								
Costa Rica	Ad valorem excise tax base, VAT tax base and Inder tax base for the most sold brand	1.5 (522.4)								
Guatemala	75% of the suggested retail price, net of the VAT and the excise	100%								
Panama	Individual pack	3.4 (1.5)								

Note: Blank cells mean that there is no excise tax floor for the corresponding tobacco product. The following countries are not presented in this table as they do not have excise tax floors in place: Bolivia, Chile, Colombia, the Dominican Republic, Ecuador, El Salvador, Honduras, Jamaica, Mexico, Nicaragua, Paraguay, Peru, Uruguay, and Venezuela. Specific taxes are converted into USD PPP with the implied PPP conversion rate available in the IMF World Economic Outlook Database (October 2023). Specific excise taxes have been standardized to a 20-unit pack to allow the comparison across countries with different tax bases. To compute the specific tax for an equivalent 20-unit pack of RYO tobacco in Argentina, it is assumed that the median cigarette in terms of weight contains 0.75 gram of tobacco (Gallus et al., 2014[10]). The minimum specific tax in Costa Rica is equivalent to 85% of the indirect tax liabilities of the most sold brand, including the ad valorem excise tax, the VAT and the Inder. In Brazil, the minimum excise tax payable per 20-unit pack is calculated by applying the specific and ad valorem rates of the special excise tax regime (BRL 1.5 + 66.7% levied on 15% of the retail price) to the minimum legal price of BRL 5.0 for a 20-unit pack of cigarettes.
Source: National legislation listed in Annex Table 3.B.1; and IMF World Economic Outlook Database (IMF, 2023[7]).

Annex Table 3.B.5. National legislation of other indirect taxes on cigarettes, 2022

	VAT legislation	Other indirect taxes	
		Official name	Legislation
Argentina	Decreto No. 280/1997	Impuesto adicional de emergencia sobre cigarrillos (IAE)	Ley No. 24625 y sus modificaciones
		Fondo especial del tabaco (FET)	Ley No. 25465 y sus modificaciones
Bolivia	Ley No. 843		
Brazil	Lei complementar No. 87-96	Programas de integração Social e de formação do patrimônio do servidor público (PIS/Pasep)	RFB NORMATIVE INSTRUCTION NO. 2121
		Contribuições para os financiamento da seguridade social (Cofins)	
Chile	Decreto Ley 825 sobre impuesto a las ventas y servicios		

	VAT legislation	Other indirect taxes	
		Official name	Legislation
Colombia	Decreto Nacional No. 624-89 y sus modificaciones, Estatuto Tributario Libro III		
Costa Rica	Ley No. 6826 y sus modificaciones	Impuesto a favor del Instituto de Desarrollo Rural (Inder)	Ley No. 9036
Dominican Republic	Ley 253-12 y sus modificaciones		
Ecuador	Ley de Régimen Tributario Interno y sus modificaciones		
El Salvador	Decreto Legislativo No. 296 y sus modificaciones		
Guatemala	Decreto No. 27-92 y sus modificaciones		
Honduras	Decreto ley No. 24-1963 y sus modificaciones		
Jamaica	General Consumption Tax act	Environmental Protection Levy	Provisional Collection of Tax Order 2015
		Standard compliance fee (SCF)	Jamaica Customs Agency webpage
		Administration fee (CAF)	
Mexico	Ley del Impuesto al Valor Agregado y normas modificatorias DECRETO por el que se modifica el diverso de estímulos fiscales región fronteriza norte DECRETO de estímulos fiscales región fronteriza sur		
Nicaragua	Ley No. 822 y sus modificaciones		
Panama	Ley No. 06-2005 y sus modificaciones		
Paraguay	Ley No. 6380 y sus modificaciones		
Peru	Texto único ordenado de la Ley del Impuesto General a las Ventas		
Uruguay	Ley No. 18.083 y sus modificaciones, arts. 30º a 32º		
Venezuela	Decreto Constituyente de Reforma Parcial del Decreto con Rango, Valor y Fuerza de Ley que establece el Impuesto al Valor Agregado		

Note: Blank cells indicate that the category does not apply.
Source: National legislation.

Annex 3.C. Detailed tables on tobacco excise tax administration

Annex Table 3.C.1. Processes to report and pay excise tax liabilities levied on tobacco products, 2022

	Tax filing			Time limits for payments	
	Excise tax returns include detailed information on tobacco transactions	Format	Frequency	Number of days	Calendar/ Business days
Argentina	No	Digital	Monthly	20	Calendar
Bolivia	No	Paper	Monthly	10	Calendar
Brazil	No	Digital	Monthly	10	Calendar
Chile	No	Digital	Monthly	15	Calendar
Colombia	Yes	Digital	Biweekly	5	Calendar
Costa Rica	No	Digital	Monthly	15	Calendar
Dominican Republic	No	Digital	Monthly	20	Calendar
Ecuador	No	Digital	Monthly	30	Calendar
El Salvador	No	Digital	Monthly	10	Business
Guatemala	No	Digital	Monthly	10	Business
Honduras	No	Paper	Monthly	10	Business
Jamaica	No	Digital	...	...	...
Mexico	Yes	Digital	Monthly	17	Calendar
Nicaragua	No	Digital	Monthly	15	Calendar
Panama	No	Digital	Monthly	15	Calendar
Paraguay	No	Digital	Monthly	30	Calendar
Peru	No	Digital	Monthly	14 – 22	Calendar
Uruguay	No	Digital	Monthly	10	Calendar

Note: Cells with "..." indicate that the information is not available. Blank cells indicate that the category does not apply. Excise tax returns are considered to include detailed information on tobacco transactions when taxpayers are required to provide information that goes beyond the total value and/or volume of tobacco transactions.
Source: National legislation listed in Annex Table 3.B.1.

Annex Table 3.C.2. Use of tax stamps against excise duty payments in LAC countries, 2022

	Excise taxpayers required to purchase tax stamps	
	For cigarettes	For other tobacco products
Argentina	Yes	Yes
Bolivia	Yes	Yes
Brazil	Yes	No
Chile	Yes	No
Colombia	No	...
Costa Rica	No	...
Dominican Republic	Yes	No
Ecuador	Yes	No

	Excise taxpayers required to purchase tax stamps	
	For cigarettes	For other tobacco products
El Salvador	No	No
Guatemala	No	No
Honduras	No	No
Jamaica	No	No
Mexico	Yes	Yes
Nicaragua	No	No
Panama	No	No
Paraguay	Yes	Yes
Peru	No	No
Uruguay	No	No

Note: Cells with "..." indicate that the information is not available. "Other tobacco products" refers to cigars, cigarillos and Roll-Your-Own (RYO) tobacco products. Tax stamps are labels or marks placed on certain types of consumer goods to show that the applicable excise tax has been paid (WHO, 2021[2]). In Mexico, handmade tobacco products other than cigarettes do not require the purchase and affixing of tax stamps.
Source: Annex 9.5 "Supplementary information on taxation" of the WHO report on the global tobacco epidemic (WHO, 2023[3]).

Annex Table 3.C.3. Practices implemented by tax administrations in LAC to assess tobacco excise tax compliance, 2022

	Regular assessment of excise tax returns (Yes/No)	Cross-checks of excise tax returns		Tax audits based on risk analysis (Yes/No)	Physical controls (Yes/No)
		with declarations of other taxes (Yes/No)	with third-parties information (Yes/No)		
Argentina	...	...	...	...	...
Bolivia	...	...	...	...	...
Brazil	...	...	...	...	...
Chile	...	...	...	...	...
Colombia	...	...	...	...	...
Costa Rica	...	...	...	...	...
Dominican Republic	...	...	...	...	...
Ecuador	...	...	...	...	...
El Salvador	...	...	...	...	...
Guatemala	Yes	No	No	No	Yes
Honduras	...	...	...	...	...
Jamaica	...	...	...	...	...
Mexico	Yes	Yes	Yes	Yes	Yes
Nicaragua	...	...	...	...	...
Panama	...	...	...	...	...
Paraguay	Yes	Yes	No	Yes	No
Peru	Yes	Yes	Yes	Yes	Yes
Uruguay	...	...	...	...	...

Note: Cells with "..." indicate that the information is not available.
Source: Replies from the OECD questionnaire sent to LAC countries in August 2023.

4 Assessing tobacco tax policy performance in Latin America and the Caribbean

This chapter finds that countries in Latin America and Caribbean (LAC) have gradually aligned their tobacco tax system with the best practices of the World Health Organisation (WHO). Nevertheless, there remains significant scope to further implement tobacco tax best practices across countries in the region that would strengthen the effectiveness of tobacco excise tax and other policies.

4.1. Framework to assess countries' tobacco tax policy performance

The MPOWER policy package has successfully contributed to setting tobacco control reforms in motion. The MPOWER framework has been successful in evaluating country progress in the implementation of a broad set of tobacco control policies based on a few indicators, including the tobacco tax share (see Table 1.3 in Chapter 1).

However, the good performance with respect to the tobacco tax share target (i.e. the R component) is not a sufficient condition for a tobacco tax design and policy that is successful in reducing smoking prevalence (Drope, Siu and Chaloupka, 2022[1]). In countries where the tobacco tax share is substantial and at WHO best practice level, the tax share does not necessarily imply that cigarettes are expensive. While a high tax share can result in high prices, this is not necessarily the case when pre-tax prices are low (see Figure 1.13 in Chapter 1). Therefore, the tobacco tax share has to be evaluated jointly with the price level and the affordability of tobacco products.

As a response to the limitations of relying on a single indicator (i.e. the tobacco tax share), the cigarette tax scorecard was developed to capture the strengths and weaknesses of countries' tobacco tax structures. The cigarette tax scorecard assesses countries' cigarette tax systems with respect to their consistency with the four established best practices for cigarette taxation: 1) cigarette price of the most sold brand of cigarette, 2) changes in cigarette affordability, 3) tax shares (average between the proportion of total indirect taxes and excise tax in the retail price of the most sold brand of cigarette), 4) tax structure (i.e. design of excise taxes applied to cigarettes) (Chaloupka et al., 2020[2]; Chaloupka et al., 2021[3]; Drope et al., 2024[4]).

To evaluate a country's tobacco tax policy, the OECD builds on the WHO's existing tobacco tax policy best practices (BP) summarised in Box 4.1. It assesses the extent to which LAC countries have implemented some of the WHO tobacco tax policy best practices, following the same (criteria and colour-based) approach as MPOWER. The selected best practices all relate to core tobacco excise tax design and follow closely the topics discussed in Chapter 3. The evaluation criteria and the country information that is used to assess the implementation of tobacco tax best practices in countries in LAC are presented in Annex 4.A and Box 4.2. The summary scores for each country are included in Table 4.1.

The Framework presented in this report is a complement to the MPOWER framework and the cigarette tax scorecard that has as objective to identify opportunities for reform in individual countries. Rather than tracking reform progress over time, the aim of this report's framework is to identify opportunities for country tobacco tax design and administrative reform.

Box 4.1. WHO tobacco tax policy best practices

- **BP1**: Increase tobacco taxes significantly to reduce the affordability of tobacco products. To reduce affordability, tax increases need to result in nominal retail price increases that exceed the increase in nominal incomes (**affordability**).
- **BP2**: Rely more on tobacco excise tax increases over other general indirect (and direct) taxes as they are most effective in raising both absolute and relative prices of tobacco products (**type of taxes**).
- **BP3**: Rely more on specific tobacco taxes over ad valorem taxes, and in mixed tax structures, give more weight to the specific tax component than to the ad valorem tax component (**tobacco excise tax structure**).
- **BP4**: Tax all traditional tobacco products (i.e. cigarettes, cigars, cigarillos, Roll-Your-Own (RYO) tobacco) with a tobacco excise tax (**taxable products**).

- **BP5**: Tax new and emerging tobacco and nicotine products (i.e. electronic nicotine delivery systems (ENDS), electronic non-nicotine delivery systems (ENNDS) and heated tobacco products (HTP)) with an excise tax when their sales are not banned (**taxable products**).
- **BP6**: For ad valorem tax structures, set the retail price as the tax base rather than, for instance, the cost, insurance and freight (CIF) value or the producer price (**tobacco excise tax base**).
- **BP7**: For specific excise taxes, clearly define the tax base (for cigarettes, cigars and bidis, it is the number of sticks; for other tobacco products, such as smokeless tobacco or RYO tobacco, it is the weight of tobacco) (**tobacco excise tax base**).
- **BP8**: Tax all tobacco and nicotine products similarly (e.g. similar tax structure, similar tax rates) (**tobacco excise tax rates**).
- **BP9**: Rely more on uniform excise tax rates over tiered rates (**tobacco excise tax rates**).
- **BP10**: Adjust specific tobacco taxes for inflation and real income growth on a regular basis (prices are not decreased at times of deflation) (**indexation**).
- **BP11**: Complement the ad valorem excise tax with an excise tax floor (e.g. a minimum excise tax, a minimum retail price) (**excise tax floors**).
- **BP12**: Implement non-tax policies affecting price levels of tobacco products (e.g. sale restriction for single stick of cigarettes, bans of promotional discounts for tobacco products, minimum number of cigarettes per pack) to support the effectiveness of tobacco tax policies (**sale regulations that affect tobacco tax policy design**).

Note: Some key sale regulations (BP12) have been included in the list of best practices on tobacco tax policy design because they closely interact with the other best practices, in particular those related to the tax base (BP6 and BP7). For instance, countries may have decided to comply strongly with BP6 and BP7 because they underperform on BP12. Strong compliance of BP12 might support high scores for BP6 and BP7.

Source: WHO technical manual on tobacco tax policy and administration (WHO, 2021[5]).

4.2. Applying the tobacco taxation policy performance framework to countries in LAC

While significant country differences can be observed, many countries have implemented tobacco taxes that are completely or moderately aligned with a large selection of WHO best practices (Figure 4.1). A large majority of LAC countries (15 out of 18) have designed their tobacco tax regime such that it meets more than half of the WHO tobacco tax best practices either completely or moderately. Five out of 18 countries (Chile, Colombia, Ecuador, Mexico and Panama) meet 50% or more of the WHO best practices in a complete manner.

In some countries, however, the tobacco tax regime is only weakly aligned with WHO best practices. In four countries (Bolivia, the Dominican Republic, Guatemala and Honduras) the tobacco tax design meets less than 30% of the WHO best practices at complete level of implementation. Some LAC countries (Mexico, Peru and Uruguay) have a polarised tobacco tax policy design in that they completely meet a significant number of best practices but also fail to meet many of them.

Figure 4.1. Overview of the implementation of the WHO tax policy best practices

Percentage of best practices, 2022

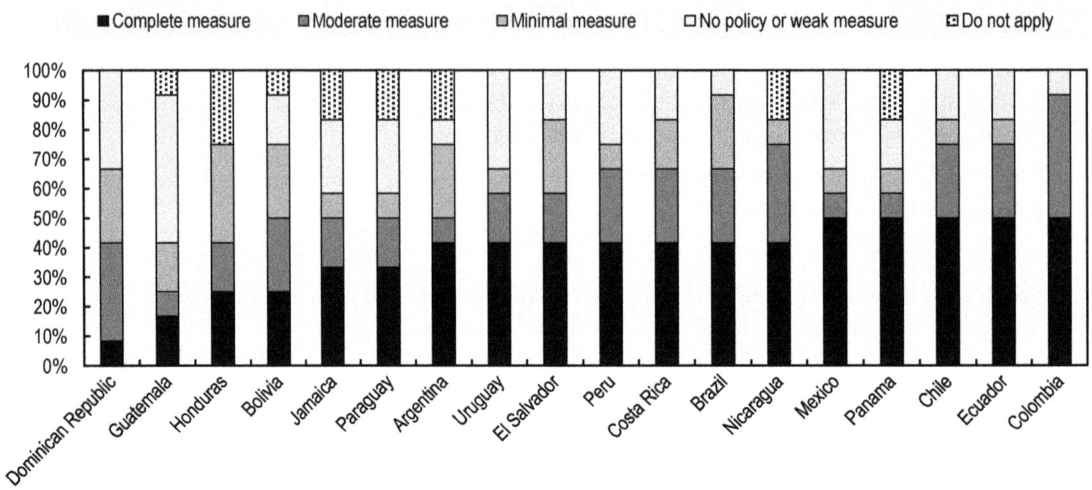

Note: WHO best practices in tobacco tax policy design are those listed in Box 4.1. For an explanation of the criteria used to classify each country's compliance with the WHO best practices, see Box 4.2 and Annex Table 4.A.1.
Source: OECD based on WHO technical manual on tobacco tax policy and administration (WHO, 2021[5]); WHO report on the global tobacco epidemic (WHO, 2023[6]); and information listed in Chapter 3.

Box 4.2. The OECD tobacco tax policy evaluation framework

The OECD tobacco tax policy evaluation framework identifies the extent to which a country's tobacco tax policy aligns with the WHO tobacco tax policy best practices. The framework follows a criteria and colour-based methodology that is aligned with the MPOWER framework. The overview of country alignment with the WHO best practices is presented in Figure 4.1. The detailed evaluation is included in Table 4.1. More detailed guidance on the methodology is included in Annex 4.A: Annex Table 4.A.1 presents the tax criteria used to assess the implementation of the WHO tobacco tax policy best practices; Annex Table 4.A.2 provides country information regarding the implementation of each best practice.

The evaluation of country tobacco tax policies based on the WHO best practices provides an objective basis that allows for country comparisons. Nevertheless, country specific settings may require policies that slightly deviate from these BPs. Hence, the evaluation framework is not meant to replace country specific tobacco tax policy analysis but has to be complemented with it.

Additional guidance with respect to the interpretation of some best practices (BP) is included below:

- BP1 calls for ambitious tax reforms that reduce affordability and, therefore, induce behavioural change. If increases in tobacco tax rates are modest, they will have to be continued over several years in order to induce behavioural change. The criteria to assess compliance with BP1 are the trends in the tobacco tax share and the affordability of the most sold brand of cigarettes. The tobacco tax share corresponds to the share of total indirect taxes levied on a 20-cigarette pack (i.e., tobacco excise taxes, VAT, import duties, and any other indirect taxes). To assess whether affordability changed on average since 2012, the average annual percentage change in affordability is calculated as the least squares growth rate for each country with four or more years of data. The affordability of cigarettes is considered unchanged if the least squares trend in GDP per capita that is required to purchase 2 000 cigarettes (that is, 100 packs of 20 cigarettes) is not significant at the 5% level. Cigarettes are considered to have become less (more) affordable on average if the least squares trend in GDP per capita required to purchase 2 000 cigarettes is positive (negative) and significantly different from zero at the 5% level (WHO, 2023[6]).

- BP2 states that tobacco excise taxes are more effective than other indirect taxes to raise absolute and relative tobacco prices. To assess the extent to which countries are compliant with BP2, the share of excise tax in the total tobacco tax mix is calculated. The tobacco tax mix expresses the share of all tobacco taxes as a percentage of the retail price of the most sold brand of cigarettes. Thresholds for BP2 have been set to allow classification in four categories that show the relative reliance on tobacco excise taxes: no reliance (0% of total tobacco tax mix), less reliance than on other indirect taxes (<50%); more than half but less than two thirds reliance on excise taxes (50%< reliance <66%); more than two thirds reliance on excise taxes (>66%).
- BP3 signals that specific excise taxes are preferred over ad valorem tobacco taxes, as they are more effective in reducing tobacco consumption and raising tax revenues. The excise tax structure assessed in this chapter is that applied to cigarettes.
- BP4 calls for the taxation of all traditional tobacco products (i.e. cigarettes, cigars, cigarillos and RYO tobacco) as they are equally harmful for health.
- BP5: Following the WHO report on the global tobacco epidemic (WHO, 2021[7]), new tobacco and nicotine products include ENDS, ENNDS and HTP. In decision FCTC/COP8(22), Parties recognized those emerging products as tobacco products and were reminded to apply the measures agreed in the WHO Framework Convention on Tobacco Control (FTCT) (including Article 6 relative to taxation) in the same way as for conventional tobacco products.
- BP7 signals that specific excise taxes should be levied on a legally defined tax base and that a "disaggregated" tax base (such as the use of single sticks of cigarettes) is preferred over a more aggregated tax base (e.g. kilograms, 1 000 sticks) especially for tobacco products that do not have standard packaging (e.g. cigars, RYO tobacco). The use of single sticks as the tax base prevents packaging strategies that aim at manipulating the tax base to reduce tax liabilities. Levying the specific excise tax per single stick is particularly critical in countries with no regulation regarding the minimum/maximum number of sticks per pack of tobacco products. Even in countries that forbid the sale of single stick cigarettes, single sticks can be used as the tax base.
- BP10: Regular indexation could be annual when inflation is low, or more regular at times of high inflation.
- BP12: The three key sale regulations that impact pricing behaviour considered in BP12 are sale restriction for single stick of cigarettes, bans of promotional discounts for tobacco products, and minimum number of cigarettes per pack.

Source: OECD.

Table 4.1. The implementation of the WHO tax policy best practices, 2022

	Affordability (BP1)	Type of taxes (BP2)	Excise tax structure (BP3)	Taxable products		Excise tax base		Excise tax rate		Indexation (BP10)	Tax floor (BP11)	Sale regulation (BP12)
				(BP4)	(BP5)	(BP6)	(BP7)	(BP8)	(BP9)			
Argentina							–			–		
Bolivia	...											
Brazil												
Chile												
Colombia												
Costa Rica												
Dominican Republic												
Ecuador												
El Salvador												
Guatemala										–		
Honduras						–		–			–	
Jamaica						–					–	
Mexico												
Nicaragua						–					–	
Panama							–			–		
Paraguay							–			–		
Peru												
Uruguay												

Note: Cells with "..." mean data not reported/not available. Cells with " – " means the best practice does not apply because of the absence of specific or ad valorem excise tax. For an explanation of the criteria used to classify each country's compliance with the WHO best practices, see Box 4.2 and Annex Table 4.A.1. The ad valorem tax base (BP6) for non-cigarette tobacco products in Mexico is the final (observed) retail price net of taxes (see Table 3.2 in Chapter 3 and Table 6.51 in Chapter 6). However, BP6 in Mexico is considered weak since the ad valorem tax base for cigarettes (i.e., the most popular tobacco product, see Table 6.49 in Chapter 6 and Figure 1.2 in Chapter 1) is the ex-factory price net of tax.

Source: OECD based on WHO technical manual on tobacco tax policy and administration (WHO, 2021[5]); WHO report on the global tobacco epidemic (WHO, 2023[6]); and information listed in Chapter 3.

The MPOWER R indicator is positively correlated with the implementation of the WHO best practices. Figure 4.2 indicates that LAC countries that perform better on the MPOWER R indicator also perform better on the broader set of WHO tobacco tax best practices, on average. This finding is supported by the tobacco tax literature that finds that well-designed tobacco taxes are effective in increasing the tax burden on tobacco products (Ngo et al., 2022[8]; Hutchinson et al., 2022[9]; Paraje et al., 2023[10]; Ghebreyesus and Clark, 2023[11]).

While the overall correlation is positive, there are large differences across countries. For instance, El Salvador meets more than 40% of the tobacco best practices completely but has a relatively low tax share compared to other countries that meet 40% of the best practices, such as Argentina, Brazil, Nicaragua and Peru. The Dominican Republic and Guatemala meet less than 20% of the tobacco tax best practices completely but have a tax share similar to the tax share in Costa Rica and Panama.

Figure 4.2. Correlation between the implementation of the WHO tobacco tax policy best practices and the MPOWER R tax share measure

Complete WHO best practices as a share of total best practices and tobacco tax share as a percentage of the retail price of the most sold brand of cigarettes, 2022

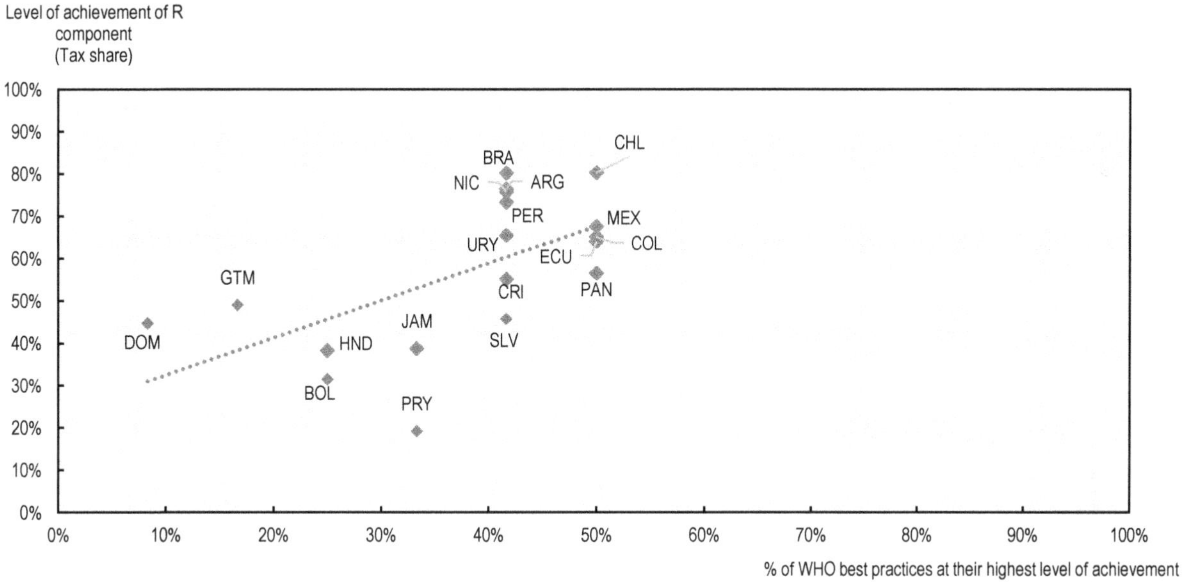

Note: The percentage of complete WHO best practices is included in Figure 4.1. The R component tax share is the share of total tobacco taxes as a percentage of the retail price of the most sold brand of cigarettes (see Figure 1.12, Chapter 1).
Source: OECD based on WHO technical manual on tobacco tax policy and administration (WHO, 2021[5]); WHO report on the global tobacco epidemic (WHO, 2023[6]); and information listed in Chapter 3.

On average, LAC countries perform well with respect to a significant number of WHO tobacco tax best practices (Figure 4.3). The OECD tobacco tax policy evaluation framework identifies the best practices that are broadly followed or implemented in a more limited manner across countries. On average, LAC countries perform well with respect to:

- BP2 (countries rely more on excise taxes than on other indirect taxes to raise the absolute and relative price of tobacco products)
- BP3 (specific taxes are more common than ad valorem tobacco taxes)
- BP4 (all traditional tobacco products are taxed)
- BP7 (specific taxes are levied on a tax base per unit of tobacco product)
- BP9 (uniform rates are more common than tiered rates)
- BP12 (sale regulations are in place that support the effectiveness of tobacco taxes).

However, some best practices are implemented moderately or not at all (Figure 4.3). On average, LAC countries perform weakly with respect to:

- BP1 (tobacco excise tax rates are set too low and the affordability of tobacco products increased overtime) (see Table 1.4 in Chapter 1)
- BP5 (when their sales are allowed, new tobacco and nicotine products are often not taxed) (ECLAC, 2019[12])
- BP6 (ad valorem tobacco taxes are levied on a narrow base)
- BP8 (tax rates vary significantly across tobacco products, which runs the risk that consumers substitute one tobacco product for another, thereby undermining the overall effectiveness of tobacco tax policy)
- BP10 (specific taxes are not regularly adjusted based on changes in the CPI and income growth to ensure tobacco products become less affordable over time)
- BP11 (the absence of an excise tax floor in countries with an ad valorem tobacco tax).

The weak implementation of certain best practices can explain why, on average, cigarettes remain relatively affordable in countries in LAC (see Table 1.4 in Chapter 1). This is reflected in BP1 that shows that tobacco tax reform to reduce tobacco affordability remains a reform priority across countries in LAC (Figure 4.3).

The affordability of cigarettes is also explained by the fact that tobacco tax policy design is not sufficiently embedded within the broader functioning of the tobacco market. Market factors, such as the price level, the dispersion of prices across different brands, the purchasing power of smokers across the income distribution, and the industry's strategic response to tobacco tax policy (both reforms and the absence thereof), also have an impact on a country's performance with the R-component and the extent to which tobacco products are affordable (IARC, 2008[13]). On average in LAC, these factors are not sufficiently incorporated in tobacco tax policy evaluation and reform (see Chapter 5 for a detailed discussion).

Figure 4.3. Overview of LAC compliance with WHO best practices on tobacco tax policy design

Percentage of LAC countries, 2022

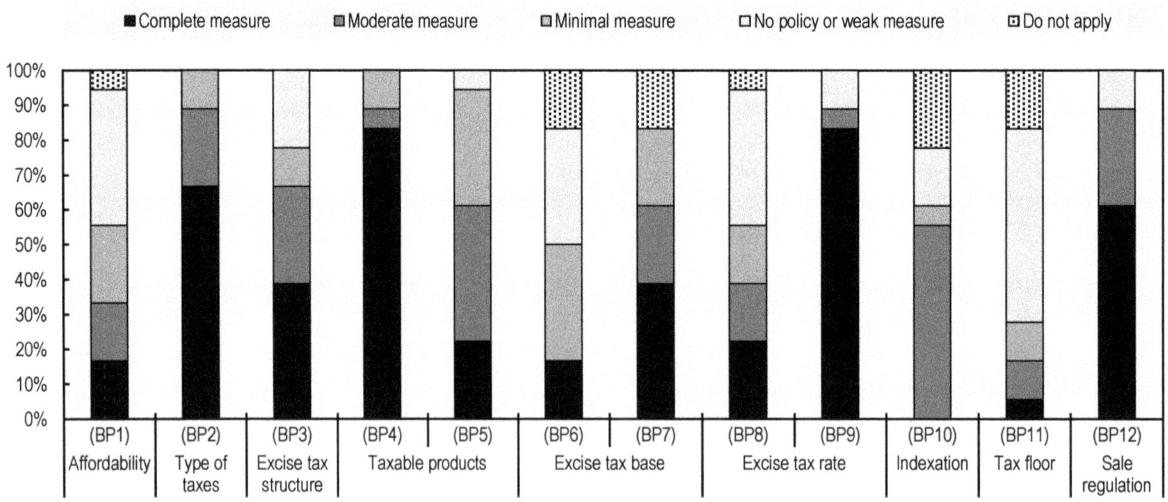

Note: The following countries are included: Argentina, Bolivia, Brazil, Chile, Colombia, Costa Rica, the Dominican Republic, Ecuador, El Salvador, Guatemala, Honduras, Jamaica, Mexico, Nicaragua, Panama, Paraguay, Peru and Uruguay. For an explanation of the criteria used to classify each country's compliance with the WHO best practices, see Box 4.2 and Annex Table 4.A.1.

Source: OECD based on WHO technical manual on tobacco tax policy and administration (WHO, 2021[5]); WHO report on the global tobacco epidemic (WHO, 2023[6]); and information listed in Chapter 3.

References

Chaloupka, F. et al. (2021), *Cigarette Tax Scorecard (2nd Edition)*, Tobacconomics, https://tobacconomics.org/research/cigarette-tax-scorecard-2nd-edition/. [3]

Chaloupka, F. et al. (2020), "Tobacconomics cigarette tax scorecard", *Tobacconomics*, https://www.tobacconomics.org/files/research/636/uic-tobacco-scorecard-report-eng-v7.1.pdf. [2]

Drope, J. et al. (2024), *Tobacconomics cigarette tax scorecard (3rd ed.)*, Bloomberg School of Public Health, Johns Hopkins University, https://tobacconomics.org/research/cigarette-tax-scorecard-3rd-edition/. [4]

Drope, J., E. Siu and F. Chaloupka (2022), "Perseverance is innovation: the journey to successful tobacco tax reform", *Tobacco Control*, Vol. 31/2, pp. 241-242, https://doi.org/10.1136/tobaccocontrol-2021-057088. [1]

ECLAC (2019), *Fiscal Panorama of Latin America and the Caribbean 2019: Tax policies for resource mobilization in the framework of the 2030 Agenda for Sustainable Development*, Economic Commission for Latin America and the Caribbean, https://www.cepal.org/en/publications/44517-fiscal-panorama-latin-america-and-caribbean-2019-tax-policies-resource. [12]

Ghebreyesus, T. and H. Clark (2023), "Health taxes for healthier lives: an opportunity for all governments", *BMJ Global Health*, Vol. 8/Suppl 8, p. e013761, https://doi.org/10.1136/bmjgh-2023-013761. [11]

Hutchinson, B. et al. (2022), "The case for investment in tobacco control: lessons from four countries in the Americas", *Revista Panamericana de Salud Pública*, Vol. 46, p. 1, https://doi.org/10.26633/rpsp.2022.174. [9]

IARC (2008), *Methods for Evaluating Tobacco Control Policies*, International Agency for Research on Cancer, https://www.iarc.who.int/wp-content/uploads/2018/07/Tobacco_vol12.pdf. [13]

Ngo, A. et al. (2022), "As countries improve their cigarette tax policy, cigarette consumption declines", *Tobacco Control*, Vol. 33/e1, https://doi.org/10.1136/tc-2022-057486. [8]

Paraje, G. et al. (2023), "Taxation of tobacco, alcohol, and sugar-sweetened beverages: reviewing the evidence and dispelling the myths", *BMJ Global Health*, Vol. 8/Suppl 8, p. e011866, https://doi.org/10.1136/bmjgh-2023-011866. [10]

WHO (2023), *WHO report on the global tobacco epidemic 2023: Protect people from tobacco smoke*, World Health Organization, https://www.who.int/publications/i/item/9789240077164. [6]

WHO (2021), *WHO report on the global tobacco epidemic 2021: Addressing new and emerging products*, World Health Organization, https://www.who.int/publications/i/item/9789240032095. [7]

WHO (2021), *WHO technical manual on tobacco tax policy and administration*, World Health Organization, https://www.who.int/publications/i/item/9789240019188. [5]

Annex 4.A. Assessing compliance with WHO tobacco tax policy design best practices

Annex Table 4.A.1. Criteria used to assess LAC countries' compliance with WHO tobacco tax policy design best practices

		No policy or weak measure	Minimal measure	Moderate measure	Complete measure
Affordability	BP1	Cigarettes are not less affordable since 2012 and the tax share has not increased.	Cigarettes are not less affordable since 2012 despite an increase in the tax share.	Cigarettes are less affordable since 2012 but the tax share has not increased.	Cigarettes are less affordable since 2012 and the tax share has increased.
Type of taxes	BP2	The excise tax share in the tobacco tax mix is equal to 0%.	The excise tax share in the tobacco tax mix is below 50%.	The excise tax share in the tobacco tax mix is between 50% and 66%.	The excise tax share in the tobacco tax mix is above 66%.
Excise tax structure	BP3	The excise tax structure is ad valorem only.	The excise tax structure is mixed, with a lower reliance on the specific component.	The excise tax structure is mixed, with a greater reliance on the specific component.	The excise tax structure is specific only.
Taxable products	BP4	None of the traditional tobacco products are subject to excise tax.	Up to two out of four traditional tobacco products are subject to excise tax.	Three out of four traditional tobacco products are subject to excise tax.	All traditional tobacco products are subject to a tobacco excise tax.
	BP5	Sales of new tobacco and nicotine products are authorised, and the products are not subject to an excise tax.	The sale of new tobacco and nicotine products is regulated but the products are not taxed with an excise tax.	At least one type of new tobacco and nicotine products is taxed. If more than one new tobacco and nicotine products are taxed, the rate at which they are taxed is lower than the one applied to conventional cigarettes. If they are not taxed, the sales of at least one type of new tobacco and nicotine products are banned.	At least two types of new tobacco and nicotine products are taxed at a rate that is similar to the one applied to conventional cigarettes. If they are not taxed, the sales of new tobacco and nicotine products are banned.
Excise tax base	BP6	The ad valorem excise tax is levied on the tax-exclusive ex-factory price/CIF value.	The ad valorem excise tax is levied on the tax-exclusive retail price suggested by the manufacturer/importer.	The ad valorem excise tax is levied on the tax-inclusive retail price suggested by the manufacturer/importer.	The ad valorem excise tax is levied on the tax-inclusive final (observed) retail price.
	BP7	The specific excise tax is levied on weight or one of the characteristics of the tobacco products (e.g. quality, or length).	The specific excise tax is levied on a unit: a pack of tobacco products (without specifying the number of sticks per pack), or 1 000 sticks.	The specific excise tax is levied on a unit: a pack of tobacco products with a number of sticks per pack sets out in the law.	The specific excise tax is levied on a unit: a single stick of tobacco products, whose characteristics are defined in the law.
Excise tax rate	BP8	Excise tax structures differ across tobacco and nicotine products.	Tobacco and nicotine products are subject to the same excise tax structure but to different statutory tax rates.	Tobacco and nicotine products are subject to the same excise tax structure and to the same statutory tax rates. However, when levied on weight, the tax rates per 20-unit packs differ significantly.	Tobacco and nicotine products are subject to the same excise tax structure and to the same tax rates per 20-unit packs.
	BP9	Tiered taxation for most tobacco products.	Tiered taxation for few tobacco products.	Tiered taxation for one tobacco product.	Uniform tax rates for all tobacco products.

		No policy or weak measure	Minimal measure	Moderate measure	Complete measure
Indexation	BP10	No indexation.	Regular adjustments but not necessarily annual indexation for inflation.	Indexation for inflation only, preferably automatic.	Annual indexation for inflation and real income growth.
Tax floor	BP11	No excise tax floor.	Excise tax floor for some tobacco products, but not expressed as a fixed amount (i.e., specific).	Excise tax floor for some tobacco products and expressed as a fixed amount (i.e., specific).	Excise tax floor for all tobacco products and expressed as a fixed amount (i.e., specific).
Sale regulation	BP12	There are no sale regulations.	One out of three key sale regulations is in place.	Two out of three key sale regulations are in place.	All the three key sale regulations are in place.

Note: Data for all Best Practices (BPs) are for 2022. See Box 4.2 for further explanation on the indicators used to classify countries according to the criteria.
Source: OECD based on WHO technical manual on tobacco tax policy and administration (WHO, 2021[5]); WHO report on the global tobacco epidemic (WHO, 2023[6]); and information listed in Chapter 3.

Annex Table 4.A.2. Data supporting the assessment of country compliance with the WHO tobacco tax policy best practices

	Trends in affordability and tax burden (BP1)	Excise tax share in the tobacco tax mix (%) (BP2)	Excise tax structure and specific excise tax share over excise tax mix (%) (BP3)	Taxable tobacco products		Excise tax base		Excise tax rate		Indexation (BP10)	Tax floor (BP11)	Number of key sale regulations in place (BP12)
				Traditional tobacco products (BP4)	New tobacco and nicotine products (BP5)	Ad valorem tax base (BP6)	Specific tax base (BP7)	Comparable tax rates across tobacco products (BP8)	Uniform tax rates (BP9)			
Argentina	Least square trend in affordability is not significant and tax share increased by 6.5 p.p.	81%	Ad valorem only (0%)	4	Sales of ENDS and ENNDS banned Sales of HTP are not banned nor taxed	Tax-excl. SRP	N/A	Different statutory tax rates	Yes, for all tobacco products	N/A	Specific for all tobacco products	3
Bolivia	…	63%	Specific only (100%)	4	Sales regulated but not taxed	Tax-excl. SRP	1 000 sticks	Different tax structures	Tiered for cigarettes only	Annually on CPI	No	3
Brazil	Least square trend in affordability is negative and tax share increased by 17.1 p.p.	46%	Mixed, greater reliance on specific (73%)	4	Sales banned	Tax-incl. FRP	Pack of 20 sticks	Different statutory tax rates	Yes, for all tobacco products	No	Specific and for cigarettes only	3
Chile	Least square trend in affordability is positive but tax share reduced by 1.7 p.p.	80%	Mixed, greater reliance on specific (53%)	4	Sales regulated but not taxed	Tax-incl. FRP	Single stick	Different tax structures	Yes, for all tobacco products	Monthly on CPI	No	3
Colombia	Least square trend in affordability is positive and tax share increased by 14.6 p.p.	76%	Mixed, greater reliance on specific (80%)	4	HTPs taxed at similar rate Sales of ENDS and ENNDS are not banned nor taxed	Tax-incl. FRP	Individual pack of 20 sticks/ gram	Same structure, but tax rates per 20-unit packs differ	Yes, for all tobacco products	Annually on CPI	No	3

	Trends in affordability and tax burden (BP1)	Excise tax share in the tobacco tax mix (%) (BP2)	Excise tax structure and specific excise tax share over excise tax mix (%) (BP3)	Taxable tobacco products		Excise tax base		Excise tax rate		Indexation (BP10)	Tax floor (BP11)	Number of key sale regulations in place (BP12)
				Traditional tobacco products (BP4)	New tobacco and nicotine products (BP5)	Ad valorem tax base (BP6)	Specific tax base (BP7)	Comparable tax rates across tobacco products (BP8)	Uniform tax rates (BP9)			
Costa Rica	Least square trend in affordability is not significant and tax share reduced by 3.3 p.p.	83%	Mixed, greater reliance on specific (56%)	4	Taxed with lower rate	Tax-excl. EFP	Single stick	Different statutory tax rates	Yes, for all tobacco products	Annually on CPI	Non-specific and for cigarettes only	3
Dominican Republic	Least square trend in affordability is not significant and tax share reduced by 13.9 p.p.	66%	Mixed, greater reliance on specific (62%)	2	Sales regulated but not taxed	Tax-excl. SRP	Individual pack of 20 sticks	Different tax structures	Yes, for all tobacco products	Quarterly on CPI	No	0
Ecuador	Least square trend in affordability is positive but tax share reduced by 9 p.p.	83%	Specific only (100%)	4	Taxed with similar rate	Tax-excl. SRP	Single stick	Different tax structures	Yes, for all tobacco products	Annually on CPI	No	2
El Salvador	Least square trend in affordability is positive but tax share reduced by 7.2 p.p.	75%	Mixed, lower reliance on specific (38%)	4	Sales regulated but not taxed	Tax-excl. SRP	Single stick	Same structure, but tax rates per 20-unit packs differ	Yes, for all tobacco products	No	No	3
Guatemala	Least square trend in affordability is not significant and tax share did not change	78%	Ad valorem only (0%)	4	Sales not regulated or taxed	Tax-excl. EFP	Single stick/ kilogram	Different tax structures	Yes, for cigarettes Tiered for non-cigarettes	N/A	Non-specific and for cigarettes only	2

	Trends in affordability and tax burden (BP1)	Excise tax share in the tobacco tax mix (%) (BP2)	Excise tax structure and specific excise tax share over excise tax mix (%) (BP3)	Taxable tobacco products		Excise tax base		Excise tax rate		Indexation (BP10)	Tax floor (BP11)	Number of key sale regulations in place (BP12)
				Traditional tobacco products (BP4)	New tobacco and nicotine products (BP5)	Ad valorem tax base (BP6)	Specific tax base (BP7)	Comparable tax rates across tobacco products (BP8)	Uniform tax rates (BP9)			
Honduras	Least square trend in affordability is positive and tax share increased by 4.3 p.p.	40%	Specific only (100%)	1	Sales regulated but not taxed	N/A	1 000 sticks	N/A	Yes, for all tobacco products	Annually on CPI	N/A	2
Jamaica	Least square trend in affordability is not significant and tax share reduced by 7.3 p.p.	63%	Specific only (100%)	3	Sales regulated but not taxed	N/A	Single stick	Same structure and tax rates	Yes, for all tobacco products	No	N/A	0
Mexico	Least square trend in affordability is not significant and tax share reduced by 0.8 p.p.	80%	Mixed, lower reliance on specific (29%)	4	Sales banned	Tax-excl. EFP (for cigarettes) Tax-excl. FRP (for non-cigarettes)	Single stick	Same structure and tax rates	Yes, for cigarettes Tiered for non-cigarettes, based on the manufacturing process	Annually on CPI	No	3
Nicaragua	Least square trend in affordability is positive and tax share increased by 46.6 p.p.	83%	Specific only (100%)	4	Sales of ENDS and ENNDS banned Sales of HTPs are not banned nor taxed	N/A	1 000 sticks/ kilogram	Same structure, but tax rates per 20-unit packs differ	Yes, for all tobacco products	Annually on CPI	N/A	2
Panama	Least square trend in affordability is not significant and tax share did not change	77%	Ad valorem only (0%)	4	Sales banned	Tax-excl. SRP	N/A	Same structure and tax rates	Yes, for all tobacco products	N/A	Specific and for cigarettes only	3

	Trends in affordability and tax burden (BP1)	Excise tax share in the tobacco tax mix (%) (BP2)	Excise tax structure and specific excise tax share over excise tax mix (%) (BP3)	Taxable tobacco products		Excise tax base		Excise tax rate		Indexation (BP10)	Tax floor (BP11)	Number of key sale regulations in place (BP12)
				Traditional tobacco products (BP4)	New tobacco and nicotine products (BP5)	Ad valorem tax base (BP6)	Specific tax base (BP7)	Comparable tax rates across tobacco products (BP8)	Uniform tax rates (BP9)			
Paraguay	Least square trend in affordability is not significant and tax share increased by 1.9 p.p.	53%	Ad valorem only (0%)	4	HTPs taxed at similar rate Sales of ENDS and ENNDS are not banned nor taxed	Tax-excl. EFP	N/A	Same structure and tax rates	Yes, for all tobacco products	N/A	No	3
Peru	Least square trend in affordability is not significant and tax share increased by 31.1 p.p.	79%	Specific only (100%)	4	HTPs taxed at lower rate Sales of ENDS and ENNDS are not banned nor taxed	Tax-excl. EFP	Single stick	Different tax structures	Yes, for all tobacco products	Annually on CPI	No	2
Uruguay	Least square trend in affordability is not significant and tax share reduced by 3.2 p.p.	72%	Specific only (100%)	2	Sales of ENDS and ENNDS banned Sales of HTPs are not banned nor taxed	Tax-excl. EFP	Individual pack	Different tax structures	Yes, for all tobacco products	Regular adjustments but no indexation for inflation	No	3

Note: Cells with "N/A" means the BP does not apply for the corresponding country because of the absence of specific or ad valorem excise tax. BP1 is assessed for the 2012 – 2022 period. The excise tax share indicator (BP2 and BP3) corresponds to the share of excise tax in the tobacco tax mix, which is defined as the sum of all tobacco taxes expressed as a percentage of the retail price of the most sold brand of cigarettes. For more detailed information on excise tax rates across tobacco products (BP8), see Table 3.2 and Annex 3.B in Chapter 3. Tax bases and tax rates (BP6 – BP9) correspond to the design of excise taxes levied on all tobacco products. Countries can levy the specific excise tax per stick of cigarettes, and per kilogram or gram for other tobacco products (e.g. Colombia, Nicaragua). Ad-valorem tax base "EFP" means "Ex-factory price/CIF value"; "SRP" means "Suggested retail price by the manufacturer/importer"; "FRP" means "Final (observed) retail price"; "CPI" means consumer price index. The ad valorem tax base (BP6) for non-cigarette tobacco products in Mexico is the final (observed) retail price net of taxes (see Table 3.2 in Chapter 3 and Table 6.51 in Chapter 6). However, BP6 in Mexico is considered weak since the ad valorem tax base for cigarettes (i.e, the most popular tobacco product, see Table 6.49 in Chapter 6 and Figure 1.2 in Chapter 1) is the ex-factory price net of tax.
Source: OECD based on WHO technical manual on tobacco tax policy and administration (WHO, 2021[5]); and information listed in Chapter 3.

5 The need for tobacco tax reform in Latin America and the Caribbean

This chapter finds that LAC countries have to increase their efforts to reduce tobacco use prevalence through the introduction of tobacco tax reforms. Countries introduced a wide range of tobacco excise tax reforms before 2011, but reform progress has been slower since then. In order to advance reform, policy makers have to take account of the responses of tobacco businesses to tobacco tax policy and, if necessary, introduce additional measures to maintain the effectiveness of tobacco excise taxes. Countries have to align their tobacco tax administration and tobacco tax design, strengthen the coherence between tobacco excise and income tax policy, and improve domestic and regional tobacco tax cooperation.

5.1. Tobacco excise tax reforms in LAC since 2000

Since 2000, all LAC countries have implemented at least one tobacco excise tax reform. Since 2000, the 18 LAC countries covered in this chapter have adopted 93 tobacco excise tax reforms (changes in the tobacco excise tax rates, and/or the introduction of indexation mechanisms or tax floors, and/or adjustments to the excise tax base) (Figure 5.1). These reforms typically entail the enactment of new laws or decrees.

Figure 5.1. Tobacco excise tax reforms

Number of tobacco excise tax reform measures adopted in LAC countries, 2000 – 2022

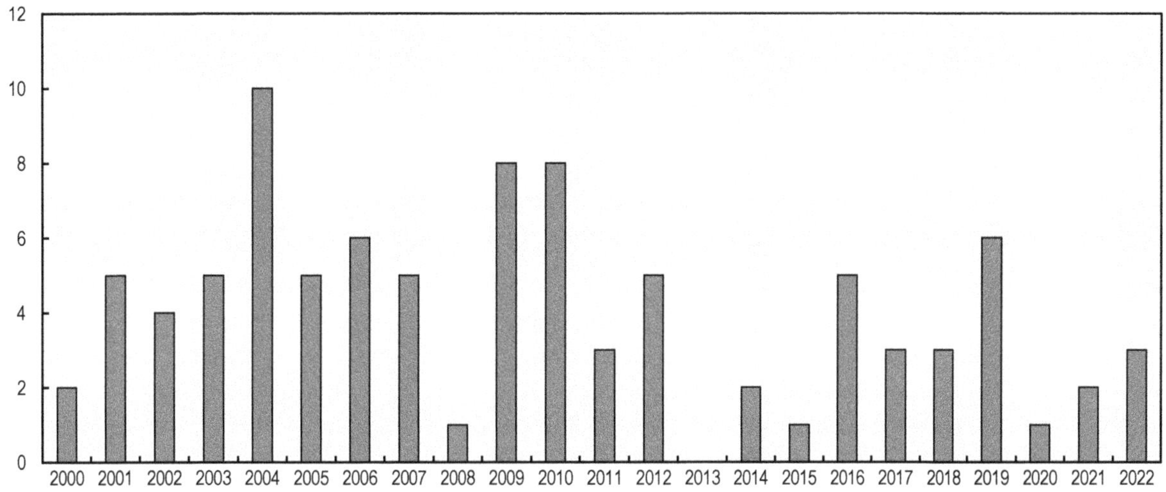

Note: The following countries are included: Argentina, Bolivia, Brazil, Chile, Colombia, Costa Rica, the Dominican Republic, Ecuador, El Salvador, Guatemala, Honduras, Jamaica, Mexico, Nicaragua, Panama, Paraguay, Peru and Uruguay. Venezuela has been excluded due to missing data. Tobacco excise tax reform refers to changes in the tobacco excise tax rates, and/or the introduction of indexation mechanisms or tax floors, and/or adjustments to the excise tax base. These reforms typically entail the enactment of new laws or decrees. The figure does not refer to recurrent tax changes that result from the indexation for inflation of tax brackets and price floors. Tobacco excise tax reforms do not include the introduction of sale regulations (BP12, see Box 4.1 in Chapter 4). The year reflects the enactment of new legislation, not when the tobacco tax reform is implemented. Bans on new tobacco and nicotine products are also included in the figure to reflect country's efforts aligned with BP5 ("taxable products", see Box 4.1 in Chapter 4): Argentina, Brazil, Mexico, Nicaragua, Panama and Uruguay.
Source: Based on national legislation listed in the country profiles available in Chapter 6.

Many tobacco excise tax reforms took place before 2011. The number of tobacco excise tax reforms peaked in 2004 with the ratification of the WHO Framework Convention on Tobacco Control (WHO FCTC) by many LAC countries (Sandoval et al., 2022[1]). Guiding principles for the implementation of Article 6 of the WHO FCTC on price and tax measures to reduce the demand for tobacco helped countries in implementing tobacco excise tax reforms. It peaked again in 2009-2010 following the global financial crisis (Figure 5.1). However, the COVID-19 pandemic did not (yet) result in a new wave of tobacco tax reforms.

The most significant changes in tobacco tax policy design in LAC took place following the global financial crisis (Figure 5.2). Between 2009 and 2011, countries have implemented reforms that follow the WHO tobacco tax design best practices. Four countries moved from an ad valorem to a specific tax structure (Nicaragua 2009, Peru 2010, Honduras 2010, and Ecuador 2011) (BP3). Two countries moved from an ad valorem to a mixed tax structure (Mexico 2009, Chile 2010), although two countries moved from a specific only to a mixed excise tax structure (Colombia 2010, Brazil 2011). Specific excise taxes started to be levied on single sticks of tobacco products (BP7). Chile (2010), Ecuador (2011), Honduras (2010) and Nicaragua (2009) started indexing specific excises for inflation (BP10). Tiered taxation was widely abolished in 2010 (BP9), except in Bolivia where tiered rates are still in force for cigarettes, and in Guatemala and Mexico for non-cigarette tobacco products. Excise tax rates were gradually aligned (BP8) (Figure 5.2, Panel B), although excise tax rates still vary significantly across tobacco products in LAC (Figure 4.1 in Chapter 4 and Table 3.2 in Chapter 3). The sales of some types of new tobacco and nicotine products have been banned in Argentina (2011), Brazil (2009), and Uruguay (2009) (Figure 5.2, Panel B).

The pace and scale of tobacco excise tax reform in LAC has somewhat decreased since 2012. Between 2012 and 2022, 31 tobacco tax reforms were adopted, which is significantly below the 62 tobacco tax reforms that were implemented between 2000 and 2011 (Figure 5.1). Moreover, the tobacco tax reforms that were implemented were less wide in scope. Between 2000 and 2011, 28 excise tax increases were enacted that allowed some countries to reach at least 50% of tobacco excise taxes in the tobacco tax mix by 2022 (BP2) (Figure 5.2, Panel A). Since 2012, the number of such tax increases has been more limited (15 measures), while the increases in statutory tax rates have also been more modest than in the previous period (see Box 5.1). Over the last decade, only one country shifted from an ad valorem to a specific tax structure (Bolivia 2017), and one country from an ad valorem to a mixed tax structure (Costa Rica 2012) (BP3) (Figure 5.2, Panel C). After 2018, tobacco excise tax reforms primarily focused on indexing specific taxes for inflation (BP10) (Figure 5.2, Panel C). Regarding new tobacco and nicotine products, their sales have been banned in Mexico (2022), Nicaragua (ENDS and ENNDS only, 2021), Panama (2022) while they started to be taxed in Colombia (HTPs only, 2018), Costa Rica (2022), Ecuador (2019), Paraguay (HTPs only, 2019) and Peru (HTPs only, 2019) (BP5) (Figure 5.2, Panel B).

Figure 5.2. Implementation of the WHO tobacco tax policy best practices over time

Cumulated number of tobacco tax reforms at moderate/complete level of compliance with WHO best practices

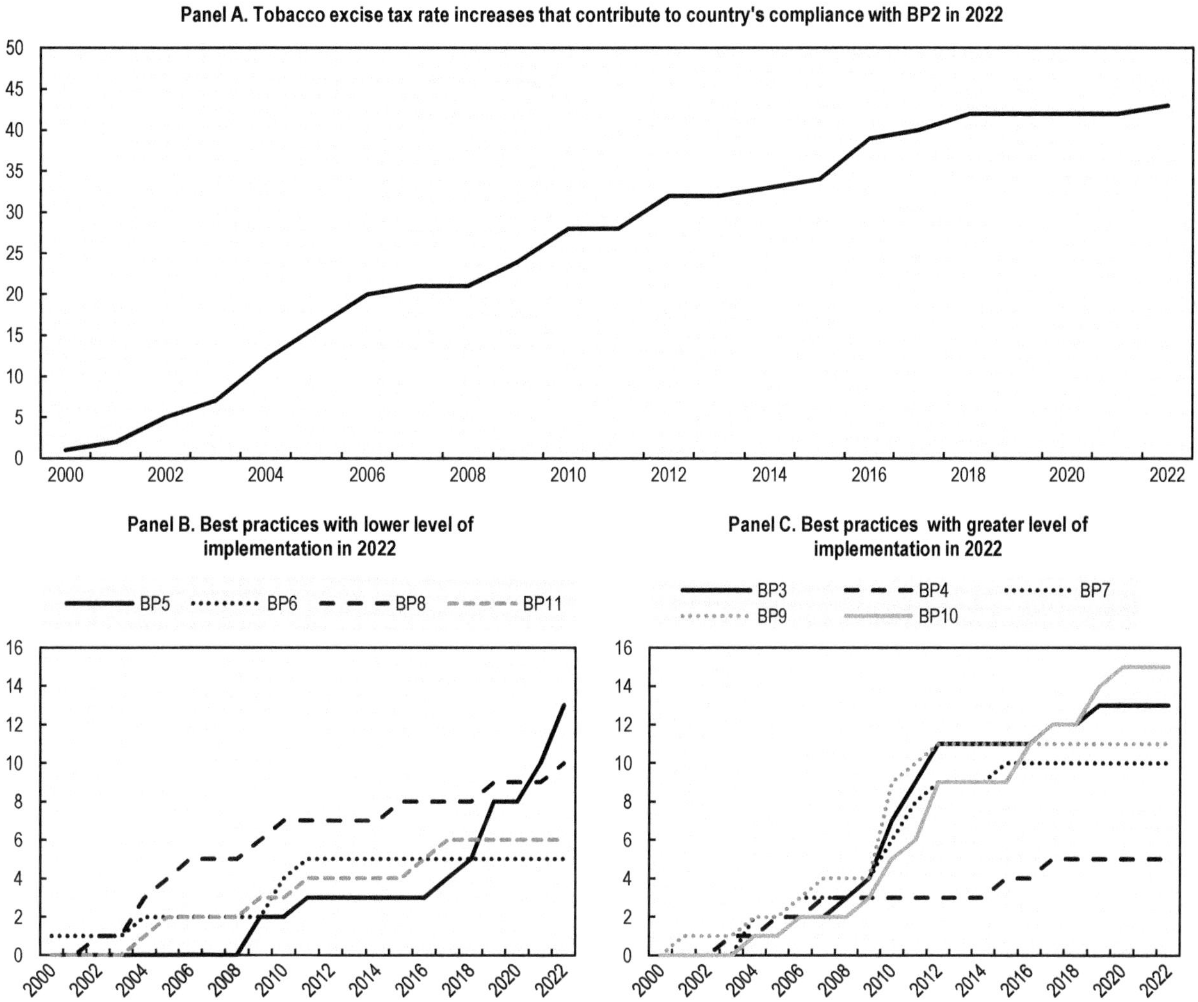

Note: LAC countries included in the figure are Argentina, Bolivia, Brazil, Chile, Colombia, Costa Rica, the Dominican Republic, Ecuador, El Salvador, Guatemala, Honduras, Jamaica, Mexico, Nicaragua, Panama, Paraguay, Peru and Uruguay. Venezuela has been excluded due to missing data. The number of tobacco tax reforms is cumulative, starting from zero for the base year (2000) and showing, for each year, the total number of reforms adopted since the base year. For an explanation of the criteria that are used to classify and evaluate tobacco tax reforms' alignment with the WHO tobacco tax policy best practices, see Box 4.2, Table 4.A.1 and Table 4.A.2 in Chapter 4. Annex Table 5.A.1 provides country specific information on best practices implementation overtime. BP1 (affordability) and BP12 (sale regulations) have not been included in the figure because affordability is related to a wide range of tax and non-tax measures and the regulation of sales is not directly related to tobacco tax design. Progress on BP4 has been comparatively slower than other best practices over the 2000 – 2022 period because traditional tobacco products were already taxed in most countries prior to the year 2000. Tobacco tax reforms aligned with BP5 correspond to the ban of sales in the following countries: Argentina, Brazil, Mexico, Nicaragua, Panama and Uruguay.

Source: OECD based on national legislation listed in the country profiles available in Chapter 6; WHO technical manual on tobacco tax policy and administration (WHO, 2021[2]); WHO report on the global tobacco epidemic (WHO, 2023[3]).

Box 5.1. Evolution of tobacco excise tax rates

A comparison of statutory tobacco excise tax rates over the 2008-2022 period shows a slowdown in tax rate increases in recent years.

Between 2008 and 2015, ad valorem excise tax rates increased in five countries (Figure 5.3, Panel A). The most significant ad valorem tax rate increase took place in Panama, which raised the tax rate from 32.5% to 100% in 2009 on the retail price suggested by the manufacturer/importer net of the VAT. The introduction of a specific rate in Chile in 2010 was accompanied by a reduction in the ad valorem excise tax rate between 2008 and 2015, while in Costa Rica and Mexico the introduction of a specific excise tax (in 2012 and 2009, respectively) did not result in a reduction of the ad valorem tax rates. Between 2015 and 2022, ad valorem tax rates increased slightly in Argentina, Brazil, and Paraguay.

Increases in the amount of the specific taxes have been modest in recent years (Figure 5.3, Panel B). In the Dominican Republic, El Salvador, and Jamaica, the tax increases were larger between 2008 and 2015 than they were between 2015 and 2022. Following the introduction of a specific tax in the period 2009-2012, subsequent increases in the specific tax on cigarettes in Chile, Costa Rica, Honduras and Mexico have been modest and reflect only the increase with inflation as a result of indexation. In Brazil, the absence of indexation for inflation of the specific tax since 2016 has led to its relative drop in real value. In contrast, in Colombia, Nicaragua, Peru and Uruguay, the increases in the specific taxes have been more significant between 2015 and 2022 than in other countries that levy a specific excise tax on cigarettes.

Figure 5.3. Evolution and comparison of statutory excise rates

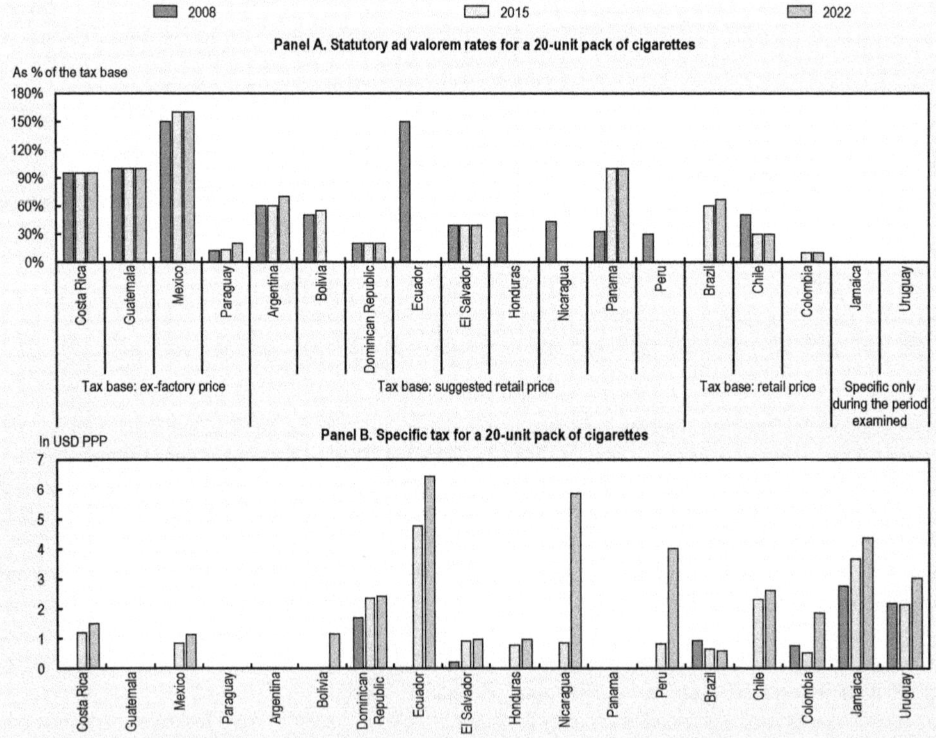

Note: Countries are grouped according to the excise tax design set in 2008. Specific tax for Brazil (BRA) and Colombia (COL) in 2008 correspond to the highest tiered rate, as well as for Bolivia (BOL) in 2022. Specific taxes in Panel B are converted into USD PPP with the implied PPP conversion rate available in the IMF World Economic Outlook Database (October 2023). Argentina, Guatemala, Panama and Paraguay do not levy a specific tax. Jamaica and Uruguay do not levy an ad valorem excise tax. Specific excise taxes have been standardized to a 20-unit pack to allow the comparison across countries with different tax bases.

Source: National legislation listed in the country profile of each country (Chapter 6); IMF World Economic Outlook Database (IMF, 2023[4]).

Tobacco tax reforms have gradually widened the relative wedge between pre-tax and retail prices over time across different tobacco tax structures. The panels in Figure 5.4 present the average change in pre-tax and retail prices over time for different tax structures, taking the pre-tax and retail price in 2008 as the base. The difference between pre-tax and retail price levels provides an indication about the impact of tobacco taxes on prices (Partos et al., 2020[5]; Sheikh, Branston and Gilmore, 2021[6]). However, the price evolution in Figure 5.4 does not separately identify the impact of a tobacco tax reform and the industry's response to the reform (e.g. tobacco producers may have lowered pre-tax prices in response to a tax increase, which would have widened the gap) so the data needs to be interpreted with caution. The country notes of this report provide more insight on country specific trends (see Chapter 6).

Figure 5.4. Inflation-adjusted change in pre-tax and retail prices of cigarettes for different tax structures

Percentage change from base year, 2008 – 2022

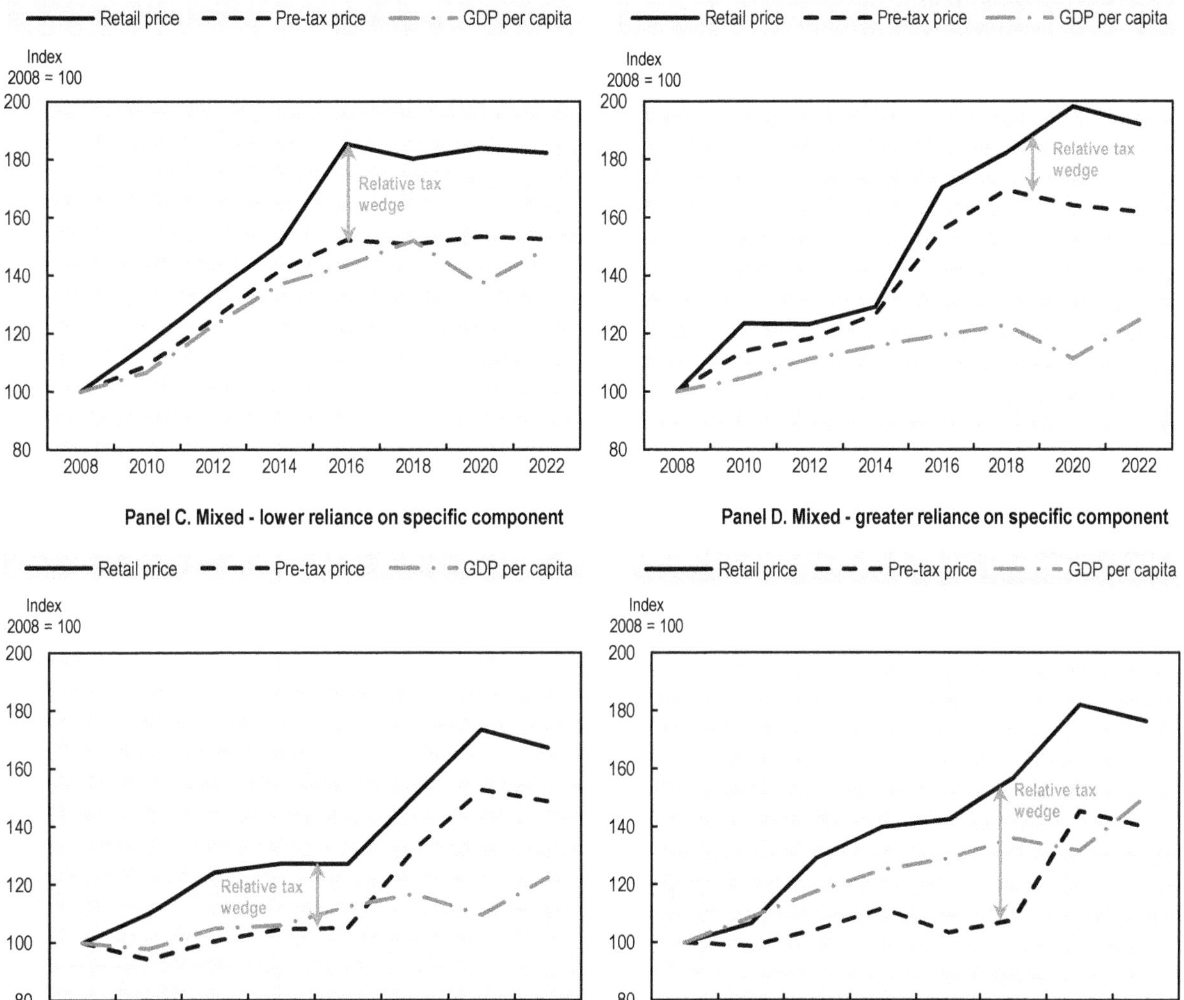

Note: The following countries are included in the averages: Argentina, Bolivia, Brazil, Chile, Colombia, Costa Rica, the Dominican Republic, Ecuador, El Salvador, Guatemala, Honduras, Jamaica, Mexico, Nicaragua, Panama, Paraguay, Peru, and Uruguay. Countries have been included in the average that is presented in a particular panel according to their excise tax structure in place. Hence, countries are included in a different panel if they have changed their tobacco excise tax structure at a particular year during the 2008 – 2022 period. Tax policy indicators have been computed using national currency and have been adjusted for inflation; therefore, the data presents inflation-adjusted trends. Tobacco prices indicators are based on data for the most sold brand of cigarettes. "Pre-tax price" corresponds to the retail price of the most sold brand of cigarettes net of the indirect taxes levied on this brand (tobacco excise taxes, VAT, import duties and other indirect taxes). The "relative tax wedge" is defined as the difference between the change in the pre-tax price and the retail price.

Source: WHO report on the global tobacco epidemic (WHO, 2023[3]); World Bank World Development Indicators (World Bank, 2024[7]); IMF International Financial Statistics (IMF, 2024[8]).

5.2. Reasons for further tobacco tax reform in LAC

Despite progress being made over the last decades, LAC countries need to continue to introduce tobacco tax reform measures. As described in this section, there are four main reasons for tobacco tax reform (Sandoval et al., 2022[9]):

1. Smoking prevalence can be reduced further.
2. Tobacco use leads to high economic and social costs.
3. Cigarettes remain affordable.
4. Countries are not fully tapping into their tobacco tax revenue potential.

Tobacco use prevalence remains high in some countries and amongst young people. Overall, tobacco prevalence remains high, and even in countries where prevalence is lower, there remains scope to reduce it further (Blanco Marquizo et al., 2022[10]; Hutchinson et al., 2022[11]) (see also Figure 1.6 in Chapter 1). In several countries, tobacco consumption has increased since the COVID-19 pandemic (see Chapter 1). Finally, the increasing use of new tobacco and nicotine products introduces new consumers to the tobacco market (Perucic et al., 2022[12]).

The economic and social costs of tobacco use are high. The economic and social costs include the direct health costs, the loss in economic productivity and the caregiver's related costs (Goodchild, Nargis and Tursan d'Espaignet, 2017[13]; Pichon-Riviere et al., 2023[14]). These costs are high and outweigh largely the revenues raised from tobacco excise taxes (see Table 1.2 in Chapter 1). While difficult to quantify, the loss in well-being for people who suffer from a smoking-caused disease and their families, caused by active and/or passive smoking, provides an additional strong rationale for tobacco tax reform.

Cigarettes remain affordable. The affordability of tobacco products depends on the tobacco tax share, tobacco prices, the level of income within the country, and the evolution of the income level with inflation and real income growth compared to the evolution of prices and tobacco taxes (Blecher, 2020[15]). Since 2012, cigarettes have not become less affordable in 23 out of 33 countries (Table 1.4 in Chapter 1) and the affordability of the most sold brand of cigarettes in LAC has remained fairly stable (Figure 5.5). More recently, from 2020 to 2022, the average cigarette prices have decreased across regions, including in LAC where the prices of cigarettes have not even been keeping up with inflation or income growth in most countries (Drope et al., 2024[16]).

Countries could raise more revenue from tobacco taxes (Goodchild, Sandoval and Belausteguigoitia, 2017[17]). Tobacco tax revenue varies across countries in LAC. Revenue from all indirect taxes levied on tobacco range from 0.01% of total tax revenue and GDP in Barbados to 2.58% of total tax revenue in Chile (0.67% of GDP) (Figure 2.4 in Chapter 2). Tobacco excise taxes raise, on average, 0.12% of GDP (0.50% of total tax revenue) in LAC (Figure 2.5 in Chapter 2). This is reflected in the substantial variation across LAC countries in the average excise tax revenue collected per pack of legal cigarettes sold, ranging from USD PPP 0.5 in Bolivia to USD PPP 4.5 in Chile (Figure 2.12 in Chapter 2). The extent to which a country can raise more revenue from tobacco taxes will depend on a number of factors, including the current tobacco tax design, tobacco use prevalence, the pre-tax prices for tobacco and the price elasticity of demand (South American Network on Applied Economics/Red Sur, 2019[18]; Blecher, Ozer and Bloom, 2023[19]; Petit and Nagy, 2016[20]).

Figure 5.5. Affordability of the most sold brand of cigarettes over time

As a percentage of GDP per capita required to purchase 100 packs of 20 cigarettes

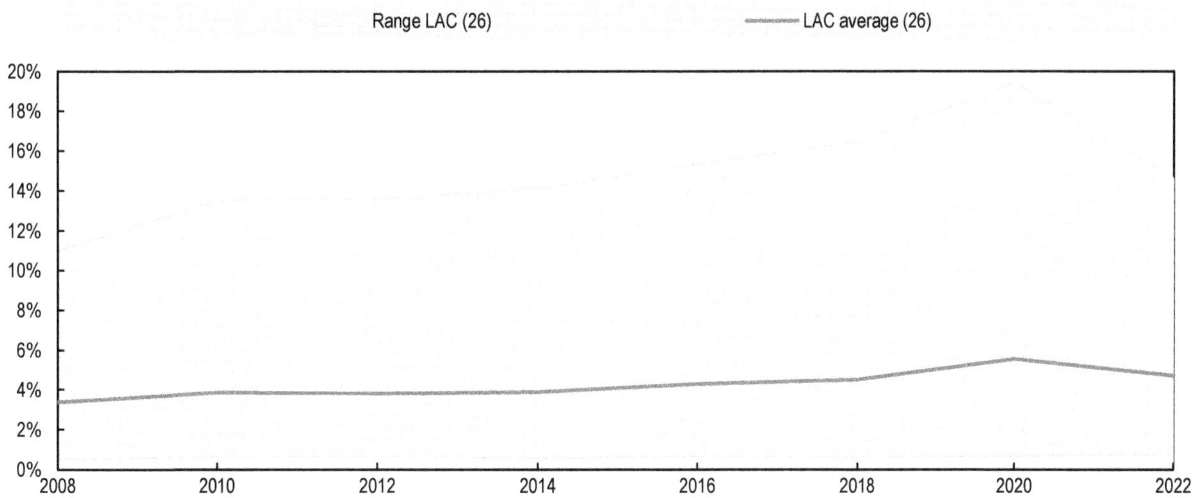

Note: The figure includes the following countries: Argentina, Belize, Bolivia, Brazil, Chile, Colombia, Costa Rica, Dominica, the Dominican Republic, Ecuador, El Salvador, Guatemala, Guyana, Honduras, Jamaica, Mexico, Nicaragua, Panama, Paraguay, Peru, Saint Lucia, Saint Vincent and the Grenadines, Suriname, Trinidad and Tobago, Uruguay, Venezuela. The affordability indicator measures the percentage of the country's GDP per capita required to purchase 100 packs of 20 cigarettes. A higher (lower) percentage means lower (higher) affordability of cigarettes. To ensure comparability of average affordability across LAC countries over time, countries for which there was no information for one or multiple years have been excluded.
Source: WHO report on the global tobacco epidemic (WHO, 2023[3]).

Increases in tobacco tax rates have positive impacts on tax revenue in the short run. Between 2008 and 2016, the average excise tax revenue collected per pack of legal cigarettes sold increased from USD PPP 1.2 to USD PPP 2.0 (Figure 5.6), in line with increases in the tobacco tax rates, which have been more significant before 2016 (see Box 5.1). Since 2017, the average revenue ratio per pack of cigarettes has increased only slightly (from USD PPP 2.1 to 2.4 in 2022) which is consistent with the relative lack of tobacco tax increases in recent years (Figure 5.1 and Figure 5.2). This illustrates the fact that, because of inelastic tobacco demand, tobacco tax increases have a positive impact on tax revenue on average (Jawad et al., 2018[21]; Guindon, Paraje and Chaloupka, 2018[22]).

In the long run also, increases in tobacco tax rates have a positive net fiscal impact. Tobacco tax rates increases aim to reduce tobacco consumption which in turn may reduce tobacco tax revenue. However, the reduction in tax revenue tends to be smaller than the additional revenue generated by the tax increase. In addition, a reduction in tobacco consumption decreases the social and economic costs of smoking. Given that the costs of tobacco use outweigh the tobacco tax revenue across countries in LAC, the net effect of a free-smoking society would always remain positive (Fuchs et al., 2019[23]).

Figure 5.6. Average excise tax revenue collected per pack of 20 cigarettes sold over time

Tobacco excise tax revenue in USD PPP collected per pack of legal cigarettes sold

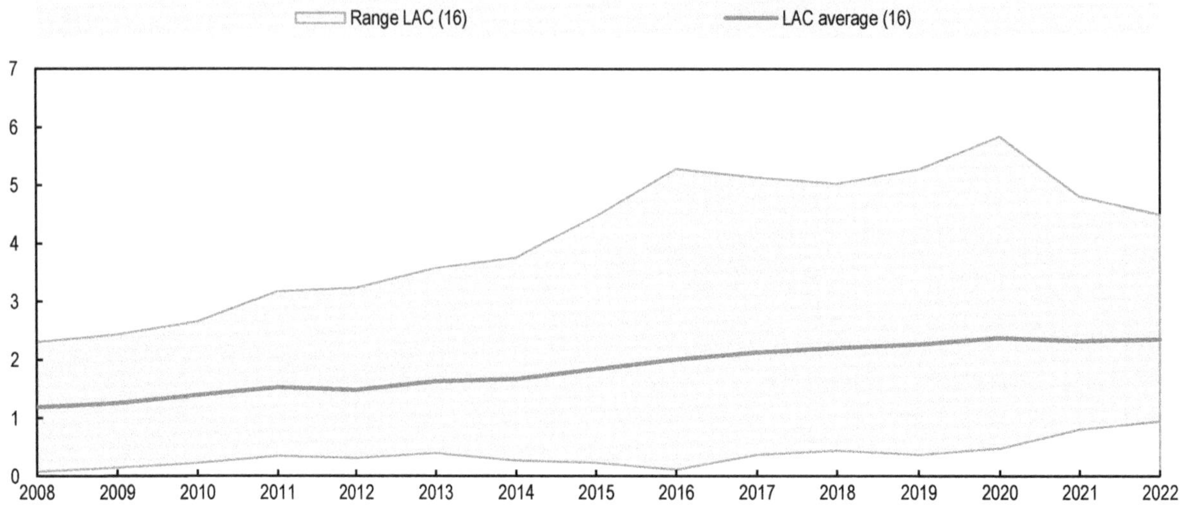

Note: See Box 2.1 (Chapter 2) for more information on tobacco tax revenue (source of information and calculations). The following countries are included: Argentina, Bolivia, Brazil, Chile, Colombia, Costa Rica, the Dominican Republic, Ecuador, El Salvador, Guatemala, Honduras, Mexico, Panama, Paraguay, Peru and Uruguay. The country selection is provided by the availability of data on sales of cigarettes in Euromonitor International Tobacco Industry edition, 2023 © All rights reserved (Euromonitor International, 2023[24]).
Source: OECD Revenue Statistics (OECD, 2024[25]); National data; IMF World Economic Outlook Database (IMF, 2023[4]); and OECD own calculations based on Euromonitor International's Tobacco Industry edition (Euromonitor International, 2023[24]).

5.3. Options to strengthen tobacco taxes design and administration in LAC

Scope exists to further align the design of the tobacco tax policies in LAC countries with WHO tobacco tax best practices. Despite reform progress over the last decades (Figure 5.2), there remains significant scope to further strengthen the design of tobacco taxes, increase the tobacco tax rates and tax share and improve the tobacco tax administration (Chaloupka et al., 2021[26]). The increase of specific tobacco excise tax amounts and its indexation to inflation and real income growth, and the introduction of minimum tax or price floor in countries with a large ad valorem tobacco tax component are priority reform measures (see Figure 4.3 in Chapter 4), which will have significant and immediate reform impacts.

In order to strengthen the effectiveness of tobacco taxes in reducing smoking prevalence, LAC countries will have to introduce a set of complementary tobacco tax policy and administration measures. The tobacco excise tax administration and enforcement have an impact on the effectiveness of tobacco excise taxes. This chapter therefore introduces a number of additional best practices that are currently not sufficiently addressed by LAC countries. Box 5.2 lists those additional tobacco tax best practices, while the rest of the chapter will discuss them one by one.

Box 5.2. OECD tobacco tax policy and administration best practices

Accounting for the strategic response of tobacco businesses when designing tobacco tax policy

- **BP13**: Evaluate the impact of tobacco tax increases on pre-tax and retail prices over time and follow-up with additional tax measures as necessary.

Aligning tobacco tax administration and tax policy design

- **BP14**: Select the tobacco excise tax point that facilitates the tobacco excise tax administration.
- **BP15**: Given the choice of the excise taxing point, introduce measures to limit fraud and illicit trade:
  - Use modern fiscal markings.
  - Collect more detailed tobacco transaction information within the excise tax declarations.
  - Enforce mandatory licencing for all parts of the tobacco value chain.
- **BP16**: Align the tobacco excise tax structure with the excise taxing point.
- **BP17**: In countries with an ad valorem tobacco tax component, introduce a minimum tax or price floor; levy the ad valorem tax on the suggested or actual retail price rather than on the ex-factory price. Use information from the VAT administration to ensure that the tobacco tax base is aligned with the retail price.
- **BP18**: Levy the VAT on the tobacco excise tax-inclusive price.

Strengthening tobacco excise and income tax policy coherence

- **BP19**: Implement Article 5.3 of the WHO FCTC so that direct and indirect (tax and non-tax) subsidies are not provided to tobacco companies to prevent these subsidies from undermining the effectiveness of tobacco tax policies.

Strengthening domestic and regional tobacco tax cooperation

- **BP20**: Reinforce the cooperation between Ministries of Finance and Ministries of Health to ensure that tobacco tax policies are effective in significantly reducing tobacco use prevalence. Include other parts of government to participate in such a dialogue, such as the tax administration and the customs authorities.
- **BP21**: Engage in regional coordination and cooperation on tobacco tax policy and exchange information on tobacco-related information to avoid that weak tobacco control policies in one country create a hurdle for effective tobacco tax policies in other countries.

Source: OECD.

5.3.1. Accounting for strategic response of tobacco businesses when designing tobacco tax policy

Tobacco companies respond strategically to tobacco tax increases to maximise their profits. As any other businesses, tobacco companies aim at maximising their profits. A tobacco tax reform, by aiming at reducing demand for tobacco products, will put the profits of tobacco companies under pressure. In response, tobacco companies adjust their behaviour to minimise the impact, and therefore the effectiveness, of the tobacco tax reform (Partos et al., 2020[5]; Sheikh, Branston and Gilmore, 2021[6]).

Tobacco companies respond in varies ways to tobacco tax reform, including by:

1. **Limiting the pass-through of a tobacco tax increase by lowering the pre-tax price, in particular in the short run**. By absorbing partly (or fully) the tax increase, tobacco companies will limit (or avoid) the price increase to minimise the number of smokers that reduce or quit smoking. The extent to which tobacco businesses will absorb a tobacco tax increase will depend on many factors, including the profitability of the business (the more profitable is a tobacco company, the more it can engage in strategies that absorb, even if it is only temporarily, a tax increase), the degree of competition in the tobacco market, and the level of the tax increase (a more ambitious tax increase will be more difficult to fully absorb as it will be more costly for tobacco companies).
2. **Gradually increasing pre-tax retail prices in response to a tobacco tax increase**, so that the year-to-year change in the tobacco price is such that consumers do not change their smoking behaviour. When tobacco companies are successful in limiting the behavioural response of smokers, they may even decide to continue to increase the price of tobacco products even if the tobacco tax has been fully passed through into retail prices.
3. **Adjusting the pre-tax price of brands differently** aligned with the price elasticity of demand that may vary across brands. For instance, if demand for premium brands is less price elastic than the demand for cheaper brands, tobacco companies may decide to under-pass through the tax increase for cheaper products and, in order to offset the loss in profits, to over-pass through the tax increase in the price of premium brands.
4. **Creating cheaper new brands that allow smokers to trade down** (i.e. to smoke cheaper tobacco products) **rather than reduce or quit smoking**. If new brands are registered outside the country where the products are smoked, the tobacco business may shift part of its profits to that jurisdiction. Tax avoidance strategies increase after-income tax profitability (Vermeulen, Dillen and Branston, 2020[27]), which may further increase the financial resources that can be used to undermine the effectiveness of tobacco tax increases.

To tackle tobacco companies' strategic responses, countries have to implement dynamic tobacco tax reform and to evaluate the impact of a tax increase on tobacco product retail prices. If necessary, countries can introduce additional tobacco tax measures, including tax rate increases to have a greater impact on reducing consumption (Tauras et al., 2014[28]). Hence an additional best practice is to *Evaluate the impact of tobacco tax increases on pre-tax and retail prices over time and follow-up with additional tax measures as necessary* (BP 13 see Box 5.2).

From the country-specific information included in this report, LAC countries are, at best, only modestly aligned with BP13. On average, countries that have introduced a tobacco tax reform in the last decade have not introduced additional measures based on an evaluation of the impact of the tax increase on tobacco retail prices in the following years. As tobacco tax reform success of the past does not necessarily extend over time, the lack of (or insufficient) follow-up reform measures may undermine the effectiveness of tobacco tax reform.

5.3.2. Aligning tobacco tax administration and tax policy design

The tobacco excise tax administration and enforcement have an impact on the effectiveness of tobacco excise taxes. This section introduces important tax administration issues, including the choice of the excise taxing point and the order in which tobacco taxes are levied, and identifies how they are implemented in countries in LAC.

The excise taxing point

Governments need to select the excise taxing point. The excise taxing point is "the point at which the legislation provides for the liability over the excisable goods or services to be recognized and brought to account for the purposes of payment of the appropriate duty" (Preece, 2008[29]).

Tobacco excise taxes can be levied at different taxing points (Figure 5.7):

- At the input stage (i.e. inputs used in the production of tobacco products).
- At the manufacture point (i.e. on the producer or importer of tobacco products, which are supposed to pass through the tax in the final retail price that the smoker pays).
- At the domestic distribution (i.e. wholesale) stage.
- At the retail point (i.e. at the point of sale to the smoker).

The "optimal" (i.e. most effective) excise taxing point will be the point in the value chain where:

- Tobacco excise taxes have the greatest probability that they will be passed through into retail prices and reduce the affordability of tobacco products (to meet health and revenue objectives).
- The tax administration can keep track of volume and the value of tobacco transactions and has to engage with a relatively limited number of agents (to ease the enforcement of the tax).
- Taxpayers have the resources and knowledge to comply with tobacco excise tax regulations (to ease voluntary compliance).

With respect to the import and export of tobacco products:

- Excises on importation are meant to align the tax treatment of imported tobacco products with the tax treatment of domestically produced tobacco products.
- Tobacco excises are remitted when tobacco products are exported (in case they have been taxed as they may also have remained under the suspension regime applied within the tax warehouse – see below). The Contracting Parties to the General Agreement on Tariffs and Trade may, but are not required, exempt or remit taxes on exported tobacco products. In practice, LAC countries do exempt exported tobacco products from domestic tobacco excise taxes, but do not facilitate the compliance with the tobacco tax rules in the country that imports the products (see below).

Figure 5.7. Tobacco supply chain and excise taxing point options

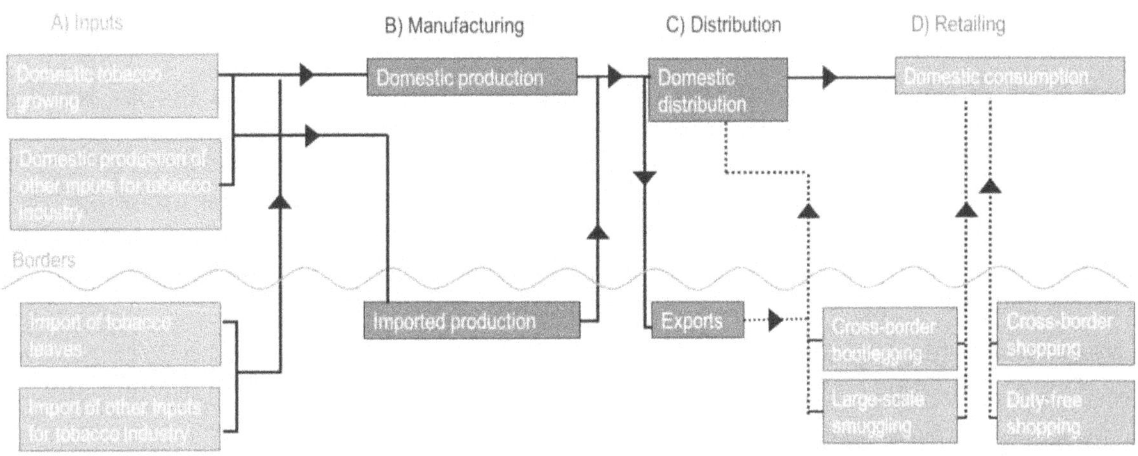

Source: OECD based on (Hiscock and Bloomfield, 2021[30]).

All countries in LAC levy tobacco excise taxes at the manufacturing point and at the border when tobacco products are imported (see Chapter 3). This approach implies that the excise tax administration has to interact with a relatively limited number of tobacco producers and importers. These companies need to be registered and provide information to the tax administration, which facilitates the control of the value chain by the tax administration. However, this taxing point may create challenges in terms of the choice of the tax base (see below). Moreover, if tobacco manufacturers control (or own) the distribution of tobacco products, they may be able to transfer part of their margin to their distributors to reduce the tobacco excise taxable base. Given limited tax administrative resources in LAC countries, the advantages of having to interact with a small number of taxpayers outweighs the challenges that are related to the choice of the manufacturing/importing level as the taxing point, in particular if additional measures are implemented that protect the tax base.

This discussion leads to an additional tobacco tax policy best practice for which LAC countries perform strongly (BP 14 see Box 5.2): *Select the tobacco excise tax point that facilitates the administration tobacco excise taxes.*

The use of fiscal marking

Tax administrations need to define a series of rules with respect to:

- Actions that lead to a taxable event (e.g. the production or importation of cigarettes).
- The agent who is liable to pay the tax.
- The point in time the tobacco excise tax becomes chargeable (i.e. when the tobacco tax can be claimed from the agent who is liable to pay the tax).

Similarly, customs legislation will have to define a wide set of rules that determine how tobacco products can move within the territory and the rules that need to be followed when they are exported.

Countries also need to establish rules regarding tax warehouses. Production, processing and holding of tobacco products can only take place in a tax warehouse. Tax warehouses should receive authorisation of competent authorities to operate the warehouse, provide all the required documentation and follow the procedures as defined by the tobacco excise tax administration. Under "suspension arrangements", produced or imported tobacco products may be held in a tax warehouse without tobacco excise tax becoming chargeable. Tobacco excise taxes are chargeable when they are released for consumption or when shortages (that have to be defined by the law) are recorded by the tax administration. The tax administration also has to define clear rules of what is understood under "shortages". Lost tobacco products that are attributable to force majeure (e.g., a warehouse fire) should not trigger taxation. Theft, on the other hand, is often considered a taxable event in order to avoid that the tax warehouse does not comply strictly with the regulations in place.

To keep track of tobacco products that have paid tax when released from the tax warehouse, countries can apply fiscal markings. Fiscal markings are traditional or modern tax stamps which are labels or marks placed on goods to show that the applicable excise tax has been paid (WHO, 2021[2]). Traditional tax stamps provide information on the country of origin and whether the excise tax has been paid. Modern tax stamps (i.e. a unique identifier) provide information that signals that producers and importers of tobacco products comply with tax payment requirements, help detect illicit tobacco products, and provide detailed information on the product and production process.

This discussion leads to an additional tobacco taxation best practice (BP 15 see Box 5.2): *Given the choice of the excise taxing point, introduce measures to limit fraud and illicit trade:*

- *Use modern fiscal markings*
- *Collect more detailed tobacco transaction information within the excise tax declarations*
- *Enforce mandatory licencing for all parts of the tobacco value chain.*

LAC countries underperform with respect to BP15. Although information on how countries organise their tobacco excise tax administration is limited, there seems to be scope to strengthen the regulations to facilitate the administration of tobacco excise taxes and to prevent fraud and illicit trade, including through the use of fiscal markings and tax stamps. Information shows that only 8 out of 19 countries apply fiscal markings for cigarettes (often traditional tax stamps) and only 4 for other tobacco products (Figure 5.8). Other measures could be better implemented, such as more detailed excise tax declarations and mandatory licencing for all parts of the tobacco value chain (see Table 3.10 and Table 3.11 in Chapter 3).

Figure 5.8. Use of tax stamps by type of tobacco product

Number of LAC countries, 2022

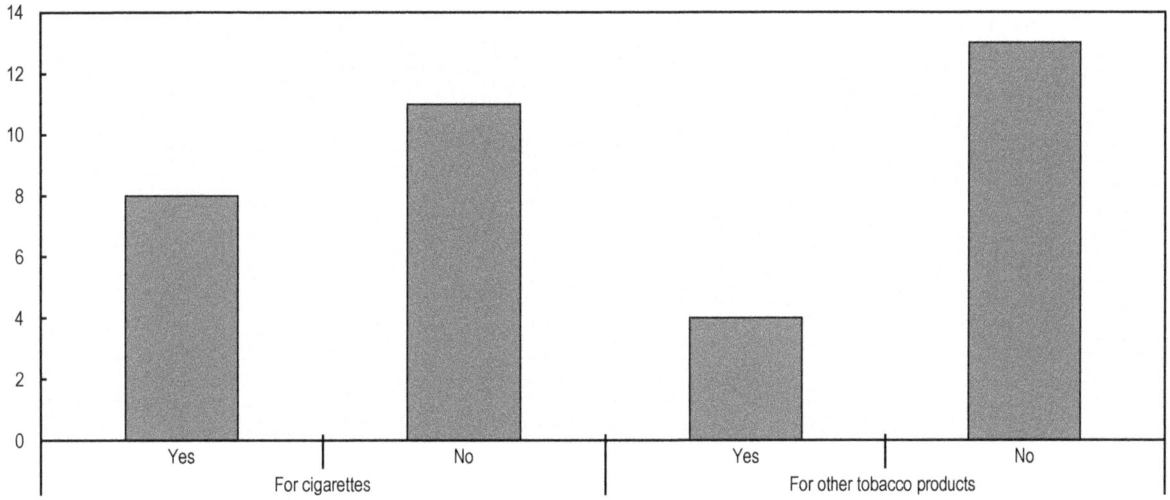

Note: The following countries are included: Argentina, Bolivia, Brazil, Chile, Colombia, Costa Rica, the Dominican Republic, Ecuador, El Salvador, Guatemala, Honduras, Jamaica, Mexico, Nicaragua, Panama, Paraguay, Peru, Uruguay and Venezuela. The category "other tobacco products" refers to cigars, cigarillos and Roll-Your-Own (RYO) tobacco products.
Source: WHO report on the global tobacco epidemic (WHO, 2023[3]).

Choice of the tax base

From a tax administrative perspective, the choice of the excise taxing point at the manufacturing and import level strengthens the preference for specific excise taxes over ad valorem taxes. Specific excise taxes can easily be implemented at the producer or importer stage as no price information is required. Ad valorem taxes, on the other hand, should be levied on the retail price, but this information is not immediately available at the producer or importer level. The use of ad valorem taxes therefore creates additional complexity from a tax administrative perspective (Petit and Nagy, 2016[20]). This leads to an additional best practice (BP 16 see Box 5.2): *Align the tobacco excise tax structure with the excise taxing point.* Given the significant use of ad valorem excise taxes, LAC countries perform moderately on BP16.

The information available to the tobacco excise tax administration may have an impact on the ad valorem tax base. LAC countries differ in their choice of the ad valorem tax base. For cigarettes, the excise tax base is the producer (ex-factory) price in four countries, the suggested retail price in five countries, and the retail price in three countries (Figure 5.9). Information about producer (ex-factory) prices is readily available at the manufacturer level, but the price will be lower than the final retail price (and even more so if tobacco operators further down the supply chain are affiliated to the manufacturer), which will result in a lower tax share if the tax rates are not adjusted upward accordingly. Information about the final (observed) retail price might not be available at the excise taxing point. Some countries therefore apply the retail price that is suggested by the producers or importers as the ad valorem tax base. This tax base is easier to enforce but implies that the tax administration has to verify whether the "suggested" price is sufficiently similar (within error margin) to the final (observed) retail price in order to avoid that tobacco businesses "suggest" a price that is too low. The excise tax administration may rely on information from the VAT administration in case VAT is levied on the retail price to enforce a suggested retail price that is close to (or equal to) the (actual) retail price that consumers pay. Finally, in order to avoid that ad valorem taxes result in low tax burdens for cheaper tobacco products, countries that levy an ad valorem tax only will have to complement the tax with a price floor or minimum tax to ensure that a minimum amount of tax is paid. This price floor would be triggered when the ad valorem tax base would be below the floor.

Figure 5.9. The ad valorem tobacco excise tax base in LAC across tobacco products

Number of countries, 2022

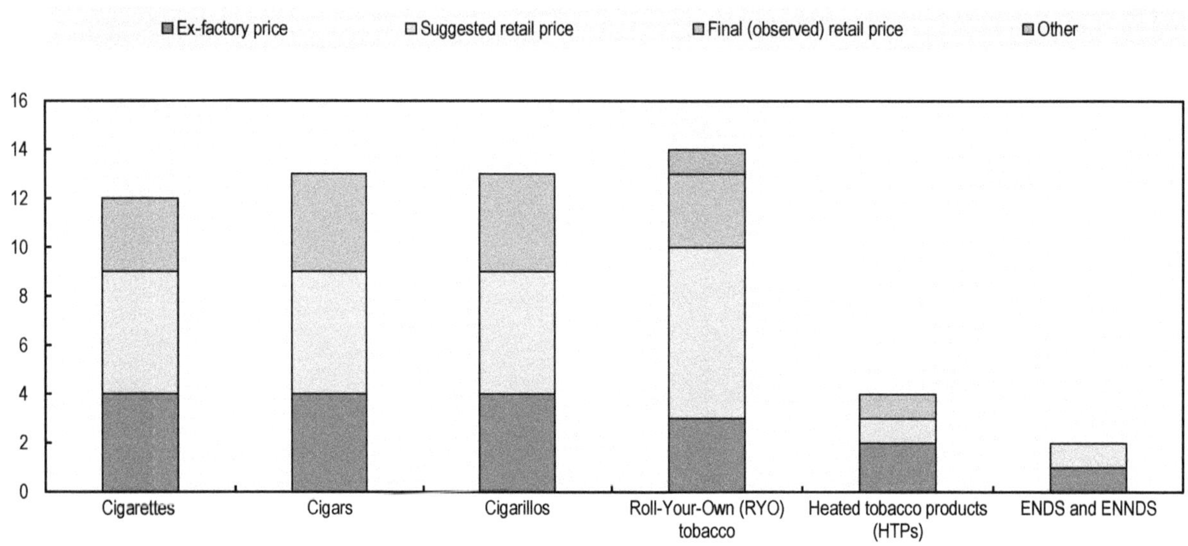

Note: The following countries are included: Argentina, Bolivia, Brazil, Chile, Colombia, Costa Rica, the Dominican Republic, Ecuador, El Salvador, Guatemala, Honduras, Jamaica, Mexico, Nicaragua, Panama, Paraguay, Peru, Uruguay and Venezuela. Following the WHO report on the global tobacco epidemic (WHO, 2021[31]), new tobacco and nicotine products in this report include ENDS, ENNDS and HTPs. Argentina, Brazil, Mexico, Nicaragua, Panama, Uruguay, and Venezuela do not levy an excise tax on ENDS or ENNDS because their sales are banned. In Brazil, Mexico and Panama, the sales of HTPs are also banned (WHO, 2023[3]). "Other" refers to the tax base for RYO tobacco products in Colombia which is 10% of the specific excise tax.
Source: National legislation listed in Annex Table 3.B.1 in Chapter 3.

This leads to an additional tobacco taxation best practice (BP 17 see Box 5.2): *In countries with an ad valorem tobacco tax component, introduce a minimum tax or price floor; levy the tax on the suggested or actual retail price rather than on the ex-factory price. Use information from the VAT administration to ensure that the tobacco tax base is aligned with the retail price.* The narrower is the tax base, the higher should be the ad valorem rate (for a given tax share).

LAC countries seem to follow BP17 relatively well. Although limited information is available, countries seem to have aligned the choice of the ad valorem tax base with their existing administrative capacities and access to information. In general, countries that apply the ad valorem rate for cigarettes on the producer price tend to levy higher rates than countries that levy the tax on the retail price (Figure 5.10). For instance, the Dominican Republic and El Salvador (mixed excise tax structure) have lower rates than Argentina, Panama and Venezuela (ad valorem tax only) (Figure 5.10). Before its dual VAT reform, Brazil levied a relatively high statutory tax rate (66.7%) on a narrow tax base (15% of the tax-inclusive retail price).

Figure 5.10. Ad valorem excise tax rates levied on cigarettes across different tax bases

As a percentage of the tax base and as a percentage of the retail price, 2022

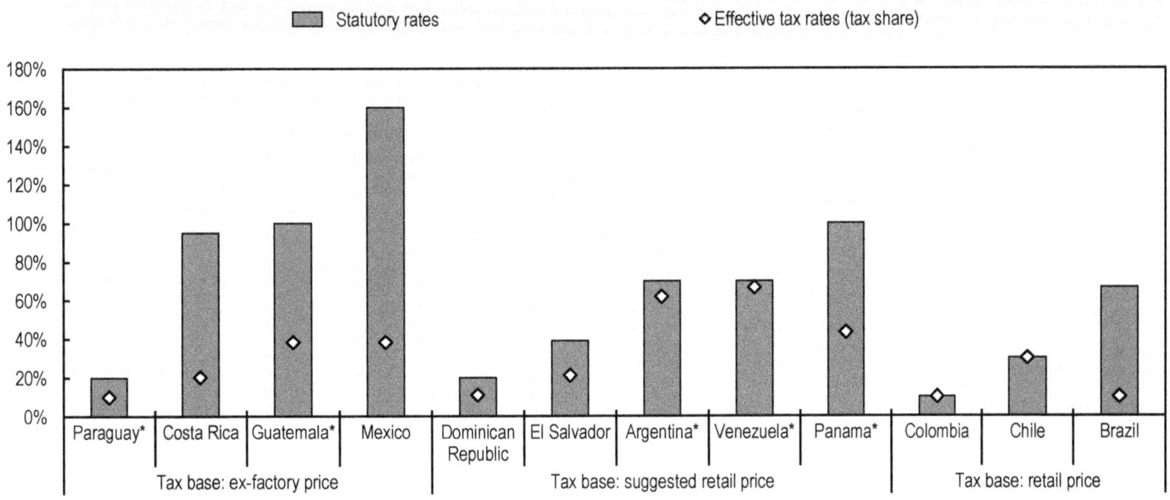

Note: Countries with an asterisk (*) implement an ad valorem only excise tax structure, while the other countries have a mixed excise tax structure. The ad valorem tax base is tax exclusive in Argentina, Costa Rica, the Dominican Republic, El Salvador, Guatemala, Mexico, Panama; and tax inclusive in Brazil, Chile, Colombia and Venezuela. In Brazil, the ad valorem excise tax base is narrowed as it is 15% of the tax-inclusive retail price. Retail prices for a 20-unit pack of cigarettes of the most sold brand.
Source: National legislation listed in Annex Table 3.B.1 in Chapter 3.

Tobacco excise taxes and the VAT are administered separately in countries in LAC. The fact that excises have a different taxing point than the VAT implies that countries need a separate VAT and excise tax administration that have their own rules and procedures. This is the case in LAC countries. However, the fact that both taxes are administered separately will require that protocols are set in place to ensure that both administrations cooperate and exchange information to avoid fraud.

The sequence in which tobacco taxes are levied

The sequence of the tobacco taxes that are levied has an impact on the tobacco tax share, except if the tax level is adjusted accordingly. The sequence of the tobacco taxes (i.e. whether taxes are levied on tax-exclusive or tax-inclusive prices) has an impact on whether the tax base is broad or narrow, which finally has an impact on the total tobacco tax share. However, this effect can be mitigated by adjusting the level of the taxes that are levied. Insofar tobacco excise taxes internalise negative external effects and make smokers pay for the social costs of smoking and because the VAT is a general tax on consumption, one could argue that tobacco excise taxes should be levied first, and the VAT should be levied on the tobacco excise tax-inclusive price. This leads to an additional tobacco taxation best practice (BP18, see Box 5.2): *Levy the VAT on the tobacco excise tax-inclusive price.*

LAC countries differ in the tobacco tax sequence that they apply, although most countries levy the VAT on top of the excise tax-inclusive retail price (Table 5.1). The sequence in which tobacco taxes are levied can vary. For instance, ad valorem tobacco excise taxes can be levied on the price that includes or excludes the specific tobacco tax. Ad valorem tobacco taxes can be levied before the VAT is applied, or after. Table 5.1 provides available information on the taxing order that is applied in countries in LAC. Most LAC countries levy the VAT on top of the tobacco excise tax inclusive price (Table 5.1). In Costa Rica, the Dominican Republic, El Salvador and Mexico, the ad valorem component applies first (i.e. the ad valorem tobacco tax is levied on a narrow specific tax and VAT-exclusive retail price), the specific tobacco excise tax is applied next (i.e. the tax is added to the price that includes the ad valorem tax), and the VAT is levied on top (i.e. the VAT is levied on the tobacco excise tax-inclusive price). In contrast, in Brazil and

Colombia, the specific component applies first, and the ad valorem tax is levied on the price that includes the specific tax. However, these countries levy VAT on a tobacco excise tax-exclusive retail price.

Table 5.1. Sequence of the indirect taxes levied on cigarettes by type of excise tax structure

Excise tax structure	Sequence of the excise taxes in mixed structures	Sequence of the excise taxes with respect to the VAT		
		Ad valorem tobacco excise tax is levied on top of the VAT	VAT is levied on top of the tobacco excise tax	Countries for which the tax sequence is unclear to the OECD team
Specific			Ecuador Honduras Jamaica Nicaragua Peru Uruguay	Bolivia
Ad valorem			Guatemala Panama Paraguay	Argentina
Mixed	Specific excise tax is added to the price that includes the ad valorem tax		Costa Rica Dominican Republic El Salvador Mexico	
	Ad valorem excise tax is levied on top of the specific tax	Brazil Colombia		Chile

Source: National legislation listed in Annex Table 3.B.5 from Annex 3.B (Chapter 3).

5.3.3. Strengthening tobacco excise and income tax policy coherence

The WHO Framework Convention on Tobacco Control (WHO FCTC) is designed to protect present and future generations from the health, social, environmental and economic consequences and harm cause by tobacco consumption and exposure to tobacco smoke. Article 5.3 of the WHO FCTC states: "*In setting and implementing their public health policies with respect to tobacco control, Parties shall act to protect these policies from commercial and other vested interests of the tobacco industry in accordance with national law*". Article 5.3 Guidelines recommend that WHO FCTC Parties do not provide subsidies to tobacco companies.

The use of (direct and indirect) tax incentives targeted at tobacco companies, or that they benefit from, is not aligned with the WHO FCTC as they provide a subsidy. The WHO FCTC implies that direct and indirect subsidies, including subsidies provided through the tax system, are not aligned with Article 5.3 of the WHO FCTC. The Guidelines to the implementation of Article 5.3 of the FCTC explicitly state: "*Do not give preferential treatment to the tobacco industry*". Tax expenditures and tax incentives can be considered as subsidies provided through the tax system. They can come in different forms, including tax allowances (provisions that narrow the tax base), tax credits (provisions that reduce the tax liability), tax exemptions or exclusions, and reduced tax rates (Campos Vázquez, 2022[32]). They can range from profit-based tax incentives that reduce or exempt a certain amount of profits (e.g. free trade zones, tax holidays) to cost-based tax incentives that reduce the cost of investment or stimulate innovation (e.g. tax credits, accelerated tax depreciation allowances).

Weak tobacco control policies in one country create negative spillovers/external effects for other countries in the LAC region. Policies in individual countries that support and subsidise the cultivation of tobacco, the production and/or the distribution of tobacco products, including through the use of tax incentives, will have a negative impact on other countries, as these subsidies will allow tobacco business to sell tobacco products at a cheaper price.

Countries in LAC need to ensure that their income tax system does not undermine the effectiveness of tobacco excise tax and other tobacco control policies that are in place. The case for tobacco companies to operate in free trade zones, which is the case in a number of LAC countries, where businesses are exempted from income tax and where they do not have to comply with information provisions and regulations that apply to other businesses, is particularly weak (WHO, 2021[33]). This leads to the additional BP19: *Implement Article 5.3 of the WHO FCTC so that direct and indirect (tax and non-tax) subsidies are not provided to tobacco companies to prevent these subsidies from undermining the effectiveness of tobacco tax policies.*

Across countries in the world, the direct tax implications of Article 5.3 of the WHO FCTC have not resulted in income tax reform. This is also the case in countries in LAC.

5.3.4. Strengthening domestic and regional tobacco tax cooperation

Domestic tobacco tax cooperation

As shown by the MPOWER policy package, efficient tobacco control policies require coherent measures to be implemented by different stakeholders, in particular Health and Finance Ministries. Traditionally, the main objective of the Ministry of Health is to reduce tobacco use prevalence, while the Ministry of Finance aims at raising tobacco tax revenue and reducing the net fiscal impact of tobacco use. Achieving both objectives requires that both Ministries are actively engaged in a dialogue and collaborate (BP 20 see Box 5.2). However, the priority for tobacco tax reform is the reduction in the tobacco use prevalence as this will allow both ministries to meet their objectives. First, because decreasing tobacco consumption will reduce health expenditure. Second, because tobacco tax policy will not decrease tobacco tax revenues in the short run due to the inelastic demand for tobacco products. In the long run, a successful tobacco tax reform that would significantly reduce smoking would indeed result in a drop in tobacco tax revenues. However, the drop in the health, economic and social costs of smoking would outweigh the drop in tobacco tax revenue: the net effect on the budget will therefore always be positive (Marquez and Moreno-Dodson, 2017[34]).

In practice, there are many countries in LAC where the Ministries of Health and Finance have to establish, or reinforce, their dialogue and collaboration. The collaboration can focus on the two objectives cited above (decreasing tobacco use prevalence; raising tobacco tax revenue and reducing the net fiscal impact of tobacco use) and be expanded to other tobacco-related topics such as the cost of smoking, the economic footprint of the tobacco sector (in terms of employment in particular), the effectiveness of tobacco control policies in place, the industry response to tobacco control policies, illicit trade in tobacco products, etc. (Lwin et al., 2023[35]). Across-government collaboration and coordination should involve other government departments, including the tax administration and the customs authorities.

There possibly is a role for other Ministries, such as the Ministry of Industry, Trade, Agriculture or Labour, to maximise the effectiveness of tobacco tax policy. For instance, subsidies to the raw tobacco sector will undermine the effectiveness of tobacco control policies; rather than subsidizing the tobacco agricultural sector, it would be more effective to stimulate farmers to diversify their activities into other crops. An integrated policy approach would allow countries to develop cross cutting policies (Sandoval et al., 2022[9]), such as providing training to former tobacco workers financed through the revenues raised from tobacco excise taxes.

This leads to an additional best practice (BP 20 see Box 5.2): *Reinforce the cooperation between Ministries of Finance and Ministries of Health to ensure that tobacco tax policies are effective in significantly reducing tobacco use prevalence. Include other part of government to participate in such a dialogue, such as the tax administration and the customs authorities.*

Regional tobacco tax coordination and cooperation

The design and administration of a country's tobacco tax policy can generate negative cross-country spill-over effects. For instance, weak tobacco tax enforcement and administration in one country can increase illicit trade opportunities that will negatively affect other countries. Countries that allow tobacco companies to operate in tax-free economic zones will provide a windfall gain to these companies. These profits may then be used strategically to limit the behavioural response of smokers as a result of a tax increase in other countries.

The LAC region lacks regional coordination and cooperation on tobacco tax policy and administration. For example, tobacco tax rates are set in isolation from neighbouring countries. Not all countries tax all traditional tobacco products (cigars, cigarillos, and RYO tobacco) and new tobacco and nicotine products. There is no analysis of the volumes and characteristics of manufactured tobacco products in tax-free economic zones nor whether the products will be sold in the domestic or a foreign market. When countries have an effective domestic track and trace system (which is rather the exception than the rule in LAC) information on tobacco production and (illicit) trade tends not to be shared across countries, which does not facilitate the fight against illicit trade at the regional level (Joossens and Raw, 2012[36]; OECD, 2018[37]; WHO, 2018[38]). Regional coordination and cooperation of tobacco tax policies is therefore one of the key reform priorities for the LAC region (Sandoval et al., 2022[9]).

There is scope to strengthen the coordination and cooperation across LAC countries using the mechanisms that are already in place. First, only seven countries in LAC have ratified the WHO Protocol to Eliminate Illicit Trade in Tobacco Products, adopted in 2012, that aims to eliminate all forms of illicit trade in tobacco products (WHO, 2013[39]). Second, LAC countries have experience in exchanging financial account information for tax purposes, both upon request and automatically, which allows countries to tax capital income more effectively (OECD, 2022[40]). The effective cooperation on income taxes should inspire countries to start exchanging tobacco tax and non-tax information, such as volumes of domestic tobacco production (tobacco leaves, manufactured products), exported tobacco products and destination of tobacco exports. Finally, the Regional Tax Cooperation Platform for LAC created in 2023 is an excellent opportunity to discuss tobacco taxation, both from the policy and administration side, and to strengthen tobacco collaboration at the regional level (ECLAC, 2024[41]).

This leads to an additional best practice (BP 21 see Box 5.2): *Engage in regional coordination and cooperation on tobacco tax policy and exchange information on tobacco-related information to avoid that weak tobacco control policies in one country create a hurdle for effective tobacco tax policies in other countries.* In particular, make a greater use of existing mechanisms, such as the WHO Protocol to Eliminate Illicit Trade in Tobacco Products and the Regional Tax Cooperation Platform for LAC, and build on the experience that countries have in sharing tax information.

References

Blanco Marquizo, A. et al. (2022), "Moving forward in the Americas: tobacco control fosters sustainable development", *Revista Panamericana de Salud Pública*, Vol. 46, p. 1, https://doi.org/10.26633/rpsp.2022.139. [10]

Blecher, E. (2020), "Affordability of Tobacco Products: The Case of Cigarettes", *Tobacconomics*, https://tobacconomics.org/research/affordability-of-tobacco-products-the-case-of-cigarettes/. [15]

Blecher, E., C. Ozer and D. Bloom (2023), *Knowledge Note: Unpacking the empirics behind health tax revenue*, World Bank, https://thedocs.worldbank.org/en/doc/f1f068e38935e2f5d92b7edf365d5089-0350032023/original/KN-4-Unpacking-the-empirics-behind-health-tax-revenues.pdf. [19]

Campos Vázquez, R. (2022), *Measurement of tax expenditures in Latin America*, Economic Commission for Latin America and the Caribbean, https://www.cepal.org/en/publications/48526-measurement-tax-expenditures-latin-america. [32]

Chaloupka, F. et al. (2021), *Cigarette Tax Scorecard (2nd Edition)*, Tobacconomics, https://tobacconomics.org/research/cigarette-tax-scorecard-2nd-edition/. [26]

Drope, J. et al. (2024), *Tobacconomics cigarette tax scorecard (3rd ed.)*, Bloomberg School of Public Health, Johns Hopkins University, https://tobacconomics.org/research/cigarette-tax-scorecard-3rd-edition/. [16]

ECLAC (2024), *The Regional Tax Cooperation Platform for Latin America and the Caribbean is ready*, Economic Commission for Latin America and the Caribbean, https://www.cepal.org/en/notes/regional-tax-cooperation-platform-latin-america-and-caribbean-ready. [41]

Euromonitor International (2023), *Euromonitor International's Tobacco Industry edition*, https://www.euromonitor.com/tobacco (accessed on 1 August 2023). [24]

Fuchs, A. et al. (2019), *Is Tobacco Taxation Regressive? Evidence on Public Health, Domestic Resource Mobilization, and Equity Improvements*, World Bank Group, https://doi.org/10.1596/31575. [23]

Goodchild, M., N. Nargis and E. Tursan d'Espaignet (2017), "Global economic cost of smoking-attributable diseases", *Tobacco Control*, Vol. 27/1, pp. 58-64, https://doi.org/10.1136/tobaccocontrol-2016-053305. [13]

Goodchild, M., R. Sandoval and I. Belausteguigoitia (2017), "Generating revenue by raising tobacco taxes in Latin America and the Caribbean", *Revista Panamericana de Salud Pública*, pp. 1-7, https://doi.org/10.26633/rpsp.2017.151. [17]

Guindon, G., G. Paraje and F. Chaloupka (2018), "The Impact of Prices and Taxes on the Use of Tobacco Products in Latin America and the Caribbean", *American Journal of Public Health*, Vol. 108/S6, pp. S492-S502, https://doi.org/10.2105/ajph.2014.302396r. [22]

Hiscock, R. and M. Bloomfield (2021), "The value of studying supply chains for tobacco control", *Tobacco Prevention & Cessation*, Vol. 7/February, pp. 1-7, https://doi.org/10.18332/tpc/131811. [30]

Hutchinson, B. et al. (2022), "The case for investment in tobacco control: lessons from four countries in the Americas", *Revista Panamericana de Salud Pública*, Vol. 46, p. 1, https://doi.org/10.26633/rpsp.2022.174. [11]

IMF (2024), *International Financial Statistics (IFS)*, International Monetary Fund, https://data.imf.org/?sk=4c514d48-b6ba-49ed-8ab9-52b0c1a0179b&sId=1390030341854 (accessed on 13 January 2024). [8]

IMF (2023), *World Economic Outlook Database*, International Monetary Fund, https://www.imf.org/en/Publications/WEO/weo-database/2023/October (accessed on 13 January 2024). [4]

Jawad, M. et al. (2018), "Price elasticity of demand of non-cigarette tobacco products: a systematic review and meta-analysis", *Tobacco Control*, Vol. 27/6, pp. 689-695, https://doi.org/10.1136/tobaccocontrol-2017-054056. [21]

Joossens, L. and M. Raw (2012), "From cigarette smuggling to illicit tobacco trade: Table 1", *Tobacco Control*, Vol. 21/2, pp. 230-234, https://doi.org/10.1136/tobaccocontrol-2011-050205. [36]

Lwin, K. et al. (2023), "Framing health taxes: learning from low- and middle-income countries", *BMJ Global Health*, Vol. 8/Suppl 8, p. e012955, https://doi.org/10.1136/bmjgh-2023-012955. [35]

Marquez, P. and B. Moreno-Dodson (2017), *Tobacco Tax Reform at the Crossroads of Health and Development: A Multisectoral Perspective*, World Bank, https://openknowledge.worldbank.org/entities/publication/3d81d739-30aa-5092-9c5b-e0b4b68d40e1. [34]

OECD (2024), *Global Revenue Statistics Database*, Organisation for Economic Co-operation and Development, https://www.oecd.org/tax/tax-policy/global-revenue-statistics-database.htm (accessed on 13 August 2023). [25]

OECD (2022), *Peer Review of the Automatic Exchange of Financial Account Information 2022*, OECD Publishing, Paris, https://doi.org/10.1787/36e7cded-en. [40]

OECD (2018), *Governance Frameworks to Counter Illicit Trade*, Illicit Trade, OECD Publishing, Paris, https://doi.org/10.1787/9789264291652-en. [37]

Partos, T. et al. (2020), "Impact of tobacco tax increases and industry pricing on smoking behaviours and inequalities: a mixed-methods study", *Public Health Research*, Vol. 8/6, https://doi.org/10.3310/phr08060. [5]

Perucic, A. et al. (2022), "Taxation of novel and emerging nicotine and tobacco products (HTPs, ENDS, and ENNDS) globally and in Latin America", *Revista Panamericana de Salud Publica/Pan American Journal of Public Health*, Vol. 46, https://doi.org/10.26633/RPSP.2022.175. [12]

Petit, P. and J. Nagy (2016), "How to Design and Enforce Tobacco Excises?" How-To Note No. 2016/003, https://doi.org/10.5089/9781475546651.061. [20]

Pichon-Riviere, A. et al. (2023), "Health, economic and social burden of tobacco in Latin America and the expected gains of fully implementing taxes, plain packaging, advertising bans and smoke-free environments control measures: a modelling study", *Tobacco Control*, pp. tc-2022-057618, https://doi.org/10.1136/tc-2022-057618. [14]

Preece, R. (2008), "Key controls in the administration of excise duties", *World Customs Journal*, Vol. 2/1, https://worldcustomsjournal.org/Archives/Volume%202%2C%20Number%201%20(Apr%202008)/08%20key_controls_in_the_administration_of_excise_duties.pdf. [29]

Sandoval, R. et al. (2022), "Advances in Tobacco Control in the Region of the Americas, 2020", *Revista Panamericana de Salud Pública*, Vol. 46, p. 1, https://doi.org/10.26633/rpsp.2022.202. [1]

Sandoval, R. et al. (2022), "Lessons learned from fostering tobacco taxes in the Americas and implications for other health taxes", *Revista Panamericana de Salud Pública*, Vol. 46, p. 1, https://doi.org/10.26633/rpsp.2022.188. [9]

Sheikh, Z., J. Branston and A. Gilmore (2021), "Tobacco industry pricing strategies in response to excise tax policies: a systematic review", *Tobacco Control*, Vol. 32/2, pp. 239-250, https://doi.org/10.1136/tobaccocontrol-2021-056630. [6]

South American Network on Applied Economics/Red Sur (2019), *Effective Tobacco Taxes in Latin America: Obstacles and Recommendations Based on National Experiences*, Tobacconomics, https://www.tobacconomics.org/files/research/539/Regional-REPORT-ENG-WEB-1.pdf. [18]

Tauras, J. et al. (2014), *Is the Cigarette Price Effect Nonlinear?*, Tobacconomics, https://tobacconomics.org/files/research/164/Tauras_PriceLinear_SCTC_Sept2014.pdf. [28]

Vermeulen, S., M. Dillen and J. Branston (2020), *Big Tobacco, Big Avoidance*, The Investigative Desk, https://www.bath.ac.uk/publications/big-tobacco-big-avoidance/attachments/Big_Tobacco_Big_Avoidance.pdf. [27]

WHO (2023), *WHO report on the global tobacco epidemic 2023: Protect people from tobacco smoke*, World Health Organization, https://www.who.int/publications/i/item/9789240077164. [3]

WHO (2021), *Examples of current practices in the implementation of Article 12 (free zones and international transit) of the protocol to eliminate illicit trade in tobacco products*, World Health Organization, https://iris.who.int/handle/10665/340212. [33]

WHO (2021), *WHO report on the global tobacco epidemic 2021: Addressing new and emerging products*, World Health Organization, https://www.who.int/publications/i/item/9789240032095. [31]

WHO (2021), *WHO technical manual on tobacco tax policy and administration*, World Health Organization, https://www.who.int/publications/i/item/9789240019188. [2]

WHO (2018), *Report of the Panel of Experts on the Protocol to Eliminate Illicit Trade in Tobacco Products*, World Health Organization, https://fctc.who.int/publications/m/item/report-of-the-panel-of-experts-on-the-protocol-to-eliminate-illicit-trade-in-tobacco-products-technical-documents. [38]

WHO (2013), *Protocol to eliminate illicit trade in tobacco products*, World Health Organization, https://iris.who.int/bitstream/handle/10665/80873/9789241505246_eng.pdf?sequence=1. [39]

World Bank (2024), *World Bank Open Data*, World Bank, https://data.worldbank.org/ (accessed on 13 January 2024). [7]

Annex 5.A. Year of introduction of excise tax measures

Annex Table 5.A.1. Year of introduction of measures that follow WHO tobacco tax policy best practices moderately or completely since 2000

Year of measure introduction (year of measure reform)

	Type of taxes (BP2)	Excise tax structure (BP3)	Taxable products		Excise tax base		Excise tax rate		Indexation (BP10)	Tax floor (BP11)
			(BP4)	(BP5)	(BP6)	(BP7)	(BP8)	(BP9)		
Argentina	(2016)			2011						2004 (2017)
Bolivia	(2004)	2017	2017					2006	2017	
Brazil		2011		2009	2011	2011		2011		2011 (2016)
Chile	(2010) (2012) (2014)	2010 (2012)			(2010)	2010		(2010)	2010	
Colombia	(2006) (2010) (2016)	2006		2018	2010	2006	2006	2010	2006 (2016)	
Costa Rica		2012		2022		2012		(2012)	2012	
Dominican Republic	(2000) (2004) (2005) (2006) (2012)	2004				2004			2004 (2012)	
Ecuador	(2004) (2006) (2016)	2011	(2007)	2019		2011		2007	2011 (2016)	
El Salvador	(2004) (2009)					2004	2004	2004		
Guatemala										
Honduras		2010			(2004)			(2010)	2010	
Jamaica	(2005) (2007) (2009) (2012) (2016) (2017)	2008	2015			2015	2015			(2005)
Mexico	(2002) (2006) (2010)			2021 (2022)		2009	2002 (2009)		2019	
Nicaragua	(2002) (2003) (2012)	2009 (2019)	2003	2021	2000		2019		2009 (2012)	
Panama	(2005) (2009)		2005	2022			(2005)			2009

	Type of taxes (BP2)	Excise tax structure (BP3)	Taxable products		Excise tax base		Excise tax rate		Indexation (BP10)	Tax floor (BP11)
			(BP4)	(BP5)	(BP6)	(BP7)	(BP8)	(BP9)		
Paraguay	(2004) (2010) (2015) (2018) (2022)			2019			(2004) (2010) (2022)			
Peru	(2001) (2003) (2016) (2018)	2010		2019		2010		2001 (2010)	2001 (2019) (2020)	
Uruguay	(2002) (2005)			2009 (2017)				2010		

Note: BP1 (affordability) and BP12 (sale regulations) have not been included in the table. Blank cells indicate that there were no measures introduced that align the tobacco tax system with the WHO tobacco tax policy best practices in a moderate or complete manner between 2000 and 2022. Some countries have implemented measures that align moderately with one or multiple BPs and then have later in time introduced measures that weaken the implementation of the BP. As a result, there are some measures included in the table, while the country scores below the moderate level of compliance in 2022 in Table 4.1 of Chapter 4 (e.g., Bolivia for BP9). The information for BP2 corresponds to a tobacco excise tax increase that contributes to country's compliance with an excise tax share of at least 50% of the total tobacco tax share in 2022. Progress on BP5 corresponds to the ban of sales of new tobacco and nicotine products in the following countries: Argentina (ENDS and ENNDS only, 2011), Brazil (2009), Mexico (2022), Nicaragua (ENDS and ENNDS only, 2021), Panama (2022) and Uruguay (ENDS and ENNDS only, 2009). Costa Rica started to levy an excise tax on e-cigarettes in 2022, and Ecuador in 2019. Heated tobacco products are taxed in Colombia (since 2018), Paraguay (since 2019) and Peru (since 2019).
Source: OECD based on national legislation listed in country notes (Chapter 6); WHO report on the global tobacco epidemic (WHO, 2023[3]).

6 Tobacco taxation country profiles

This chapter is a collection of country profiles for 18 countries in Latin America and the Caribbean (LAC). Subject to data availability, each country profile provides information on tobacco use prevalence, MPOWER measures, taxes and prices of the most sold brand of cigarettes, trends in retail prices of cigarettes by brand category, affordability of cigarettes, the design of tobacco excise taxes across tobacco products, tobacco tax reforms, tobacco excise tax revenue, the average excise tax revenue collected per pack of 20 cigarettes sold, and the change in tobacco tax policy indicators over time.

Argentina

Figure 6.1. Argentina - Trends in tobacco use prevalence

Percentage of the population aged 15 years and over who currently use any tobacco product (smoked and/or smokeless tobacco) on a daily or non-daily basis, 2000-2020

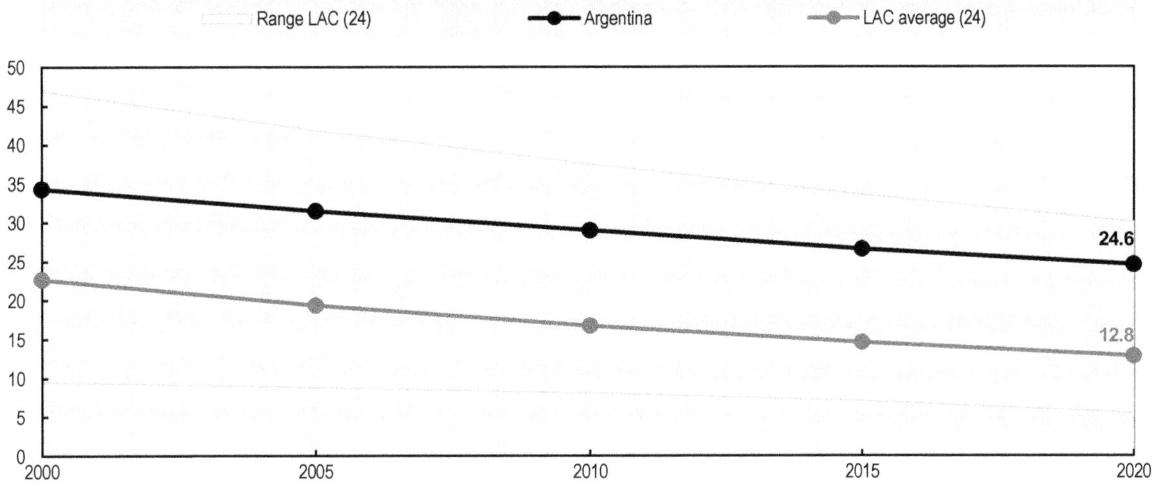

Note: Tobacco products include cigarettes, pipes, cigars, cigarillos, waterpipes (hookah, shisha), bidis, kretek, heated tobacco products (HTP), and all forms of smokeless (oral and nasal) tobacco. Tobacco products exclude e-cigarettes (which do not contain tobacco), e-cigars, e-hookahs, and e-pipes. The rates are age-standardized to the World Health Organisation (WHO) standard population. The LAC average was calculated as the average of Argentina, Bahamas, Barbados, Belize, Bolivia, Brazil, Chile, Colombia, Costa Rica, Cuba, the Dominican Republic, Ecuador, El Salvador, Guatemala, Guyana, Haiti, Honduras, Jamaica, Mexico, Panama, Paraguay, Peru, Saint Lucia, and Uruguay.
Source: WHO Global Health Observatory Data Repository (WHO, 2024[1]).

Table 6.1. Argentina - Tobacco use prevalence by sex and age groups

Percentage of the population group, latest year available

	Tobacco use prevalence (all tobacco products)	Cigarette smoking prevalence (cigarettes only)
Students aged 13-15 years		
Total	**16.0**	**14.6**
Males	13.7	12.1
Females	18.0	16.8
People aged 15 and over		
Total	**24.6**	**22.4**
Males	29.5	26.9
Females	19.7	17.9

Note: Tobacco use prevalence is defined as the percentage of the population group who currently use any tobacco product (smoked and/or smokeless tobacco) on a daily or non-daily basis. Tobacco products exclude e-cigarettes (which do not contain tobacco), e-cigars, e-hookahs, and e-pipes. Data for students aged 13-15 years are from 2018 and taken from the Global School-based Student Health Survey. Data for people aged 15 and over correspond to 2020.
Source: WHO Global Health Observatory Data Repository (WHO, 2024[1]); Global School-based Student Health Survey (WHO, 2018[2]).

Table 6.2. Argentina - Summary of MPOWER measures, 2022

M Monitoring	P Smoking bans	O Cessation programmes	W Health warnings	E Advertising bans	R Taxation	WHO Frawework Convention on Tobacco Control		Protocol to eliminate illicit trade in tobacco products	
						Date of signature	Date of ratification	Date of signature	Date of ratification
						25-09-2003			

... Not categorized/ No data; No policy or weak measure; Minimal measure; Moderate measure; Complete measure

Source: WHO report on the global tobacco epidemic (WHO, 2023[3]).

Figure 6.2. Argentina - Taxes and prices of the most sold brand of cigarettes

Panel A. Indirect taxes levied on cigarettes in Argentina and LAC | **Panel B. Tobacco tax share and price of cigarettes in Argentina**

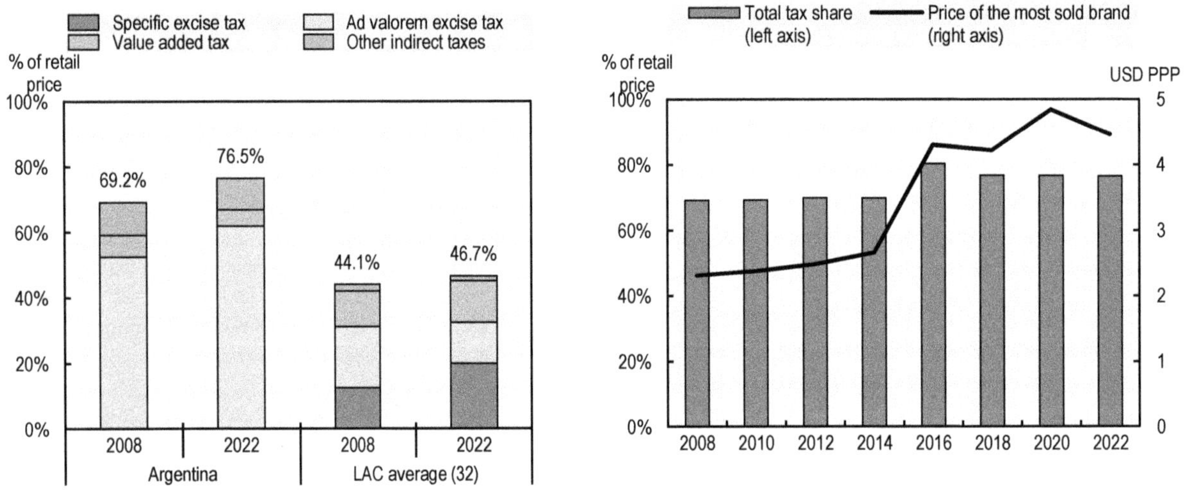

Note: Prices correspond to a 20-cigarette pack of the most sold brand. Retail prices in USD PPP are based on the implied purchasing power parity (PPP) conversion rate from the International Monetary Fund (IMF) World Economic Outlook Database (October 2023). The most sold brand of cigarettes is determined based on national market share information and can vary over time (i.e. the most sold brand of cigarettes in year 1 can be different from year 2).

Source: WHO report on the global tobacco epidemic (WHO, 2023[3]); IMF World Economic Outlook Database (IMF, 2023[4]).

Figure 6.3. Argentina - Trends in retail prices of cigarettes by brand category

In USD PPP per pack of 20 cigarettes, 2008-2022

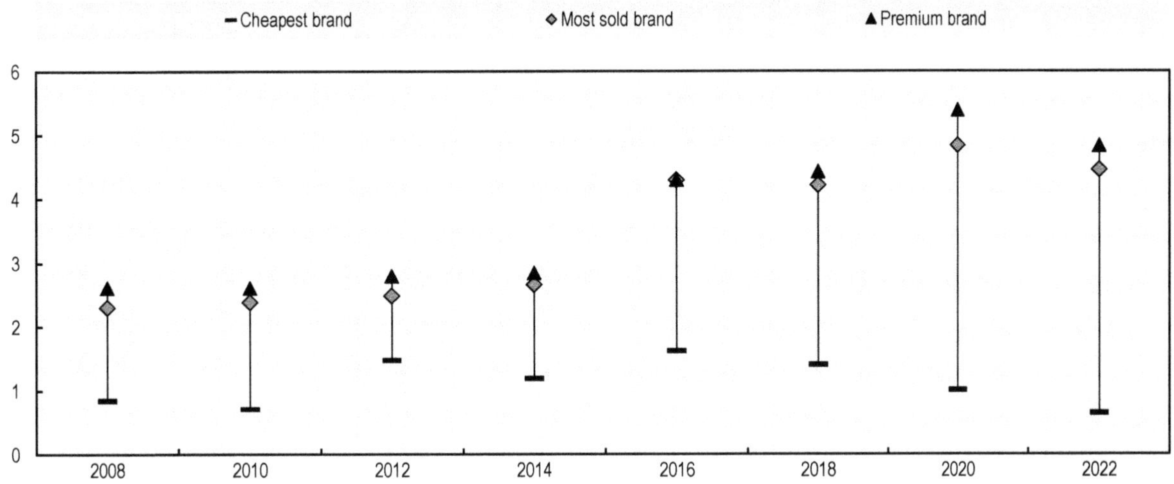

Note: Prices correspond to a 20-cigarette pack of the cheapest, most sold and premium brands. The cheapest, most sold and premium brands of cigarettes are determined based on national market share information and can vary over time (i.e. the cheapest/most sold/premium brands of cigarettes in year 1 can be different from year 2). Retail prices in USD PPP are based on the implied PPP conversion rate from the IMF World Economic Outlook Database (October 2023).
Source: WHO reports on the global tobacco epidemic (WHO, 2009[5]; WHO, 2011[6]; WHO, 2013[7]; WHO, 2015[8]; WHO, 2017[9]; WHO, 2019[10]; WHO, 2021[11]); IMF World Economic Outlook Database (IMF, 2023[4]).

Figure 6.4. Argentina - Affordability of cigarettes

Percentage of GDP per capita required to purchase 100 packs of 20 cigarettes

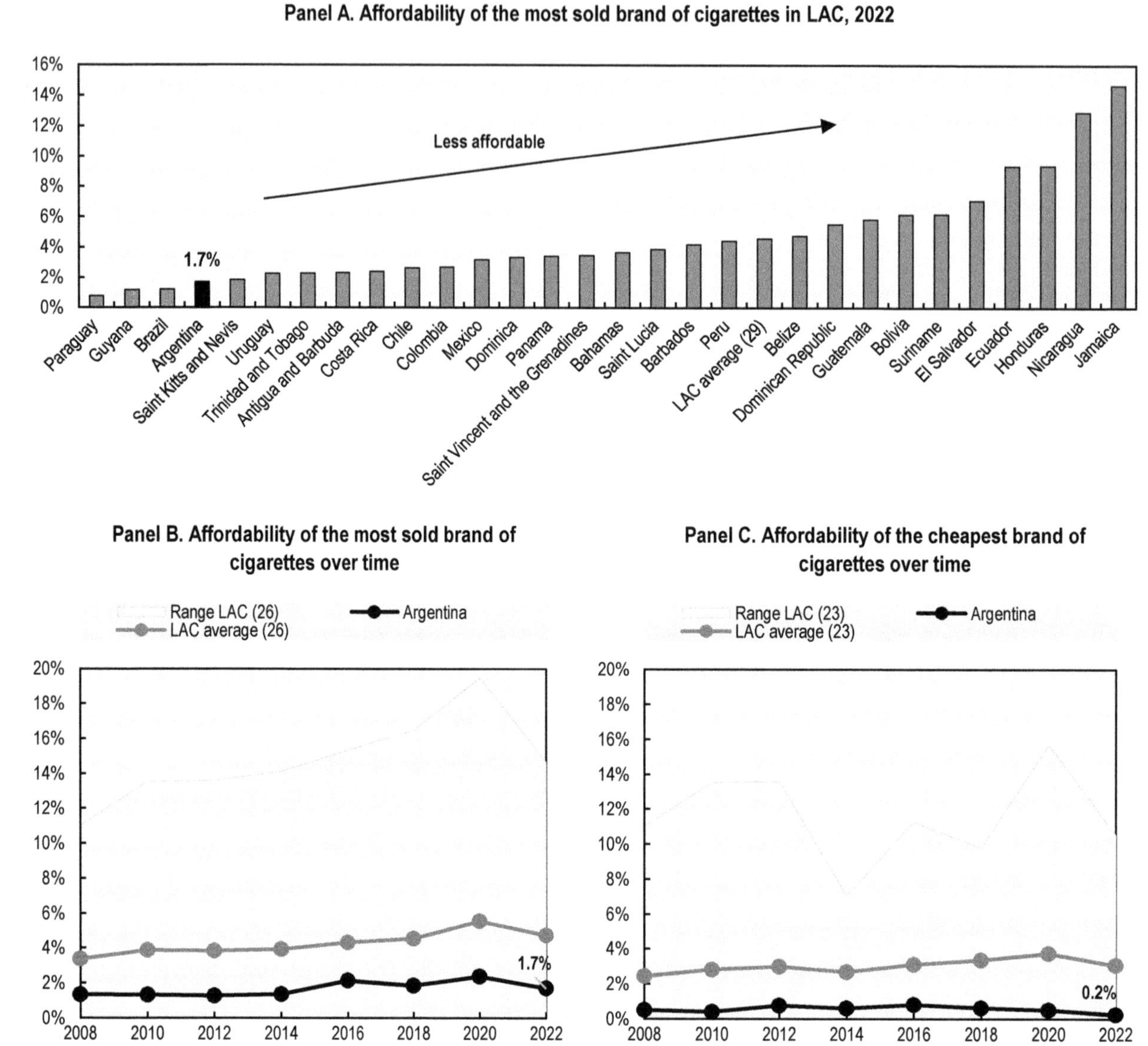

Note: The affordability indicator measures the percentage of the country's GDP per capita required to purchase 100 packs of 20 cigarettes. A higher percentage means lower affordability of cigarettes while a lower percentage means higher affordability. To ensure comparability of average affordability across LAC over time, countries where information was unavailable for certain years have been excluded from the calculation. Data for Panel C are OECD calculations based on WHO reports on the global tobacco epidemic (2009-2023 editions). The cheapest and most sold brands of cigarettes are determined based on national market share information and can vary over time (i.e. the cheapest/most sold brand of cigarettes in year 1 can be different from year 2).

Source: WHO reports on the global tobacco epidemic (WHO, 2009[5]; WHO, 2011[6]; WHO, 2013[7]; WHO, 2015[8]; WHO, 2017[9]; WHO, 2019[10]; WHO, 2021[11]).

Table 6.3. Argentina - Design of tobacco excise taxes across tobacco products, 2022

	Excise tax structure	Specific excise tax				Ad valorem excise tax			Excise tax floor			
		Yes / No	Tax base	Rate per 20-unit pack USD PPP (local currency)	Indexation mechanisms	Yes / No	Tax base	Statutory rate	Yes / No	Tax base	Rate per 20-unit pack USD PPP (local currency)	Indexation mechanisms
Cigarettes	Ad valorem only	No				Yes	SRP excl. VAT	70%	Yes	Ind. pack	2.5 (169.3)	CPI
Cigars	Ad valorem only	No				Yes	SRP excl. VAT	20%	Yes	Sticks	23.1 (1 550.2)	CPI
Cigarillos	Ad valorem only	No				Yes	SRP excl. VAT	20%	Yes	Ind. pack	2.3 (155.0)	CPI
Roll-Your-Own (RYO) tobacco	Ad valorem only	No				Yes	SRP excl. VAT	25%	Yes	Weight	2.5 (165.4)	CPI
Heated tobacco products (HTPs)	No excise											
ENDS and ENNDS	No excise											

Note: "SRP" means "Suggested retail price by the manufacturer/importer"; blank cells mean that there is no excise tax for the corresponding tobacco product; "VAT" means "Value added tax"; "CPI" means consumer price index. Following the WHO report on the global tobacco epidemic (WHO, 2021[11]), new tobacco and nicotine products in this report include electronic nicotine delivery systems (ENDS), electronic non-nicotine delivery systems (ENNDS), and heated tobacco products (HTP). Argentina does not levy an excise tax on ENDS or ENNDS their sales are banned (WHO, 2023[3]). Specific taxes are converted into USD PPP with the implied PPP conversion rate available in the IMF World Economic Outlook Database (October 2023). Specific excise taxes have been standardized to a 20-unit pack to allow the comparison across countries with different tax bases. To compute the minimum specific tax for an equivalent 20-unit pack of Roll-Your-Own (RYO) tobacco product, it is assumed that the median cigarette in terms of weight contains 0.75 gram of tobacco (Gallus et al., 2014[12]).
Source: Decreto 626/2016; Ley N° 27430; IMF World Economic Outlook Database (IMF, 2023[4]).

Table 6.4. Argentina - Tobacco tax reforms since 2000

Year of adoption	Specific excise taxes	Ad valorem excise taxes	Other
2004	No	No	Cigarettes: introduction of a minimum tax equivalent to 75% of the ad valorem excise tax levied on the most sold brand of cigarettes.
2016	No	Cigarettes: increase in the tax rate from 60% to 75% levied on the retail price suggested by the manufacturer/importer, excluding VAT.	No
2017	No	Cigarettes: reduction in the tax rate from 75% to 70% levied on the retail price suggested by the manufacturer/importer, excluding VAT. Cigars and cigarillos: increase in the tax rate from 16% to 20% levied on the retail price suggested by the manufacturer/importer, excluding VAT. RYO tobacco products: increase in the tax rate from 20% to 25% levied on the retail price suggested by the manufacturer/importer, excluding VAT.	All tobacco products: introduction of a tax floor and a limit to temporary tax increases motivated by exceptional economic circumstances. The increased tax shall be the lowest between a 25% increased tax and 75% of the tax base.

Note: "Tobacco tax reform" refers to changes in the tobacco excise tax rates, the introduction of indexation mechanisms or minimum taxes, as well as adjustments to the tax base. These reforms typically entail the enactment of new laws or decrees. The table does not refer to recurrent tax changes that result from the indexation for inflation of tax brackets and price floors (if implemented). Tobacco tax reforms included reflect changes in the legislation, but not whether or when the reforms have been implemented.
Source: Decreto 296/2004; Decreto 626/2016; Ley N° 27430.

Figure 6.5. Argentina - Tobacco excise tax revenue

Percentage of GDP, latest year available

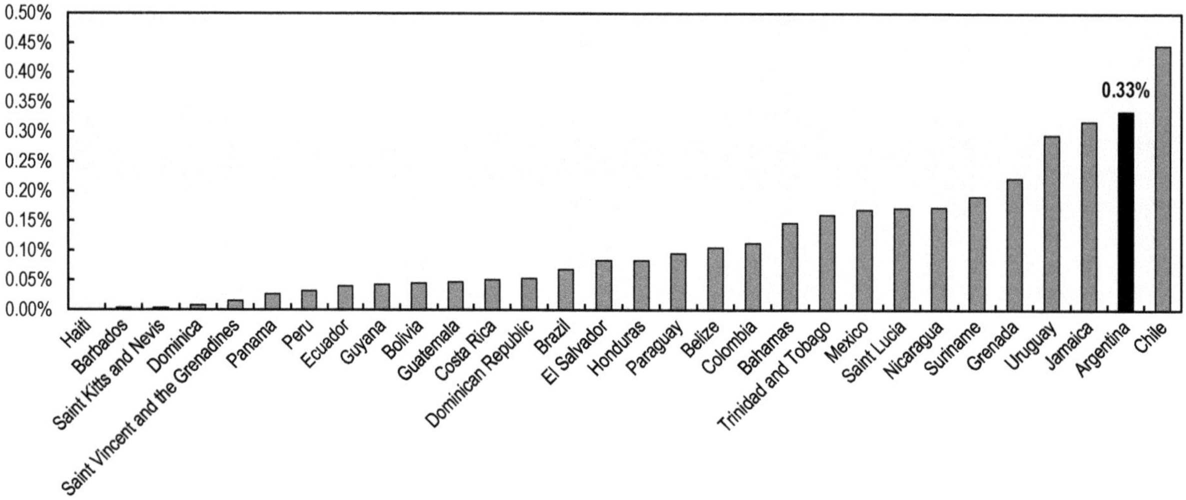

Note: See Box 2.1 (Chapter 2) for more information on tobacco tax revenue (source of information and calculations) and country selection. The latest year available is 2022 for Argentina, Brazil, Chile, Colombia, Costa Rica, the Dominican Republic, El Salvador, Guatemala, Guyana, Honduras, Mexico, Nicaragua, Panama, Paraguay, Peru, Saint Kitts and Nevis, Suriname, and Uruguay; 2021 for Belize, Dominica, Ecuador, Grenada, Saint Lucia, Saint Vincent and the Grenadines; 2020 for Bahamas, Bolivia, Jamaica and Trinidad and Tobago; 2015 for Haiti; 2014 for Barbados.
Source: OECD Revenue Statistics (OECD, 2024[13]); WHO report on the global tobacco epidemic (WHO, 2023[3]); National data.

Figure 6.6. Argentina - Trends in tobacco excise tax revenue

Percentage of GDP, 2000-2022

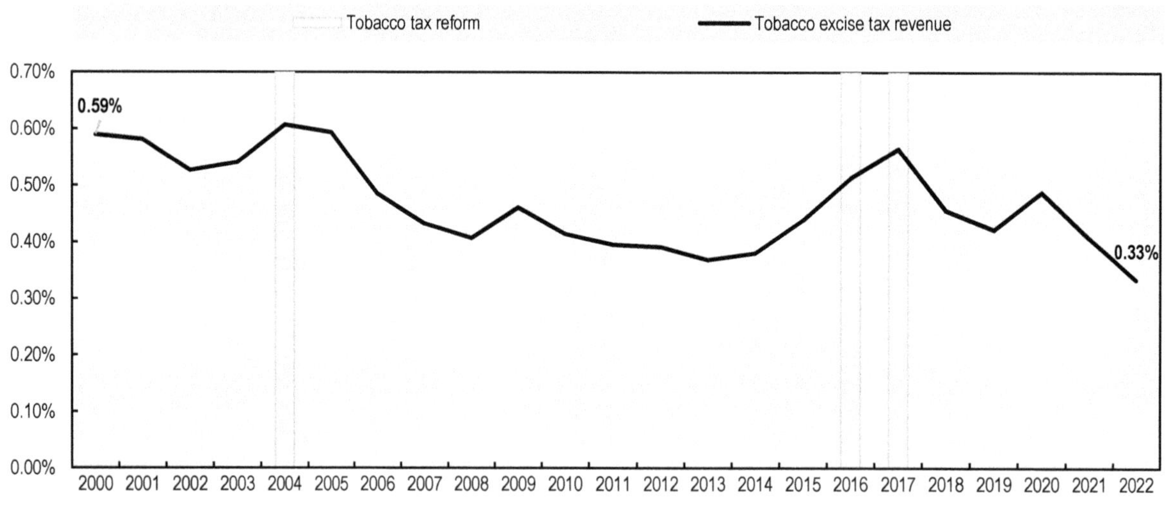

Note: "Tobacco tax reform" refers to the measures included in Table 6.4.
Source: OECD Revenue Statistics (OECD, 2024[13]); Decreto 296/2004; Decreto 626/2016; Ley N° 27430.

Figure 6.7. Argentina - Average excise tax revenue collected per pack of 20 cigarettes sold

Tobacco excise tax revenue in USD PPP collected per pack of legal cigarettes sold, latest year available

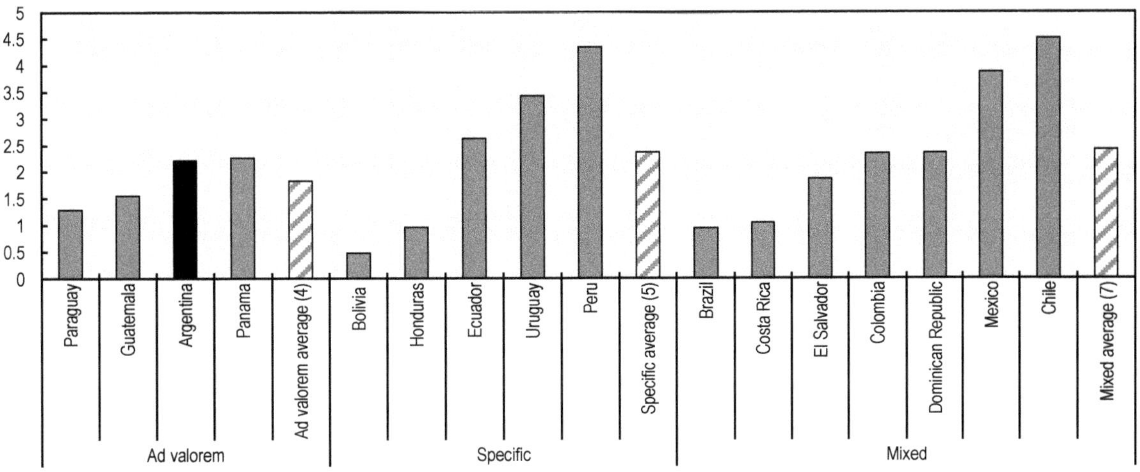

Note: See Box 2.1 (Chapter 2) for more information on tobacco tax revenue (source of information and calculations). The latest year available is 2022 for Argentina, Brazil, Chile, Colombia, Costa Rica, the Dominican Republic, El Salvador, Guatemala, Honduras, Mexico, Panama, Paraguay, Peru and Uruguay; 2021 for Ecuador; 2020 for Bolivia. The country selection is provided by the availability of data on sales of cigarettes in Euromonitor International Tobacco Industry edition, 2023 © All rights reserved (Euromonitor International, 2023[14]).
Source: OECD Revenue Statistics (OECD, 2024[13]); WHO report on the global tobacco epidemic (WHO, 2023[3]); National data; IMF World Economic Outlook Database (IMF, 2023[4]); and OECD calculations based on Euromonitor International's Tobacco Industry edition (Euromonitor International, 2023[14]).

Figure 6.8. Argentina - Change in tobacco tax policy indicators

Percentage change from base year, 2008-2022

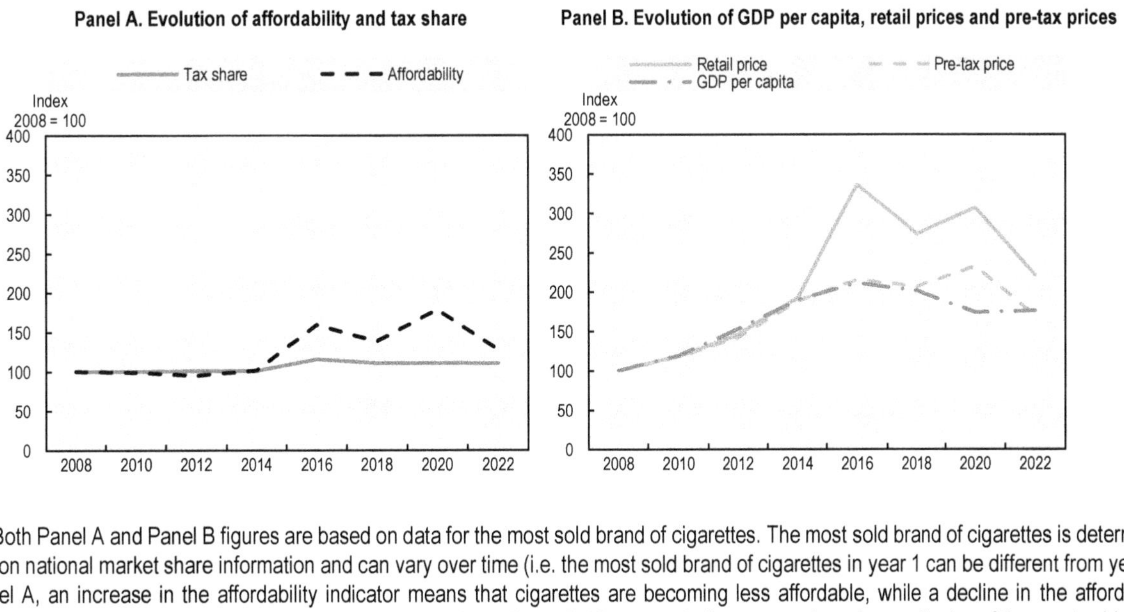

Note: Both Panel A and Panel B figures are based on data for the most sold brand of cigarettes. The most sold brand of cigarettes is determined based on national market share information and can vary over time (i.e. the most sold brand of cigarettes in year 1 can be different from year 2). In Panel A, an increase in the affordability indicator means that cigarettes are becoming less affordable, while a decline in the affordability indicator means that cigarettes are becoming more affordable. In Panel B, "Pre-tax price" corresponds to the retail price of the most sold brand of cigarettes minus the indirect taxes levied on this brand, namely excise taxes, VAT, import duties and other. Indicators in Panel B have been computed using national currency and have been adjusted for inflation; therefore, present inflation-adjusted trends.
Source: WHO report on the global tobacco epidemic (WHO, 2023[3]); World Bank Open Data (World Bank, 2024[15]); Banco Central de la República de Argentina for CPI (Central Bank of Argentina, 2024[16]).

References

Central Bank of Argentina (2024), *Publicaciones y Estadísticas - Principales variables - Inflación interanual (variación en i.a.)*, https://www.bcra.gob.ar/PublicacionesEstadisticas/Principales_variables_datos.asp?serie=7932&detalle=Inflaci%F3n%20interanual%A0(variaci%F3n%20en%20%%20i.a.) (accessed on 13 January 2024). [16]

Euromonitor International (2023), *Euromonitor International's Tobacco Industry edition*, https://www.euromonitor.com/tobacco (accessed on 1 August 2023). [14]

Gallus, S. et al. (2014), "Roll-your-own cigarettes in Europe", *European Journal of Cancer Prevention*, Vol. 23/3, pp. 186-192, https://doi.org/10.1097/cej.0000000000000010. [12]

IMF (2023), *World Economic Outlook Database*, International Monetary Fund, https://www.imf.org/en/Publications/WEO/weo-database/2023/October (accessed on 13 January 2024). [4]

OECD (2024), *Global Revenue Statistics Database*, Organisation for Economic Co-operation and Development, https://www.oecd.org/tax/tax-policy/global-revenue-statistics-database.htm (accessed on 13 August 2023). [13]

WHO (2024), *Global Health Observatory: Age-standardized estimates of current tobacco use, tobacco smoking and cigarette smoking (Tobacco control: Monitor)*, World Health Organization, https://www.who.int/data/gho/data/indicators/indicator-details/GHO/gho-tobacco-control-monitor-current-tobaccouse-tobaccosmoking-cigarrettesmoking-agestd-tobagestdcurr (accessed on 20 February 2024). [1]

WHO (2023), *WHO report on the global tobacco epidemic 2023: protect people from tobacco smoke*, World Health Organization, https://www.who.int/publications/i/item/9789240077164. [3]

WHO (2021), *WHO report on the global tobacco epidemic 2021: Addressing new and emerging products*, World Health Organization, https://www.who.int/publications/i/item/9789240032095. [11]

WHO (2019), *WHO report on the global tobacco epidemic 2019: Offer help to quit tobacco use*, World Health Organization, https://www.who.int/publications/i/item/9789241516204. [10]

WHO (2018), *Global School-based Student Health Survey. Argentina 2018 Fact Sheet*, World Health Organization, https://cdn.who.int/media/docs/default-source/ncds/ncd-surveillance/data-reporting/argentina/arg2018-gshs-fact-sheet.pdf?sfvrsn=c4927d2b_1&download=true (accessed on 13 January 2024). [2]

WHO (2017), *WHO report on the global tobacco epidemic 2017: Monitoring tobacco use and prevention policies*, World Health Organization, https://www.who.int/publications/i/item/9789241512824. [9]

WHO (2015), *WHO report on the global tobacco epidemic 2015: Raising taxes on tobacco*, World Health Organization, https://www.who.int/publications/i/item/9789241509121. [8]

WHO (2013), *WHO report on the global tobacco epidemic 2013: Enforcing bans on tobacco advertising, promotion and sponsorship*, World Health Organization, https://www.who.int/publications/i/item/9789241505871. [7]

WHO (2011), *WHO report on the global tobacco epidemic 2011: Warning about the dangers of tobacco*, World Health Organization, https://www.who.int/publications/i/item/9789244564264. [6]

WHO (2009), *WHO report on the global tobacco epidemic 2009: Implementing smoke-free environments*, World Health Organization, https://www.who.int/publications/i/item/9789241563918. [5]

World Bank (2024), *World Bank Open Data*, World Bank, https://data.worldbank.org/ (accessed on 13 January 2024). [15]

Bolivia

Figure 6.9. Bolivia - Trends in tobacco use prevalence

Percentage of the population aged 15 years and over who currently use any tobacco product (smoked and/or smokeless tobacco) on a daily or non-daily basis, 2000-2020

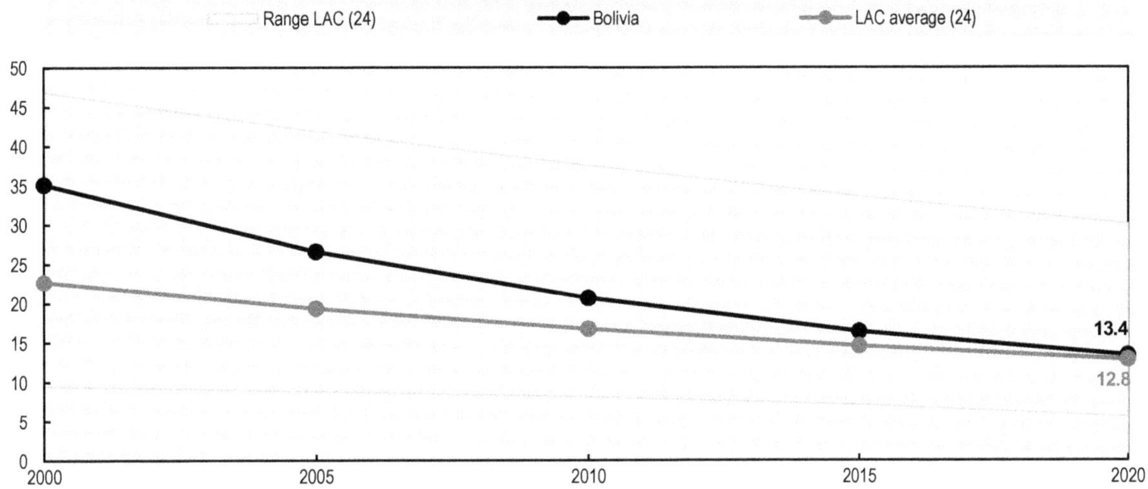

Note: Tobacco products include cigarettes, pipes, cigars, cigarillos, waterpipes (hookah, shisha), bidis, kretek, heated tobacco products (HTP), and all forms of smokeless (oral and nasal) tobacco. Tobacco products exclude e-cigarettes (which do not contain tobacco), e-cigars, e-hookahs, and e-pipes. The rates are age-standardized to the World Health Organisation (WHO) standard population. The LAC average was calculated as the average of Argentina, Bahamas, Barbados, Belize, Bolivia, Brazil, Chile, Colombia, Costa Rica, Cuba, the Dominican Republic, Ecuador, El Salvador, Guatemala, Guyana, Haiti, Honduras, Jamaica, Mexico, Panama, Paraguay, Peru, Saint Lucia, and Uruguay.
Source: WHO Global Health Observatory Data Repository (WHO, 2024[1]).

Table 6.5. Bolivia - Tobacco use prevalence by sex and age groups

Percentage of the population group, latest year available

	Tobacco use prevalence (all tobacco products)	Cigarette smoking prevalence (cigarettes only)
Students aged 13-15 years		
Total	**10.9**	**6.9**
Males	13.6	8.6
Females	8.1	5.2
People aged 15 and over		
Total	**13.4**	**11.2**
Males	21.9	18.0
Females	4.9	4.5

Note: Tobacco use prevalence is defined as the percentage of the population group who currently use any tobacco product (smoked and/or smokeless tobacco) on a daily or non-daily basis. Tobacco products exclude e-cigarettes (which do not contain tobacco), e-cigars, e-hookahs, and e-pipes. Data for students aged 13-15 years are from 2018 and taken from the Global School-based Student Health Survey. Data for people aged 15 and over correspond to 2020.
Source: WHO Global Health Observatory Data Repository (WHO, 2024[1]); Global School-based Student Health Survey (WHO, 2018[17]).

Table 6.6. Bolivia - Summary of MPOWER measures, 2022

M Monitoring	P Smoking bans	O Cessation programmes	W Health warnings	E Advertising bans	R Taxation	WHO Frawework Convention on Tobacco Control		Protocol to eliminate illicit trade in tobacco products	
						Date of signature	Date of ratification	Date of signature	Date of ratification
						27-02-2004	15-09-2005		

... Not categorized/ No data — No policy or weak measure — Minimal measure — Moderate measure — Complete measure

Source: WHO report on the global tobacco epidemic (WHO, 2023[3]).

Figure 6.10. Bolivia - Taxes and prices of the most sold brand of cigarettes

Panel A. Indirect taxes levied on cigarettes in Bolivia and LAC — **Panel B. Tobacco tax share and price of cigarettes in Bolivia**

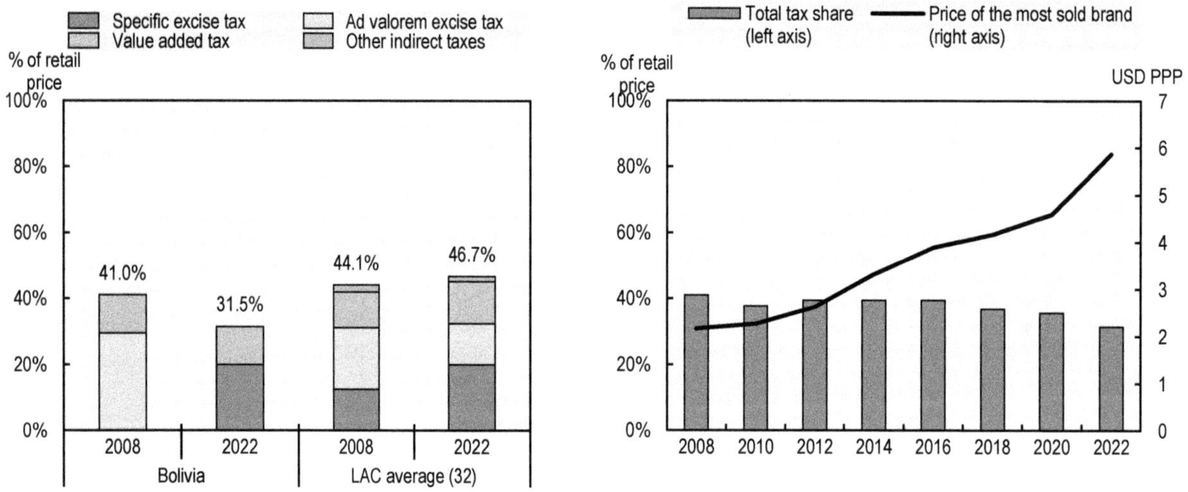

Note: Prices correspond to a 20-cigarette pack of the most sold brand. Retail prices in USD PPP are based on the implied purchasing power parity (PPP) conversion rate from the International Monetary Fund (IMF) World Economic Outlook Database (October 2023). The most sold brand of cigarettes is determined based on national market share information and can vary over time (i.e. the most sold brand of cigarettes in year 1 can be different from year 2).
Source: WHO report on the global tobacco epidemic (WHO, 2023[3]); IMF World Economic Outlook Database (IMF, 2023[4]).

Figure 6.11. Bolivia - Trends in retail prices of cigarettes by brand category

In USD PPP per pack of 20 cigarettes, 2008-2022

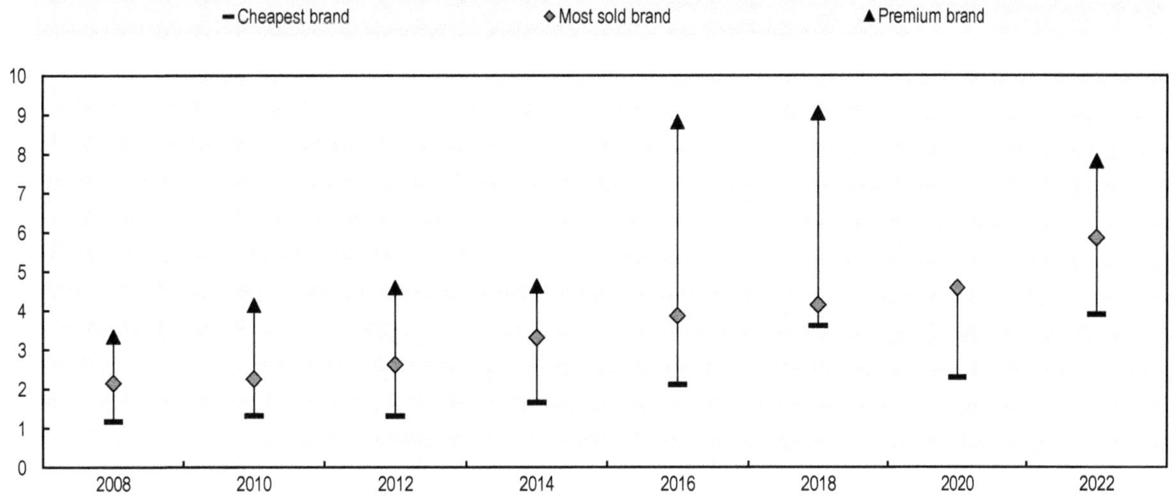

Note: Prices correspond to a 20-cigarette pack of the cheapest, most sold and premium brands. The cheapest, most sold and premium brands of cigarettes are determined based on national market share information and can vary over time (i.e. the cheapest/most sold/premium brands of cigarettes in year 1 can be different from year 2). Retail price of the premium brand is not available for 2020. Retail prices in USD PPP are based on the implied PPP conversion rate from the IMF World Economic Outlook Database (October 2023).
Source: WHO reports on the global tobacco epidemic (WHO, 2009[5]; WHO, 2011[6]; WHO, 2013[7]; WHO, 2015[8]; WHO, 2017[9]; WHO, 2019[10]; WHO, 2021[11]); IMF World Economic Outlook Database (IMF, 2023[4]).

Figure 6.12. Bolivia - Affordability of cigarettes

Percentage of GDP per capita required to purchase 100 packs of 20 cigarettes

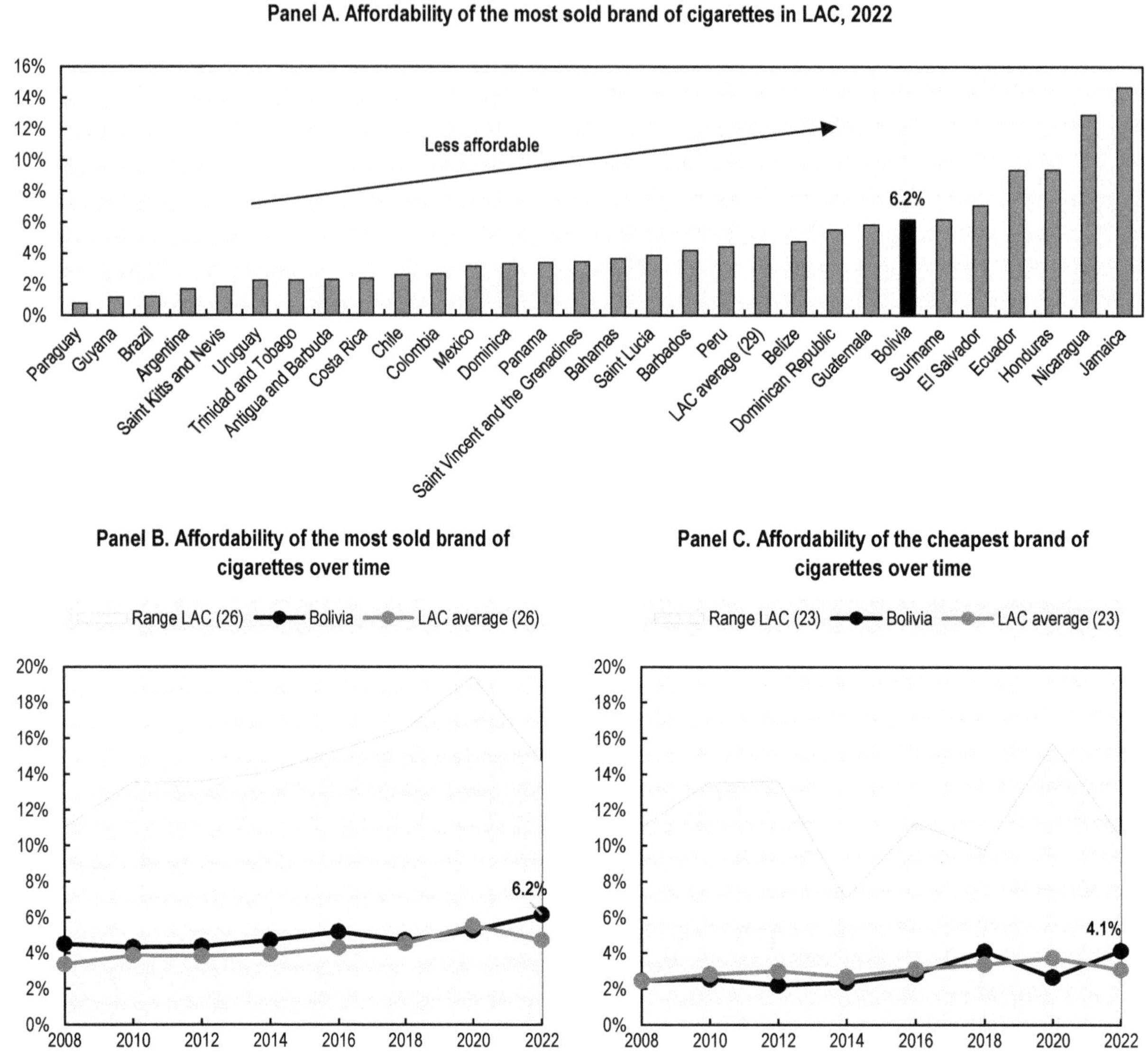

Note: The affordability indicator measures the percentage of the country's GDP per capita required to purchase 100 packs of 20 cigarettes. A higher percentage means lower affordability of cigarettes while a lower percentage means higher affordability. To ensure comparability of average affordability across LAC over time, countries where information was unavailable for certain years have been excluded from the calculation. Data for Panel C are OECD calculations based on WHO reports on the global tobacco epidemic (2009-2023 editions). The cheapest and most sold brands of cigarettes are determined based on national market share information and can vary over time (i.e. the cheapest/most sold brand of cigarettes in year 1 can be different from year 2).

Source: WHO reports on the global tobacco epidemic (WHO, 2009[5]; WHO, 2011[6]; WHO, 2013[7]; WHO, 2015[8]; WHO, 2017[9]; WHO, 2019[10]; WHO, 2021[11]).

Table 6.7. Bolivia - Design of tobacco excise taxes across tobacco products, 2022

	Excise tax structure	Specific excise tax				Ad valorem excise tax			Excise tax floor			
		Yes / No	Tax base	Rate per 20-unit pack USD PPP (local currency)	Indexation mechanisms	Yes / No	Tax base	Statutory rate	Yes / No	Tax base	Rate per 20-unit pack USD PPP (local currency)	Indexation mechanisms
Cigarettes	Specific only	Yes	1 000 sticks	0.6 - 1.2 (1.6 - 3.0)	Unidad de Fomento de Vivienda	No			No			
Cigars	Specific only	Yes	1 000 sticks	1.2 (3.0)	Unidad de Fomento de Vivienda	No			No			
Cigarillos	Specific only	Yes	1 000 sticks	1.2 (3.0)	Unidad de Fomento de Vivienda	No			No			
Roll-Your-Own (RYO) tobacco	Ad valorem only	No				Yes	SRP excl. VAT	50%	No			
Heated tobacco products (HTPs)	No excise											
ENDS and ENNDS	No excise											

Note: "SRP" means "Suggested retail price by the manufacturer/importer"; blank cells mean that there is no excise tax for the corresponding tobacco product; "VAT" means "Value added tax". Following the WHO report on the global tobacco epidemic (WHO, 2021[11]), new tobacco and nicotine products in this report include electronic nicotine delivery systems (ENDS), electronic non-nicotine delivery systems (ENNDS), and heated tobacco products (HTP). Specific taxes are converted into USD PPP with the implied PPP conversion rate available in the IMF World Economic Outlook Database (October 2023). Specific excise taxes have been standardized to a 20-unit pack to allow the comparison across countries with different tax bases.
Source: Ley Nº 1006 (2017), RND 1021-29 (2021); IMF World Economic Outlook Database (IMF, 2023[4]).

Table 6.8. Bolivia - Tobacco tax reforms since 2000

Year of adoption	Specific excise taxes	Ad valorem excise taxes	Other
2004	No	Cigarettes: changes to the tiered tax rates: 50% tax rate for cigarettes that consist of brown tobacco and 55% tax rate for cigarettes that consist of blond tobacco.	No
2006	No	Cigarettes: introduction of a uniform tax rate of 50% levied on the retail price suggested by the manufacturer/importer, excluding VAT.	No
2010	No	Cigarettes: re-introduction of a tiered tax based on tobacco content. The tax rate is 50% for cigarettes that consist of brown tobacco and 55% for cigarettes that consist of blond tobacco.	No
2017	Cigarettes: introduction of a specific excise tax indexed for inflation (Unidad de Fomento de Vivienda) and levied on each 1 000 sticks. The specific tax is tiered according to the type of tobacco that cigarettes contain (brown/blond). Cigars and cigarillos: introduction of a uniform specific excise tax levied on each 1 000 sticks.	Cigarettes, cigars and cigarillos: the ad valorem excise tax is abolished.	No

Note: "Tobacco tax reform" refers to changes in the tobacco excise tax rates, the introduction of indexation mechanisms or minimum taxes, as well as adjustments to the tax base. These reforms typically entail the enactment of new laws or decrees. The table does not refer to recurrent tax changes that result from the indexation for inflation of tax brackets and price floors (if implemented). Tobacco tax reforms included reflect changes in the legislation, but not whether or when the reforms have been implemented.
Source: Ley No. 843 (2004); Ley No. 3467 (2006); Ley No. 66 (2010); Ley No. 1006 (2017).

Figure 6.13. Bolivia - Tobacco excise tax revenue

Percentage of GDP, latest year available

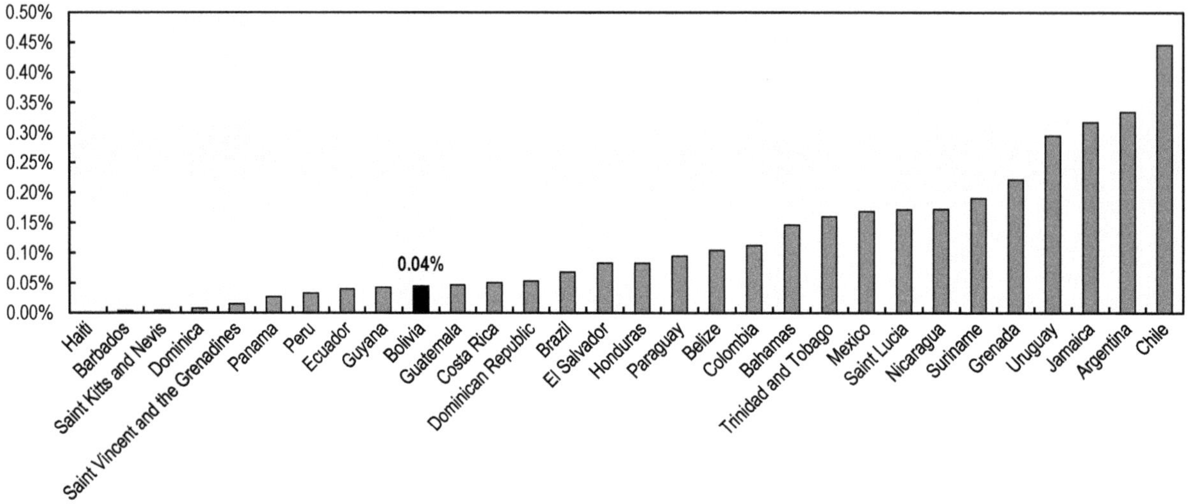

Note: See Box 2.1 (Chapter 2) for more information on tobacco tax revenue (source of information and calculations) and country selection. The latest year available is 2022 for Argentina, Brazil, Chile, Colombia, Costa Rica, the Dominican Republic, El Salvador, Guatemala, Guyana, Honduras, Mexico, Nicaragua, Panama, Paraguay, Peru, Saint Kitts and Nevis, Suriname, and Uruguay; 2021 for Belize, Dominica, Ecuador, Grenada, Saint Lucia, Saint Vincent and the Grenadines; 2020 for Bahamas, Bolivia, Jamaica and Trinidad and Tobago; 2015 for Haiti; 2014 for Barbados.
Source: OECD Revenue Statistics (OECD, 2024[13]); WHO report on the global tobacco epidemic (WHO, 2023[3]); National data.

Figure 6.14. Bolivia - Trends in tobacco excise tax revenue

Percentage of GDP, 2000-2020

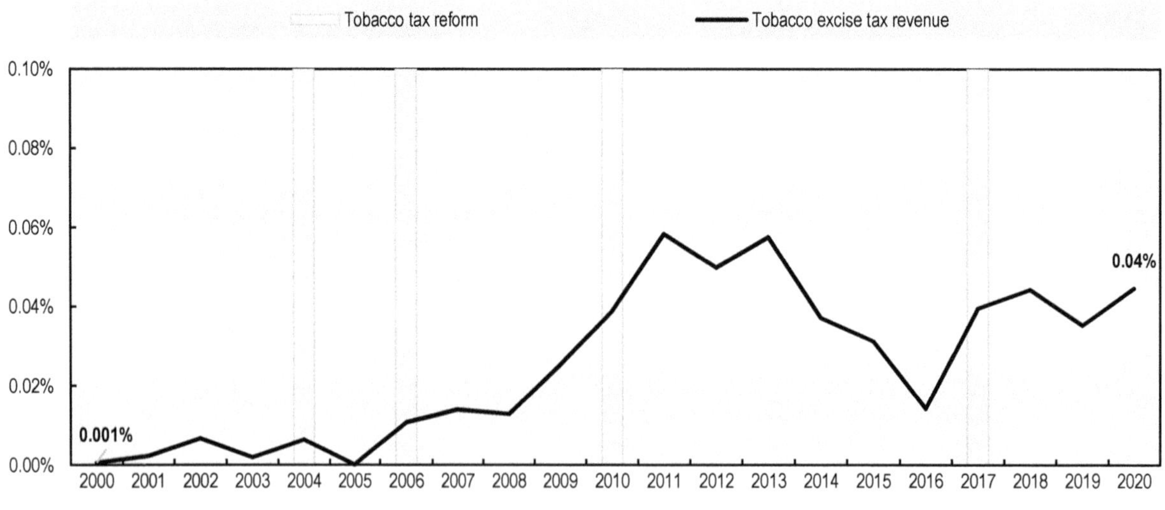

Note: "Tobacco tax reform" refers to the measures included in Table 6.8.
Source: Boletín Económico: Ingresos Tributarios al Primer Semestre 2021 (Plurinational State of Bolivia, 2021[18]); Ley 843 de Reforma Tributaria (Decreto Supremo 27947); Ley Nº 3467 (2010), Ley Nº 66 (2010), Ley Nº 1006 (2017).

Figure 6.15. Bolivia - Average excise tax revenue collected per pack of 20 cigarettes sold

Tobacco excise tax revenue in USD PPP collected per pack of legal cigarettes sold, latest year available

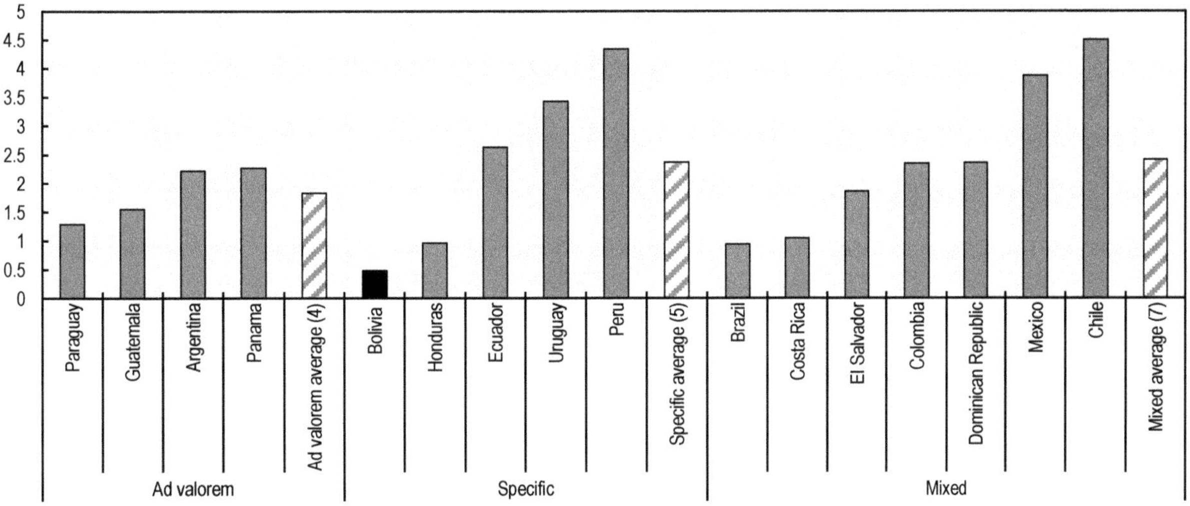

Note: See Box 2.1 (Chapter 2) for more information on tobacco tax revenue (source of information and calculations). The latest year available is 2022 for Argentina, Brazil, Chile, Colombia, Costa Rica, the Dominican Republic, El Salvador, Guatemala, Honduras, Mexico, Panama, Paraguay, Peru and Uruguay; 2021 for Ecuador; 2020 for Bolivia. The country selection is provided by the availability of data on sales of cigarettes in Euromonitor International Tobacco Industry edition, 2023 © All rights reserved (Euromonitor International, 2023[14]).
Source: OECD Revenue Statistics (OECD, 2024[13]); WHO report on the global tobacco epidemic (WHO, 2023[3]); National data; IMF World Economic Outlook Database (IMF, 2023[4]); and OECD calculations based on Euromonitor International's Tobacco Industry edition (Euromonitor International, 2023[14]).

Figure 6.16. Bolivia - Change in tobacco tax policy indicators

Percentage change from base year, 2008-2022

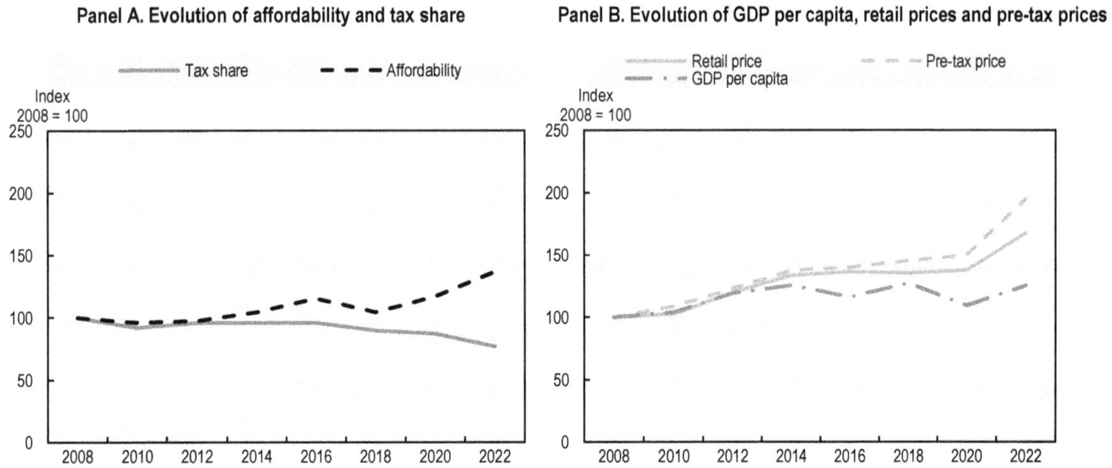

Note: Both Panel A and Panel B figures are based on data for the most sold brand of cigarettes. The most sold brand of cigarettes is determined based on national market share information and can vary over time (i.e. the most sold brand of cigarettes in year 1 can be different from year 2). In Panel A, an increase in the affordability indicator means that cigarettes are becoming less affordable, while a decline in the affordability indicator means that cigarettes are becoming more affordable. In Panel B, "Pre-tax price" corresponds to the retail price of the most sold brand of cigarettes minus the indirect taxes levied on this brand, namely excise taxes, VAT, import duties and other. Indicators in Panel B have been computed using national currency and have been adjusted for inflation; therefore, present inflation-adjusted trends.
Source: WHO report on the global tobacco epidemic (WHO, 2023[3]); World Bank Open Data (World Bank, 2024[15]); IMF International Financial Statistics (IMF, 2024[19]).

References

Euromonitor International (2023), *Euromonitor International's Tobacco Industry edition*, https://www.euromonitor.com/tobacco (accessed on 1 August 2023). [14]

IMF (2023), *World Economic Outlook Database*, International Monetary Fund, https://www.imf.org/en/Publications/WEO/weo-database/2023/October (accessed on 13 January 2024). [4]

IMF (2024), *International Financial Statistics (IFS)*, International Monetary Fund, https://data.imf.org/?sk=4c514d48-b6ba-49ed-8ab9-52b0c1a0179b&sId=1390030341854 (accessed on 13 January 2024). [19]

OECD (2024), *Global Revenue Statistics Database*, Organisation for Economic Co-operation and Development, https://www.oecd.org/tax/tax-policy/global-revenue-statistics-database.htm (accessed on 13 August 2023). [13]

Plurinational State of Bolivia (2021), *Boletín Económico: Ingresos Tributarios al Primer Semestre 2021*, Ministry of Economy and Public Finance, https://repositorio.economiayfinanzas.gob.bo/documentos/2018/VPT/DIRECCIONES/DGET/BOLETIN_BEIGT/2021/Boletin%20Economico%20de%20Ingresos%20Tributarios%201%20semestre%202021.pdf. [18]

WHO (2024), *Global Health Observatory: Age-standardized estimates of current tobacco use, tobacco smoking and cigarette smoking (Tobacco control: Monitor)*, World Health Organization, https://www.who.int/data/gho/data/indicators/indicator-details/GHO/gho-tobacco-control-monitor-current-tobaccouse-tobaccosmoking-cigarrettesmoking-agestd-tobagestdcurr (accessed on 20 February 2024). [1]

WHO (2023), *WHO report on the global tobacco epidemic 2023: protect people from tobacco smoke*, World Health Organization, https://www.who.int/publications/i/item/9789240077164. [3]

WHO (2021), *WHO report on the global tobacco epidemic 2021: Addressing new and emerging products*, World Health Organization, https://www.who.int/publications/i/item/9789240032095. [11]

WHO (2019), *WHO report on the global tobacco epidemic 2019: Offer help to quit tobacco use*, World Health Organization, https://www.who.int/publications/i/item/9789241516204. [10]

WHO (2018), *Global school-based student health survey. Bolivia 2018 Fact Sheet*, World Health Organization, https://cdn.who.int/media/docs/default-source/ncds/ncd-surveillance/data-reporting/bolivia/2018_bolivia_fact_sheet.pdf?sfvrsn=ed616383_1&download=true (accessed on 13 January 2024). [17]

WHO (2017), *WHO report on the global tobacco epidemic 2017: Monitoring tobacco use and prevention policies*, World Health Organization, https://www.who.int/publications/i/item/9789241512824. [9]

WHO (2015), *WHO report on the global tobacco epidemic 2015: Raising taxes on tobacco*, World Health Organization, https://www.who.int/publications/i/item/9789241509121. [8]

WHO (2013), *WHO report on the global tobacco epidemic 2013: Enforcing bans on tobacco advertising, promotion and sponsorship*, World Health Organization, https://www.who.int/publications/i/item/9789241505871. [7]

WHO (2011), *WHO report on the global tobacco epidemic 2011: Warning about the dangers of tobacco*, World Health Organization, https://www.who.int/publications/i/item/9789244564264. [6]

WHO (2009), *WHO report on the global tobacco epidemic 2009: Implementing smoke-free environments*, World Health Organization, https://www.who.int/publications/i/item/9789241563918. [5]

World Bank (2024), *World Bank Open Data*, World Bank, https://data.worldbank.org/ (accessed on 13 January 2024). [15]

Brazil

Figure 6.17. Brazil - Trends in tobacco use prevalence

Percentage of the population aged 15 years and over who currently use any tobacco product (smoked and/or smokeless tobacco) on a daily or non-daily basis, 2000-2020

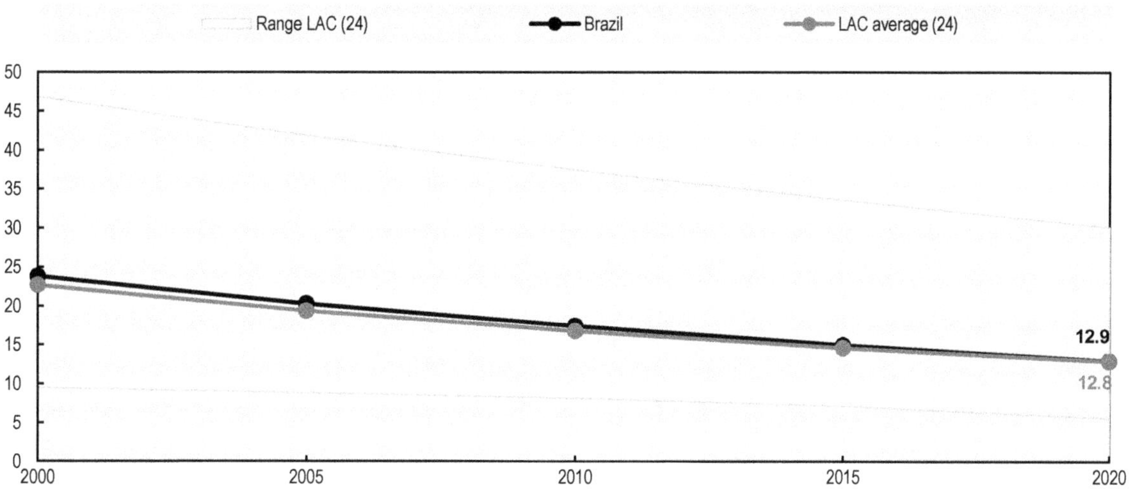

Note: Tobacco products include cigarettes, pipes, cigars, cigarillos, waterpipes (hookah, shisha), bidis, kretek, heated tobacco products (HTP), and all forms of smokeless (oral and nasal) tobacco. Tobacco products exclude e-cigarettes (which do not contain tobacco), e-cigars, e-hookahs, and e-pipes. The rates are age-standardized to the World Health Organisation (WHO) standard population. The LAC average was calculated as the average of Argentina, Bahamas, Barbados, Belize, Bolivia, Brazil, Chile, Colombia, Costa Rica, Cuba, the Dominican Republic, Ecuador, El Salvador, Guatemala, Guyana, Haiti, Honduras, Jamaica, Mexico, Panama, Paraguay, Peru, Saint Lucia, and Uruguay.
Source: WHO Global Health Observatory Data Repository (WHO, 2024[1]).

Table 6.9. Brazil - Tobacco use prevalence by sex and age groups

Percentage of the population group, latest year available

	Tobacco use prevalence (all tobacco products)	**Cigarette smoking prevalence (cigarettes only)**
Students aged 13-15 years		
Total	**11.3**	**5.0**
Males	...	4.5
Females	...	5.6
People aged 15 and over		
Total	**12.8**	**12.3**
Males	16.2	15.5
Females	9.8	9.4

Note: Tobacco use prevalence is defined as the percentage of the population group who currently use any tobacco product (smoked and/or smokeless tobacco) on a daily or non-daily basis. Tobacco products exclude e-cigarettes (which do not contain tobacco), e-cigars, e-hookahs, and e-pipes. Data for students aged 13-15 years are from 2019 and taken from the Pesquisa Nacional de Saúde do Escolar. Data for people aged 15 and over correspond to 2019 and were taken from Pesquisa Nacional de Saúde. For comparability purposes across countries, the Figure 6.17 uses another source of information (WHO Global Health Observatory Data Repository) which explains the small difference with figures included in this table. Cells with "..." indicate that the information is not available.
Source: Pesquisa Nacional de Saúde (Government of Brazil, 2019[20]); Pesquisa Nacional de Saúde do Escolar (Government of Brazil, 2021[21]); (OECD/The World Bank, 2023[22]).

Table 6.10. Brazil - Summary of MPOWER measures, 2022

M Monitoring	P Smoking bans	O Cessation programmes	W Health warnings	E Advertising bans	R Taxation	WHO Frawework Convention on Tobacco Control		Protocol to eliminate illicit trade in tobacco products	
						Date of signature	Date of ratification	Date of signature	Date of ratification
						16-06-2003	03-11-2005	-	14-06-2018

... Not categorized/ No data | No policy or weak measure | Minimal measure | Moderate measure | Complete measure

Source: WHO report on the global tobacco epidemic (WHO, 2023[3]).

Figure 6.18. Brazil - Taxes and prices of the most sold brand of cigarettes

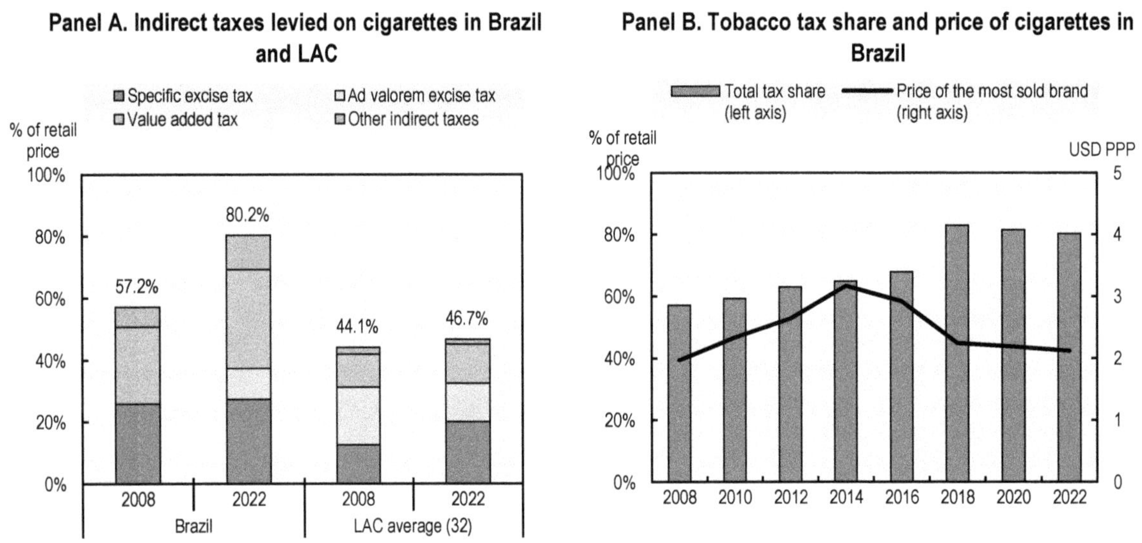

Note: Prices correspond to a 20-cigarette pack of the most sold brand. Retail prices in USD PPP are based on the implied purchasing power parity (PPP) conversion rate from the International Monetary Fund (IMF) World Economic Outlook Database (October 2023). The most sold brand of cigarettes is determined based on national market share information and can vary over time (i.e. the most sold brand of cigarettes in year 1 can be different from year 2).

Source: WHO report on the global tobacco epidemic (WHO, 2023[3]); IMF World Economic Outlook Database (IMF, 2023[4]).

Figure 6.19. Brazil - Trends in retail prices of cigarettes by brand category

In USD PPP per pack of 20 cigarettes, 2008-2022

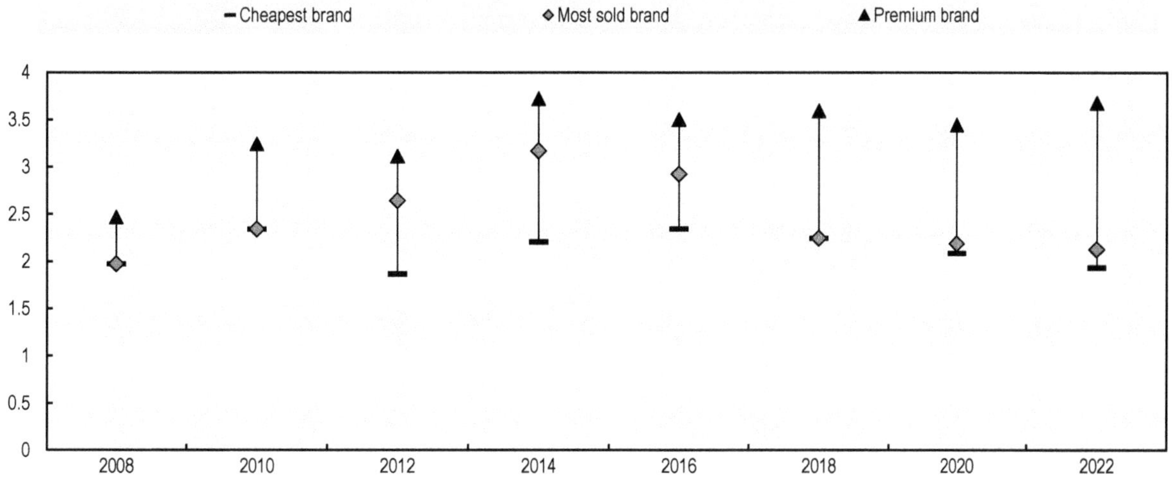

Note: Prices correspond to a 20-cigarette pack of the cheapest, most sold and premium brands. The cheapest, most sold and premium brands of cigarettes are determined based on national market share information and can vary over time (i.e. the cheapest/most sold/premium brands of cigarettes in year 1 can be different from year 2). Retail prices in USD PPP are based on the implied PPP conversion rate from the IMF World Economic Outlook Database (October 2023).
Source: WHO reports on the global tobacco epidemic (WHO, 2009[5]; WHO, 2011[6]; WHO, 2013[7]; WHO, 2015[8]; WHO, 2017[9]; WHO, 2019[10]; WHO, 2021[11]); IMF World Economic Outlook Database (IMF, 2023[4]).

Figure 6.20. Brazil - Affordability of cigarettes

Percentage of GDP per capita required to purchase 100 packs of 20 cigarettes

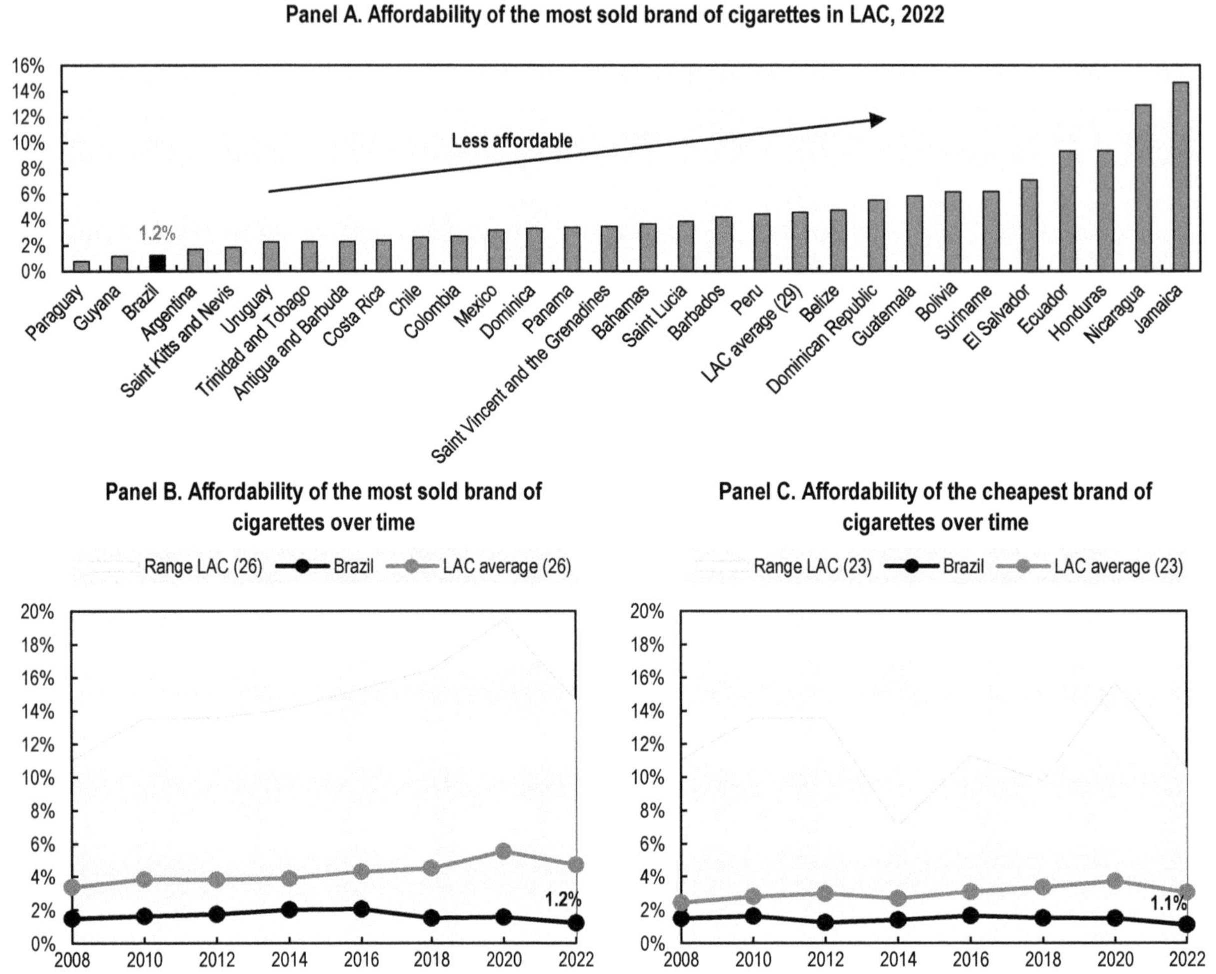

Note: The affordability indicator measures the percentage of the country's GDP per capita required to purchase 100 packs of 20 cigarettes. A higher percentage means lower affordability of cigarettes while a lower percentage means higher affordability. To ensure comparability of average affordability across LAC over time, countries where information was unavailable for certain years have been excluded from the calculation. Data for Panel C are OECD calculations based on WHO reports on the global tobacco epidemic (2009-2023 editions). The cheapest and most sold brands of cigarettes are determined based on national market share information and can vary over time (i.e. the cheapest/most sold brand of cigarettes in year 1 can be different from year 2).

Source: WHO reports on the global tobacco epidemic (WHO, 2009[5]; WHO, 2011[6]; WHO, 2013[7]; WHO, 2015[8]; WHO, 2017[9]; WHO, 2019[10]; WHO, 2021[11]).

Table 6.11. Brazil - Design of tobacco excise taxes across tobacco products, 2022

	Excise tax structure	Specific excise tax				Ad valorem excise tax			Excise tax floor			
		Yes / No	Tax base	Rate per 20-unit pack USD PPP (local currency)	Indexation mechanisms	Yes / No	Tax base	Statutory rate	Yes / No	Tax base	Rate per 20-unit pack USD PPP (local currency)	Indexation mechanisms
Cigarettes	Mixed	Yes	Individual pack	0.6 (1.5)	No	Yes	15% of FRP Incl. VAT	66.7%	Yes	Minimum price	0.8 (2.0)	No
Cigars	Ad valorem only	No					15% of FRP Incl. VAT	30%	No			
Cigarillos	Ad valorem only	No					15% of FRP Incl. VAT	300%	No			
Roll-Your-Own (RYO) tobacco	Ad valorem only	No					15% of FRP Incl. VAT	30%	No			
Heated tobacco products (HTPs)	No excise											
ENDS and ENNDS	No excise											

Note: "FRP" means "Final (observed) retail price"; blank cells mean that there is no excise tax for the corresponding tobacco product; "VAT" means "Value added tax". Following the WHO report on the global tobacco epidemic (WHO, 2021[11]), new tobacco and nicotine products in this report include electronic nicotine delivery systems (ENDS), electronic non-nicotine delivery systems (ENNDS), and heated tobacco products (HTP). Brazil does not levy an excise tax on new tobacco and nicotine products because their sales are banned (WHO, 2023[3]). Specific taxes are converted into USD PPP with the implied PPP conversion rate available in the IMF World Economic Outlook Database (October 2023). Specific excise taxes have been standardized to a 20-unit pack to allow the comparison across countries with different tax bases.
Source: Decreto Nº 8.656 (2016); IMF World Economic Outlook Database (IMF, 2023[4]).

Table 6.12. Brazil - Tobacco tax reforms since 2000

Year of adoption	Specific excise taxes	Ad valorem excise taxes	Other
2002	Cigarettes: increase tiered rates to BRL 0.385 - 0.760 per pack of 20 cigarettes.	No	No
2003	Cigarettes: increase tiered rates to BRL 0.469 - 0.884 per pack of 20 cigarettes.	No	No
2007	Cigarettes: increase tiered rates to BRL 0.619 – 1.131 per pack of 20 cigarettes.	No	No
2009	Cigarettes: increase tiered rates to BRL 0.764 – 1.397 per pack of 20 cigarettes.	No	No
2011	Cigarettes: introduction of two excise tax regimes that taxpayers can choose from. The Special Regime includes a specific excise tax component which has two tiered rates (BRL 0.80 - 1.15) levied on a pack of 20 cigarettes, where the rates vary across different types of packaging. The two-tiered specific tax is gradually increased each following year; by BRL 0.15 for the lower rate, and by BRL 0.05 for the higher rate. In 2015, the specific tax will be uniform at BRL 1.3 per pack of 20 cigarettes.	Cigarettes: introduction of two excise tax regimes that taxpayers can choose from. The General Regime levies only an ad valorem tax of 300% on 15% of the retail price (incl. VAT). The Special regime is mixed and includes an ad valorem tax rate of 40% levied on 15% of the retail price (incl. VAT). The ad valorem rate will be gradually increase by 7% annually to reach 60% in 2015.	Cigarettes: introduction of a minimum (legal) retail price. Initially set at BRL 3.0 per pack of 20 cigarettes, the minimum price is increased gradually by BRL 0.5 each year to reach BRL 4.5 in 2015.

Year of adoption	Specific excise taxes	Ad valorem excise taxes	Other
2016	Cigarettes: increase the specific tax by BRL 0.1 in two steps to reach BRL1.5 per pack of 20 cigarettes as of December 2016.	Cigarettes: increase in the ad valorem tax rate of the Special Regime in two steps to reach 66.7% levied on retail price (incl. VAT) as of December 2016	Cigarettes: increase in the minimum retail price from BRL 4.5 to BRL 5.0 per pack of 20 cigarettes.

Note: "Tobacco tax reform" refers to changes in the tobacco excise tax rates, the introduction of indexation mechanisms or minimum taxes, as well as adjustments to the tax base. These reforms typically entail the enactment of new laws or decrees. The table does not refer to recurrent tax changes that result from the indexation for inflation of tax brackets and price floors (if implemented). Tobacco tax reforms included reflect changes in the legislation, but not whether or when the reforms have been implemented.
Source: Decreto Nº 4.542 (2002); Decreto Nº 4.924 (2003); Decreto Nº 6.072 (2007); Decreto Nº 6.809 (2009); Decreto Nº 7.555 (2011); Decreto Nº 8.656 (2016).

Figure 6.21. Brazil - Tobacco excise tax revenue

Percentage of GDP, latest year available

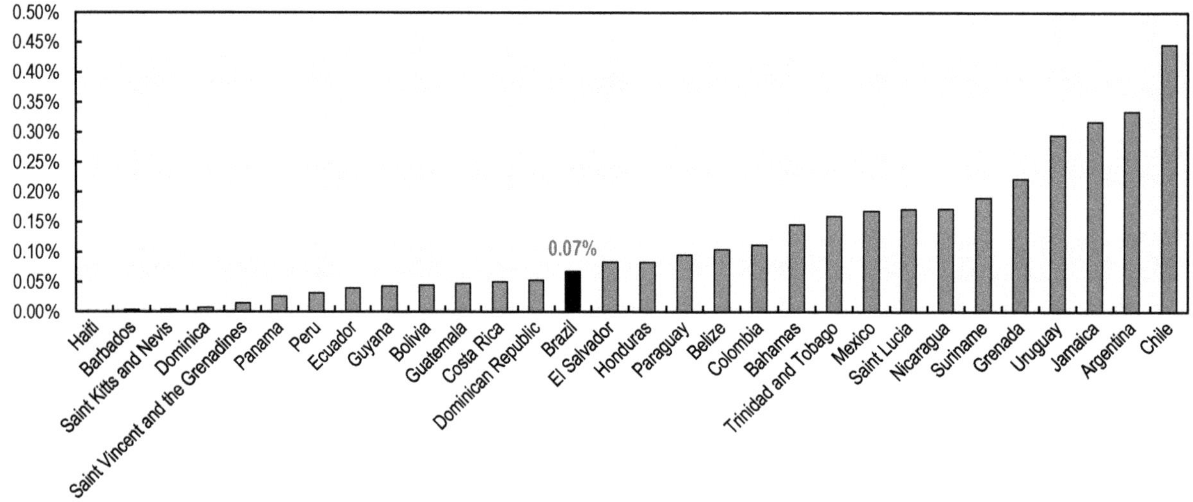

Note: See Box 2.1 (Chapter 2) for more information on tobacco tax revenue (source of information and calculations). For Brazil, the tobacco excise tax is the Imposto sobre productos industrializados (IPI). Hence, revenue from other indirect taxes is not considering in this figure. The latest year available is 2022 for Argentina, Brazil, Chile, Colombia, Costa Rica, the Dominican Republic, El Salvador, Guatemala, Guyana, Honduras, Mexico, Nicaragua, Panama, Paraguay, Peru, Saint Kitts and Nevis, Suriname, and Uruguay; 2021 for Belize, Dominica, Ecuador, Grenada, Saint Lucia, Saint Vincent and the Grenadines; 2020 for Bahamas, Bolivia, Jamaica and Trinidad and Tobago; 2015 for Haiti; 2014 for Barbados.
Source: OECD Revenue Statistics (OECD, 2024[13]); WHO report on the global tobacco epidemic (WHO, 2023[3]); National data.

Figure 6.22. Brazil - Trends in tobacco excise tax revenue

Percentage of GDP, 2000-2022

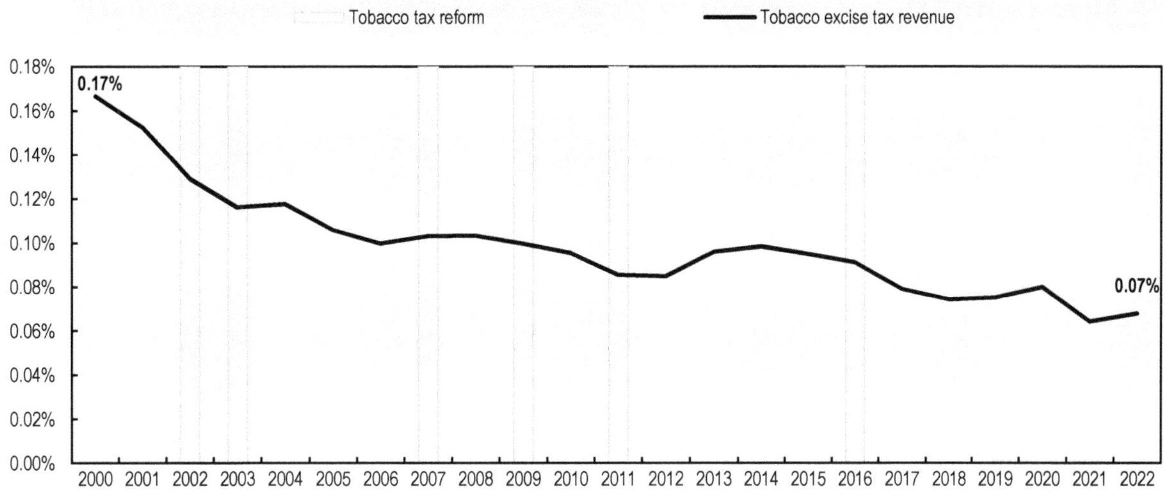

Note: "Tobacco tax reform" refers to the measures included in Table 6.12. The tobacco excise tax is the Imposto sobre productos industrializados (IPI). Hence, revenue from other indirect taxes is not considered in this figure.
Source: OECD Revenue Statistics (OECD, 2024[13]); Decreto Nº 4.542 (2002); Decreto Nº 4.924 (2003); Decreto Nº 6.072 (2007); Decreto Nº 6.809 (2009), Decreto Nº 7.555 (2011); Decreto Nº 8.656 (2016).

Figure 6.23. Brazil - Average excise tax revenue collected per pack of 20 cigarettes sold

Tobacco excise tax revenue in USD PPP collected per pack of legal cigarettes sold, latest year available

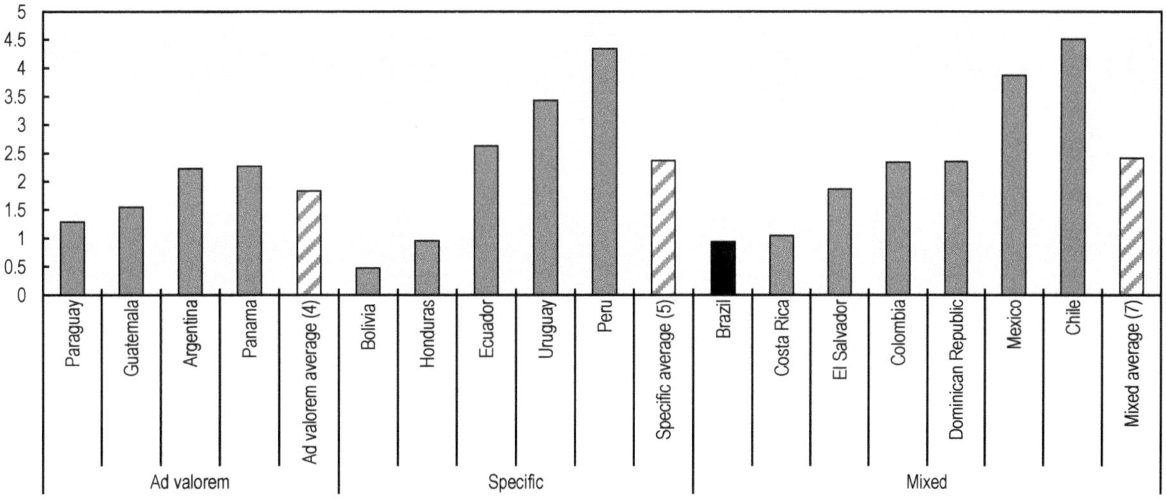

Note: See Box 2.1 (Chapter 2) for more information on tobacco tax revenue (source of information and calculations). For Brazil, the tobacco excise tax is the Imposto sobre productos industrializados (IPI). Hence, revenue from other indirect taxes is not considering in this figure. The latest year available is 2022 for Argentina, Brazil, Chile, Colombia, Costa Rica, the Dominican Republic, El Salvador, Guatemala, Honduras, Mexico, Panama, Paraguay, Peru and Uruguay; 2021 for Ecuador; 2020 for Bolivia. The country selection is provided by the availability of data on sales of cigarettes in Euromonitor International Tobacco Industry edition, 2023 © All rights reserved (Euromonitor International, 2023[14]).
Source: OECD Revenue Statistics (OECD, 2024[13]); WHO report on the global tobacco epidemic (WHO, 2023[3]); National data; IMF World Economic Outlook Database (IMF, 2023[4]); and OECD calculations based on Euromonitor International's Tobacco Industry edition (Euromonitor International, 2023[14]).

Figure 6.24. Brazil - Change in tobacco tax policy indicators

Percentage change from base year, 2008-2022

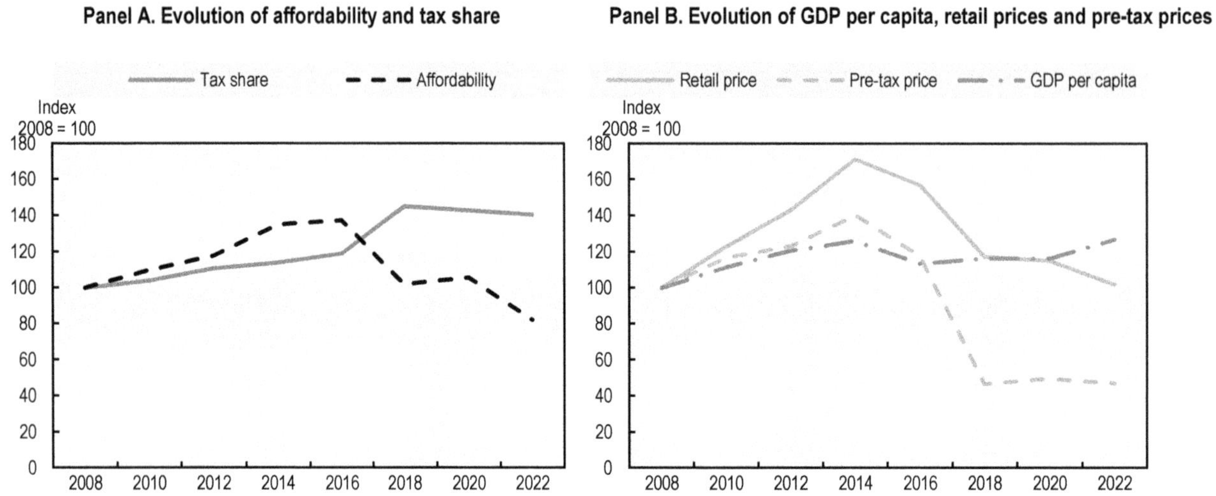

Note: Both Panel A and Panel B figures are based on data for the most sold brand of cigarettes. The most sold brand of cigarettes is determined based on national market share information and can vary over time (i.e. the most sold brand of cigarettes in year 1 can be different from year 2). In Panel A, an increase in the affordability indicator means that cigarettes are becoming less affordable, while a decline in the affordability indicator means that cigarettes are becoming more affordable. In Panel B, "Pre-tax price" corresponds to the retail price of the most sold brand of cigarettes minus the indirect taxes levied on this brand, namely excise taxes, VAT, import duties and other. Indicators in Panel B have been computed using national currency and have been adjusted for inflation; therefore, present inflation-adjusted trends.
Source: WHO report on the global tobacco epidemic (WHO, 2023[3]); World Bank Open Data (World Bank, 2024[15]); IMF International Financial Statistics (IMF, 2024[19]).

References

Euromonitor International (2023), *Euromonitor International's Tobacco Industry edition*, https://www.euromonitor.com/tobacco (accessed on 1 August 2023). [14]

Government of Brazil (2019), *Pesquisa Nacional de Saúde, Tabelas Completas*, Brazilian Institute of Geography and Statistics, https://www.ibge.gov.br/estatisticas/sociais/saude/9160-pesquisa-nacional-de-saude.html?lang=pt-BR (accessed on 13 June 2024). [20]

Government of Brazil (2021), *Pesquisa nacional de saúde do escolar*, Brazilian Institute of Geography and Statistics, https://www.ibge.gov.br/estatisticas/sociais/educacao/9134-pesquisa-nacional-de-saude-do-escolar.html. [21]

IMF (2023), *World Economic Outlook Database*, International Monetary Fund, https://www.imf.org/en/Publications/WEO/weo-database/2023/October (accessed on 13 January 2024). [4]

IMF (2024), *International Financial Statistics (IFS)*, International Monetary Fund, https://data.imf.org/?sk=4c514d48-b6ba-49ed-8ab9-52b0c1a0179b&sId=1390030341854 (accessed on 13 January 2024). [19]

OECD (2024), *Global Revenue Statistics Database*, Organisation for Economic Co-operation and Development, https://www.oecd.org/tax/tax-policy/global-revenue-statistics-database.htm (accessed on 13 August 2023). [13]

OECD/The World Bank (2023), *Health at a Glance: Latin America and the Caribbean 2023*, OECD Publishing, Paris, https://doi.org/10.1787/532b0e2d-en. [22]

WHO (2024), *Global Health Observatory: Age-standardized estimates of current tobacco use, tobacco smoking and cigarette smoking (Tobacco control: Monitor)*, World Health Organization, https://www.who.int/data/gho/data/indicators/indicator-details/GHO/gho-tobacco-control-monitor-current-tobaccouse-tobaccosmoking-cigarrettesmoking-agestd-tobagestdcurr (accessed on 20 February 2024). [1]

WHO (2023), *WHO report on the global tobacco epidemic 2023: protect people from tobacco smoke*, World Health Organization, https://www.who.int/publications/i/item/9789240077164. [3]

WHO (2021), *WHO report on the global tobacco epidemic 2021: Addressing new and emerging products*, World Health Organization, https://www.who.int/publications/i/item/9789240032095. [11]

WHO (2019), *WHO report on the global tobacco epidemic 2019: Offer help to quit tobacco use*, World Health Organization, https://www.who.int/publications/i/item/9789241516204. [10]

WHO (2017), *WHO report on the global tobacco epidemic 2017: Monitoring tobacco use and prevention policies*, World Health Organization, https://www.who.int/publications/i/item/9789241512824. [9]

WHO (2015), *WHO report on the global tobacco epidemic 2015: Raising taxes on tobacco*, World Health Organization, https://www.who.int/publications/i/item/9789241509121. [8]

WHO (2013), *WHO report on the global tobacco epidemic 2013: Enforcing bans on tobacco advertising, promotion and sponsorship*, World Health Organization, https://www.who.int/publications/i/item/9789241505871. [7]

WHO (2011), *WHO report on the global tobacco epidemic 2011: Warning about the dangers of tobacco*, World Health Organization, https://www.who.int/publications/i/item/9789244564264. [6]

WHO (2009), *WHO report on the global tobacco epidemic 2009: Implementing smoke-free environments*, World Health Organization, https://www.who.int/publications/i/item/9789241563918. [5]

World Bank (2024), *World Bank Open Data*, World Bank, https://data.worldbank.org/ (accessed on 13 January 2024). [15]

Chile

Figure 6.25. Chile - Trends in tobacco use prevalence

Percentage of the population aged 15 years and over who currently use any tobacco product (smoked and/or smokeless tobacco) on a daily or non-daily basis, 2000-2020

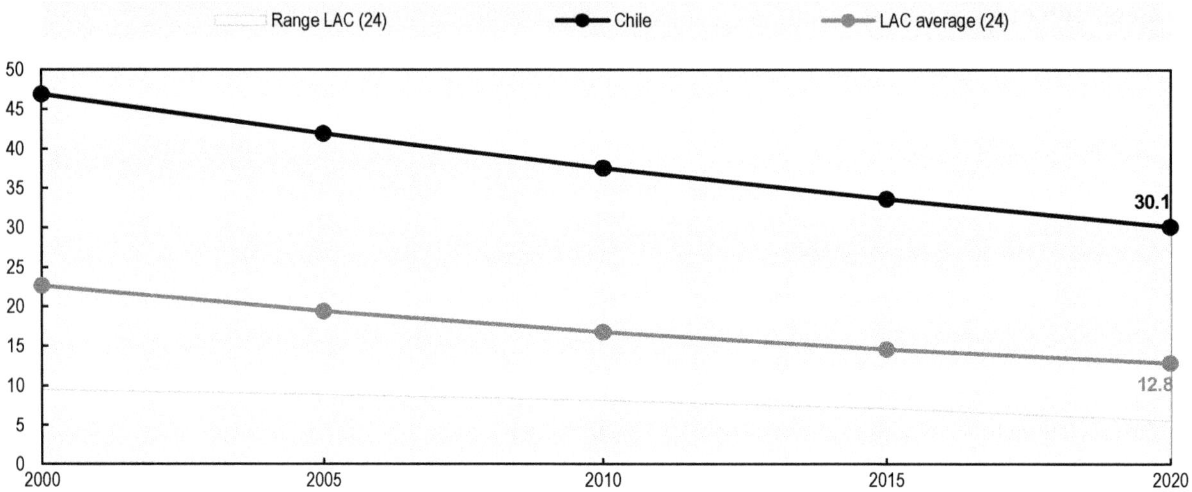

Note: Tobacco products include cigarettes, pipes, cigars, cigarillos, waterpipes (hookah, shisha), bidis, kretek, heated tobacco products (HTP), and all forms of smokeless (oral and nasal) tobacco. Tobacco products exclude e-cigarettes (which do not contain tobacco), e-cigars, e-hookahs, and e-pipes. The rates are age-standardized to the World Health Organisation (WHO) standard population. The LAC average was calculated as the average of Argentina, Bahamas, Barbados, Belize, Bolivia, Brazil, Chile, Colombia, Costa Rica, Cuba, the Dominican Republic, Ecuador, El Salvador, Guatemala, Guyana, Haiti, Honduras, Jamaica, Mexico, Panama, Paraguay, Peru, Saint Lucia, and Uruguay.
Source: WHO Global Health Observatory Data Repository (WHO, 2024[1]).

Table 6.13. Chile - Tobacco use prevalence by sex and age groups

Percentage of the population group, latest year available

	Tobacco use prevalence (all tobacco products)	**Cigarette smoking prevalence (cigarettes only)**
Students aged 13-17 years		
Total	**15.2**	**...**
Males	13.1	...
Females	17.3	...
People aged 15 and over		
Total	**30.1**	**27.6**
Males	32.3	29.9
Females	27.9	25.4

Note: Tobacco use prevalence is defined as the percentage of the population group who currently use any tobacco product (smoked and/or smokeless tobacco) on a daily or non-daily basis. Tobacco products exclude e-cigarettes (which do not contain tobacco), e-cigars, e-hookahs, and e-pipes. Data for students aged 13-17 years are from 2019 and taken from the Estudio Nacional de Drogas en Población Escolar de Chile. Data for people aged 15 and over correspond to 2020. Cells with "..." indicate that the information is not available.
Source: WHO Global Health Observatory Data Repository (WHO, 2024[1]); Décimo Tercer Estudio Nacional de Drogas en Población Escolar de Chile, 2019 (Government of Chile, 2020[23]).

Table 6.14. Chile - Summary of MPOWER measures, 2022

M Monitoring	P Smoking bans	O Cessation programmes	W Health warnings	E Advertising bans	R Taxation	WHO Frawework Convention on Tobacco Control		Protocol to eliminate illicit trade in tobacco products	
						Date of signature	Date of ratification	Date of signature	Date of ratification
						25-09-2003	13-06-2005		

... Not categorized/ No data; No policy or weak measure; Minimal measure; Moderate measure; Complete measure

Source: WHO report on the global tobacco epidemic (WHO, 2023[3]).

Figure 6.26. Chile - Taxes and prices of the most sold brand of cigarettes

Panel A. Indirect taxes levied on cigarettes in Chile and LAC **Panel B. Tobacco tax share and price of cigarettes in Chile**

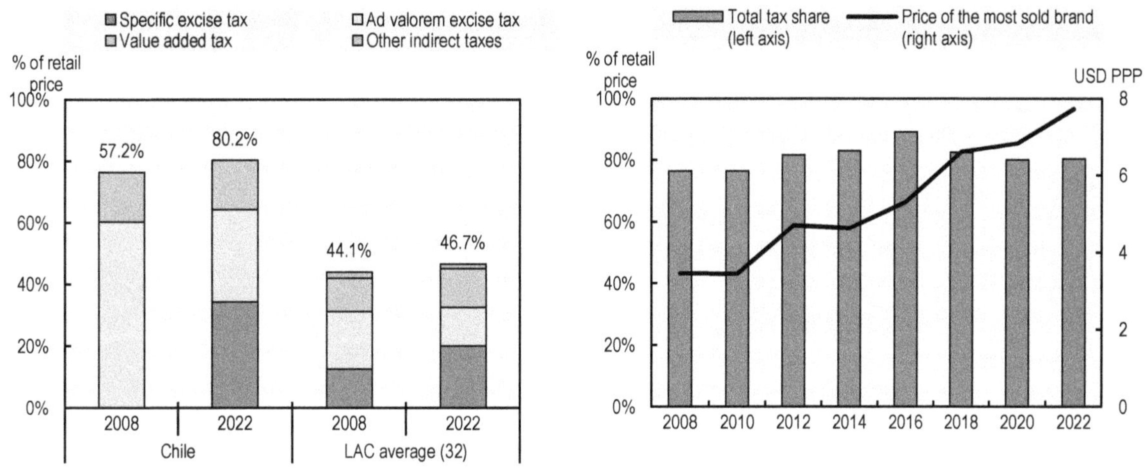

Note: Prices correspond to a 20-cigarette pack of the most sold brand. The most sold brand of cigarettes is determined based on national market share information and can vary over time (i.e. the most sold brand of cigarettes in year 1 can be different from year 2). Retail prices in USD PPP are based on the implied purchasing power parity (PPP) conversion rate from the International Monetary Fund (IMF) World Economic Outlook Database (October 2023).

Source: WHO report on the global tobacco epidemic (WHO, 2023[3]); IMF World Economic Outlook Database (IMF, 2023[4]).

Figure 6.27. Chile - Trends in retail prices of cigarettes by brand category

In USD PPP per pack of 20 cigarettes, 2008-2022

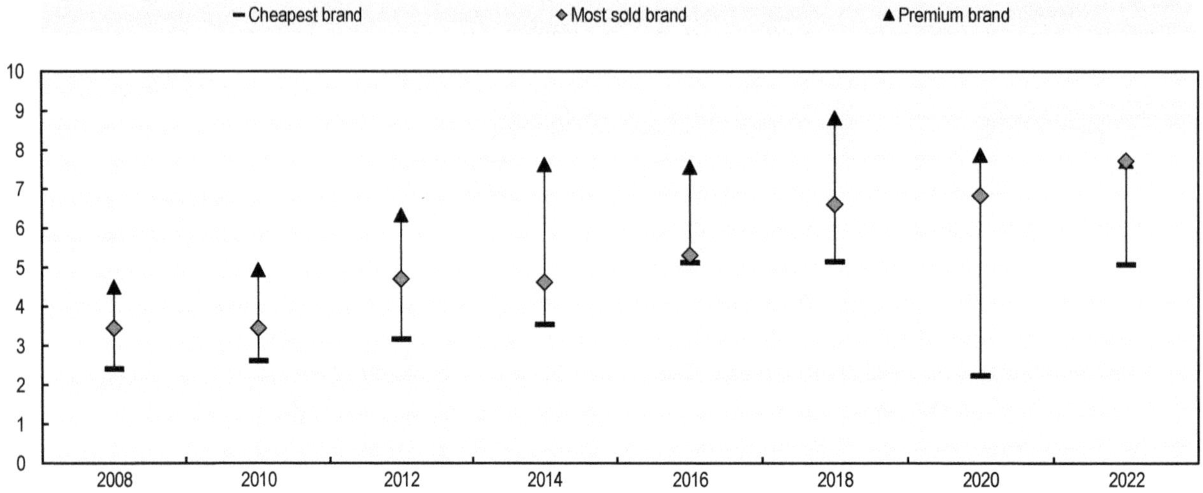

Note: Prices correspond to a pack of 20 cigarettes of the cheapest, most sold and premium brands. Retail prices in USD PPP are based on the implied PPP conversion rate from the IMF World Economic Outlook Database (October 2023). The cheapest, most sold and premium brands of cigarettes are determined based on national market share information and can vary over time (i.e. the cheapest/most sold/premium brands of cigarettes in year 1 can be different from year 2).

Source: WHO reports on the global tobacco epidemic (WHO, 2009[5]; WHO, 2011[6]; WHO, 2013[7]; WHO, 2015[8]; WHO, 2017[9]; WHO, 2019[10]; WHO, 2021[11]); IMF World Economic Outlook Database (IMF, 2023[4]).

Figure 6.28. Chile - Affordability of cigarettes

Percentage of GDP per capita required to purchase 100 packs of 20 cigarettes

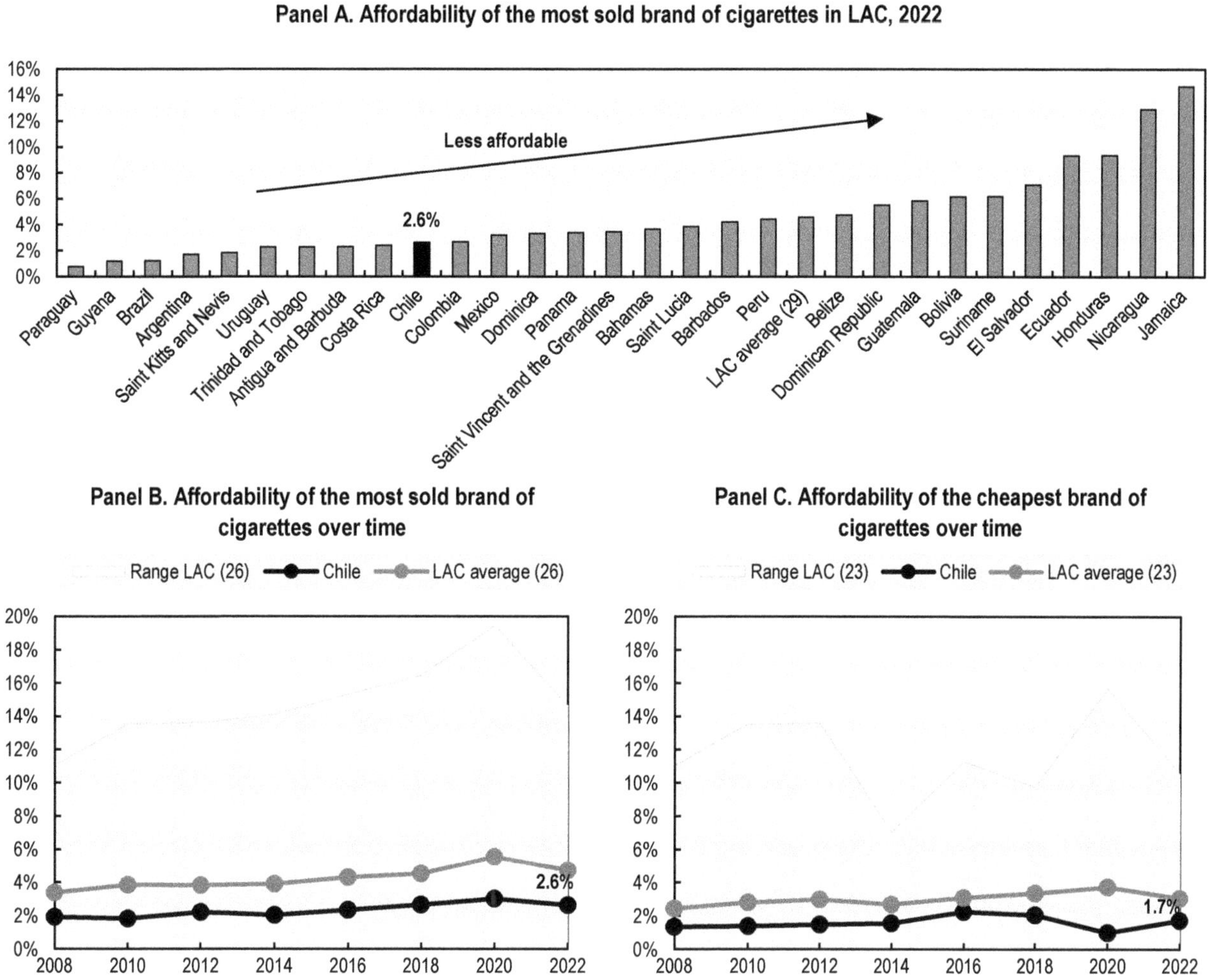

Note: The affordability indicator measures the percentage of the country's GDP per capita required to purchase 100 packs of 20 cigarettes. A higher percentage means lower affordability of cigarettes while a lower percentage means higher affordability. To ensure comparability of average affordability across LAC over time, countries where information was unavailable for certain years have been excluded from the calculation. Data for Panel C are OECD calculations based on WHO reports on the global tobacco epidemic (2009-2023 editions). The cheapest and most sold brands of cigarettes are determined based on national market share information and can vary over time (i.e. the cheapest/most sold brand of cigarettes in year 1 can be different from year 2).

Source: WHO reports on the global tobacco epidemic (WHO, 2009[5]; WHO, 2011[6]; WHO, 2013[7]; WHO, 2015[8]; WHO, 2017[9]; WHO, 2019[10]; WHO, 2021[11]).

Table 6.15. Chile - Design of tobacco excise taxes across tobacco products, 2022

	Excise tax structure	Specific excise tax				Ad valorem excise tax			Excise tax floor			
		Yes / No	Tax base	Rate per 20-unit pack USD PPP (local currency)	Indexation mechanisms	Yes / No	Tax base	Statutory rate	Yes / No	Tax base	Rate per 20-unit pack USD PPP (local currency)	Indexation mechanisms
Cigarettes	Mixed	Yes	Single stick	2.6 (1 186.9)	Unidades Tributarias Mensuales	Yes	FRP Incl. VAT	30%	No			
Cigars	Ad valorem only	No					FRP Incl. VAT	52.6%	No			
Cigarillos	Ad valorem only	No					FRP Incl. VAT	52.6%	No			
Roll-Your-Own (RYO) tobacco	Ad valorem only	No					FRP Incl. VAT	59.7%	No			
Heated tobacco products (HTPs)	No excises											
ENDS and ENNDS	No excise											

Note: "SRP" means "Suggested retail price by the manufacturer/importer"; "FRP" means "Final (observed) retail price"; blank cells mean that there is no excise tax for the corresponding tobacco product; "VAT" means "Value added tax". Following the WHO report on the global tobacco epidemic (WHO, 2021[11]), new tobacco and nicotine products in this report include electronic nicotine delivery systems (ENDS), electronic non-nicotine delivery systems (ENNDS), and heated tobacco products (HTP). Specific excise taxes have been standardized to a 20-unit pack to allow the comparison across countries with different tax bases. They are converted into USD PPP with the implied PPP conversion rate available in the IMF World Economic Outlook Database (October 2023). The specific tax levied on cigarettes in this table corresponds to the annual unweighted average of the tax rate which is adjusted monthly based on CPI.
Source: Decreto Ley 828 y sus reformas (2016); IMF World Economic Outlook Database (IMF, 2023[4]).

Table 6.16. Chile - Tobacco tax reforms since 2000

Year of adoption	Specific excise taxes	Ad valorem excise taxes	Other
2010	Cigarettes: introduction of a specific excise tax of 0.0000675 Unidades Tributarias Mensuales levied on each single stick.	Cigarettes: increase in the tax rate from 50.4% to 62.3% levied on the retail price (incl. VAT). Cigars and cigarillos: increase in the tax rate from 51% to 52.6% levied on the retail price (incl. VAT). RYO tobacco: increase in the tax rate from 47.9% to 59.7% levied on the retail price (incl. VAT).	No
2012	Cigarettes: increase in the specific tax from 0.0000675 to 0.000128803 Unidades Tributarias Mensuales levied on each single stick.	Cigarettes: reduction in the tax rate from 62.3% to 60.5% levied on the retail price (incl. VAT).	No
2014	Cigarettes: increase in the specific tax from 0.000128803 to 0.0010304240 Unidades Tributarias Mensuales levied on each single stick.	Cigarettes: reduction in the tax rate from 60.5% to 30% levied on the retail price (incl. VAT).	No

Note: "Tobacco tax reform" refers to changes in the tobacco excise tax rates, the introduction of indexation mechanisms or minimum taxes, as well as adjustments to the tax base. These reforms typically entail the enactment of new laws or decrees. The table does not refer to recurrent tax changes that result from the indexation for inflation of tax brackets and price floors (if implemented). Tobacco tax reforms included reflect changes in the legislation, but not whether or when the reforms have been implemented.
Source: Ley 20455 – Art. 6 (2010); Ley 20630 – Art. 6 (2012); Ley 20780 – Art. 4 (2014).

Figure 6.29. Chile - Tobacco excise tax revenue

Percentage of GDP, latest year available

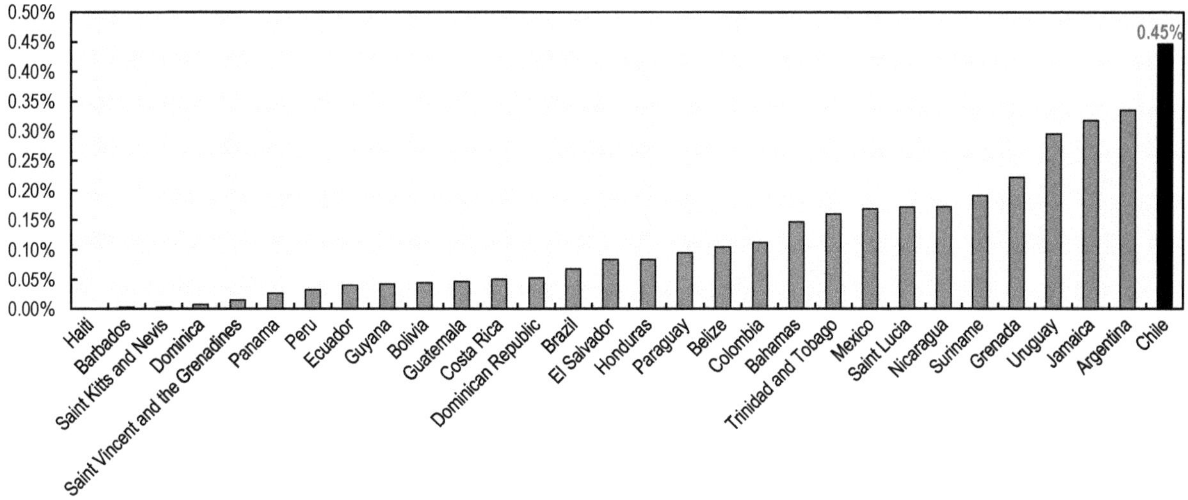

Note: See Box 2.1 (Chapter 2) for more information on tobacco tax revenue (source of information and calculations) and country selection. The latest year available is 2022 for Argentina, Brazil, Chile, Colombia, Costa Rica, the Dominican Republic, El Salvador, Guatemala, Guyana, Honduras, Mexico, Nicaragua, Panama, Paraguay, Peru, Saint Kitts and Nevis, Suriname, and Uruguay; 2021 for Belize, Dominica, Ecuador, Grenada, Saint Lucia, Saint Vincent and the Grenadines; 2020 for Bahamas, Bolivia, Jamaica and Trinidad and Tobago; 2015 for Haiti; 2014 for Barbados.
Source: OECD Revenue Statistics (OECD, 2024[13]); WHO report on the global tobacco epidemic (WHO, 2023[3]); National data.

Figure 6.30. Chile - Trends in tobacco excise tax revenue

Percentage of GDP, 2000-2022

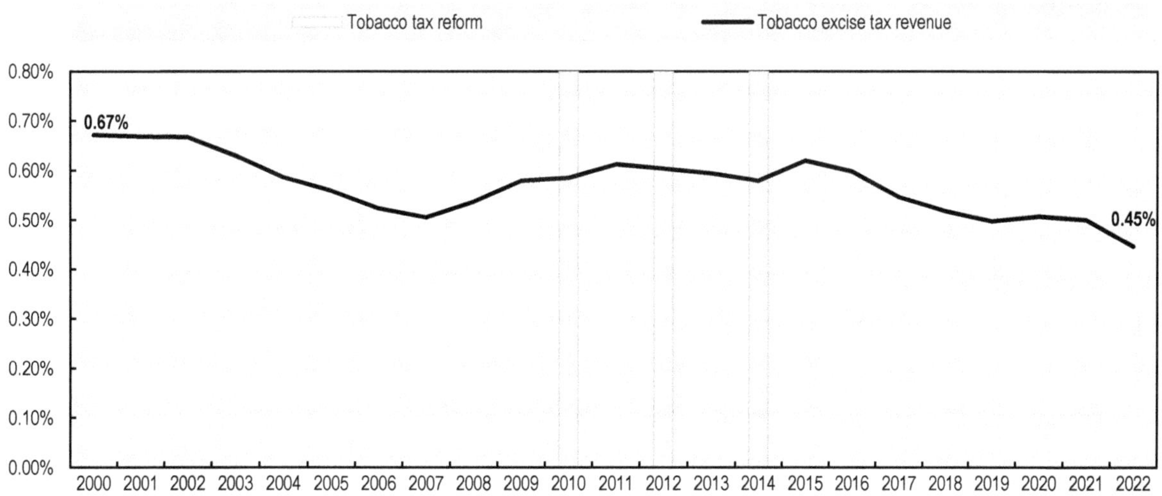

Note: "Tobacco tax reform" refers to the measures included in Table 6.16.
Source: OECD Revenue Statistics (OECD, 2024[13]); Ley 20455 – Art. 6 (2010); Ley 20630 – Art. 6 (2012); Ley 20780 – Art. 4 (2014).

Figure 6.31. Chile - Average excise tax revenue collected per pack of 20 cigarettes sold

Tobacco excise tax revenue in USD PPP collected per pack of legal cigarettes sold, latest year available

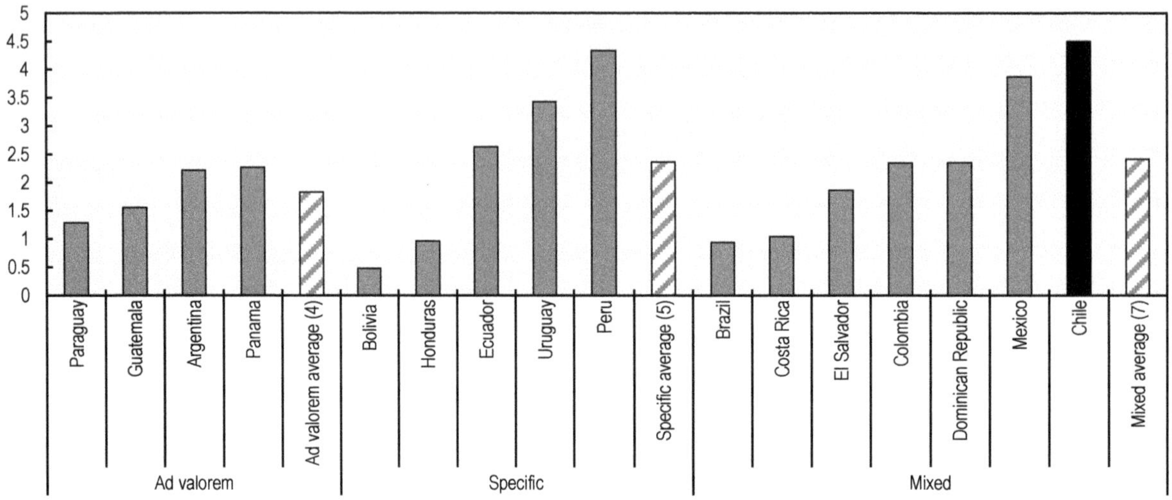

Note: See Box 2.1 (Chapter 2) for more information on tobacco tax revenue (source of information and calculations). The latest year available is 2022 for Argentina, Brazil, Chile, Colombia, Costa Rica, the Dominican Republic, El Salvador, Guatemala, Honduras, Mexico, Panama, Paraguay, Peru and Uruguay; 2021 for Ecuador; 2020 for Bolivia. The country selection is provided by the availability of data on sales of cigarettes in Euromonitor International Tobacco Industry edition, 2023 © All rights reserved (Euromonitor International, 2023[14]).
Source: OECD Revenue Statistics (OECD, 2024[13]); WHO report on the global tobacco epidemic (WHO, 2023[3]); National data; IMF World Economic Outlook Database (IMF, 2023[4]); and OECD calculations based on Euromonitor International's Tobacco Industry edition (Euromonitor International, 2023[14]).

Figure 6.32. Chile - Change in tobacco tax policy indicators

Percentage change from base year, 2008-2022

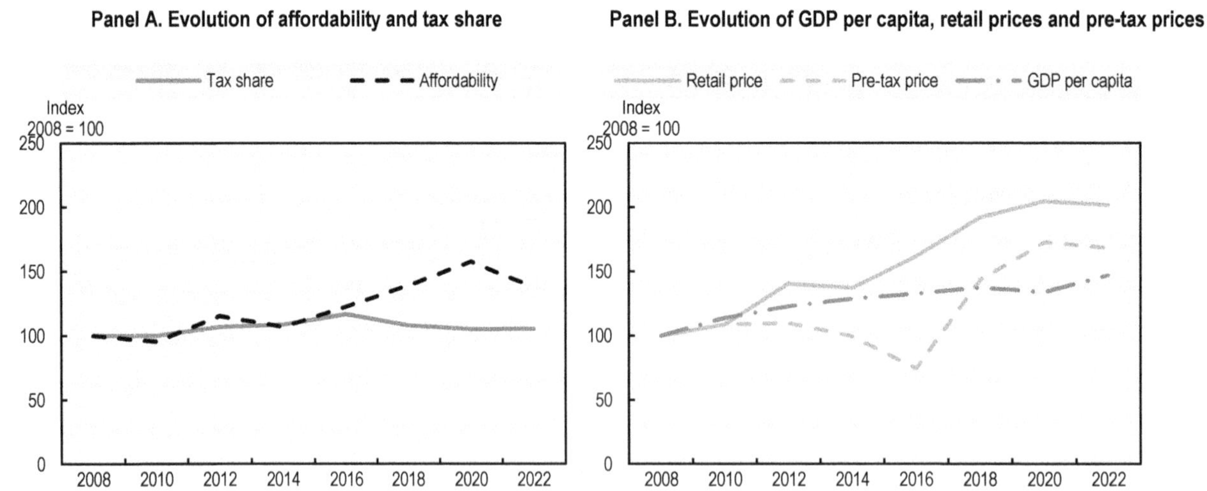

Note: Both Panel A and Panel B figures are based on data for the most sold brand of cigarettes. The most sold brand of cigarettes is determined based on national market share information and can vary over time (i.e. the most sold brand of cigarettes in year 1 can be different from year 2). In Panel A, an increase in the affordability indicator means that cigarettes are becoming less affordable, while a decline in the affordability indicator means that cigarettes are becoming more affordable. In Panel B, "Pre-tax price" corresponds to the retail price of the most sold brand of cigarettes minus the indirect taxes levied on this brand, namely excise taxes, VAT, import duties and other. Indicators in Panel B have been computed using national currency and have been adjusted for inflation; therefore, present inflation-adjusted trends.
Source: WHO report on the global tobacco epidemic (WHO, 2023[3]); World Bank Open Data (World Bank, 2024[15]); IMF International Financial Statistics (IMF, 2024[19]).

References

Euromonitor International (2023), *Euromonitor International's Tobacco Industry edition*, https://www.euromonitor.com/tobacco (accessed on 1 August 2023). [14]

Government of Chile (2020), *Décimo Tercer Estudio Nacional de Drogas en Población Escolar de Chile, 2019. 8º Básico a 4º Medio*, National Service for the Prevention and Rehabilitation of Drug and Alcohol Consumption, https://bibliodrogas.gob.cl/wp-content/uploads/2022/04/ENPE-2019-30-12-20.pdf. [23]

IMF (2023), *World Economic Outlook Database*, International Monetary Fund, https://www.imf.org/en/Publications/WEO/weo-database/2023/October (accessed on 13 January 2024). [4]

IMF (2024), *International Financial Statistics (IFS)*, International Monetary Fund, https://data.imf.org/?sk=4c514d48-b6ba-49ed-8ab9-52b0c1a0179b&sId=1390030341854 (accessed on 13 January 2024). [19]

OECD (2024), *Global Revenue Statistics Database*, Organisation for Economic Co-operation and Development, https://www.oecd.org/tax/tax-policy/global-revenue-statistics-database.htm (accessed on 13 August 2023). [13]

WHO (2024), *Global Health Observatory: Age-standardized estimates of current tobacco use, tobacco smoking and cigarette smoking (Tobacco control: Monitor)*, World Health Organization, https://www.who.int/data/gho/data/indicators/indicator-details/GHO/gho-tobacco-control-monitor-current-tobaccouse-tobaccosmoking-cigarrettesmoking-agestd-tobagestdcurr (accessed on 20 February 2024). [1]

WHO (2023), *WHO report on the global tobacco epidemic 2023: protect people from tobacco smoke*, World Health Organization, https://www.who.int/publications/i/item/9789240077164. [3]

WHO (2021), *WHO report on the global tobacco epidemic 2021: Addressing new and emerging products*, World Health Organization, https://www.who.int/publications/i/item/9789240032095. [11]

WHO (2019), *WHO report on the global tobacco epidemic 2019: Offer help to quit tobacco use*, World Health Organization, https://www.who.int/publications/i/item/9789241516204. [10]

WHO (2017), *WHO report on the global tobacco epidemic 2017: Monitoring tobacco use and prevention policies*, World Health Organization, https://www.who.int/publications/i/item/9789241512824. [9]

WHO (2015), *WHO report on the global tobacco epidemic 2015: Raising taxes on tobacco*, World Health Organization, https://www.who.int/publications/i/item/9789241509121. [8]

WHO (2013), *WHO report on the global tobacco epidemic 2013: Enforcing bans on tobacco advertising, promotion and sponsorship*, World Health Organization, https://www.who.int/publications/i/item/9789241505871. [7]

WHO (2011), *WHO report on the global tobacco epidemic 2011: Warning about the dangers of tobacco*, World Health Organization, https://www.who.int/publications/i/item/9789244564264. [6]

WHO (2009), *WHO report on the global tobacco epidemic 2009: Implementing smoke-free environments*, World Health Organization, https://www.who.int/publications/i/item/9789241563918. [5]

World Bank (2024), *World Bank Open Data*, World Bank, https://data.worldbank.org/ (accessed on 13 January 2024). [15]

Colombia

Figure 6.33. Colombia - Trends in tobacco use prevalence

Percentage of the population aged 15 years and over who currently use any tobacco product (smoked and/or smokeless tobacco) on a daily or non-daily basis, 2000-2020

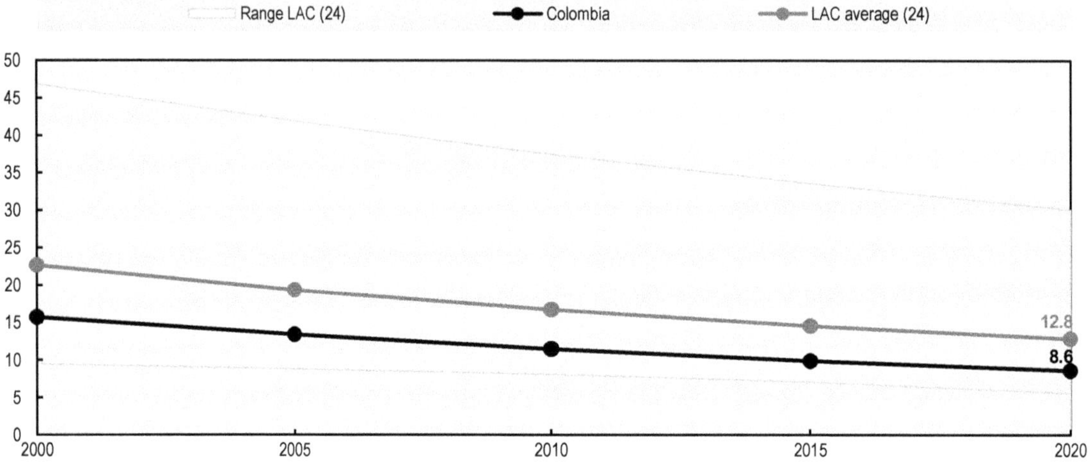

Note: Tobacco products include cigarettes, pipes, cigars, cigarillos, waterpipes (hookah, shisha), bidis, kretek, heated tobacco products (HTP), and all forms of smokeless (oral and nasal) tobacco. Tobacco products exclude e-cigarettes (which do not contain tobacco), e-cigars, e-hookahs, and e-pipes. The rates are age-standardized to the World Health Organisation (WHO) standard population. The LAC average was calculated as the average of Argentina, Bahamas, Barbados, Belize, Bolivia, Brazil, Chile, Colombia, Costa Rica, Cuba, the Dominican Republic, Ecuador, El Salvador, Guatemala, Guyana, Haiti, Honduras, Jamaica, Mexico, Panama, Paraguay, Peru, Saint Lucia, and Uruguay.
Source: WHO Global Health Observatory Data Repository (WHO, 2024[1]).

Table 6.17. Colombia - Tobacco use prevalence by sex and age groups

Percentage of the population group, latest year available

	Tobacco use prevalence (all tobacco products)	Cigarette smoking prevalence (cigarettes only)
Youths aged 13-15 years		
Total	**20.2**	**9.0**
Males	20.6	9.2
Females	19.6	8.6
People aged 15 and over		
Total	**8.6**	**7.5**
Males	12.6	11.0
Females	4.6	4.1

Note: Current tobacco use prevalence is defined as the percentage of the populations who used a tobacco product at least once during the past 30 days. Data for youths aged 13-15 years are from 2017 and taken from the Encuesta Nacional de Tabaquismo en Jóvenes. Data for people aged 15 and over correspond to 2020. Tobacco use includes all types of tobacco products but excludes e-cigarettes (which do not contain tobacco), e-cigars, e-hookahs, and e-pipes.
Source: WHO Global Health Observatory Data Repository (WHO, 2024[1]); Encuesta Nacional de Tabaquismo en Jóvenes, 2017 (Government of Colombia, 2018[24]).

Table 6.18. Colombia - Summary of MPOWER measures, 2022

M Monitoring	P Smoking bans	O Cessation programmes	W Health warnings	E Advertising bans	R Taxation	WHO Frawework Convention on Tobacco Control		Protocol to eliminate illicit trade in tobacco products	
						Date of signature	Date of ratification	Date of signature	Date of ratification
							10-04-2008	21-02-2013	

... Not categorized/ No data; No policy or weak measure; Minimal measure; Moderate measure; Complete measure

Source: WHO report on the global tobacco epidemic (WHO, 2023[3]).

Figure 6.34. Colombia - Taxes and prices of the most sold brand of cigarettes

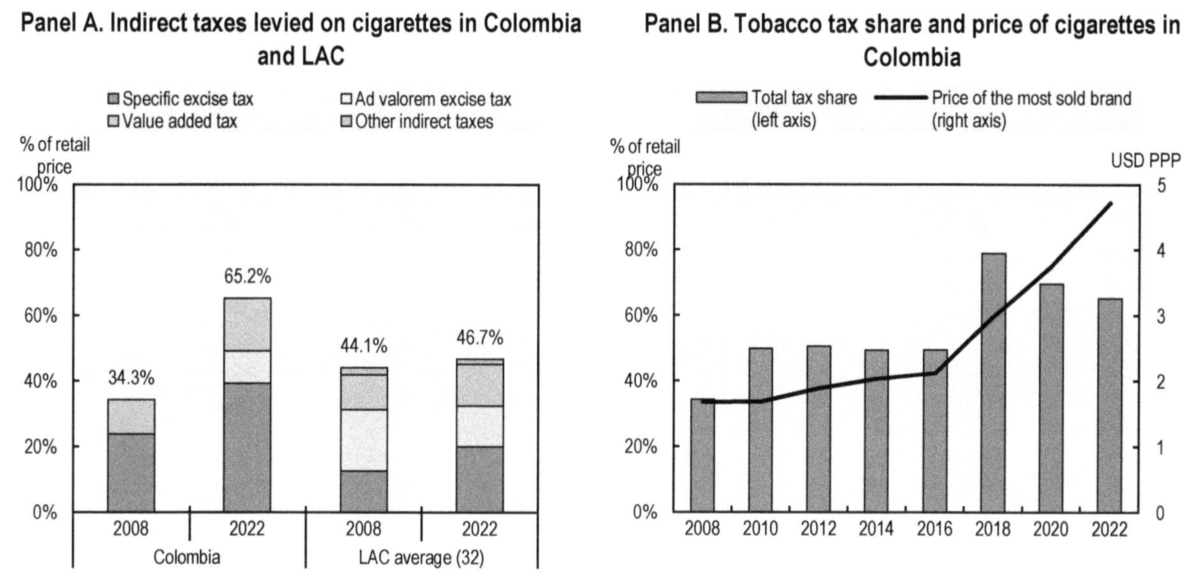

Note: Prices correspond to a 20-cigarette pack of the most sold brand. The most sold brand of cigarettes is determined based on national market share information and can vary over time (i.e. the most sold brand of cigarettes in year 1 can be different from year 2). Retail prices in USD PPP are based on the implied purchasing power parity (PPP) conversion rate from the International Monetary Fund (IMF) World Economic Outlook Database (October 2023).
Source: WHO report on the global tobacco epidemic (WHO, 2023[3]); IMF World Economic Outlook Database (IMF, 2023[4]).

Figure 6.35. Colombia - Trends in retail prices of cigarettes by brand category

In USD PPP per pack of 20 cigarettes, 2008-2022

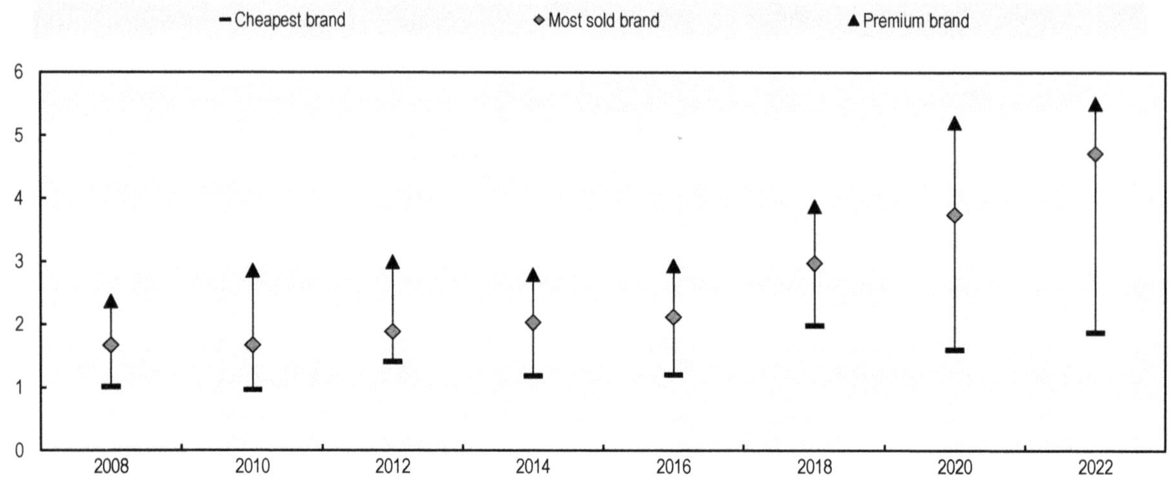

Note: Prices correspond to a 20-cigarette pack of the cheapest, most sold and premium brands. The cheapest, most sold and premium brands of cigarettes are determined based on national market share information and can vary over time (i.e. the cheapest/most sold/premium brands of cigarettes in year 1 can be different from year 2). Retail prices in USD PPP are based on the implied PPP conversion rate from the IMF World Economic Outlook Database (October 2023).

Source: WHO reports on the global tobacco epidemic (WHO, 2009[5]; WHO, 2011[6]; WHO, 2013[7]; WHO, 2015[8]; WHO, 2017[9]; WHO, 2019[10]; WHO, 2021[11]); IMF World Economic Outlook Database (IMF, 2023[4]).

Figure 6.36. Colombia - Affordability of cigarettes

Percentage of GDP per capita required to purchase 100 packs of 20 cigarettes

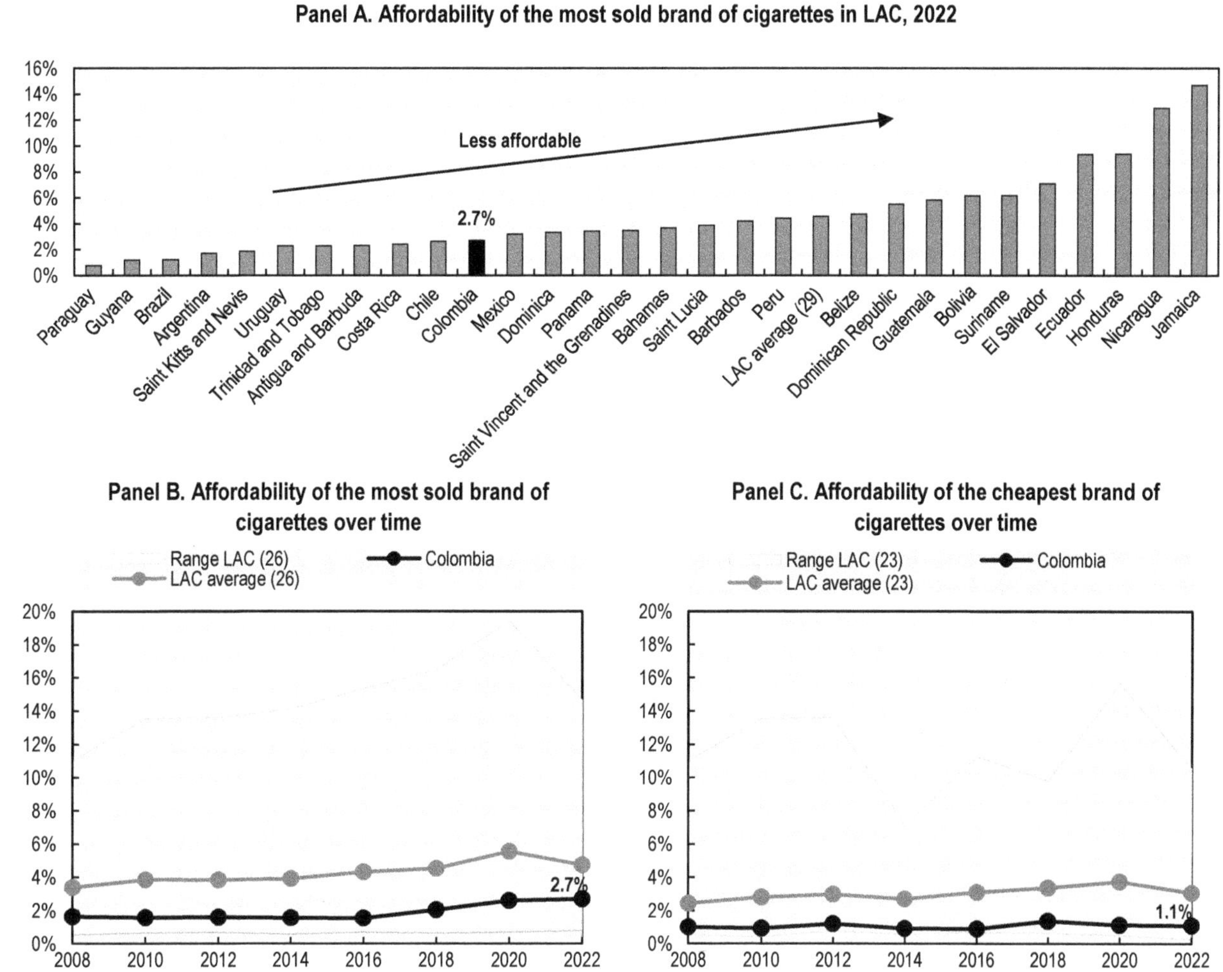

Note: The affordability indicator measures the percentage of the country's GDP per capita required to purchase 100 packs of 20 cigarettes. A higher percentage means lower affordability of cigarettes while a lower percentage means higher affordability. To ensure comparability of average affordability across LAC over time, countries where information was unavailable for certain years have been excluded from the calculation. Data for Panel C are OECD calculations based on WHO reports on the global tobacco epidemic (2009-2023 editions). The cheapest and most sold brands of cigarettes are determined based on national market share information and can vary over time (i.e. the cheapest/most sold brand of cigarettes in year 1 can be different from year 2).

Source: WHO reports on the global tobacco epidemic (WHO, 2009[5]; WHO, 2011[6]; WHO, 2013[7]; WHO, 2015[8]; WHO, 2017[9]; WHO, 2019[10]; WHO, 2021[11]).

Table 6.19. Colombia - Design of tobacco excise taxes across tobacco products, 2022

	Excise tax structure	Specific excise tax				Ad valorem excise tax			Excise tax floor			
		Yes / No	Tax base	Rate per 20-unit pack USD PPP (local currency)	Indexation mechanisms	Yes / No	Tax base	Statutory rate	Yes / No	Tax base	Rate per 20-unit pack USD PPP (local currency)	Indexation mechanisms
Cigarettes	Mixed	Yes	Individual pack	1.8 (2 800)	CPI + 4 pp	Yes	FRP incl. VAT	10%	No			
Cigars	Mixed	Yes	Individual pack	1.8 (2 800)	CPI + 4 pp	Yes	FRP incl. VAT	10%	No			
Cigarillos	Mixed	Yes	Individual pack	1.8 (2 800)	CPI + 4 pp	Yes	FRP incl. VAT	10%	No			
Roll-Your-Own (RYO) tobacco	Mixed	Yes	Gram	3.9 (5 946.7)	CPI + 4 pp	Yes	Other	10%	No			
Heated tobacco products (HTPs)	Mixed	Yes	Individual pack	1.8 (2 800)	CPI + 4 pp	Yes	FRP incl. VAT	10%	No			
ENDS and ENNDS	No excise											

Note: "FRP" means "Final (observed) retail price"; blank cells mean that there is no excise tax for the corresponding tobacco product; "VAT" means "Value added tax". "Other" refers to the ad valorem tax base for Roll-Your-Own (RYO) tobacco, which is the amount of the specific excise tax applied to RYO tobacco according to Art. 348, Ley 1819 (2016). Following the WHO report on the global tobacco epidemic (WHO, 2021[11]), new tobacco and nicotine products in this report include electronic nicotine delivery systems (ENDS), electronic non-nicotine delivery systems (ENNDS), and heated tobacco products (HTP). The mixed excise tax levied on new tobacco products in Colombia applies only to HTP (DIAN, Memorando 000153-2018). Specific taxes are converted into USD PPP with the implied PPP conversion rate available in the IMF World Economic Outlook Database (October 2023). Specific excise taxes have been standardized to a 20-unit pack to allow the comparison across countries with different tax bases. Specific tax for RYO tobacco in Colombia is levied on each gram of RYO tobacco. To compute the specific tax for an equivalent 20-unit pack of RYO tobacco, it is assumed that the median cigarette in terms of weight contains 0.75 gram of tobacco (Gallus et al., 2014[12]).

Source: DIAN Memorando 000153-2018; Ley 1819, Art. 347y sus reformas (2016); IMF World Economic Outlook Database (IMF, 2023[4]).

Table 6.20. Colombia - Tobacco tax reforms since 2000

Year of adoption	Specific excise taxes	Ad valorem excise taxes	Other
2006	Cigarettes, cigars and cigarillos: introduction of a specific excise tax with two-tiered rates based on the retail price. For packs of 20 units below COP 2 000, the specific tax is COP 400 per 20-unit pack. For packs with a price exceeding COP 2 000, the specific tax is COP 800 per 20-unit pack. RYO tobacco: introduction of a uniform specific excise tax of COP 30 levied on each gram. All tobacco products: the specific tax is annually adjusted based on changes in CPI.	All tobacco products: the ad valorem excise tax is abolished.	No
2010	Cigarettes, cigars and cigarillos: uniformize and increase in the specific tax to COP 570 levied on each pack of 20 units. RYO tobacco: increase in the specific tax to COP 36 levied on each gram. All tobacco products: the specific tax is annually adjusted based on changes in CPI.	Cigarettes, cigars and cigarillos: introduction of an ad valorem tax component levied at a rate of 10% on the retail price (incl. VAT). RYO tobacco: introduction of an ad valorem tax component levied at a rate of 10% on the value of the specific excise tax.	No

Year of adoption	Specific excise taxes	Ad valorem excise taxes	Other
2016	Cigarettes, cigars and cigarillos: increase in the specific tax to COP 1 700 in 2017 and to COP 2 100 in 2018 levied on each pack of 20 units. RYO tobacco: increase in the specific tax to COP 90 in 2017 and to COP 167 in 2018 levied on each gram. All tobacco products: the specific tax is annually adjusted based on changes in CPI + 4 pp. starting from 2019.	No	No
2018	Heated tobacco products: introduction of a specific excise tax levied at a similar rate than cigarettes, cigars and cigarillos.	Heated tobacco products: introduction of an ad valorem excise tax levied at a similar rate than cigarettes, cigars and cigarillos.	

Note: "Tobacco tax reform" refers to changes in the tobacco excise tax rates, the introduction of indexation mechanisms or minimum taxes, as well as adjustments to the tax base. These reforms typically entail the enactment of new laws or decrees. The table does not refer to recurrent tax changes that result from the indexation for inflation of tax brackets and price floors (if implemented). Tobacco tax reforms included reflect changes in the legislation, but not whether or when the reforms have been implemented.
Source: Ley 1111 - Art. 76 (2006); Ley 1393 - Art. 5 (2010); Ley 1819 - Art. 347 (2016); DIAN Memorando 000153-2018.

Figure 6.37. Colombia - Tobacco excise tax revenue

Percentage of GDP, latest year available

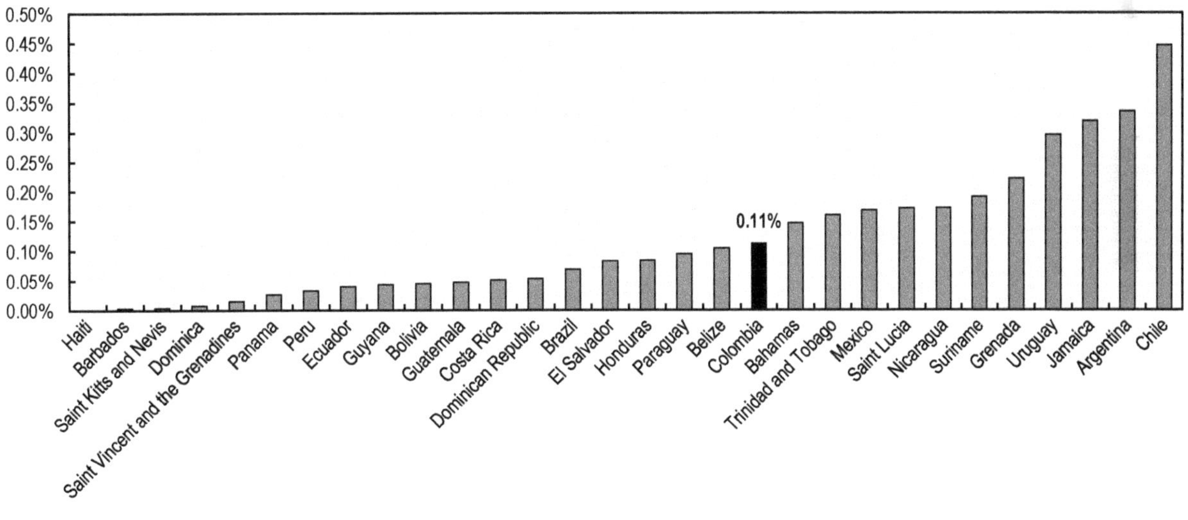

Note: See Box 2.1 (Chapter 2) for more information on tobacco tax revenue (source of information and calculations) and country selection. The latest year available is 2022 for Argentina, Brazil, Chile, Colombia, Costa Rica, the Dominican Republic, El Salvador, Guatemala, Guyana, Honduras, Mexico, Nicaragua, Panama, Paraguay, Peru, Saint Kitts and Nevis, Suriname, and Uruguay; 2021 for Belize, Dominica, Ecuador, Grenada, Saint Lucia, Saint Vincent and the Grenadines; 2020 for Bahamas, Bolivia, Jamaica and Trinidad and Tobago; 2015 for Haiti; 2014 for Barbados.
Source: OECD Revenue Statistics (OECD, 2024[13]); WHO report on the global tobacco epidemic (WHO, 2023[3]); National data.

Figure 6.38. Colombia - Trends in tobacco excise tax revenue

Percentage of GDP, 2000-2022

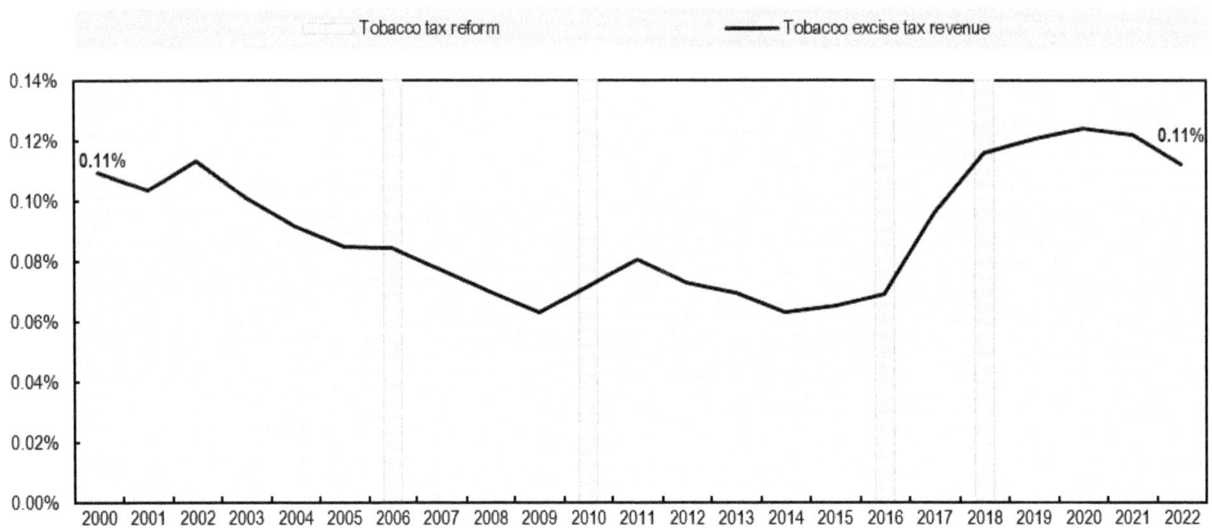

Note: "Tobacco tax reform" refers to the measures included in Table 6.20.
Source: OECD Revenue Statistics (OECD, 2024[13]); Ley 1111 - Art. 76 (2006); Ley 1393 - Art. 5 (2010); Ley 1819 - Art. 347 (2016).

Figure 6.39. Colombia - Average excise tax revenue collected per pack of 20 cigarettes sold

Tobacco excise tax revenue in USD PPP collected per pack of legal cigarettes sold, latest year available

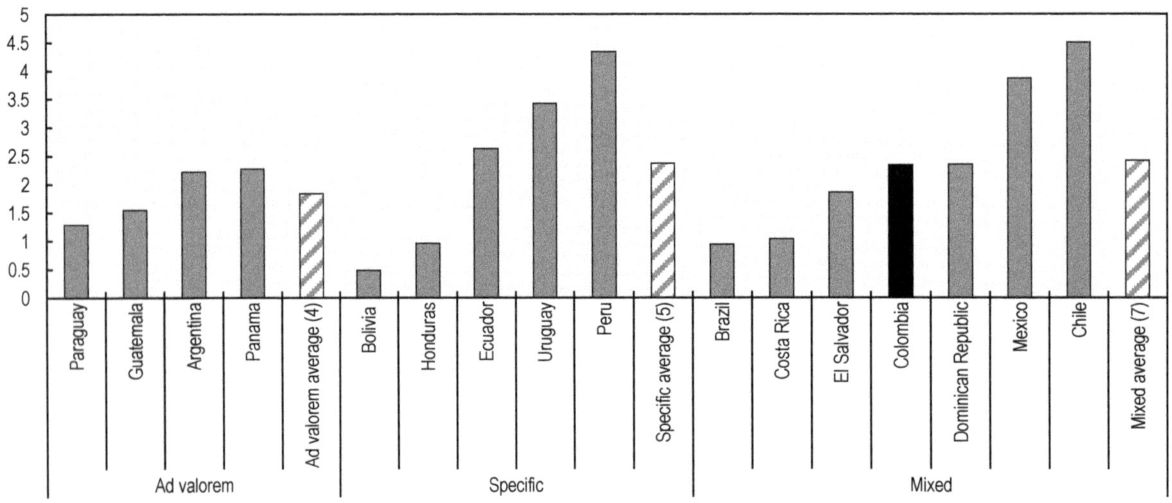

Note: See Box 2.1 (Chapter 2) for more information on tobacco tax revenue (source of information and calculations). The latest year available is 2022 for Argentina, Brazil, Chile, Colombia, Costa Rica, the Dominican Republic, El Salvador, Guatemala, Honduras, Mexico, Panama, Paraguay, Peru and Uruguay; 2021 for Ecuador; 2020 for Bolivia. The country selection is provided by the availability of data on sales of cigarettes in Euromonitor International Limited © All rights reserved (Euromonitor International, 2023[14]).
Source: OECD Revenue Statistics (OECD, 2024[13]); WHO report on the global tobacco epidemic (WHO, 2023[3]); National data; IMF World Economic Outlook Database (IMF, 2023[4]); and OECD calculations based on Euromonitor International's Tobacco Industry edition (Euromonitor International, 2023[14]).

Figure 6.40. Colombia - Change in tobacco tax policy indicators

Percentage change from base year, 2008-2022

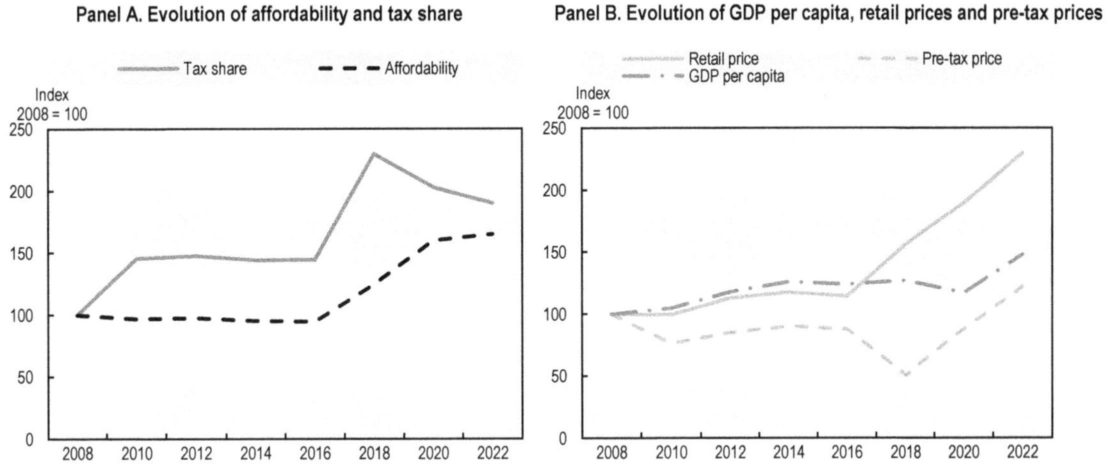

Note: Both Panel A and Panel B figures are based on data for the most sold brand of cigarettes. The most sold brand of cigarettes is determined based on national market share information and can vary over time (i.e. the most sold brand of cigarettes in year 1 can be different from year 2). In Panel A, an increase in the affordability indicator means that cigarettes are becoming less affordable, while a decline in the affordability indicator means that cigarettes are becoming more affordable. In Panel B, "Pre-tax price" corresponds to the retail price of the most sold brand of cigarettes minus the indirect taxes levied on this brand, namely excise taxes, VAT, import duties and other. Indicators in Panel B have been computed using national currency and have been adjusted for inflation; therefore, present inflation-adjusted trends.
Source: WHO report on the global tobacco epidemic (WHO, 2023[3]); World Bank Open Data (World Bank, 2024[15]); IMF International Financial Statistics (IMF, 2024[19]).

References

Euromonitor International (2023), *Euromonitor International's Tobacco Industry edition*, https://www.euromonitor.com/tobacco (accessed on 1 August 2023). [14]

Gallus, S. et al. (2014), "Roll-your-own cigarettes in Europe", *European Journal of Cancer Prevention*, Vol. 23/3, pp. 186-192, https://doi.org/10.1097/cej.0000000000000010. [12]

Government of Colombia (2018), *Encuesta Nacional de Tabaquismo en Jóvenes, 2017*, Ministry of Health and Social Protection, https://www.minsalud.gov.co/salud/publica/epidemiologia/Paginas/Estudios-y-encuestas.aspx. [24]

IMF (2023), *World Economic Outlook Database*, International Monetary Fund, https://www.imf.org/en/Publications/WEO/weo-database/2023/October (accessed on 13 January 2024). [4]

IMF (2024), *International Financial Statistics (IFS)*, International Monetary Fund, https://data.imf.org/?sk=4c514d48-b6ba-49ed-8ab9-52b0c1a0179b&sId=1390030341854 (accessed on 13 January 2024). [19]

OECD (2024), *Global Revenue Statistics Database*, Organisation for Economic Co-operation and Development, https://www.oecd.org/tax/tax-policy/global-revenue-statistics-database.htm (accessed on 13 August 2023). [13]

WHO (2024), *Global Health Observatory: Age-standardized estimates of current tobacco use, tobacco smoking and cigarette smoking (Tobacco control: Monitor)*, World Health Organization, https://www.who.int/data/gho/data/indicators/indicator-details/GHO/gho-tobacco-control-monitor-current-tobaccouse-tobaccosmoking-cigarrettesmoking-agestd-tobagestdcurr (accessed on 20 February 2024). [1]

WHO (2023), *WHO report on the global tobacco epidemic 2023: protect people from tobacco smoke*, World Health Organization, https://www.who.int/publications/i/item/9789240077164. [3]

WHO (2021), *WHO report on the global tobacco epidemic 2021: Addressing new and emerging products*, World Health Organization, https://www.who.int/publications/i/item/9789240032095. [11]

WHO (2019), *WHO report on the global tobacco epidemic 2019: Offer help to quit tobacco use*, World Health Organization, https://www.who.int/publications/i/item/9789241516204. [10]

WHO (2017), *WHO report on the global tobacco epidemic 2017: Monitoring tobacco use and prevention policies*, World Health Organization, https://www.who.int/publications/i/item/9789241512824. [9]

WHO (2015), *WHO report on the global tobacco epidemic 2015: Raising taxes on tobacco*, World Health Organization, https://www.who.int/publications/i/item/9789241509121. [8]

WHO (2013), *WHO report on the global tobacco epidemic 2013: Enforcing bans on tobacco advertising, promotion and sponsorship*, World Health Organization, https://www.who.int/publications/i/item/9789241505871. [7]

WHO (2011), *WHO report on the global tobacco epidemic 2011: Warning about the dangers of tobacco*, World Health Organization, https://www.who.int/publications/i/item/9789244564264. [6]

WHO (2009), *WHO report on the global tobacco epidemic 2009: Implementing smoke-free environments*, World Health Organization, https://www.who.int/publications/i/item/9789241563918. [5]

World Bank (2024), *World Bank Open Data*, World Bank, https://data.worldbank.org/ (accessed on 13 January 2024). [15]

Costa Rica

Figure 6.41. Costa Rica - Trends in tobacco use prevalence

Percentage of the population aged 15 years and over who currently use any tobacco product (smoked and/or smokeless tobacco) on a daily or non-daily basis, 2000-2020

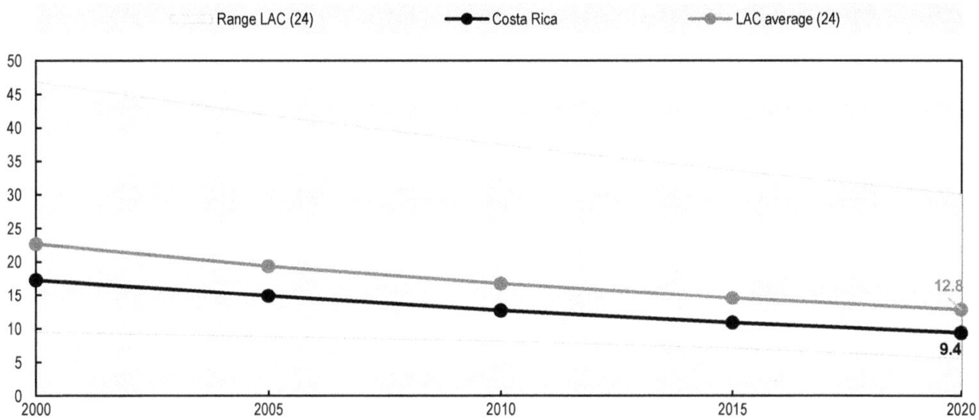

Note: Tobacco products include cigarettes, pipes, cigars, cigarillos, waterpipes (hookah, shisha), bidis, kretek, heated tobacco products (HTP), and all forms of smokeless (oral and nasal) tobacco. Tobacco products exclude e-cigarettes (which do not contain tobacco), e-cigars, e-hookahs, and e-pipes. The rates are age-standardized to the World Health Organisation (WHO) standard population. The LAC average was calculated as the average of Argentina, Bahamas, Barbados, Belize, Bolivia, Brazil, Chile, Colombia, Costa Rica, Cuba, the Dominican Republic, Ecuador, El Salvador, Guatemala, Guyana, Haiti, Honduras, Jamaica, Mexico, Panama, Paraguay, Peru, Saint Lucia, and Uruguay.
Source: WHO Global Health Observatory Data Repository (WHO, 2024[1]).

Table 6.21. Costa Rica - Tobacco use prevalence by sex and age groups

Percentage of the population group, latest year available

	Tobacco use prevalence (all tobacco products)	Cigarette smoking prevalence (cigarettes only)
Students aged 13-15 years		
Total	**2.6**	**...**
Males	3.4	...
Females	1.8	...
People aged 15 and over		
Total	**8.7**	**8.2**
Males	13.1	12.5
Females	4.3	4.0

Note: Tobacco use prevalence is defined as the percentage of the population group who currently use any tobacco product (smoked and/or smokeless tobacco) on a daily or non-daily basis. Tobacco products exclude e-cigarettes (which do not contain tobacco), e-cigars, e-hookahs, and e-pipes. Data for students aged 13-15 years are from 2018 and taken from the Encuesta Nacional sobre Consumo de Drogas en población de Educación Secundaria. Data for people aged 15 and over correspond to 2022 and are taken from the Global Adult Tobacco Survey (GATS). For comparability purposes across countries, the Figure 6.41 uses another source of information (WHO Global Health Observatory Data Repository) which explains the small difference with figures included in this table. Cells with "..." indicate that the information is not available.
Source: Global Adult Tobacco Survey Fact Sheet, Costa Rica (Government of Costa Rica, 2023[25]); Encuesta Nacional sobre Consumo de Drogas en población de Educación Secundaria, 2018 (Government of Costa Rica, 2019[26]).

Table 6.22. Costa Rica - Summary of MPOWER measures, 2022

M Monitoring	P Smoking bans	O Cessation programmes	W Health warnings	E Advertising bans	R Taxation	WHO Frawework Convention on Tobacco Control		Protocol to eliminate illicit trade in tobacco products	
						Date of signature	Date of ratification	Date of signature	Date of ratification
						03-07-2003	21-08-2008	21-03-2013	07-03-2017

... Not categorized/ No data; No policy or weak measure; Minimal measure; Moderate measure; Complete measure

Source: WHO report on the global tobacco epidemic (WHO, 2023[3]).

Figure 6.42. Costa Rica - Taxes and prices of the most sold brand of cigarettes

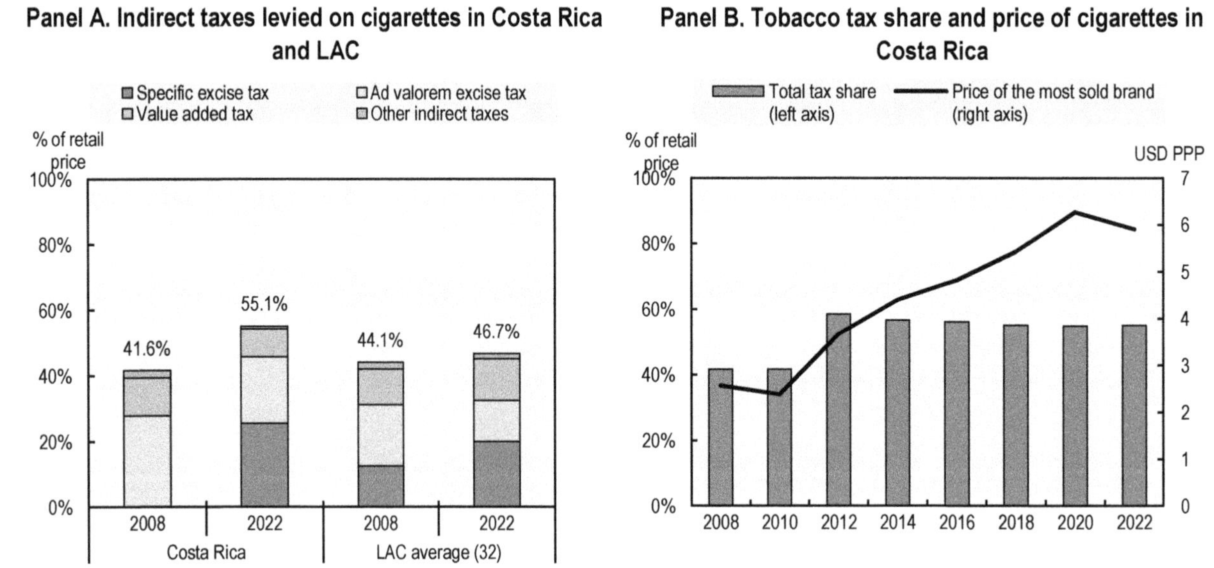

Note: Prices correspond to a 20-cigarette pack of the most sold brand. The most sold brand of cigarettes is determined based on national market share information and can vary over time (i.e. the most sold brand of cigarettes in year 1 can be different from year 2). Retail prices in USD PPP are based on the implied purchasing power parity (PPP) conversion rate from the International Monetary Fund (IMF) World Economic Outlook Database (October 2023).
Source: WHO report on the global tobacco epidemic (WHO, 2023[3]); IMF World Economic Outlook Database (IMF, 2023[4]).

Figure 6.43. Costa Rica - Trends in retail prices of cigarettes by brand category

In USD PPP per pack of 20 cigarettes, 2008-2022

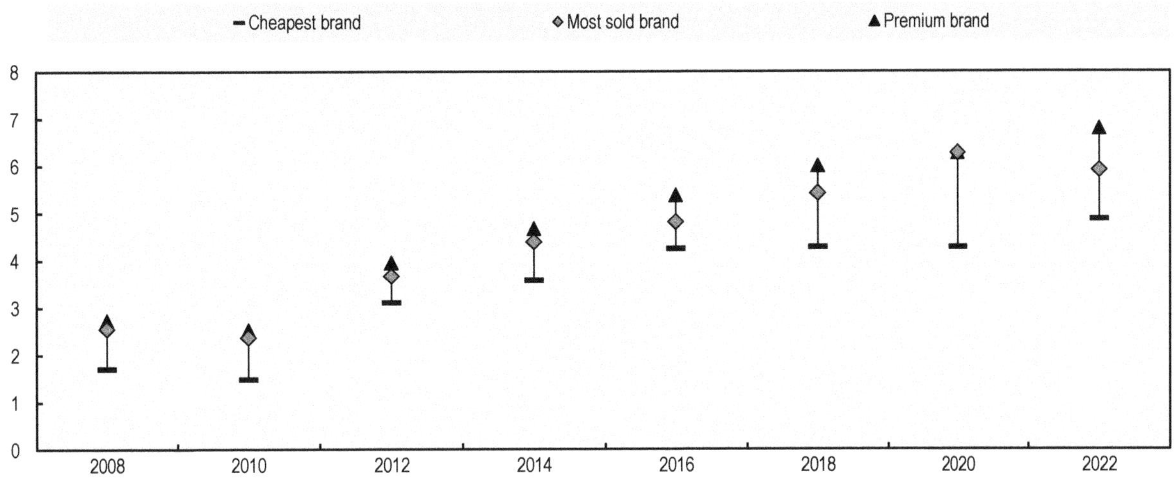

Note: Prices correspond to a 20-cigarette pack of the cheapest, most sold and premium brands. The cheapest, most sold and premium brands of cigarettes are determined based on national market share information and can vary over time (i.e. the cheapest/most sold/premium brands of cigarettes in year 1 can be different from year 2). Retail prices in USD PPP are based on the implied PPP conversion rate from the IMF World Economic Outlook Database (October 2023).

Source: WHO reports on the global tobacco epidemic (WHO, 2009[5]; WHO, 2011[6]; WHO, 2013[7]; WHO, 2015[8]; WHO, 2017[9]; WHO, 2019[10]; WHO, 2021[11]); IMF World Economic Outlook Database (IMF, 2023[4]).

Figure 6.44. Costa Rica - Affordability of cigarettes

Percentage of GDP per capita required to purchase 100 packs of 20 cigarettes

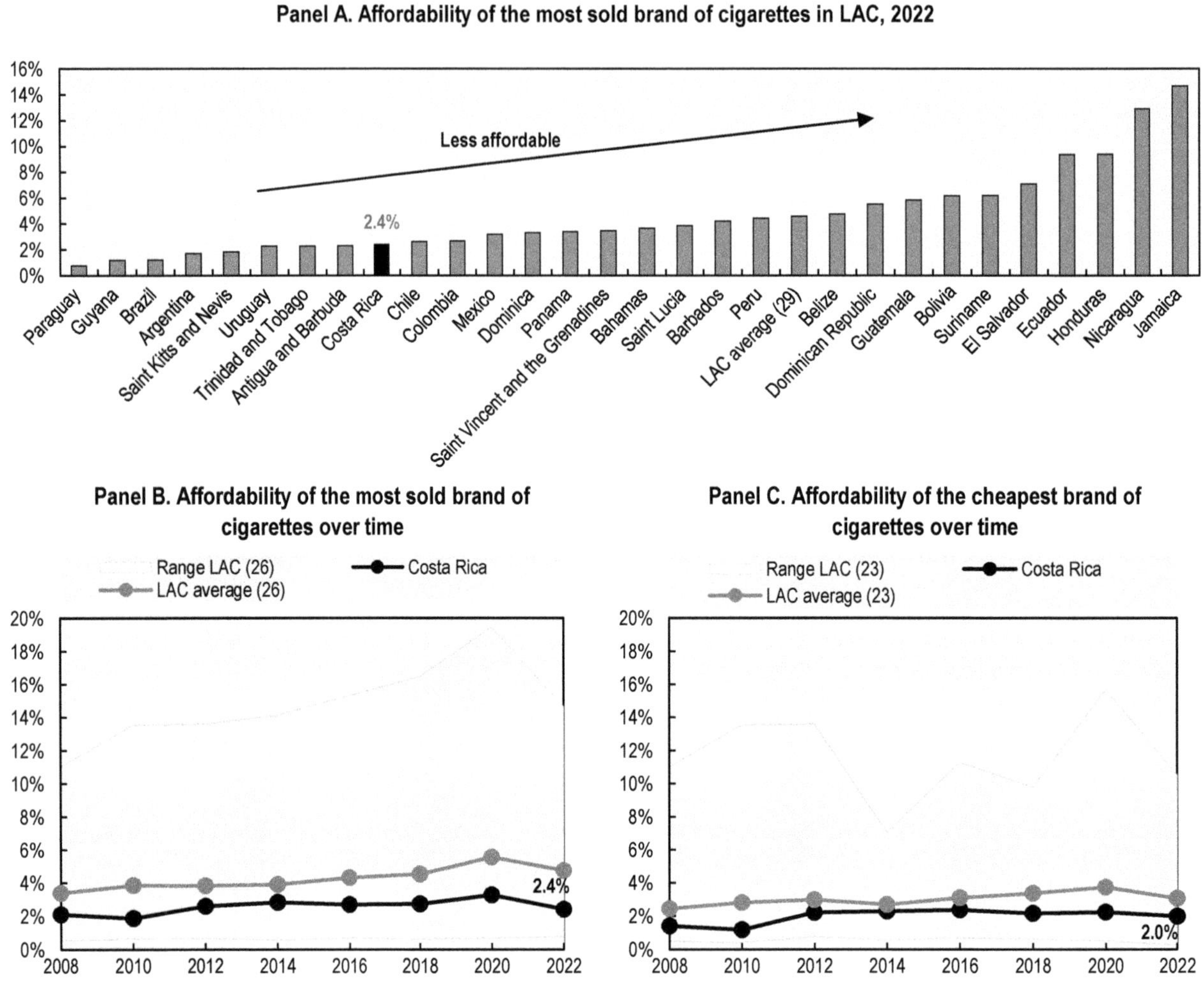

Note: The affordability indicator measures the percentage of the country's GDP per capita required to purchase 100 packs of 20 cigarettes. A higher percentage means lower affordability of cigarettes while a lower percentage means higher affordability. To ensure comparability of average affordability across LAC over time, countries where information was unavailable for certain years have been excluded from the calculation. Data for Panel C are OECD calculations based on WHO reports on the global tobacco epidemic (2009-2023 editions). The cheapest and most sold brands of cigarettes are determined based on national market share information and can vary over time (i.e. the cheapest/most sold brand of cigarettes in year 1 can be different from year 2).

Source: WHO reports on the global tobacco epidemic (WHO, 2009[5]; WHO, 2011[6]; WHO, 2013[7]; WHO, 2015[8]; WHO, 2017[9]; WHO, 2019[10]; WHO, 2021[11]).

Table 6.23. Costa Rica - Design of tobacco excise taxes across tobacco products, 2022

	Excise tax structure	Specific excise tax				Ad valorem excise tax			Excise tax floor			
		Yes / No	Tax base	Rate per 20-unit pack USD PPP (local currency)	Indexation mechanisms	Yes / No	Tax base	Statutory rate	Yes / No	Tax base	Rate per 20-unit pack USD PPP (local currency)	Indexation mechanisms
Cigarettes	Mixed	Yes	Single stick	1.5 (509.4)	CPI	Yes	EFP excl. VAT	95%	Yes	Ad valorem excise tax base, VAT tax base and Inder tax base for the most sold brand	1.5 (522.4)	85% of the ad valorem excise, the VAT and the Inder tax liability levied on the most sold brand during the previous year
Cigars	Mixed	Yes	Single stick	1.5 (509.4)	CPI	Yes	EFP excl. VAT	95%	No			
Cigarillos	Mixed	Yes	Single stick	1.5 (509.4)	CPI	Yes	EFP excl. VAT	95%	No			
Roll-Your-Own (RYO) tobacco	Mixed	Yes	Single stick	1.5 (509.4)	CPI	Yes	EFP excl. VAT	65%	No			
Heated Tobacco Products (HTPs)	Ad valorem only	No				Yes	EFP excl. VAT	20%	No			
ENDS and ENNDS	Ad valorem only	No				Yes	EFP excl. VAT	20%	No			

Note: Ad valorem tax base "EFP" means "Ex-factory price/CIF value"; blank cells mean that there is no excise tax for the corresponding tobacco product; "VAT" means "Value added tax"; "CPI" means consumer price index. Following the WHO report on the global tobacco epidemic (WHO, 2021[11]), new tobacco and nicotine products in this report include electronic nicotine delivery systems (ENDS), electronic non-nicotine delivery systems (ENNDS), and heated tobacco products (HTP). Specific taxes are converted into USD PPP with the implied PPP conversion rate available in the IMF World Economic Outlook Database (October 2023). Specific excise taxes have been standardized to a 20-unit pack to allow the comparison across countries with different tax bases.
Source: Ley N° 9028 (2012) y sus reformas; IMF World Economic Outlook Database (IMF, 2023[4]).

Table 6.24. Costa Rica - Tobacco tax reforms since 2000

Year of adoption	Specific excise taxes	Ad valorem excise taxes	Other
2012	Cigarettes, cigars, cigarillos and RYO tobacco: introduction of a specific component levied at a rate of CRC 20.0 on each single stick. The specific tax is annually adjusted based on changes in CPI.	Cigarettes, cigars, cigarillos and RYO tobacco: the ad valorem excise tax that was in force is maintained.	Cigarettes: introduction of a minimum tax which applies to the ad valorem excise tax, the VAT and the Inder tax. The total tax liability per pack of cigarettes derived from these three taxes cannot be lower than 85% of the analogous tax liability (i.e. that derived from the ad valorem excise tax, the VAT and the Inder) levied on the most sold brand of cigarettes.
2022	No	New tobacco and nicotine products: introduction of an ad valorem excise tax levied at a rate of 20% on the ex-factory price, excluding VAT.	No

Note: "Tobacco tax reform" refers to changes in the tobacco excise tax rates, the introduction of indexation mechanisms or minimum taxes, as well as adjustments to the tax base. These reforms typically entail the enactment of new laws or decrees. The table does not refer to recurrent tax changes that result from the indexation for inflation of tax brackets and price floors (if implemented). Tobacco tax reforms included reflect changes in the legislation, but not whether or when the reforms have been implemented.
Source: Ley N° 9028 (2012); Ley N° 10066 (2022).

Figure 6.45. Costa Rica - Tobacco excise tax revenue

Percentage of GDP, latest year available

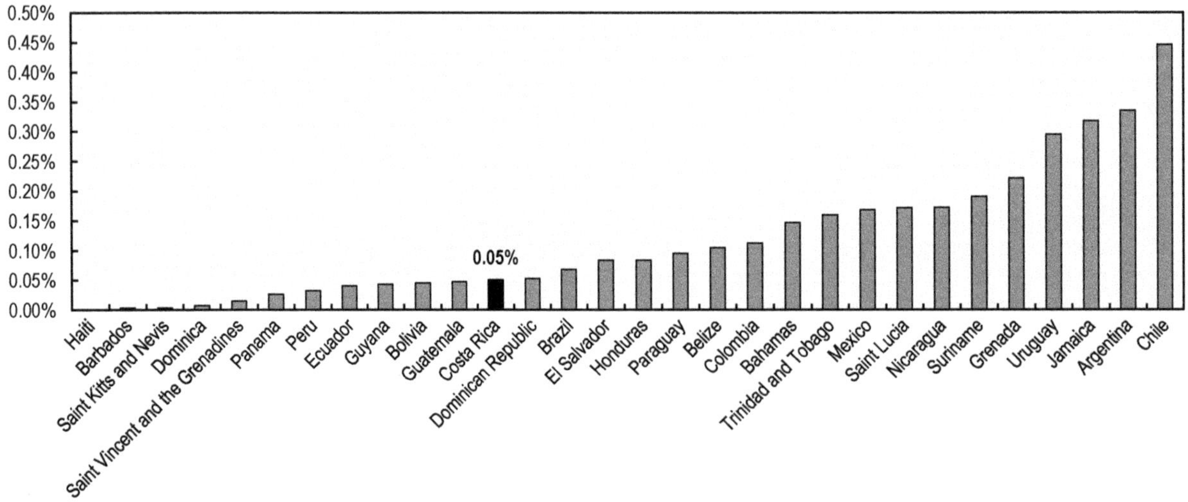

Note: See Box 2.1 (Chapter 2) for more information on tobacco tax revenue (source of information and calculations) and country selection. The latest year available is 2022 for Argentina, Brazil, Chile, Colombia, Costa Rica, the Dominican Republic, El Salvador, Guatemala, Guyana, Honduras, Mexico, Nicaragua, Panama, Paraguay, Peru, Saint Kitts and Nevis, Suriname, and Uruguay; 2021 for Belize, Dominica, Ecuador, Grenada, Saint Lucia, Saint Vincent and the Grenadines; 2020 for Bahamas, Bolivia, Jamaica and Trinidad and Tobago; 2015 for Haiti; 2014 for Barbados. Data on excise tax revenue for Costa Rica include only the revenue from the specific component since tax revenue data for the "selective" (ad valorem) excise tax are missing.
Source: OECD Revenue Statistics (OECD, 2024[13]); WHO report on the global tobacco epidemic (WHO, 2023[3]); National data.

Figure 6.46. Costa Rica - Trends in tobacco excise tax revenue

Percentage of GDP, 2012-2022

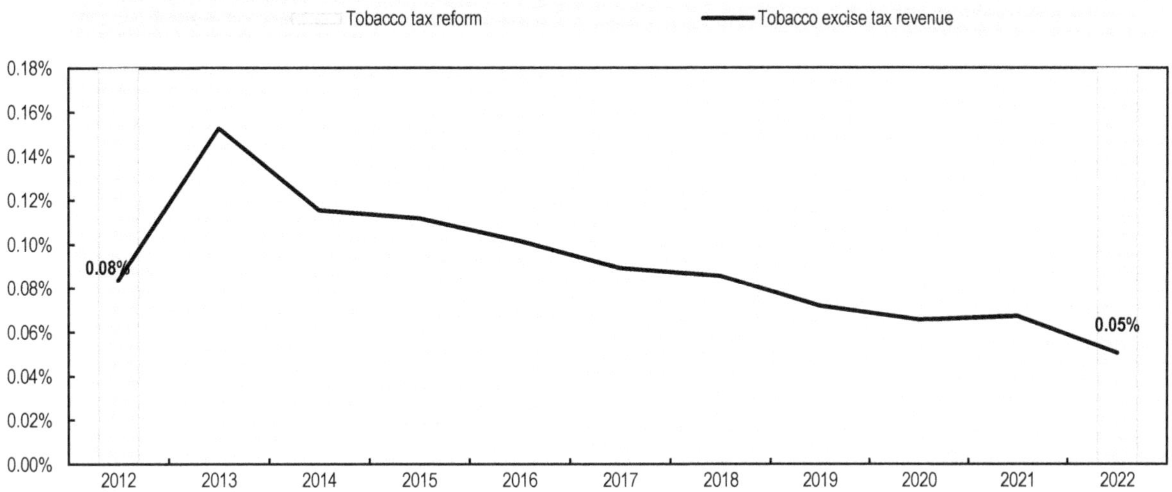

Note: "Tobacco tax reform" refers to the measures included in Table 6.24. Data on excise tax revenue include only the revenue from the specific component since tax revenue data for the "selective" (ad valorem) excise tax are missing. Data on excise tax revenue prior 2012 are not available.

Source: OECD Revenue Statistics (OECD, 2024[13]); Ley N° 9028 (2012); Ley N° 10066 (2022).

Figure 6.47. Costa Rica - Average excise tax revenue collected per pack of 20 cigarettes sold

Tobacco excise tax revenue in USD PPP collected per pack of legal cigarettes sold, latest year available

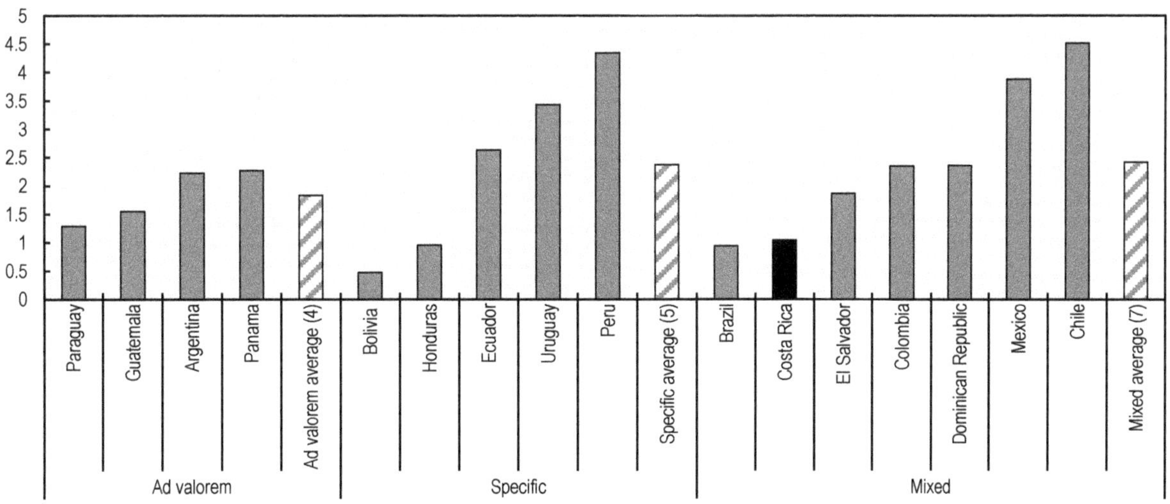

Note: See Box 2.1 (Chapter 2) for more information on tobacco tax revenue (source of information and calculations). The latest year available is 2022 for Argentina, Brazil, Chile, Colombia, Costa Rica, the Dominican Republic, El Salvador, Guatemala, Honduras, Mexico, Panama, Paraguay, Peru and Uruguay; 2021 for Ecuador;2020 for Bolivia. Data on excise tax revenue for Costa Rica include only the revenue from the specific component since tax revenue data for the "selective" (ad valorem) excise tax are missing. The country selection is provided by the availability of data on sales of cigarettes in Euromonitor International Limited © All rights reserved (Euromonitor International, 2023[14]).

Source: OECD Revenue Statistics (OECD, 2024[13]); WHO report on the global tobacco epidemic (WHO, 2023[3]); National data; IMF World Economic Outlook Database (IMF, 2023[4]); and OECD calculations based on Euromonitor International's Tobacco Industry edition (Euromonitor International, 2023[14]).

Figure 6.48. Costa Rica - Change in tobacco tax policy indicators

Percentage change from base year, 2008-2022

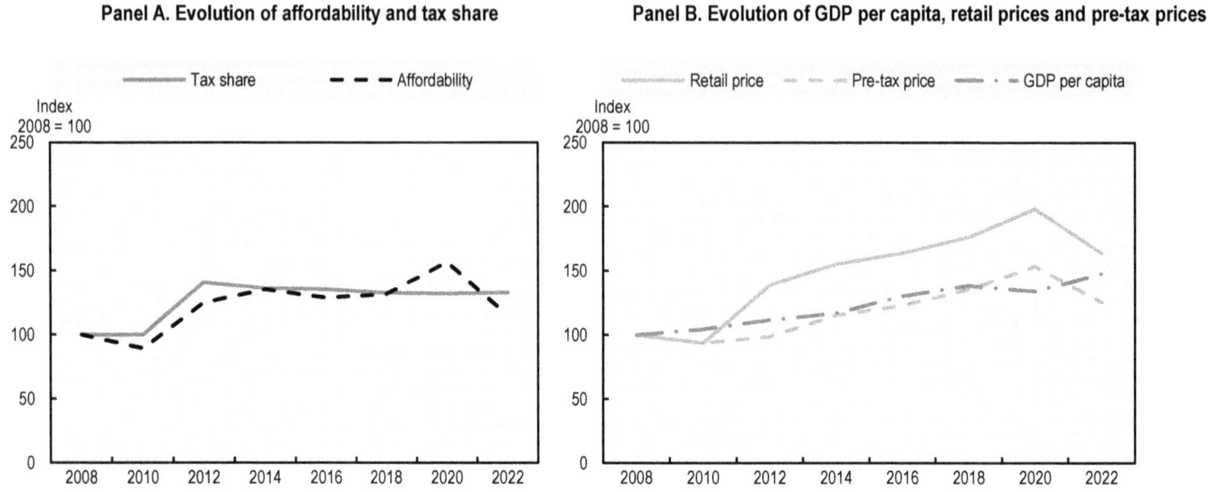

Note: Both Panel A and Panel B figures are based on data for the most sold brand of cigarettes. The most sold brand of cigarettes is determined based on national market share information and can vary over time (i.e. the most sold brand of cigarettes in year 1 can be different from year 2). In Panel A, an increase in the affordability indicator means that cigarettes are becoming less affordable, while a decline in the affordability indicator means that cigarettes are becoming more affordable. In Panel B, "Pre-tax price" corresponds to the retail price of the most sold brand of cigarettes minus the indirect taxes levied on this brand, namely excise taxes, VAT, import duties and other. Indicators in Panel B have been computed using national currency and have been adjusted for inflation; therefore, present inflation-adjusted trends.
Source: WHO report on the global tobacco epidemic (WHO, 2023[3]); World Bank Open Data (World Bank, 2024[15]); IMF International Financial Statistics (IMF, 2024[19]).

References

Euromonitor International (2023), *Euromonitor International's Tobacco Industry edition*, https://www.euromonitor.com/tobacco (accessed on 1 August 2023). [14]

Government of Costa Rica (2019), *Encuesta Nacional sobre Consumo de Drogas en población de Educación Secundaria, 2018*, Institute on Alcoholism and Drug Dependence, https://www.iafa.go.cr/wp-content/uploads/2022/05/iafa-encuenstanacional-adolescentes-2019.pdf. [26]

Government of Costa Rica (2023), *GATS Global Adult Tobacco Survey Fact Sheet : Costa Rica 2022*, Ministry of Health, https://stacks.cdc.gov/view/cdc/148219 (accessed on 13 June 2024). [25]

IMF (2023), *World Economic Outlook Database*, International Monetary Fund, https://www.imf.org/en/Publications/WEO/weo-database/2023/October (accessed on 13 January 2024). [4]

IMF (2024), *International Financial Statistics (IFS)*, International Monetary Fund, https://data.imf.org/?sk=4c514d48-b6ba-49ed-8ab9-52b0c1a0179b&sId=1390030341854 (accessed on 13 January 2024). [19]

OECD (2024), *Global Revenue Statistics Database*, Organisation for Economic Co-operation and Development, https://www.oecd.org/tax/tax-policy/global-revenue-statistics-database.htm (accessed on 13 August 2023). [13]

WHO (2024), *Global Health Observatory: Age-standardized estimates of current tobacco use, tobacco smoking and cigarette smoking (Tobacco control: Monitor)*, World Health Organization, https://www.who.int/data/gho/data/indicators/indicator-details/GHO/gho-tobacco-control-monitor-current-tobaccouse-tobaccosmoking-cigarrettesmoking-agestd-tobagestdcurr (accessed on 20 February 2024). [1]

WHO (2023), *WHO report on the global tobacco epidemic 2023: protect people from tobacco smoke*, World Health Organization, https://www.who.int/publications/i/item/9789240077164. [3]

WHO (2021), *WHO report on the global tobacco epidemic 2021: Addressing new and emerging products*, World Health Organization, https://www.who.int/publications/i/item/9789240032095. [11]

WHO (2019), *WHO report on the global tobacco epidemic 2019: Offer help to quit tobacco use*, World Health Organization, https://www.who.int/publications/i/item/9789241516204. [10]

WHO (2017), *WHO report on the global tobacco epidemic 2017: Monitoring tobacco use and prevention policies*, World Health Organization, https://www.who.int/publications/i/item/9789241512824. [9]

WHO (2015), *WHO report on the global tobacco epidemic 2015: Raising taxes on tobacco*, World Health Organization, https://www.who.int/publications/i/item/9789241509121. [8]

WHO (2013), *WHO report on the global tobacco epidemic 2013: Enforcing bans on tobacco advertising, promotion and sponsorship*, World Health Organization, https://www.who.int/publications/i/item/9789241505871. [7]

WHO (2011), *WHO report on the global tobacco epidemic 2011: Warning about the dangers of tobacco*, World Health Organization, https://www.who.int/publications/i/item/9789244564264. [6]

WHO (2009), *WHO report on the global tobacco epidemic 2009: Implementing smoke-free environments*, World Health Organization, https://www.who.int/publications/i/item/9789241563918. [5]

World Bank (2024), *World Bank Open Data*, World Bank, https://data.worldbank.org/ (accessed on 13 January 2024). [15]

Dominican Republic

Figure 6.49. Dominican Republic - Trends in tobacco use prevalence

Percentage of the population aged 15 years and over who currently use any tobacco product (smoked and/or smokeless tobacco) on a daily or non-daily basis, 2000-2020

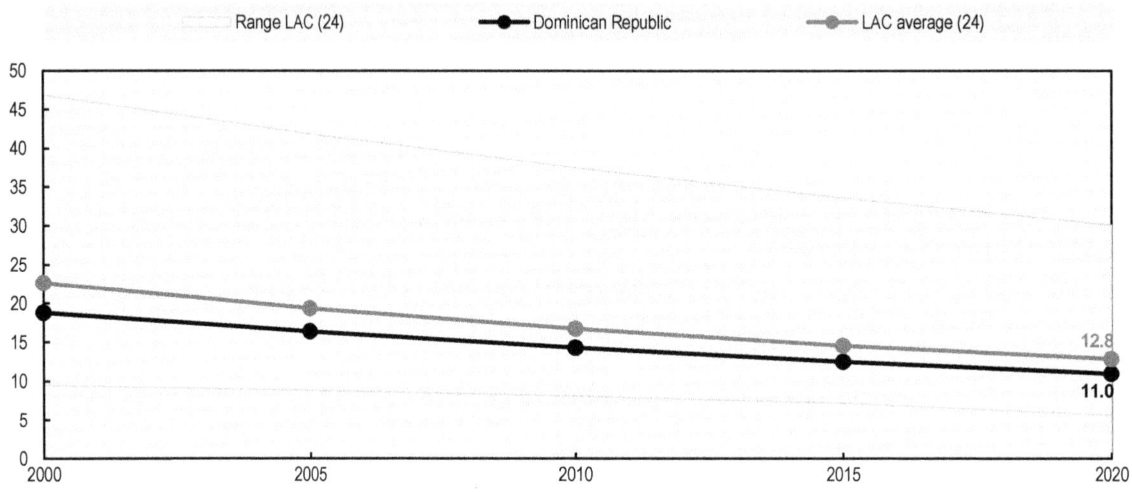

Note: Tobacco products include cigarettes, pipes, cigars, cigarillos, waterpipes (hookah, shisha), bidis, kretek, heated tobacco products (HTP), and all forms of smokeless (oral and nasal) tobacco. Tobacco products exclude e-cigarettes (which do not contain tobacco), e-cigars, e-hookahs, and e-pipes. The rates are age-standardized to the World Health Organisation (WHO) standard population. The LAC average was calculated as the average of Argentina, Bahamas, Barbados, Belize, Bolivia, Brazil, Chile, Colombia, Costa Rica, Cuba, the Dominican Republic, Ecuador, El Salvador, Guatemala, Guyana, Haiti, Honduras, Jamaica, Mexico, Panama, Paraguay, Peru, Saint Lucia, and Uruguay.
Source: WHO Global Health Observatory Data Repository (WHO, 2024[1]).

Table 6.25. Dominican Republic - Tobacco use prevalence by sex and age groups

Percentage of the population group, latest year available

	Tobacco use prevalence (all tobacco products)	Cigarette smoking prevalence (cigarettes only)
Youths aged 13-15 years		
Total	**7.4**	**2.4**
Males	8.3	2.4
Females	6.0	1.8
People aged 15 and over		
Total	**11.0**	**7.2**
Males	14.9	10.2
Females	7.1	4.2

Note: Tobacco use prevalence is defined as the percentage of the population group who currently use any tobacco product (smoked and/or smokeless tobacco) on a daily or non-daily basis. Tobacco products exclude e-cigarettes (which do not contain tobacco), e-cigars, e-hookahs, and e-pipes. Data for students aged 13-15 years are from 2016 and taken from the Global Youth Tobacco Survey. Data for people aged 15 and over correspond to 2020.
Source: WHO Global Health Observatory Data Repository (WHO, 2024[1]); Global Youth Tobacco Survey (WHO, 2016[27]).

Table 6.26. Dominican Republic - Summary of MPOWER measures, 2022

M Monitoring	P Smoking bans	O Cessation programmes	W Health warnings	E Advertising bans	R Taxation	WHO Frawework Convention on Tobacco Control		Protocol to eliminate illicit trade in tobacco products	
						Date of signature	Date of ratification	Date of signature	Date of ratification

... Not categorized/ No data; No policy or weak measure; Minimal measure; Moderate measure; Complete measure

Source: WHO report on the global tobacco epidemic (WHO, 2023[3]).

Figure 6.50. Dominican Republic - Taxes and prices of the most sold brand of cigarettes

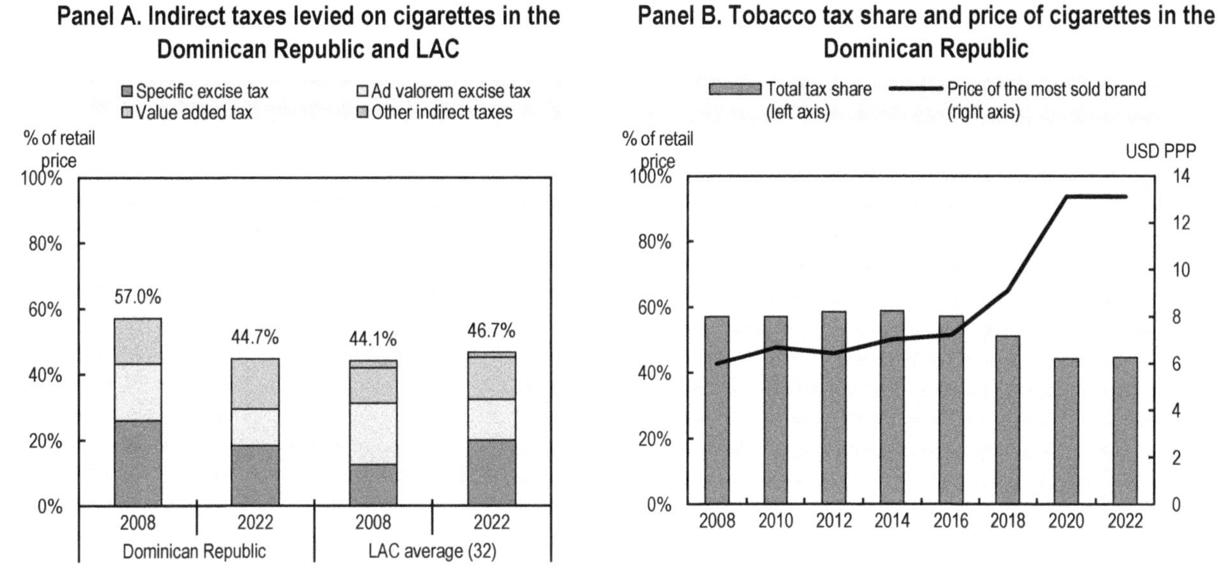

Note: Prices correspond to a 20-cigarette pack of the most sold brand. The most sold brand of cigarettes is determined based on national market share information and can vary over time (i.e. the most sold brand of cigarettes in year 1 can be different from year 2). Retail prices in USD PPP are based on the implied purchasing power parity (PPP) conversion rate from the International Monetary Fund (IMF) World Economic Outlook Database (October 2023).

Source: WHO report on the global tobacco epidemic (WHO, 2023[3]); IMF World Economic Outlook Database (IMF, 2023[4]).

Figure 6.51. Dominican Republic - Trends in retail prices of cigarettes by brand category

In USD PPP per pack of 20 cigarettes, 2008-2022

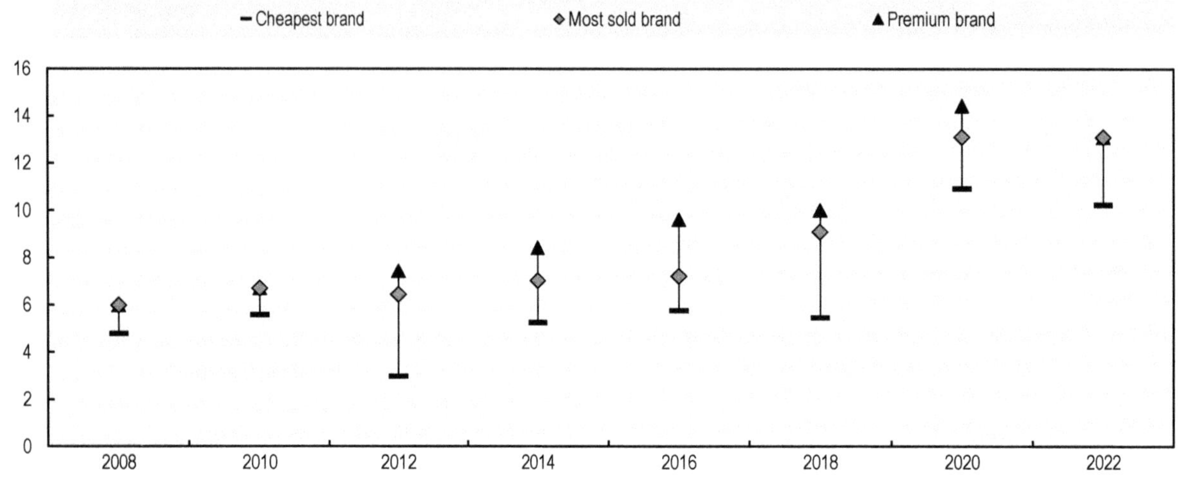

Note: Prices correspond to a 20-cigarette pack of the cheapest, most sold and premium brands. The cheapest, most sold and premium brands of cigarettes are determined based on national market share information and can vary over time (i.e. the cheapest/most sold/premium brands of cigarettes in year 1 can be different from year 2). Retail prices in USD PPP are based on the implied PPP conversion rate from the IMF World Economic Outlook Database (October 2023).
Source: WHO reports on the global tobacco epidemic (WHO, 2009[5]; WHO, 2011[6]; WHO, 2013[7]; WHO, 2015[8]; WHO, 2017[9]; WHO, 2019[10]; WHO, 2021[11]); IMF World Economic Outlook Database (IMF, 2023[4]).

Figure 6.52. Dominican Republic - Affordability of cigarettes

Percentage of GDP per capita required to purchase 100 packs of 20 cigarettes

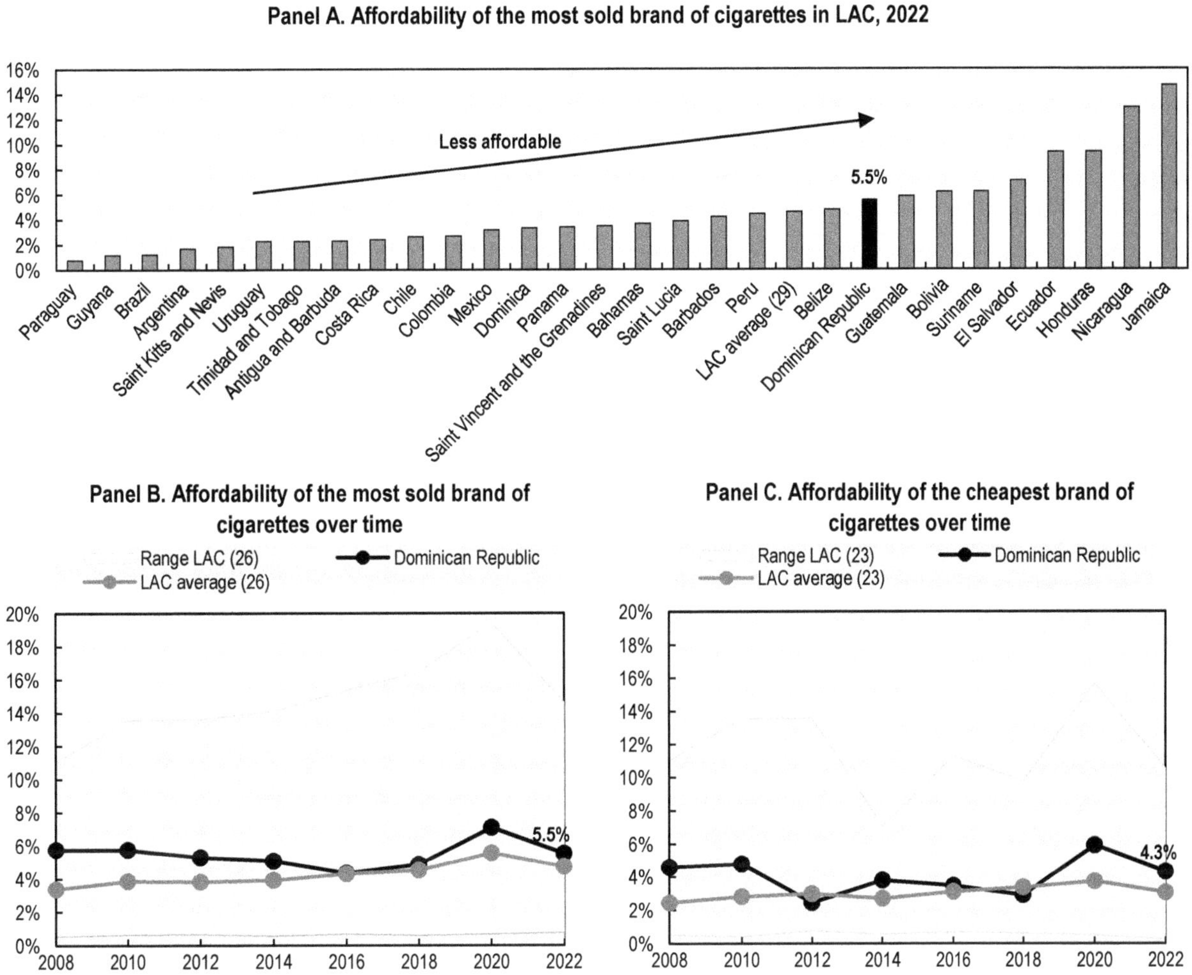

Note: The affordability indicator measures the percentage of the country's GDP per capita required to purchase 100 packs of 20 cigarettes. A higher percentage means lower affordability of cigarettes while a lower percentage means higher affordability. To ensure comparability of average affordability across LAC over time, countries where information was unavailable for certain years have been excluded from the calculation. Data for Panel C are OECD calculations based on WHO reports on the global tobacco epidemic (2009-2023 editions). The cheapest and most sold brands of cigarettes are determined based on national market share information and can vary over time (i.e. the cheapest/most sold brand of cigarettes in year 1 can be different from year 2).

Source: WHO reports on the global tobacco epidemic (WHO, 2009[5]; WHO, 2011[6]; WHO, 2013[7]; WHO, 2015[8]; WHO, 2017[9]; WHO, 2019[10]; WHO, 2021[11]).

Table 6.27. Dominican Republic - Design of tobacco excise taxes across tobacco products, 2022

	Excise tax structure	Specific excise tax				Ad valorem excise tax			Excise tax floor			
		Yes / No	Tax base	Rate per 20-unit pack USD PPP (local currency)	Indexation mechanisms	Yes / No	Tax base	Statutory rate	Yes / No	Tax base	Rate per 20-unit pack USD PPP (local currency)	Indexation mechanisms
Cigarettes	Mixed	Yes	Individual pack	2.4 (59.3)	CPI	Yes	SRP excl. VAT	20%	No			
Cigars	No excise											
Cigarillos	No excise											
Roll-Your-Own (RYO) tobacco	Ad valorem only	No				Yes	SRP excl. VAT	20%	No			
Heated tobacco products (HTPs)	No excise											
ENDS and ENNDS	No excise											

Note: "SRP" means "Suggested retail price by the manufacturer/importer"; blank cells mean that there is no excise tax for the corresponding tobacco product; "VAT" means "Value added tax". Following the WHO report on the global tobacco epidemic (WHO, 2021[11]), new tobacco and nicotine products in this report include electronic nicotine delivery systems (ENDS), electronic non-nicotine delivery systems (ENNDS), and heated tobacco products (HTP). The specific tax levied on cigarettes corresponds to the rate in force at the 4th quarter of 2022. It is converted into USD PPP with the implied PPP conversion rate available in the IMF World Economic Outlook Database (October 2023). Specific excise taxes have been standardized to a 20-unit pack to allow the comparison across countries with different tax bases.
Source: Ley No. 253-12 y sus reformas (2012); IMF World Economic Outlook Database (IMF, 2023[4]).

Table 6.28. Dominican Republic - Tobacco tax reforms since 2000

Year of adoption	Specific excise taxes	Ad valorem excise taxes	Other
2000	No	Cigarettes and RYO tobacco: introduction of an ad valorem tax levied at a uniform tax rate of 50% on the ex-factory price (CIF). Cigars and cigarillos: introduction of an ad valorem tax levied at a uniform tax rate of 25% on ex-factory price (CIF).	No
2004	Cigarettes: introduction of a specific excise tax of DOP 9.6 levied on each pack of 20 cigarettes or its equivalent if the number of cigarettes per pack is different. The specific tax is annually adjusted based on changes in the CPI.	Cigars and cigarillos: increase in the tax rate to 32.5% levied on the ex-factory price (CIF). RYO tobacco: increase in the tax rate to 65% levied on the ex-factory price (CIF).	No
2004	Cigarettes: increase in the specific tax to DOP 13.44 levied on each pack of 20 cigarettes or its equivalent if the number of cigarettes per pack is different. The indexation of the specific tax on the CPI is changed from annually to quarterly.	Cigars and cigarillos: the ad valorem excise tax is abolished. RYO tobacco: increase in the tax rate to 130% levied on the ex-factory price (CIF).	
2005	Cigarettes: increase in the specific tax to DOP 16.25 levied on each pack of 20 cigarettes or its equivalent if the number of cigarettes per pack is different. The specific tax is quarterly adjusted based on changes in the CPI.	No	No

Year of adoption	Specific excise taxes	Ad valorem excise taxes	Other
2006	Cigarettes: increase in the specific tax to DOP 16.82 levied on each pack of 20 cigarettes or its equivalent if the number of cigarettes per pack is different. The indexation of the specific tax on the CPI is changed from quarterly to annually.	Cigarettes: introduction of an ad valorem component levied at a rate of 100% on the retail price suggested by the manufacturer/ importer (excl. VAT). RYO tobacco: increase in the tax rate to 100% of the retail price suggested by the manufacturer/ importer (excl. VAT).	No
2007	Cigarettes: increase in the specific tax to DOP 26.0 levied on each pack of 20 cigarettes or its equivalent if the number of cigarettes per pack is different. The specific tax is annually adjusted based on changes in the CPI.	Cigarettes and RYO tobacco: reduction in the tax rate to 20% of the retail price suggested by the manufacturer/ importer (excl. VAT).	No
2012	Cigarettes: increase in the specific tax in three steps according to a projected CPI of 5%: to DOP 40 in 2013; to DOP 45 in 2014 and to DOP 50 in 2015. The specific tax is levied on each pack of 20 cigarettes or its equivalent if the number of cigarettes per pack is different. From 2017, the specific tax is quarterly adjusted based on changes in the CPI.	No	No

Note: "Tobacco tax reform" refers to changes in the tobacco excise tax rates, the introduction of indexation mechanisms or minimum taxes, as well as adjustments to the tax base. These reforms typically entail the enactment of new laws or decrees. The table does not refer to recurrent tax changes that result from the indexation for inflation of tax brackets and price floors (if implemented). Tobacco tax reforms included reflect changes in the legislation, but not whether or when the reforms have been implemented.
Source: Ley No. 147-00; Ley No. 3-04; Ley No. 288-04; Ley No. 557-05; Ley No. 495-06; Ley No. 175-07; Ley No. 253-12.

Figure 6.53. Dominican Republic - Tobacco excise tax revenue

Percentage of GDP, latest year available

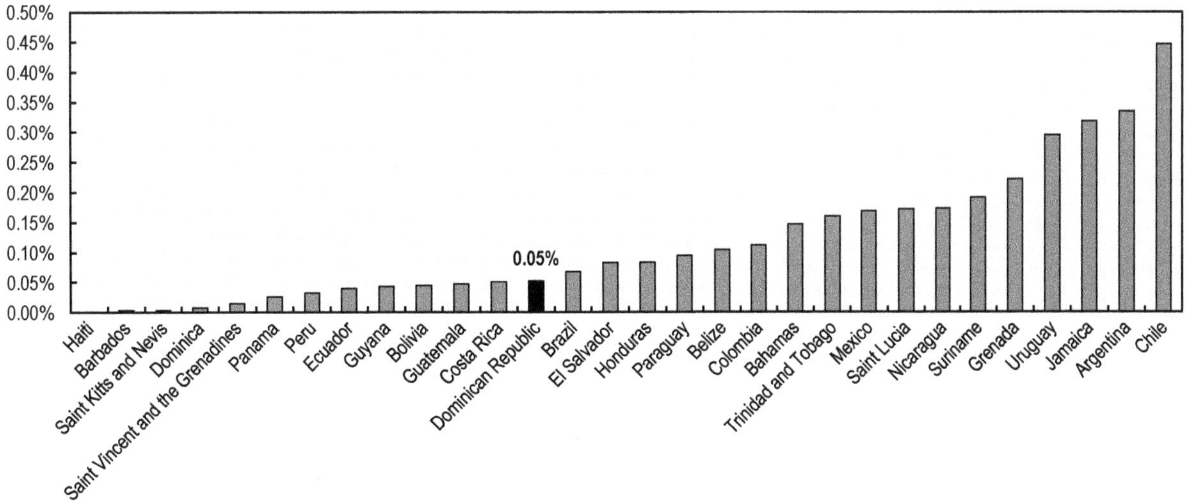

Note: See Box 2.1 (Chapter 2) for more information on tobacco tax revenue (source of information and calculations) and country selection. The latest year available is 2022 for Argentina, Brazil, Chile, Colombia, Costa Rica, the Dominican Republic, El Salvador, Guatemala, Guyana, Honduras, Mexico, Nicaragua, Panama, Paraguay, Peru, Saint Kitts and Nevis, Suriname, and Uruguay; 2021 for Belize, Dominica, Ecuador, Grenada, Saint Lucia, Saint Vincent and the Grenadines; 2020 for Bahamas, Bolivia, Jamaica and Trinidad and Tobago; 2015 for Haiti; 2014 for Barbados.
Source: OECD Revenue Statistics (OECD, 2024[13]); WHO report on the global tobacco epidemic (WHO, 2023[3]); National data.

Figure 6.54. Dominican Republic - Trends in tobacco excise tax revenue

Percentage of GDP, 2000-2022

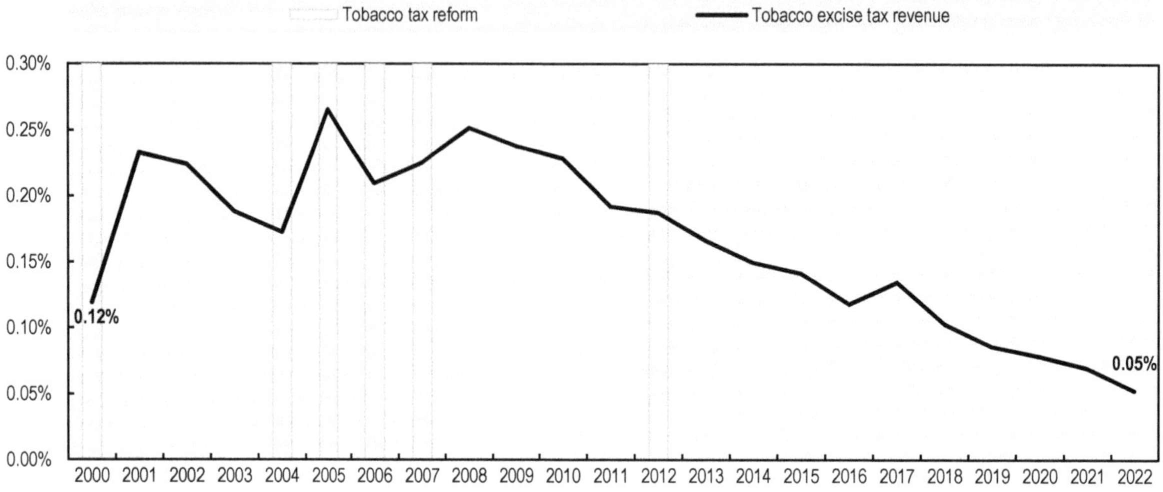

Note: "Tobacco tax reform" refers to the measures included in Table 6.28.
Source: OECD Revenue Statistics (OECD, 2024[13]); Ley No. 147-00; Ley No. 3-04; Ley No. 288-04; Ley No. 557-05; Ley No. 495-06; Ley No. 175-07; Ley No. 253-12.

Figure 6.55. Dominican Republic - Average excise tax revenue collected per pack of 20 cigarettes sold

Tobacco excise tax revenue in USD PPP collected per pack of legal cigarettes sold, latest year available

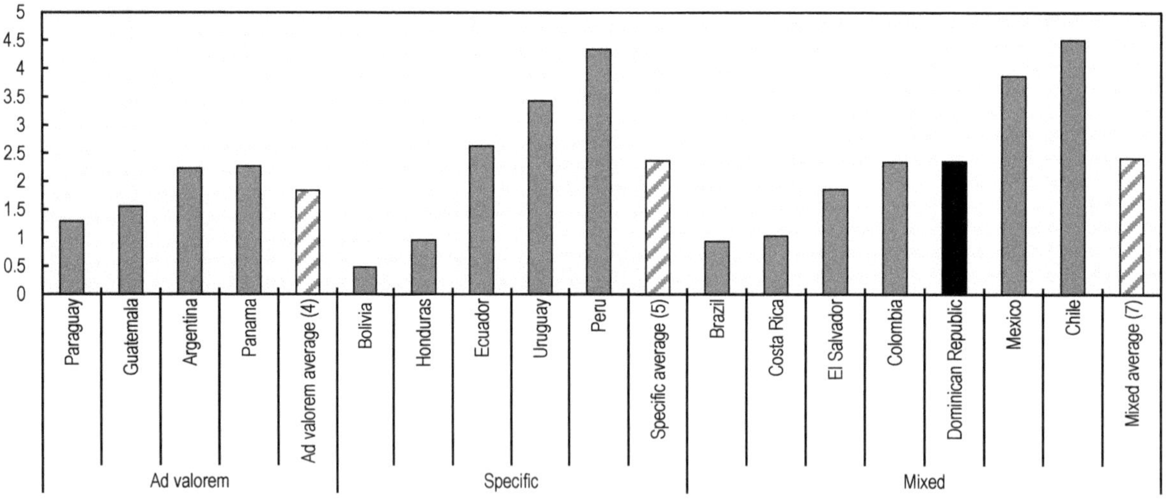

Note: See Box 2.1 (Chapter 2) for more information on tobacco tax revenue (source of information and calculations). The latest year available is 2022 for Argentina, Brazil, Chile, Colombia, Costa Rica, the Dominican Republic, El Salvador, Guatemala, Honduras, Mexico, Panama, Paraguay, Peru and Uruguay; 2021 for Ecuador;2020 for Bolivia. The country selection is provided by the availability of data on sales of cigarettes in Euromonitor International Tobacco Industry edition, 2023 © All rights reserved (Euromonitor International, 2023[14]).
Source: OECD Revenue Statistics (OECD, 2024[13]); WHO report on the global tobacco epidemic (WHO, 2023[3]) National data; IMF World Economic Outlook Database (IMF, 2023[4]); and OECD calculations based on Euromonitor International's Tobacco Industry edition (Euromonitor International, 2023[14]).

Figure 6.56. Dominican Republic - Change in tobacco tax policy indicators

Percentage change from base year, 2008-2022

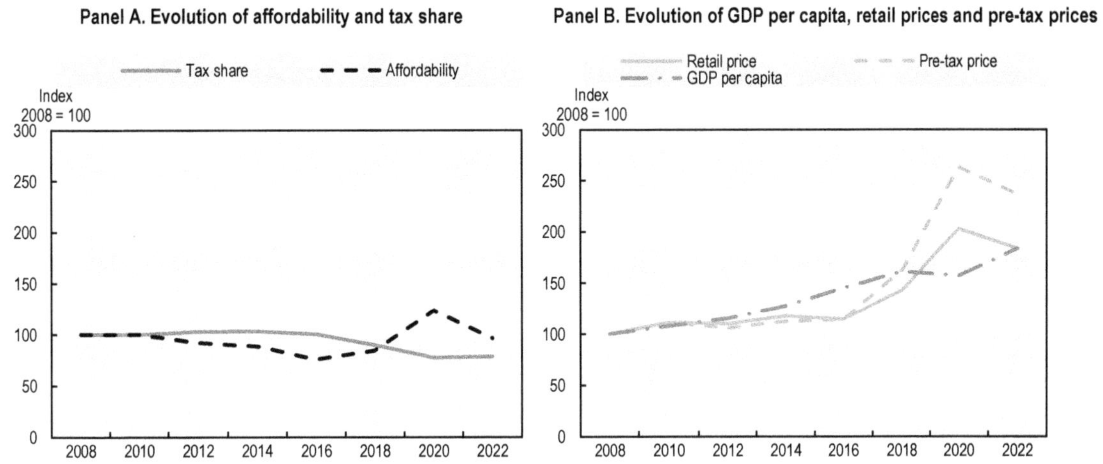

Note: Both Panel A and Panel B figures are based on data for the most sold brand of cigarettes. The most sold brand of cigarettes is determined based on national market share information and can vary over time (i.e. the most sold brand of cigarettes in year 1 can be different from year 2). In Panel A, an increase in the affordability indicator means that cigarettes are becoming less affordable, while a decline in the affordability indicator means that cigarettes are becoming more affordable. In Panel B, "Pre-tax price" corresponds to the retail price of the most sold brand of cigarettes minus the indirect taxes levied on this brand, namely excise taxes, VAT, import duties and other. Indicators in Panel B have been computed using national currency and have been adjusted for inflation; therefore, present inflation-adjusted trends.
Source: WHO report on the global tobacco epidemic (WHO, 2023[3]); World Bank Open Data (World Bank, 2024[15]); IMF International Financial Statistics (IMF, 2024[19]).

References

Euromonitor International (2023), *Euromonitor International's Tobacco Industry edition*, https://www.euromonitor.com/tobacco (accessed on 1 August 2023). [14]

IMF (2023), *World Economic Outlook Database*, International Monetary Fund, https://www.imf.org/en/Publications/WEO/weo-database/2023/October (accessed on 13 January 2024). [4]

IMF (2024), *International Financial Statistics (IFS)*, International Monetary Fund, https://data.imf.org/?sk=4c514d48-b6ba-49ed-8ab9-52b0c1a0179b&sId=1390030341854 (accessed on 13 January 2024). [19]

OECD (2024), *Global Revenue Statistics Database*, Organisation for Economic Co-operation and Development, https://www.oecd.org/tax/tax-policy/global-revenue-statistics-database.htm (accessed on 13 August 2023). [13]

WHO (2024), *Global Health Observatory: Age-standardized estimates of current tobacco use, tobacco smoking and cigarette smoking (Tobacco control: Monitor)*, World Health Organization, https://www.who.int/data/gho/data/indicators/indicator-details/GHO/gho-tobacco-control-monitor-current-tobaccouse-tobaccosmoking-cigarrettesmoking-agestd-tobagestdcurr (accessed on 20 February 2024). [1]

WHO (2023), *WHO report on the global tobacco epidemic 2023: protect people from tobacco smoke*, World Health Organization, https://www.who.int/publications/i/item/9789240077164. [3]

WHO (2021), *WHO report on the global tobacco epidemic 2021: Addressing new and emerging products*, World Health Organization, https://www.who.int/publications/i/item/9789240032095. [11]

WHO (2019), *WHO report on the global tobacco epidemic 2019: Offer help to quit tobacco use*, World Health Organization, https://www.who.int/publications/i/item/9789241516204. [10]

WHO (2017), *WHO report on the global tobacco epidemic 2017: Monitoring tobacco use and prevention policies*, World Health Organization, https://www.who.int/publications/i/item/9789241512824. [9]

WHO (2016), *Global school-based student health survey. Dominican Republic 2016 Fact Sheet*, World Health Organization, https://cdn.who.int/media/docs/default-source/ncds/ncd-surveillance/data-reporting/dominican-republic/gshs/dominican-republic-2016-gshs-fs.pdf?sfvrsn=44ba7479_2&download=true. [27]

WHO (2015), *WHO report on the global tobacco epidemic 2015: Raising taxes on tobacco*, World Health Organization, https://www.who.int/publications/i/item/9789241509121. [8]

WHO (2013), *WHO report on the global tobacco epidemic 2013: Enforcing bans on tobacco advertising, promotion and sponsorship*, World Health Organization, https://www.who.int/publications/i/item/9789241505871. [7]

WHO (2011), *WHO report on the global tobacco epidemic 2011: Warning about the dangers of tobacco*, World Health Organization, https://www.who.int/publications/i/item/9789244564264. [6]

WHO (2009), *WHO report on the global tobacco epidemic 2009: Implementing smoke-free environments*, World Health Organization, https://www.who.int/publications/i/item/9789241563918. [5]

World Bank (2024), *World Bank Open Data*, World Bank, https://data.worldbank.org/ (accessed on 13 January 2024). [15]

Ecuador

Figure 6.57. Ecuador - Trends in tobacco use prevalence

Percentage of the population aged 15 years and over who currently use any tobacco product (smoked and/or smokeless tobacco) on a daily or non-daily basis, 2000-2020

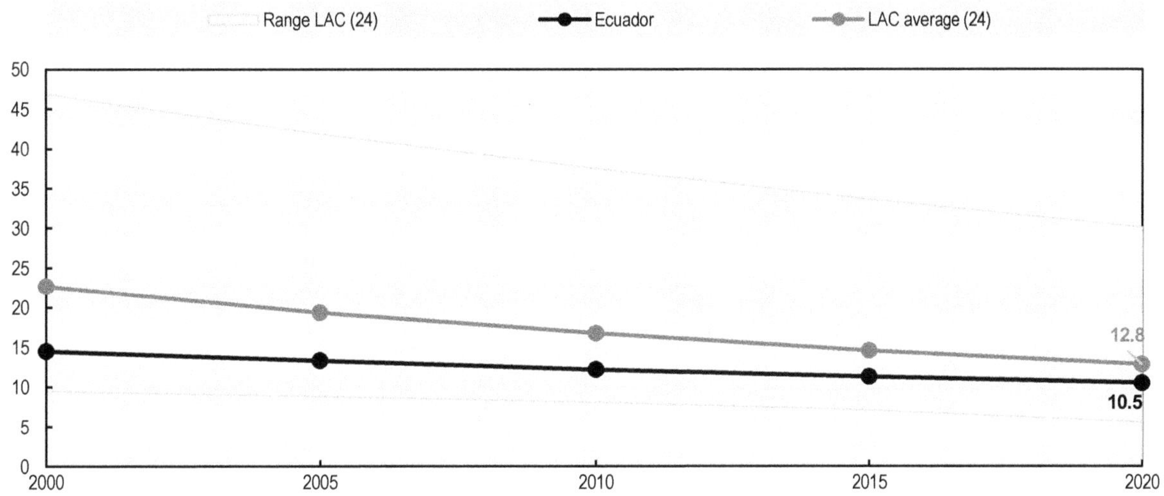

Note: Tobacco products include cigarettes, pipes, cigars, cigarillos, waterpipes (hookah, shisha), bidis, kretek, heated tobacco products (HTP), and all forms of smokeless (oral and nasal) tobacco. Tobacco products exclude e-cigarettes (which do not contain tobacco), e-cigars, e-hookahs, and e-pipes. The rates are age-standardized to the World Health Organisation (WHO) standard population. The LAC average was calculated as the average of Argentina, Bahamas, Barbados, Belize, Bolivia, Brazil, Chile, Colombia, Costa Rica, Cuba, the Dominican Republic, Ecuador, El Salvador, Guatemala, Guyana, Haiti, Honduras, Jamaica, Mexico, Panama, Paraguay, Peru, Saint Lucia, and Uruguay.
Source: WHO Global Health Observatory Data Repository (WHO, 2024[1]).

Table 6.29. Ecuador - Tobacco use prevalence by sex and age groups

Percentage of the population group, latest year available

	Tobacco use prevalence (all tobacco products)	Cigarette smoking prevalence (cigarettes only)
Youths aged 13-15 years		
Total	**13.0**	**8.9**
Males	15.3	7.0
Females	10.7	8.0
People aged 15 and over		
Total	**10.5**	**9.0**
Males	18.1	15.7
Females	2.8	2.4

Note: Tobacco use prevalence is defined as the percentage of the population group who currently use any tobacco product (smoked and/or smokeless tobacco) on a daily or non-daily basis. Tobacco products exclude e-cigarettes (which do not contain tobacco), e-cigars, e-hookahs, and e-pipes. Data for students aged 13-15 years are from 2016 and taken from the Global Youth Tobacco Survey. Data for people aged 15 and over correspond to 2020.
Source: WHO Global Health Observatory Data Repository (WHO, 2024[1]); Global Youth Tobacco Survey (WHO, 2016[28]).

Table 6.30. Ecuador - Summary of MPOWER measures, 2022

M Monitoring	P Smoking bans	O Cessation programmes	W Health warnings	E Advertising bans	R Taxation	WHO Frawework Convention on Tobacco Control		Protocol to eliminate illicit trade in tobacco products	
						Date of signature	Date of ratification	Date of signature	Date of ratification
						22-03-2004	25-07-2006	25-09-2013	15-10-2015

... Not categorized/ No data; No policy or weak measure; Minimal measure; Moderate measure; Complete measure

Source: WHO report on the global tobacco epidemic (WHO, 2023[3]).

Figure 6.58. Ecuador - Taxes and prices of the most sold brand of cigarettes

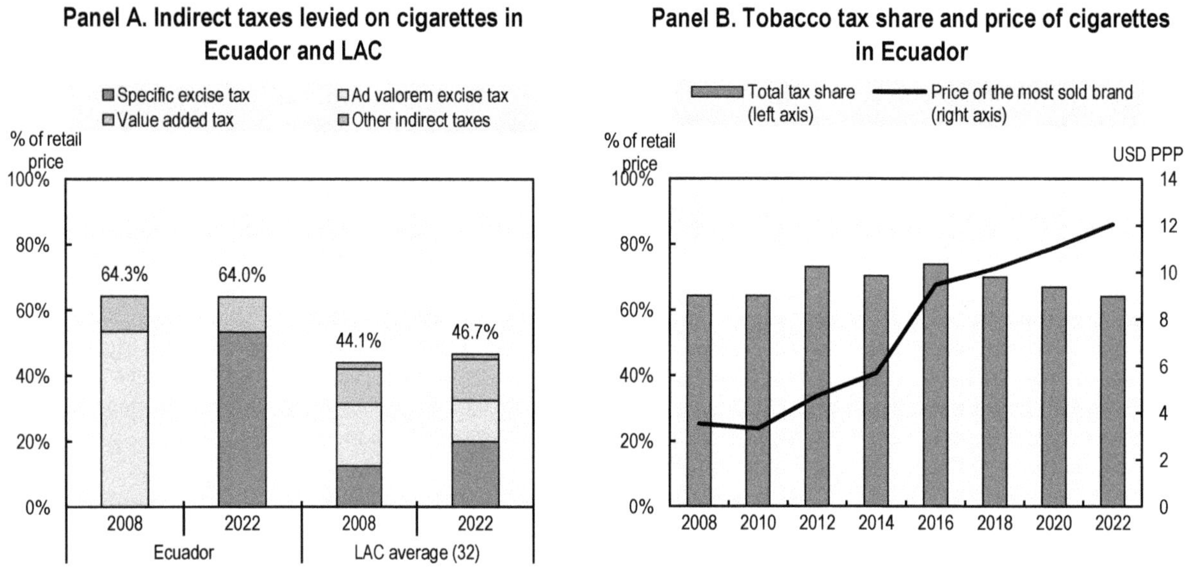

Note: Prices correspond to a 20-cigarette pack of the most sold brand. The most sold brand of cigarettes is determined based on national market share information and can vary over time (i.e. the most sold brand of cigarettes in year 1 can be different from year 2). Retail prices in USD PPP are based on the implied purchasing power parity (PPP) conversion rate from the International Monetary Fund (IMF) World Economic Outlook Database (October 2023).
Source: WHO report on the global tobacco epidemic (WHO, 2023[3]); IMF World Economic Outlook Database (IMF, 2023[4]).

Figure 6.59. Ecuador - Trends in retail prices of cigarettes by brand category

In USD PPP per pack of 20 cigarettes, 2008-2022

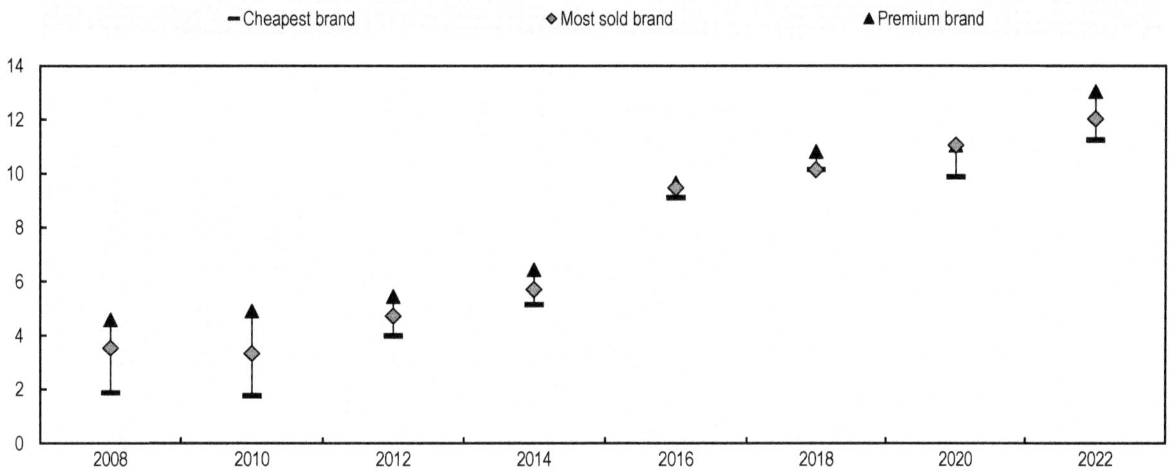

Note: Prices correspond to a 20-cigarette pack of the cheapest, most sold and premium brands. The cheapest, most sold and premium brands of cigarettes are determined based on national market share information and can vary over time (i.e. the cheapest/most sold/premium brands of cigarettes in year 1 can be different from year 2). Retail prices in USD PPP are based on the implied PPP conversion rate from the IMF World Economic Outlook Database (October 2023).
Source: WHO reports on the global tobacco epidemic (WHO, 2009[5]; WHO, 2011[6]; WHO, 2013[7]; WHO, 2015[8]; WHO, 2017[9]; WHO, 2019[10]; WHO, 2021[11]); IMF World Economic Outlook Database (IMF, 2023[4]).

Figure 6.60. Ecuador - Affordability of cigarettes

Percentage of GDP per capita required to purchase 100 packs of 20 cigarettes

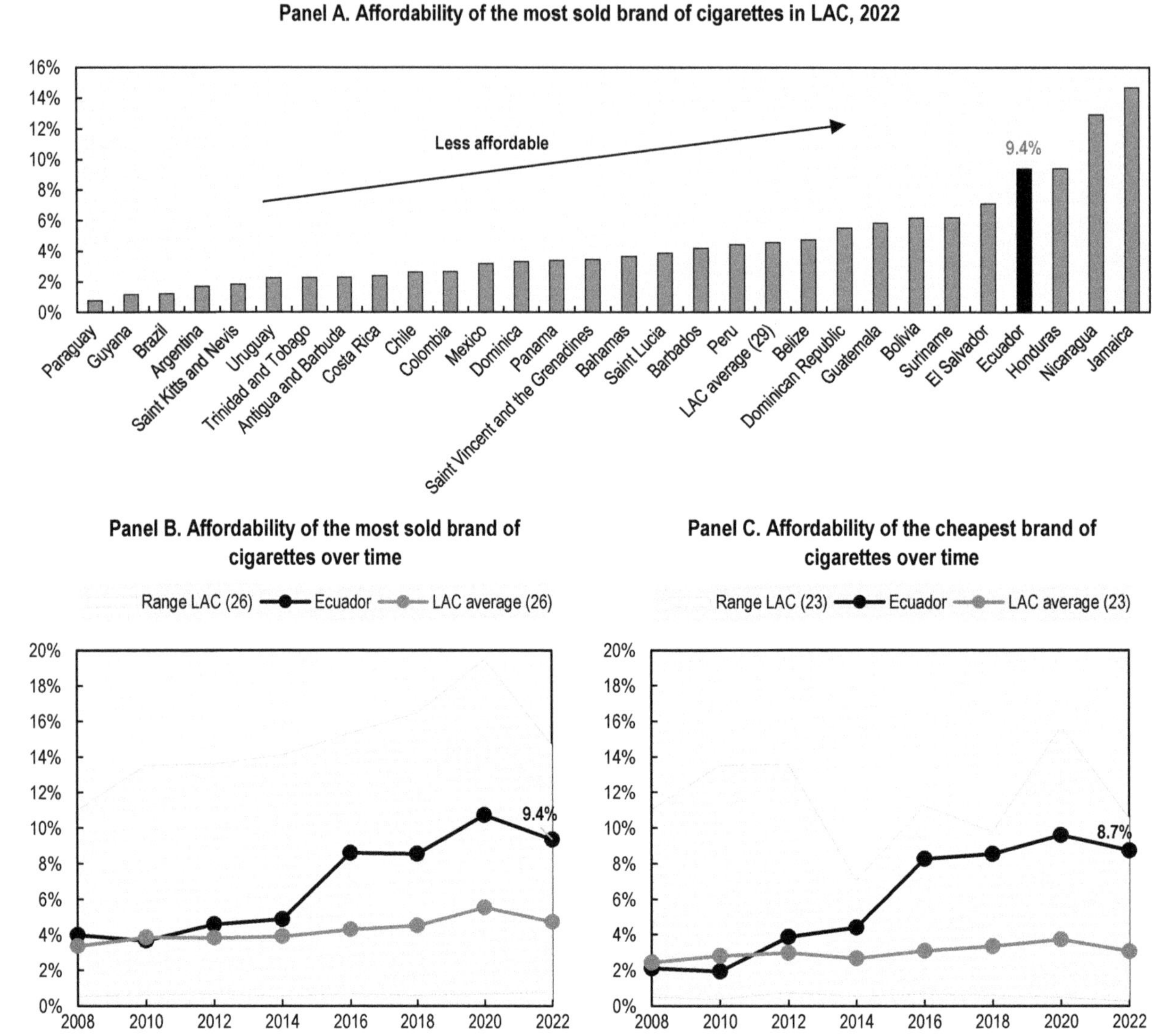

Note: The affordability indicator measures the percentage of the country's GDP per capita required to purchase 100 packs of 20 cigarettes. A higher percentage means lower affordability of cigarettes while a lower percentage means higher affordability. To ensure comparability of average affordability across LAC over time, countries where information was unavailable for certain years have been excluded from the calculation. Data for Panel C are OECD calculations based on WHO reports on the global tobacco epidemic (2009-2023 editions). The cheapest and most sold brands of cigarettes are determined based on national market share information and can vary over time (i.e. the cheapest/most sold brand of cigarettes in year 1 can be different from year 2).

Source: WHO reports on the global tobacco epidemic (WHO, 2009[5]; WHO, 2011[6]; WHO, 2013[7]; WHO, 2015[8]; WHO, 2017[9]; WHO, 2019[10]; WHO, 2021[11]).

Table 6.31. Ecuador - Design of tobacco excise taxes across tobacco products, 2022

	Excise tax structure	Specific excise tax				Ad valorem excise tax			Excise tax floor			
		Yes / No	Tax base	Rate per 20-unit pack USD PPP (local currency)	Indexation mechanisms	Yes / No	Tax base	Statutory rate	Yes / No	Tax base	Rate per 20-unit pack USD PPP (local currency)	Indexation mechanisms
Cigarettes	Specific only	Yes	Single stick	6.4 (3.2)	CPI	No			No			
Cigars	Ad valorem only	No				Yes	SRP excl. VAT	150%	No			
Cigarillos	Ad valorem only	No				Yes	SRP excl. VAT	150%	No			
Roll-Your-Own (RYO) tobacco	Ad valorem only	No				Yes	SRP excl. VAT	150%	No			
Heated tobacco products (HTPs)	Ad valorem only	No				Yes	SRP excl. VAT	150%	No			
ENDS and ENNDS	Ad valorem only	No				Yes	SRP excl. VAT	150%	No			

Note: "SRP" means "Suggested retail price by the manufacturer/importer"; blank cells mean that there is no excise tax for the corresponding tobacco product; "VAT" means "Value added tax"; "CPI" means consumer price index. Following the WHO report on the global tobacco epidemic (WHO, 2021[11]), new tobacco and nicotine products in this report include electronic nicotine delivery systems (ENDS), electronic non-nicotine delivery systems (ENNDS), and heated tobacco products (HTP). The excise tax levied on e-cigarettes in Ecuador applies only to those containing nicotine (i.e., ENDS). Specific taxes are converted into USD PPP with the implied PPP conversion rate available in the IMF World Economic Outlook Database (October 2023). Specific excise taxes have been standardized to a 20-unit pack to allow the comparison across countries with different tax bases.

Source: Ley Orgánica de Simplificación y Progresividad Tributaria (2019); IMF World Economic Outlook Database (IMF, 2023[4]).

Table 6.32. Ecuador - Tobacco tax reforms since 2000

Year of adoption	Specific excise taxes	Ad valorem excise taxes	Other
2004	No	Cigarettes: increase in the tiered rates to 18.64% for cigarettes containing brown tobacco and to 77.25% for cigarettes containing blond tobacco. The ad valorem excise tax is levied on the retail price suggested by the manufacturer/ importer (excl. VAT).	Cigarettes: earmarking of the excise tax revenue to the Social Security Fund (IESS).
2006	No	Cigarettes: increase in the tiered rates to 98% for cigarettes containing blond tobacco.	No
2007	No	Cigarettes, cigars, cigarillos, RYO tobacco: introduction of an ad valorem tax levied at a uniform tax rate of 150%. The tax base calculation is changed, but remains based upon the retail price suggested by the manufacturer/ importer, excluding VAT.	No
2011	Cigarettes: introduction of a specific excise tax of USD 0.08 levied per stick. The specific tax is adjusted semi-annually in accordance with changes in the CPI.	Cigarettes: the ad valorem excise tax is abolished.	No

Year of adoption	Specific excise taxes	Ad valorem excise taxes	Other
2016	Cigarettes: the specific tax is increased to USD 0.16 per stick and is annually adjusted based on changes in the CPI.	No	No
2019	No	ENDS: introduction of an ad valorem excise tax levied at a rate of 150% on the retail price suggested by the manufacturer/ importer, excluding VAT.	No

Note: "Tobacco tax reform" refers to changes in the tobacco excise tax rates, the introduction of indexation mechanisms or minimum taxes, as well as adjustments to the tax base. These reforms typically entail the enactment of new laws or decrees. The table does not refer to recurrent tax changes that result from the indexation for inflation of tax brackets and price floors (if implemented). Tobacco tax reforms included reflect changes in the legislation, but not whether or when the reforms have been implemented.
Source: Ley de Régimen Tributario Interno, Art. 82 (2004); Ley de Régimen Tributario Interno (2006); Registro Oficial Suplemento 242 (2007); Registro Oficial Suplemento 583 (2011); Ley Orgánica para el Equilibrio de las Finanzas Públicas (2016); Ley Orgánica de Simplificación y Progresividad Tributaria (2019).

Figure 6.61. Ecuador - Tobacco excise tax revenue

Percentage of GDP, latest year available

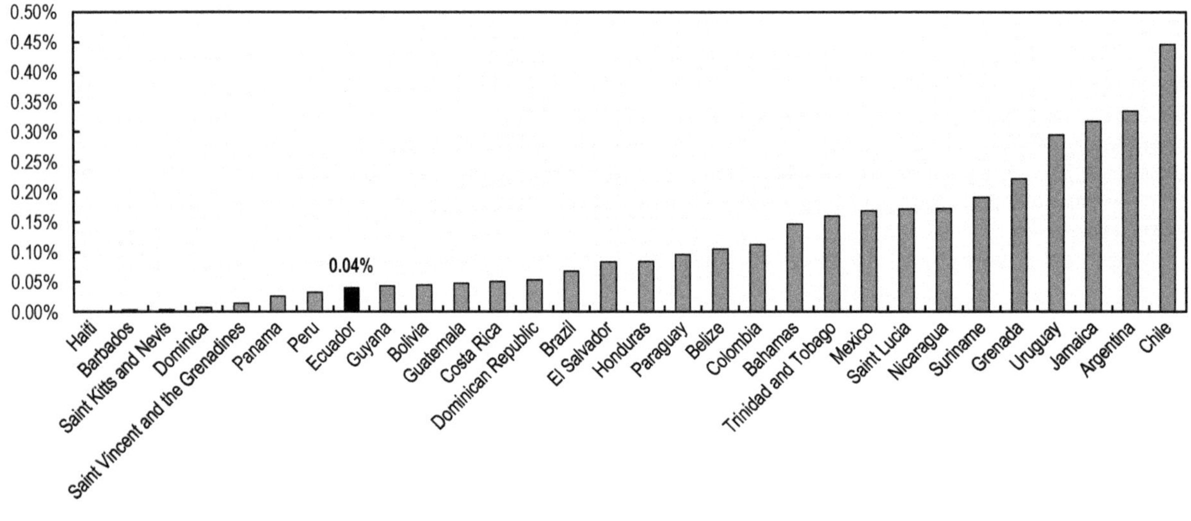

Note: See Box 2.1 (Chapter 2) for more information on tobacco tax revenue (source of information and calculations) and country selection. The latest year available is 2022 for Argentina, Brazil, Chile, Colombia, Costa Rica, the Dominican Republic, El Salvador, Guatemala, Guyana, Honduras, Mexico, Nicaragua, Panama, Paraguay, Peru, Saint Kitts and Nevis, Suriname, and Uruguay; 2021 for Belize, Dominica, Ecuador, Grenada, Saint Lucia, Saint Vincent and the Grenadines; 2020 for Bahamas, Bolivia, Jamaica and Trinidad and Tobago; 2015 for Haiti; 2014 for Barbados.
Source: OECD Revenue Statistics (OECD, 2024[13]); WHO report on the global tobacco epidemic (WHO, 2023[3]); National data.

Figure 6.62. Ecuador - Tobacco excise tax revenue

Percentage of GDP, 2000-2021

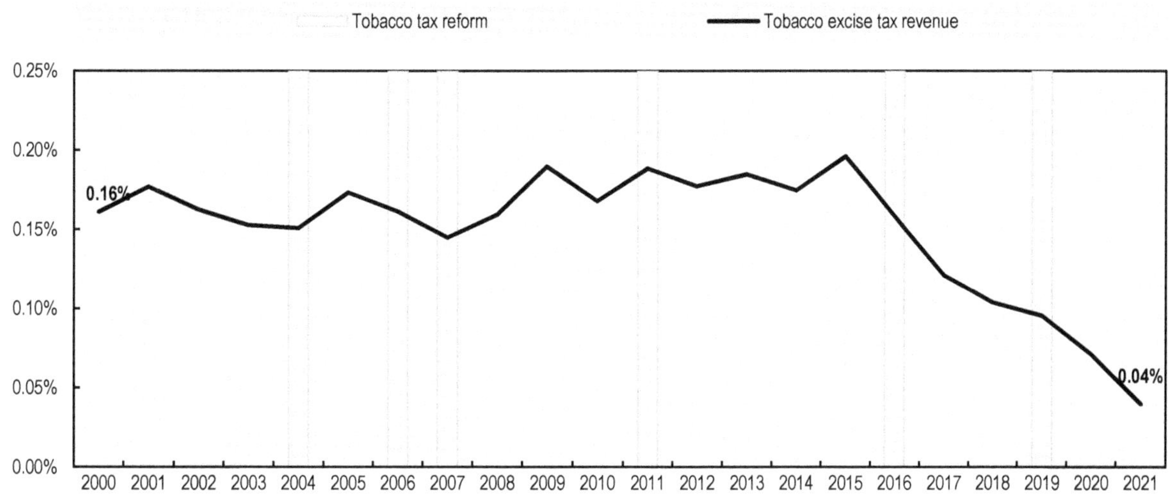

Note: "Tobacco tax reform" refers to the measures included in Table 6.32.
Source: OECD Revenue Statistics (OECD, 2024[13]); Ley de Régimen Tributario Interno, Art. 82 (2004); Ley de Régimen Tributario Interno (2006); Registro Oficial Suplemento 242 (2007); Registro Oficial Suplemento 583 (2011); Ley Orgánica para el Equilibrio de las Finanzas Públicas (2016); Ley Orgánica de Simplificación y Progresividad Tributaria (2019).

Figure 6.63. Ecuador - Average excise tax revenue collected per pack of 20 cigarettes sold

Tobacco excise tax revenue in USD PPP collected per pack of legal cigarettes sold, latest year available

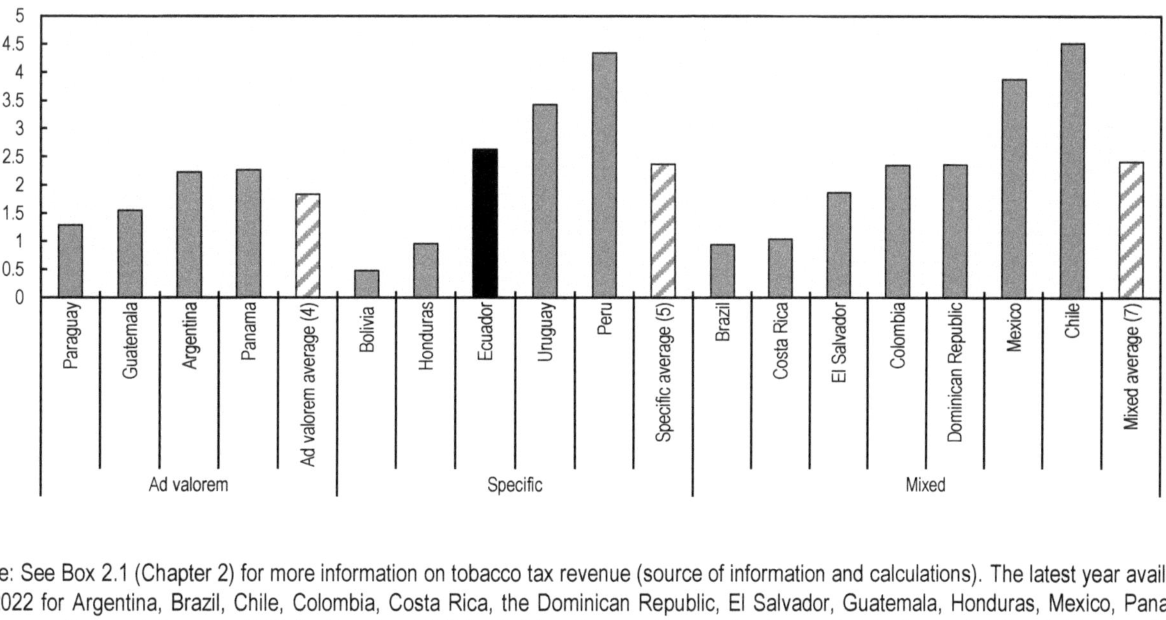

Note: See Box 2.1 (Chapter 2) for more information on tobacco tax revenue (source of information and calculations). The latest year available is 2022 for Argentina, Brazil, Chile, Colombia, Costa Rica, the Dominican Republic, El Salvador, Guatemala, Honduras, Mexico, Panama, Paraguay, Peru and Uruguay; 2021 for Ecuador; 2020 for Bolivia. The country selection is provided by the availability of data on sales of cigarettes in Euromonitor International Tobacco Industry edition, 2023 © All rights reserved (Euromonitor International, 2023[14]).
Source: OECD Revenue Statistics (OECD, 2024[13]); WHO report on the global tobacco epidemic (WHO, 2023[3]); National data; IMF World Economic Outlook Database (IMF, 2023[4]); and OECD calculations based on Euromonitor International's Tobacco Industry edition (Euromonitor International, 2023[14]).

Figure 6.64. Ecuador - Change in tobacco tax policy indicators

Percentage change from base year, 2008-2022

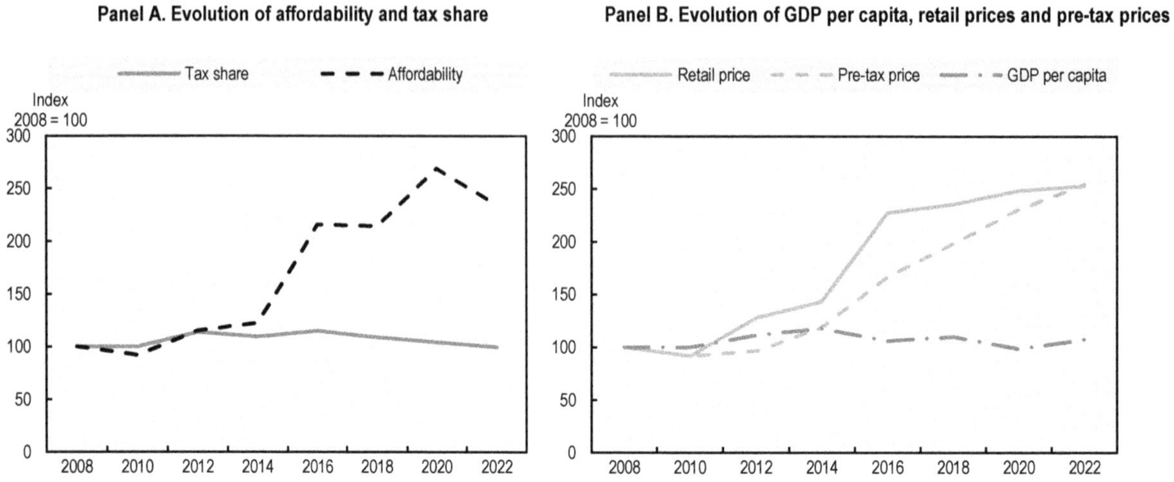

Note: Both Panel A and Panel B figures are based on data for the most sold brand of cigarettes. The most sold brand of cigarettes is determined based on national market share information and can vary over time (i.e. the most sold brand of cigarettes in year 1 can be different from year 2). In Panel A, an increase in the affordability indicator means that cigarettes are becoming less affordable, while a decline in the affordability indicator means that cigarettes are becoming more affordable. In Panel B, "Pre-tax price" corresponds to the retail price of the most sold brand of cigarettes minus the indirect taxes levied on this brand, namely excise taxes, VAT, import duties and other. Indicators in Panel B have been computed using national currency and have been adjusted for inflation; therefore, present inflation-adjusted trends.
Source: WHO report on the global tobacco epidemic (WHO, 2023[3]); World Bank Open Data (World Bank, 2024[15]); IMF International Financial Statistics (IMF, 2024[19]).

References

Euromonitor International (2023), *Euromonitor International's Tobacco Industry edition*, https://www.euromonitor.com/tobacco (accessed on 1 August 2023). [14]

IMF (2023), *World Economic Outlook Database*, International Monetary Fund, https://www.imf.org/en/Publications/WEO/weo-database/2023/October (accessed on 13 January 2024). [4]

IMF (2024), *International Financial Statistics (IFS)*, International Monetary Fund, https://data.imf.org/?sk=4c514d48-b6ba-49ed-8ab9-52b0c1a0179b&sId=1390030341854 (accessed on 13 January 2024). [19]

OECD (2024), *Global Revenue Statistics Database*, Organisation for Economic Co-operation and Development, https://www.oecd.org/tax/tax-policy/global-revenue-statistics-database.htm (accessed on 13 August 2023). [13]

WHO (2024), *Global Health Observatory: Age-standardized estimates of current tobacco use, tobacco smoking and cigarette smoking (Tobacco control: Monitor)*, World Health Organization, https://www.who.int/data/gho/data/indicators/indicator-details/GHO/gho-tobacco-control-monitor-current-tobaccouse-tobaccosmoking-cigarrettesmoking-agestd-tobagestdcurr (accessed on 20 February 2024). [1]

WHO (2023), *WHO report on the global tobacco epidemic 2023: Protect people from tobacco smoke*, World Health Organization, https://www.who.int/publications/i/item/9789240077164. [3]

WHO (2021), *WHO report on the global tobacco epidemic 2021: Addressing new and emerging products*, World Health Organization, https://www.who.int/publications/i/item/9789240032095. [11]

WHO (2019), *WHO report on the global tobacco epidemic 2019: Offer help to quit tobacco use*, World Health Organization, https://www.who.int/publications/i/item/9789241516204. [10]

WHO (2017), *WHO report on the global tobacco epidemic 2017: Monitoring tobacco use and prevention policies*, World Health Organization, https://www.who.int/publications/i/item/9789241512824. [9]

WHO (2016), *Global Youth Tobacco Survey. Ecuador 2016 Fact Sheet*, World Health Organization, https://cdn.who.int/media/docs/default-source/ncds/ncd-surveillance/data-reporting/ecuador/ecuador-gyts-2016-factsheet-(ages-13-15)-final-26april2018_508tagged.pdf?sfvrsn=ac39d9d6_1&download=true. [28]

WHO (2015), *WHO report on the global tobacco epidemic 2015: Raising taxes on tobacco*, World Health Organization, https://www.who.int/publications/i/item/9789241509121. [8]

WHO (2013), *WHO report on the global tobacco epidemic 2013: Enforcing bans on tobacco advertising, promotion and sponsorship*, World Health Organization, https://www.who.int/publications/i/item/9789241505871. [7]

WHO (2011), *WHO report on the global tobacco epidemic 2011: Warning about the dangers of tobacco*, World Health Organization, https://www.who.int/publications/i/item/9789244564264. [6]

WHO (2009), *WHO report on the global tobacco epidemic 2009: Implementing smoke-free environments*, World Health Organization, https://www.who.int/publications/i/item/9789241563918. [5]

World Bank (2024), *World Bank Open Data*, World Bank, https://data.worldbank.org/ (accessed on 13 January 2024). [15]

El Salvador

Figure 6.65. El Salvador - Trends in tobacco use prevalence

Percentage of the population aged 15 years and over who currently use any tobacco product (smoked and/or smokeless tobacco) on a daily or non-daily basis, 2000-2020

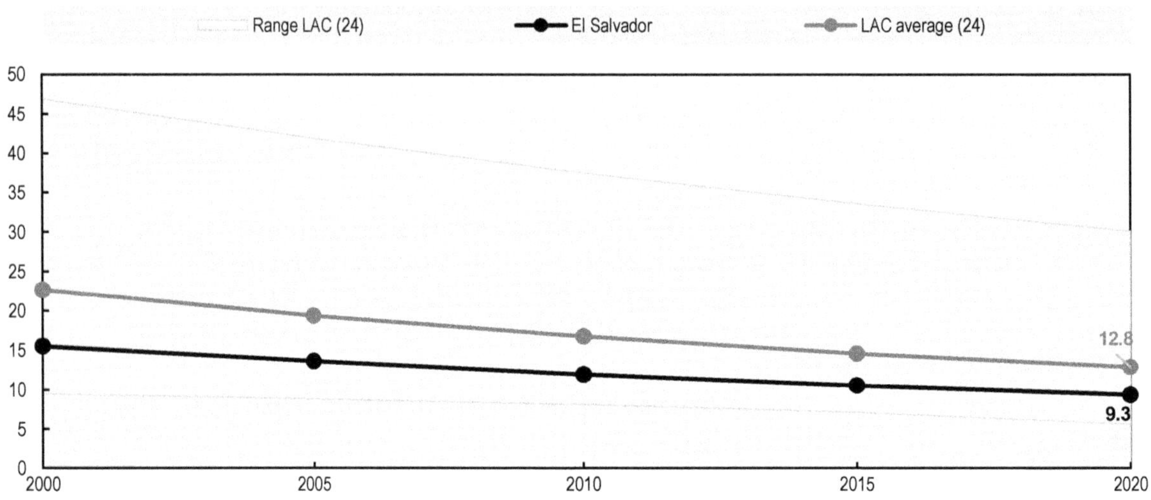

Note: Tobacco products include cigarettes, pipes, cigars, cigarillos, waterpipes (hookah, shisha), bidis, kretek, heated tobacco products (HTP), and all forms of smokeless (oral and nasal) tobacco. Tobacco products exclude e-cigarettes (which do not contain tobacco), e-cigars, e-hookahs, and e-pipes. The rates are age-standardized to the World Health Organisation (WHO) standard population. The LAC average was calculated as the average of Argentina, Bahamas, Barbados, Belize, Bolivia, Brazil, Chile, Colombia, Costa Rica, Cuba, the Dominican Republic, Ecuador, El Salvador, Guatemala, Guyana, Haiti, Honduras, Jamaica, Mexico, Panama, Paraguay, Peru, Saint Lucia, and Uruguay.
Source: WHO Global Health Observatory Data Repository (WHO, 2024[1]).

Table 6.33. El Salvador - Tobacco use prevalence by sex and age groups

Percentage of the population group, latest year available

	Tobacco use prevalence (all tobacco products)	Cigarette smoking prevalence (cigarettes only)
Youths aged 13-15 years		
Total	**0.9**	**0.9**
Males	1.0	1.0
Females	0.9	0.9
People aged 15 and over		
Total	**9.3**	**8.0**
Males	16.6	14.4
Females	2.0	1.7

Note: Tobacco use prevalence is defined as the percentage of the population group who currently use any tobacco product (smoked and/or smokeless tobacco) on a daily or non-daily basis. Tobacco products exclude e-cigarettes (which do not contain tobacco), e-cigars, e-hookahs, and e-pipes. Data for students aged 13-15 years are from 2021 and taken from the Global Youth Tobacco Survey. Data for people aged 15 and over correspond to 2020.
Source: WHO Global Health Observatory Data Repository (WHO, 2024[1]); Global Youth Tobacco Survey (WHO, 2021[29]).

Table 6.34. El Salvador - Summary of MPOWER measures, 2022

M Monitoring	P Smoking bans	O Cessation programmes	W Health warnings	E Advertising bans	R Taxation	WHO Frawework Convention on Tobacco Control		Protocol to eliminate illicit trade in tobacco products	
						Date of signature	Date of ratification	Date of signature	Date of ratification
						18-03-2004	21-07-2014		

... Not categorized/ No data; No policy or weak measure; Minimal measure; Moderate measure; Complete measure

Source: WHO report on the global tobacco epidemic (WHO, 2023[3]).

Figure 6.66. El Salvador - Taxes and prices of the most sold brand of cigarettes

Panel A. Indirect taxes levied on cigarettes in El Salvador and LAC | **Panel B. Tobacco tax share and price of cigarettes in El Salvador**

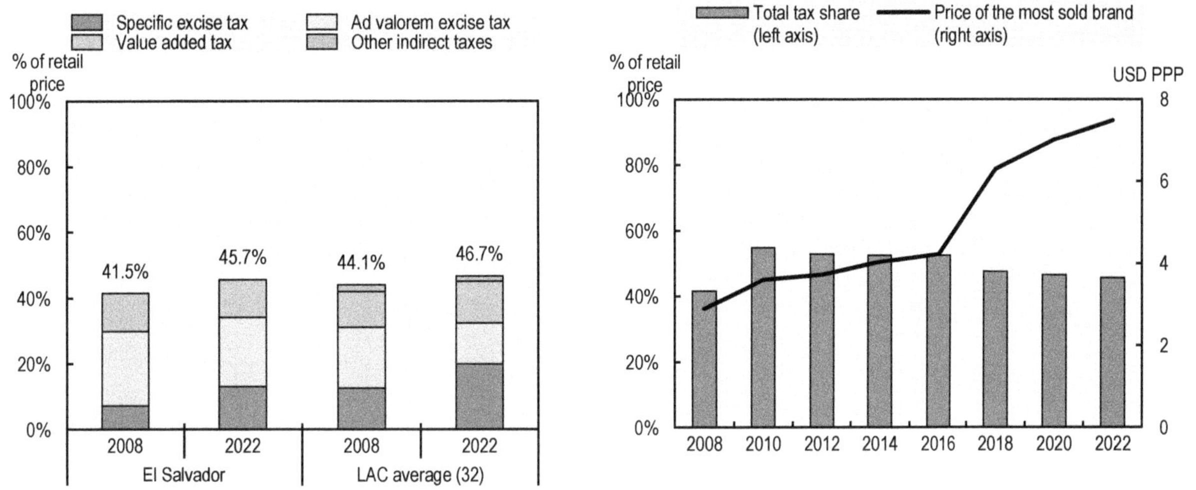

Note: Prices correspond to a 20-cigarette pack of the most sold brand. The most sold brand of cigarettes is determined based on national market share information and can vary over time (i.e. the most sold brand of cigarettes in year 1 can be different from year 2). Retail prices in USD PPP are based on the implied purchasing power parity (PPP) conversion rate from the International Monetary Fund (IMF) World Economic Outlook Database (October 2023).
Source: WHO report on the global tobacco epidemic (WHO, 2023[3]); IMF World Economic Outlook Database (IMF, 2023[4]).

Figure 6.67. El Salvador - Trends in retail prices of cigarettes by brand category

In USD PPP per pack of 20 cigarettes, 2008-2022

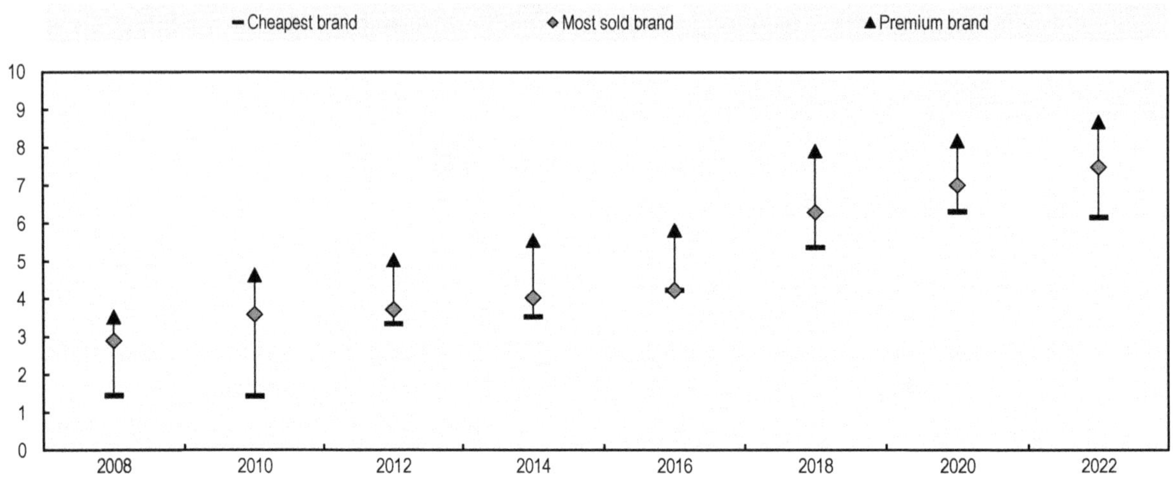

Note: Prices correspond to a 20-cigarette pack of the cheapest, most sold and premium brands. The cheapest, most sold and premium brands of cigarettes are determined based on national market share information and can vary over time (i.e. the cheapest/most sold/premium brands of cigarettes in year 1 can be different from year 2). Retail prices in USD PPP are based on the implied PPP conversion rate from the IMF World Economic Outlook Database (October 2023).
Source: WHO reports on the global tobacco epidemic (WHO, 2009[5]; WHO, 2011[6]; WHO, 2013[7]; WHO, 2015[8]; WHO, 2017[9]; WHO, 2019[10]; WHO, 2021[11]); IMF World Economic Outlook Database (IMF, 2023[4]).

Figure 6.68. El Salvador - Affordability of cigarettes

Percentage of GDP per capita required to purchase 100 packs of 20 cigarettes

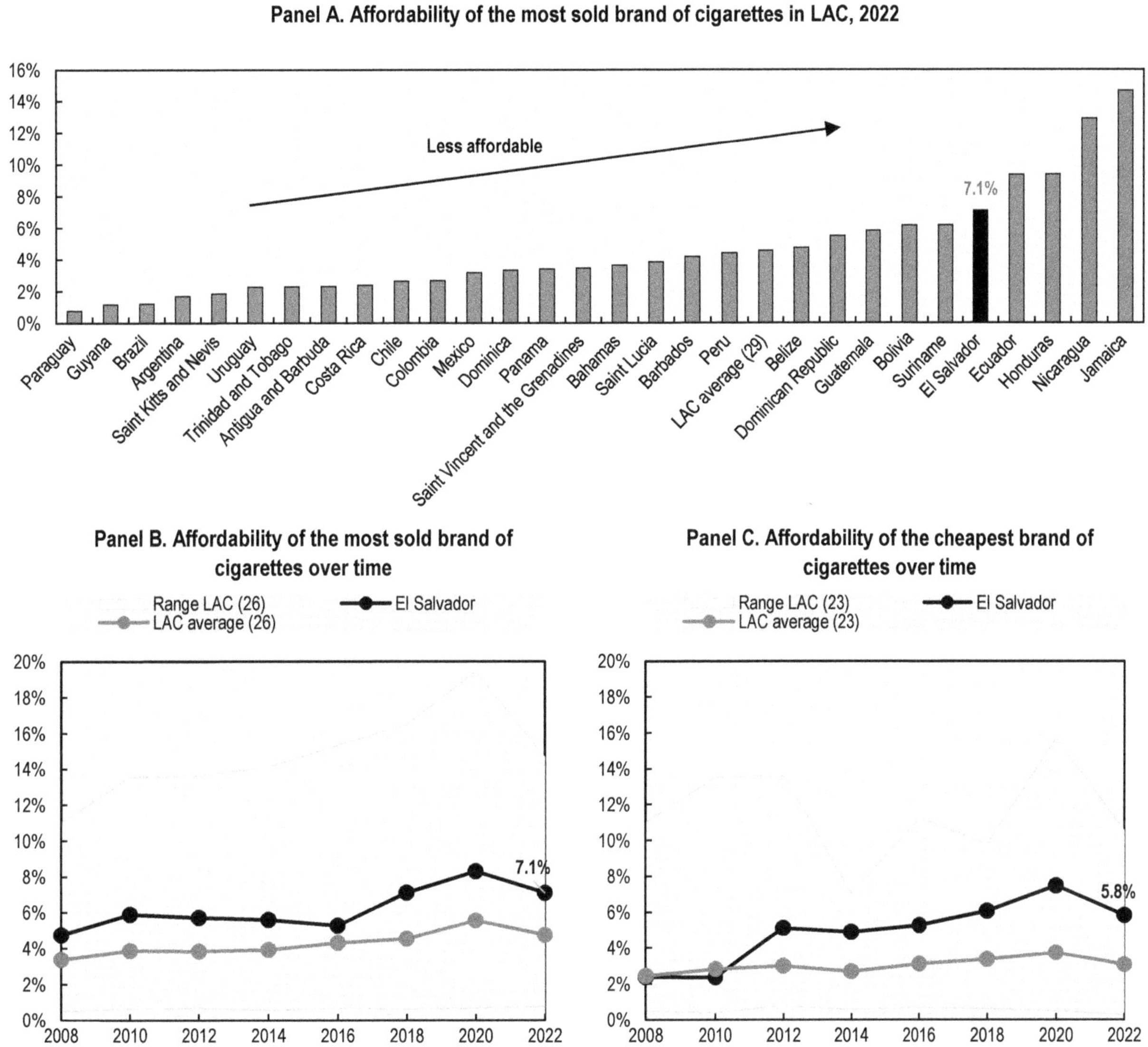

Note: The affordability indicator measures the percentage of the country's GDP per capita required to purchase 100 packs of 20 cigarettes. A higher percentage means lower affordability of cigarettes while a lower percentage means higher affordability. To ensure comparability of average affordability across LAC over time, countries where information was unavailable for certain years have been excluded from the calculation. Data for Panel C are OECD calculations based on WHO reports on the global tobacco epidemic (2009-2023 editions). The cheapest and most sold brands of cigarettes are determined based on national market share information and can vary over time (i.e. the cheapest/most sold brand of cigarettes in year 1 can be different from year 2).

Source: WHO reports on the global tobacco epidemic (WHO, 2009[5]; WHO, 2011[6]; WHO, 2013[7]; WHO, 2015[8]; WHO, 2017[9]; WHO, 2019[10]; WHO, 2021[11]).

Table 6.35. El Salvador - Design of tobacco excise taxes across tobacco products, 2022

	Excise tax structure	Specific excise tax				Ad valorem excise tax			Excise tax floor			
		Yes / No	Tax base	Rate per 20-unit pack USD PPP (local currency)	Indexation mechanisms	Yes / No	Tax base	Statutory rate	Yes / No	Tax base	Rate per 20-unit pack USD PPP (local currency)	Indexation mechanisms
Cigarettes	Mixed	Yes	Single stick	1.0 (0.5)	No	Yes	SRP excl. VAT	39%	No			
Cigars	Mixed	Yes	Single stick	1.0 (0.5)	No	Yes	SRP excl. VAT	100%	No			
Cigarillos	Mixed	Yes	Single stick	1.0 (0.5)	No	Yes	SRP excl. VAT	39%	No			
Roll-Your-Own (RYO) tobacco	Mixed	Yes	Gram	1.3 (0.6)	No	Yes	SRP excl. VAT	39%	No			
Heated tobacco products (HTPs)	No excise											
ENDS and ENNDS	No excise											

Note: "SRP" means "Suggested retail price by the manufacturer/importer"; blank cells mean that there is no excise tax for the corresponding tobacco product; "VAT" means "Value added tax". Following the WHO report on the global tobacco epidemic (WHO, 2021[11]), new tobacco and nicotine products in this report include electronic nicotine delivery systems (ENDS), electronic non-nicotine delivery systems (ENNDS), and heated tobacco products (HTP). Specific taxes are converted into USD PPP with the implied PPP conversion rate available in the IMF World Economic Outlook Database (October 2023). Specific excise taxes have been standardized to a 20-unit pack to allow the comparison across countries with different tax bases. The specific excise tax is levied on each gram of RYO tobacco in El Salvador. To compute the specific tax for an equivalent 20-unit pack of RYO tobacco it is assumed that the median cigarette in terms of weight contains 0.75 gram of tobacco (Gallus et al., 2014[12]).

Source: Decreto Legislativo No. 235 (2009); IMF World Economic Outlook Database (IMF, 2023[4]).

Table 6.36. El Salvador - Tobacco tax reforms since 2000

Year of adoption	Specific excise taxes	Ad valorem excise taxes	Other
2004	All tobacco products: introduction of a uniform specific excise tax of USD 0.005 on each stick.	All tobacco products: introduction of an ad valorem component levied at a uniform tax rate of 39% on the retail price suggested by the manufacturer/importer, excluding VAT.	Earmarking the tobacco tax revenue for the Solidarity Fund for Public Health (Fondo Solidario para la Salud).
2005	No	All tobacco products: exclude the specific excise tax from the ad valorem tax base.	No
2009	All tobacco products: increase in the specific tax to USD 0.0225 levied on each stick. For RYO tobacco, the tax is levied on each gram.	Cigars: increase in the ad valorem tax rate to 100% levied on the retail price suggested by the manufacturer/ importer, excluding VAT and the specific excise tax.	No

Note: "Tobacco tax reform" refers to changes in the tobacco excise tax rates, the introduction of indexation mechanisms or minimum taxes, as well as adjustments to the tax base. These reforms typically entail the enactment of new laws or decrees. The table does not refer to recurrent tax changes that result from the indexation for inflation of tax brackets and price floors (if implemented). Tobacco tax reforms included reflect changes in the legislation, but not whether or when the reforms have been implemented.

Source: Ley Especial para la Constitución del Fondo Solidario para la Salud (Decreto No. 538, 2004); Ley de Impuesto sobre productos del tabaco (Decreto No. 539, 2004); Decreto Legislativo No. 643 (2005); Decreto Legislativo No. 235 (2009).

Figure 6.69. El Salvador - Tobacco excise tax revenue

Percentage of GDP, latest year available

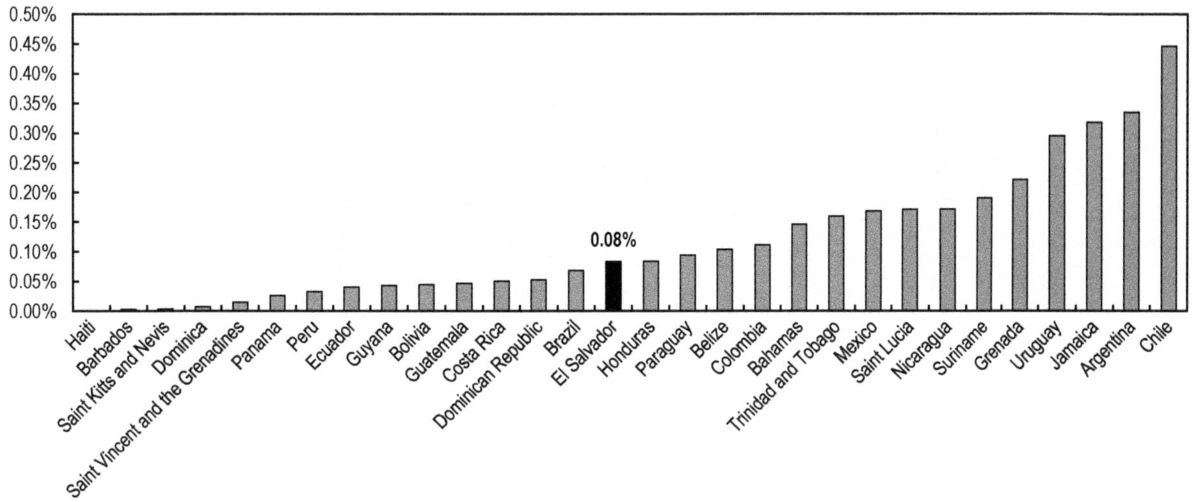

Note: See Box 2.1 (Chapter 2) for more information on tobacco tax revenue (source of information and calculations) and country selection. The latest year available is 2022 for Argentina, Brazil, Chile, Colombia, Costa Rica, the Dominican Republic, El Salvador, Guatemala, Guyana, Honduras, Mexico, Nicaragua, Panama, Paraguay, Peru, Saint Kitts and Nevis, Suriname, and Uruguay; 2021 for Belize, Dominica, Ecuador, Grenada, Saint Lucia, Saint Vincent and the Grenadines; 2020 for Bahamas, Bolivia, Jamaica and Trinidad and Tobago; 2015 for Haiti; 2014 for Barbados.
Source: OECD Revenue Statistics (OECD, 2024[13]); WHO report on the global tobacco epidemic (WHO, 2023[3]); National data.

Figure 6.70. El Salvador - Trends in tobacco excise tax revenue

Percentage of GDP, 2001-2022

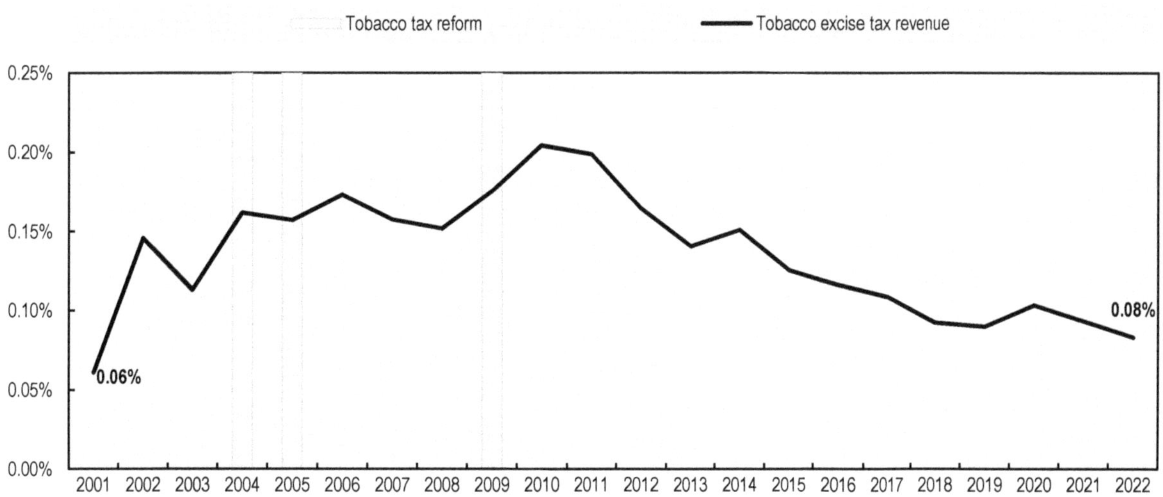

Note: "Tobacco tax reform" refers to the measures included in Table 6.36. Tobacco excise tax revenue for 2000 are not available.
Source: OECD Revenue Statistics (OECD, 2024[13]); Ley Especial para la Constitución del Fondo Solidario para la Salud (Decreto No. 538, 2004); Ley de Impuesto sobre productos del tabaco (Decreto No. 539, 2004); Decreto Legislativo No. 643 (2005); Decreto Legislativo No. 235 (2009).

Figure 6.71. El Salvador - Average excise tax revenue collected per pack of 20 cigarettes sold

Tobacco excise tax revenue in USD PPP collected per pack of legal cigarettes sold, latest year available

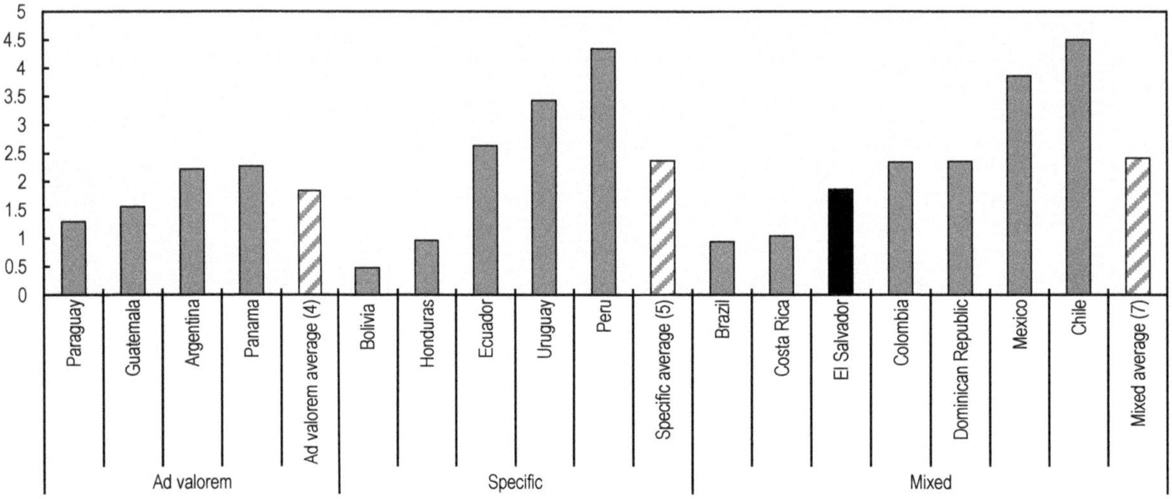

Note: See Box 2.1 (Chapter 2) for more information on tobacco tax revenue (source of information and calculations). The latest year available is 2022 for Argentina, Brazil, Chile, Colombia, Costa Rica, the Dominican Republic, El Salvador, Guatemala, Honduras, Mexico, Panama, Paraguay, Peru and Uruguay; 2021 for Ecuador;2020 for Bolivia. The country selection is provided by the availability of data on sales of cigarettes in Euromonitor International Tobacco Industry edition, 2023 © All rights reserved (Euromonitor International, 2023[14]).

Source: OECD Revenue Statistics (OECD, 2024[13]); WHO report on the global tobacco epidemic (WHO, 2023[3]); National data; IMF World Economic Outlook Database (IMF, 2023[4]); and OECD calculations based on Euromonitor International's Tobacco Industry edition (Euromonitor International, 2023[14]).

Figure 6.72. El Salvador - Change in tobacco tax policy indicators

Percentage change from base year, 2008-2022

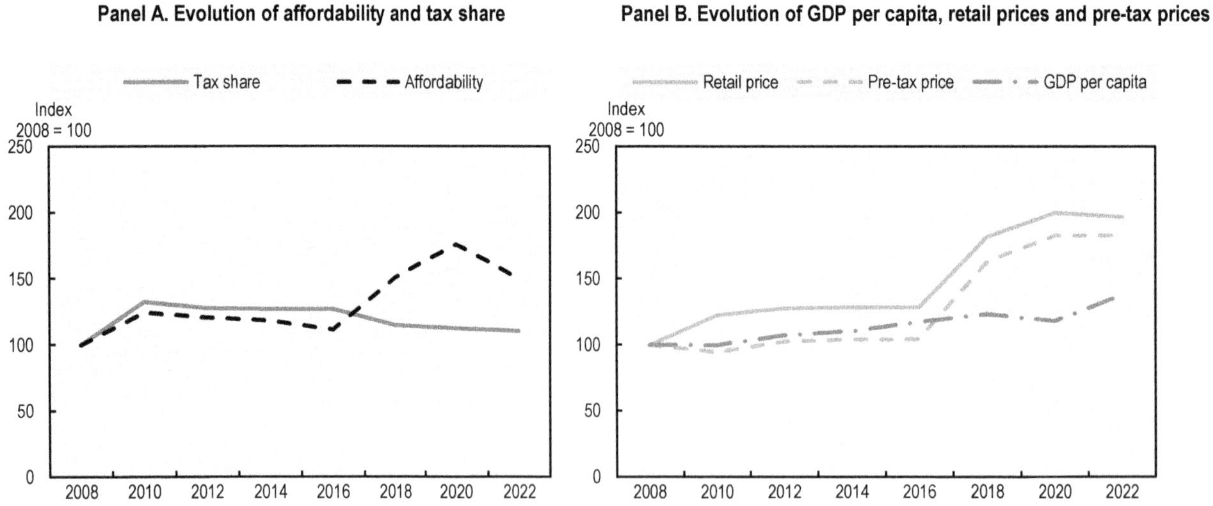

Note: Both Panel A and Panel B figures are based on data for the most sold brand of cigarettes. The most sold brand of cigarettes is determined based on national market share information and can vary over time (i.e. the most sold brand of cigarettes in year 1 can be different from year 2). In Panel A, an increase in the affordability indicator means that cigarettes are becoming less affordable, while a decline in the affordability indicator means that cigarettes are becoming more affordable. In Panel B, "Pre-tax price" corresponds to the retail price of the most sold brand of cigarettes minus the indirect taxes levied on this brand, namely excise taxes, VAT, import duties and other. Indicators in Panel B have been computed using national currency and have been adjusted for inflation; therefore, present inflation-adjusted trends.

Source: WHO report on the global tobacco epidemic (WHO, 2023[3]); World Bank Open Data (World Bank, 2024[15]); IMF International Financial Statistics (IMF, 2024[19]).

References

Euromonitor International (2023), *Euromonitor International's Tobacco Industry edition*, https://www.euromonitor.com/tobacco (accessed on 1 August 2023). [14]

Gallus, S. et al. (2014), "Roll-your-own cigarettes in Europe", *European Journal of Cancer Prevention*, Vol. 23/3, pp. 186-192, https://doi.org/10.1097/cej.0000000000000010. [12]

IMF (2023), *World Economic Outlook Database*, International Monetary Fund, https://www.imf.org/en/Publications/WEO/weo-database/2023/October (accessed on 13 January 2024). [4]

IMF (2024), *International Financial Statistics (IFS)*, International Monetary Fund, https://data.imf.org/?sk=4c514d48-b6ba-49ed-8ab9-52b0c1a0179b&sId=1390030341854 (accessed on 13 January 2024). [19]

OECD (2024), *Global Revenue Statistics Database*, Organisation for Economic Co-operation and Development, https://www.oecd.org/tax/tax-policy/global-revenue-statistics-database.htm (accessed on 13 August 2023). [13]

WHO (2024), *Global Health Observatory: Age-standardized estimates of current tobacco use, tobacco smoking and cigarette smoking (Tobacco control: Monitor)*, World Health Organization, https://www.who.int/data/gho/data/indicators/indicator-details/GHO/gho-tobacco-control-monitor-current-tobaccouse-tobaccosmoking-cigarrettesmoking-agestd-tobagestdcurr (accessed on 20 February 2024). [1]

WHO (2023), *WHO report on the global tobacco epidemic 2023: protect people from tobacco smoke*, World Health Organization, https://www.who.int/publications/i/item/9789240077164. [3]

WHO (2021), *WHO report on the global tobacco epidemic 2021: Addressing new and emerging products*, World Health Organization, https://www.who.int/publications/i/item/9789240032095. [11]

WHO (2021), *Global Youth Tobacco Survey. El Salvador 2021 Fact Sheet*, World Health Organization, https://www.who.int/publications/m/item/2021-gyts-fact-sheet-el-salvador. [29]

WHO (2019), *WHO report on the global tobacco epidemic 2019: Offer help to quit tobacco use*, World Health Organization, https://www.who.int/publications/i/item/9789241516204. [10]

WHO (2017), *WHO report on the global tobacco epidemic 2017: Monitoring tobacco use and prevention policies*, World Health Organization, https://www.who.int/publications/i/item/9789241512824. [9]

WHO (2015), *WHO report on the global tobacco epidemic 2015: Raising taxes on tobacco*, World Health Organization, https://www.who.int/publications/i/item/9789241509121. [8]

WHO (2013), *WHO report on the global tobacco epidemic 2013: Enforcing bans on tobacco advertising, promotion and sponsorship*, World Health Organization, https://www.who.int/publications/i/item/9789241505871. [7]

WHO (2011), *WHO report on the global tobacco epidemic 2011: Warning about the dangers of tobacco*, World Health Organization, https://www.who.int/publications/i/item/9789244564264. [6]

WHO (2009), *WHO report on the global tobacco epidemic 2009: Implementing smoke-free environments*, World Health Organization, https://www.who.int/publications/i/item/9789241563918. [5]

World Bank (2024), *World Bank Open Data*, World Bank, https://data.worldbank.org/ (accessed on 13 January 2024). [15]

Guatemala

Figure 6.73. Guatemala - Trends in tobacco use prevalence

Percentage of the population aged 15 years and over who currently use any tobacco product (smoked and/or smokeless tobacco) on a daily or non-daily basis, 2000-2020

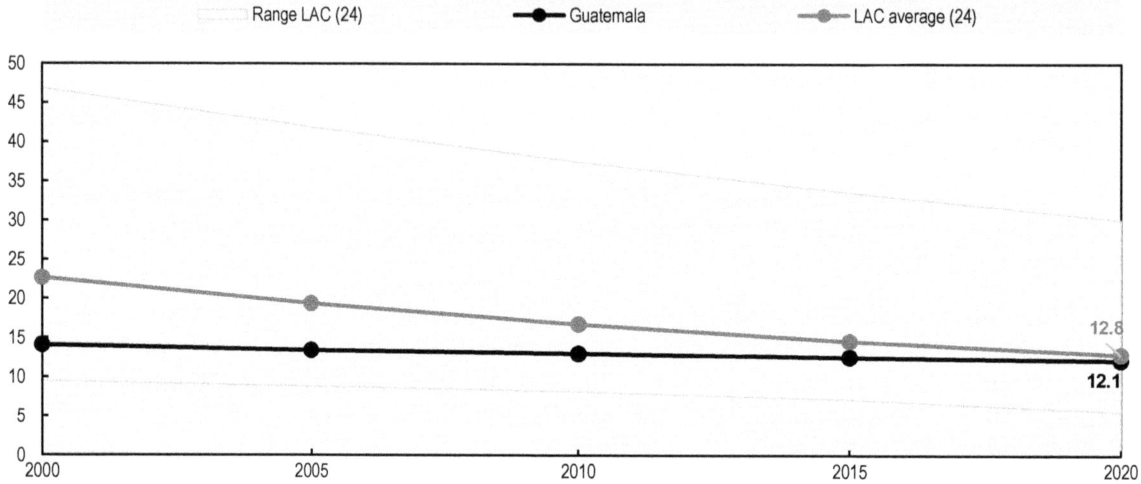

Note: Tobacco products include cigarettes, pipes, cigars, cigarillos, waterpipes (hookah, shisha), bidis, kretek, heated tobacco products (HTP), and all forms of smokeless (oral and nasal) tobacco. Tobacco products exclude e-cigarettes (which do not contain tobacco), e-cigars, e-hookahs, and e-pipes. The rates are age-standardized to the World Health Organisation (WHO) standard population. The LAC average was calculated as the average of Argentina, Bahamas, Barbados, Belize, Bolivia, Brazil, Chile, Colombia, Costa Rica, Cuba, the Dominican Republic, Ecuador, El Salvador, Guatemala, Guyana, Haiti, Honduras, Jamaica, Mexico, Panama, Paraguay, Peru, Saint Lucia, and Uruguay.
Source: WHO Global Health Observatory Data Repository (WHO, 2024[11]).

Table 6.37. Guatemala - Tobacco use prevalence by sex and age groups

Percentage of the population group, latest year available

	Tobacco use prevalence (all tobacco products)	Cigarette smoking prevalence (cigarettes only)
Youths aged 13-15 years		
Total	**17.1**	**12.9**
Males	19.5	14.7
Females	14.4	11.1
People aged 15 and over		
Total	**12.1**	**10.4**
Males	22.5	19.4
Females	1.8	1.4

Note: Tobacco use prevalence is defined as the percentage of the population group who currently use any tobacco product (smoked and/or smokeless tobacco) on a daily or non-daily basis. Tobacco products exclude e-cigarettes (which do not contain tobacco), e-cigars, e-hookahs, and e-pipes. Data for students aged 13-15 years are from 2015 and taken from the Global Youth Tobacco Survey. Data for people aged 15 and over correspond to 2020.
Source: WHO Global Health Observatory Data Repository (WHO, 2024[11]); Global Youth Tobacco Survey (WHO, 2015[30]).

Table 6.38. Guatemala - Summary of MPOWER measures, 2022

M Monitoring	P Smoking bans	O Cessation programmes	W Health warnings	E Advertising bans	R Taxation	WHO Frawework Convention on Tobacco Control		Protocol to eliminate illicit trade in tobacco products	
						Date of signature	Date of ratification	Date of signature	Date of ratification
						25-09-2003	16-11-2005		

... Not categorized/ No data; No policy or weak measure; Minimal measure; Moderate measure; Complete measure

Source: WHO report on the global tobacco epidemic (WHO, 2023[3]).

Figure 6.74. Guatemala - Taxes and prices of the most sold brand of cigarettes

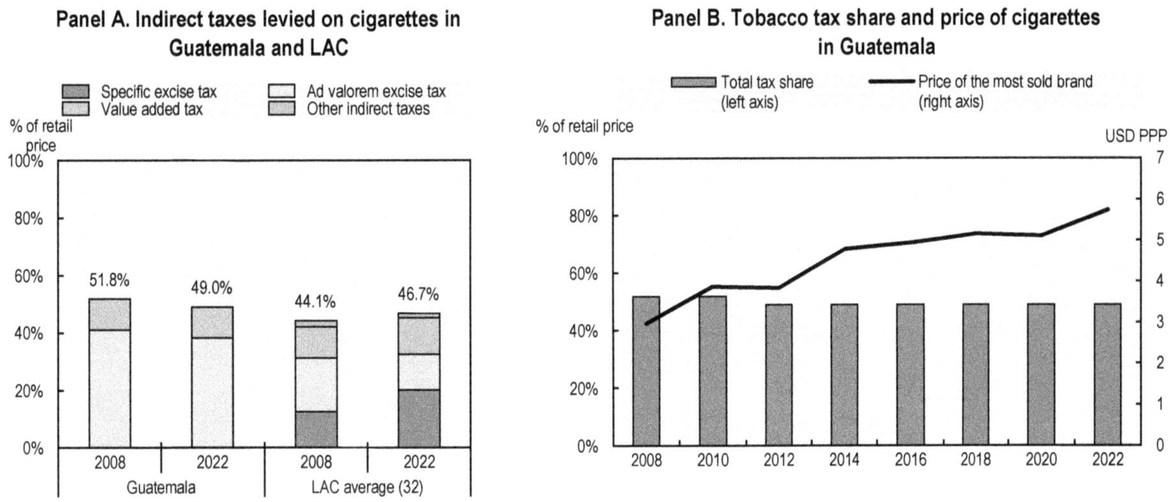

Note: Prices correspond to a 20-cigarette pack of the most sold brand. The most sold brand of cigarettes is determined based on national market share information and can vary over time (i.e. the most sold brand of cigarettes in year 1 can be different from year 2). Retail prices in USD PPP are based on the implied purchasing power parity (PPP) conversion rate from the International Monetary Fund (IMF) World Economic Outlook Database (October 2023).

Source: WHO report on the global tobacco epidemic (WHO, 2023[3]); IMF World Economic Outlook Database (IMF, 2023[4]).

Figure 6.75. Guatemala - Trends in retail prices of cigarettes by brand category

In USD PPP per pack of 20 cigarettes, 2008-2022

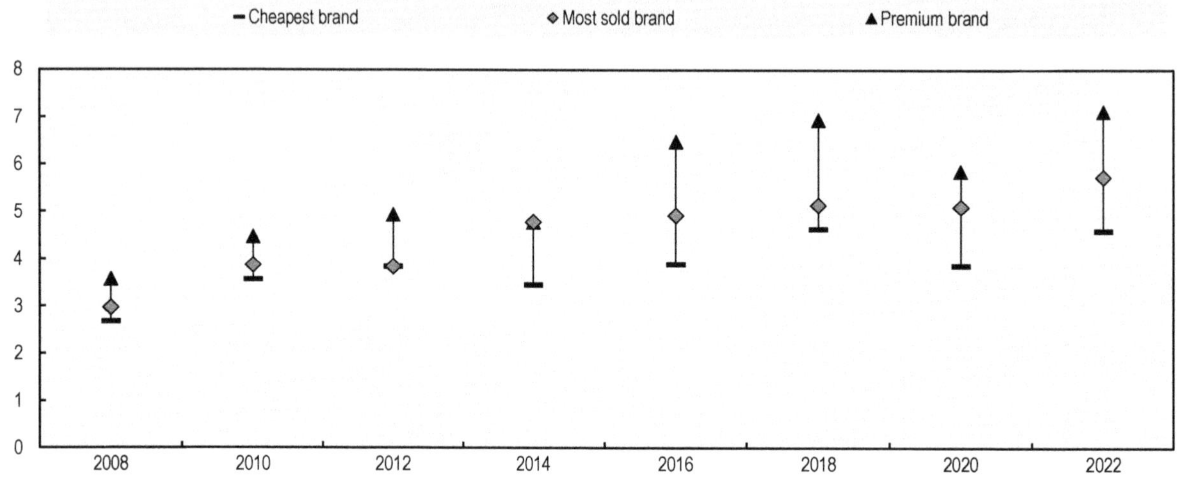

Note: Prices correspond to a 20-cigarette pack of the cheapest, most sold and premium brands. The cheapest, most sold and premium brands of cigarettes are determined based on national market share information and can vary over time (i.e. the cheapest/most sold/premium brands of cigarettes in year 1 can be different from year 2). Retail prices in USD PPP are based on the implied PPP conversion rate from the IMF World Economic Outlook Database (October 2023).
Source: WHO reports on the global tobacco epidemic (WHO, 2009[5]; WHO, 2011[6]; WHO, 2013[7]; WHO, 2015[8]; WHO, 2017[9]; WHO, 2019[10]; WHO, 2021[11]); IMF World Economic Outlook Database (IMF, 2023[4]).

Figure 6.76. Guatemala - Affordability of cigarettes

Percentage of GDP per capita required to purchase 100 packs of 20 cigarettes

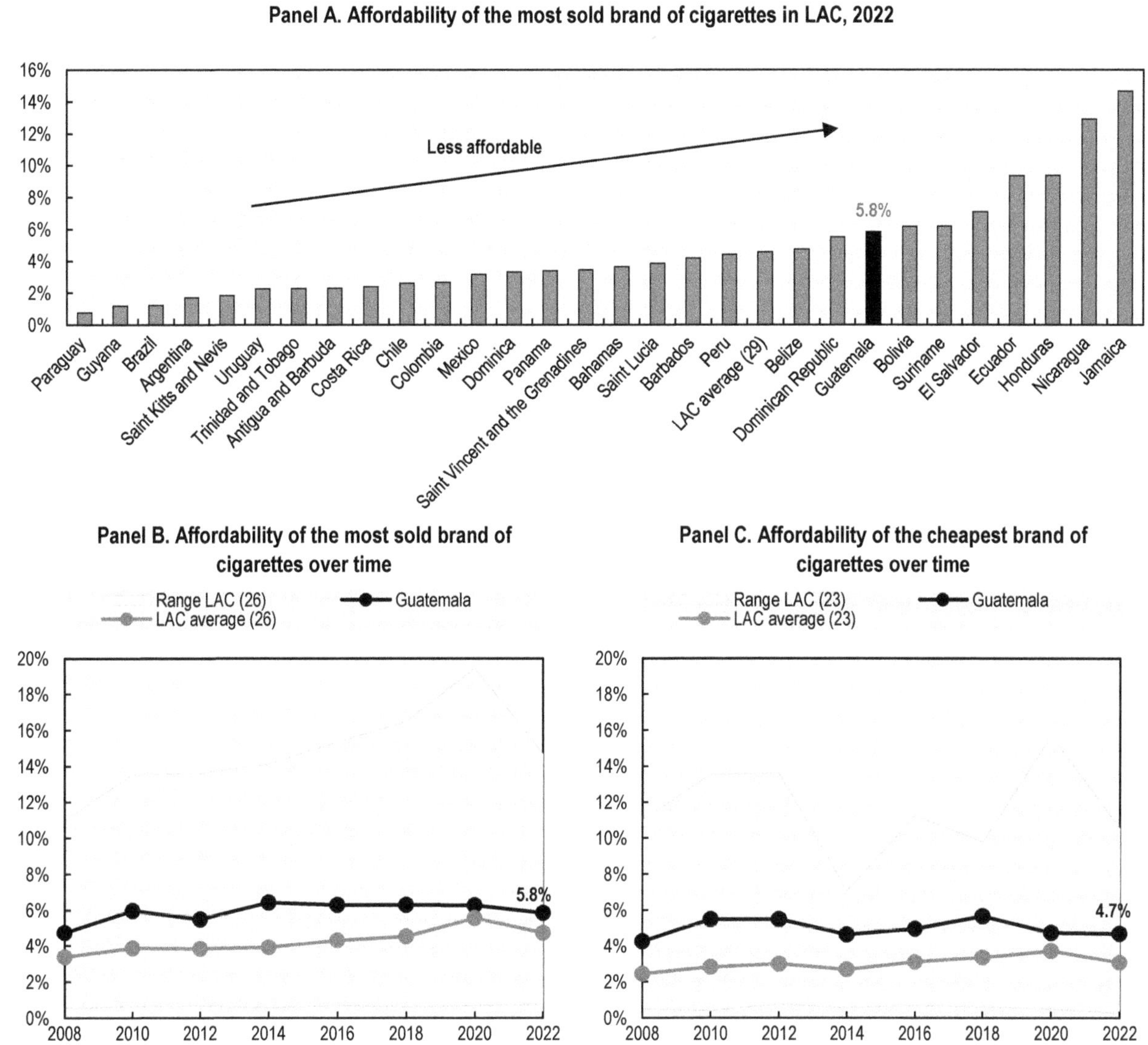

Note: The affordability indicator measures the percentage of the country's GDP per capita required to purchase 100 packs of 20 cigarettes. A higher percentage means lower affordability of cigarettes while a lower percentage means higher affordability. To ensure comparability of average affordability across LAC over time, countries where information was unavailable for certain years have been excluded from the calculation. Data for Panel C are OECD calculations based on WHO reports on the global tobacco epidemic (2009-2023 editions). The cheapest and most sold brands of cigarettes are determined based on national market share information and can vary over time (i.e. the cheapest/most sold brand of cigarettes in year 1 can be different from year 2).

Source: WHO reports on the global tobacco epidemic (WHO, 2009[5]; WHO, 2011[6]; WHO, 2013[7]; WHO, 2015[8]; WHO, 2017[9]; WHO, 2019[10]; WHO, 2021[11]).

Table 6.39. Guatemala - Design of tobacco excise taxes across tobacco products, 2022

	Excise tax structure	Specific excise tax				Ad valorem excise tax			Excise tax floor			
		Yes / No	Tax base	Rate per 20-unit pack USD PPP (local currency)	Indexation mechanisms	Yes / No	Tax base	Statutory rate	Yes / No	Tax base	Rate per 20-unit pack USD PPP (local currency)	Indexation mechanisms
Cigarettes	Ad valorem only	No				Yes	EFP excl. VAT	100%	Yes	75% of the suggested retail price, net of the VAT and the excise	100%	No
Cigars	Specific only	Yes	Single stick	0.005 - 0.26 (0.02 - 1.0)	No	No			No			
Cigarillos	Specific only	Yes	Single stick	0.008 - 0.013 (0.03 - 0.05)	No	No			No			
Roll-Your-Own (RYO) tobacco	Specific only	Yes	Net kilogram	0.005 - 0.015 (0.02 - 0.06)	No	No			No			
Heated tobacco products (HTPs)	No excise											
ENDS and ENNDS	No excise											

Note: Ad valorem tax base "EFP" means "Ex-factory price/CIF value"; blank cells mean that there is no excise tax for the corresponding tobacco product; "VAT" means "Value added tax". Following the WHO report on the global tobacco epidemic (WHO, 2021[11]), new tobacco and nicotine products in this report include electronic nicotine delivery systems (ENDS), electronic non-nicotine delivery systems (ENNDS), and heated tobacco products (HTP). Specific taxes are converted into USD PPP with the implied PPP conversion rate available in the IMF World Economic Outlook Database (October 2023). Specific excise taxes have been standardized to a 20-unit pack to allow the comparison across countries with different tax bases. The specific excise tax is levied on net kilogram of RYO tobacco in Guatemala. To compute the specific tax for an equivalent 20-unit pack of RYO tobacco it is assumed that the median cigarette in terms of weight contains 0.75 gram of tobacco (Gallus et al., 2014[12]). Cigars are levied with a five-tiered tax rate based on the size and the country of production. Cigarillos and RYO tobacco are levied with a two-tiered tax rate based on the country of production.
Source: Decreto No. 61-77 y sus reformas (2012); IMF World Economic Outlook Database (IMF, 2023[4]).

Table 6.40. Guatemala - Tobacco tax reforms since 2000

Year of adoption	Specific excise taxes	Ad valorem excise taxes	Other
2001	No	No	Cigarettes: the minimum tax base for the ad valorem component is raised to 46% of the suggested retail price, excluding VAT and the excise.
2012	No	No	Cigarettes: the minimum tax base for the ad valorem component is raised to 75% of the suggested retail price, excluding VAT and the excise.

Note: "Tobacco tax reform" refers to changes in the tobacco excise tax rates, the introduction of indexation mechanisms or minimum taxes, as well as adjustments to the tax base. These reforms typically entail the enactment of new laws or decrees. The table does not refer to recurrent tax changes that result from the indexation for inflation of tax brackets and price floors (if implemented). Tobacco tax reforms included reflect changes in the legislation, but not whether or when the reforms have been implemented.
Source: Decreto No. 65-2001 (art. 1); Decreto No. 4-2012 (art. 69).

Figure 6.77. Guatemala - Tobacco excise tax revenue

Percentage of GDP, latest year available

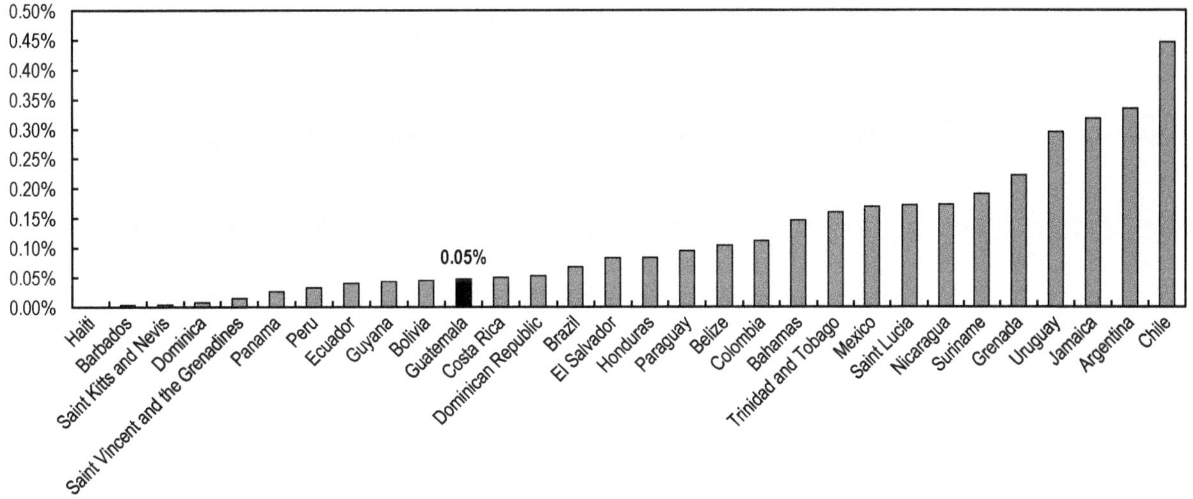

Note: See Box 2.1 (Chapter 2) for more information on tobacco tax revenue (source of information and calculations) and country selection. The latest year available is 2022 for Argentina, Brazil, Chile, Colombia, Costa Rica, the Dominican Republic, El Salvador, Guatemala, Guyana, Honduras, Mexico, Nicaragua, Panama, Paraguay, Peru, Saint Kitts and Nevis, Suriname, and Uruguay; 2021 for Belize, Dominica, Ecuador, Grenada, Saint Lucia, Saint Vincent and the Grenadines; 2020 for Bahamas, Bolivia, Jamaica and Trinidad and Tobago; 2015 for Haiti; 2014 for Barbados.
Source: OECD Revenue Statistics (OECD, 2024[13]); WHO report on the global tobacco epidemic (WHO, 2023[3]); National data.

Figure 6.78. Guatemala - Trends in tobacco excise tax revenue

Percentage of GDP, 2000-2022

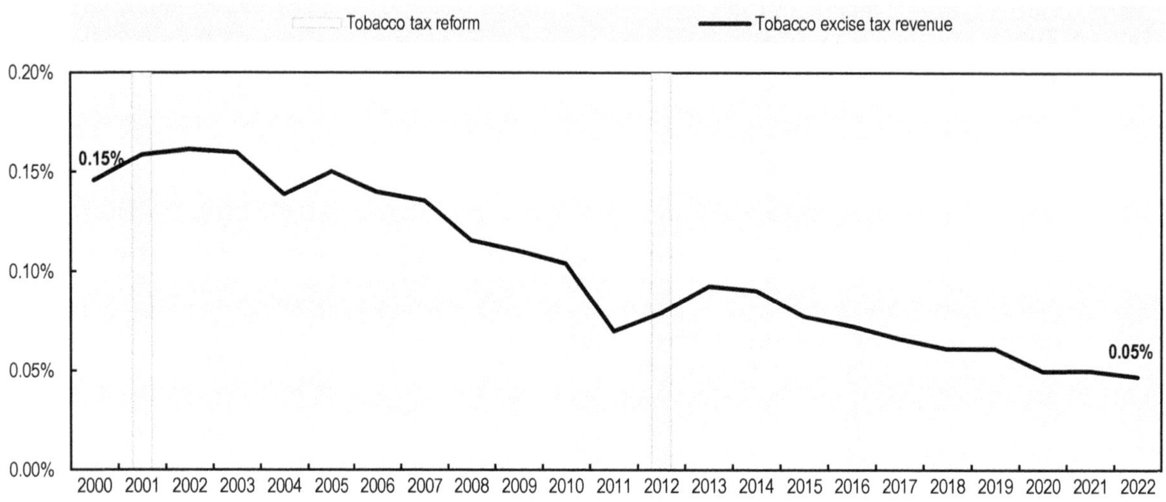

Note: "Tobacco tax reform" refers to the measures included in Table 6.40.
Source: OECD Revenue Statistics (OECD, 2024[13]); Decreto No. 65-2001 (art. 1); Decreto No. 4-2012 (art. 69).

Figure 6.79. Guatemala - Average excise tax revenue collected per pack of 20 cigarettes sold

Tobacco excise tax revenue in USD PPP collected per pack of legal cigarettes sold, latest year available

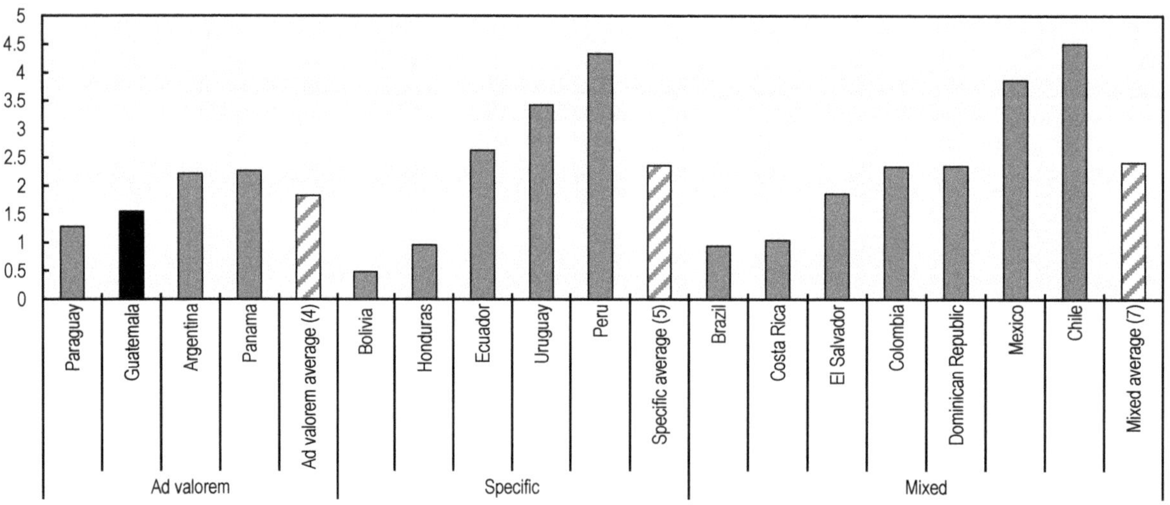

Note: See Box 2.1 (Chapter 2) for more information on tobacco tax revenue (source of information and calculations). The latest year available is 2022 for Argentina, Brazil, Chile, Colombia, Costa Rica, the Dominican Republic, El Salvador, Guatemala, Honduras, Mexico, Panama, Paraguay, Peru and Uruguay; 2021 for Ecuador; 2020 for Bolivia. The country selection is provided by the availability of data on sales of cigarettes in Euromonitor International Tobacco Industry edition, 2023 © All rights reserved (Euromonitor International, 2023[14]).
Source: OECD Revenue Statistics (OECD, 2024[13]); WHO report on the global tobacco epidemic (WHO, 2023[3]); National data; IMF World Economic Outlook Database (IMF, 2023[4]); and OECD calculations based on Euromonitor International's Tobacco Industry edition (Euromonitor International, 2023[14]).

Figure 6.80. Guatemala - Change in tobacco tax policy indicators

Percentage change from base year, 2008-2022

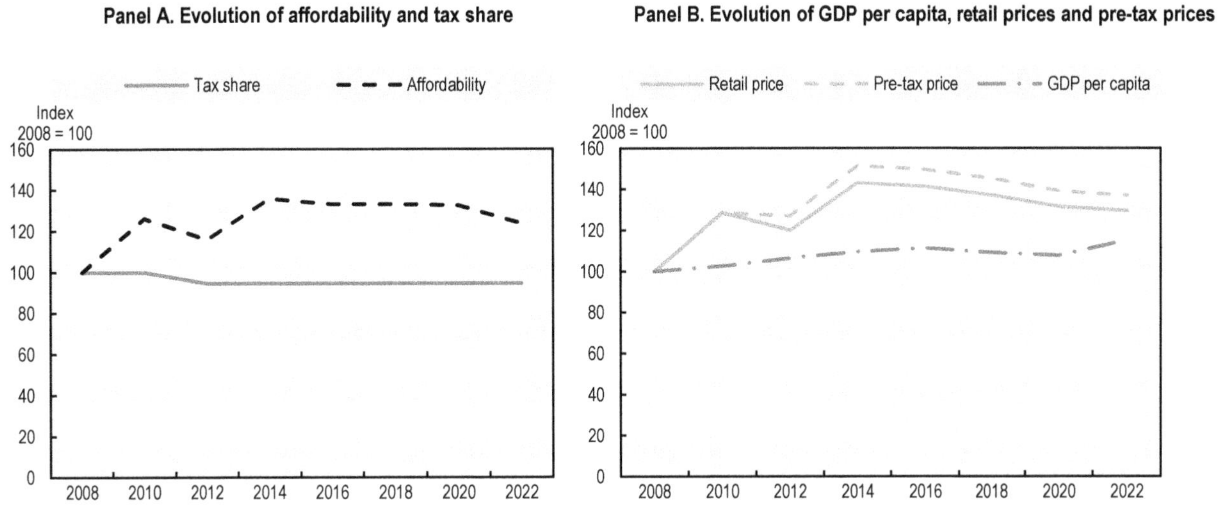

Note: Both Panel A and Panel B figures are based on data for the most sold brand of cigarettes. The most sold brand of cigarettes is determined based on national market share information and can vary over time (i.e. the most sold brand of cigarettes in year 1 can be different from year 2). In Panel A, an increase in the affordability indicator means that cigarettes are becoming less affordable, while a decline in the affordability indicator means that cigarettes are becoming more affordable. In Panel B, "Pre-tax price" corresponds to the retail price of the most sold brand of cigarettes minus the indirect taxes levied on this brand, namely excise taxes, VAT, import duties and other. Indicators in Panel B have been computed using national currency and have been adjusted for inflation; therefore, present inflation-adjusted trends.
Source: WHO report on the global tobacco epidemic (WHO, 2023[3]); World Bank Open Data (World Bank, 2024[15]); IMF International Financial Statistics (IMF, 2024[19]).

References

Euromonitor International (2023), *Euromonitor International's Tobacco Industry edition*, https://www.euromonitor.com/tobacco (accessed on 1 August 2023). [14]

Gallus, S. et al. (2014), "Roll-your-own cigarettes in Europe", *European Journal of Cancer Prevention*, Vol. 23/3, pp. 186-192, https://doi.org/10.1097/cej.0000000000000010. [12]

IMF (2023), *World Economic Outlook Database*, International Monetary Fund, https://www.imf.org/en/Publications/WEO/weo-database/2023/October (accessed on 13 January 2024). [4]

IMF (2024), *International Financial Statistics (IFS)*, International Monetary Fund, https://data.imf.org/?sk=4c514d48-b6ba-49ed-8ab9-52b0c1a0179b&sId=1390030341854 (accessed on 13 January 2024). [19]

OECD (2024), *Global Revenue Statistics Database*, Organisation for Economic Co-operation and Development, https://www.oecd.org/tax/tax-policy/global-revenue-statistics-database.htm (accessed on 13 August 2023). [13]

WHO (2024), *Global Health Observatory: Age-standardized estimates of current tobacco use, tobacco smoking and cigarette smoking (Tobacco control: Monitor)*, World Health Organization, https://www.who.int/data/gho/data/indicators/indicator-details/GHO/gho-tobacco-control-monitor-current-tobaccouse-tobaccosmoking-cigarrettesmoking-agestd-tobagestdcurr (accessed on 20 February 2024). [1]

WHO (2023), *WHO report on the global tobacco epidemic 2023: protect people from tobacco smoke*, World Health Organization, https://www.who.int/publications/i/item/9789240077164. [3]

WHO (2021), *WHO report on the global tobacco epidemic 2021: Addressing new and emerging products*, World Health Organization, https://www.who.int/publications/i/item/9789240032095. [11]

WHO (2019), *WHO report on the global tobacco epidemic 2019: Offer help to quit tobacco use*, World Health Organization, https://www.who.int/publications/i/item/9789241516204. [10]

WHO (2017), *WHO report on the global tobacco epidemic 2017: Monitoring tobacco use and prevention policies*, World Health Organization, https://www.who.int/publications/i/item/9789241512824. [9]

WHO (2015), *WHO report on the global tobacco epidemic 2015: Raising taxes on tobacco*, World Health Organization, https://www.who.int/publications/i/item/9789241509121. [8]

WHO (2015), *Global school-based student health survey. Guatemala 2015 Fact Sheet*, World Health Organization, https://www.who.int/publications/m/item/2015-gshs-fact-sheet-guatemala. [30]

WHO (2013), *WHO report on the global tobacco epidemic 2013: Enforcing bans on tobacco advertising, promotion and sponsorship*, World Health Organization, https://www.who.int/publications/i/item/9789241505871. [7]

WHO (2011), *WHO report on the global tobacco epidemic 2011: Warning about the dangers of tobacco*, World Health Organization, https://www.who.int/publications/i/item/9789244564264. [6]

WHO (2009), *WHO report on the global tobacco epidemic 2009: Implementing smoke-free environments*, World Health Organization, https://www.who.int/publications/i/item/9789241563918. [5]

World Bank (2024), *World Bank Open Data*, World Bank, https://data.worldbank.org/ (accessed on 13 January 2024). [15]

Honduras

Figure 6.81. Honduras - Trends in tobacco use prevalence

Percentage of the population aged 15 years and over who currently use any tobacco product (smoked and/or smokeless tobacco) on a daily or non-daily basis, 2000-2020

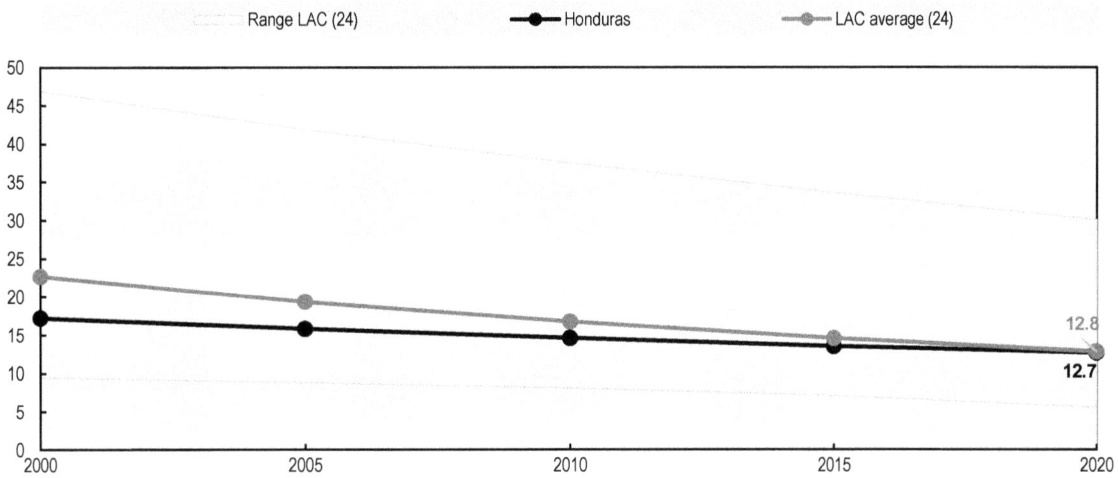

Note: Tobacco products include cigarettes, pipes, cigars, cigarillos, waterpipes (hookah, shisha), bidis, kretek, heated tobacco products (HTP), and all forms of smokeless (oral and nasal) tobacco. Tobacco products exclude e-cigarettes (which do not contain tobacco), e-cigars, e-hookahs, and e-pipes. The rates are age-standardized to the World Health Organisation (WHO) standard population. The LAC average was calculated as the average of Argentina, Bahamas, Barbados, Belize, Bolivia, Brazil, Chile, Colombia, Costa Rica, Cuba, the Dominican Republic, Ecuador, El Salvador, Guatemala, Guyana, Haiti, Honduras, Jamaica, Mexico, Panama, Paraguay, Peru, Saint Lucia, and Uruguay.
Source: WHO Global Health Observatory Data Repository (WHO, 2024[1]).

Table 6.41. Honduras - Tobacco use prevalence by sex and age groups

Percentage of the population group, latest year available

	Tobacco use prevalence (all tobacco products)	Cigarette smoking prevalence (cigarettes only)
Youths aged 13-15 years		
Total	**7.9**	**5.2**
Males	9.6	6.1
Females	6.4	4.4
People aged 15 and over		
Total	**12.7**	**11.2**
Males	23.5	20.9
Females	1.8	1.6

Note: Tobacco use prevalence is defined as the percentage of the population group who currently use any tobacco product (smoked and/or smokeless tobacco) on a daily or non-daily basis. Tobacco products exclude e-cigarettes (which do not contain tobacco), e-cigars, e-hookahs, and e-pipes. Data for students aged 13-15 years are from 2016 and taken from the Global Youth Tobacco Survey. Data for people aged 15 and over correspond to 2020.
Source: WHO Global Health Observatory Data Repository (WHO, 2024[1]); Global Youth Tobacco Survey (WHO, 2016[31]).

Table 6.42. Honduras - Summary of MPOWER measures, 2022

M Monitoring	P Smoking bans	O Cessation programmes	W Health warnings	E Advertising bans	R Taxation	WHO Frawework Convention on Tobacco Control		Protocol to eliminate illicit trade in tobacco products	
						Date of signature	Date of ratification	Date of signature	Date of ratification
						18-06-2004	16-02-2005		

... Not categorized/ No data; No policy or weak measure; Minimal measure; Moderate measure; Complete measure

Source: WHO report on the global tobacco epidemic (WHO, 2023[3]).

Figure 6.82. Honduras - Taxes and prices of the most sold brand of cigarettes

Panel A. Indirect taxes levied on cigarettes in Honduras and LAC

Panel B. Tobacco tax share and price of cigarettes in Honduras

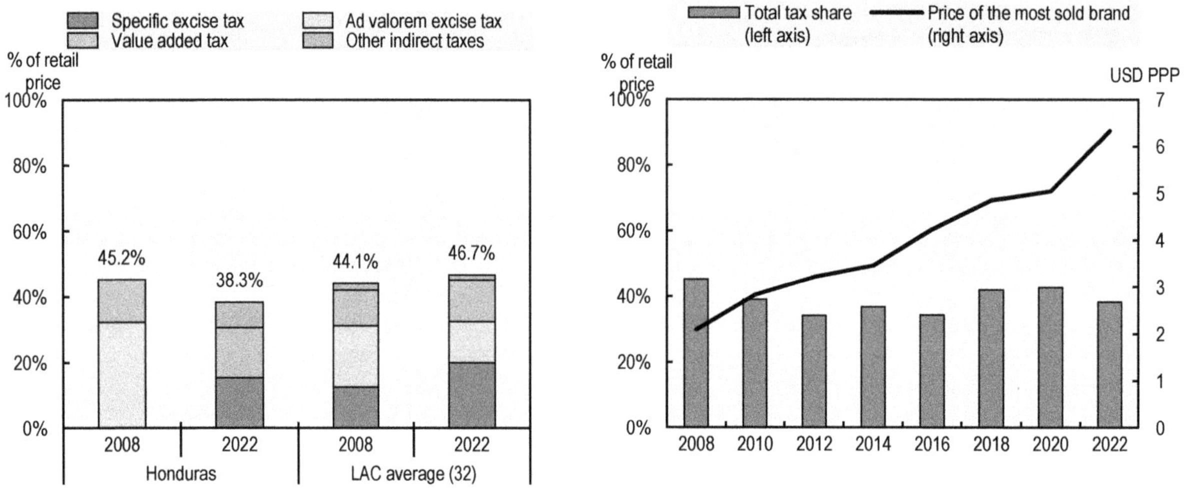

Note: Prices correspond to a 20-cigarette pack of the most sold brand. The most sold brand of cigarettes is determined based on national market share information and can vary over time (i.e. the most sold brand of cigarettes in year 1 can be different from year 2). Retail prices in USD PPP are based on the implied purchasing power parity (PPP) conversion rate from the International Monetary Fund (IMF) World Economic Outlook Database (October 2023).
Source: WHO report on the global tobacco epidemic (WHO, 2023[3]); IMF World Economic Outlook Database (IMF, 2023[4]).

Figure 6.83. Honduras - Trends in retail prices of cigarettes by brand category

In USD PPP per pack of 20 cigarettes, 2008-2022

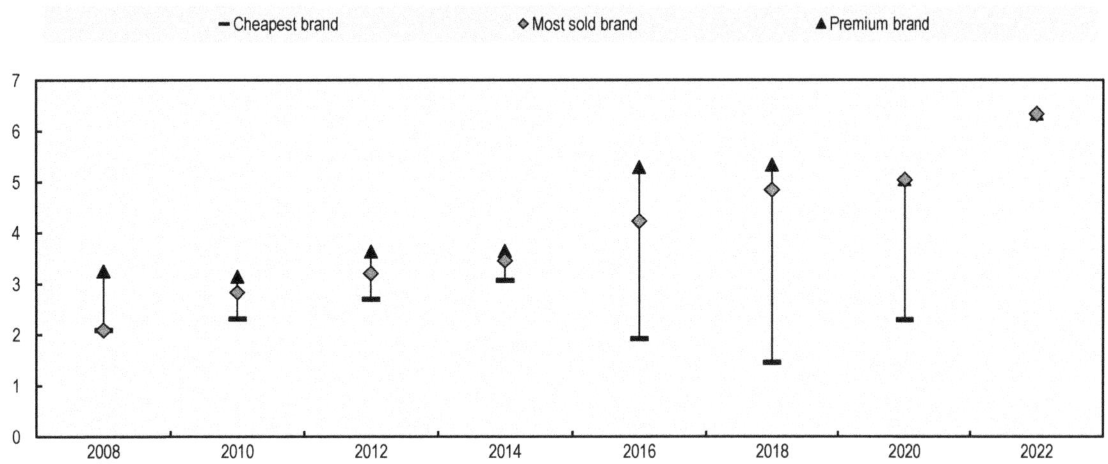

Note: Prices correspond to a 20-cigarette pack of the cheapest, most sold and premium brands. The cheapest, most sold and premium brands of cigarettes are determined based on national market share information and can vary over time (i.e. the cheapest/most sold/premium brands of cigarettes in year 1 can be different from year 2). Retail prices in USD PPP are based on the implied PPP conversion rate from the IMF World Economic Outlook Database (October 2023). Retail price of the cheapest brand is not available for 2022.

Source: WHO reports on the global tobacco epidemic (WHO, 2009[5]; WHO, 2011[6]; WHO, 2013[7]; WHO, 2015[8]; WHO, 2017[9]; WHO, 2019[10]; WHO, 2021[11]); IMF World Economic Outlook Database (IMF, 2023[4]).

Figure 6.84. Honduras - Affordability of cigarettes

Percentage of GDP per capita required to purchase 100 packs of 20 cigarettes

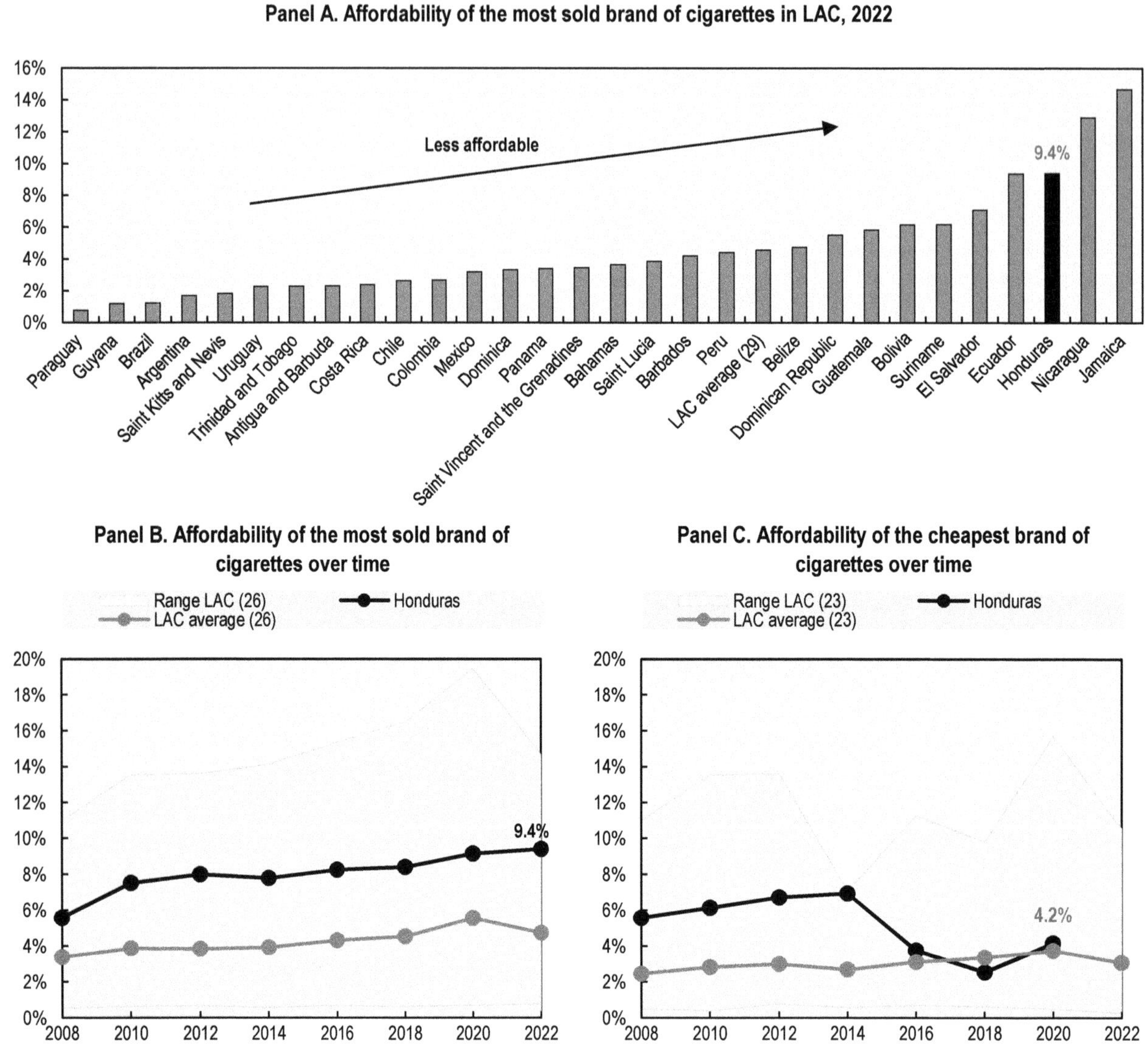

Note: Affordability of the cheapest brand in Honduras is not available for 2022. The affordability indicator measures the percentage of the country's GDP per capita required to purchase 100 packs of 20 cigarettes. A higher percentage means lower affordability of cigarettes while a lower percentage means higher affordability. To ensure comparability of average affordability across LAC over time, countries where information was unavailable for certain years have been excluded from the calculation. Data for Panel C are OECD calculations based on WHO reports on the global tobacco epidemic (2009-2023 editions). The cheapest and most sold brands of cigarettes are determined based on national market share information and can vary over time (i.e. the cheapest/most sold brand of cigarettes in year 1 can be different from year 2).

Source: WHO reports on the global tobacco epidemic (WHO, 2009[5]; WHO, 2011[6]; WHO, 2013[7]; WHO, 2015[8]; WHO, 2017[9]; WHO, 2019[10]; WHO, 2021[11]).

Table 6.43. Honduras - Design of tobacco excise taxes across tobacco products, 2022

	Excise tax structure	Specific excise tax				Ad valorem excise tax			Excise tax floor			
		Yes / No	Tax base	Rate per 20-unit pack USD PPP (local currency)	Indexation mechanisms	Yes / No	Tax base	Statutory rate	Yes / No	Tax base	Rate per 20-unit pack USD PPP (local currency)	Indexation mechanisms
Cigarettes	Specific only	Yes	1 000 sticks	1.0 (10.8)	CPI	No			No			
Cigars	No excise											
Cigarillos	No excise											
Roll-Your-Own (RYO) tobacco	No excise											
Heated tobacco products (HTPs)	No excise											
ENDS and ENNDS	No excise											

Note: Blank cells mean that there is no excise tax for the corresponding tobacco product; "CPI" means consumer price index. Following the WHO report on the global tobacco epidemic (WHO, 2021[11]), new tobacco and nicotine products in this report include electronic nicotine delivery systems (ENDS), electronic non-nicotine delivery systems (ENNDS), and heated tobacco products (HTP). Specific taxes are converted into USD PPP with the implied PPP conversion rate available in the IMF World Economic Outlook Database (October 2023). Specific excise taxes have been standardized to a 20-unit pack to allow the comparison across countries with different tax bases.
Source: Decreto No. 17-2010; Acuerdo No. 172-2022; IMF World Economic Outlook Database (IMF, 2023[4]).

Table 6.44. Honduras - Tobacco tax reforms since 2000

Year of adoption	Specific excise taxes	Ad valorem excise taxes	Other
2004	No	Cigarettes: increase in the tax rate to 47.5% levied on the retail price, excluding all indirect taxes.	No
2010	Cigarettes: introduction of a specific excise tax levied at a rate of HNL 350 per 1 000 sticks. From 2013, the specific excise tax is adjusted annually based on changes in CPI. The year-on-year increase of the indexed specific excise tax cannot exceed 6%, irrespective of changes in CPI.	Cigarettes: the ad valorem excise tax is abolished.	No

Note: "Tobacco tax reform" refers to changes in the tobacco excise tax rates, the introduction of indexation mechanisms or minimum taxes, as well as adjustments to the tax base. These reforms typically entail the enactment of new laws or decrees. The table does not refer to recurrent tax changes that result from the indexation for inflation of tax brackets and price floors (if implemented). Tobacco tax reforms included reflect changes in the legislation, but not whether or when the reforms have been implemented.
Source: Decreto No.219-2003; Decreto No. 17-2010 (art. 23).

Figure 6.85. Honduras - Tobacco excise tax revenue

Percentage of GDP, latest year available

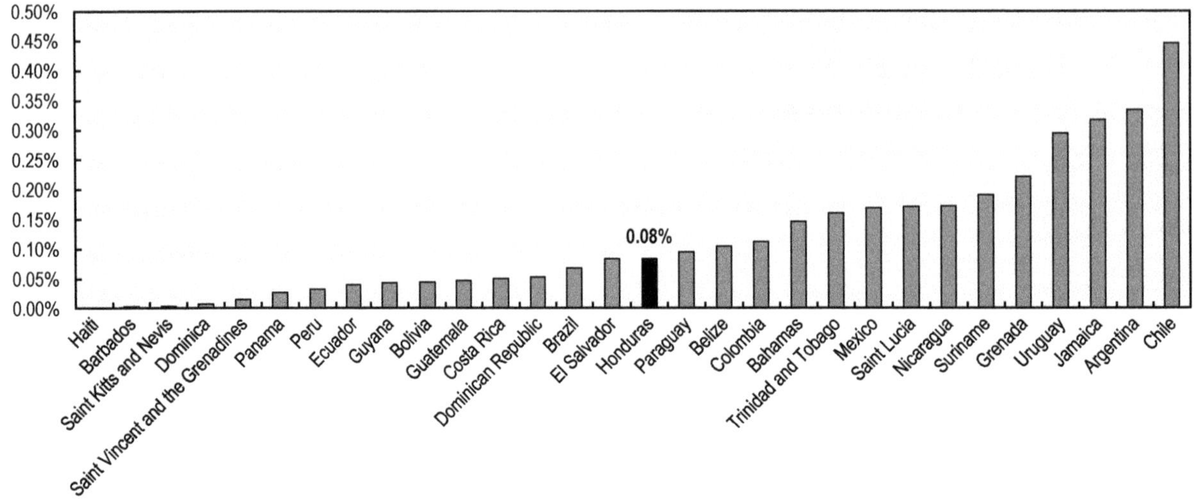

Note: See Box 2.1 (Chapter 2) for more information on tobacco tax revenue (source of information and calculations) and country selection. The latest year available is 2022 for Argentina, Brazil, Chile, Colombia, Costa Rica, the Dominican Republic, El Salvador, Guatemala, Guyana, Honduras, Mexico, Nicaragua, Panama, Paraguay, Peru, Saint Kitts and Nevis, Suriname, and Uruguay; 2021 for Belize, Dominica, Ecuador, Grenada, Saint Lucia, Saint Vincent and the Grenadines; 2020 for Bahamas, Bolivia, Jamaica and Trinidad and Tobago; 2015 for Haiti; 2014 for Barbados.
Source: OECD Revenue Statistics (OECD, 2024[13]); WHO report on the global tobacco epidemic (WHO, 2023[3]); National data.

Figure 6.86. Honduras - Trends in tobacco excise tax revenue

Percentage of GDP, 2000-2022

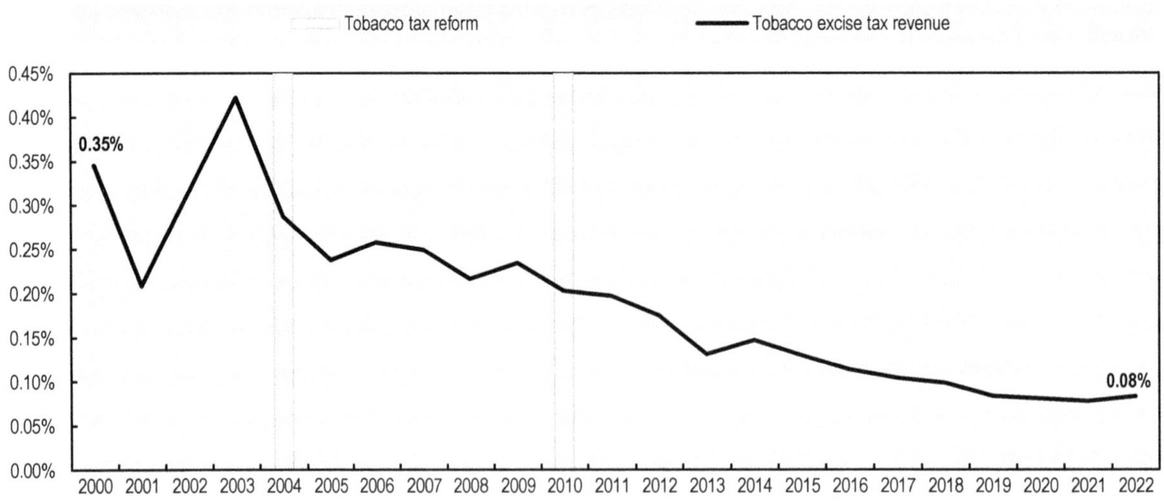

Note: "Tobacco tax reform" refers to the measures included in Table 6.44.
Source: OECD Revenue Statistics (OECD, 2024[13]); Decreto No.219-2003; Decreto No. 17-2010 (art. 23).

Figure 6.87. Honduras - Average excise tax revenue collected per pack of 20 cigarettes sold

Tobacco excise tax revenue in USD PPP collected per pack of legal cigarettes sold, latest year available

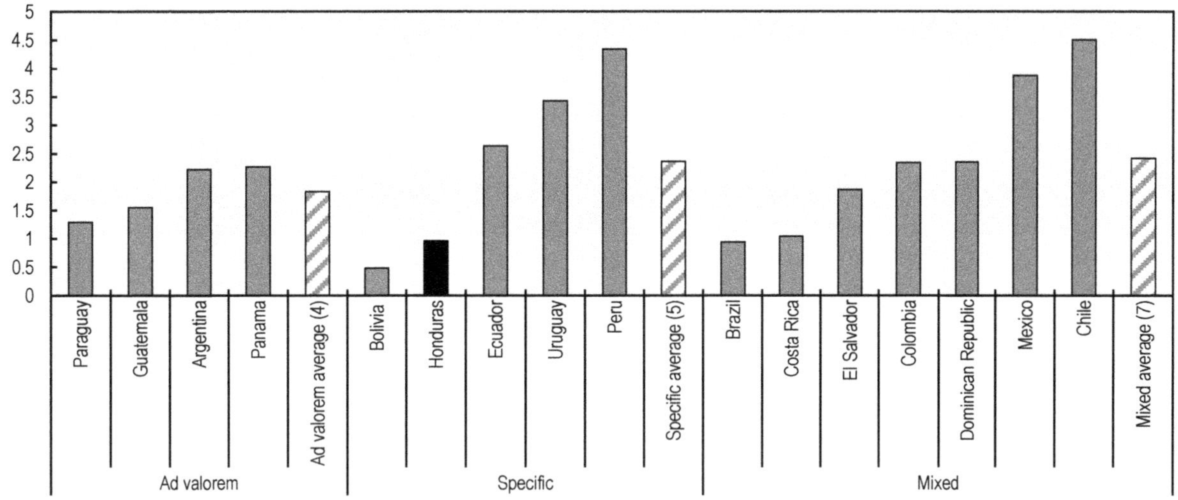

Note: See Box 2.1 (Chapter 2) for more information on tobacco tax revenue (source of information and calculations). The latest year available is 2022 for Argentina, Brazil, Chile, Colombia, Costa Rica, the Dominican Republic, El Salvador, Guatemala, Honduras, Mexico, Panama, Paraguay, Peru and Uruguay; 2021 for Ecuador;2020 for Bolivia. The country selection is provided by the availability of data on sales of cigarettes in Euromonitor International Tobacco Industry edition, 2023 © All rights reserved (Euromonitor International, 2023[14]).

Source: OECD Revenue Statistics (OECD, 2024[13]); WHO report on the global tobacco epidemic (WHO, 2023[3]); National data; IMF World Economic Outlook Database (IMF, 2023[4]); and OECD calculations based on Euromonitor International's Tobacco Industry edition (Euromonitor International, 2023[14]).

Figure 6.88. Honduras - Change in tobacco tax policy indicators

Percentage change from base year, 2008-2022

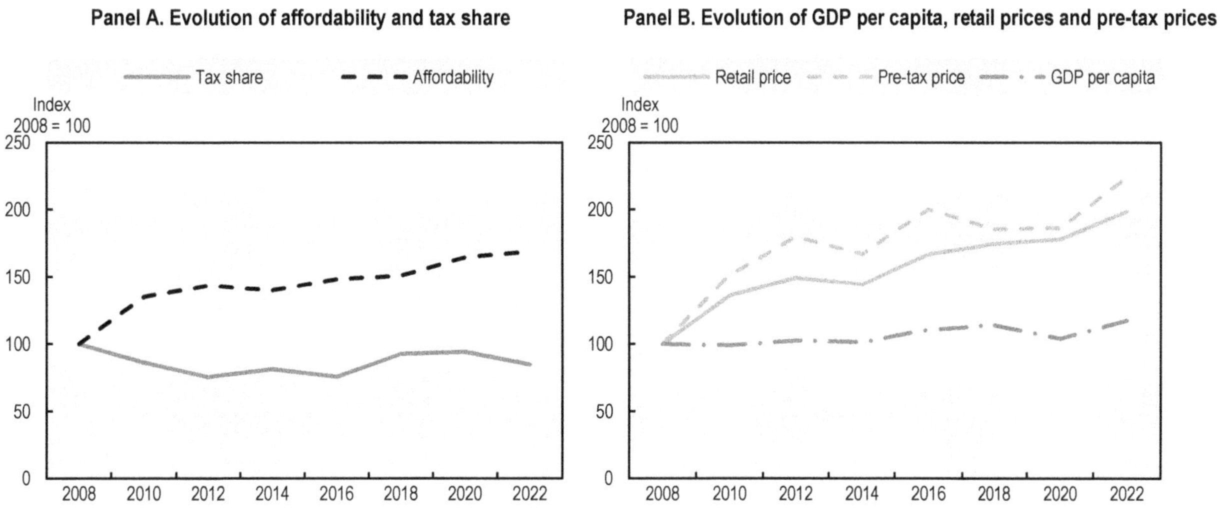

Note: Both Panel A and Panel B figures are based on data for the most sold brand of cigarettes. The most sold brand of cigarettes is determined based on national market share information and can vary over time (i.e. the most sold brand of cigarettes in year 1 can be different from year 2). In Panel A, an increase in the affordability indicator means that cigarettes are becoming less affordable, while a decline in the affordability indicator means that cigarettes are becoming more affordable. In Panel B, "Pre-tax price" corresponds to the retail price of the most sold brand of cigarettes minus the indirect taxes levied on this brand, namely excise taxes, VAT, import duties and other. Indicators in Panel B have been computed using national currency and have been adjusted for inflation; therefore, present inflation-adjusted trends.

Source: WHO report on the global tobacco epidemic (WHO, 2023[3]); World Bank Open Data (World Bank, 2024[15]); IMF International Financial Statistics (IMF, 2024[19]).

References

Euromonitor International (2023), *Euromonitor International's Tobacco Industry edition*, https://www.euromonitor.com/tobacco (accessed on 1 August 2023). [14]

IMF (2023), *World Economic Outlook Database*, International Monetary Fund, https://www.imf.org/en/Publications/WEO/weo-database/2023/October (accessed on 13 January 2024). [4]

IMF (2024), *International Financial Statistics (IFS)*, International Monetary Fund, https://data.imf.org/?sk=4c514d48-b6ba-49ed-8ab9-52b0c1a0179b&sId=1390030341854 (accessed on 13 January 2024). [19]

OECD (2024), *Global Revenue Statistics Database*, Organisation for Economic Co-operation and Development, https://www.oecd.org/tax/tax-policy/global-revenue-statistics-database.htm (accessed on 13 August 2023). [13]

WHO (2024), *Global Health Observatory: Age-standardized estimates of current tobacco use, tobacco smoking and cigarette smoking (Tobacco control: Monitor)*, World Health Organization, https://www.who.int/data/gho/data/indicators/indicator-details/GHO/gho-tobacco-control-monitor-current-tobaccouse-tobaccosmoking-cigarrettesmoking-agestd-tobagestdcurr (accessed on 20 February 2024). [1]

WHO (2023), *WHO report on the global tobacco epidemic 2023: protect people from tobacco smoke*, World Health Organization, https://www.who.int/publications/i/item/9789240077164. [3]

WHO (2021), *WHO report on the global tobacco epidemic 2021: Addressing new and emerging products*, World Health Organization, https://www.who.int/publications/i/item/9789240032095. [11]

WHO (2019), *WHO report on the global tobacco epidemic 2019: Offer help to quit tobacco use*, World Health Organization, https://www.who.int/publications/i/item/9789241516204. [10]

WHO (2017), *WHO report on the global tobacco epidemic 2017: Monitoring tobacco use and prevention policies*, World Health Organization, https://www.who.int/publications/i/item/9789241512824. [9]

WHO (2016), *Global Youth Tobacco Survey. Honduras 2016 Fact Sheet*, World Health Organization, https://cdn.who.int/media/docs/default-source/ncds/ncd-surveillance/data-reporting/honduras/honduras-gyts-2016-factsheet-(ages-13-15)_508tagged.pdf?sfvrsn=660b614a_1&download=true. [31]

WHO (2015), *WHO report on the global tobacco epidemic 2015: Raising taxes on tobacco*, World Health Organization, https://www.who.int/publications/i/item/9789241509121. [8]

WHO (2013), *WHO report on the global tobacco epidemic 2013: Enforcing bans on tobacco advertising, promotion and sponsorship*, World Health Organization, https://www.who.int/publications/i/item/9789241505871. [7]

WHO (2011), *WHO report on the global tobacco epidemic 2011: Warning about the dangers of tobacco*, World Health Organization, https://www.who.int/publications/i/item/9789244564264. [6]

WHO (2009), *WHO report on the global tobacco epidemic 2009: Implementing smoke-free environments*, World Health Organization, https://www.who.int/publications/i/item/9789241563918. [5]

World Bank (2024), *World Bank Open Data*, World Bank, https://data.worldbank.org/ (accessed on 13 January 2024). [15]

Jamaica

Figure 6.89. Jamaica - Trends in tobacco use prevalence

Percentage of the population aged 15 years and over who currently use any tobacco product (smoked and/or smokeless tobacco) on a daily or non-daily basis, 2000-2020

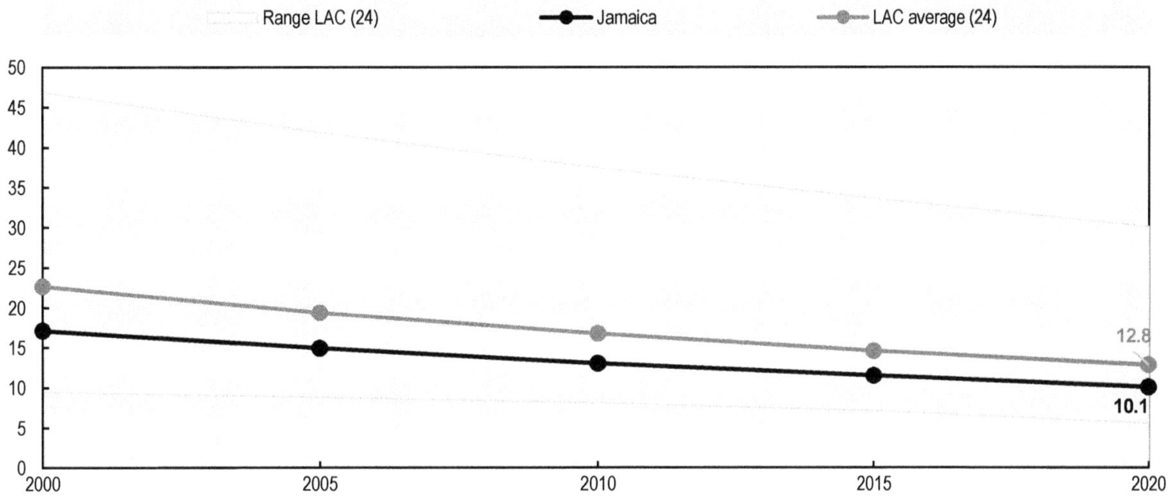

Note: Tobacco products include cigarettes, pipes, cigars, cigarillos, waterpipes (hookah, shisha), bidis, kretek, heated tobacco products (HTP), and all forms of smokeless (oral and nasal) tobacco. Tobacco products exclude e-cigarettes (which do not contain tobacco), e-cigars, e-hookahs, and e-pipes. The rates are age-standardized to the World Health Organisation (WHO) standard population. The LAC average was calculated as the average of Argentina, Bahamas, Barbados, Belize, Bolivia, Brazil, Chile, Colombia, Costa Rica, Cuba, the Dominican Republic, Ecuador, El Salvador, Guatemala, Guyana, Haiti, Honduras, Jamaica, Mexico, Panama, Paraguay, Peru, Saint Lucia, and Uruguay.
Source: WHO Global Health Observatory Data Repository (WHO, 2024[1]).

Table 6.45. Jamaica - Tobacco use prevalence by sex and age groups

Percentage of the population group, latest year available

	Tobacco use prevalence (all tobacco products)	Cigarette smoking prevalence (cigarettes only)
Youths aged 13-15 years		
Total	**15.6**	**11.2**
Males	15.9	11.1
Females	15.0	10.9
People aged 15 and over		
Total	**10.1**	**9.0**
Males	16.5	14.9
Females	3.8	3.2

Note: Tobacco use prevalence is defined as the percentage of the population group who currently use any tobacco product (smoked and/or smokeless tobacco) on a daily or non-daily basis. Tobacco products exclude e-cigarettes (which do not contain tobacco), e-cigars, e-hookahs, and e-pipes. Data for students aged 13-15 years are from 2017 and taken from the Global Youth Tobacco Survey. Data for people aged 15 and over correspond to 2020.
Source: WHO Global Health Observatory Data Repository (WHO, 2024[1]); Global Youth Tobacco Survey (WHO, 2017[32]).

Table 6.46. Jamaica - Summary of MPOWER measures, 2022

M Monitoring	P Smoking bans	O Cessation programmes	W Health warnings	E Advertising bans	R Taxation	WHO Frawework Convention on Tobacco Control		Protocol to eliminate illicit trade in tobacco products	
						Date of signature	Date of ratification	Date of signature	Date of ratification
						25-09-2004	07-07-2005		

... Not categorized/ No data; No policy or weak measure; Minimal measure; Moderate measure; Complete measure

Source: WHO report on the global tobacco epidemic (WHO, 2023[3]).

Figure 6.90. Jamaica - Taxes and prices of the most sold brand of cigarettes

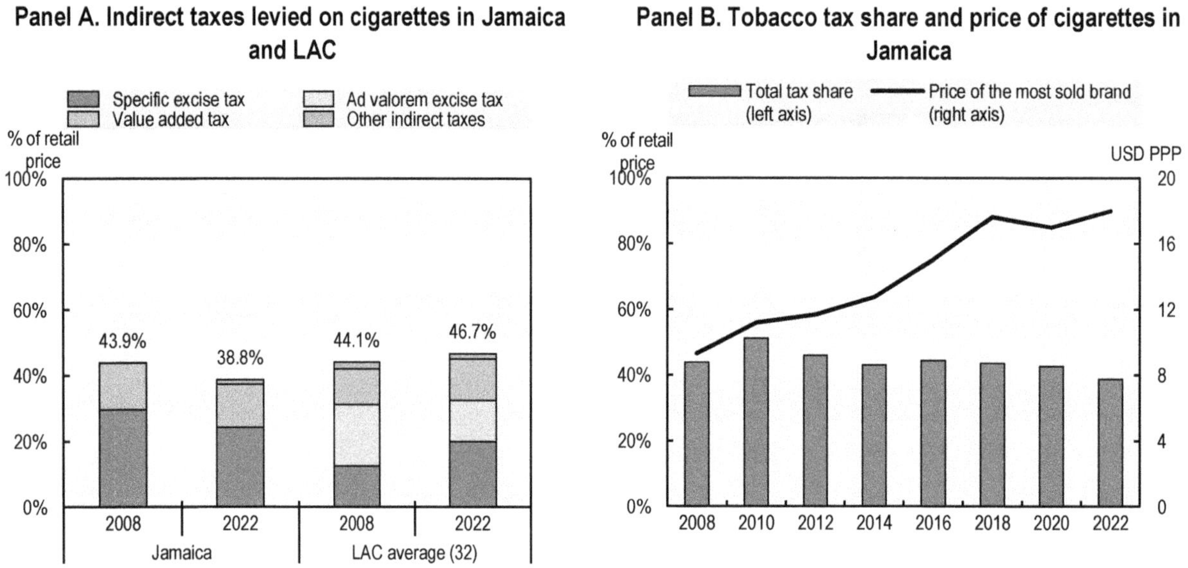

Note: Prices correspond to a 20-cigarette pack of the most sold brand. The most sold brand of cigarettes is determined based on national market share information and can vary over time (i.e. the most sold brand of cigarettes in year 1 can be different from year 2). Retail prices in USD PPP are based on the implied purchasing power parity (PPP) conversion rate from the International Monetary Fund (IMF) World Economic Outlook Database (October 2023).
Source: WHO report on the global tobacco epidemic (WHO, 2023[3]); IMF World Economic Outlook Database (IMF, 2023[4]).

Figure 6.91. Jamaica - Trends in retail prices of cigarettes by brand category

In USD PPP per pack of 20 cigarettes, 2008-2022

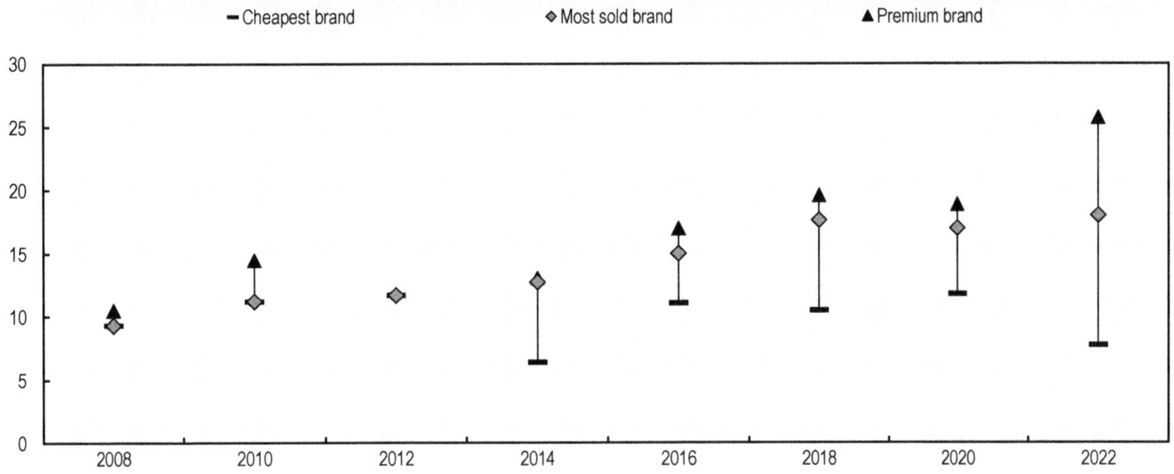

Note: Prices correspond to a 20-cigarette pack of the cheapest, most sold and premium brands. The cheapest, most sold and premium brands of cigarettes are determined based on national market share information and can vary over time (i.e. the cheapest/most sold/premium brands of cigarettes in year 1 can be different from year 2). Retail prices in USD PPP are based on the implied PPP conversion rate from the IMF World Economic Outlook Database (October 2023).
Source: WHO reports on the global tobacco epidemic (WHO, 2009[5]; WHO, 2011[6]; WHO, 2013[7]; WHO, 2015[8]; WHO, 2017[9]; WHO, 2019[10]; WHO, 2021[11]); IMF World Economic Outlook Database (IMF, 2023[4]).

Figure 6.92. Jamaica - Affordability of cigarettes

Percentage of GDP per capita required to purchase 100 packs of 20 cigarettes

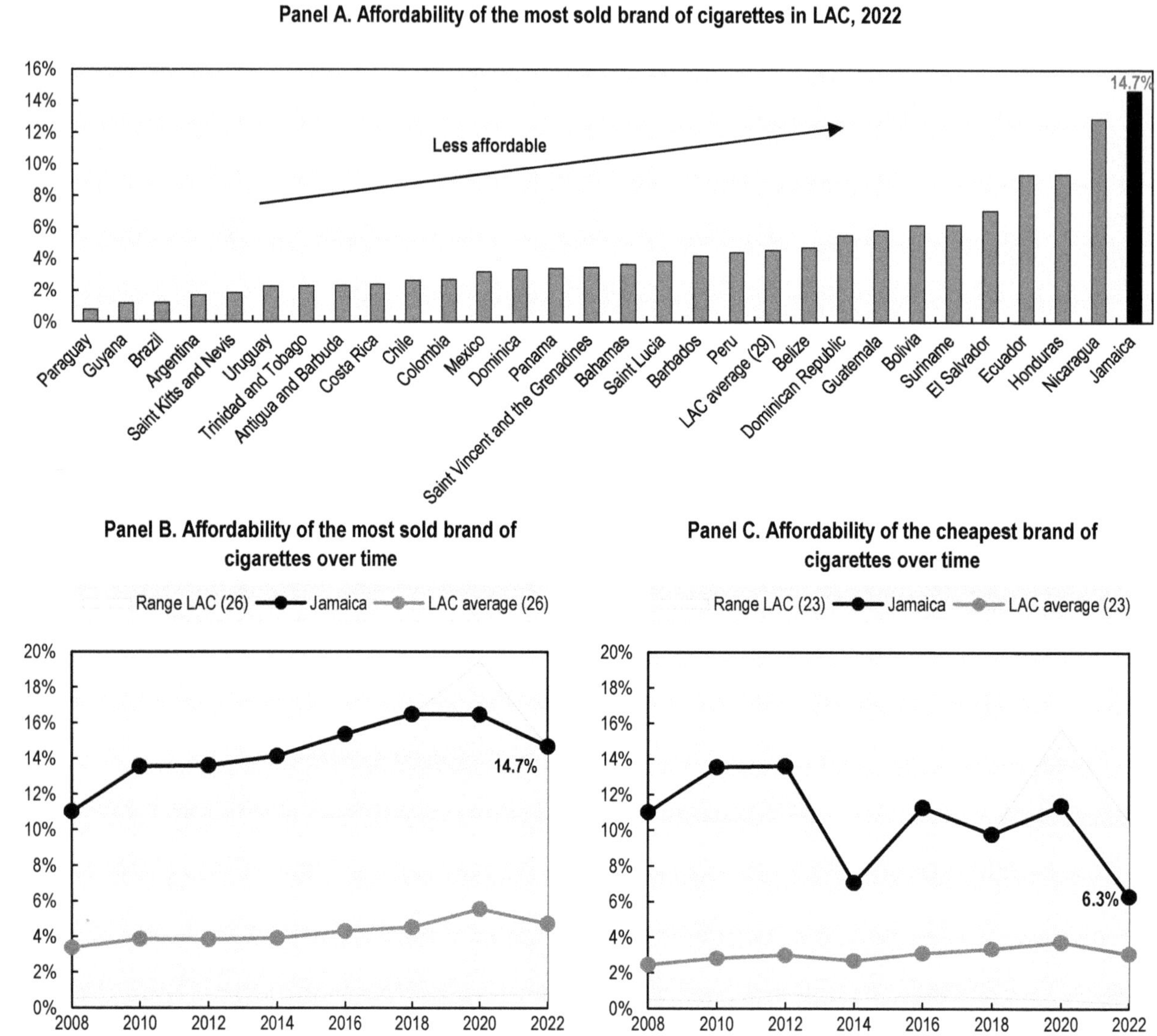

Note: The affordability indicator measures the percentage of the country's GDP per capita required to purchase 100 packs of 20 cigarettes. A higher percentage means lower affordability of cigarettes while a lower percentage means higher affordability. To ensure comparability of average affordability across LAC over time, countries where information was unavailable for certain years have been excluded from the calculation. Data for Panel C are OECD calculations based on WHO reports on the global tobacco epidemic (2009-2023 editions). The cheapest and most sold brands of cigarettes are determined based on national market share information and can vary over time (i.e. the cheapest/most sold brand of cigarettes in year 1 can be different from year 2).

Source: WHO reports on the global tobacco epidemic (WHO, 2009[5]; WHO, 2011[6]; WHO, 2013[7]; WHO, 2015[8]; WHO, 2017[9]; WHO, 2019[10]; WHO, 2021[11]).

Table 6.47. Jamaica - Design of tobacco excise taxes across tobacco products, 2022

	Excise tax structure	Specific excise tax				Ad valorem excise tax			Excise tax floor			
		Yes / No	Tax base	Rate per 20-unit pack USD PPP (local currency)	Indexation mechanisms	Yes / No	Tax base	Statutory rate	Yes / No	Tax base	Rate per 20-unit pack USD PPP (local currency)	Indexation mechanisms
Cigarettes	Specific only	Yes	Single stick	4.4 (340.0)	No	No			No			
Cigars	Specific only	Yes	Single stick	4.4 (340.0)	No	No			No			
Cigarillos	Specific only	Yes	Single stick	4.4 (340.0)	No	No			No			
Roll-Your-Own (RYP) tobacco	No excise											
Heated tobacco products (HTPs)	No excise											
ENDS and ENNDS	No excise											

Note: Blank cells mean that there is no excise tax for the corresponding tobacco product. Following the WHO report on the global tobacco epidemic (WHO, 2021[11]), new tobacco and nicotine products in this report include electronic nicotine delivery systems (ENDS), electronic non-nicotine delivery systems (ENNDS), and heated tobacco products (HTP). Specific taxes are converted into USD PPP with the implied PPP conversion rate available in the IMF World Economic Outlook Database (October 2023). Specific excise taxes have been standardized to a 20-unit pack to allow the comparison across countries with different tax bases.
Source: Revenue Measures FY 2017/2018; IMF World Economic Outlook Database (IMF, 2023[4]).

Table 6.48. Jamaica - Tobacco tax reforms since 2000

Year of adoption	Specific excise taxes	Ad valorem excise taxes	Other
2005	Cigarettes: increase in the specific tax to JMD 1 920 levied per 1 000 sticks.	Cigarettes: increase in the floor price to JMD 4 338.13 upon which the ad valorem excise tax of 39.9% is applied.	No
2007	Cigarettes: increase in the specific tax to JMD 2 300 levied per 1 000 sticks.	No	No
2008	Cigarettes: increase in the specific tax to JMD 6 000 levied per 1 000 sticks.	Cigarettes: the ad valorem excise tax is abolished.	Earmark 20% of the tobacco excise tax revenue to the National Health Fund.
2009	Cigarettes: increase in the specific tax to JMD 9 000 per 1 000 sticks.	No	No
2010	Cigarettes: increase in the specific tax to JMD 10 500 levied per 1 000 sticks.	No	No
2015	Cigarettes: increase in the specific tax and modification of the tax base, setting the specific excise tax at JMD 12.0 levied on each single stick. Cigars and cigarillos: introduction of a specific excise tax of JMD 12.0 levied on each single stick.	No	No
2016	Cigarettes, cigars, cigarillos: increase in the specific tax to JMD 14.0 levied on each single stick.	No	No
2017	Cigarettes, cigars, cigarillos: increase in the tax to JMD 17.0 levied on each single stick.	No	No

Note: "Tobacco tax reform" refers to changes in the tobacco excise tax rates, the introduction of indexation mechanisms or minimum taxes, as well as adjustments to the tax base. These reforms typically entail the enactment of new laws or decrees. The table does not refer to recurrent tax changes that result from the indexation for inflation of tax brackets and price floors (if implemented). Tobacco tax reforms included reflect changes in the legislation, but not whether or when the reforms have been implemented.
Source: Revenue Measures FY 2005/2006; Revenue Measures FY 2008/2009; Enhanced Revenue Measures for the balance of FY 2009/2010 and Medium term; Revenue Measures FY 2015/2016; Revenue Measures FY 2016/2017; Revenue Measures FY 2017/2018; and (Lewis and Edwards, 2017[33]).

Figure 6.93. Jamaica - Tobacco excise tax revenue

Percentage of GDP, latest year available

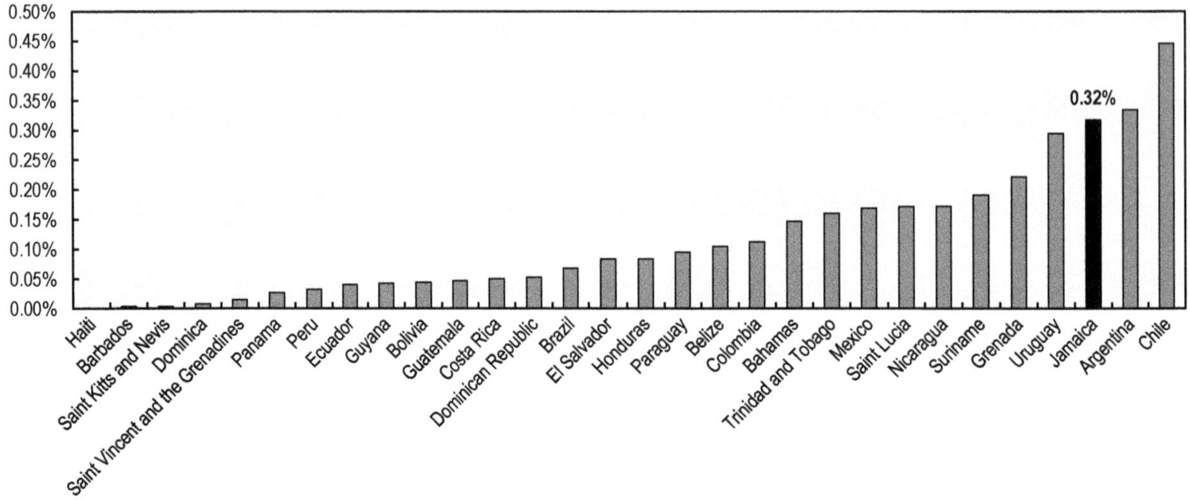

Note: See Box 2.1 (Chapter 2) for more information on tobacco tax revenue (source of information and calculations) and country selection. The latest year available is 2022 for Argentina, Brazil, Chile, Colombia, Costa Rica, the Dominican Republic, El Salvador, Guatemala, Guyana, Honduras, Mexico, Nicaragua, Panama, Paraguay, Peru, Saint Kitts and Nevis, Suriname, and Uruguay; 2021 for Belize, Dominica, Ecuador, Grenada, Saint Lucia, Saint Vincent and the Grenadines; 2020 for Bahamas, Bolivia, Jamaica and Trinidad and Tobago; 2015 for Haiti; 2014 for Barbados.
Source: OECD Revenue Statistics (OECD, 2024[13]); WHO report on the global tobacco epidemic (WHO, 2023[3]); National data.

Figure 6.94. Jamaica - Trends in tobacco excise tax revenue

Percentage of GDP, 2010-2020

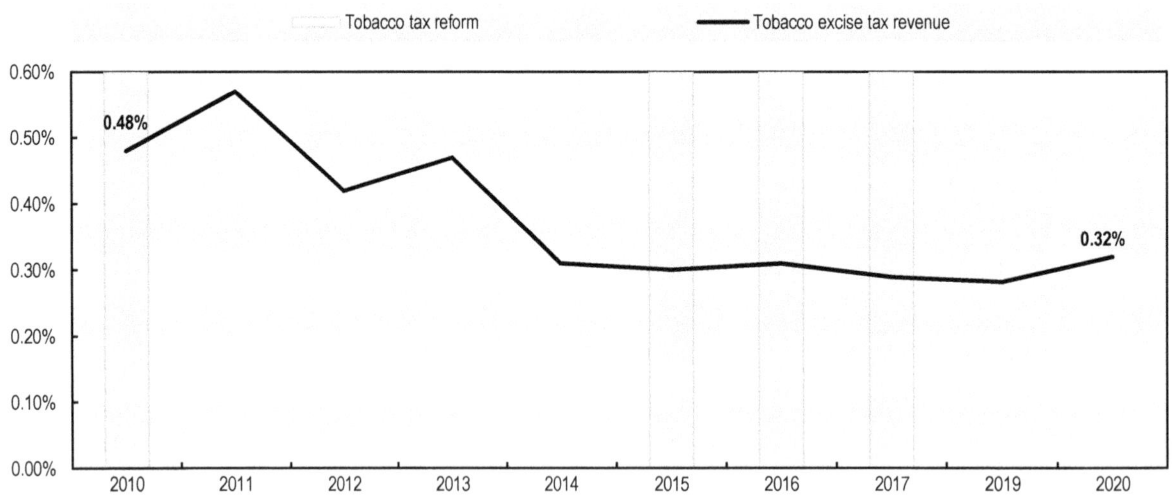

Note: "Tobacco tax reform" refers to the measures included in Table 6.48. Tobacco excise tax revenue data prior 2010 and for 2018 are not available. Tobacco tax revenue data from 2010 to 2016 were taken from the presentation ""Evolution of Jamaica's Excise Tax Regime for Alcohol and Tobacco Products" (Lewis and Edwards, 2017[33]).
Source: WHO report on the global tobacco epidemic (WHO, 2023[3]); (Lewis and Edwards, 2017[33]).

Figure 6.95. Jamaica - Change in tobacco tax policy indicators

Percentage change from base year, 2008-2022

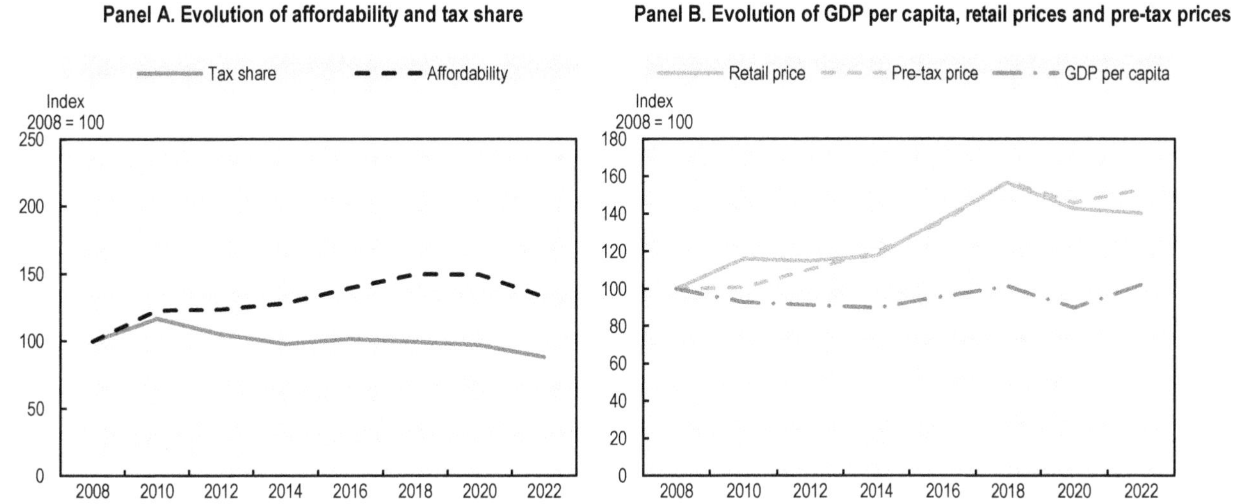

Note: Both Panel A and Panel B figures are based on data for the most sold brand of cigarettes. The most sold brand of cigarettes is determined based on national market share information and can vary over time (i.e. the most sold brand of cigarettes in year 1 can be different from year 2). In Panel A, an increase in the affordability indicator means that cigarettes are becoming less affordable, while a decline in the affordability indicator means that cigarettes are becoming more affordable. In Panel B, "Pre-tax price" corresponds to the retail price of the most sold brand of cigarettes minus the indirect taxes levied on this brand, namely excise taxes, VAT, import duties and other. Indicators in Panel B have been computed using national currency and have been adjusted for inflation; therefore, present inflation-adjusted trends.
Source: WHO report on the global tobacco epidemic (WHO, 2023[3]); World Bank Open Data (World Bank, 2024[15]); IMF International Financial Statistics (IMF, 2024[19]).

References

IMF (2023), *World Economic Outlook Database*, International Monetary Fund, https://www.imf.org/en/Publications/WEO/weo-database/2023/October (accessed on 13 January 2024). [4]

IMF (2024), *International Financial Statistics (IFS)*, International Monetary Fund, https://data.imf.org/?sk=4c514d48-b6ba-49ed-8ab9-52b0c1a0179b&sId=1390030341854 (accessed on 13 January 2024). [19]

Lewis, F. and S. Edwards (2017), *Evolution of Jamaica's Excise Tax Regime for Alcohol and Tobacco Products*, https://www.paho.org/spc-crb/dmdocuments/day-2/5-Jamaica-experience-tobacco-alcohol-taxation.pdf. [33]

OECD (2024), *Global Revenue Statistics Database*, Organisation for Economic Co-operation and Development, https://www.oecd.org/tax/tax-policy/global-revenue-statistics-database.htm (accessed on 13 August 2023). [13]

WHO (2024), *Global Health Observatory: Age-standardized estimates of current tobacco use, tobacco smoking and cigarette smoking (Tobacco control: Monitor)*, World Health Organization, https://www.who.int/data/gho/data/indicators/indicator-details/GHO/gho-tobacco-control-monitor-current-tobaccouse-tobaccosmoking-cigarrettesmoking-agestd-tobagestdcurr (accessed on 20 February 2024). [1]

WHO (2023), *WHO report on the global tobacco epidemic 2023: protect people from tobacco smoke*, World Health Organization, https://www.who.int/publications/i/item/9789240077164. [3]

WHO (2021), *WHO report on the global tobacco epidemic 2021: Addressing new and emerging products*, World Health Organization, https://www.who.int/publications/i/item/9789240032095. [11]

WHO (2019), *WHO report on the global tobacco epidemic 2019: Offer help to quit tobacco use*, World Health Organization, https://www.who.int/publications/i/item/9789241516204. [10]

WHO (2017), *WHO report on the global tobacco epidemic 2017: Monitoring tobacco use and prevention policies*, World Health Organization, https://www.who.int/publications/i/item/9789241512824. [9]

WHO (2017), *Global Youth Tobacco Survey. Jamaica 2017 Fact Sheet*, World Health Organization, https://www.who.int/publications/m/item/2017-gyts-fact-sheet-jamaica. [32]

WHO (2015), *WHO report on the global tobacco epidemic 2015: Raising taxes on tobacco*, World Health Organization, https://www.who.int/publications/i/item/9789241509121. [8]

WHO (2013), *WHO report on the global tobacco epidemic 2013: Enforcing bans on tobacco advertising, promotion and sponsorship*, World Health Organization, https://www.who.int/publications/i/item/9789241505871. [7]

WHO (2011), *WHO report on the global tobacco epidemic 2011: Warning about the dangers of tobacco*, World Health Organization, https://www.who.int/publications/i/item/9789244564264. [6]

WHO (2009), *WHO report on the global tobacco epidemic 2009: Implementing smoke-free environments*, World Health Organization, https://www.who.int/publications/i/item/9789241563918. [5]

World Bank (2024), *World Bank Open Data*, World Bank, https://data.worldbank.org/ (accessed on 13 January 2024). [15]

Mexico

Figure 6.96. Mexico - Trends in tobacco use prevalence

Percentage of the population aged 15 years and over who currently use any tobacco product (smoked and/or smokeless tobacco) on a daily or non-daily basis, 2000-2020

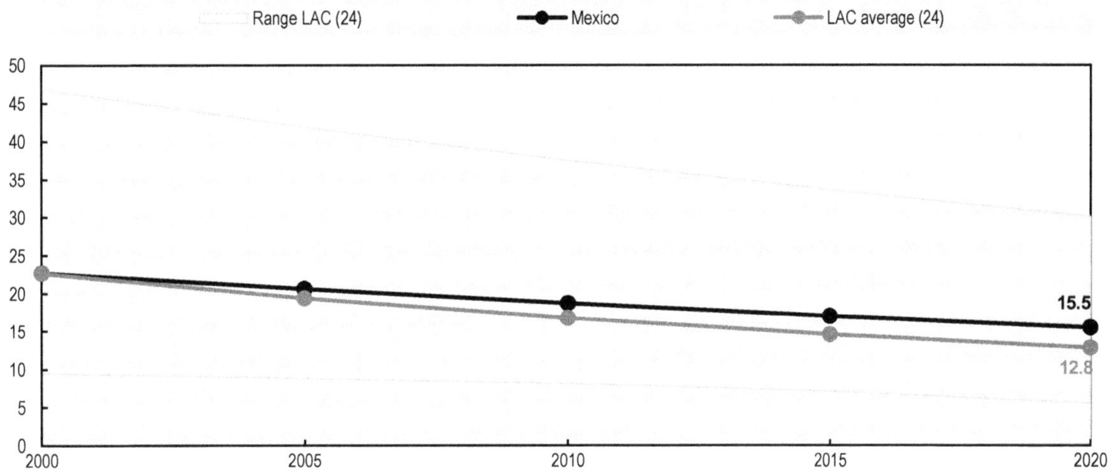

Note: Tobacco products include cigarettes, pipes, cigars, cigarillos, waterpipes (hookah, shisha), bidis, kretek, heated tobacco products (HTP), and all forms of smokeless (oral and nasal) tobacco. Tobacco products exclude e-cigarettes (which do not contain tobacco), e-cigars, e-hookahs, and e-pipes. The rates are age-standardized to the World Health Organisation (WHO) standard population. The LAC average was calculated as the average of Argentina, Bahamas, Barbados, Belize, Bolivia, Brazil, Chile, Colombia, Costa Rica, Cuba, the Dominican Republic, Ecuador, El Salvador, Guatemala, Guyana, Haiti, Honduras, Jamaica, Mexico, Panama, Paraguay, Peru, Saint Lucia, and Uruguay.
Source: WHO Global Health Observatory Data Repository (WHO, 2024[11]).

Table 6.49. Mexico - Tobacco use prevalence by sex and age groups

Percentage of the population group, latest year available

	Tobacco use prevalence (all tobacco products)	Cigarette smoking prevalence (cigarettes only)
Students aged 13-15 years		
Total	**19.8**	**14.6**
Males	21.6	15.8
Females	17.7	12.9
People aged 15 and over		
Total	**15.6**	**15.0**
Males	24.3	23.2
Females	7.4	7.3

Note: Tobacco use prevalence is defined as the percentage of the population group who currently use any tobacco product (smoked and/or smokeless tobacco) on a daily or non-daily basis. Tobacco products exclude e-cigarettes (which do not contain tobacco), e-cigars, e-hookahs, and e-pipes. Data for students aged 13-15 years are from 2011 and taken from the Global Youth Tobacco Survey. Data for people aged 15 and over correspond to 2023 and are taken from the Global Adult Tobacco Survey (GATS). For comparability purposes, the Figure 6.96 uses another source of information (WHO Global Health Observatory Data Repository) which explains the small difference with figures included in this table.
Source: Encuesta Global de Tabaquismo en Adultos, México (Government of Mexico, 2023[34]); Global Youth Tobacco Survey (WHO, 2011[35]).

Table 6.50. Mexico - Summary of MPOWER measures, 2022

M Monitoring	P Smoking bans	O Cessation programmes	W Health warnings	E Advertising bans	R Taxation	WHO Frawework Convention on Tobacco Control		Protocol to eliminate illicit trade in tobacco products	
						Date of signature	Date of ratification	Date of signature	Date of ratification
						12-08-2003	28-05-2004		

... Not categorized/ No data; No policy or weak measure; Minimal measure; Moderate measure; Complete measure

Source: WHO report on the global tobacco epidemic (WHO, 2023[3]).

Figure 6.97. Mexico - Taxes and prices of the most sold brand of cigarettes

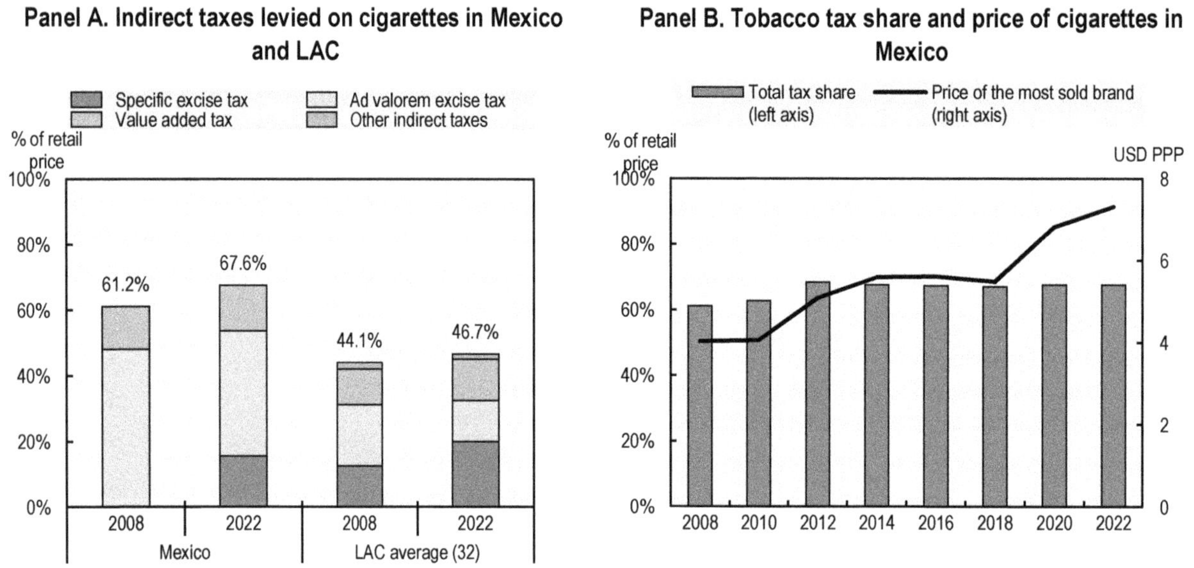

Note: Prices correspond to a 20-cigarette pack of the most sold brand. The most sold brand of cigarettes is determined based on national market share information and can vary over time (i.e. the most sold brand of cigarettes in year 1 can be different from year 2). Retail prices in USD PPP are based on the implied purchasing power parity (PPP) conversion rate from the International Monetary Fund (IMF) World Economic Outlook Database (October 2023).
Source: WHO report on the global tobacco epidemic (WHO, 2023[3]); IMF World Economic Outlook Database (IMF, 2023[4]).

Figure 6.98. Mexico - Trends in retail prices of cigarettes by brand category

In USD PPP per pack of 20 cigarettes, 2008-2022

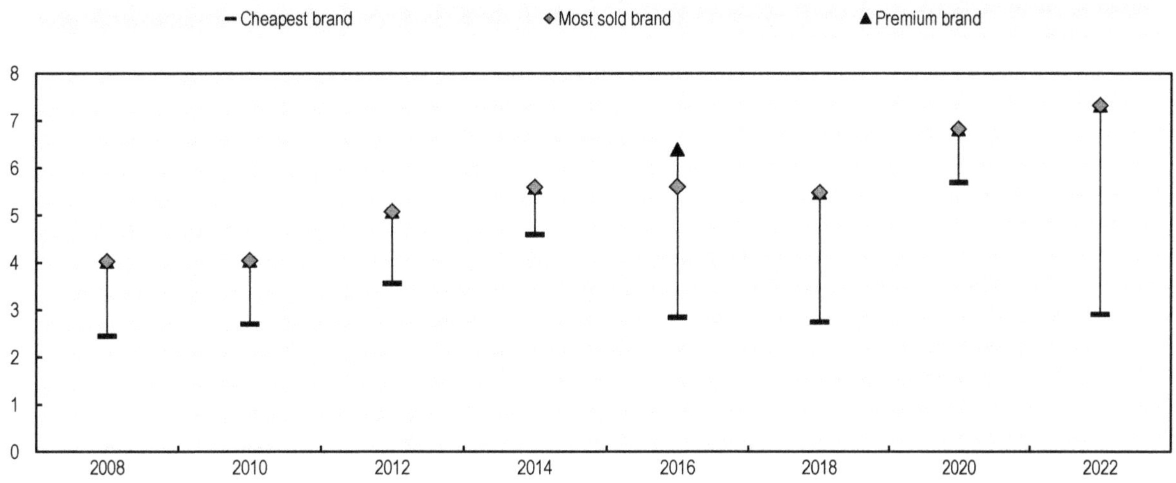

Note: Prices correspond to a 20-cigarette pack of the cheapest, most sold and premium brands. The cheapest, most sold and premium brands of cigarettes are determined based on national market share information and can vary over time (i.e. the cheapest/most sold/premium brands of cigarettes in year 1 can be different from year 2). Retail prices in USD PPP are based on the implied PPP conversion rate from the IMF World Economic Outlook Database (October 2023).
Source: WHO reports on the global tobacco epidemic (WHO, 2009[5]; WHO, 2011[6]; WHO, 2013[7]; WHO, 2015[8]; WHO, 2017[9]; WHO, 2019[10]; WHO, 2021[11]); IMF World Economic Outlook Database (IMF, 2023[4]).

Figure 6.99. Mexico - Affordability of cigarettes

Percentage of GDP per capita required to purchase 100 packs of 20 cigarettes

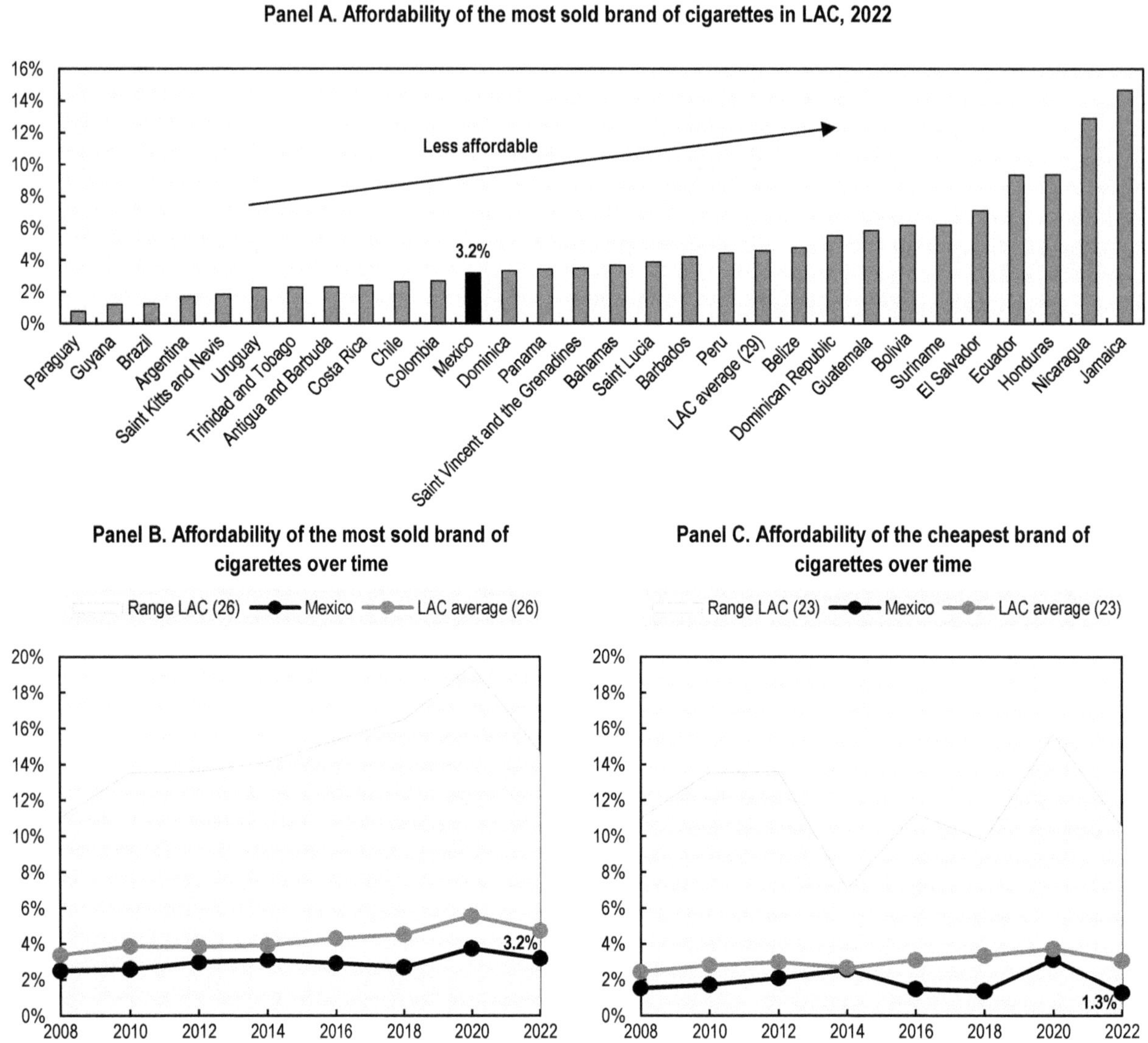

Note: The affordability indicator measures the percentage of the country's GDP per capita required to purchase 100 packs of 20 cigarettes. A higher percentage means lower affordability of cigarettes while a lower percentage means higher affordability. To ensure comparability of average affordability across LAC over time, countries where information was unavailable for certain years have been excluded from the calculation. Data for Panel C are OECD calculations based on WHO reports on the global tobacco epidemic (2009-2023 editions). The cheapest and most sold brands of cigarettes are determined based on national market share information and can vary over time (i.e. the cheapest/most sold brand of cigarettes in year 1 can be different from year 2).

Source: WHO reports on the global tobacco epidemic (WHO, 2009[5]; WHO, 2011[6]; WHO, 2013[7]; WHO, 2015[8]; WHO, 2017[9]; WHO, 2019[10]; WHO, 2021[11]).

Table 6.51. Mexico - Design of tobacco excise taxes across tobacco products, 2022

	Excise tax structure	Specific excise tax				Ad valorem excise tax			Excise tax floor			
		Yes / No	Tax base	Rate per 20-unit pack USD PPP (local currency)	Indexation mechanisms	Yes / No	Tax base	Statutory rate	Yes / No	Tax base	Rate per 20-unit pack USD PPP (local currency)	Indexation mechanisms
Cigarettes	Mixed	Yes	Single stick	1.1 (11.0)	CPI	Yes	EFP excl. VAT	160%	No			
Cigars	Mixed	Yes	Single stick	1.1 (11.0)	CPI	Yes	FRP excl. VAT	30.4% - 160%	No			
Cigarillos	Mixed	Yes	Single stick	1.1 (11.0)	CPI	Yes	FRP excl. VAT	30.4% - 160%	No			
Roll-Your-Own (RYO) tobacco	Mixed	Yes	Single stick (0.75 g)	1.1 (11.0)	CPI	Yes	FRP excl. VAT	30.4% - 160%	No			
Heated tobacco products (HTPs)	No excise											
ENDS and ENNDS	No excise											
New tobacco and nicotine products	No excise											

Note: Ad valorem tax base "EFP" means "Ex-factory price/CIF value"; "FRP" means "Final (observed) retail price"; blank cells mean that there is no excise tax for the corresponding tobacco product; "VAT" means "Value added tax". In Mexico, handmade tobacco products other than cigarettes are taxed with a reduced ad valorem rate of 30.4% and are not subject to the specific excise tax. Following the WHO report on the global tobacco epidemic (WHO, 2021[11]), new tobacco and nicotine products in this report include electronic nicotine delivery systems (ENDS), electronic non-nicotine delivery systems (ENNDS), and heated tobacco products (HTP). Mexico does not levy an excise tax on new tobacco and nicotine products because their sales are banned (WHO, 2023[3]). Specific taxes are converted into USD PPP with the implied PPP conversion rate available in the IMF World Economic Outlook Database (October 2023). Specific excise taxes have been standardized to a 20-unit pack to allow the comparison across countries with different tax bases. Ad valorem tax rates for cigars, cigarillos and RYO tobacco are tiered based on the manufacturing process. The products entirely handmade are levied at a lower rate of 30.4% and are not subject to the specific excise tax.

Source: DOF 23-12-2021; IMF World Economic Outlook Database (IMF, 2023[4])).

Table 6.52. Mexico - Tobacco tax reforms since 2000

Year of adoption	Specific excise taxes	Ad valorem excise taxes	Other
2002	No	Cigarettes: introduction of an ad valorem excise tax with a uniform tax rate of 110% effective as 2005. The tax rate increased to 105% in 2002 and then continues to increase each year to reach 110% in 2005. The ad valorem tax base remains the retail price. Cigars, cigarillos and RYO tobacco: introduction of an ad valorem excise tax levied at a rate of 20.9% on retail price.	No
2006	No	All tobacco products: introduction of tiered ad valorem tax rates based on manufacturing processes. Products entirely handmade are taxed at a rate of 30.4%, while other products are taxed at a rate of 160%. The ad valorem tax is levied on the tax-exclusive ex-factory price for cigarettes and the tax-exclusive final retail price for non-cigarette tobacco products. The tax rate increased to 140% in 2007, to 150% in 2008 and to 160% in 2009. For the handmade tobacco products, the tax rate is raised to 26.6% in 2007, to 28.5% in 2008 and to 30.4% in 2009.	No
2009	All tobacco products: introduction of a specific excise tax levied at a rate of MXN 0.04 on each single stick. For the RYO tobacco products, the weight is divided by 0.75 to reflect the tobacco content of a cigarette stick.	No	No
2010	All tobacco products: increase in the specific tax to MXN 0.35 levied on each single stick. The specific excise tax on handmade tobacco products other than cigarettes is abolished from 2014.	No	No
2019	All tobacco products: the specific excise tax is adjusted annually based on the change in the CPI. For 2020, the specific excise tax is raised to MXN 0.4944, accounting for the cumulated CPI between November 2010 and November 2019.		

Note: "Tobacco tax reform" refers to changes in the tobacco excise tax rates, the introduction of indexation mechanisms or minimum taxes, as well as adjustments to the tax base. These reforms typically entail the enactment of new laws or decrees. The table does not refer to recurrent tax changes that result from the indexation for inflation of tax brackets and price floors (if implemented). Tobacco tax reforms included reflect changes in the legislation, but not whether or when the reforms have been implemented.
Source: DOF 01-01-2002; DOF 27-12-2006; DOF 27-11-2009; DOF 19-11-2010; DOF 09-12-2019.

Figure 6.100. Mexico - Tobacco excise tax revenue

Percentage of GDP, latest year available

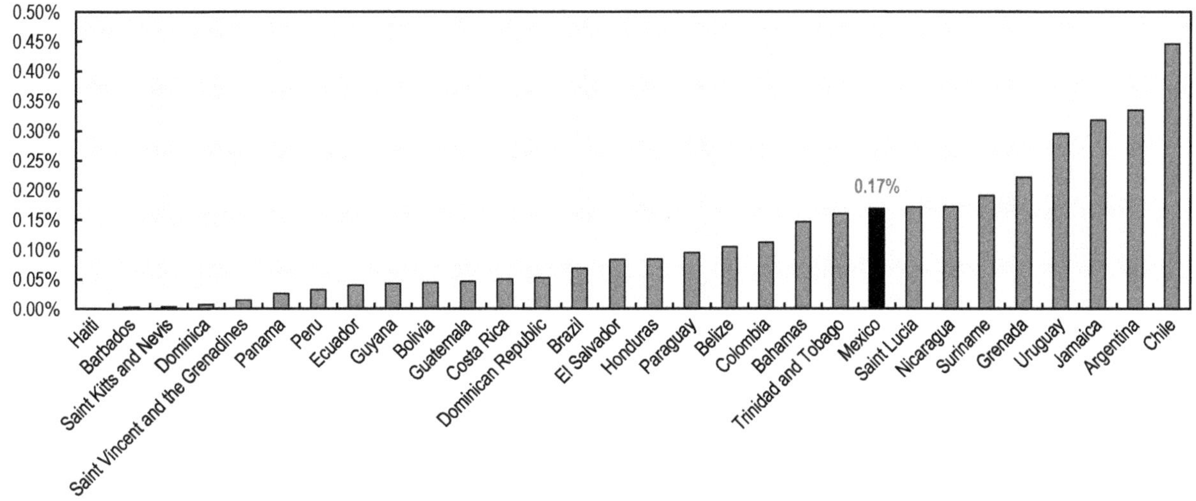

Note: See Box 2.1 (Chapter 2) for more information on tobacco tax revenue (source of information and calculations) and country selection. The latest year available is 2022 for Argentina, Brazil, Chile, Colombia, Costa Rica, the Dominican Republic, El Salvador, Guatemala, Guyana, Honduras, Mexico, Nicaragua, Panama, Paraguay, Peru, Saint Kitts and Nevis, Suriname, and Uruguay; 2021 for Belize, Dominica, Ecuador, Grenada, Saint Lucia, Saint Vincent and the Grenadines; 2020 for Bahamas, Bolivia, Jamaica and Trinidad and Tobago; 2015 for Haiti; 2014 for Barbados.
Source: OECD Revenue Statistics (OECD, 2024[13]); WHO report on the global tobacco epidemic (WHO, 2023[3]); National data.

Figure 6.101. Mexico - Trends in tobacco excise tax revenue

Percentage of GDP, 2000-2022

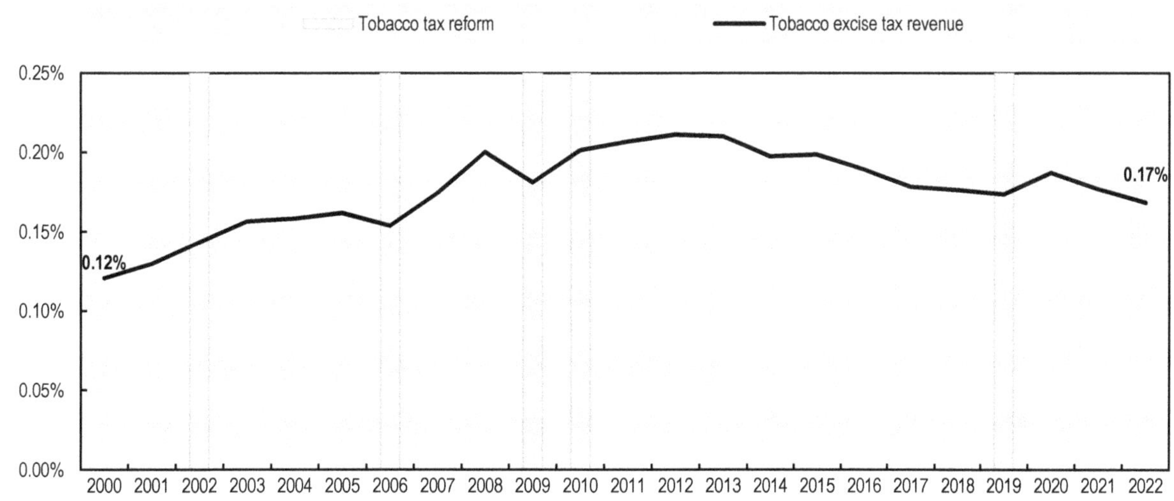

Note: "Tobacco tax reform" refers to the measures included in Table 6.52.
Source: Ingresos Presupuestarios del Gobierno Federal (Resumen Artículo 1 LIF) (Government of Mexico, 2023[36]); DOF 01-01-2002; DOF 27-12-2006; DOF 27-11-2009; DOF 19-11-2010; DOF 09-12-2019.

Figure 6.102. Mexico - Average excise tax revenue collected per pack of 20 cigarettes sold

Tobacco excise tax revenue in USD PPP collected per pack of legal cigarettes sold, latest year available

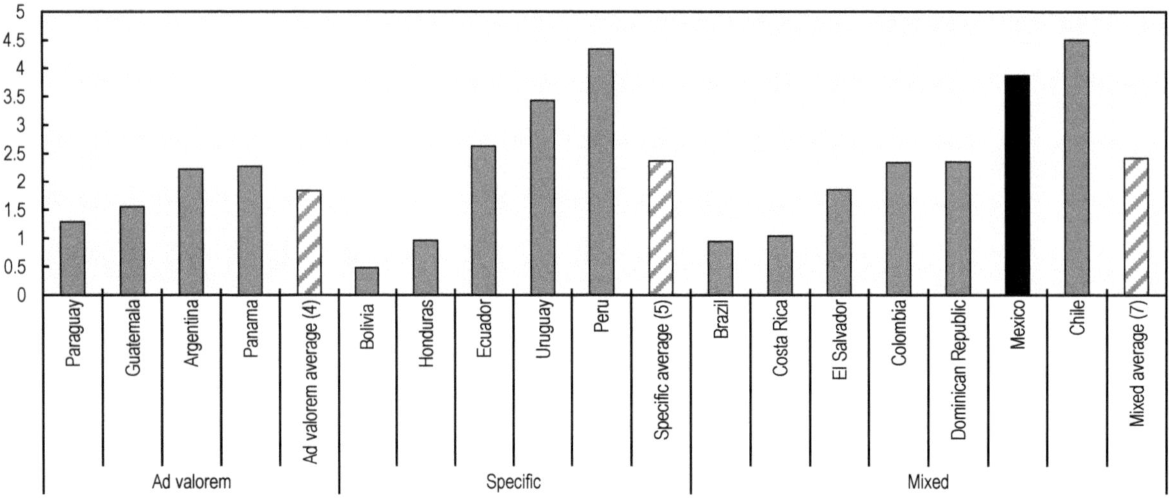

Note: See Box 2.1 (Chapter 2) for more information on tobacco tax revenue (source of information and calculations). The latest year available is 2022 for Argentina, Brazil, Chile, Colombia, Costa Rica, the Dominican Republic, El Salvador, Guatemala, Honduras, Mexico, Panama, Paraguay, Peru and Uruguay; 2021 for Ecuador; 2020 for Bolivia. The country selection is provided by the availability of data on sales of cigarettes in Euromonitor International Tobacco Industry edition, 2023 © All rights reserved (Euromonitor International, 2023[14]).

Source: OECD Revenue Statistics (OECD, 2024[13]); WHO report on the global tobacco epidemic (WHO, 2023[3]); National data; IMF World Economic Outlook Database (IMF, 2023[4]); and OECD calculations based on Euromonitor International's Tobacco Industry edition (Euromonitor International, 2023[14]).

Figure 6.103. Mexico - Change in tobacco tax policy indicators

Percentage change from base year, 2008-2022

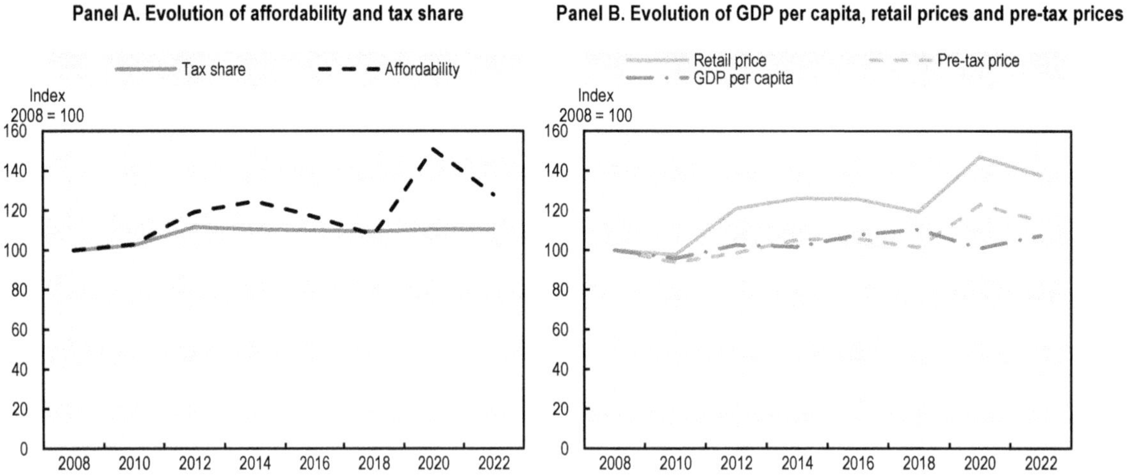

Note: Both Panel A and Panel B figures are based on data for the most sold brand of cigarettes. The most sold brand of cigarettes is determined based on national market share information and can vary over time (i.e. the most sold brand of cigarettes in year 1 can be different from year 2). In Panel A, an increase in the affordability indicator means that cigarettes are becoming less affordable, while a decline in the affordability indicator means that cigarettes are becoming more affordable. In Panel B, "Pre-tax price" corresponds to the retail price of the most sold brand of cigarettes minus the indirect taxes levied on this brand, namely excise taxes, VAT, import duties and other. Indicators in Panel B have been computed using national currency and have been adjusted for inflation; therefore, present inflation-adjusted trends.

Source: WHO report on the global tobacco epidemic (WHO, 2023[3]); World Bank Open Data (World Bank, 2024[15]); IMF International Financial Statistics (IMF, 2024[19]).

References

Euromonitor International (2023), *Euromonitor International's Tobacco Industry edition*, https://www.euromonitor.com/tobacco (accessed on 1 August 2023). [14]

Government of Mexico (2023), *Encuesta Global de Tabaquismo en Adultos (GATS)*, National Commission on Mental Health and Addictions, https://www.gob.mx/salud/conadic/documentos/encuesta-global-de-tabaquismo-en-adultos-gats-2023-359138 (accessed on 13 June 2024). [34]

Government of Mexico (2023), *Ingresos Presupuestarios del Gobierno Federal (Resumen Artículo 1 LIF) Pesos corrientes multianual (2000-2022), Millones de pesos (Flujos Acumulados)*, Secretariat of Finance and Public Credit, http://presto.hacienda.gob.mx/EstoporLayout/estadisticas.jsp (accessed on 13 August 2023). [36]

IMF (2023), *World Economic Outlook Database*, International Monetary Fund, https://www.imf.org/en/Publications/WEO/weo-database/2023/October (accessed on 13 January 2024). [4]

IMF (2024), *International Financial Statistics (IFS)*, International Monetary Fund, https://data.imf.org/?sk=4c514d48-b6ba-49ed-8ab9-52b0c1a0179b&sId=1390030341854 (accessed on 13 January 2024). [19]

OECD (2024), *Global Revenue Statistics Database*, Organisation for Economic Co-operation and Development, https://www.oecd.org/tax/tax-policy/global-revenue-statistics-database.htm (accessed on 13 August 2023). [13]

WHO (2024), *Global Health Observatory: Age-standardized estimates of current tobacco use, tobacco smoking and cigarette smoking (Tobacco control: Monitor)*, World Health Organization, https://www.who.int/data/gho/data/indicators/indicator-details/GHO/gho-tobacco-control-monitor-current-tobaccouse-tobaccosmoking-cigarrettesmoking-agestd-tobagestdcurr (accessed on 20 February 2024). [1]

WHO (2023), *WHO report on the global tobacco epidemic 2023: protect people from tobacco smoke*, World Health Organization, https://www.who.int/publications/i/item/9789240077164. [3]

WHO (2021), *WHO report on the global tobacco epidemic 2021: Addressing new and emerging products*, World Health Organization, https://www.who.int/publications/i/item/9789240032095. [11]

WHO (2019), *WHO report on the global tobacco epidemic 2019: Offer help to quit tobacco use*, World Health Organization, https://www.who.int/publications/i/item/9789241516204. [10]

WHO (2017), *WHO report on the global tobacco epidemic 2017: Monitoring tobacco use and prevention policies*, World Health Organization, https://www.who.int/publications/i/item/9789241512824. [9]

WHO (2015), *WHO report on the global tobacco epidemic 2015: Raising taxes on tobacco*, World Health Organization, https://www.who.int/publications/i/item/9789241509121. [8]

WHO (2013), *WHO report on the global tobacco epidemic 2013: Enforcing bans on tobacco advertising, promotion and sponsorship*, World Health Organization, https://www.who.int/publications/i/item/9789241505871. [7]

WHO (2011), *WHO report on the global tobacco epidemic 2011: Warning about the dangers of tobacco*, World Health Organization, https://www.who.int/publications/i/item/9789244564264. [6]

WHO (2011), *Global Youth Tobacco Survey. Mexico 2011 Fact Sheet*, World Health Organization, https://www.who.int/publications/m/item/2011-gyts-fact-sheet-mexico. [35]

WHO (2009), *WHO report on the global tobacco epidemic 2009: Implementing smoke-free environments*, World Health Organization, https://www.who.int/publications/i/item/9789241563918. [5]

World Bank (2024), *World Bank Open Data*, World Bank, https://data.worldbank.org/ (accessed on 13 January 2024). [15]

Nicaragua

Table 6.53. Nicaragua - Tobacco use prevalence by sex and age groups

Percentage of the population group, latest year available

	Tobacco use prevalence (all tobacco products)	Cigarette smoking prevalence (cigarettes only)
Youths aged 13-15 years		
Total	**14.2**	**10.9**
Males	16.4	8.9
Females	11.8	12.9
People aged 15 and over		
Total	**...**	**...**
Males	...	...
Females	...	...

Note: Cells with "..." indicate that the information is not available. Tobacco use prevalence is defined as the percentage of the population group who currently use any tobacco product (smoked and/or smokeless tobacco) on a daily or non-daily basis. Tobacco products exclude e-cigarettes (which do not contain tobacco), e-cigars, e-hookahs, and e-pipes. Data for students aged 13-15 years are from 2019 and taken from the Global Youth Tobacco Survey.
Source: WHO Global Health Observatory Data Repository (WHO, 2024[1]); Global Youth Tobacco Survey (WHO, 2019[37]).

Table 6.54. Nicaragua - Summary of MPOWER measures, 2022

M Monitoring	P Smoking bans	O Cessation programmes	W Health warnings	E Advertising bans	R Taxation	WHO Frawework Convention on Tobacco Control		Protocol to eliminate illicit trade in tobacco products	
						Date of signature	Date of ratification	Date of signature	Date of ratification
						07-06-2004	09-04-2008	10-01-2013	20-12-2013

... Not categorized/ No data; No policy or weak measure; Minimal measure; Moderate measure; Complete measure

Source: WHO report on the global tobacco epidemic (WHO, 2023[3]).

Figure 6.104. Nicaragua - Taxes and prices of the most sold brand of cigarettes

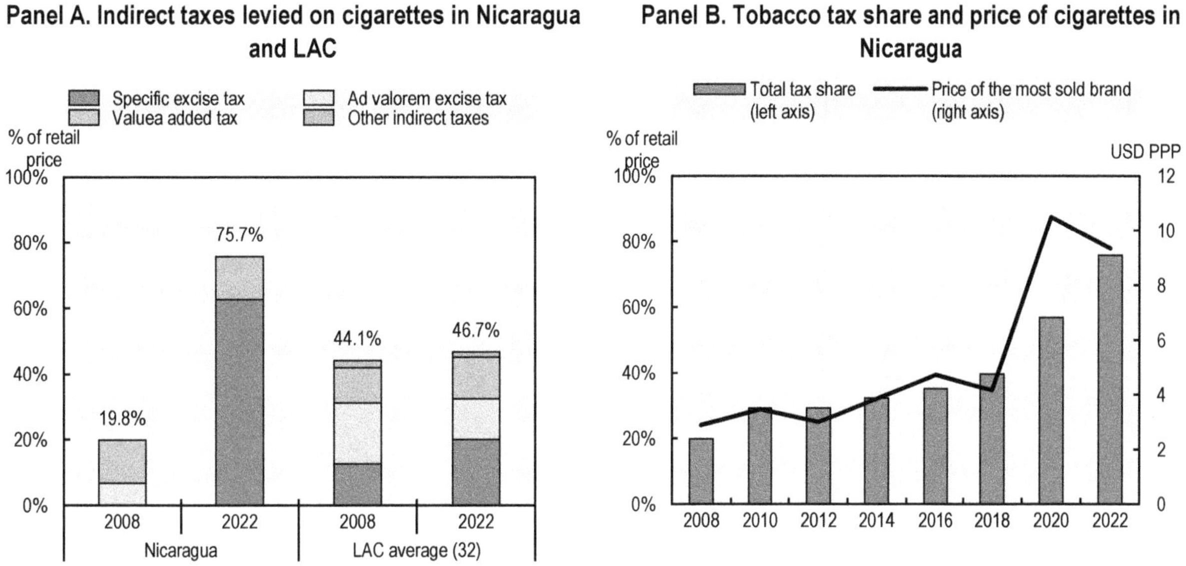

Note: Prices correspond to a 20-cigarette pack of the most sold brand. The most sold brand of cigarettes is determined based on national market share information and can vary over time (i.e. the most sold brand of cigarettes in year 1 can be different from year 2). Retail prices in USD PPP are based on the implied purchasing power parity (PPP) conversion rate from the International Monetary Fund (IMF) World Economic Outlook Database (October 2023).

Source: WHO report on the global tobacco epidemic (WHO, 2023[3]); IMF World Economic Outlook Database (IMF, 2023[4]).

Figure 6.105. Nicaragua - Trends in retail prices of cigarettes by brand category

In USD PPP per pack of 20 cigarettes, 2008-2022

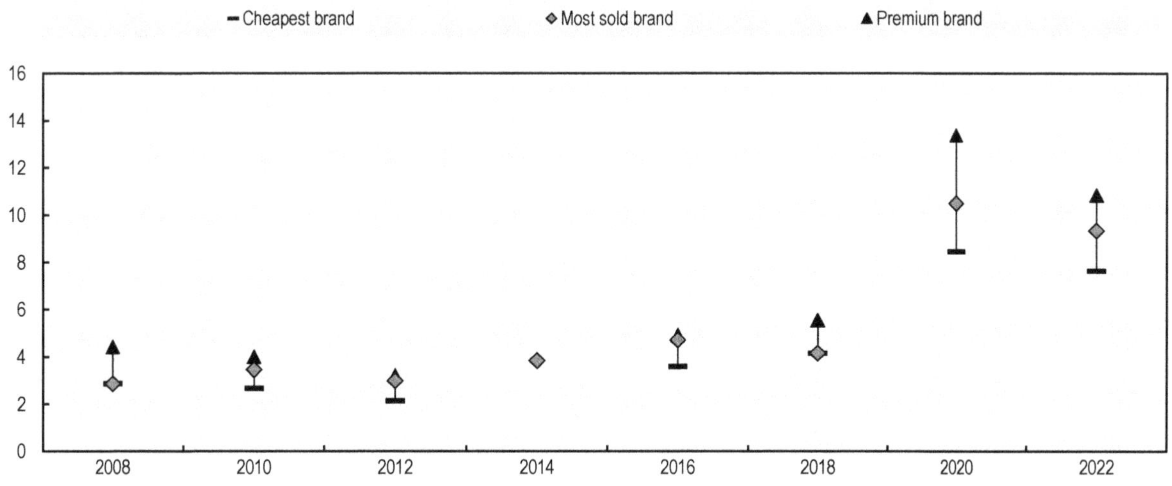

Note: Prices correspond to a 20-cigarette pack of the cheapest, most sold and premium brands. The cheapest, most sold and premium brands of cigarettes are determined based on national market share information and can vary over time (i.e. the cheapest/most sold/premium brands of cigarettes in year 1 can be different from year 2). Retail prices in USD PPP are based on the implied PPP conversion rate from the IMF World Economic Outlook Database (October 2023). Retail prices of the cheapest and premium brand are not available for 2014.

Source: WHO reports on the global tobacco epidemic (WHO, 2009[5]; WHO, 2011[6]; WHO, 2013[7]; WHO, 2015[8]; WHO, 2017[9]; WHO, 2019[10]; WHO, 2021[11]); IMF World Economic Outlook Database (IMF, 2023[4]).

Figure 6.106. Nicaragua - Affordability of cigarettes

Percentage of GDP per capita required to purchase 100 packs of 20 cigarettes

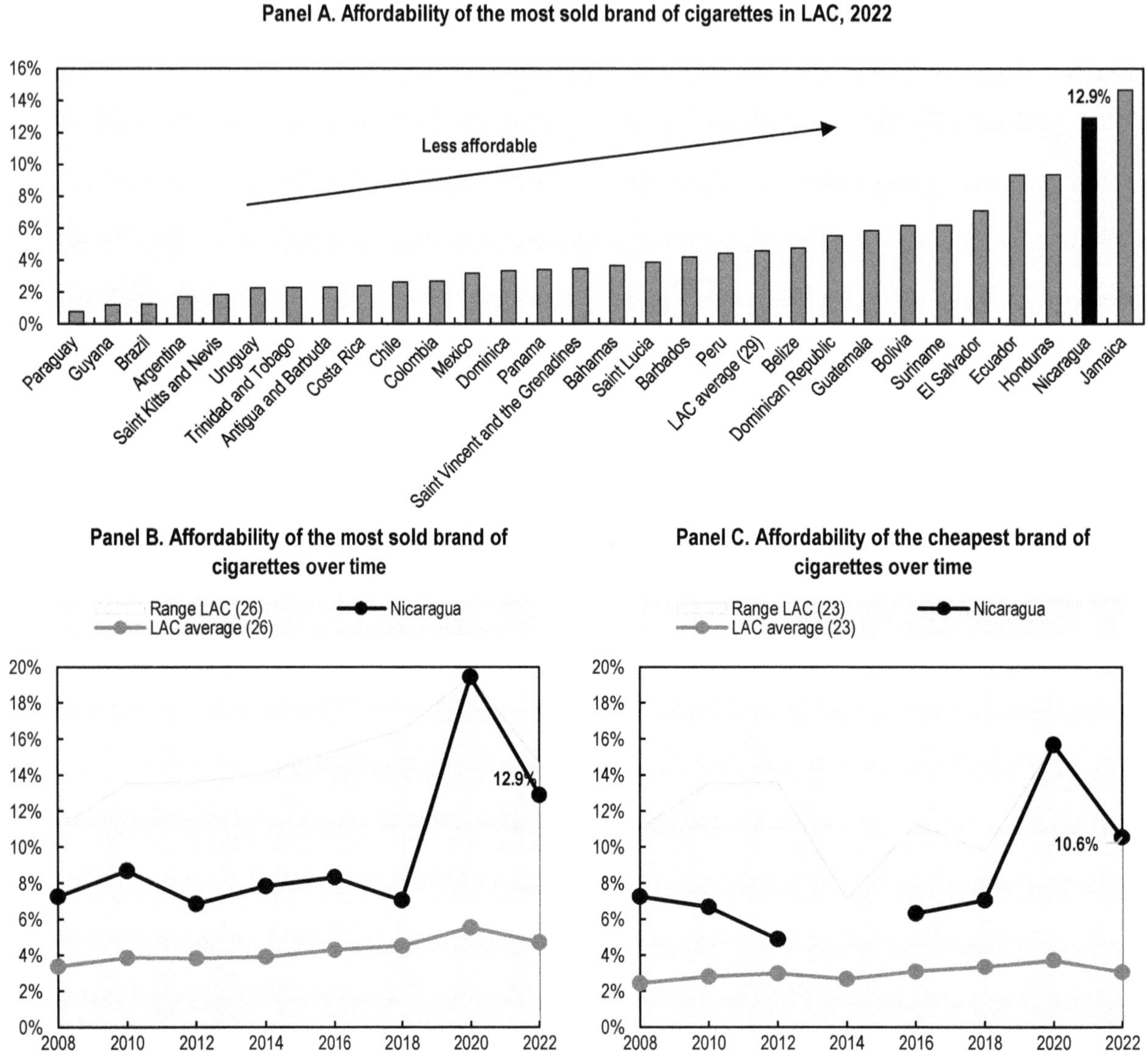

Note: The cheapest and most sold brands of cigarettes are determined based on national market share information and can vary over time (i.e. the cheapest/most sold brand of cigarettes in year 1 can be different from year 2). The affordability of the cheapest brand in Nicaragua is not available for 2014. The affordability indicator measures the percentage of the country's GDP per capita required to purchase 100 packs of 20 cigarettes. A higher percentage means lower affordability of cigarettes while a lower percentage means higher affordability. To ensure comparability of average affordability across LAC over time, countries where information was unavailable for certain years have been excluded from the calculation. Data for Panel C are OECD calculations based on WHO reports on the global tobacco epidemic (2009-2023 editions).
Source: WHO reports on the global tobacco epidemic (WHO, 2009[5]; WHO, 2011[6]; WHO, 2013[7]; WHO, 2015[8]; WHO, 2017[9]; WHO, 2019[10]; WHO, 2021[11]).

Table 6.55. Nicaragua - Design of tobacco excise taxes across tobacco products, 2022

	Excise tax structure	Specific excise tax				Ad valorem excise tax			Excise tax floor			
		Yes / No	Tax base	Rate per 20-unit pack USD PPP (local currency)	Indexation mechanisms	Yes / No	Tax base	Statutory rate	Yes / No	Tax base	Rate per 20-unit pack USD PPP (local currency)	Indexation mechanisms
Cigarettes	Specific only	Yes	1 000 sticks	5.9 (69.0)	CPI or USD exchange rate	No			No			
Cigars	Specific only	Yes	Kilogram	55.1 (648.6)	CPI or USD exchange rate	No			No			
Cigarillos	Specific only	Yes	Kilogram	10.9 (128.8)	CPI or USD exchange rate	No			No			
Roll-Your-Own (RYO) tobacco	Specific only	Yes	Kilogram	2.9 (34.5)	CPI or USD exchange rate	No			No			
Heated tobacco products (HTPs)	No excise											
ENDS and ENNDS	No excise											

Note: Blank cells mean that there is no excise tax for the corresponding tobacco product; "CPI" means consumer price index. Following the WHO report on the global tobacco epidemic (WHO, 2021[11]), new tobacco and nicotine products in this report include electronic nicotine delivery systems (ENDS), electronic non-nicotine delivery systems (ENNDS), and heated tobacco products (HTP). Specific taxes are converted into USD PPP with the implied PPP conversion rate available in the IMF World Economic Outlook Database (October 2023). Specific excise taxes have been standardized to a 20-unit pack to allow the comparison across countries with different tax bases. The specific tax is levied on kilogram of non-cigarette products in Nicaragua. To compute the specific tax levied on weight for a 20-unit pack, the median weight of cigars is assumed to be 14.1 grams while for cigarillos the median weight is 2.8 grams (Yassin S, 2022[38]). To compute the specific tax for an equivalent 20-unit pack of RYO tobacco, it is assumed that the median cigarette in terms of weight contains 0.75 gram of tobacco (Gallus et al., 2014[12]).
Source: Ley No. 987 (2019); IMF World Economic Outlook Database (IMF, 2023[4]).

Table 6.56. Nicaragua - Tobacco tax reforms since 2000

Year of adoption	Specific excise taxes	Ad valorem excise taxes	Other
2000	No	Cigarettes, cigars and cigarillos: reduction in the ad valorem tax rate to 40% in 2000, to 39% in 2001 and to 38% in 2002. The ad valorem tax is levied on the retail price, excluding VAT.	No
2002	No	Cigarettes, cigars and cigarillo: increase in the tax rate to 39% levied on the retail price, excluding VAT.	No
2003	No	Cigarettes, cigars, cigarillos: increase in the tax rate to 43% levied on the retail price, excluding VAT. RYO tobacco: introduction of an ad valorem excise tax levied at a rate of 59% on the retail price, excluding VAT.	No
2009	Cigarettes: introduction of a specific excise tax annually indexed with the average of the annual change in the USD exchange rate and the CPI. The specific tax is NIO 225.0 levied on each 1 000 sticks.	Cigarettes: the ad valorem excise tax is abolished.	No

Year of adoption	Specific excise taxes	Ad valorem excise taxes	Other
2012	Cigarettes: increase in the specific excise tax to NIO 309.22 in 2013, to NIO 374.93 in 2014, to NIO 454.61 in 2015 and to NIO 551.21 in 2016. The specific excise tax is levied per 1 000 sticks. Starting from 2017, the specific tax will be annually adjusted with the maximum of the change in the CPI and the USD exchange rate.	No	No
2019	Cigarettes: increase in the specific excise tax to NIO 2 000 in 2019, to NIO 2 500 in 2020, and to NIO 3 450 in 2021. The specific excise tax is levied on each 1 000 sticks. Cigars, cigarillos, RYO tobacco: introduction of a specific excise tax levied on each kilogram of tobacco product. Initially set at NIO 1 335 per kg in 2019, the specific tax will be increased to NIO 1 670 in 2020 and to NIO 2 300 in 2021. All tobacco products: Starting from 2022, the tax rate will be annually adjusted based on the higher changes between the CPI and the USD exchange rate.	Cigars, cigarillos, RYO tobacco: the ad valorem excise tax is abolished.	No

Note: "Tobacco tax reform" refers to changes in the tobacco excise tax rates, the introduction of indexation mechanisms or minimum taxes, as well as adjustments to the tax base. These reforms typically entail the enactment of new laws or decrees. The table does not refer to recurrent tax changes that result from the indexation for inflation of tax brackets and price floors (if implemented). Tobacco tax reforms included reflect changes in the legislation, but not whether or when the reforms have been implemented.
Source: Ley No. 343; Ley No. 439; Ley No. 453; Ley No. 712; Ley No. 822; Ley No. 987.

Figure 6.107. Nicaragua - Tobacco excise tax revenue

Percentage of GDP, latest year available

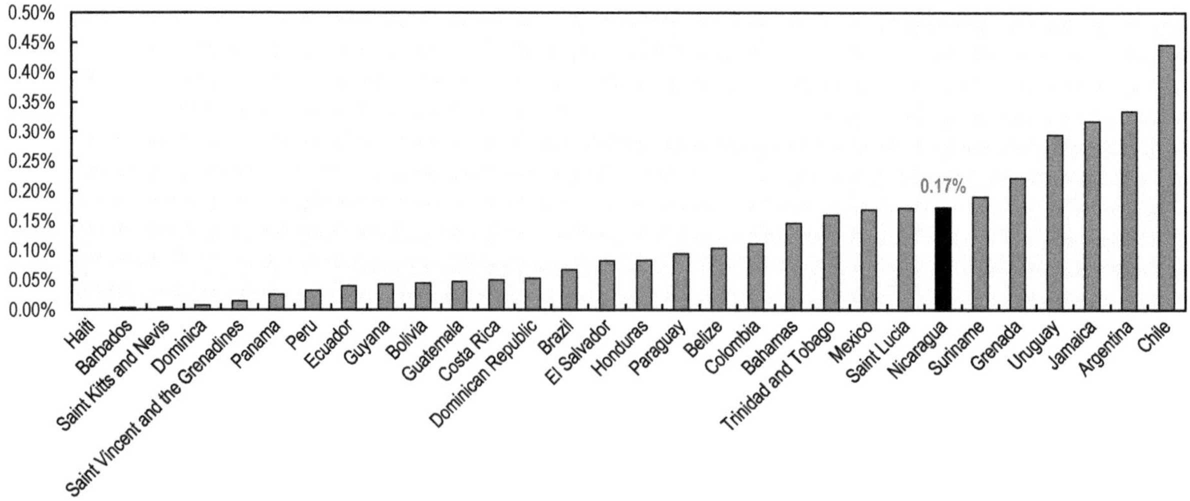

Note: See Box 2.1 (Chapter 2) for more information on tobacco tax revenue (source of information and calculations) and country selection. The latest year available is 2022 for Argentina, Brazil, Chile, Colombia, Costa Rica, the Dominican Republic, El Salvador, Guatemala, Guyana, Honduras, Mexico, Nicaragua, Panama, Paraguay, Peru, Saint Kitts and Nevis, Suriname, and Uruguay; 2021 for Belize, Dominica, Ecuador, Grenada, Saint Lucia, Saint Vincent and the Grenadines; 2020 for Bahamas, Bolivia, Jamaica and Trinidad and Tobago; 2015 for Haiti; 2014 for Barbados.
Source: OECD Revenue Statistics (OECD, 2024[13]); WHO report on the global tobacco epidemic (WHO, 2023[3]); National data.

Figure 6.108. Nicaragua - Change in tobacco tax policy indicators

Percentage change from base year, 2008-2022

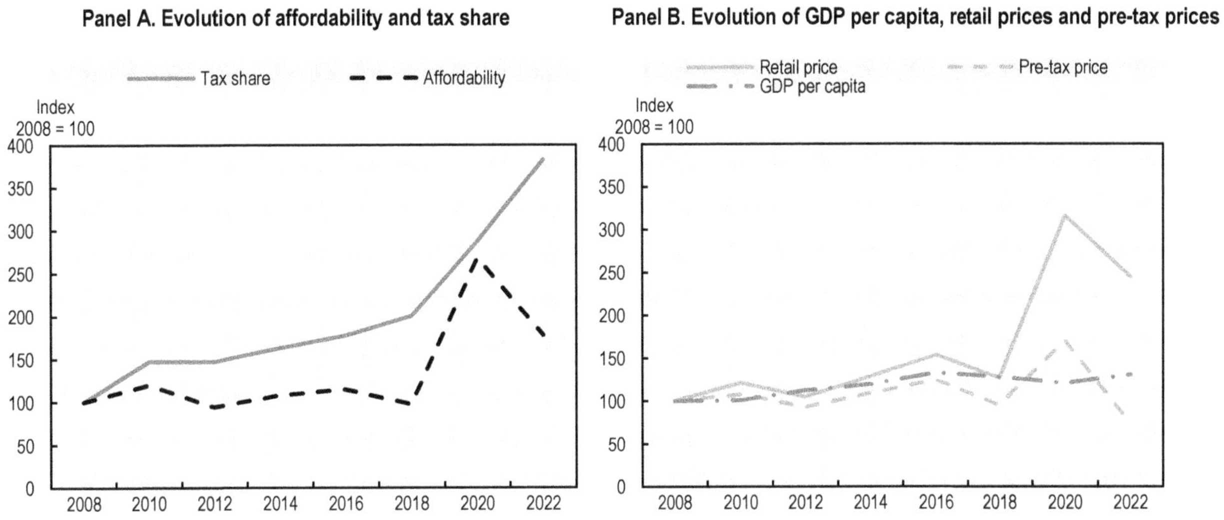

Note: Both Panel A and Panel B figures are based on data for the most sold brand of cigarettes. The most sold brand of cigarettes is determined based on national market share information and can vary over time (i.e. the most sold brand of cigarettes in year 1 can be different from year 2). In Panel A, an increase in the affordability indicator means that cigarettes are becoming less affordable, while a decline in the affordability indicator means that cigarettes are becoming more affordable. In Panel B, "Pre-tax price" corresponds to the retail price of the most sold brand of cigarettes minus the indirect taxes levied on this brand, namely excise taxes, VAT, import duties and other. Indicators in Panel B have been computed using national currency and have been adjusted for inflation; therefore, present inflation-adjusted trends.
Source: WHO report on the global tobacco epidemic (WHO, 2023[3]); World Bank Open Data (World Bank, 2024[15]); IMF International Financial Statistics (IMF, 2024[19]).

References

IMF (2023), *World Economic Outlook Database*, International Monetary Fund, https://www.imf.org/en/Publications/WEO/weo-database/2023/October (accessed on 13 January 2024). [4]

IMF (2024), *International Financial Statistics (IFS)*, International Monetary Fund, https://data.imf.org/?sk=4c514d48-b6ba-49ed-8ab9-52b0c1a0179b&sId=1390030341854 (accessed on 13 January 2024). [19]

OECD (2024), *Global Revenue Statistics Database*, Organisation for Economic Co-operation and Development, https://www.oecd.org/tax/tax-policy/global-revenue-statistics-database.htm (accessed on 13 August 2023). [13]

WHO (2024), *Global Health Observatory: Age-standardized estimates of current tobacco use, tobacco smoking and cigarette smoking (Tobacco control: Monitor)*, World Health Organization, https://www.who.int/data/gho/data/indicators/indicator-details/GHO/gho-tobacco-control-monitor-current-tobaccouse-tobaccosmoking-cigarrettesmoking-agestd-tobagestdcurr (accessed on 20 February 2024). [1]

WHO (2023), *WHO report on the global tobacco epidemic 2023: protect people from tobacco smoke*, World Health Organization, https://www.who.int/publications/i/item/9789240077164. [3]

WHO (2021), *WHO report on the global tobacco epidemic 2021: Addressing new and emerging products*, World Health Organization, https://www.who.int/publications/i/item/9789240032095. [11]

WHO (2019), *WHO report on the global tobacco epidemic 2019: Offer help to quit tobacco use*, World Health Organization, https://www.who.int/publications/i/item/9789241516204. [10]

WHO (2019), *Global Youth Tobacco Survey. Nicaragua 2019 Fact Sheet*, World Health Organization, https://www.who.int/publications/m/item/2019-gyts-fact-sheet-nicaragua. [37]

WHO (2017), *WHO report on the global tobacco epidemic 2017: Monitoring tobacco use and prevention policies*, World Health Organization, https://www.who.int/publications/i/item/9789241512824. [9]

WHO (2015), *WHO report on the global tobacco epidemic 2015: Raising taxes on tobacco*, World Health Organization, https://www.who.int/publications/i/item/9789241509121. [8]

WHO (2013), *WHO report on the global tobacco epidemic 2013: Enforcing bans on tobacco advertising, promotion and sponsorship*, World Health Organization, https://www.who.int/publications/i/item/9789241505871. [7]

WHO (2011), *WHO report on the global tobacco epidemic 2011: Warning about the dangers of tobacco*, World Health Organization, https://www.who.int/publications/i/item/9789244564264. [6]

WHO (2009), *WHO report on the global tobacco epidemic 2009: Implementing smoke-free environments*, World Health Organization, https://www.who.int/publications/i/item/9789241563918. [5]

World Bank (2024), *World Bank Open Data*, World Bank, https://data.worldbank.org/ (accessed on 13 January 2024). [15]

Yassin S, G. (2022), "Appendix F. Cigar Physical Characteristics" Premium Cigars: Patterns of Use, Marketing, and Health Effects, https://www.ncbi.nlm.nih.gov/books/NBK586235/. [38]

Panama

Figure 6.109. Panama - Trends in tobacco use prevalence

Percentage of the population aged 15 years and over who currently use any tobacco product (smoked and/or smokeless tobacco) on a daily or non-daily basis, 2000-2020

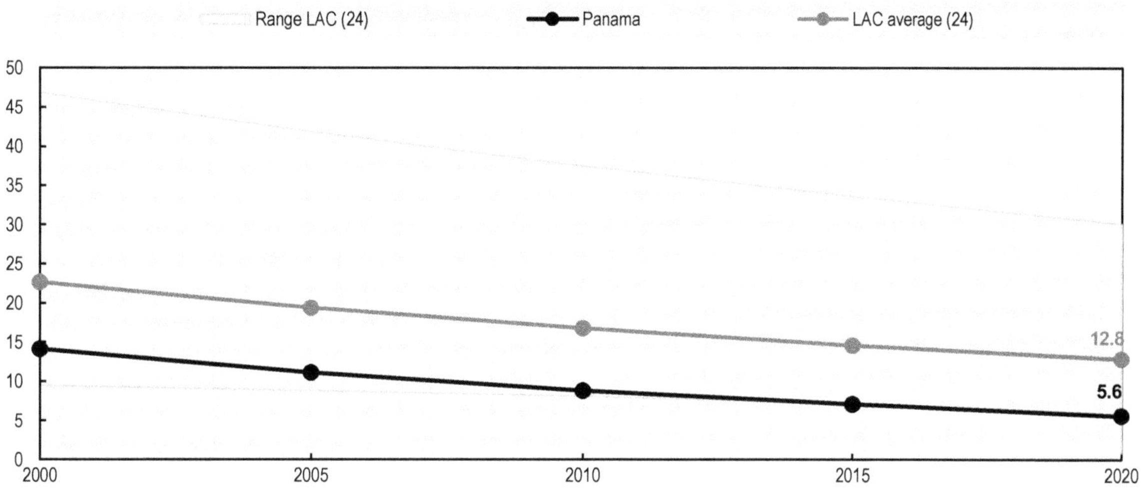

Note: Tobacco products include cigarettes, pipes, cigars, cigarillos, waterpipes (hookah, shisha), bidis, kretek, heated tobacco products (HTP), and all forms of smokeless (oral and nasal) tobacco. Tobacco products exclude e-cigarettes (which do not contain tobacco), e-cigars, e-hookahs, and e-pipes. The rates are age-standardized to the World Health Organisation (WHO) standard population. The LAC average was calculated as the average of Argentina, Bahamas, Barbados, Belize, Bolivia, Brazil, Chile, Colombia, Costa Rica, Cuba, the Dominican Republic, Ecuador, El Salvador, Guatemala, Guyana, Haiti, Honduras, Jamaica, Mexico, Panama, Paraguay, Peru, Saint Lucia, and Uruguay.
Source: WHO Global Health Observatory Data Repository (WHO, 2024[1]).

Table 6.57. Panama - Tobacco use prevalence by sex and age groups

Percentage of the population group, latest year available

	Tobacco use prevalence (all tobacco products)	Cigarette smoking prevalence (cigarettes only)
Students aged 13-15 years		
Total	**7.6**	**6.3**
Males	9.1	7.1
Females	6.2	5.5
People aged 15 and over		
Total	**5.6**	**4.7**
Males	9.1	7.6
Females	2.0	1.8

Note: Tobacco use prevalence is defined as the percentage of the population group who currently use any tobacco product (smoked and/or smokeless tobacco) on a daily or non-daily basis. Tobacco products exclude e-cigarettes (which do not contain tobacco), e-cigars, e-hookahs, and e-pipes. Data for students aged 13-15 years are from 2018 and taken from the Global School-Based Student Health Survey. Data for people aged 15 and over correspond to 2020.
Source: WHO Global Health Observatory Data Repository (WHO, 2024[1]); Global School-Based Student Health Survey (WHO, 2018[39]).

Table 6.58. Panama - Summary of MPOWER measures, 2022

M Monitoring	P Smoking bans	O Cessation programmes	W Health warnings	E Advertising bans	R Taxation	WHO Frawework Convention on Tobacco Control		Protocol to eliminate illicit trade in tobacco products	
						Date of signature	Date of ratification	Date of signature	Date of ratification
						26-09-2003	16-08-2004	10-01-2013	23-09-2016

... Not categorized/ No data; No policy or weak measure; Minimal measure; Moderate measure; Complete measure

Source: WHO report on the global tobacco epidemic (WHO, 2023[3]).

Figure 6.110. Panama - Taxes and prices of the most sold brand of cigarettes

Panel A. Indirect taxes levied on cigarettes in Panama and LAC | **Panel B. Tobacco tax share and price of cigarettes in Panama**

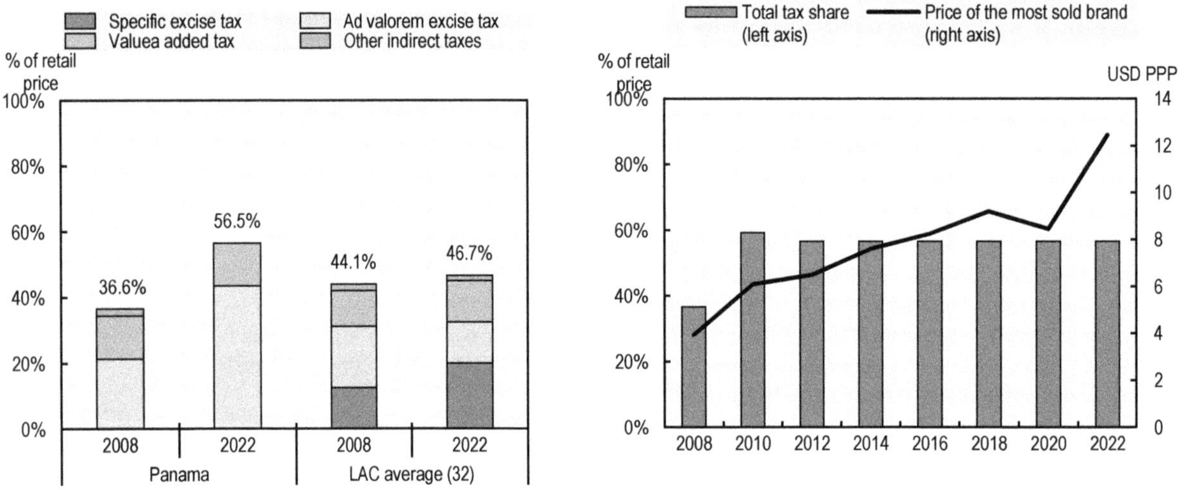

Note: Prices correspond to a 20-cigarette pack of the most sold brand. The most sold brand of cigarettes is determined based on national market share information and can vary over time (i.e. the most sold brand of cigarettes in year 1 can be different from year 2). Retail prices in USD PPP are based on the implied purchasing power parity (PPP) conversion rate from the International Monetary Fund (IMF) World Economic Outlook Database (October 2023).

Source: WHO report on the global tobacco epidemic (WHO, 2023[3]); IMF World Economic Outlook Database (IMF, 2023[4]).

Figure 6.111. Panama - Trends in retail prices of cigarettes by brand category

In USD PPP per pack of 20 cigarettes, 2008-2022

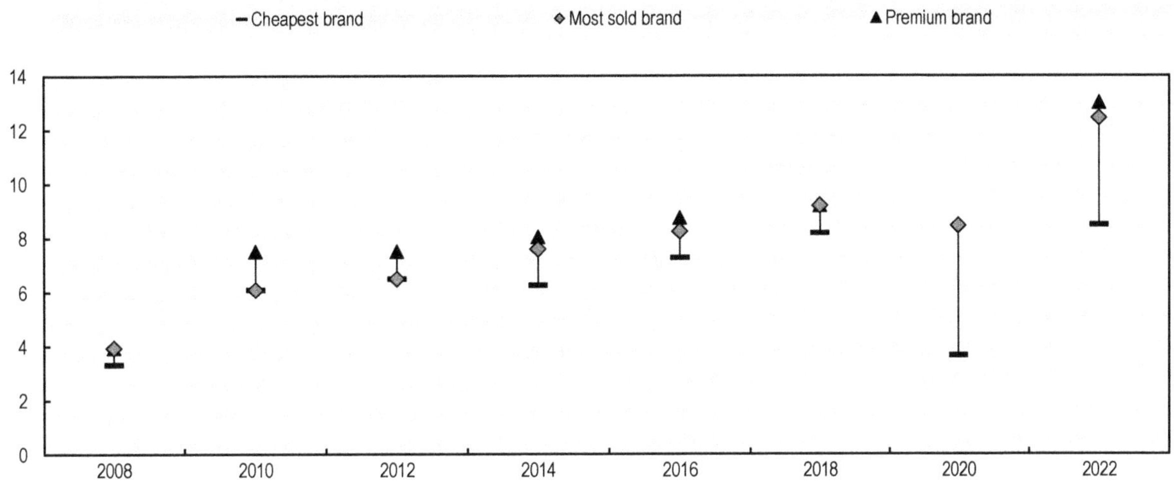

Note: Prices correspond to a 20-cigarette pack of the cheapest, most sold and premium brands. The cheapest, most sold and premium brands of cigarettes are determined based on national market share information and can vary over time (i.e. the cheapest/most sold/premium brands of cigarettes in year 1 can be different from year 2). Retail prices in USD PPP are based on the implied PPP conversion rate from the IMF World Economic Outlook Database (October 2023). Retail price of the premium brand is not available for 2020.
Source: WHO reports on the global tobacco epidemic (WHO, 2009[5]; WHO, 2011[6]; WHO, 2013[7]; WHO, 2015[8]; WHO, 2017[9]; WHO, 2019[10]; WHO, 2021[11]); IMF World Economic Outlook Database (IMF, 2023[4]).

Figure 6.112. Panama - Affordability of cigarettes

Percentage of GDP per capita required to purchase 100 packs of 20 cigarettes

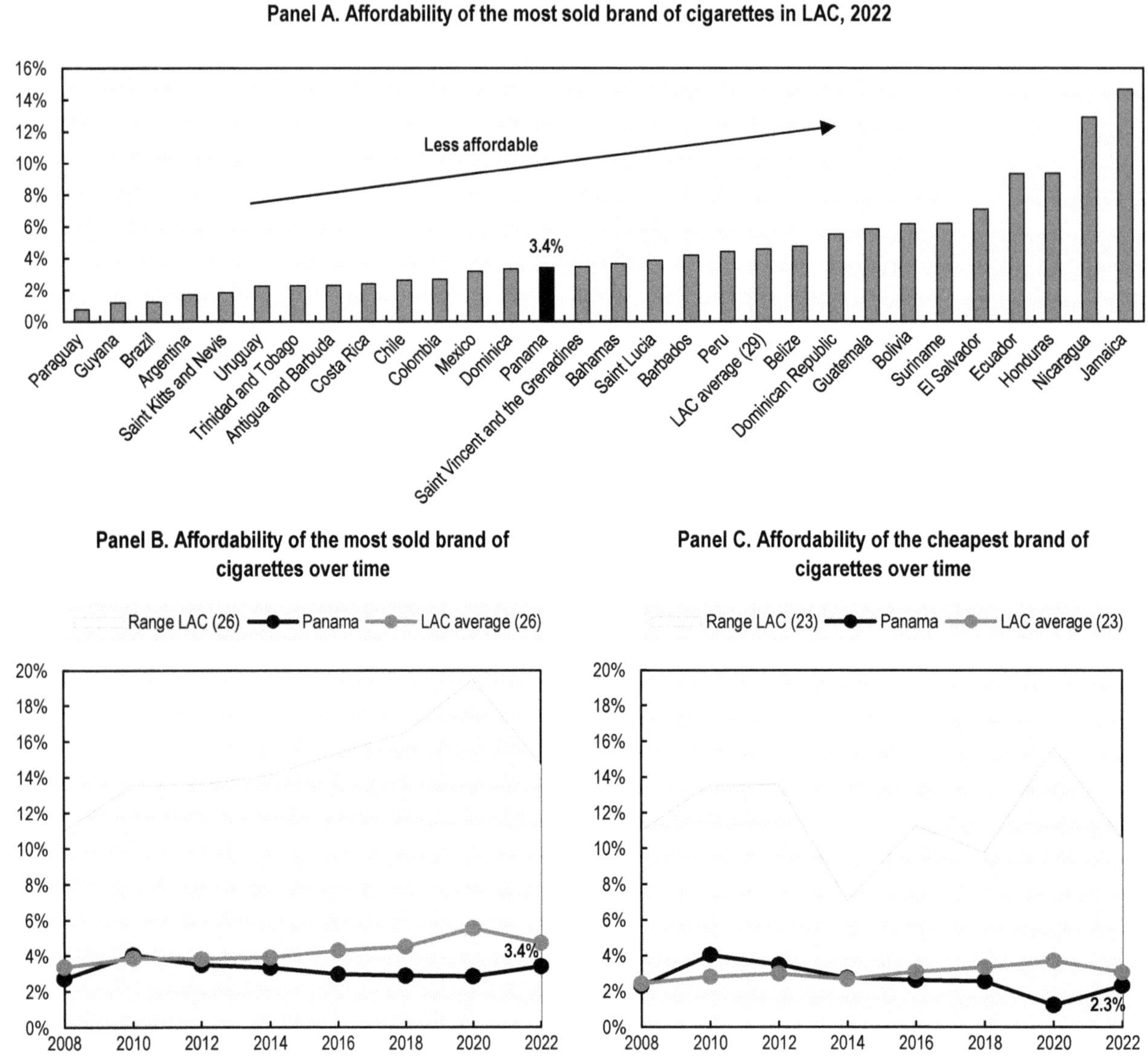

Note: The affordability indicator measures the percentage of the country's GDP per capita required to purchase 100 packs of 20 cigarettes. A higher percentage means lower affordability of cigarettes while a lower percentage means higher affordability. To ensure comparability of average affordability across LAC over time, countries where information was unavailable for certain years have been excluded from the calculation. Data for Panel C are OECD calculations based on WHO reports on the global tobacco epidemic (2009-2023 editions). The cheapest and most sold brands of cigarettes are determined based on national market share information and can vary over time (i.e. the cheapest/most sold brand of cigarettes in year 1 can be different from year 2).

Source: WHO reports on the global tobacco epidemic (WHO, 2009[5]; WHO, 2011[6]; WHO, 2013[7]; WHO, 2015[8]; WHO, 2017[9]; WHO, 2019[10]; WHO, 2021[11]).

Table 6.59. Panama - Design of tobacco excise taxes across tobacco products, 2022

	Excise tax structure	Specific excise tax				Ad valorem excise tax			Excise tax floor			
		Yes / No	Tax base	Rate per 20-unit pack USD PPP (local currency)	Indexation mechanisms	Yes / No	Tax base	Statutory rate	Yes / No	Tax base	Rate per 20-unit pack USD PPP (local currency)	Indexation mechanisms
Cigarettes	Ad valorem only	No				Yes	SRP excl. VAT	100%	Yes	Individual pack	3.4 (1.5)	No
Cigars	Ad valorem only	No				Yes	SRP excl. VAT	100%	No			
Cigarillos	Ad valorem only	No				Yes	SRP excl. VAT	100%	No			
Roll-Your-Own (RYO) tobacco	Ad valorem only	No				Yes	SRP excl. VAT	100%	No			
Heated tobacco products (HTPs)	No excise											
ENDS and ENNDS	No excise											

Note: "SRP" means "Suggested retail price by the manufacturer/importer"; blank cells mean that there is no excise tax for the corresponding tobacco product; "VAT" means "Value added tax". Following the WHO report on the global tobacco epidemic (WHO, 2021[11]), new tobacco and nicotine products in this report include electronic nicotine delivery systems (ENDS), electronic non-nicotine delivery systems (ENNDS), and heated tobacco products (HTP). Panama does not levy an excise tax on new tobacco and nicotine products because their sales are banned (WHO, 2023[3]). Specific taxes are converted into USD PPP with the implied PPP conversion rate available in the IMF World Economic Outlook Database (October 2023). Specific excise taxes have been standardized to a 20-unit pack to allow the comparison across countries with different tax bases.

Source: Ley No. 69 (2009); IMF World Economic Outlook Database (IMF, 2023[4]).

Table 6.60. Panama - Tobacco tax reforms since 2000

Year of adoption	Specific excise taxes	Ad valorem excise taxes	Other
2005	No	Cigars, cigarillos and RYO tobacco: introduction of an ad valorem excise tax levied at a rate of 32.5% on the retail price suggested by the manufacturer/ importer, excluding VAT.	All tobacco products: increase in the VAT rate applied to tobacco products to 15%.
2009	No	All tobacco products: increase in the ad valorem tax rate to 100% levied on the retail price suggested by the manufacturer/ importer, excluding VAT.	Cigarettes: introduction of a non-indexed minimum specific tax of PAB 1.5 per pack of 20 cigarettes. All tobacco products: earmark 50% of the tobacco excise tax revenue for the health budget and the customs administration to finance activities related to the control of illicit trade in tobacco products.

Note: "Tobacco tax reform" refers to changes in the tobacco excise tax rates, the introduction of indexation mechanisms or minimum taxes, as well as adjustments to the tax base. These reforms typically entail the enactment of new laws or decrees. The table does not refer to recurrent tax changes that result from the indexation for inflation of tax brackets and price floors (if implemented). Tobacco tax reforms included reflect changes in the legislation, but not whether or when the reforms have been implemented.

Source: Ley No. 6 (2005); Ley No. 69 (2009).

Figure 6.113. Panama - Tobacco excise tax revenue

Percentage of GDP, latest year available

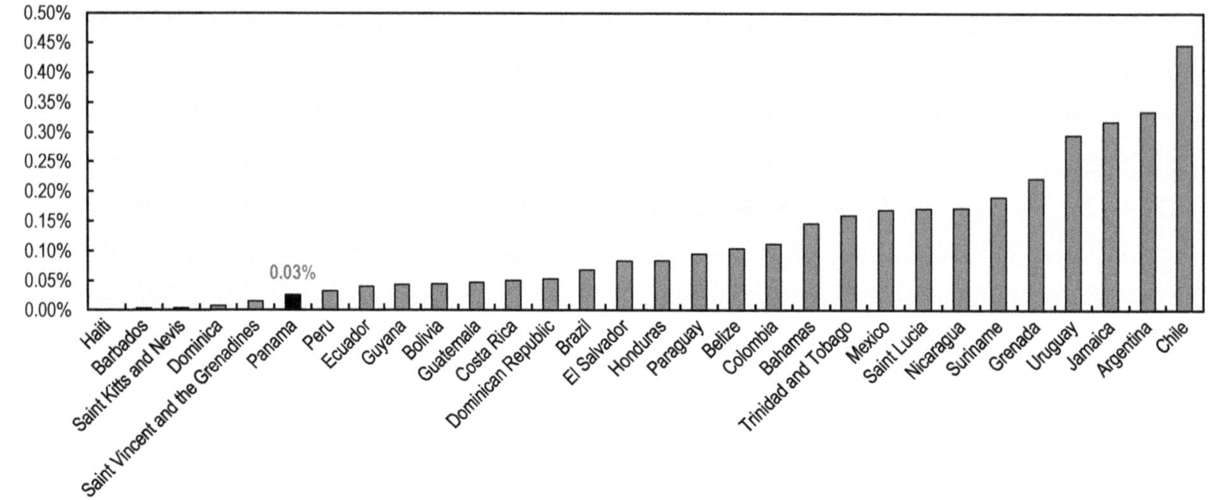

Note: See Box 2.1 (Chapter 2) for more information on tobacco tax revenue (source of information and calculations) and country selection. The latest year available is 2022 for Argentina, Brazil, Chile, Colombia, Costa Rica, the Dominican Republic, El Salvador, Guatemala, Guyana, Honduras, Mexico, Nicaragua, Panama, Paraguay, Peru, Saint Kitts and Nevis, Suriname, and Uruguay; 2021 for Belize, Dominica, Ecuador, Grenada, Saint Lucia, Saint Vincent and the Grenadines; 2020 for Bahamas, Bolivia, Jamaica and Trinidad and Tobago; 2015 for Haiti; 2014 for Barbados.
Source: OECD Revenue Statistics (OECD, 2024[13]); WHO report on the global tobacco epidemic (WHO, 2023[3]); National data.

Figure 6.114. Panama - Trends in tobacco excise tax revenue

Percentage of GDP, 2012-2022

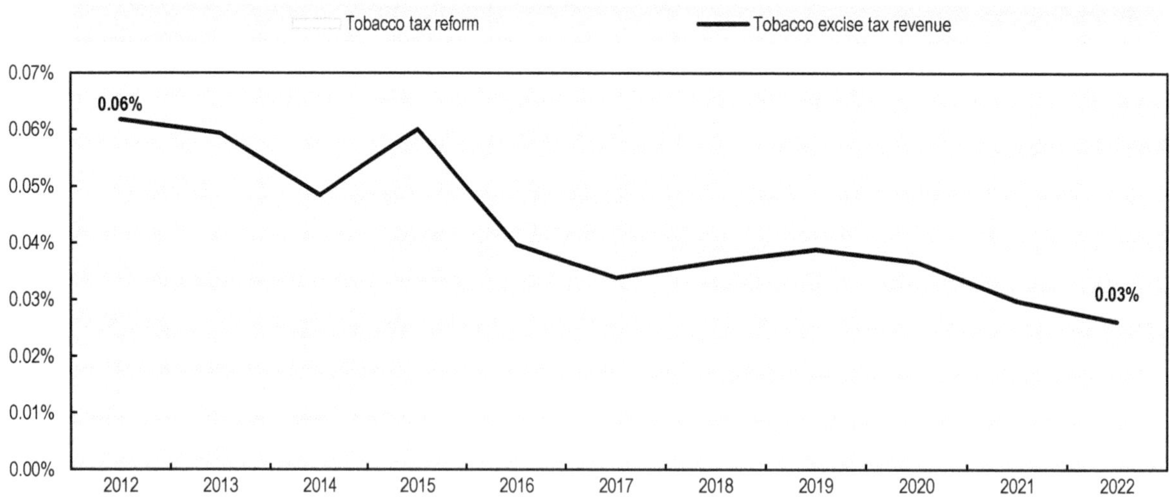

Note: Tobacco excise tax revenue data prior 2012 are not available. Tobacco tax reforms refer to those listed in Table 6.60.
Source: OECD Revenue Statistics (OECD, 2024[13]); Ley No. 6 (2005); Ley No. 69 (2009).

Figure 6.115. Panama - Average excise tax revenue collected per pack of 20 cigarettes sold

Tobacco excise tax revenue in USD PPP collected per pack of legal cigarettes sold, latest year available

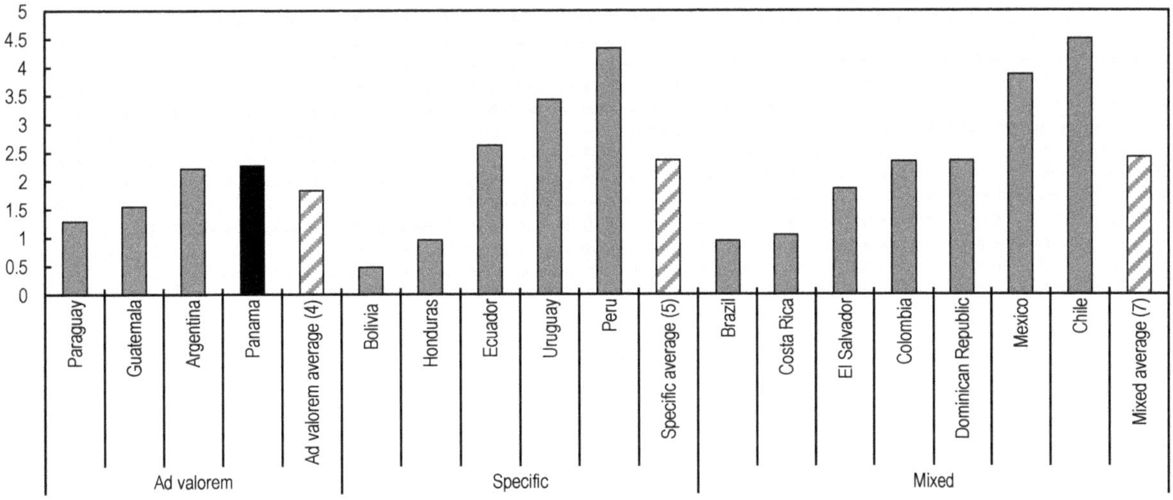

Note: See Box 2.1 (Chapter 2) for more information on tobacco tax revenue (source of information and calculations). The latest year available is 2022 for Argentina, Brazil, Chile, Colombia, Costa Rica, the Dominican Republic, El Salvador, Guatemala, Honduras, Mexico, Panama, Paraguay, Peru and Uruguay; 2021 for Ecuador; 2020 for Bolivia. The country selection is provided by the availability of data on sales of cigarettes in Euromonitor International Tobacco Industry edition, 2023 © All rights reserved (Euromonitor International, 2023[14]).
Source: OECD Revenue Statistics (OECD, 2024[13]); WHO report on the global tobacco epidemic (WHO, 2023[3]); National data; IMF World Economic Outlook Database (IMF, 2023[4]); and OECD calculations based on Euromonitor International's Tobacco Industry edition (Euromonitor International, 2023[14]).

Figure 6.116. Panama - Change in tobacco tax policy indicators

Percentage change from base year, 2008-2022

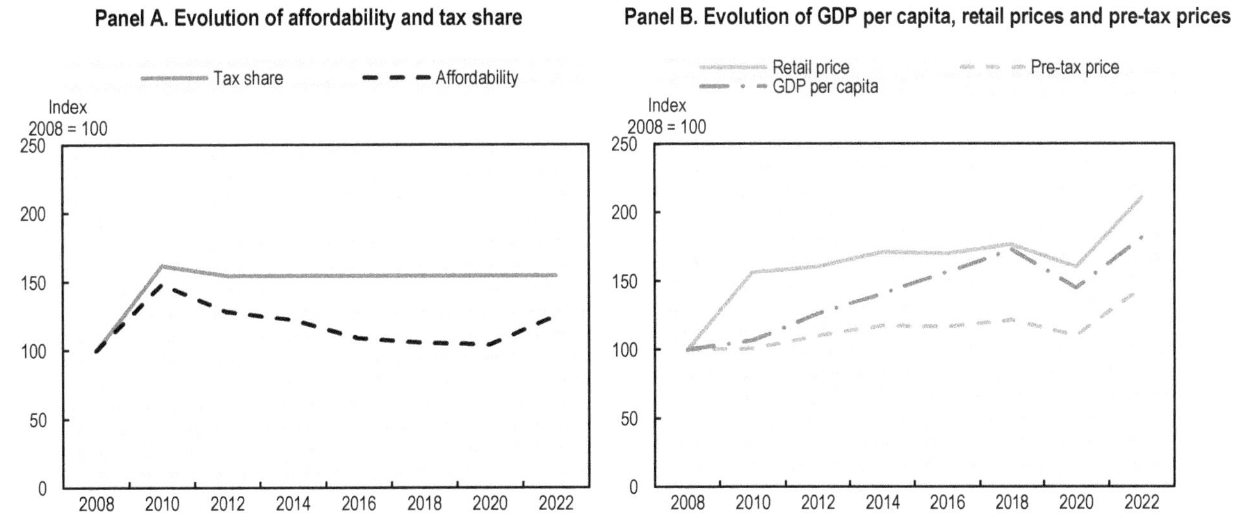

Note: Both Panel A and Panel B figures are based on data for the most sold brand of cigarettes. The most sold brand of cigarettes is determined based on national market share information and can vary over time (i.e. the most sold brand of cigarettes in year 1 can be different from year 2). In Panel A, an increase in the affordability indicator means that cigarettes are becoming less affordable, while a decline in the affordability indicator means that cigarettes are becoming more affordable. In Panel B, "Pre-tax price" corresponds to the retail price of the most sold brand of cigarettes minus the indirect taxes levied on this brand, namely excise taxes, VAT, import duties and other. Indicators in Panel B have been computed using national currency and have been adjusted for inflation; therefore, present inflation-adjusted trends.
Source: WHO report on the global tobacco epidemic (WHO, 2023[3]); World Bank Open Data (World Bank, 2024[15]); IMF International Financial Statistics (IMF, 2024[19]).

References

Euromonitor International (2023), *Euromonitor International's Tobacco Industry edition*, https://www.euromonitor.com/tobacco (accessed on 1 August 2023). [14]

IMF (2023), *World Economic Outlook Database*, International Monetary Fund, https://www.imf.org/en/Publications/WEO/weo-database/2023/October (accessed on 13 January 2024). [4]

IMF (2024), *International Financial Statistics (IFS)*, International Monetary Fund, https://data.imf.org/?sk=4c514d48-b6ba-49ed-8ab9-52b0c1a0179b&sId=1390030341854 (accessed on 13 January 2024). [19]

OECD (2024), *Global Revenue Statistics Database*, Organisation for Economic Co-operation and Development, https://www.oecd.org/tax/tax-policy/global-revenue-statistics-database.htm (accessed on 13 August 2023). [13]

WHO (2024), *Global Health Observatory: Age-standardized estimates of current tobacco use, tobacco smoking and cigarette smoking (Tobacco control: Monitor)*, World Health Organization, https://www.who.int/data/gho/data/indicators/indicator-details/GHO/gho-tobacco-control-monitor-current-tobaccouse-tobaccosmoking-cigarrettesmoking-agestd-tobagestdcurr (accessed on 20 February 2024). [1]

WHO (2023), *WHO report on the global tobacco epidemic 2023: protect people from tobacco smoke*, World Health Organization, https://www.who.int/publications/i/item/9789240077164. [3]

WHO (2021), *WHO report on the global tobacco epidemic 2021: Addressing new and emerging products*, World Health Organization, https://www.who.int/publications/i/item/9789240032095. [11]

WHO (2019), *WHO report on the global tobacco epidemic 2019: Offer help to quit tobacco use*, World Health Organization, https://www.who.int/publications/i/item/9789241516204. [10]

WHO (2018), *Global school-based student health survey. Panama 2018 Fact Sheet*, World Health Organization, https://www.who.int/publications/m/item/2018-gshs-fact-sheet-panama. [39]

WHO (2017), *WHO report on the global tobacco epidemic 2017: Monitoring tobacco use and prevention policies*, World Health Organization, https://www.who.int/publications/i/item/9789241512824. [9]

WHO (2015), *WHO report on the global tobacco epidemic 2015: Raising taxes on tobacco*, World Health Organization, https://www.who.int/publications/i/item/9789241509121. [8]

WHO (2013), *WHO report on the global tobacco epidemic 2013: Enforcing bans on tobacco advertising, promotion and sponsorship*, World Health Organization, https://www.who.int/publications/i/item/9789241505871. [7]

WHO (2011), *WHO report on the global tobacco epidemic 2011: Warning about the dangers of tobacco*, World Health Organization, https://www.who.int/publications/i/item/9789244564264. [6]

WHO (2009), *WHO report on the global tobacco epidemic 2009: Implementing smoke-free environments*, World Health Organization, https://www.who.int/publications/i/item/9789241563918. [5]

World Bank (2024), *World Bank Open Data*, World Bank, https://data.worldbank.org/ (accessed on 13 January 2024). [15]

Paraguay

Figure 6.117. Paraguay - Trends in tobacco use prevalence

Percentage of the population aged 15 years and over who currently use any tobacco product (smoked and/or smokeless tobacco) on a daily or non-daily basis, 2000-2020

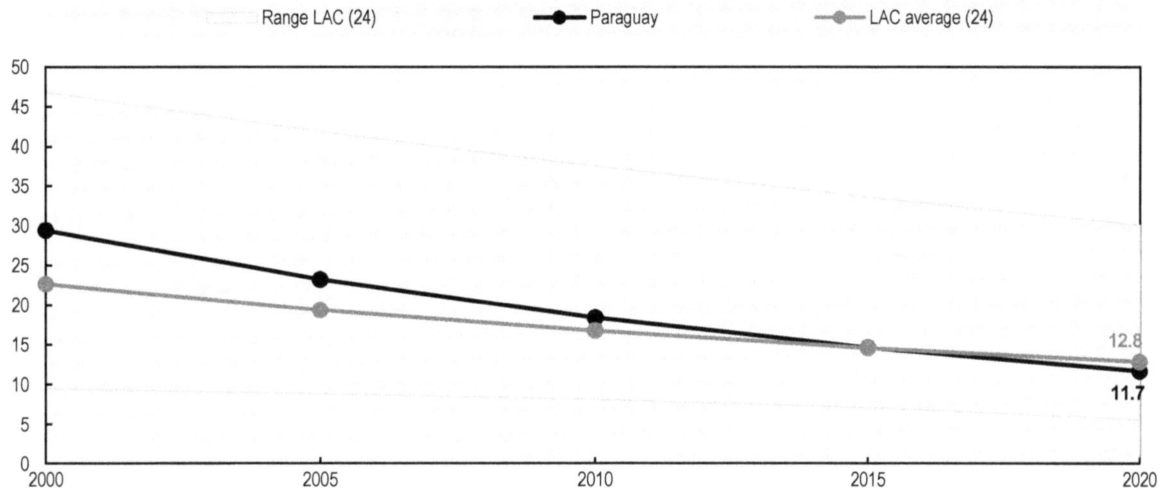

Note: Tobacco products include cigarettes, pipes, cigars, cigarillos, waterpipes (hookah, shisha), bidis, kretek, heated tobacco products (HTP), and all forms of smokeless (oral and nasal) tobacco. Tobacco products exclude e-cigarettes (which do not contain tobacco), e-cigars, e-hookahs, and e-pipes. The rates are age-standardized to the World Health Organisation (WHO) standard population. The LAC average was calculated as the average of Argentina, Bahamas, Barbados, Belize, Bolivia, Brazil, Chile, Colombia, Costa Rica, Cuba, the Dominican Republic, Ecuador, El Salvador, Guatemala, Guyana, Haiti, Honduras, Jamaica, Mexico, Panama, Paraguay, Peru, Saint Lucia, and Uruguay.
Source: WHO Global Health Observatory Data Repository (WHO, 2024[1]).

Table 6.61. Paraguay - Tobacco use prevalence by sex and age groups

Percentage of the population group, latest year available

	Tobacco use prevalence (all tobacco products)	Cigarette smoking prevalence (cigarettes only)
Students aged 13-15 years		
Total	**8.1**	**3.0**
Males	8.8	2.7
Females	7.2	3.3
People aged 15 and over		
Total	**11.7**	**9.6**
Males	19.0	15.6
Females	4.4	3.6

Note: Tobacco use prevalence is defined as the percentage of the population group who currently use any tobacco product (smoked and/or smokeless tobacco) on a daily or non-daily basis. Tobacco products exclude e-cigarettes (which do not contain tobacco), e-cigars, e-hookahs, and e-pipes. Data for students aged 13-15 years are from 2019 and taken from the Global School-Based Student Health Survey. Data for people aged 15 and over correspond to 2020.
Source: WHO Global Health Observatory Data Repository (WHO, 2024[1]); Global School-Based Student Health Survey (WHO, 2019[40]).

Table 6.62. Paraguay - Summary of MPOWER measures, 2022

M Monitoring	P Smoking bans	O Cessation programmes	W Health warnings	E Advertising bans	R Taxation	WHO Frawework Convention on Tobacco Control		Protocol to eliminate illicit trade in tobacco products	
						Date of signature	Date of ratification	Date of signature	Date of ratification
						16-06-2003	26-09-2006	-	27-09-2022

... Not categorized/ No data; No policy or weak measure; Minimal measure; Moderate measure; Complete measure

Source: WHO report on the global tobacco epidemic (WHO, 2023[3]).

Figure 6.118. Paraguay - Taxes and prices of the most sold brand of cigarettes

Panel A. Indirect taxes levied on cigarettes in Paraguay and LAC | **Panel B. Tobacco tax share and price of cigarettes in Paraguay**

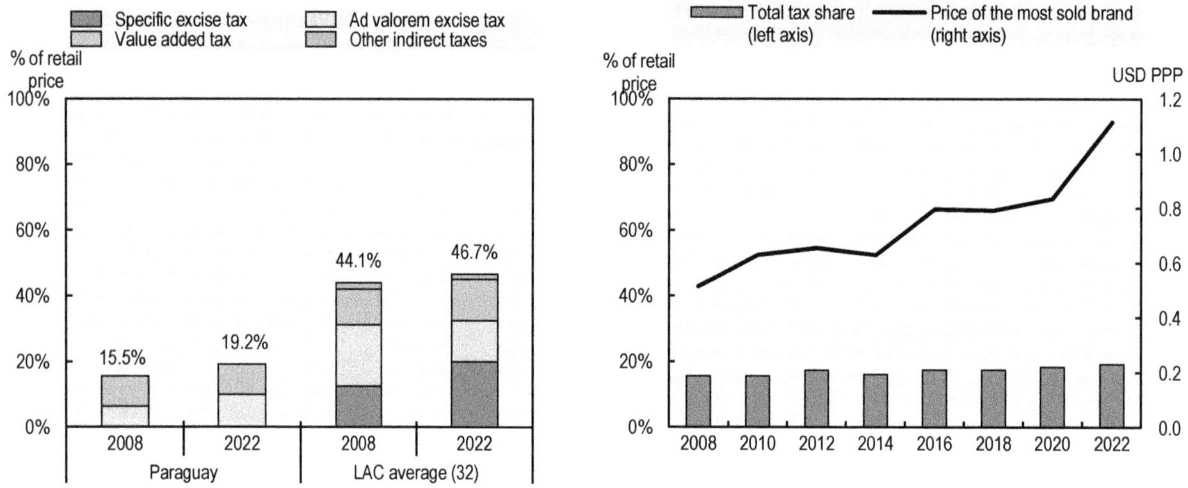

Note: Prices correspond to a 20-cigarette pack of the most sold brand. The most sold brand of cigarettes is determined based on national market share information and can vary over time (i.e. the most sold brand of cigarettes in year 1 can be different from year 2). Retail prices in USD PPP are based on the implied purchasing power parity (PPP) conversion rate from the International Monetary Fund (IMF) World Economic Outlook Database (October 2023).
Source: WHO report on the global tobacco epidemic (WHO, 2023[3]); IMF World Economic Outlook Database (IMF, 2023[4]).

Figure 6.119. Paraguay - Trends in retail prices of cigarettes by brand category

In USD PPP per pack of 20 cigarettes, 2008-2022

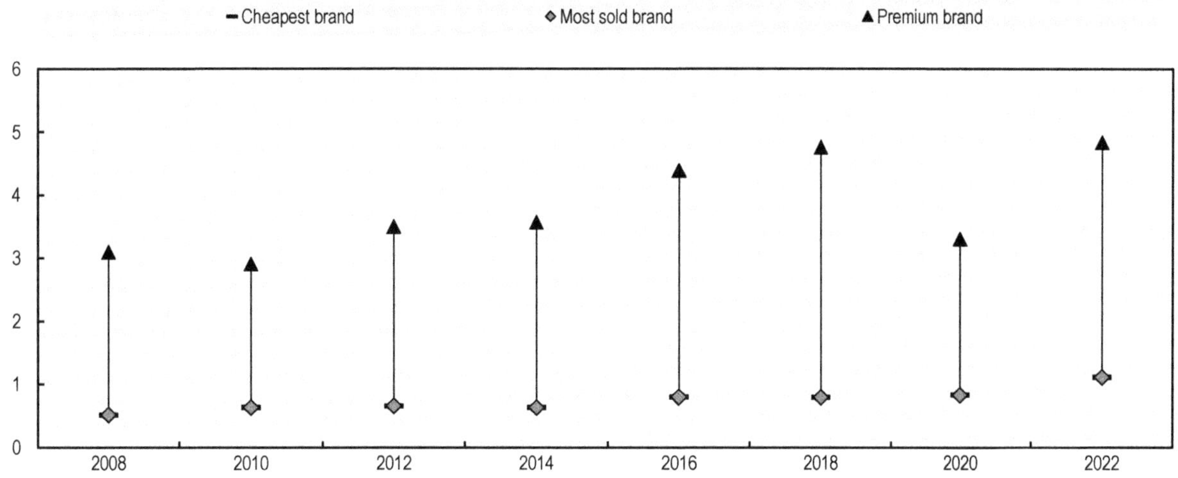

Note: Prices correspond to a 20-cigarette pack of the cheapest, most sold and premium brands. The cheapest, most sold and premium brands of cigarettes are determined based on national market share information and can vary over time (i.e. the cheapest/most sold/premium brands of cigarettes in year 1 can be different from year 2). Retail prices in USD PPP are based on the implied PPP conversion rate from the IMF World Economic Outlook Database (October 2023).
Source: WHO reports on the global tobacco epidemic (WHO, 2009[5]; WHO, 2011[6]; WHO, 2013[7]; WHO, 2015[8]; WHO, 2017[9]; WHO, 2019[10]; WHO, 2021[11]); IMF World Economic Outlook Database (IMF, 2023[4]).

Figure 6.120. Paraguay - Affordability of cigarettes

Percentage of GDP per capita required to purchase 100 packs of 20 cigarettes

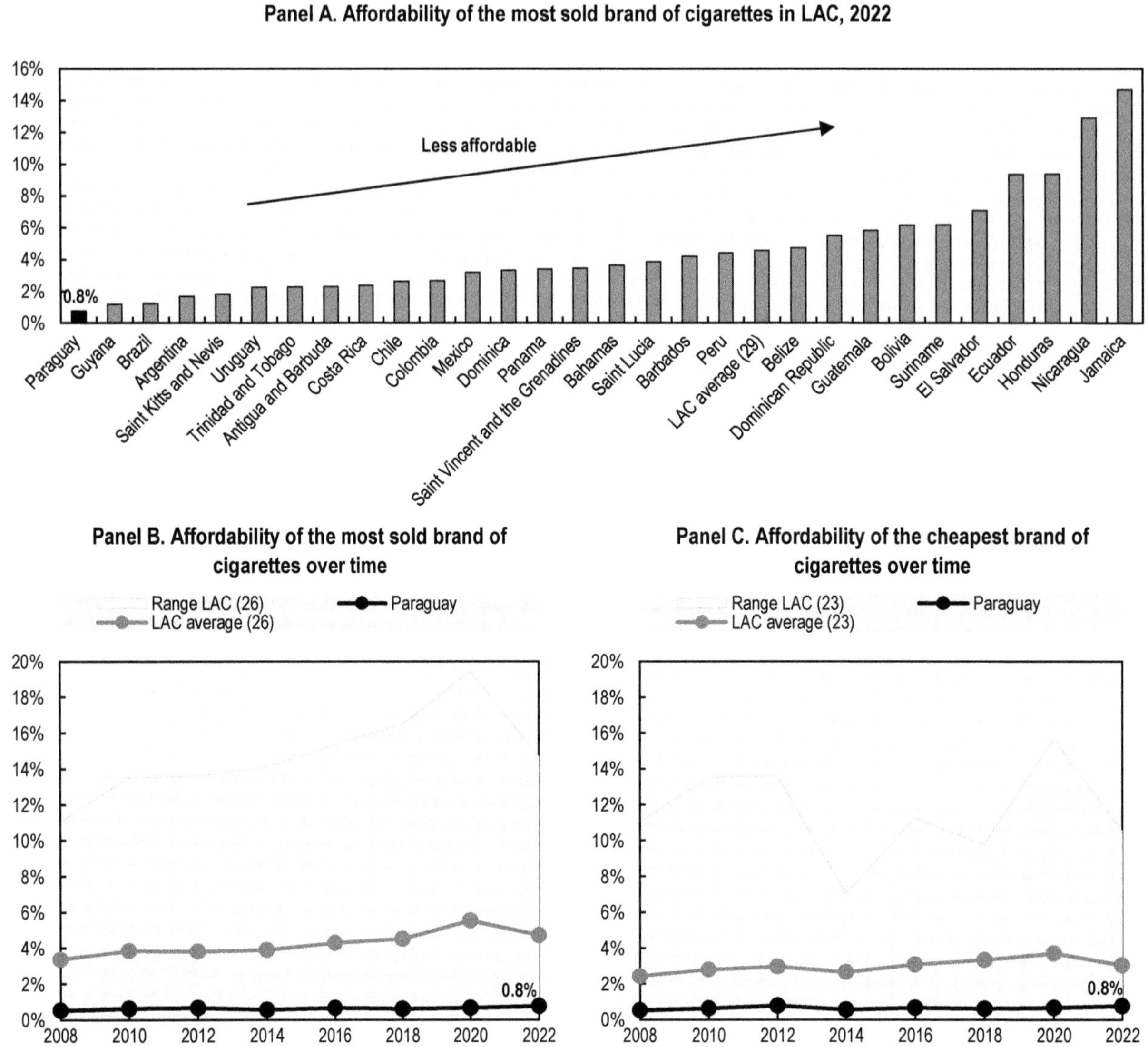

Note: The affordability indicator measures the percentage of the country's GDP per capita required to purchase 100 packs of 20 cigarettes. A higher percentage means lower affordability of cigarettes while a lower percentage means higher affordability. To ensure comparability of average affordability across LAC over time, countries where information was unavailable for certain years have been excluded from the calculation. Data for Panel C are OECD calculations based on WHO reports on the global tobacco epidemic (2009-2023 editions). The cheapest and most sold brands of cigarettes are determined based on national market share information and can vary over time (i.e. the cheapest/most sold brand of cigarettes in year 1 can be different from year 2).

Source: WHO reports on the global tobacco epidemic (WHO, 2009[5]; WHO, 2011[6]; WHO, 2013[7]; WHO, 2015[8]; WHO, 2017[9]; WHO, 2019[10]; WHO, 2021[11]).

Table 6.63. Paraguay - Design of tobacco excise taxes across tobacco products, 2022

	Excise tax structure	Specific excise tax				Ad valorem excise tax			Excise tax floor			
		Yes / No	Tax base	Rate per 20-unit pack USD PPP (local currency)	Indexation mechanisms	Yes / No	Tax base	Statutory rate	Yes / No	Tax base	Rate per 20-unit pack USD PPP (local currency)	Indexation mechanisms
Cigarettes	Ad valorem only	No				Yes	EFP excl. VAT	20%	No			
Cigars	Ad valorem only	No				Yes	EFP excl. VAT	20%	No			
Cigarillos	Ad valorem only	No				Yes	EFP excl. VAT	20%	No			
Roll-Your-Own (RYO) products	Ad valorem only	No				Yes	EFP excl. VAT	20%	No			
Heated tobacco products (HTPs)	Ad valorem only	No				Yes	EFP excl. VAT	20%	No			
ENDS and ENNDS	No excise											

Note: Ad valorem tax base "EFP" means "Ex-factory price/CIF value"; "VAT" means "Value added tax"; blank cells mean that there is no excise tax for the corresponding tobacco product. Following the WHO report on the global tobacco epidemic (WHO, 2021[11]), new tobacco and nicotine products in this report include electronic nicotine delivery systems (ENDS), electronic non-nicotine delivery systems (ENNDS), and heated tobacco products (HTP). Specific taxes are converted into USD PPP with the implied PPP conversion rate available in the IMF World Economic Outlook Database (October 2023). Specific excise taxes have been standardized to a 20-unit pack to allow the comparison across countries with different tax bases.
Source: Decreto No. 6619/2022; IMF World Economic Outlook Database (IMF, 2023[4]).

Table 6.64. Paraguay - Tobacco tax reforms since 2000

Year of adoption	Specific excise taxes	Ad valorem excise taxes	Other
2004	No	Cigarettes, cigars, cigarillos: increase in the tax rate to 12% levied on the ex-factory price, excluding VAT. RYO tobacco: increase in the tax rate to 10% levied on the ex-factory price, excluding VAT.	No
2010	No	Cigarettes, cigars, cigarillos, RYO tobacco: increase in the tax rate to 13% levied on the ex-factory price, excluding VAT.	Cigarettes, cigars, cigarillos, RYO tobacco: earmark the excise tax revenue generated from the 1% increase in the ad valorem excise tax rate for the National Fund for Sports Development.
2015	No	Cigarettes, cigars, cigarillos, RYO tobacco: increase in the tax rate to 16% levied on the ex-factory price, excluding VAT. A maximum tax rate of 20% is established.	No
2018	No	Cigarettes, cigars, cigarillos, RYO tobacco: increase in the tax rate to 18% levied on the ex-factory price, excluding VAT. The maximum tax rate of 20% is increased to 22%.	No
2019	No	Cigarettes, cigars, cigarillos, RYO tobacco: increase in the maximum tax rate to 24%. Heated Tobacco Products (HTPs): introduction of an ad valorem excise tax levied at a rate of 18% on the ex-factory price, excluding VAT.	Raw tobacco: reduction in the VAT rate to 5%.

Year of adoption	Specific excise taxes	Ad valorem excise taxes	Other
2022	No	All tobacco products: increase in the tax rate to 20% levied on the ex-factory price, excluding VAT.	No

Note: "Tobacco tax reform" refers to changes in the tobacco excise tax rates, the introduction of indexation mechanisms or minimum taxes, as well as adjustments to the tax base. These reforms typically entail the enactment of new laws or decrees. The table does not refer to recurrent tax changes that result from the indexation for inflation of tax brackets and price floors (if implemented). Tobacco tax reforms included reflect changes in the legislation, but not whether or when the reforms have been implemented.
Source: Ley No. 2421/04; Ley No. 4045/10; Decreto No. 4694/2015; Ley No. 6097/18; Ley No. 6380/19; Decreto No. 6619/2022.

Figure 6.121. Paraguay - Tobacco excise tax revenue

Percentage of GDP, latest year available

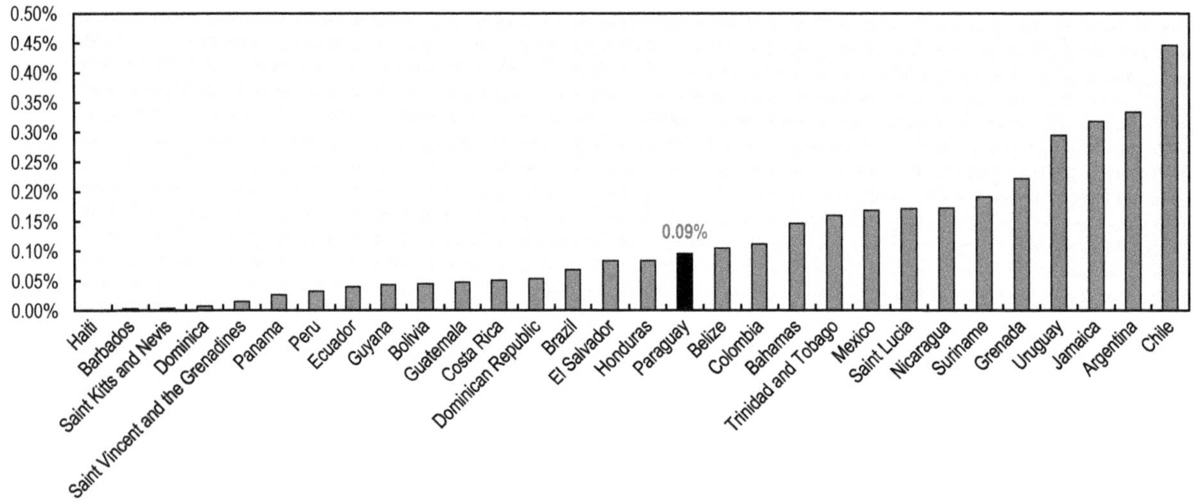

Note: See Box 2.1 (Chapter 2) for more information on tobacco tax revenue (source of information and calculations) and country selection. The latest year available is 2022 for Argentina, Brazil, Chile, Colombia, Costa Rica, the Dominican Republic, El Salvador, Guatemala, Guyana, Honduras, Mexico, Nicaragua, Panama, Paraguay, Peru, Saint Kitts and Nevis, Suriname, and Uruguay; 2021 for Belize, Dominica, Ecuador, Grenada, Saint Lucia, Saint Vincent and the Grenadines; 2020 for Bahamas, Bolivia, Jamaica and Trinidad and Tobago; 2015 for Haiti; 2014 for Barbados.
Source: OECD Revenue Statistics (OECD, 2024[13]); WHO report on the global tobacco epidemic (WHO, 2023[3]); National data.

Figure 6.122. Paraguay - Trends in tobacco excise tax revenue

Percentage of GDP, 2009-2022

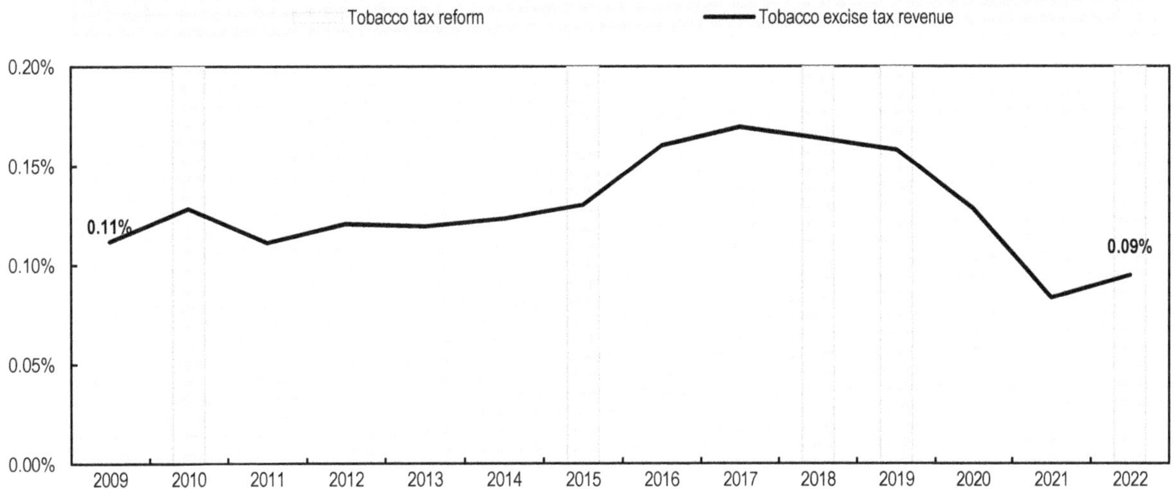

Note: "Tobacco tax reform" refers to the measures included in Table 6.64. Tobacco excise tax revenue data prior 2009 are not available.
Source: Subsecretaría de Estado de Tributación/ Sistema Marangatu (Government of Paraguay, 2023[41]); Ley No. 2421/04; Ley No. 4045/10; Decreto No. 4694/2015; Ley No. 6097/18; Ley No. 6380/19; Decreto No. 6619/2022.

Figure 6.123. Paraguay - Average excise tax revenue collected per pack of 20 cigarettes sold

Tobacco excise tax revenue in USD PPP collected per pack of legal cigarettes sold, latest year available

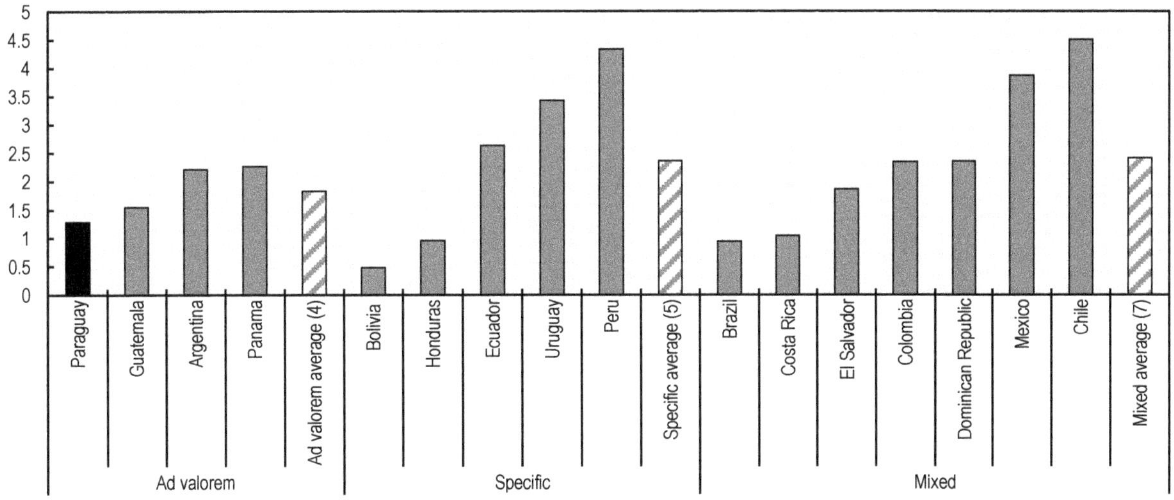

Note: See Box 2.1 (Chapter 2) for more information on tobacco tax revenue (source of information and calculations). The latest year available is 2022 for Argentina, Brazil, Chile, Colombia, Costa Rica, the Dominican Republic, El Salvador, Guatemala, Honduras, Mexico, Panama, Paraguay, Peru and Uruguay; 2021 for Ecuador; 2020 for Bolivia. The country selection is provided by the availability of data on sales of cigarettes in Euromonitor International Tobacco Industry edition, 2023 © All rights reserved (Euromonitor International, 2023[14]).
Source: OECD Revenue Statistics (OECD, 2024[13]); WHO report on the global tobacco epidemic (WHO, 2023[3]); National data; IMF World Economic Outlook Database (IMF, 2023[4]); and OECD calculations based on Euromonitor International's Tobacco Industry edition (Euromonitor International, 2023[14]).

Figure 6.124. Paraguay - Change in tobacco tax policy indicators

Percentage change from base year, 2008-2022

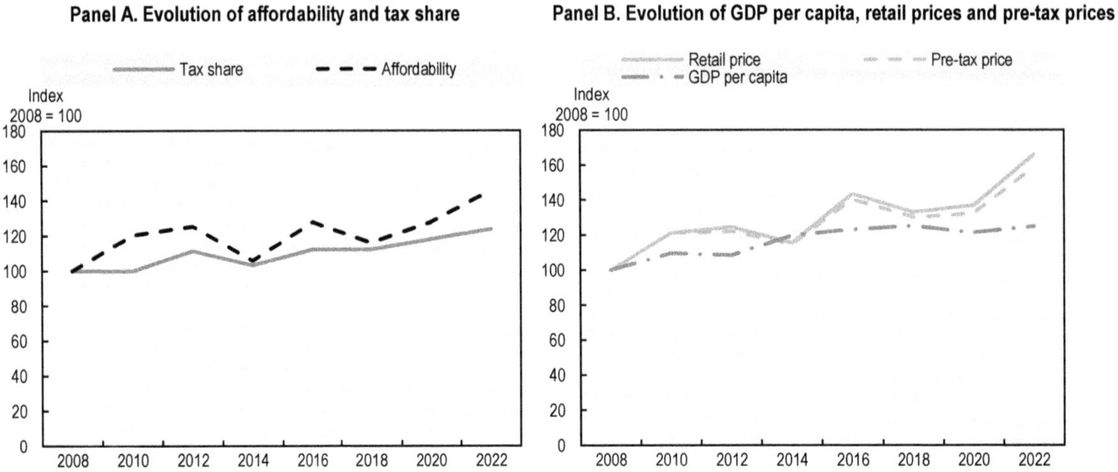

Note: Both Panel A and Panel B figures are based on data for the most sold brand of cigarettes. The most sold brand of cigarettes is determined based on national market share information and can vary over time (i.e. the most sold brand of cigarettes in year 1 can be different from year 2). In Panel A, an increase in the affordability indicator means that cigarettes are becoming less affordable, while a decline in the affordability indicator means that cigarettes are becoming more affordable. In Panel B, "Pre-tax price" corresponds to the retail price of the most sold brand of cigarettes minus the indirect taxes levied on this brand, namely excise taxes, VAT, import duties and other. Indicators in Panel B have been computed using national currency and have been adjusted for inflation; therefore, present inflation-adjusted trends.

Source: WHO report on the global tobacco epidemic (WHO, 2023[3]); World Bank Open Data (World Bank, 2024[15]); IMF International Financial Statistics (IMF, 2024[19]).

References

Euromonitor International (2023), *Euromonitor International's Tobacco Industry edition*, https://www.euromonitor.com/tobacco (accessed on 1 August 2023). [14]

Government of Paraguay (2023), *Recaudacion en concepto de ISC*, Ministry of Finance, https://www.set.gov.py/web/portal-institucional/estadisticas (accessed on 13 July 2023). [41]

IMF (2023), *World Economic Outlook Database*, International Monetary Fund, https://www.imf.org/en/Publications/WEO/weo-database/2023/October (accessed on 13 January 2024). [4]

IMF (2024), *International Financial Statistics (IFS)*, International Monetary Fund, https://data.imf.org/?sk=4c514d48-b6ba-49ed-8ab9-52b0c1a0179b&sId=1390030341854 (accessed on 13 January 2024). [19]

OECD (2024), *Global Revenue Statistics Database*, Organisation for Economic Co-operation and Development, https://www.oecd.org/tax/tax-policy/global-revenue-statistics-database.htm (accessed on 13 August 2023). [13]

WHO (2024), *Global Health Observatory: Age-standardized estimates of current tobacco use, tobacco smoking and cigarette smoking (Tobacco control: Monitor)*, World Health Organization, https://www.who.int/data/gho/data/indicators/indicator-details/GHO/gho-tobacco-control-monitor-current-tobaccouse-tobaccosmoking-cigarrettesmoking-agestd-tobagestdcurr (accessed on 20 February 2024). [1]

WHO (2023), *WHO report on the global tobacco epidemic 2023: protect people from tobacco smoke*, World Health Organization, https://www.who.int/publications/i/item/9789240077164. [3]

WHO (2021), *WHO report on the global tobacco epidemic 2021: Addressing new and emerging products*, World Health Organization, https://www.who.int/publications/i/item/9789240032095. [11]

WHO (2019), *WHO report on the global tobacco epidemic 2019: Offer help to quit tobacco use*, World Health Organization, https://www.who.int/publications/i/item/9789241516204. [10]

WHO (2019), *Global Youth Tobacco Survey. Paraguay 2019 Fact Sheet*, World Health Organization, https://www.who.int/publications/m/item/2019-gyts-fact-sheet-paraguay. [40]

WHO (2017), *WHO report on the global tobacco epidemic 2017: Monitoring tobacco use and prevention policies*, World Health Organization, https://www.who.int/publications/i/item/9789241512824. [9]

WHO (2015), *WHO report on the global tobacco epidemic 2015: Raising taxes on tobacco*, World Health Organization, https://www.who.int/publications/i/item/9789241509121. [8]

WHO (2013), *WHO report on the global tobacco epidemic 2013: Enforcing bans on tobacco advertising, promotion and sponsorship*, World Health Organization, https://www.who.int/publications/i/item/9789241505871. [7]

WHO (2011), *WHO report on the global tobacco epidemic 2011: Warning about the dangers of tobacco*, World Health Organization, https://www.who.int/publications/i/item/9789244564264. [6]

WHO (2009), *WHO report on the global tobacco epidemic 2009: Implementing smoke-free environments*, World Health Organization, https://www.who.int/publications/i/item/9789241563918. [5]

World Bank (2024), *World Bank Open Data*, World Bank, https://data.worldbank.org/ (accessed on 13 January 2024). [15]

Peru

Figure 6.125. Peru - Trends in tobacco use prevalence

Percentage of the population aged 15 years and over who currently use any tobacco product (smoked and/or smokeless tobacco) on a daily or non-daily basis, 2000-2020

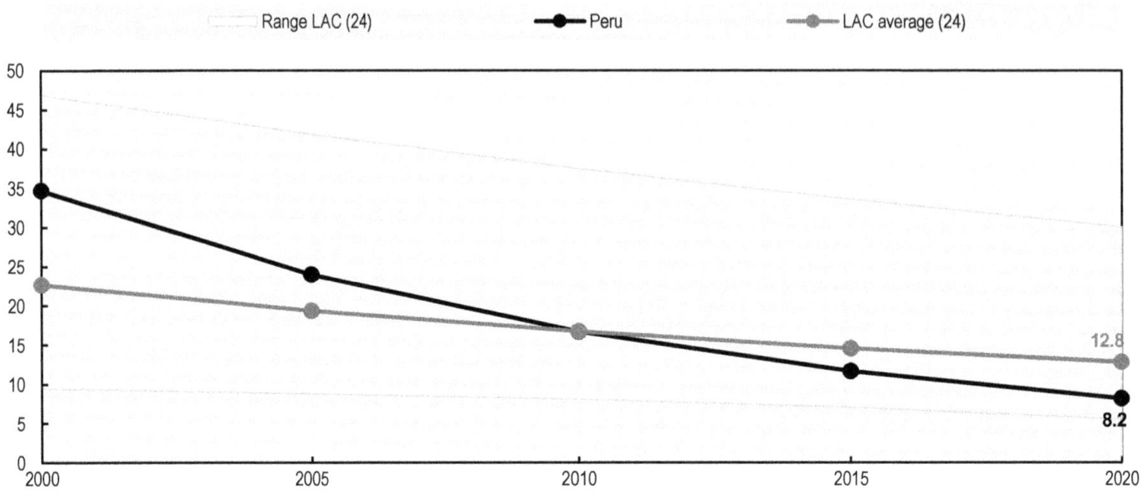

Note: Tobacco products include cigarettes, pipes, cigars, cigarillos, waterpipes (hookah, shisha), bidis, kretek, heated tobacco products (HTP), and all forms of smokeless (oral and nasal) tobacco. Tobacco products exclude e-cigarettes (which do not contain tobacco), e-cigars, e-hookahs, and e-pipes. The rates are age-standardized to the World Health Organisation (WHO) standard population. The LAC average was calculated as the average of Argentina, Bahamas, Barbados, Belize, Bolivia, Brazil, Chile, Colombia, Costa Rica, Cuba, the Dominican Republic, Ecuador, El Salvador, Guatemala, Guyana, Haiti, Honduras, Jamaica, Mexico, Panama, Paraguay, Peru, Saint Lucia, and Uruguay.
Source: WHO Global Health Observatory Data Repository (WHO, 2024[11]).

Table 6.65. Peru - Tobacco use prevalence by sex and age groups

Percentage of the population group, latest year available

	Tobacco use prevalence (all tobacco products)	Cigarette smoking prevalence (cigarettes only)
Youths aged 13-15 years		
Total	**7.2**	**4.9**
Males	8.4	5.4
Females	5.9	4.5
People aged 15 and over		
Total	**8.2**	**7.5**
Males	13.2	12.3
Females	3.1	2.7

Note: Tobacco use prevalence is defined as the percentage of the population group who currently use any tobacco product (smoked and/or smokeless tobacco) on a daily or non-daily basis. Tobacco products exclude e-cigarettes (which do not contain tobacco), e-cigars, e-hookahs, and e-pipes. Data for students aged 13-15 years are from 2019 and taken from the Global Youth Tobacco Survey. Data for people aged 15 and over correspond to 2020.
Source: WHO Global Health Observatory Data Repository (WHO, 2024[11]); Global Youth Tobacco Survey (WHO, 2019[42]).

Table 6.66. Peru - Summary of MPOWER measures, 2022

M Monitoring	P Smoking bans	O Cessation programmes	W Health warnings	E Advertising bans	R Taxation	WHO Frawework Convention on Tobacco Control		Protocol to eliminate illicit trade in tobacco products	
						Date of signature	Date of ratification	Date of signature	Date of ratification
						21-04-2004	30-11-2004		

... Not categorized/ No data; No policy or weak measure; Minimal measure; Moderate measure; Complete measure

Source: WHO report on the global tobacco epidemic (WHO, 2023[3]).

Figure 6.126. Peru - Taxes and prices of the most sold brand of cigarettes

Panel A. Indirect taxes levied on cigarettes in Peru and LAC

Panel B. Tobacco tax share and price of cigarettes in Peru

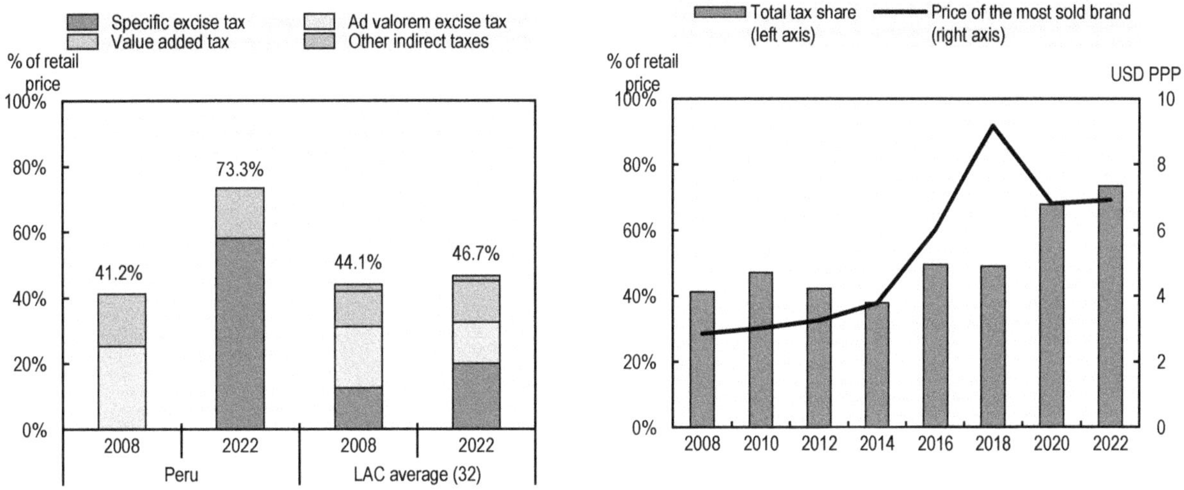

Note: Prices correspond to a 20-cigarette pack of the most sold brand. The most sold brand of cigarettes is determined based on national market share information and can vary over time (i.e. the most sold brand of cigarettes in year 1 can be different from year 2). Retail prices in USD PPP are based on the implied purchasing power parity (PPP) conversion rate from the International Monetary Fund (IMF) World Economic Outlook Database (October 2023).

Source: WHO report on the global tobacco epidemic (WHO, 2023[3]); IMF World Economic Outlook Database (IMF, 2023[4]).

Figure 6.127. Peru - Trends in retail prices of cigarettes by brand category

In USD PPP per pack of 20 cigarettes, 2008-2022

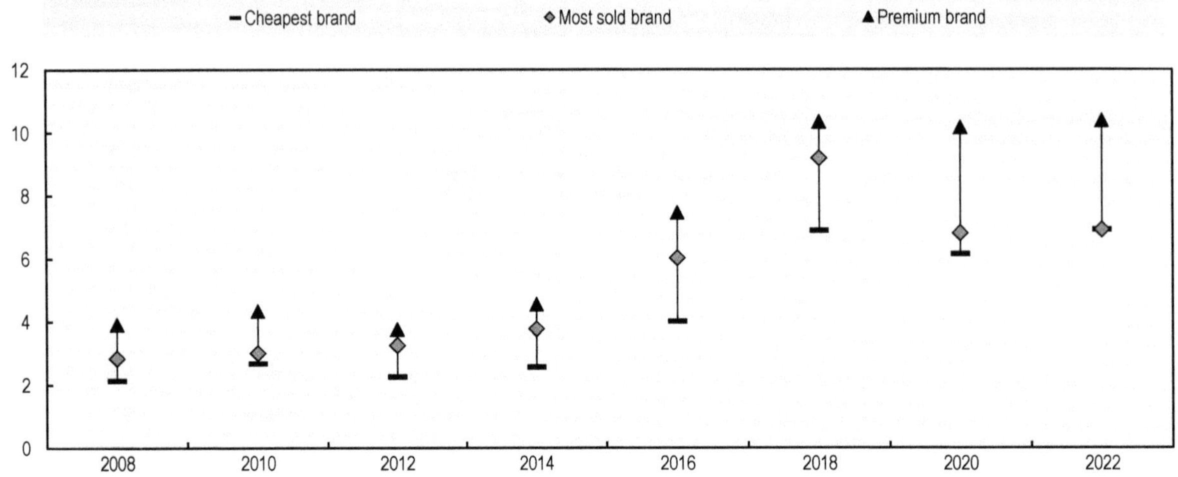

Note: Prices correspond to a 20-cigarette pack of the cheapest, most sold and premium brands. The cheapest, most sold and premium brands of cigarettes are determined based on national market share information and can vary over time (i.e. the cheapest/most sold/premium brands of cigarettes in year 1 can be different from year 2). Retail prices in USD PPP are based on the implied PPP conversion rate from the IMF World Economic Outlook Database (October 2023).
Source: WHO reports on the global tobacco epidemic (WHO, 2009[5]; WHO, 2011[6]; WHO, 2013[7]; WHO, 2015[8]; WHO, 2017[9]; WHO, 2019[10]; WHO, 2021[11]); IMF World Economic Outlook Database (IMF, 2023[4]).

Figure 6.128. Peru - Affordability of cigarettes

Percentage of GDP per capita required to purchase 100 packs of 20 cigarettes

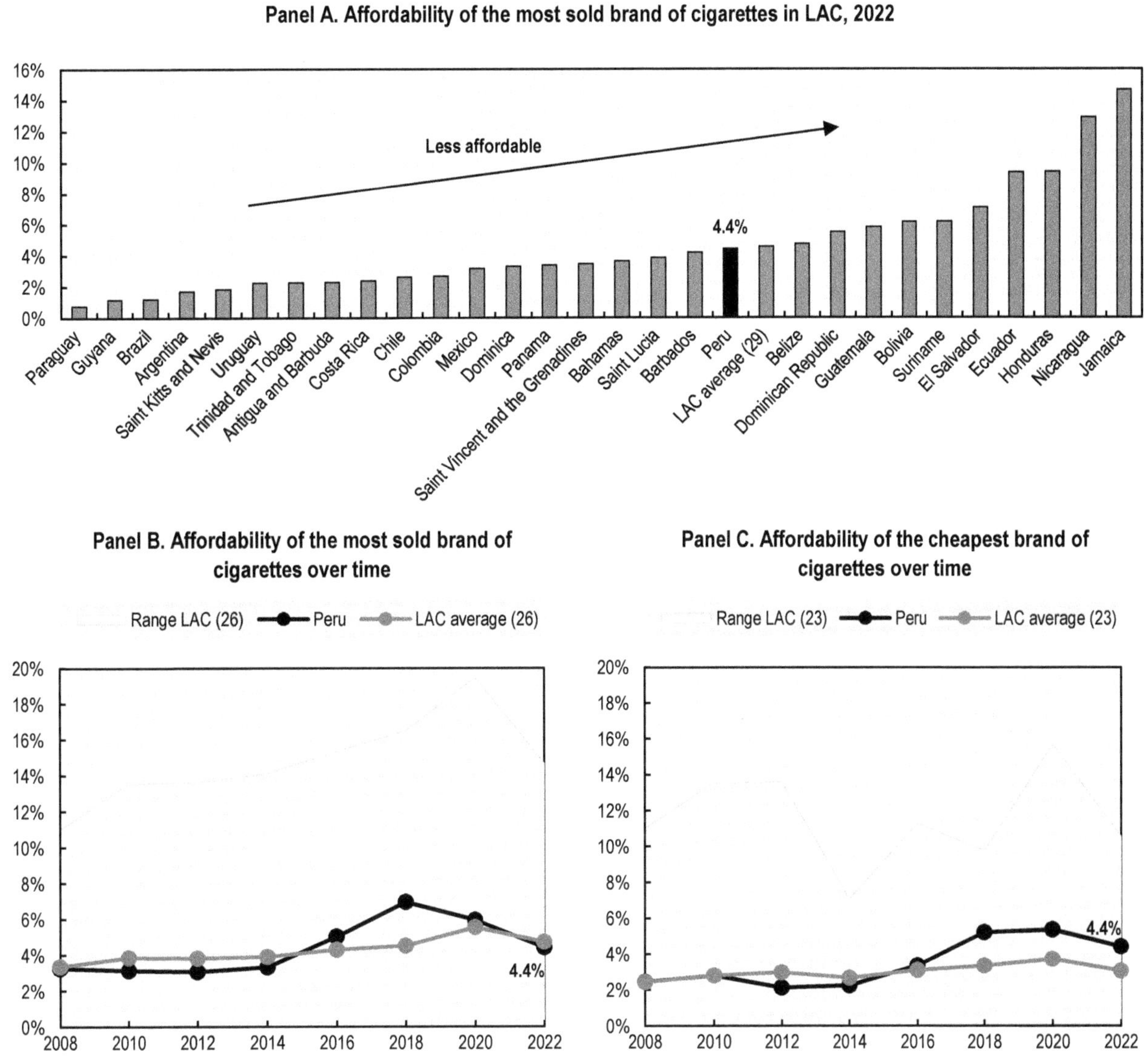

Note: The affordability indicator measures the percentage of the country's GDP per capita required to purchase 100 packs of 20 cigarettes. A higher percentage means lower affordability of cigarettes while a lower percentage means higher affordability. To ensure comparability of average affordability across LAC over time, countries where information was unavailable for certain years have been excluded from the calculation. Data for Panel C are OECD calculations based on WHO reports on the global tobacco epidemic (2009-2023 editions). The cheapest and most sold brands of cigarettes are determined based on national market share information and can vary over time (i.e. the cheapest/most sold brand of cigarettes in year 1 can be different from year 2).

Source: WHO reports on the global tobacco epidemic (WHO, 2009[5]; WHO, 2011[6]; WHO, 2013[7]; WHO, 2015[8]; WHO, 2017[9]; WHO, 2019[10]; WHO, 2021[11]).

Table 6.67. Peru - Design of tobacco excise taxes across tobacco products, 2022

	Excise tax structure	Specific excise tax				Ad valorem excise tax			Excise tax floor			
		Yes / No	Tax base	Rate per 20-unit pack USD PPP (local currency)	Indexation mechanisms	Yes / No	Tax base	Statutory rate	Yes / No	Tax base	Rate per 20-unit pack USD PPP (local currency)	Indexation mechanisms
Cigarettes	Specific only	Yes	Single stick	4.0 (7.2)	CPI-cigarette	No			No			
Cigars	Ad valorem only	No				Yes	EFP excl. VAT	50%	No			
Cigarillos	Ad valorem only	No				Yes	EFP excl. VAT	50%	No			
Roll-Your-Own (RYP) tobacco	Ad valorem only	No				Yes	EFP excl. VAT	50%	No			
Heated tobacco products (HTPs)	Specific only	Yes	Single stick	3.3 (6.0)	CPI-cigarette	No			No			
ENDS and ENNDS	No excise											

Note: Ad valorem tax base "EFP" means "Ex-factory price/CIF value"; "VAT" means "Value added tax"; blank cells mean that there is no excise tax for the corresponding tobacco product. Following the WHO report on the global tobacco epidemic (WHO, 2021[11]), new tobacco and nicotine products in this report include electronic nicotine delivery systems (ENDS), electronic non-nicotine delivery systems (ENNDS), and heated tobacco products (HTP). Specific taxes are converted into USD PPP with the implied PPP conversion rate available in the IMF World Economic Outlook Database (October 2023). Specific excise taxes have been standardized to a 20-unit pack to allow the comparison across countries with different tax bases.
Source: Resolución Ministerial N° 035-2021-EF/15; Resolución Ministerial No. 021-2022-EF/15; IMF World Economic Outlook Database (IMF, 2023[4]).

Table 6.68. Peru - Tobacco tax reforms since 2000

Year of adoption	Specific excise taxes	Ad valorem excise taxes	Other
2001	Cigarettes: the specific tax is quarterly adjusted based on the changes of the CPI.	No	No
2001	Cigarettes: increase in the tiered rates to PEN 0.026 per stick of cigarettes containing brown tobacco; to PEN 0.05 per stick of "standard" cigarettes containing blond tobacco; to PEN 0.10 per stick of "premium" cigarettes containing blond tobacco.	No	No
2001	Cigarette: the specific excise tax is abolished.	All tobacco products: introduction of an ad valorem excise tax levied at a uniform rate of 100% on the ex-factory price, excluding VAT.	No
2001	No	Cigarettes: increase in the tax rate to 125% levied on the ex-factory price, excluding VAT.	No
2003	No	Cigarettes: reduction in the tax rate to 30% and change in the tax base to the retail price (including VAT) multiplied by a factor equal to 0.847.	No
2003	No	Cigarettes: increase in the tax rate to 37.5% levied on the retail price (including VAT) multiplied by a factor 0.847.	No
2003	No	Cigarettes: reduction in the tax rate to 37.2% levied on the retail price (including VAT) multiplied by a factor 0.847.	No

Year of adoption	Specific excise taxes	Ad valorem excise taxes	Other
2004	No	Cigarettes: reduction in the tax rate to 30% levied on the retail price (including VAT). The factor by which the tax base is multiplied is changed from 0.847 to 0.84.	
2004	No	Cigars, cigarillos, RYO tobacco: reduction in the tax rate to 50% levied on the ex-factory price, excluding VAT. The multiplying factor is abolished.	
2010	Cigarettes: introduction of a uniform specific excise tax of PEN 0.07 levied on each single stick.	Cigarette: the ad valorem excise tax is abolished.	No
2016	Cigarettes: increase in the specific tax to PEN 0.18 levied on each single stick.	No	No
2018	Cigarettes: increase in the specific tax to PEN 0.27 levied on each single stick.	No	No
2019	Heated tobacco products (HTPs): introduction of a uniform specific excise tax of PEN 0.27 levied on each single stick.	No	No
2019	Cigarettes and HTPs: the specific tax is annually adjusted based on the changes of the CPI if the annual percentage variation of the CPI is equal to or greater than 1%.	No	No
2020	Cigarettes and HTPs: modification of the indexation mechanism of the specific excise tax. The specific tax is annually adjusted based on the changes of CPI-cigarette if the annual percentage variation of CPI-cigarette is equal to or greater than 1%. Cigarettes: specific tax adjusted to PEN 0.32 levied on each single stick.	No	No
2021	Cigarettes: specific tax adjusted to PEN 0.35 levied on each single stick.	No	No
2022	Cigarettes: specific tax adjusted to PEN 0.36 levied on each single stick.	No	No
2024	Cigarettes: specific tax adjusted to PEN 0.37 levied on each single stick.	No	No

Note: "Tobacco tax reform" refers to changes in the tobacco excise tax rates, the introduction of indexation mechanisms or minimum taxes, as well as adjustments to the tax base. These reforms typically entail the enactment of new laws or decrees. The table does not refer to recurrent tax changes that result from the indexation for inflation of tax brackets and price floors (if implemented). Tobacco tax reforms included reflect changes in the legislation, but not whether or when the reforms have been implemented. "CPI-cigarettes" correspond to the change of CPI index for cigarette item only.

Source: R.M. 026-2001-EF/15; R.M. 115-2001-EF/15; D.S. 128-2001-EF; D.S. 222-2001-EF; Ley 27940; D.S. 087-2003-EF; D.S.113-2003-EF; D.S. 025-2004-EF; D.S. 178-2004-EF; D.S. 004-2010-EF; D.S. 112-2016-EF; D.S. 092-2018-EF; D.S. 181-2019-EF; R.M. 234-2019-EF/15; R.M. 034-2020-EF/15; R.M. 042-2020-EF/15; R.M. 035-2021-EF/15; R.M. 021-2022-EF/15; R.M. 030-2024-EF/15.

Figure 6.129. Peru - Tobacco excise tax revenue

Percentage of GDP, latest year available

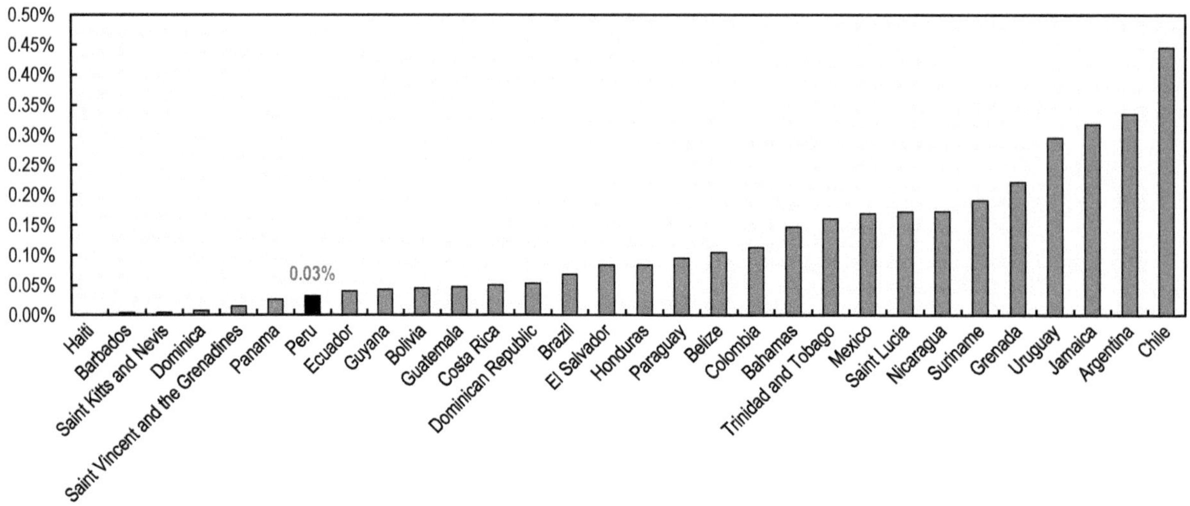

Note: See Box 2.1 (Chapter 2) for more information on tobacco tax revenue (source of information and calculations) and country selection. The latest year available is 2022 for Argentina, Brazil, Chile, Colombia, Costa Rica, the Dominican Republic, El Salvador, Guatemala, Guyana, Honduras, Mexico, Nicaragua, Panama, Paraguay, Peru, Saint Kitts and Nevis, Suriname, and Uruguay; 2021 for Belize, Dominica, Ecuador, Grenada, Saint Lucia, Saint Vincent and the Grenadines; 2020 for Bahamas, Bolivia, Jamaica and Trinidad and Tobago; 2015 for Haiti; 2014 for Barbados.
Source: OECD Revenue Statistics (OECD, 2024[13]); WHO report on the global tobacco epidemic (WHO, 2023[3]); National data.

Figure 6.130. Peru - Trends in tobacco excise tax revenue

Percentage of GDP, 2007-2023

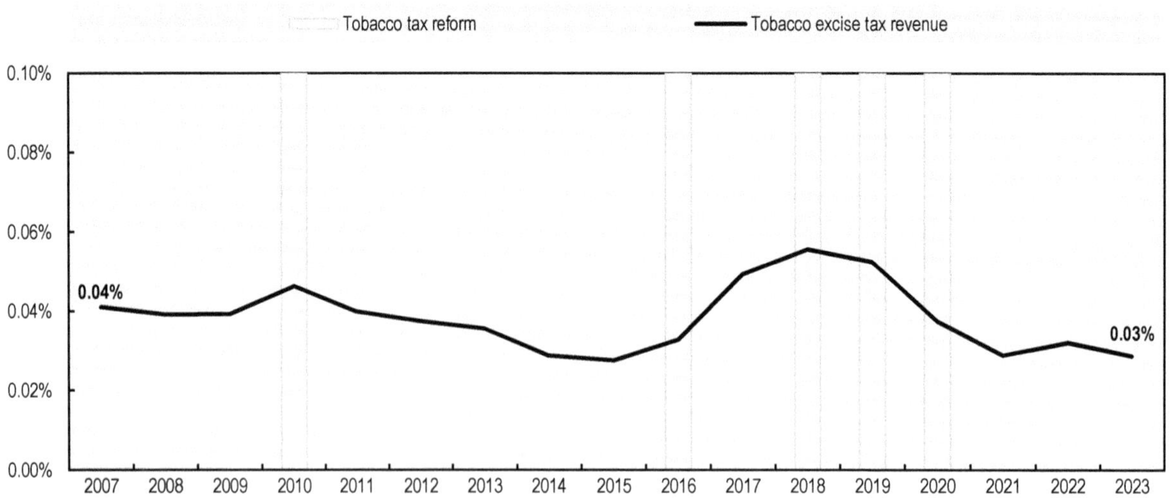

Note: "Tobacco tax reform" refers to the measures included in Table 6.68. Tobacco excise tax revenue data prior 2007 are not available.
Source: National data; Questionnaire sent to the tax administration (SUNAT) in June 2024; D.S. 004-2010-EF; D.S. 112-2016-EF; D.S. 092-2018-EF; R.M. 234-2019-EF/15; R.M. 034-2020-EF/15. R.S. 234-2019-EF/15; R.S. 034-2020-EF/15.

Figure 6.131. Peru - Average excise tax revenue collected per pack of 20 cigarettes sold

Tobacco excise tax revenue in USD PPP collected per pack of legal cigarettes sold, latest year available

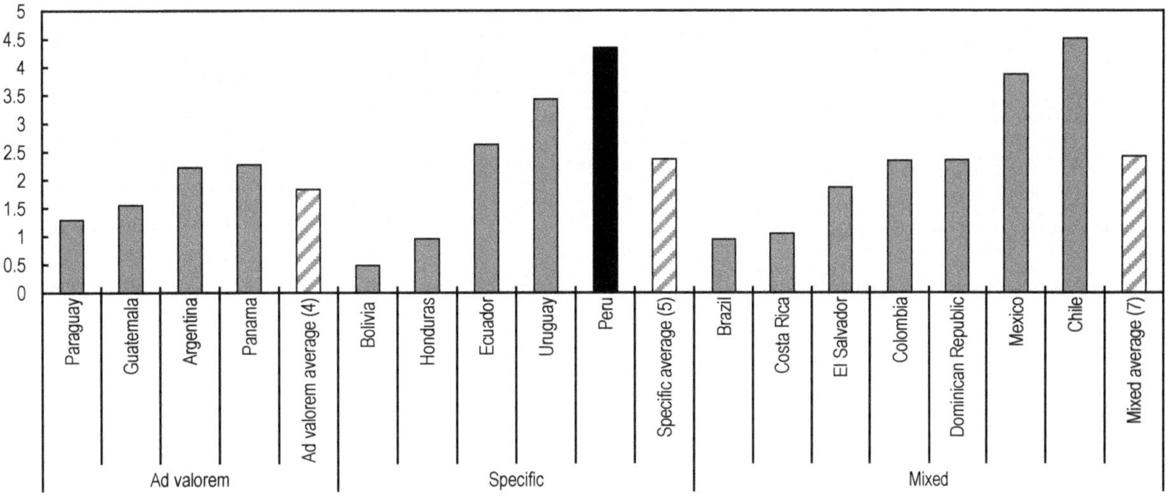

Note: See Box 2.1 (Chapter 2) for more information on tobacco tax revenue (source of information and calculations). The latest year available is 2022 for Argentina, Brazil, Chile, Colombia, Costa Rica, the Dominican Republic, El Salvador, Guatemala, Honduras, Mexico, Panama, Paraguay, Peru and Uruguay; 2021 for Ecuador and 2020 for Bolivia. The country selection is provided by the availability of data on sales of cigarettes in Euromonitor International Tobacco Industry edition, 2023 © All rights reserved (Euromonitor International, 2023[14]).
Source: OECD Revenue Statistics (OECD, 2024[13]); WHO report on the global tobacco epidemic (WHO, 2023[3]); National data; IMF World Economic Outlook Database (IMF, 2023[4]); and OECD calculations based on Euromonitor International's Tobacco Industry edition (Euromonitor International, 2023[14]).

Figure 6.132. Peru - Change in tobacco tax policy indicators

Percentage change from base year, 2008-2022

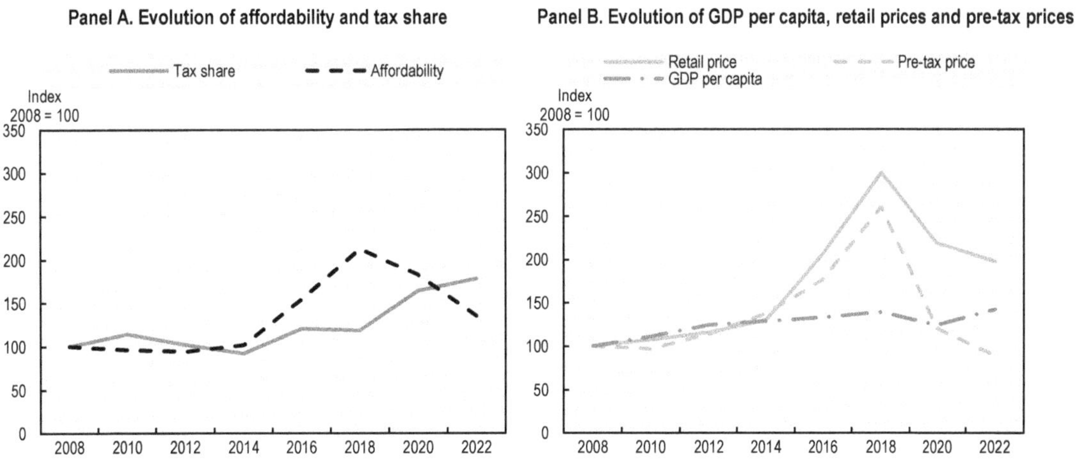

Note: Both Panel A and Panel B figures are based on data for the most sold brand of cigarettes. The most sold brand of cigarettes is determined based on national market share information and can vary over time (i.e. the most sold brand of cigarettes in year 1 can be different from year 2). In Panel A, an increase in the affordability indicator means that cigarettes are becoming less affordable, while a decline in the affordability indicator means that cigarettes are becoming more affordable. In Panel B, "Pre-tax price" corresponds to the retail price of the most sold brand of cigarettes minus the indirect taxes levied on this brand, namely excise taxes, VAT, import duties and other. Indicators in Panel B have been computed using national currency and have been adjusted for inflation; therefore, present inflation-adjusted trends.
Source: WHO report on the global tobacco epidemic (WHO, 2023[3]); World Bank Open Data (World Bank, 2024[15]); IMF International Financial Statistics (IMF, 2024[19]).

References

Euromonitor International (2023), *Euromonitor International's Tobacco Industry edition*, https://www.euromonitor.com/tobacco (accessed on 1 August 2023). [14]

IMF (2023), *World Economic Outlook Database*, International Monetary Fund, https://www.imf.org/en/Publications/WEO/weo-database/2023/October (accessed on 13 January 2024). [4]

IMF (2024), *International Financial Statistics (IFS)*, International Monetary Fund, https://data.imf.org/?sk=4c514d48-b6ba-49ed-8ab9-52b0c1a0179b&sId=1390030341854 (accessed on 13 January 2024). [19]

OECD (2024), *Global Revenue Statistics Database*, Organisation for Economic Co-operation and Development, https://www.oecd.org/tax/tax-policy/global-revenue-statistics-database.htm (accessed on 13 August 2023). [13]

WHO (2024), *Global Health Observatory: Age-standardized estimates of current tobacco use, tobacco smoking and cigarette smoking (Tobacco control: Monitor)*, World Health Organization, https://www.who.int/data/gho/data/indicators/indicator-details/GHO/gho-tobacco-control-monitor-current-tobaccouse-tobaccosmoking-cigarrettesmoking-agestd-tobagestdcurr (accessed on 20 February 2024). [1]

WHO (2023), *WHO report on the global tobacco epidemic 2023: protect people from tobacco smoke*, World Health Organization, https://www.who.int/publications/i/item/9789240077164. [3]

WHO (2021), *WHO report on the global tobacco epidemic 2021: Addressing new and emerging products*, World Health Organization, https://www.who.int/publications/i/item/9789240032095. [11]

WHO (2019), *WHO report on the global tobacco epidemic 2019: Offer help to quit tobacco use*, World Health Organization, https://www.who.int/publications/i/item/9789241516204. [10]

WHO (2019), *Global Youth Tobacco Survey. Peru 2019 Fact Sheet*, World Health Organization, https://www.who.int/publications/m/item/2019-gyts-fact-sheet-peru. [42]

WHO (2017), *WHO report on the global tobacco epidemic 2017: Monitoring tobacco use and prevention policies*, World Health Organization, https://www.who.int/publications/i/item/9789241512824. [9]

WHO (2015), *WHO report on the global tobacco epidemic 2015: Raising taxes on tobacco*, World Health Organization, https://www.who.int/publications/i/item/9789241509121. [8]

WHO (2013), *WHO report on the global tobacco epidemic 2013: Enforcing bans on tobacco advertising, promotion and sponsorship*, World Health Organization, https://www.who.int/publications/i/item/9789241505871. [7]

WHO (2011), *WHO report on the global tobacco epidemic 2011: Warning about the dangers of tobacco*, World Health Organization, https://www.who.int/publications/i/item/9789244564264. [6]

WHO (2009), *WHO report on the global tobacco epidemic 2009: Implementing smoke-free environments*, World Health Organization, https://www.who.int/publications/i/item/9789241563918. [5]

World Bank (2024), *World Bank Open Data*, World Bank, https://data.worldbank.org/ (accessed on 13 January 2024). [15]

Uruguay

Figure 6.133. Uruguay - Trends in tobacco use prevalence

Percentage of the population aged 15 years and over who currently use any tobacco product (smoked and/or smokeless tobacco) on a daily or non-daily basis, 2000-2020

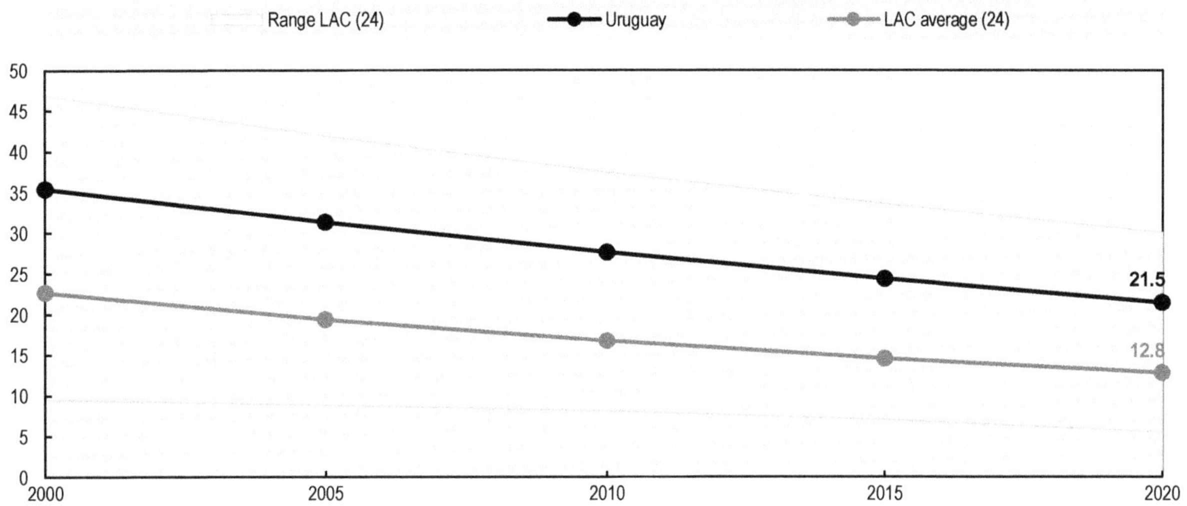

Note: Tobacco products include cigarettes, pipes, cigars, cigarillos, waterpipes (hookah, shisha), bidis, kretek, heated tobacco products (HTP), and all forms of smokeless (oral and nasal) tobacco. Tobacco products exclude e-cigarettes (which do not contain tobacco), e-cigars, e-hookahs, and e-pipes. The rates are age-standardized to the World Health Organisation (WHO) standard population. The LAC average was calculated as the average of Argentina, Bahamas, Barbados, Belize, Bolivia, Brazil, Chile, Colombia, Costa Rica, Cuba, the Dominican Republic, Ecuador, El Salvador, Guatemala, Guyana, Haiti, Honduras, Jamaica, Mexico, Panama, Paraguay, Peru, Saint Lucia, and Uruguay.
Source: WHO Global Health Observatory Data Repository (WHO, 2024[1]).

Table 6.69. Uruguay - Tobacco use prevalence by sex and age groups

Percentage of the population group, latest year available

	Tobacco use prevalence (all tobacco products)	Cigarette smoking prevalence (cigarettes only)
Students aged 13-15 years		
Total	**11.5**	**8.6**
Males	9.7	6.9
Females	13.6	10.5
People aged 15 and over		
Total	**21.6**	**21.4**
Males	25.6	25.2
Females	18.0	18.0

Note: Tobacco use prevalence is defined as the percentage of the population group who currently use any tobacco product (smoked and/or smokeless tobacco) on a daily or non-daily basis. Tobacco products exclude e-cigarettes (which do not contain tobacco), e-cigars, e-hookahs, and e-pipes. Data for students aged 13-15 years are from 2019 and taken from the Global School-based Student Health Survey. Data for people aged 15 and over correspond to 2017 and are taken from the Global Adult Tobacco Survey (GATS). For comparability purposes across countries, the Figure 6.133 uses another source of information (WHO Global Health Observatory Data Repository) which explains the small difference with figures included in this table.
Source: Global Adult Tobacco Survey, Uruguay 2017 (Government of Uruguay, 2017[43]); Global School-Based Student Health Survey (WHO, 2019[44]).

Table 6.70. Uruguay - Summary of MPOWER measures, 2022

M Monitoring	P Smoking bans	O Cessation programmes	W Health warnings	E Advertising bans	R Taxation	WHO Frawework Convention on Tobacco Control		Protocol to eliminate illicit trade in tobacco products	
						Date of signature	Date of ratification	Date of signature	Date of ratification
						19-06-2003	09-09-2004	10-01-2013	24-09-2014

... Not categorized/ No data | No policy or weak measure | Minimal measure | Moderate measure | Complete measure

Source: WHO report on the global tobacco epidemic (WHO, 2023[3]).

Figure 6.134. Uruguay - Taxes and prices of the most sold brand of cigarettes

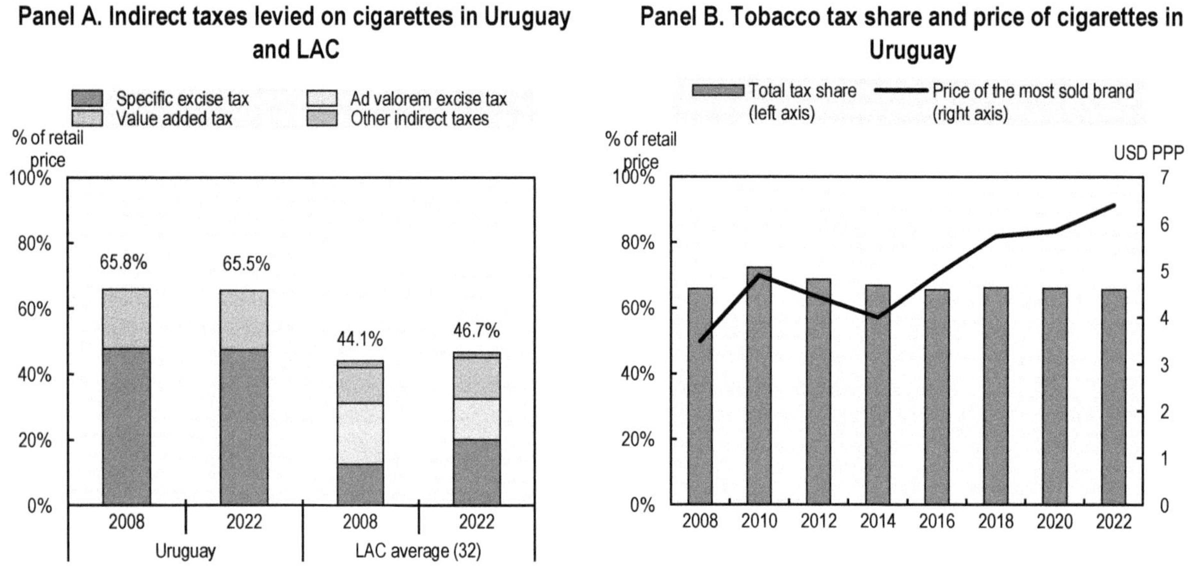

Note: Prices correspond to a 20-cigarette pack of the most sold brand. The most sold brand of cigarettes is determined based on national market share information and can vary over time (i.e. the most sold brand of cigarettes in year 1 can be different from year 2). Retail prices in USD PPP are based on the implied purchasing power parity (PPP) conversion rate from the International Monetary Fund (IMF) World Economic Outlook Database (October 2023).

Source: WHO report on the global tobacco epidemic (WHO, 2023[3]); IMF World Economic Outlook Database (IMF, 2023[4]).

Figure 6.135. Uruguay - Trends in retail prices of cigarettes by brand category

In USD PPP per pack of 20 cigarettes, 2008-2022

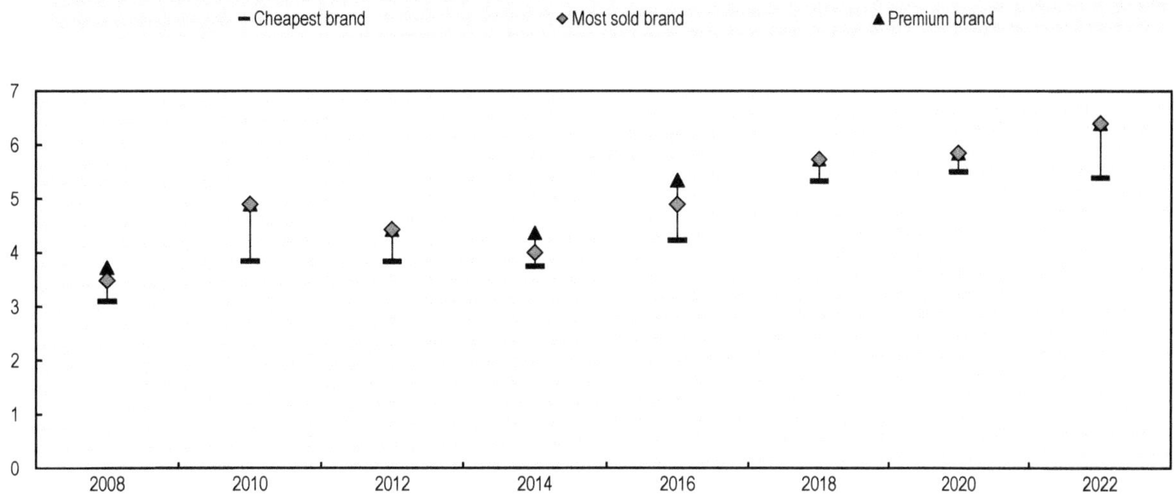

Note: Prices correspond to a 20-cigarette pack of the cheapest, most sold and premium brands. The cheapest, most sold and premium brands of cigarettes are determined based on national market share information and can vary over time (i.e. the cheapest/most sold/premium brands of cigarettes in year 1 can be different from year 2). Retail prices in USD PPP are based on the implied PPP conversion rate from the IMF World Economic Outlook Database (October 2023).

Source: WHO reports on the global tobacco epidemic (WHO, 2009[5]; WHO, 2011[6]; WHO, 2013[7]; WHO, 2015[8]; WHO, 2017[9]; WHO, 2019[10]; WHO, 2021[11]); IMF World Economic Outlook Database (IMF, 2023[4]).

Figure 6.136. Uruguay - Affordability of cigarettes

Percentage of GDP per capita required to purchase 100 packs of 20 cigarettes

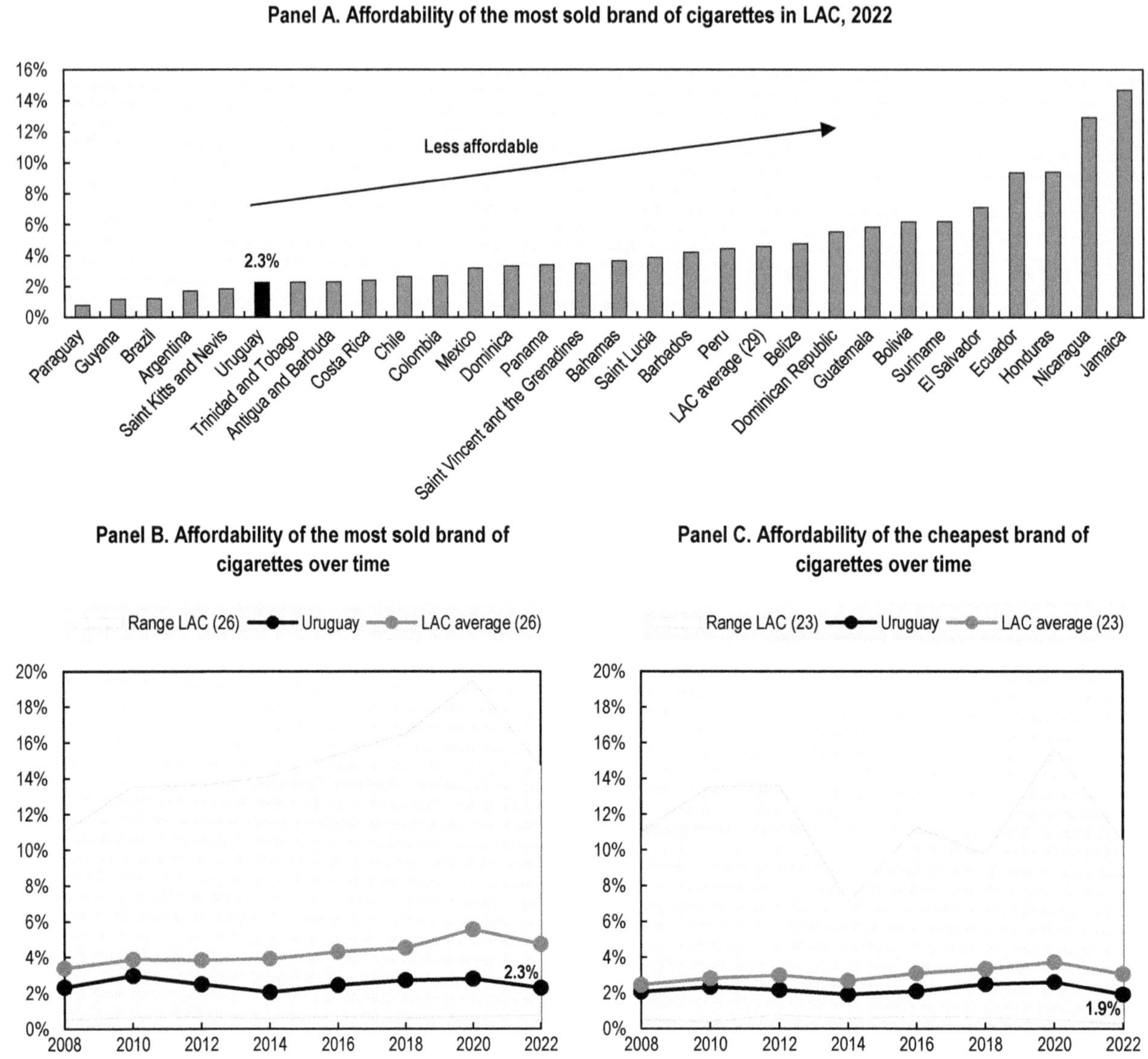

Note: The affordability indicator measures the percentage of the country's GDP per capita required to purchase 100 packs of 20 cigarettes. A higher percentage means lower affordability of cigarettes while a lower percentage means higher affordability. To ensure comparability of average affordability across LAC over time, countries where information was unavailable for certain years have been excluded from the calculation. Data for Panel C are OECD calculations based on WHO reports on the global tobacco epidemic (2009-2023 editions). The cheapest and most sold brands of cigarettes are determined based on national market share information and can vary over time (i.e. the cheapest/most sold brand of cigarettes in year 1 can be different from year 2).

Source: WHO reports on the global tobacco epidemic (WHO, 2009[5]; WHO, 2011[6]; WHO, 2013[7]; WHO, 2015[8]; WHO, 2017[9]; WHO, 2019[10]; WHO, 2021[11]).

Table 6.71. Uruguay - Design of tobacco excise taxes across tobacco products, 2022

	Excise tax structure	Specific excise tax				Ad valorem excise tax			Excise tax floor			
		Yes / No	Tax base	Rate per 20-unit pack USD PPP (local currency)	Indexation mechanisms	Yes / No	Tax base	Statutory rate	Yes / No	Tax base	Rate per 20-unit pack USD PPP (local currency)	Indexation mechanisms
Cigarettes	Specific only	Yes	Individual pack	3.0 (90.2)	No	No			No			
Cigars	Ad valorem only	No				Yes	EFP excl. VAT *1.85	70%	No			
Cigarillos	Ad valorem only	No				Yes	EFP excl. VAT *1.85	70%	No			
Roll-Your-Own (RYO) tobacco	Specific only	Yes	Individual pack (45 g)	0.5 (13.4)	No	No			No			
Heated tobacco products (HTPs)	No excise											
ENDS and ENNDS	No excise											

Note: Blank cells mean that there is no excise tax for the corresponding tobacco product. Following the WHO report on the global tobacco epidemic (WHO, 2021[11]), new tobacco and nicotine products in this report include electronic nicotine delivery systems (ENDS), electronic non-nicotine delivery systems (ENNDS), and heated tobacco products (HTP). Uruguay does not levy an excise tax on ENDs or ENNDS because their sales are banned (WHO, 2023[3]). However, the sales of HTPs are not taxed nor banned. Specific taxes are converted into USD PPP with the implied PPP conversion rate available in the IMF World Economic Outlook Database (October 2023). Specific excise taxes have been standardized to a 20-unit pack to allow the comparison across countries with different tax bases. Specific tax in Uruguay for RYO tobacco products is levied on pack of 45 grams. To compute the specific tax for an equivalent 20-unit pack of RYO tobacco, it is assumed that the median cigarette in terms of weight contains 0.75 gram of tobacco (Gallus et al., 2014[12]).
Source: Decreto No. 440/021; IMF World Economic Outlook Database (IMF, 2023[4]).

Table 6.72. Uruguay - Tobacco tax reforms since 2000

Year of adoption	Specific excise taxes	Ad valorem excise taxes	Other
2002	Cigarettes: increase in the tax rate to 68.5% levied on the price floor.	No	No
2005	Cigarettes: increase in the tax rate to 70% levied on the price floor. Cigars: increase in the tax rate to 41% levied on the price floor. RYO tobacco: increase in the tax rate to 28% levied on the price floor.	No	Cigarettes: increase in the price floor of cigarettes sold by the tobacco industry to its employees (Decree No. 276/985) to UYU 17.31 per pack of 20 cigarettes.
2006	No	No	Cigarettes: increase of the price floor of cigarettes sold by the tobacco industry to its employees (Decree No. 276/985) to UYU 19.0 per pack of 20 cigarettes.
2007	No	No	Cigarettes: increase in the price floor to UYU 30.72 per pack of 20 cigarettes.
2009	No	No	Cigarettes: increase in the price floor to UYU 40.0 per pack of 20 cigarettes; and to UYU 24.71 for cigarettes sold under Decree No. 276/985.
2010	RYO tobacco: increase in the tax rate to 70% levied on the price floor.	No	Cigarettes: increase in the price floor to UYU 54.29 per pack of 20 cigarettes. RYO tobacco: increase in the price floor to UYU 24.29 per pack of 45 grams.
2014	No	No	Cigarettes: increase in the price floor to UYU 58.71 per pack of 20 cigarettes. RYO tobacco: increase in the price floor to UYU 26.14 per pack of 45 grams.

Note: "Tobacco tax reform" refers to changes in the tobacco excise tax rates, the introduction of indexation mechanisms or minimum taxes, as well as adjustments to the tax base. These reforms typically entail the enactment of new laws or decrees. The table does not refer to recurrent tax changes that result from the indexation for inflation of tax brackets and price floors (if implemented). Increases of the price floor between 2015 and 2022 are not included in this table due to their regular nature. Tobacco tax reforms included reflect changes in the legislation, but not whether or when the reforms have been implemented.
Source: Decreto No. 99/002; Decreto No. 164/005; Decreto No. 204/005; Decreto No. 619/006; Decreto No. 232/07; Decreto No. 268/09; Decreto No. 69/010; Decreto No. 375/014.

Figure 6.137. Uruguay - Tobacco excise tax revenue

Percentage of GDP, latest year available

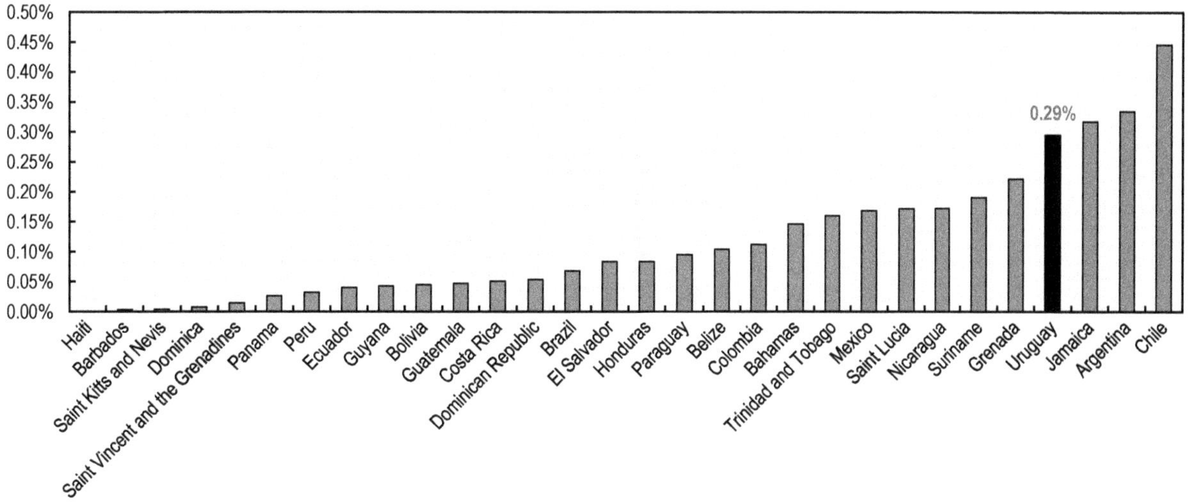

Note: See Box 2.1 (Chapter 2) for more information on tobacco tax revenue (source of information and calculations) and country selection. The latest year available is 2022 for Argentina, Brazil, Chile, Colombia, Costa Rica, the Dominican Republic, El Salvador, Guatemala, Guyana, Honduras, Mexico, Nicaragua, Panama, Paraguay, Peru, Saint Kitts and Nevis, Suriname, and Uruguay; 2021 for Belize, Dominica, Ecuador, Grenada, Saint Lucia, Saint Vincent and the Grenadines; 2020 for Bahamas, Bolivia, Jamaica and Trinidad and Tobago; 2015 for Haiti; 2014 for Barbados.
Source: OECD Revenue Statistics (OECD, 2024[13]); WHO report on the global tobacco epidemic (WHO, 2023[3]); National data.

Figure 6.138. Uruguay - Trends in tobacco excise tax revenue

Percentage of GDP, 2000-2022

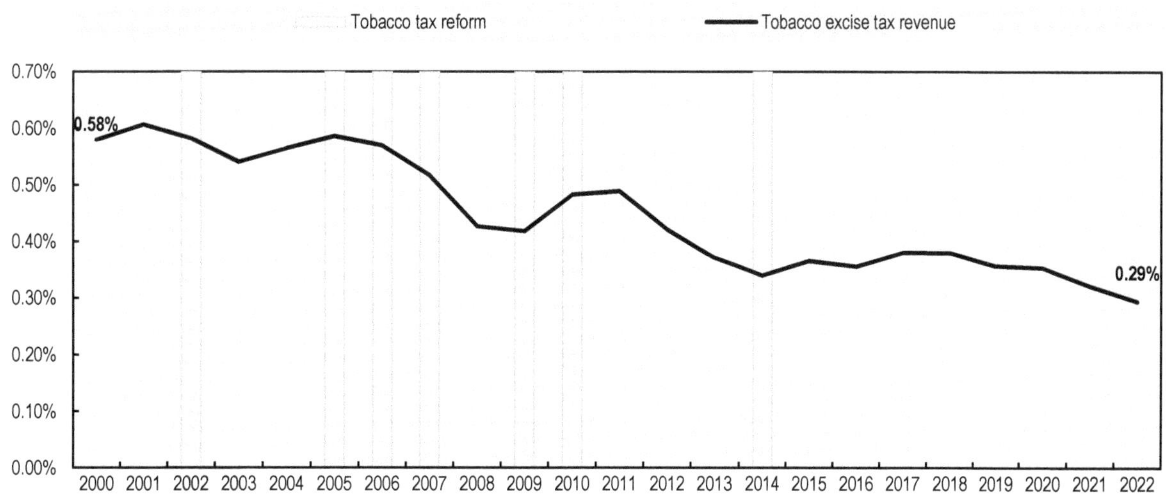

Note: "Tobacco tax reform" refers to the measures included in Table 6.72.
Source: OECD Revenue Statistics (OECD, 2024[13]); Decreto No. 99/002; Decreto No. 164/005; Decreto No. 204/005; Decreto No. 619/006; Decreto No. 232/07; Decreto No. 268/09; Decreto No. 69/010; Decreto No. 375/014.

Figure 6.139. Uruguay - Average excise tax revenue collected per pack of 20 cigarettes sold

Tobacco excise tax revenue in USD PPP collected per pack of legal cigarettes sold, latest year available

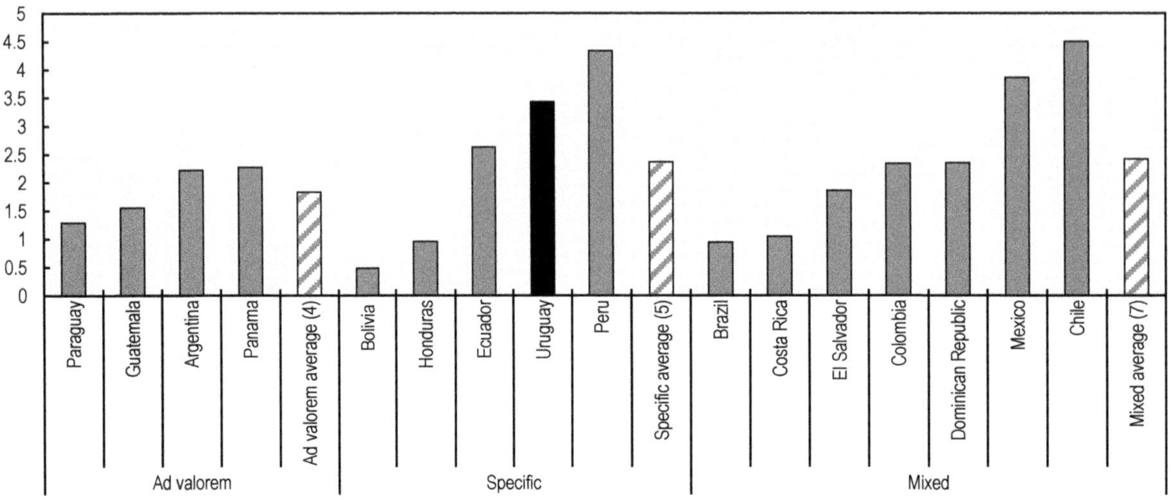

Note: See Box 2.1 (Chapter 2) for more information on tobacco tax revenue (source of information and calculations). The latest year available is 2022 for Argentina, Brazil, Chile, Colombia, Costa Rica, the Dominican Republic, El Salvador, Guatemala, Honduras, Mexico, Panama, Paraguay, Peru and Uruguay; 2021 for Ecuador; 2020 for Bolivia. The country selection is provided by the availability of data on sales of cigarettes in Euromonitor International Tobacco Industry edition, 2023 © All rights reserved (Euromonitor International, 2023[14]).
Source: OECD Revenue Statistics (OECD, 2024[13]); WHO report on the global tobacco epidemic (WHO, 2023[3]); National data; IMF World Economic Outlook Database (IMF, 2023[4]); and OECD calculations based on Euromonitor International's Tobacco Industry edition (Euromonitor International, 2023[14]).

Figure 6.140. Uruguay - Change in tobacco tax policy indicators

Percentage change from base year, 2008-2022

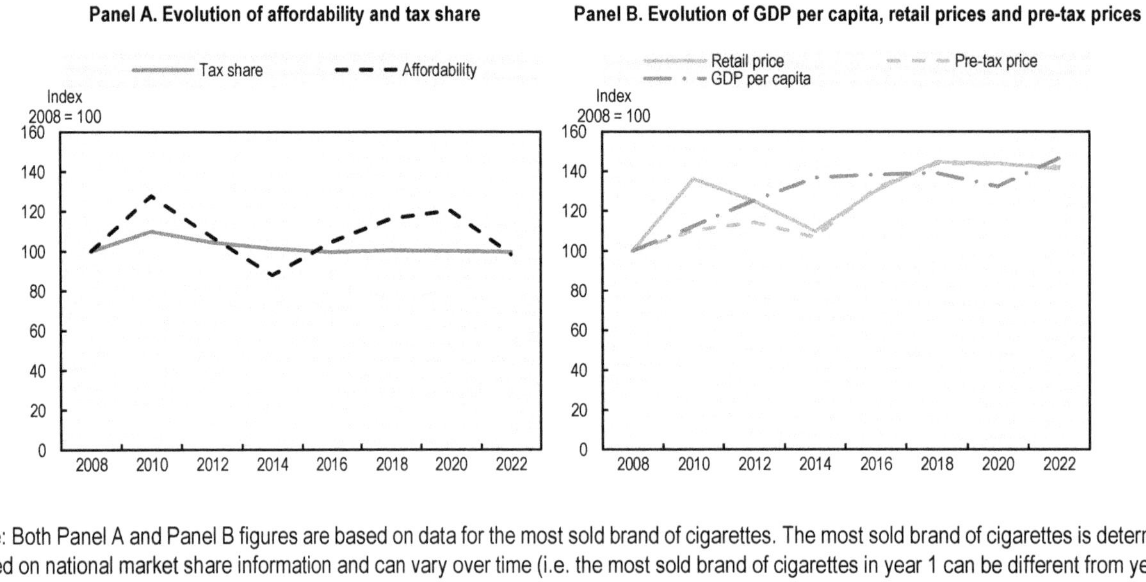

Note: Both Panel A and Panel B figures are based on data for the most sold brand of cigarettes. The most sold brand of cigarettes is determined based on national market share information and can vary over time (i.e. the most sold brand of cigarettes in year 1 can be different from year 2). In Panel A, an increase in the affordability indicator means that cigarettes are becoming less affordable, while a decline in the affordability indicator means that cigarettes are becoming more affordable. In Panel B, "Pre-tax price" corresponds to the retail price of the most sold brand of cigarettes minus the indirect taxes levied on this brand, namely excise taxes, VAT, import duties and other. Indicators in Panel B have been computed using national currency and have been adjusted for inflation; therefore, present inflation-adjusted trends.
Source: WHO report on the global tobacco epidemic (WHO, 2023[3]); World Bank Open Data (World Bank, 2024[15]); IMF International Financial Statistics (IMF, 2024[19]).

References

Euromonitor International (2023), *Euromonitor International's Tobacco Industry edition*, https://www.euromonitor.com/tobacco (accessed on 1 August 2023). [14]

Gallus, S. et al. (2014), "Roll-your-own cigarettes in Europe", *European Journal of Cancer Prevention*, Vol. 23/3, pp. 186-192, https://doi.org/10.1097/cej.0000000000000010. [12]

Government of Uruguay (2017), *Global Adult Tobacco Survey Uruguay 2017*, Ministry of Public Health of Uruguay/ National Institute of Statistics, https://cdn.who.int/media/docs/default-source/ncds/ncd-surveillance/data-reporting/uruguay/gats_uruguay_2017_countryreport.pdf?sfvrsn=3349b05b_1&download=true. [43]

IMF (2024), *International Financial Statistics (IFS)*, International Monetary Fund, https://data.imf.org/?sk=4c514d48-b6ba-49ed-8ab9-52b0c1a0179b&sId=1390030341854 (accessed on 13 January 2024). [19]

IMF (2023), *World Economic Outlook Database*, International Monetary Fund, https://www.imf.org/en/Publications/WEO/weo-database/2023/October (accessed on 13 January 2024). [4]

OECD (2024), *Global Revenue Statistics Database*, Organisation for Economic Co-operation and Development, https://www.oecd.org/tax/tax-policy/global-revenue-statistics-database.htm (accessed on 13 August 2023). [13]

WHO (2024), *Global Health Observatory: Age-standardized estimates of current tobacco use, tobacco smoking and cigarette smoking (Tobacco control: Monitor)*, World Health Organization, https://www.who.int/data/gho/data/indicators/indicator-details/GHO/gho-tobacco-control-monitor-current-tobaccouse-tobaccosmoking-cigarrettesmoking-agestd-tobagestdcurr (accessed on 20 February 2024). [1]

WHO (2023), *WHO report on the global tobacco epidemic 2023: Protect people from tobacco smoke*, World Health Organization, https://www.who.int/publications/i/item/9789240077164. [3]

WHO (2021), *WHO report on the global tobacco epidemic 2021: Addressing new and emerging products*, World Health Organization, https://www.who.int/publications/i/item/9789240032095. [11]

WHO (2019), *Global school-based student health survey. Uruguay 2019 Fact Sheet*, World Health Organization, https://www.who.int/publications/m/item/2019-gshs-fact-sheet-uruguay. [44]

WHO (2019), *WHO report on the global tobacco epidemic 2019: Offer help to quit tobacco use*, World Health Organization, https://www.who.int/publications/i/item/9789241516204. [10]

WHO (2017), *WHO report on the global tobacco epidemic 2017: Monitoring tobacco use and prevention policies*, World Health Organization, https://www.who.int/publications/i/item/9789241512824. [9]

WHO (2015), *WHO report on the global tobacco epidemic 2015: Raising taxes on tobacco*, World Health Organization, https://www.who.int/publications/i/item/9789241509121. [8]

WHO (2013), *WHO report on the global tobacco epidemic 2013: Enforcing bans on tobacco advertising, promotion and sponsorship*, World Health Organization, https://www.who.int/publications/i/item/9789241505871. [7]

WHO (2011), *WHO report on the global tobacco epidemic 2011: Warning about the dangers of tobacco*, World Health Organization, https://www.who.int/publications/i/item/9789244564264. [6]

WHO (2009), *WHO report on the global tobacco epidemic 2009: Implementing smoke-free environments*, World Health Organization, https://www.who.int/publications/i/item/9789241563918. [5]

World Bank (2024), *World Bank Open Data*, World Bank, https://data.worldbank.org/ (accessed on 13 January 2024). [15]

www.ingramcontent.com/pod-product-compliance
Ingram Content Group UK Ltd.
Pitfield, Milton Keynes, MK11 3LW, UK
UKHW051458290926
15471UKWH00008B/1280

9 789264 723962